£22·95

THE FORGOTTEN ARMY

THE FORGOTTEN ARMY

INDIA'S ARMED STRUGGLE FOR INDEPENDENCE
1942–1945

PETER WARD FAY

ANN ARBOR
THE UNIVERSITY OF MICHIGAN PRESS

Copyright © by the University of Michigan 1993

All rights reserved

Published in the United States of America by

The University of Michigan Press

Manufactured in the United States of America

1996   1995   1994   1993   4   3   2   1

The photographs that appear in this book are courtesy
of Prem and Lakshmi Sahgal, and Netaji Bhawan.

Library of Congress Cataloging-in-Publication Data

Fay, Peter Ward, 1924–
    The forgotten army: India's armed struggle for independence,
1942–1945 / Peter Ward Fay.
        p. cm.
    Includes bibliographical references and index.
    ISBN 0-472-10126-9 (alk. paper)
    1. Indian National Army—History—World War, 1939–1945.
2. India—History—Autonomy and independence movements.
3. World War, 1939–1945—India. I. Title.
D767.63.F39 1993   93-6005
954.03'59—DC20   CIP

CONTENTS

MAPS

PREFACE

Many people have lent a hand with this book. Victoria Mason managed it most capably in its manuscript stage, Lorrie LeJeune the same when it went to press. Susan Haldane made the maps. Suresht Bald, Graham Burnett, Nick Dirks, Joyce Evans, Paul Greenough, Bob Hack, Will Jones, Gita Mithal, Gyan Prakash, Robert Rosenstone, P. P. Sharma, Amita Shastri, Asiya Siddiqui, and one dear friend who prefers to remain anonymous, read parts of it and gave me their comments. My wife Mariette has read it all. I am particularly grateful to the Humanities and Social Sciences Division of the California Institute of Technology, and to its chairman David Grether, for the time off and financial assistance that enabled me to go to India more often than I otherwise could have; to Will Jones for compelling me so frequently to moderate my views; and to Nick Dirks for shaking me out of my unconsciously ethnocentric attitudes—and for introducing me to Colin Day, the director of the University of Michigan Press. The book might not exist at all had Colin not read and liked it, offered many suggestions for its improvement, encouraged me to get on with it, and reproached me delicately for the slowness with which I did.

Joyce Lebra has helped enormously over a period of years, with talk and correspondence, by reading chapters, and not least through what she has published about the Japanese and my subject. Hugh Toye has been very generous with information, much of it based on his personal recollections as a British intelligence officer in India-Burma-Malaya toward the end of the war. I am grateful to him for an extensive correspondence (from which, however, I may not quote), and for hours of conversation. Though we differ sharply on some matters of interpretation and even on some matters of fact, Hugh will perhaps find that his efforts to make me see things as he sees them have not been without effect. Philip Mason responded frankly and most usefully to an extended inquiry I sent him about the Red Fort trials. Leonard Gordon introduced me to Netaji Bhawan. There Sisir Bose and his wife Krishna have been repeatedly kind and helpful; several of the photographs in this book were supplied by them. Colonel Rashid Asuf Ali, Colonel Gurbaksh Singh Dhillon, and J. Athi Nahappan (Janaki Davar) each told me what they could remember about particular pieces of the army's story. But two persons have passed well beyond the provision of encouragement, information, and advice.

Mariette and I met Prem and Lakshmi when in 1964 we went to live in Kanpur (or Cawnpore, as the British called it), on the Ganges 250 miles southeast of Delhi. She had an obstetrical practice. He managed a mill. At the time we knew nothing about how India had obtained her independence beyond the seemingly obvious: no fighting, at least no fighting with the British, and no need for any. But in the course of two years' growing acquaintance, we learned enough about what these two had done before they married to see that there had been more to the independence process than the seemingly obvious—a whole other side to it, a body of men and women who had fought. And we came to realize that Prem Kumar Sahgal, and Lakshmi Swaminadhan (as she then was), had not simply participated. They had been principal figures.

Prem, we discovered, had been a captain with an Indian Army infantry battalion in Malaya when late in 1941, one calendar day after Pearl Harbor, the Japanese attacked. He fought the length of the peninsula, surrendered at Singapore along with everybody else, and after an interval joined the Indian National Army—the "forgotten army" of this book. Moving to Burma, he served as military secretary to the army's leader Subhas Chandra Bose. Subsequently he took command of a regiment in the field. Cornered on the Irrawaddy in late April of 1945 by a British brigade rushing for Rangoon, he became some months later the leading defendant in the first Red Fort, the trial that threw India into an uproar. Lakshmi was also in Malaya, practicing medicine, when the Japanese attacked. She, too, became one of Bose's chief lieutenants, the only woman who did. She raised a regiment of women, took it to Burma, was captured several months after Prem—

and when at last she was brought home, made it her business to let the Indian public know what this army and its leader had been all about. No less than Prem, Lakshmi speaks with great authority to the memory of the movement.

And so we listened. This book, begun much later and completed much later still, is the result. It owes a great deal to Mariette, for we have returned to Kanpur often, she knows Prem and Lakshmi as well as I do, and she has a feeling for things Indian that I cannot match. In form it is not Prem and Lakshmi's story at all. It is the story of Bose and his army, a story often involving persons and things—Quit India for example, or the beginnings of the Burmese independence movement—with which Prem and Lakshmi had nothing to do. But they were in the army from the beginning, and in the very front rank at the end. What they remember has enabled me to place them in it accurately and in considerable detail. And it is always interesting to discover how people of some significance in public life come to do what they do. So the chapters that follow begin with them, end with them, and often invite them to speak directly to the reader (I have put what they have to say, and what members of their families have to say, in italics). Their absence from long stretches of the narrative is, in any case, more apparent than real. In one sense they are always present. For it has been their willingness to talk to me that has made the writing possible. The book is for them.

Introduction

Halfway through the Second World War there appeared quite unexpectedly in Southeast Asia an army; an Indian army; an army with an adored and indomitable leader by training not a military man at all; an army that using Malaya as a base, Burma as a launching pad, and Japan as a helpmate, tried—even as the war in that part of the world wound towards its by then inevitable close—to throw the British out of India.

It did not succeed. Indeed, looked at from one point of view it may be said to have utterly failed. When on the 15th of August, 1945, Emperor Hirohito told his people that Japan could no longer go on with the war, not one inch of Indian soil was free. The army in question lay defeated, scattered, caged. Its leader had fled, and in three days would be dead. Britain's grip upon the subcontinent was outwardly as firm as it had ever been. And when, on another 15th of August two years later, India did become free, such were the auspices under which she received her independence, such was the manner in which she reached this happy state, that the army in question, though it had only recently been much in the public consciousness, was already beginning to fade. It is a process that continues to this day.

Particularly outside India, particularly in North America—though with us it is a matter less, perhaps, of forgetting than of preferring not to know. We have never wanted to be told that independence was something many Indians thought they could obtain only by fighting. We have never been anxious to admit it was reasonable of Indians to take up arms against the British. And we certainly have not wanted to admit that it was reasonable of them to do so in wartime, at a moment of great difficulty and peril for Britain elsewhere in the world. These admissions are painful. To make them is to concede the possibility that when the Second World War began, a sovereign and independent India was *not*, as we had supposed, safely in sight. That, in turn, obliges us to recast our image of India in its British period. It is an exercise we are not keen to undertake.

For we Americans are fond of British India, almost as fond as Englishmen can be. The more it recedes in time, the more we regard it with nostalgia, vicarious of course, piling our bookshelves with its recollections actual or fictional—plain and not so plain tales from the Raj. Somewhere Salman Rushdie, the novelist, calls these tales the twitchings of an amputated limb. By all the evidence they have more life to them than that. And among these tales there is one we particularly like, one we never tire of hearing: the last tale, the tale of how the Raj came to an end, the tale of Mountbatten and Nehru and "freedom at midnight."

What pleases us so much about this tale is its happy atmosphere, the good feeling that radiates from it, the absence of rancor—these, and the absence of bloodshed. There will be plenty of blood—Muslim, Sikh, Hindu blood—spilled at partition. There will be enormous carnage when Pakistan goes its separate way. But it will happen later, and be the result (a distinction most comforting to us) of violence offered by Indians to Indians, not violence offered by Indians to Englishmen or by Englishmen to Indians. At one minute past midnight on the 15th of August, 1947 (so goes the tale), India's independence arrived without any disfigurement of *that* sort. It was not fought for, patriots did not die upon the barricades to bring it about. Power was granted—or, to use the more familiar word, power was transferred.

Power transferred. It is the theme, the common thread, of twelve fat volumes you will find in every good university library and in the private study of any India buff who takes his avocation seriously and has a few hundred dollars to spare. These twelve volumes, running over three feet on the shelf, contain the more important parts of the correspondence, minutes, and other papers produced by Great Britain's terminal relationship with India. The twelfth ends, naturally, with the 15th of August, 1947. The first begins with the first day of 1942. That choice of year is somewhat arbitrary, however, for it is plain from the foreword that the editors would have been happy, if given time and print, to begin with 1940; with 1939 or 1937; even with 1919. And the arrangement within the twelve is not topical, though that had been the rule in previous official histories of Britain's external relations. It is chronological.

It is chronological because, the editors tell us,[1] in those years major questions of India policy were "in substance so closely interrelated" that they were considered by the persons who had to deal with them "not as several and separate problems but as parts of one common, underlying problem, . . . one overriding question." Government servants whose business was India had one thing on their minds. One thing preoccupied them and drew everything else in its train. And what was this poser in England's relations with India, this problem the resolution of which—as Prime Minister Harold Wilson explained when he announced the projected publication in the House of Commons on a June evening in 1967—these twelve volumes were supposed to document and trace? Not how to hang on in India. Not how to chuck everything and run. Something in between, something neither aggressive nor supine—a positive, constructive something that should be the capstone to England's imperial achievement on the subcontinent. What Wilson's predecessors worked steadily to effect, these twelve volumes assure us, was not the surrender of India but her conveyance, a planned and calculated conveyance, with all that this implies in prior purpose, studied management, and mutual consent. A measured delivery to Indians of the instruments of governance, in the manner of the father handing the car keys to his son. So there could be only one title for these twelve volumes, and it is there, in large gold letters upon the blue of each spine—*India: The Transfer of Power.*

Words and notion are pleasantly reassuring. At the same time, however, there is something odd about them. They do not altogether accord with what one expects of independence movements. Do they fit what actually occurred under the Raj?

No one, after all, applies the term transfer of power to the process by which Algeria obtained her freedom from the French. No one subsumes Ireland's experience under that rubric, or America's when we were thirteen colonies and wanted King George off our backs. Even the accumulated documents for Burma, right next door, have quite a different handle. On the spines of the Burma volumes (there are only two, as if the Burmese had been in a hurry) you read *Burma: The*

Struggle for Independence. This is not to distinguish the Burma volumes from the India set. That has already been accomplished by dressing the Burma volumes in black. The titles differ because the British look at Burma differently. Or at least Hugh Tinker, the editor of the two volumes, does.

Tinker does not see Burma as having obtained her freedom through management from above. "Power was surrendered," he writes[2]—the British gave in to pressure from below. Clear through the period of colonial rule there was restiveness and incipient violence among the Burmese, and toward the end an open willingness to fight. That is how Tinker sees it, that is how the Burmese see it: in Burma's independence myth the patriot with the gun stands heroic and alone at the center of the stage. But in the Indian equivalent he is half lost among actors of a different cast, and in the prevailing western version of India's independence story he does not appear at all, or is handed a distinctly disreputable role. For armed struggle, the twelve volumes of *The Transfer of Power* (and much else) announce, was quite unnecessary, freedom being safe and certain by another route. And if struggle was nevertheless attempted, in particular if struggle imperiled England at a moment when she fought the forces of darkness elsewhere in the world—why, then, struggle was worse than unnecessary, it was unconscionable, it was almost a criminal act. This, I think, is why Granada, the British television outfit, did what it did some years ago with the army and the leader I have mentioned. With the Indian National Army, and Subhas Chandra Bose.

❧

It was in the early 1980s. Granada was preparing to release *The Jewel in the Crown*, its long and superbly acted television version of the Raj Quartet, Paul Scott's four linked novels about British India in the middle 1940s. Now, the Raj Quartet is not a war story. Its principal scenes occur well away from any front. Scott's men—and women, the quartet is very much about European women in the twilight of the Raj—are not so much *in* the war as they are affected by it. But Scott does allow the fighting on India's eastern border to figure in his tale. There soldiers of the Indian Army, the *proper* Indian Army so to speak, battle not just Japanese but fellow Indians. And this has consequences, consequences essential to the plot.

"You know about the Jiffs?" Merrick asks Sarah from his hospital bed.

"Jiffs?"

"They're what we call Indian soldiers who were once prisoners of the Japanese in Burma and Malaya, chaps who turned coat and formed themselves into army formations to help the enemy. There were a lot of them in the attempt the Japanese made to invade India through Imphal."

"Yes, I've heard of them. Were there really a lot?"

"I'm afraid so. And officers like Teddie took it to heart. They couldn't believe Indian soldiers who'd eaten the King's salt and been proud to serve in the army generation after generation could be suborned like that, buy their way out of prison camp by turning coat, come armed hand in hand with the Japs to fight their own countrymen, fight the very officers who had trained them, cared for them and earned their respect. Well, you know. The regimental mystique. It goes deep. Teddie was always afraid of finding there were old Muzzy Guides among them. And of course that's what he did find."

It is because Teddie Bingham, Sarah Layton's brother-in-law, has been so confident he can bring the turncoats back to their true allegiance by finding them and calling them by name, that he is dead now—and Merrick talks to Sarah swathed in bandages up to the eyes. It is because Merrick subsequently pursues repatriated Jiffs with such cold-blooded intensity that we lose what little sympathy for him we have, judging him to be as twisted in mind and character as he is disfigured in the flesh. We do not meet the Indian National Army as such in Scott's pages, only stragglers and survivors. Bose does not appear at all. Both, however, make themselves felt. They are present in the wings. And so Granada put them into *The Jewel in the Crown*. But first it produced and televised a documentary film that would, it hoped, not only identify Bose and his army but lift them—and with them the entire militant wing of India's independence movement—out of a prolonged and quite undeserved obscurity.

Nehru and Gandhi do not require such treatment. Most of us are thoroughly familiar with these two. Indeed, the British have put them into their *Dictionary of National Biography* along with several maharajas, Rabindranath Tagore, and the third Aga Khan. We admire the elegance

and breeding of the Brahmin. We applaud the saintliness and shrewd-
ness of the Mahatma. We look to both for exemplary behavior under all
manner of hard knocks, and get it. We attend Sir Richard Atten-
borough's cinematic life of Gandhi expecting to be touched and
horrified by the police brutalities their nonresistance will provoke, and
are. But very few of us are able to handle Subhas Chandra Bose. We
cannot place him in Sir Richard's film because he isn't in it. (He isn't in
the *Dictionary* either, nor is George Washington, though the traitor
Benedict Arnold is.) And we know nothing, or next to nothing
(Granada rightly reasoned), about the Indian National Army. So, early
in *The War of the Springing Tiger*, as the documentary is called, Granada
gives us a shot of some INA men marching.

As they march, the commentator's voice tells us that this was a
considerable force, some forty thousand strong. Censored out of the
news when alive, painted like Trotsky out of the picture when dead
(Granada is explicit with the analogy), these men nevertheless existed.
And the fact of their existence, the commentator continues, sets at
defiance our normal, comfortable view of how India achieved independence. We have always believed that India became free by turning
the other cheek. We have always held that Indian independence was the
product of Gandhian moral force operating upon the English con-
science. In fact something else was at work, Granada tells us. These
marching soldiers were at work. *They* were not nonresisters, *they* did
not offer themselves up passively to lathi charges. They organized, took
up arms, and fought. And at this point the commentator turns, with old
film clips and stills, to the life of Subhas Chandra Bose their leader.

So far so good, I thought as I watched. (Granada's documentary
was not shown in the United States, but an English friend sent me a
video cassette.) Several INA veterans and Bose's own nephew had, I
knew, participated in the production. They had gone to England at
Granada's invitation, and been interviewed, photographed, and taped.
With their help Granada was going to give its viewers a fair, a true,
picture of Bose and his men. Surely it was.

But almost at once I smelled trouble. When Granada's commentator introduced Subhas Chandra, he did so with the remark that this was
India's *"Lost Führer."* What a curious thing to say. Why Lost Führer, why
not Lost Hero, to borrow the title of a biography of Bose just out from

a London publisher? Why pair Bose with a person whose name still evokes such feelings of anxiety, apprehension, and disgust?

It is true the men and women of the INA regularly referred to Subhas as *Netaji*. It is true the designation was devised during his wartime European stay, and that the stem *neta* translates leader. But does this make Bose another Hitler? Why did a television production that had so much to cover, and just fifty minutes to cover it in, trouble to explore at such length this connection: Bose spending a great deal of time (it is implied) in Germany, Bose accepting an engraved cigarette case from Hitler's hands, Bose taking a woman secretly to wife, a German-speaking woman, an Eva Braun no less? Were there no Garibaldis to compare him with, no Jomo Kenyattas or Mustapha Kemal Ataturks (Granada's researchers could easily have discovered that Bose had an explicit admiration for *him*) to measure him by? Was it really necessary to link him so relentlessly with Der Führer?

Yet if you took note of certain facts, and hitched to them a particular premise, the association was not so very surprising.

The facts were these. That India had fought on England's side against the Germans, and later against the Japanese, sending large armies considerable distances to do so. That some Indians had done just the contrary, had fought on Germany and Japan's side. That these contrary Indians had been beaten. And the premise was this. That in the war in question England had fought not for political or material advantage, not even simply to defend herself, but to save Europe and the rest of the world from the barbarism of Nazi Germany. And that by throwing down the challenge when others hesitated, and by persisting in that challenge though she stood alone and apparently defeated, she had made possible both the struggle and its eventual triumphant conclusion.

This was the premise, this was the proposition, that had served me (and probably most of Granada's viewers) perfectly adequately for years. Hitch it to the facts, however, and what did it do but force us to agree that any Indian who raised his hand against the British in the Second World War did more than condemn himself to lonely ineffectuality. He forfeited, by this one act, the sympathy and respect of civilized mankind. And if you protested that to allege this was beside the mark; that the said Indian, after all, was simply trying to obtain the freedom that is every people's due; more facts and assumptions moved front and center to beat your protest back. Wouldn't a world in which Germany and Japan were victorious have been hostile to democratic currents of every sort, and therefore to self-rule? Wasn't the world that *did* emerge a world by and large sympathetic to that process? Wasn't it true that India had became independent very shortly after the war was over? Wasn't it true that India had become independent not because the war had loosened Britain's grasp, but because the end of the war had permitted Britain to do what she had always planned to do?

It was in this frame of mind, I think, that the Granada people approached their subject. It was because these facts and this premise were so much a part of their intellectual baggage that they produced, in spite of best hopes and best intentions, a film that makes Bose out to be a sort of South Asian Hitler manqué, and consigns his men to the world's great fraternity of rogues, renegades, and fools.

⚬

There was a fuss, of course, angry voices raised in India's Parliament, a formal complaint lodged by India's high commissioner in London—a fuss I was reminded of when, a couple of years later, two colleagues at the place where I teach began an India-through-film course with that old RKO spectacular *Gunga Din*.

They began it tongue in cheek, of course. After *Gunga Din* the students received an almost uninterrupted dose of Satyajit Ray. But first we watched Cary Grant, Victor McClaglen, and Douglas Fairbanks, Jr. (distantly modeled, I suppose, on the trio in Kipling's *Soldiers Three*) swashbuckle their way into a remote recess of the subcontinent, surprise a band of Kali-worshippers planning the deliberate revival of *thuggee* ("kill! kill!" the high priest commands as the strangling cloths are handed around), and destroy them with a charge—a glorious charge sent home with the full weight of the grand old Indian Army. What fun, as much now as when I first saw it! Yet in February of 1946 a Punjabi soldier was brought to the Lahore Central Jail to begin a life sentence because of this film. "It is learnt," ran a news clipping of the day, "that Joginder Singh and some other Indians protested against the exhibition by the British military authorities of a film entitled 'Ganga Din' at a cinema hall in Greece. When no notice was taken of their protest, Joginder Singh visited the cinema hall and attempted to disturb the show."[3] He did more, he tried to smash the projector, and in the melee that followed shot and killed a British guard. What for me was (and still is) lightly entertaining, for Joginder Singh was simply not endurable.

For some Indians still living who remember how India got her freedom, and for many more who are too young to remember but have taken the trouble to find out, it is simply not endurable that independence should be so widely perceived, particularly outside India, as something scheduled, something certain to be granted, something that did not have to be fought for—and wasn't. It is unendurable because they know that there was, in fact, a fight. They know that there were Indians who thought Britain's professed intention grudging and the schedule sham, who believed that freedom is won not by waiting but by searching for it arms in hand, and who, finding themselves in circumstances that made such action possible, did just that.

What follows is their story, the story of the Indian National Army, of the men and women who composed it, and of its leader Subhas Chandra Bose. A story, moreover, with a point. Early in the Granada documentary there is a shot of the INA veterans I have mentioned, Prem and Lakshmi among them, getting off the plane at London's Heathrow airport on their way to be interviewed, filmed, and taped. As they disembark, the commentator remarks that these are people who fought a war of sorts for India's independence. A war of sorts. It is a small remark, almost a chance remark, dropped lightly from the commentator's tongue and likely to pass unnoticed. But there it is. And what is it supposed to convey? What kind of war is *a war of sorts*, what variety of lesser conflict, what burlesque?

It is the argument of this book that the war the Indian National Army undertook was more than a war of sorts. Though these men and women did not march to the Red Fort as they had boasted they would; though they did not ignite inside India the popular rising that was to have made that march possible; they fought. They fought at India's border, subordinate to but alongside the much more numerous Japanese. When after four desperate months their attempt to break into India failed, they withdrew to the Irrawaddy where, though the British pursued them in overwhelming numbers and it was clear the war was lost, they fought again. Of all this, India at the time knew very little. It perceived only that the British were victorious in Burma, and that the army of the Raj was the instrument of that victory. But when the war was over and the survivors of this other army came back, in handcuffs as it were, India discovered who they were and what they had attempted. India discovered, too, that there was nothing like them in the freedom movement. Curiosity gave way to surprise, surprise to passionate excitement. Public opinion hardened against any constitutional arrangement for India's future short of the complete and immediate independence these men and women had struggled to obtain. The British were weary, and anyway of two minds. Against the current of such an opinion they could not hope to stand unless they were sure of their army, the old Indian Army, and in the presence of this *other* army they discovered, one day, that they were not. So they let the current lift them. Let it lift them and carry them away.

The war the Indian National Army undertook was, then, more than a war of sorts. It was the real thing, a true war of independence, entitled as such wars are to our attention and respect. Whether it became the decisive agent of Britain's precipitate departure is a question that is perhaps best argued later in these pages, and will be. But something can be said with confidence at once. In India's pantheon there is space reserved, high, ample, and honorable space, for those men and women who, when certain accidents of time and place gave them the opportunity, seized it and went out to do battle for India's freedom.

CHAPTER I

PREM'S YOUTH

We are Punjabi Hindus, from a village near Jullundur called Mehatpur. I was born in Hoshiarpur, close by, on the 25th of March, 1917, but my official birth date is two months earlier, because when I was born my father remembered that March is the month of the school-leaving examination.

To sit for that examination you had to be fifteen. Achhru Ram (as Prem's father preferred to be called) calculated that unless he shifted the date of birth, his son would almost certainly lose a year. So the date was moved forward to January 25.

Prem grew up in Jullundur, a pleasant manufacturing and market town on the Grand Trunk Road seventy-five miles east of Lahore. His father practiced law. From the beginning Prem was the apple of the family's eye. *My grandparents,* a younger sister Raj explains, *were very, very keen to have a grandson. In fact my grandfather died praying that he would see a grandson, and Prem was born just nine months after he died. So Prem was really indulged. My grandmother especially used to dote on him.* And then, without a pause, *I am much younger, but as far as I can remember, even when he was a schoolboy he was being taken to Congress functions. People had all their hopes on the Congress. There was this agitation, public meetings and all. I think he was hardly ten when he would go out and address them.*

In fact Prem's memories go back to 1921, when he was four. *I remember going with my father and mother to meetings in Jullundur and its neighboring villages. I remember the Akalis, in their uniforms, with blue turbans and huge swords.* The Akali Dal (army of immortals) had been formed the year before to recover Sikh gurdwaras (shrines) from priests who over the years had come to regard those places as their private property.

Early in 1921 a large body of Akalis trying to reoccupy the gurdwara at Nankana, birthplace of Guru Nanak, the founder of the Sikh religion, had been set upon by hired thugs and massacred. The uproar that followed, which lasted several years and threw up a terrorist wing of the Akalis known as Babbar Akalis (immortal lions), ranged a large part of the Sikh community against the British, partly because the British were insensitive to the gurdwara issue and tended to side with the priests, partly because many of the Babbars had links with the Ghadr movement—and during the First World War that movement (*ghadr* means rebellion) had tried to raise the Punjab against British rule. But of course a small boy did not sort all this out.

The Babbars fascinated him. It was said they concealed gold sovereigns in a pouch in their throats like the pouch in which a monkey collects grain, and used these coins to bribe their way out of prison. It was said they fought single-handed against whole companies of police and soldiers, and defeated them; or if captured, broke free at their trials, striking the judges and escaping in spite of the guards.

I used to beg my father's clerks to take me to the court to see these supermen. But the clerks always put me off on one excuse or the other. One day I learned that a couple were actually hiding in our house. Nobody would tell me where they were, and I lay awake at night hoping I might hear some sound when they came out of hiding. But I never did.

It was the time of the boycott. *I remember huge bonfires of foreign goods, particularly foreign cloth. They were great fun for children. We used to go round from house to house collecting goods to be burned.* Then there were revolutionary songs to be learned and sung. His mother's favorite, in Punjabi, assured the patriot that though he might lose his life he could not be defeated. And one day Prem was witness to something much more serious, a little Amritsar Massacre almost.

Our house in Jullundur was near the main park, the Company Bagh. A big Congress meeting was to be held in this park and my father, who was the secretary of the city Congress Committee, was to be one of the speakers. We children were not allowed inside the park; we were playing just outside, at the junction of two roads. After the meeting had been going for a while we saw a regiment of British cavalry trotting along the road from the cantonment. I had never seen cavalry before. It was magnificent. The leading squadrons rode past the gate. Then the whole regiment turned and charged the meeting. It took me a little while to realize what was happening, and when I did I ran home crying. I found my mother with a number of her friends and masses of bandages and medicines. They had set up a sort of first aid post, and soon the casualties began to arrive. Some were brought on stretchers. Others walked. We children were kept busy fetching buckets of water from a hand pump outside. When the medicines were exhausted, someone said that ashes of darai, a handwoven silk that is a specialty of Jullundur, were very effective to stop bleeding and as an antiseptic. My mother went to her room, brought out a few of her beautiful darai saris, burned them, and used the ashes.

His father was not among the injured, but Prem never forgot the incident.

His next involvement in politics occurred at the end of 1929, when he was not quite thirteen. That year the annual national session of the Congress assembled at Lahore. Prem was taken to watch. An enormous camp blossomed on the banks of the Ravi. On the first day Jawaharlal Nehru, the new president of the Congress, passed on horseback through streets canopied with bunting, thousands of excited Congressmen about him, a small herd of elephants behind. And if the arrangements for the session were dramatic, the events that had led up to it were more dramatic still.

Since the arrival of the Simon Commission the year before, the temperature of Indian politics had risen noticeably. Appointed to consider what should follow the first small measure of self-government granted by the Government of India Act of 1919, the Simon Commission had advertised its emptiness and fatuity by failing to include a single Indian. It was received everywhere with black flags and *hartals* (work stoppages). The authorities responded with lathi charges. At Lucknow, Nehru was hit and bloodied; at Lahore the elderly, beloved Lala Lajpat Rai was struck across the chest, and subsequently died. Two months later the English police officer thought responsible for that outrage was shot dead. This was alleged to be the work of a certain Bhagat Singh, who some months later still entered the balcony of the Central Legislative Assembly at Delhi accompanied by a companion, scattered leaflets, and tossed a couple of bombs—not to kill, the leaflets explained, but to make the deaf hear. The two were arrested. Searches uncovered several clandestine bomb factories. Bhagat Singh became the central figure in what came to be known as the Lahore Conspiracy Case. In September 1929 one of the accused died after a long hunger strike. His funeral procession drew angry demonstrators by the thousands. Nor did the violence cease, for in December, shortly before the Congress assembled at Lahore, the Viceroy, Lord Irwin, narrowly escaped death when a bomb exploded under his special train.

This last affair confronted the Congress session with the question Bhagat Singh had been trying to raise, the question that regularly divided the independence movement. Should patriots pursue the path of nonviolence? Or should they turn to direct action? When Gandhi asked the delegates to express their relief at the Viceroy's escape, he was hotly opposed; and though his motion passed, it passed narrowly—for the moment at least, Congress party was set on a militant course. In 1928, at the annual session held that year in Calcutta, it had been agreed that if India was not granted dominion status by the end of 1929, civil disobedience, which Gandhi had brought the country to the brink of six years before, would begin in earnest. Now a resolution framed by Gandhi himself, and adopted, announced civil disobedience as soon as a time and an appropriate tactic could be determined. Dominion status would no longer suffice. India must have *purna swaraj*, complete independence, and she must have it at once.

It was therefore to a Lahore galvanized by a direct challenge to British rule that young Prem was brought. The consequence was predictable. *I was so impressed by what I saw that when we returned to Jullundur I jumped right into the student movement.* The dramatic steps that followed the Lahore session—the unfurling at midnight on the 31st of December, 1929, of the green, white, and saffron flag, the simultaneous reading all over India on January 26 (now Republic Day) of the declaration of independence, the mass resignations of Congress legislators, Gandhi's march to the sea to pick up salt—these figure in Prem's recollections only vaguely. As for the riots at Peshawar, at the height of which two platoons of Garhwali Rifles refused to fire, press censorship may have kept him from hearing about them at all. But the Lahore Conspiracy Case was another matter. Bhagat Singh had been the leader

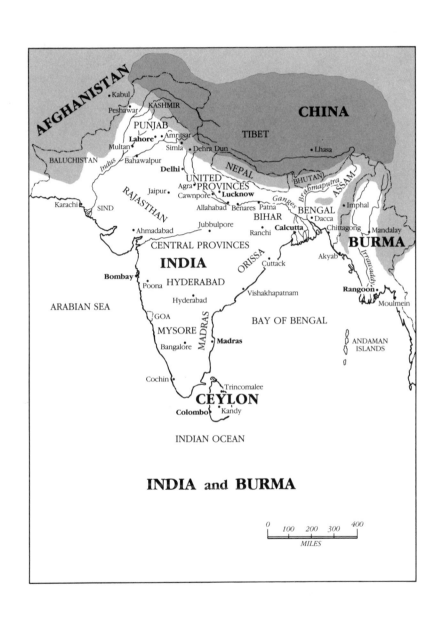

INDIA and BURMA

of the youth movement in the Punjab. The little act of bravado on the balcony of the Legislative Assembly, the arrests on charges of plotting violence against the British, gave terrorism an appeal it had not had before. In many parts of India Bhagat Singh was as well known as the Mahatma himself. Schoolboys longed to imitate him. Prem was no exception.

> *I was friendly with boys who were much older than I, and some of them were involved. I don't think they took me seriously. I was too young. But they used to talk to me about what they were doing. The idea was to organize revolutionaries all over India, men who were prepared to fight the British one life for one life. You shot a British officer and then gave yourself up, because if you gave yourself up you would be the only accused.*

But sometimes a man got caught, and talked, and then the police obtained evidence against others. So it was best

> *to meet these people individually. I never went to their headquarters. I didn't even know where it was. I used to go to their houses, and at somebody's house I went through the test of putting your elbow over a burning candle and holding it there until the flesh burned. If you jerked your hand or sighed or anything, you were out. You see, the Indian police are well known for torturing people. In the droppings of a horse there is a boring insect. The police put it in your navel and tie a bandage over it and fasten your hands behind your back. The little thing starts boring into you with the most excruciating pain. There's nothing you can do, just roll and roll on the ground.*

Prem passed the candle test. He was not, however, entrusted with the group's secrets. *I used to talk to them about what they were doing. I used to hear of their mishaps—this thing had blown up, and the like. But I never saw a bomb made.* It did not prevent the police from taking notice.

In a field near his school there was a hut. Often Prem and his friends hung out there. The hut was completely open, there was nothing in it, but the police knew Prem by now; they knew whom he was associating with; they put it under observation. They did more. One day they picked Prem and his friends up, took them a few miles out of Jullundur, beat them, and left them to walk back. Prem did not tell his father. From a friend in the police, however, Achhru Ram learned that there was a file on his son. So he spoke to him. "*Look*," Prem said, "*I'm not involved in anything. But I know some of the people who are.*" This did not wholly reassure Achhru Ram. He knew the police might fabricate a case against the boy; it was something they did all the time. So it was with relief that he moved his family to Lahore. There he could practice regularly before the High Court.

Lahore was then caught up in the climax of the conspiracy case. Appeals to the Viceroy had failed to stay the sentence passed upon Bhagat Singh. Early one morning a friend of Prem's family whose bungalow adjoined the Central Jail heard commotion and shouting, guessed that Bhagat Singh and his companions were being hanged, and gave the alarm. Young Congress party members surprised a police van leaving the jail compound, followed it into the country, saw several bodies taken out and burned, and brought the remains back. Lahore awoke. A procession miles long carried the remains to the banks of the Ravi. Tension gripped the city, tension so acute that for twenty-four hours the police kept deliberately out of sight.

This was in March 1931. Then, gradually, Prem lost interest in politics. Perhaps this was because he left the Central Model High School and entered Government College, where studies were taken seriously and political activity was discouraged. Perhaps it was because all across India the fierce excitement and high hopes of a spring and summer of civil disobedience had been replaced, as 1930 gave way to 1931, by uncertainty.

Released from the prison term that followed close on his march to the sea, Gandhi had gone to Delhi. There he closeted himself with Lord Irwin, and at the end of a series of talks agreed to discontinue civil disobedience if the government would release all political prisoners and make certain other concessions. These did not include the abolition of the salt monopoly. And if Tories were, in Churchill's unfortunate phrase, nauseated by the spectacle of this curious fellow "striding half-naked up the steps of the viceregal palace . . . to parley on equal terms with the representative of the King-Emperor,"[1] Nehru was utterly disconcerted by his acceptance of a clause expressly reserving to Britain the defense and external relations of the subcontinent. How could this be consonant with *purna swaraj*? A week after Bhagat Singh and his companions died, a sullen and divided Congress meeting in annual session at Karachi reluctantly ratified the Delhi Pact. By the end of 1931 Gandhi had changed course again and once more threatened civil disobedience. But Irwin was gone, and this time the government struck so swiftly, arresting every Congressman of consequence, seizing funds and proscribing sympathetic organizations, that the second round of civil disobedience never got started. For two years Congress barely functioned. In these circumstances a Government College student would have been hard pressed to violate his undertaking not to dabble in politics even had he wanted to. And Prem did not want to. He was turning in another direction. He had decided to enter the army.

ᴥ

The army he had in mind was the Indian Army. And here a peculiar thing cries out for notice. Should Prem enter the Indian Army, it would be regarded as a step, a perceptible step, in the Indianization of that body. But how could this be? How could an Indian army possibly stand in need of *Indianization*?

The answer, of course, was that the Indian Army was not Indian in the way the Japanese Army was Japanese or the German Army German. It was a British creation. Right through the eighteenth century it had been one among many armies on the Indian subcontinent, the military arm of Britain-in-India, maneuvering on the chessboard of Indian politics (the phrase is Philip Mason's) just as the French did, just as Mysore, the Mahratta confederacy, and the Nawabs of Bengal and the Carnatic did. In the course of time, however, Britain became the paramount power. Tentatively at the beginning of the nineteenth century, irreversibly soon after, she made herself master of the subcontinent; until at last her army became the sole Indian army (for the armed forces of the surviving princely states were little more than ornamental), *the* Indian Army, ready and able to impose its will from Karachi to Chittagong, from Kashmir to Cape Comorin. But still Britain's instrument. Indian only in what it guarded, and where it served and fought.

Indian, too, in the men who composed it. Europeans had early discovered that sepoys (native Indian troops) drilled and handled in the European manner were almost as effective as their own soldiers, and much more formidable than the men most Indian princes led. It was not arms that made them so. It was training; training, and the political stability of their employer, which meant regular service and pay. Small bodies of sepoys regularly defeated princely armies that were many times larger, far more magnificent, just as well armed, and in the skill and prowess of their horsemen absolutely without equal. It was the sepoy who gave Britain the mastery of the subcontinent.

This sepoy was led by men of his own language and community. Though his overall direction lay with the British, his day-to-day management rested with Indian officers roughly equivalent to the lieutenants, captains, and majors of European battalions. The young subaltern fresh from Ireland, Scotland, or England, the King's commissioned officer (KCO) as he would one day be designated, learned his trade from these older and more experienced Viceroy's commissioned officers (VCOs), and came to know his men through them. The sepoy for his part made VCOs his model, a thing he could not possibly do with Europeans. Here, in this layer of jemadars, subadars, and subadar-majors interposed between foreign officers and native other ranks, lay a special feature of the Indian Army.

There was another. The commitment of KCO, VCO, and sepoy was to the unit. India as a nation did not exist. The King-Emperor, so very far away, meant little to the subadar and nothing to the sepoy. So the unit took the nation and the King-Emperor's place. A man's highest obligation was to his regiment. The chief object of his veneration were the regimental colors, carried on parade or in battle not for prince or government but for the regiment itself. As the army was in body the sum of its regiments, so was it in spirit the sum of its regimental colors. The Indian Army, to borrow again from Philip Mason, was "a matter of honour."[2]

European armies had once been like this too. The Hessians who fought for the British at Saratoga, the very British themselves, could not have been made to face the overwhelming American rabble-in-arms on the pine slopes north of Albany that day, had they not been stiffened by just such regimental loyalty and pride. But that had been in the eighteenth century. With the French Revolution the armies of continental Europe began to change. In the nineteenth century, particularly when war swelled their numbers with reservists and volunteers, it was for hearth and country that men served, and what bound them to duty and perhaps to death was less often the regiment and its colors than the nation and its flag. In Britain, however, partly because year after year her wars remained glorious excursions in distant places, this substitution was much slower in arriving. Even in the First World War, Robert Graves tells us, it was regimental pride, not patriotism or religion, that kept the Royal Welch with whom he served from breaking. And in India things went on exactly as before—with one shocking interruption.

In 1857 occurred the Sepoy Rebellion, or what in Britain is still sometimes called "The Mutiny." Confident that regimental loyalty, discipline, and pay would always keep Indians steady, the British had paid less and less attention to the caste differences among their men. At the same time they had begun to move openly toward a refashioning of Indian society along western lines. Then came the business of the Enfield rifle, introduced to replace the smooth-bore Brown Bess of a century's use. To load it you first tore the paper cartridge, which held powder and bullet, open with your teeth. The cartridge was greased to keep the contents dry. Rumor had it that the grease used was mixed cow and pig fat. Much of it probably was. The cow is sacred to the Hindu. No Muslim can touch pork. A mixture more offensive to both could hardly have been invented—and now an army consisting almost entirely of Hindus and Muslims was asked to put its lips to the suspicious substance every time it prepared to fire.

For many it was too much. In the Bengal Army, largest of the three components of the Indian Army, the men rose cantonment by cantonment all the way from Meerut to Patna. Delhi fell. Cawnpore, as Kanpur was then called, fell. At Lucknow the rebels took everything except the Residency. In hundreds of places the British paid with their lives for their indifference and their confidence. But the rebellion, sudden and ferocious in its onset, was with the help of sepoys from unaffected parts of India slowly and pitilessly suppressed. And when this was done, things went back to the old basis. It seems odd, but what was the alternative?

There was no thought of replacing the Indian Army with an army of Englishmen. There was no thought of holding India with native soldiers from other colonies, black sepoys from Africa perhaps (as the

French in their empire were soon to do), or of drastically increasing the British complement in Indian battalions. The shadow of the 1857 uprising remained. But the British took a matter-of-fact view of what had occurred. The Bengal sepoy had proved unreliable. Very well, he would be replaced with men who had shown they were trustworthy. The Sikhs, for example, had given the Raj their unwavering support right through that dreadful summer of insurrection and massacre, and by keeping the Punjab quiet had made the recovery of Delhi possible. At the same time they had demonstrated, in open and manly warfare with the British only ten years before, that they were tenacious and aggressive. Let others with equally admirable qualities be added.

Add the proud Pathan, the stolid Jat, the cheerful and bloodthirsty Gurkha. (Characterizations with some basis in fact eventually shaped recruits in the manner of a self-fulfilling prophecy.) It had been a mistake to mix communities; or, as in the case of the Bengal Army, to enlist men so proud of their position, so conscious of their caste. Simpler village yeomen made better and more faithful soldiers, provided always that they were left undisturbed in their religion, and in their eating and other social habits. The communities from which these men came, possessing fewer avenues for advancement, could be depended upon for a steady flow of recruits. From these "martial races," as they were termed, the Indian Army of the future should be raised.

Many of these communities were north Indian. And as the north had the only frontier on which fighting regularly took place, and where real soldiering was possible, the army's center of gravity inevitably shifted in that direction. The southern component, recruited from what many British came to believe were "effeminate races," withered away. In 1857 there had been fifty-two Madras infantry battalions in the Indian Army. In 1914 twenty-six remained, in 1939 none. To state the matter thus is to acknowledge that it was by its battalions that the army was measured. It moved and fought by battalions—you did not encounter a regiment on the march, or read later that a certain regiment *qua* regiment had been in action against Afghans at the Khyber Pass or Turkish levies barring the road to Kut. In a purely operational sense a regiment existed only to recruit and train battalions. Thereafter the battalions went their separate ways. But it was the regiment that carried the colors. It was the regiment that bore the proud name. It was the regiment that attracted the indispensable loyalty of officers and men.

The battalions in a given regiment—the 5th Mahratta, the 8th Punjab, the 12th Frontier Force—contained men whose common origins were often reflected in the regiment's name (though the designation could be out of date, as with the 10th Baluch which by Prem's time no longer recruited Baluchis). One might be a "class regiment," meaning that it drew entirely from one community or "class." In another, a "class company regiment," the communities would vary from company to company. But within a company no mixing occurred. If there were Dogras in A Company and Punjabi Muslims in B Company, there were never any of the one in the other. And this was equally so among the VCOs: where the men were Garhwali the jemadars and subadars were Garhwali, where Jat they were Jat. When a regimental party went looking for replacements, a VCO of the appropriate class or subclass led it, calling first at his own birthplace, the noncommissioned officers and other ranks spreading out to theirs; talking to sons, brothers, and cousins of men already enlisted; sometimes urging, often appraising and choosing, since years of association had taught the peasants that service in the regiment was an honorable career, or at least a refuge for a man who had lost his land or been falsely accused by the powerful in his locality. Driven, then, by tradition, ambition, or necessity, more recruits came forward than the army could take. Indeed, selectivity in the presence of great numbers gradually narrowed the definition of what constituted an acceptable soldier, so that the roster of the martial classes and subclasses grew steadily shorter, the pool from which the army drew smaller, the Indian Army less representative of India than ever.

Philip Mason, the historian of that army, is probably right when he argues that in all this the British did not pursue, even unconsciously, a policy of divide and rule. Better to call it a policy of *separate* and rule. For what the British were doing was to cut the Indian Army off from ordinary Indians, not in the usual sense that standing armies are hidden away from the rest of us in barracks or training camps, but in the extraordinary sense that there were no personal links between it and them. The communities deemed nonmartial made up perhaps nine-tenths of the Indian population. To nine Indians out of ten the British declared, "no son of yours shall be an officer, no son of yours shall be a jawan"—the term, which means heroic young man, was slowly taking the place of sepoy—"no son shall even dream of such." And to the tenth they said, "send your son to serve the regiment, the old regiment; it shall be father and mother to him as it was to you." This was segregation, total and complete.

Without an army, without access to one, without the faintest trace of a tradition of citizens in arms, how could India ever rise and throw Britain out? This was the British answer to the frightening business of 1857 in its political dimension, if, indeed, the rebellion had been political at all, which it was convenient to doubt. As for the "mutiny" aspect, that would be managed by making the Indian Army even more "a matter of honour." Punjabi Muslims, Gurkhas, Pathans, Dogras were politically backward to begin with. Their Indian officers rose from their own ranks. Their British officers had no use for "Indian" politics, never talked it—and made sure that any subadar, havildar, or jawan who did talk it was expelled.

They took other measures too. They were careful now to observe, with separate kitchens and the rest, the caste and religious practices of their men. They cultivated a genuine fraternity with their jawans, the fraternity of the playing field, rank signifying nothing when men play field hockey together. They became knowledgeable and ardent partisans of the communities from which their regiments were raised. In return they expected loyalty and fidelity. And they very largely got it, so far as anyone looking back at the marvelous anachronism of the pre-1914 Indian Army can tell. Over all those sixty years nothing like a second 1857 ever threatened.

✦

In 1914, however, came the First World War. It transformed the Indian Army from a small professional force of 150,000 engaged in police actions and brisk punitive campaigns across India's northwest frontier and elsewhere from Khartoum to Peking, into an army almost four times the size, committed months at a time to siege and trench warfare in Mesopotamia, Egypt, Gallipoli, and distant France.

Three-quarters of a million Indians served at one time or another during these four years—and the strain on the recruiting system was almost beyond bearing. The roster of the martial classes lengthened, it is true, then lengthened again. But it was impossible to maintain the class character of battalions that passed through the meat grinder of this dreadful war. The machinery, as Mason puts it, simply could not spit out a fresh Rajput for every casualty in a Rajput company, a Dogra for every Dogra. After the war the army shrank to its former, then to less than its former, size. The wartime practice of raising units from among the Bengalis and the Bhils, the Tamils, the Mahars, and the Mazbhi Sikhs, ceased. Class regiments and class company regiments linked to a limited number of communities became again the rule. It was, indeed, in the years between the wars that the identification of the Indian Army with particular martial classes assumed the authority of a received truth. But thoughtful men knew this arrangement could not survive the breaking out of another war like the last. And a few saw that a warrior elite led by foreigners was incompatible with what was happening in the rest of Indian life.

In 1886, at the annual session of the Congress (which in those days did not talk independence and was sometimes led by Englishmen), Britain had been reproached "for degrading our natures, for systematically crushing out of us all martial spirit, for converting a race of soldiers and heroes into a timid flock of quill-driving sheep."[3] The reproach, though passionate, had been delivered by an Indian educated in England who, like many of his sort, was a loyal subject of the Raj, and who had simultaneously suggested that in the army volunteers replace long-service professionals. They would, he said, be as effective against the Russians, and much cheaper. By 1914, however, the Indian middle classes were a good deal larger and decidedly less loyal. They wanted self-government. That implied an army not for imperial use but for India's defense, an army, moreover, truly Indian in composition. On the civil side Indians had been filling judicial and administrative posts for years. Surely it was time to Indianize the officer corps as well.

So in 1917, the year Britain at last made the eventual realization of dominion status its official policy for the subcontinent, it was announced that at the Royal Military College at Sandhurst ten places each year would be reserved for Indian candidates. Those who passed out and became King's commissioned officers were not, however, posted like ordinary KCOs. After the usual first year with a British battalion, they went to one of just eight Indian Army battalions designated for Indianization. And to these eight no new British officers were assigned. Otherwise a British subaltern might someday find himself serving under a native—a word that could still be heard, though officially out of use.

Later the Sandhurst quota was raised from ten to twenty, the eight battalions to fifteen. Arrangements were made to train Indian officers for the artillery and other specialized services. More important, it was recognized that sending Indians halfway around the world to compete with English boys fresh from public school, and very much on their own turf, led to frequent failure or withdrawal—which discouraged others who might follow. No one thought to ask whether a public school preparation was really necessary. (In British officer training it was as if the war, and French and American experience, had never happened.) Let the public school ethos be reproduced on Indian soil. So arrangements were made. A military academy was opened at the hill station of Dehra Dun. The first cadets entered with the monsoon in 1932. Two and a half years later they emerged with their commissions. Indianization was no longer a promise or a token, it was beginning to take place.

Yet it did not amount to much. Forty, fifty, sixty Indian commissioned officers (as they were called) was a great improvement over ten or twenty. But each year twice that number of new KCOs arrived from England, so that when the Second World War broke out the proportion of Indian to British officers was still only one to ten. After his apprentice year with a British battalion, the new ICO was assigned to one of the fifteen Indianizing battalions, which together made up only one-eighth of the Indian Army. There he took a subadar's place, at a level of command distinctly lower than that of his British equivalent, and was paid less—on the grounds that he was at home while the Englishman, Scotsman, or Irishman was not.

What really mattered, however, was what his arrival did to the army of which he was now a full (if not fully equal) part. It did little. That army continued to draw its recruits from the same narrow circle of martial communities. Even at Dehra Dun, half the seats were reserved for serving soldiers and the sons of serving soldiers, only half filled by open competitive examination. An inscription in bold letters upon the academy's walls instructed the candidate that as an officer he must put his own comfort and safety behind the comfort and safety of his men, and both behind the honor and welfare of his country, "always and every time." But neither the inscription nor the training told him what his country was. In the mess he might drink the King-Emperor's health night after night and be no nearer an answer. The mess, indeed, taught him another loyalty altogether. After the last war the testimonials to India's casualties (there were, of course, no village memorials of the sort that sprang up all over Europe) had usually invoked the regiment. It was the regiment the dead had died for, it being difficult to think of anything else for which they could have given their lives. In the mess it was the same. Whatever they said they drank to, British and Indian officers in fact drank to the regiment. It was their only common ground.

This was what Prem was about to join. Viewed politically and socially, the Indian Army in the 1930s was as much an anachronism as it had been in 1914. Indianization at the pace it was occurring would not alter that soon. Gandhi would have put the army to nation building and cleaning latrines. Nehru would have abolished it altogether. The army paid attention to neither. What Gandhi and Nehru thought and did was politics, and politics, like women, was not the subject of conversation in the mess. C Company's performance on the rifle range, the prospects for the regimental hockey team, the likelihood of the battalion seeing a little action in Waziristan—these were the things that occupied the Indian Army in peacetime. These were the things that would occupy Prem too.

That Prem chose an army career at all is not easily explained. In spite of the old saying that the Punjab is India's spear, sword, and shield, the military was an unlikely occupation for a person of his background. No one in his family had ever pursued it. Why, then, did he?

Subhashini, Prem's eldest daughter, believes her father was disgusted by the direction Congress party was taking, and particularly by Gandhi's failure (for lack of trying) to save Bhagat Singh's life. Perhaps this turned him from civil life. On the positive side there was the enthusiasm of Colonel Garrett, the Principal of Government College, who was keen for Dehra Dun and had started a special army class. It may be, too, that to a boy as confident and spirited as Prem the very novelty of a military career was appealing—that, and the sheer improbability of the thing. *My father was certain that with my background and the police records against me, I would never get in. "All right," he said, "if you want to try, try."* Prem's sister Raj remembers that Achhru Ram, who hoped Prem would follow him into the law, planned a party to be held when his son was *not* selected. But Colonel Garrett prepared his candidates well. Prem sat for the examination and passed with high marks. When the police made inquiries about him, as they were bound to do, they made them in Lahore. All the records were in Jullundur. So Prem got a favorable report, and in August 1936 went up to Dehra Dun.

The terms ran from late August to Christmas, and from February to early June. During the first two the cadets did a great deal of English and mathematics. Prem discovered that he was as well prepared as any of the examination entrants, and a good deal better prepared than the men who had come up from the ranks by way of Kitchener College, or those who were intended for the States Forces (the little armies of the princely states). Perhaps for this reason, what he chiefly remembers is not the curriculum—in the third and fourth terms they were introduced to conventional warfare, in the fifth to the mountain warfare peculiar to the Northwest Frontier—but the sports. The cadets rode. They played hockey, tennis, soccer, cricket. Prem boxed and ran cross-country for his company. In his last term the company did so well that it won the Viceroy's banner, the King's banner, *and practically all the cups there were.*

Prem also learned to drink. *Once a year the Viceroy or the Commander-in-Chief paid us a visit. My final term the Viceroy came, and we gave a big parade. My father and mother were there. Then they went away. The next day there was to be a cricket match. Four of us decided to have lunch together. But first we had a party. We drank sixty-four bottles of Allsop's beer. Empty bottles were lined up all along the sides of our canteen.* One of the four was Henry Ranganadhan, already a pilot in the Indian Air Force, later killed flying in formation when the plane next to him chewed into his tail. Another was Henry's brother Mark, who was going into the artillery.

He came from an Anglicized family, a Christian family, which was why his name was Mark. He had one sister. She married an English officer. That upset Mark terribly, he didn't like the idea of his sister marrying a foreigner. Overnight he became rabidly anti-British. This was during the war, after he had been commissioned, and the result was, poor chap, he was court-martialed and thrown out. Then he became a planter in Malaya. It didn't work out. Eventually he went to England—that's the funny part of it, he went and settled down in England, and got a small job in a hospital. He died there.

The third was Kazim Hussain, who went into the Hyderabad State Forces. One day he quarreled with a brother officer,

got very angry, went home, picked up a shotgun, and shot the chap dead. He was put in prison, escaped, and has been missing ever since. Most people think he went away to Pakistan. Out of the four of us, one was killed in an accident, one died in England, one is missing, and I ended up in Kanpur. So [with a laugh] *all four of us came to a bad end.*

But not yet.

During the vacations, five weeks in winter, ten during the hot weather, Prem's fellow cadets often went home with him, a practice his family encouraged. *Even if their families were living in town,* his sister Raj remembers, *they preferred to be with us* because the household was so warm, so lively. Achhru Ram and Prem's mother Ratan Devi had a wide circle of acquaintances. People of all sorts came and went, took their meals with the family, made conversation. It was an education to be around them.

An education, among other things, in tolerance. Many were Sikhs or Christians. *The atmosphere in the house,* says Prem, *was such that we hardly ever felt ourselves different from friends who were not Hindus.* But for the seven children—three boys, four girls, Prem third in line and oldest of the boys—perhaps their best friends were their parents. Achhru Ram was much occupied with his law practice before the High Court, from which he was beginning to derive a considerable income. *He did not spend much time with us. But whenever we were together, we were more like friends than children.* "You should be my best friends," he used to say, "and I yours." So we were always very free with him.

And he was generous with them. *I think Prem was one of the few students who had a car,* continues Raj. *Even when he was in college he had one, a little Austin. And Prem himself was always very large-hearted.* Sometimes cadets visiting the house found themselves short in the purse. With perfect confidence in Achhru Ram, Prem knew at once what they should do. *When these friends were scared to ask their own parents for money, they signed their bills in his name—and my father paid. Of course Prem had an allowance too,* she adds. It did not cease when he completed his two and a half years at the academy and became a second lieutenant.

He was commissioned on the 1st of February, 1939, and went for his first attachment to the Argyll and Sutherland Highlanders, at Secunderabad just outside Hyderabad. Secunderabad was a lovely cantonment. British units, Indian units, and units of the Nizam's army lived side by side with much mutual hospitality. Prem's months there taught him to be thoroughly at ease with British officers. This was partly a matter of knowing how to drink. But Prem did more than raise a glass with these men, he rode with them, played polo with them—for he could ride. When for lack of advanced math he had failed to qualify for the gunners' wing at Dehra Dun, he might have opted for the cavalry, had not cavalry life been too expensive even for a man with his allowance. An infantry officer, however, could keep horses.

> *We used to get from the cavalry regiments what we called seven-eighters, meaning seven rupees eight annas. The cavalry regiment gave you the horse. You paid seven and eight as insurance, in case you damaged it. I took two of these horses, paid fifteen rupees a month for them, and engaged two syces [grooms]. That cost me forty rupees. Another twenty-five or so went for equipment and extras. So for under a hundred rupees a month I could play polo.*

What with this, his general assurance, and (though he says nothing about it) his natural talent for command, *I was all right. I got on pretty well in the regiment. In fact, when the Argylls were posted to Singapore they wanted to take me with them. But the Government of India wouldn't allow.* Newly commissioned Indian Army officers spent their year's attachment in India, and Prem's was only half over. He remained at Secunderabad with the West Yorks. At the end of the year, after a month's leave with his family at Lahore, he was posted to the 5th Battalion of the 10th Baluch Regiment (the 5/10th Baluch), at Peshawar on the Northwest Frontier.

The 10th Baluch, five active battalions plus a training battalion, was a class company regiment recruiting (in the words of the Indian Army List) "Punjabi Musalmans, Pathans, and Dogra Brahmins." It prided itself on a long association with Sind Province, a skill at Northwest Frontier operations derived from close and continuous experience, and the distinction of having won the first Victoria Cross awarded to an Indian (it went posthumously to a jawan who in 1914 showed extreme bravery in Flanders). The 5th was one of fifteen battalions designated for Indianization. By the time Prem joined, it had very few English officers left.

Indianization did not, however, affect regimental style, which right up to the outbreak of the war remained what it had always been. At Secunderabad Prem had kept several horses. His Peshawar stable was more modest—polo was not a 5th Battalion sport. But he rode. *Our Colonel was very keen on hunting. There were lots of foxes, and every Thursday and Sunday we went fox hunting. The master of the hunt was a lady. I think she was a civil officer's wife. She was a remarkable horsewoman, she used to ride sidesaddle.* But the heart of regimental life was the mess. Breakfast was a working meal, you went in when you liked. So was lunch. Supper nights you put on a dinner jacket (to the Anglicized families of Lahore the dinner jacket was a perfectly familiar article) and went in between such and such hours. But on mess nights you went in a group. The mess kit consisted of tight trousers, called overalls, worn over Wellington boots. In the Baluch Regiment the overalls were cherry colored (*we were known as the cherry bottoms*), and the jackets were rifle green, worn with a waistcoat, stiff-fronted shirt, and side cap. Each officer was served by a bearer he hired and paid himself. When the mess sat down to dinner, behind each chair stood a bearer in a long white coat, sash, and turban. It was magnificent. And it was cheap. A bearer cost twenty-five rupees a month (not quite two pounds sterling, or eight dollars). A bottle of scotch cost ten.

The battalion took its turn going on column into the hills. Though under orders to travel light, it made a point of being able to produce, when needed, an extra section of machine guns or the apparatus for making soda water. At one point Prem was detached to command the Jamrud Fort, overlooking the Khyber Pass—a curious structure *shaped like a battleship. The officers' quarters were the bridge, very high, with windows all around. When the wind blew, it swayed.* Later the battalion moved to a place on the Afghan border where defenses were being built. Rumor had it there were Germans on the other side, helping the Afghans. *It was summer, very hot, and I remember there was not a blade of grass.* In fact it was the summer of 1940. France had fallen. The war was coming closer.

In July the battalion returned to Peshawar. The army was expanding again. Regiments were adding battalions. Indianization was at last general, and battalions contained once more a full complement of VCOs. The 2nd Battalion was short of officers, and as Prem knew it was going overseas, he volunteered—he thought the 5th might be stuck on the Northwest Frontier. Overseas, it was understood, meant the Middle East and desert war against the Italians. Prem was given leave to visit his family before reporting.

I remember so well, his sister Raj says, *the day he came home.* Prem was afraid to break the news, but a letter with his orders came to the house, and somehow Achhru Ram saw it. *After reading that letter,* Raj remembers, *my father must have sat in his office for some time, thinking how to tell my mother. When he came out he was so upset! You could see from his face that something serious had happened. So he told us, and my mother was absolutely stunned.* Prem was to leave the next day. His married sisters were informed. *From outstation they came immediately. We all went to see him off. Some wanted to go with garlands,* but Prem did not want garlands. After he had left Raj packed his things away, she knew the sight of them distressed her mother so.

Prem spent his last night with the 5th drinking champagne with G. G. Bewoor, two years his senior and much later to be Chief of the Army Staff. Next morning, nursing a headache and absentmindedly without his revolver, he set off for the 2nd Battalion at Bareilly. A week later the battalion was aboard the passenger ship *Amara.* Prem was a full lieutenant now, and had a single-berth cabin to himself. Officially the 2/10th was not to be told its destination until it was some days at sea, but everyone knew what it was—and it was not Suez. On the 11th of November, 1940, the *Amara* docked at Singapore.

CHAPTER 2

LAKSHMI'S YOUTH

I was born in Madras on the 24th of October, 1914. My father was one of the leading criminal lawyers of Madras. I think I have never met a man of my father's caliber and intelligence and understanding. He was in no way limited by his background or his upbringing; he was an absolutely clear-thinking, independent person. He was born into a very poor family in Kerala, a Brahmin family but very, very poor. He was so poor he used to support himself and his younger brother by tutoring boys of a class higher than himself, because he was very intelligent, and his learning was far above the class of which he was.

The poverty was relative. Subharama Swaminadhan's forebears had settled in a village near Palghat, some fifty miles northeast of Cochin, and become village headmen. Swaminadhan's father managed a large estate. Local Nair landholders came to him for help and advice. Among them was a certain Govinda Menon. Menon and his wife took a fancy to young Swaminadhan. They encouraged him to learn English. Then Swaminadhan's father died suddenly, and his mother too, leaving him to support a grandmother, a younger brother, and two sisters. Menon and his wife drew closer to the boy.

They urged him to enter the provincial college at Calicut. It was there he did the tutoring Lakshmi mentions, in the homes of rich Gujaratis, because his scholarship barely met his fees. When his classmates graduated and went off to Madras, he followed with a few annas in his pocket, sat for the entrance examinations at two colleges, topped the list at both, and entered one—again on a scholarship, which obliged him to tutor on the side. Physics was his interest. For a time he worked towards a science degree. But his family position (the brother to educate and one sister still to marry) dictated a more prudent choice of career, so he turned to the law, entered the Madras Law College, and just before the turn of the century won a Gilchrist Scholarship for higher studies at the University of Edinburgh.

The prospect of a voyage across the black water (as pious Hindus held the ocean to be) outraged his relations and friends as it had outraged Gandhi's a decade before. Swaminadhan paid no attention, took passage, and on arrival arranged to read science and law simultaneously: science at Edinburgh, law at Gray's Inn in London. Academically this was perfectly possible. Swaminadhan's eldest son Govind, himself a product of Oxford and the Inner Temple, assured me once that the bar exams *even in my time were a mere formality for one with my father's education.* There is no reason why so enterprising a young man should not have solved the physical problem of double attendance, as Govind believes he did, by periodically working his way down from Edinburgh on a coaster, eating the required dinners while she lay at a London dock, then working his way back up again. In any case it is recorded at Gray's Inn that he was called to the bar in June 1899. It is equally certain that he received Edinburgh's L.L.B. in 1898, and the B.Sc. one year later.[1]

He spent the greater part of his three years in the Scottish city, and it is of Edinburgh that Lakshmi remembers the following tale. *There was a big bank crash in Madras. My father lost all the money he had saved. But he had a Scottish landlady, and somehow she heard about this and gave him her life's savings. "So don't let me hear anything about the Scots being stingy," he always said.* The tale is engaging, and not altogether apocryphal, for there *was* a bank crash several years later that ruined people all over south India and wiped out the earnings of Swaminadhan's first few years of practice.

After London and Edinburgh he might have come home.

But he had part of the scholarship left. So he went to America, to Harvard. There he took another degree. He finished the thesis in six months. When he submitted it, Harvard said, "but you have two and a half years to go!" "I'm sorry," he replied, "if I stay I'll be wasting your money and my time, especially my time. I've got to get back and start earning my living. Here's your thesis."

In Lakshmi's memory the subject is astronomy. Science had always been her father's true love, the law was simply something to make a living by, and at Harvard, she believes, for the last time he allowed his heart to lead his head. But Harvard avers that in 1900 it conferred on one Subharama Swaminadhan a Ph.D. for a thesis entitled "Custom in its Juridical Aspect with Special Reference to the Administration of Oriental Law by British Tribunals."

By then Swaminadhan was over thirty, and thought it time to settle down and raise a family. For this he needed a wife. So a few years after his return he set about finding one. As his indifference to Brahmin ways was by now well known—it was his habit, something Lakshmi continues to this day, to hire servants without respect to caste or community—most Brahmin families in Madras no longer considered him an eligible bachelor. But he remembered his surrogate family in Kerala. In Kerala it was altogether usual for Brahmins to marry well-bred Nair girls. *So he went to our village*, to Kuttipuram and the Menon house.

> *There he found that my grandfather was dead. But he met my grandmother and asked her if she had any marriageable daughters. "All my elder daughters are married," she said, "there is only this one who is fourteen. And since I've grown old I've come to live in the village, so she hasn't had much schooling. She only knows how to read and write Malayalam; she doesn't know anything else." "Can I see her?" my father asked. "Of course you can," my grandmother said. So he met Ammu, my mother, and was very taken with her. And she also agreed, though he was so much older than she.*

He was older by twenty-three years. They were married toward the end of 1908 and came at once to Madras. *There my father had my mother educated. He had an English governess to teach her English. And a few years after they were married he took her to England, where he made her stay with an English family so that she could learn to speak English as it is really spoken.* He introduced Ammu to the theater, which so excited her that once home she began to act in amateur theatricals. She learned to play tennis, she learned to ride; *we have a picture of her somewhere*, says Govind, *all dolled up in her riding habit, taken in Rotten Row.* Years later she became, he believes, the first Indian woman in Madras to drive a car.

Meanwhile there were children. Govind, born in 1909, when Ammu was only fifteen, was followed by Lakshmi; a second son, Subrama Krishna; and a second daughter, Mrinalini. Their house, named Gilchrist Gardens in honor of Swaminadhan's benefactor, stood on a large tree-filled piece of ground along one side of which ran the silver and blue trains of the suburban Chetput line. The poet Harindranath Chattopadhyaya visited the compound in or about 1918 with his older sister Mrinalini. (Their father, Aghorenath Chatto-padhyaya, had been one of the first recipients of the Gilchrist Scholarship, and it was after this Mrinalini that Swaminadhan's second daughter was named.) Chattopadhyaya remembers being met by a small, shy young woman dressed entirely in white, with a cataract of black hair running down her back—this was Ammu; remembers Ammu's two older children, Govind alert with smiling eyes, Lakshmi very sweet; remembers being shown a room filled with law books. But Swaminadhan was not there. He did not appear until the evening.

For work was everything to Swaminadhan. Though he was active in the university and the Madras city corporation, and served twice as president of the Madras Law College, it was as a barrister practicing before the High Court that he made his mark and his money. He delighted in his large and growing family, but spent few daylight hours with them. Early each morning he left by train for his office in Armenian Street, and it was there that he pursued his practice, kept his large and meticulously ordered private library, and entertained his friends.

In personal habits he was abstemious. *I remember Daddy eating hardly anything but curds,* Mrinalini says. *He never served drinks, of course. He never smoked.* In the hot weather he took the family to a hill station, but stayed with them only a few days. He had no interest in Madras society, did not visit his Brahmin relatives (he did not feel at home with them), and went to the cinema only to please his children. Almost every waking moment was occupied with work. Mrinalini, who keeps his memory with a small girl's devotion, recalls the day she didn't practice the piano. *We were a British household, remember, so I had to learn the piano, which was the bane of my life. It was the only time he was ever angry with me. "Child," he said, "you must work hard in the world, that is the only thing that really has meaning.*" To an observer it is an injunction his children seem hardly to have needed.

There was therefore a certain sobriety about Gilchrist Gardens. Ammu, though in age so much nearer her children than her husband, was nevertheless not close to them. Mrinalini thinks she must have absorbed from Miss Jordan, the governess, a quite un-Indian notion of how children should be raised. Bring them up strictly. *Never show them any love. I don't think I kissed Mummy until after I was thirty.* Ammu, though, was indulged. *Daddy indulged her, he indulged her like a child. I remember he used to bring her coffee in the morning, make it and bring it up, which no Indian husband normally would do.*

Just as he had made her learn England's language and England's ways, so he insisted that his sons receive a proper English education. For Govind that meant boarding school at Darjeeling, then off to public school in England at the age of twelve. His younger brother went directly to England when he was seven. *All during school,* Lakshmi remembers, *they couldn't come home, the holidays weren't long enough. Those were the days of traveling by ship.* Indeed, Govind did not see Madras again until he was almost twenty. Though no one knew it, his father had by then only a few months to live.

But for all the enforced absences, the attention to work, the Englishness, in some ways perhaps because of them, Gilchrist Gardens was an exciting place. Lakshmi's mother loved society, particularly the westernized society of clubs and tennis parties, and threw into social life the energy another woman might have directed at her children and her household. *My mother was a tremendous hostess,* Govind says. *She was very, very popular, the Queen of Madras,* is how Mrinalini remembers her. And though her husband did not share this enthusiasm, and would not absent himself long from work, he was far from a recluse. So to the house, attracted by the exuberance and grace of the one, and by the intelligence and sophistication of the other, came all sorts of people, interesting people, men and women of this accomplishment and that distinction.

Among them were Englishmen. Swaminadhan treated them with some ambivalence. *He had lots of English friends,* Lakshmi says, *and was always telling them to their faces they were firangi rascals,* white rascals. He was not a member of the Congress, and of politics in general, Govind believes, harbored a certain suspicion. But he made it a point towards the end of his life to wear only khadi (hand-spun cloth). Even his law robes were made of khadi. Every Englishman knew what that meant.

Once he had to defend on a murder charge a boy who was heir to some valuable landed property. Because of his youth, the boy had been placed by the Court of Wards in the Newington Institute. Delahaye, the Englishman who ran the institute, was notorious for his rough manner and for the contempt in which he held Indians. As Lakshmi heard the tale, Delahaye

> *must have said something to the boy, I don't know what it was. One night the boy took a revolver and shot the poor man dead. By every logic he should have been hanged. But my father had the case transferred to a court where there were two Indian judges and one English judge. And he so played upon the feelings of the Indian judges, making it appear so much a case of an Indian boy who had killed a Britisher and so was not going to receive justice, that he got the boy off.*

In the memoir of him by his younger brother, Ranganadha Iyar,[2] we read that while Swaminadhan did indeed have the case shifted—to Bombay—he won acquittal by demonstrating that the chief prosecution witness had been coached. The two accounts are not incompatible. And they certainly permit us to believe that when occasion offered, Swaminadhan was not above playing on anti-British sentiment. *But he had nothing against English people,* continues Lakshmi. *He sent both my brothers to England. "The English have some admirable qualities which you can only discover when you go there," he said. "They don't show those qualities in India, they show a different side." He wanted me to go too, but I refused.*

From the age of twelve she had wanted to be a doctor. It was not that she found medicine particularly exciting. Literature and history attracted her more. At school she regularly carried off prizes for the best essay, the best poem; her house today is full of books. *But I wanted to take up a profession that I could use. And somehow I felt that as a doctor I could be most useful. At that time the only professions really open to women were teaching and medicine. It wasn't as it is now.*

From a Madras convent school she passed to the school attached to Lady Willingdon Training College, took her school leaving certificate, and did two years of pre-medical work at Queen Mary's College. By now it was 1932. Her father had died on the first day of 1930. Lakshmi could see that if she followed his wishes and took her medical degree in England, interning and specializing there, she might be away for as long as ten years. The thought dismayed her. *I had the feeling that something was going to happen in India, that revolution was just around the corner. I wanted to be part of it.* Her mother was of like mind. *She also had that feeling. She would have sent me if I had wanted to go, but she didn't oppose me when I said I didn't.* Ammu took her two daughters to England, but it was only for a visit; Lakshmi did not stay.

Instead her life took a political turn. In the early twenties her mother had met the Irish suffragette and Theosophist Margaret Cousins, who from her home in Madras had organized a local organization that concerned itself with the disabilities under which Indian women labored: the practice of treating a young widow as if she were dead, the crippling dowries, the child marriages.

Ammu's own marriage at age fourteen was to a degree one of these. *But she was one of the lucky ones*, Lakshmi says. Lucky in the man she married, a circumstance more than ever apparent when he died. For *my father had made his will in such a way that my mother was completely independent. She had her own income, the house was in her name. As for us, he had left equal shares to his two sons and his two daughters, which at that time was very unusual. If he hadn't made a will, my brothers would have got everything and we wouldn't have got a thing.* Ammu went regularly to the meetings of this local women's association. When the All-India Women's Conference was formed, she joined it too, and began attending its annual conferences. In this way Lakshmi got her first glimpse of Subhas Chandra Bose.

It was in December 1928, at Calcutta, on the occasion of one of these conferences. The Congress, too, was holding its annual session in that city. To control the crowds a force of Congress Volunteers had been put together. They dressed in khaki, which gave them a martial air. They drilled as soldiers drill. And it was Bose who drilled them—early every morning Lakshmi stole out to watch him march and counter-march the men before sending them off to the enormous temporary pavilion at Park Circus and the duties of the day. Her mother had no use for the young Bengali. "*He's an upstart,*" Lakshmi remembers her saying, "*he's showing off, strutting about in that uniform!*" All her life Ammu remained a devoted and uncritical follower of Gandhi. Nevertheless she was beginning to see, in Lakshmi's words, that *it wasn't enough to hold meetings and pass resolutions*, as the All-India Women's Conference tended to do. *To get things made into law you had to go further. You had to reach the legislators.*

That meant getting involved in politics. In 1930, a few months after her husband's death, in the year of civil disobedience and the salt march, Ammu joined the Congress. A few years later she was sitting on the Madras municipal corporation; a few years later still she was contesting a seat in the Central Legislative Assembly at Delhi. But what her children remember best about her involvement with Congress party is the way she put Gilchrist Gardens at its service. More than ever it hummed with activity, activity in which her children shared. Though her second son was constantly away in England, Govind came home for the long holidays, and in 1935 came home for good. Mrinalini was too young to be sent away. Lakshmi was always there.

If we may see Lakshmi through the eyes of a brother and a sister, she was now, at twenty, a person in her own right, someone decidedly to be reckoned with. *She was the beauty of the family*, says Mrinalini, herself an exquisite woman with the figure and manner of the dancer—which she is, for Mrinalini Sarabhai, widow of the physicist Vikram Sarabhai, is an internationally recognized interpreter of classical Indian dance. *She had all that south Indian beauty.* And in Govind's recollections you detect the surprise and pleasure of the elder brother discovering, after a long absence, what time has made of his little sister.

No doubt she made a good deal of him. *I was five years older*, Govind remembers, *and I'd just come back from Christ Church. I had the aura, and all the rest of it. We used to have a tremendous time.* But what strikes one today is how taken he was with her after those years of separation. He noticed her appearance, of course. *She was terrific in her looks.* He noticed also, and puts more stress upon, a quality he has some trouble expressing. Outgoing. Extrovert. Govind uses both and is satisfied with neither. *She's a difficult person to describe*, he will say, *because she had no complexes, no complexes of any kind,* and this permitted her to meet and engage people in an absolutely unreserved way. *She was friendly with everyone, and it was a genuine friendship, not a friendship for the*

*sake of furthering her own ends. She would trust anybody, and because of her
lovely nature and her beauty nobody took advantage of her.* She was interested
in many things. She was *full of enthusiasms* (on the tape the plural is
unmistakable). She was ready for anything.

*We had this lovely house. We were all independent of each other financially.
There was nothing to worry about. So she just blossomed.* Of course a good
part of Lakshmi's life was devoted to her medical training. *When I came
back she was settled into it, she was working very hard.* But more than any
of the others, she had (and still has) the sort of interest in and
commitment to public causes that turns a person toward politics—at
least in societies where politics are possible.

In India in the thirties politics were possible, as in Dutch Java and
French Indochina they were not. Gandhi, Nehru, and others spent as
much time in prison as they spent in the state of normal civil liberty.
There were moments when almost the entire upper echelon of the
Indian National Congress joined them behind bars. But they were not
met with a categorical ban on political dialogue—not asked, as
Solzhenitsyn in another time and place was asked, to choose between
forever keeping still and leaving the country. What they encountered
was the cat-and-mouse use of Section 144 of the Criminal Procedure
Code to silence a person here, detain a person there. Section 144
slowed, confused, sometimes deflected the independence initiative. But
the cat never closed in for the kill. That was never the intention.
Besides there were, if you will, too many mice.

Many of these passed through Gilchrist Gardens, men and women
both, great names in the register of independence politics and
enlightened thought. Rajagopalachari ("Rajaji" as he was called) of the
Madras Congress party came. Margaret Sanger, the American birth
control pioneer, was a visitor. So was the firebrand Aruna Asaf Ali, and
Nehru's sister Vijaya Lakshmi Pandit. So was the poetess and Congress
leader Sarojini Naidu, Harindranath Chattopadhyaya's sister. So was
Harindranath's wife Kamaladevi Chattopadhyaya.

Sometimes the visitors brought a touch of danger with them.
When, at the height of the renewed civil disobedience campaign in
1932, Margaret Cousins deliberately violated a prohibition on assemblies of five persons or more, it was to Gilchrist Gardens that the
arresting party came.[3] Mrinalini remembers Suhashini Nambiar, an-

other of Harindranath's sisters and the most radical of the three. She was under surveillance for allegedly having given refuge to some of the accused in the Meerut Conspiracy Case; there were police outside; a search must have seemed imminent—for suddenly *a whole bundle of letters was given to me to tuck into my pavadai.* (Since the affair of Delahaye's murder the girls had abandoned their English frocks and wore the more comfortable south Indian pavadai, or ankle-length skirt, with a blouse.) *I remember feeling terribly important, as though I was part of some exciting plot.* Afterwards Suhashini came often to the house. She had a powerful voice, and used it to taunt the detectives posted outside. *She would send cups of tea out to them, and sing "wherever you go, whatever you do, I want you to know I'm following you."*

Comrade Suhashini, as Lakshmi calls her, had lived in Germany before Hitler came to power and had developed an interest in Marxism and the Communist movement, an interest she conveyed to Lakshmi. *I used to sit up night after night and listen to her, while the rest of the household slept.* Suhashini was suspicious of Gandhi and Nehru. Do not to be swept off your feet by the spirituality of the one and the charm and sophistication of the other, she warned. Their patriotism was genuine. So was Gandhi's concern for untouchables. *But they looked backward, not forward. Nowhere in their program was there a word about the revolution that would once and for all destroy the old decaying feudal structure and build a new society.* Lakshmi listened, read what she could about Russia and the glorious socialist world being built there, and devoured Edgar Snow's *Red Star Over China* when it appeared. She did not, however, turn her back upon the Congress, as Suhashini would perhaps have wished her to do. In the Madras colleges *we used to have debates. Whenever any of the political leaders came to Madras, I would invite them to one college or another* (being Ammu's daughter surely gave such invitations weight). And though *we wouldn't get the permission unless we gave a guarantee that the person invited would give a general sort of speech*, not an inflammatory one, often these people came. In this way Lakshmi heard Gandhi and Nehru. Always, however, she put her medicine first.

> *There was this youth movement. It was a wing of the Congress. You joined as an individual, it had nothing to do with your college, so your college couldn't feel responsible for you or take action against you. This was*

particularly true after the first noncooperation movement that Gandhi started. He encouraged students to leave their colleges, join the movement, and go to jail. Hundreds and thousands of students did. But I didn't. I was keen to finish my studies. I thought I would be much more useful if I was qualified in some way.

The thirties advanced. Mrinalini went off to school in Switzerland. An English university ought logically to have followed, but as resolutely as Lakshmi and at an even earlier age, Mrinalini knew what she wanted to do. She wanted to dance. At Shantiniketan, Tagore's university, she could begin her training while she completed her education. Meanwhile Lakshmi took her degree from Madras Medical College, followed it with a diploma in gynecology and obstetrics, and went to work in the Victoria Caste and Gosha Hospital. She explained to me once what this meant. *High caste women had a prejudice against going to hospitals. They had no qualms over being killed in their homes by untrained midwives, but their relatives felt they would be polluted if they went to ordinary hospitals,* so they came to the Victoria where they were kept in special wards. *Gosha is the Tamil word for purdah. This hospital had a completely female staff. Even the stretcher bearers and the messengers were women. This was to encourage Muslim women to come.*

Lakshmi also married. *It wasn't arranged. I married a pilot in Tata Airlines. I stayed with him in Bombay for six months, but we didn't get on at all, so I came back to Madras and finished my studies. Meanwhile I fell in love with a classfellow of mine who was a year senior to me. But my husband refused to give me a divorce.*

In 1939 Ammu took Mrinalini on a world tour, Java and Bali first, then the United States. Much interested in Margaret Sanger's work, she spent six months in Chicago while Mrinalini studied drama in New York. Meanwhile Govind married and brought his bride to Gilchrist Gardens. Lakshmi lived with them. But she was growing restless. The house seemed half empty. Her classfellow "K", already a doctor, had gone off to Singapore. In June 1940 she followed him there.

❦

At Singapore she had relations: Kutty, and his wife Padmini. Kutty was a first cousin, Padmini a little more distant. They asked her to stay with them and their small child. "K" was already in practice. Lakshmi joined him at his clinic in Geylang, east of the city. *He did the general side, and I did the gynecology and obstetrics.*

Delivering babies quickly brought her into contact with the various communities on the island. From the start she respected the Chinese. As patients they were remarkable. They listened, did what they were told, and bore pain without crying. In the month she spent at a missionary hospital in the heart of Singapore's Chinese district, she was only once woken by the din she had accepted as normal in a Madras maternity ward. Rushing down to see who the exception could be, she found it was no Chinese at all *but the wife of a Tamil laborer who thought it her duty to make known to the world that she was bringing forth new life and that it was no easy matter.* Not that the Chinese were never noisy. Facing her bedroom window was a three-story building that housed hundreds. All night lights blazed, men and women talked, smoked, and played mah jong, baskets dropped empty to food vendors in the street below and came up full. But in the morning the building was deserted. Everyone had gone off to a job. The Chinese, she decided, slept less and worked harder than any other people.

Indeed, on first sight Singapore was a Chinese city. From ricksha puller to prosperous businessman they dominated the place. Malays were hardly to be seen—a few policemen, a few chauffeurs, a few gardeners—otherwise you encountered them only if you went into their villages, where they lived in little thatched houses built on stilts. They roused in Lakshmi an odd combination of pity and exasperation. Her Chinese patients came to her because, businesslike as ever, they had something they expected her to cure. With Indians, because she was Indian herself and because so many were from Madras or Kerala, *it was more of a social business. If you went to their houses even on a professional visit, you often stayed for dinner or tea.* But the Malays? *Poor things, they never came to you, we usually had to go to them. Someone would call you and say this or that woman was in desperate need, and off you'd go, wading flooded lanes to a one-room hut, to find her in labor attended by an old hag of a dai* [midwife]. Malay women married young, bore endlessly, and surrendered such infants as survived to wet nurses—which killed a further proportion (it was usual to buy Chinese babies to take their place). Lakshmi was horrified. She also cared. Mrinalini recalls visiting the

SINGAPORE

❶ The Padang
❷ Cathay Building
❸ Farrer Park
❹ Kallang Airport
❺ Mount Pleasant

0 1 2 3 4

clinic when she and her mother passed through Singapore in the autumn of 1940. It was doing well; Lakshmi and "K" had plenty of patients who could pay. But she particularly remembers her sister's kindness and effectiveness. *She had this gift, that people had faith in her. In a doctor, especially in India, you have to have a certain faith. I know that a lot of people now will say, "Doctor Lakshmi is here, we don't have to fear anything." I think that touch was there even then.*

The Indians on the island were of two sorts. Most worked in the rubber plantations or on the roads. They came from south India, Tamils and a few Malayalese and Telugus. Though assisted emigration was supposed now to be illegal, Lakshmi's ship had stopped at Nagappattinam, below Madras, and she had watched as scores of men were brought out in small boats and put into steerage. The great majority of these wretched fellows were from the depressed castes. Everybody looked down on them, they were willing to work for so little. Other Indians drove trams, clerked, taught school. Sikhs filled the police. For some reason the milk vendors came from the United Provinces and Bihar.

Then there were the Indian businessmen, Gujaratis and Marwaris and Parsees from north India, Chettiars and others from the south. They seemed to Lakshmi wholly occupied with their jobs and the money they were making. Over public issues they showed very little spirit, as Lakshmi discovered one day when trouble broke out in the Selangor rubber plantations two hundred miles to the north. The war in Europe had driven rubber prices up, giving the owners excellent profits. Aware of this the Tamil tappers, who earned fifty cents a day, and were quartered one family to a room, asked for an extra ten cents. The owners refused. The tappers struck. Troops were called out and given the order to fire. Several tappers were killed. In Singapore the local Indian Association met. Lakshmi attended, the only woman who did. She fully expected a vigorous condemnation of the government's action. Instead, the members debated whether an official inquiry might be useful, and whether one could be requested without giving offense.

She and "K" mixed with these Indians, of course. Some were professional people like themselves, friendly enough and obviously successful. Every house was well furnished, often with a refrigerator as well as a radio. *But there was something vital lacking*, she writes. (Lakshmi has put a good deal of what she remembers in writing, and I have not hesitated to mix this in with what she has told me.) For the first time in her life she was encountering *the middle class mind*, and she found it *barren*. Social gatherings followed a predictable pattern. Men and women separated, *the men taking possession of the drawing room while the women were relegated to the back. After the first few inquiries about children, servants, the cost of living, and the like, it was just a question of marking time till the inevitable tea arrived, after which one beat a hasty retreat.* Never had Ammu, her daughters, or the women who visited Gilchrist Gardens, been asked to put up with such a routine as this. At Gilchrist Gardens, moreover, the conversation had been filled with books, music, politics. But though Singapore was in many ways more of a crossroads than Madras, the Indians Lakshmi met had no interest whatever in happenings elsewhere. While she was on board ship, France had fallen, Dunkirk been evacuated. Her Indian acquaintances were unmoved. *The war in Europe and our own national struggle for independence made no dent in the armor of their indifference.*

As for Europeans, she met none except the few missionaries who ran the hospital. For Singapore, she discovered, raised more racial barriers than Madras did, and raised them higher. In Madras Rajagopalachari had headed a ministry responsible to a popularly elected legislature. Through his ministers he had directed not just the provincial civil servants, who were Indian like himself, but the Indian Civil Service men assigned to the province, many of whom were British. In Malaya this was impossible. In Malaya no Malay or Indian directed whites. *Whites.* That was exactly what they were called. Never had Lakshmi been so conscious of being Asian.

In spite of its reputation as the gateway to the east, in spite of its wide streets, tall buildings, and generally modern air, Singapore, she decided, had no character. *Its god was money.* She could practice medicine there, and live well, but she wondered whether she might not be bored to death. What saved her was K. P. Keshava Menon.

K. P. K. was a Kerala barrister who had come to Malaya in 1927 after serving a prison term for trying in aggressive ways to put an end to the south Indian practice of barring untouchables from public roads and paths near temples. But this assault on prejudice was not the only arrow in K. P. K.'s political quiver. Educated like Lakshmi's father in Madras and England, K. P. K. had entered practice in Calicut early in the First World War, and almost at once had opened a branch of Annie Besant's Home Rule League. In Madras, to which he moved for a time, he had helped start a New Fabian Society for the study of public questions while simultaneously organizing a ricksha pullers' union. Returning to Kerala at the personal request of Rajagopalachari, he had left his law practice to take part in Gandhi's noncooperation movement, and when it became apparent that the local press would not publish Congress party news, had founded his own Malayalam daily.

His imprisonment, followed by financial and domestic calamities (his wife and then his eldest daughter died), discouraged him. He was invited to practice law in Malaya. Eventually he settled in Singapore with his still considerable family. Lakshmi's parents had known him well. His son Unni, a civilian employee of the RAF, was a close friend of "K". So Lakshmi met him at once, discovered that his interest in what was going on in the world was as lively as her own, and came to look forward to Saturday evenings at his house in Paya Lebar. After a week at the office the old fellow was full of the latest political gossip. Conversation turned these evenings into *the only really stimulating kind of a time we had.*

K. P. K. made a point, too, of listening to the news broadcasts, especially the German and Italian ones when he could get them, and did not conceal his delight as the Allies stumbled from one defeat to another. Nor did Lakshmi. It was not that she wanted the fascists to win. She had supported the Loyalists in the Spanish Civil War, and she sympathized now with Chiang Kaishek in his fight against the Japanese. But she wanted the British to lose. In Singapore they were so smug and unassailable. It was a pleasure to hear about the lickings they were taking, *British army having to retreat from here, British army having to retreat from there. I wished to see them taste the bitter fruit of defeat.*

The days and weeks went by, almost unvarying, since at that latitude it rains or it does not, otherwise there is little to distinguish December from July. Saturday evenings, after a full day at the clinic, she and "K" passed at K. P. K.'s. On Sundays they closed at noon, picked up Unni, and if the tide was right went for a swim somewhere along the coast, then took in a movie. Padmini had another baby. Ammu and Mrinalini passed through on their way home from America. Ammu tried to persuade Lakshmi to return to Madras. In New York people were sure the war would spread. Lakshmi refused. The practice was going well. She and "K" had almost finished paying the installments on their little Morris car. For the house she shared with Kutty and Padmini she planned the extravagance of new furniture.

By early 1941 there was talk of trouble with the Japanese. Air raid drills were called and the garrison received reinforcements. (Among them were Indian troops. It began to dawn on the Singapore British that not all Indians were coolies or moneylenders. Observing a group of Sikh officers at a dance, one English girl went up and exclaimed in evident astonishment, "you people dance!")[4] But Lakshmi did not think war would come. When a *Statesman* correspondent by the name of Nair told her "nothing's going to happen here," she did not argue.

In Kuala Lumpur, where at about the same time Prem spent a few days' leave, a friend in the police was sure the Japanese would attack before Christmas. He was right, of course, and Nair wrong.

CHAPTER 3

THE FALL OF MALAYA

By the late autumn of 1941, Prem's battalion had been in Malaya for a little over a year. It had spent two weeks on Singapore Island, then moved by rail three hundred miles north to Kelantan Province, where it went into camp and waited uncomfortably for the northeast monsoon rains to abate. The battalion was part of the first Indian formation to reach Kelantan. And it was there because this was what was called for in the plan for the defense of the peninsula. The plan left the officers uneasy.

They knew perfectly well that the great naval base on the north shore of Singapore Island had been built to support a battle fleet England had never dispatched and could not now provide. England's difficulties in this respect were longstanding and well advertised, and none but the credulous supposed that they would soon be overcome. Malaya would have to defend itself without the help of the Royal Navy. Everybody understood that.

What worried the officers of the 2/10th Baluch was not the absence of ships but the state of the ground forces. In numbers these were formidable. By the late autumn Lt. Gen. Arthur E. Percival, General Officer Commanding, had thirty-one infantry battalions (seventeen Indian, one Malay, the rest British and Australian) in three infantry divisions and four independent brigades, with Indian States Forces besides. But there were no tanks and very few antitank and antiaircraft guns. The Indian battalions had been milked of experienced officers and men for the expanded army training in India. The Australian battalions were green through and through.

Worse, the troops were scattered all over the peninsula. Aware that a true battle fleet was utterly unavailable, and that the army's equipment shortages could be made good only in driblets, the Chiefs of Staff had resolved to defend Malaya from the air. Defense by air power. It was a novel and interesting idea, made persuasive by the Battle of Britain. Aircraft, of course, would be required. In Singapore they estimated that 600 first-line planes would do the job. But in London the Chiefs, their eyes on desperate shortages in other theatres, cut this figure in half. And since Churchill insisted that modern fighters as they became available must be sent to the Russians, 300 was twice the number actually provided. On the fateful Monday morning in December there were some 150 serviceable aircraft in Malaya, not one a Hurricane, Spitfire, or remotely their equivalents. Airfields were another matter. There were plenty of airfields. They need only be defended.

That was why Brigadier Key's 8th Indian Brigade, to which Lt. Colonel Frith's 2/10th belonged, was way up in Kelantan, on the northeast coast where the peninsula begins to narrow towards the Thai frontier. *We went on expanding our airfields,* Prem remembers, *and as the airfields were built our troops were sent to defend them and cover the beaches in front. Kota Bharu used to have a small civilian airport. This was being turned into an air force base, new runways built—we were there to defend it.* There was a second field at Gong Kedah, thirty miles to the southeast, and a third at Machang, twenty miles due south. 8th Brigade's job was to see that aircraft could operate safely from these three fields. But when Prem looked about him, he had difficulty finding any aircraft.

At Kota Bharu there were eleven Hudson bombers and a handful of Brewster Buffaloes. Gong Kedah had nine Wildebeeste torpedo bombers, ancient biplanes with fixed landing gear and open cockpits, of which it was later said that if they hurt the enemy at all it can only have been when Japanese pilots, catching sight of them, died laughing. At Machang there were no planes at all. Was it for this that an entire brigade was stationed in an area so remote—between Kelantan and the rest of Malaya lay rain forest pierced by a single decrepit railroad line— that the Japanese, if ever they did land, would be well advised to stay where they were? *We were too young and too ignorant to realize what was happening. We got on with the job,* and let work cover their unease.

By then Prem was at Bachok, at the upper end of the twenty-three miles of coast for which the 2/10th had responsibility. *I had an independent command of my own. I was an acting captain, commanding nearly*

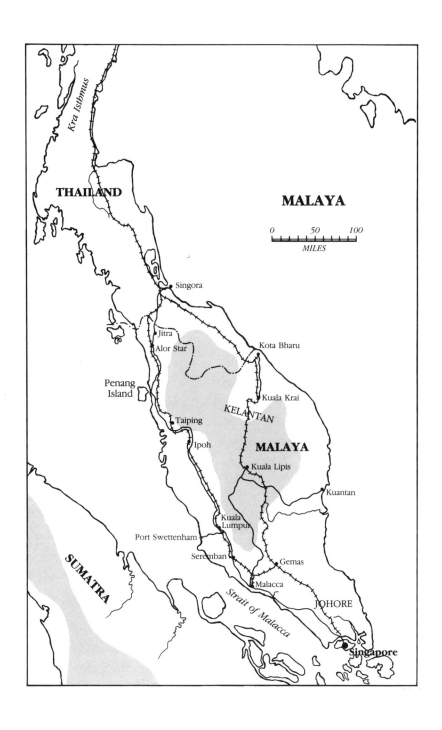

THAILAND

MALAYA

0   50   100
MILES

Kra Isthmus

Singora

Jitra

Alor Star

Kota Bharu

Penang
Island

Kuala Krai

Taiping

KELANTAN

Ipoh

MALAYA

Kuala Lipis

Kuantan

Kuala
Lumpur

Port Swettenham

Seremban

Gemas

SUMATRA

Malacca

JOHORE

Strait of Malacca

Singapore

half the battalion. He does not remember exactly when he reached Bachok, but the battalion's war diary tells us that on the 17th of May C Company began work on beach defenses there.[1] Prem had commanded the company for some time. He also had the overall direction of B Company, on Melawi Beach to his south, because its commander was an emergency commissioned officer of little experience. Still farther south, beyond a wooded and swampy area that was thought to be impassable, A Company held the beach in front of Gong Kedah. To the north the 3/17th Dogra worked on the ten miles that sweep northwest and west to the mouths of the Kelantan River. Within that arc lay Kota Bharu town and airfield. Brigadier Key had two more battalions between Kota Bharu and Kuala Krai forty miles to the south. At Kuala Krai the road stopped and only the railroad continued.

Bachok village was a charming place with a beach of clean, white sand. Europeans regularly swam there—the Kelantan Club maintained a branch for that purpose. Because they did, Prem discovered how color conscious the British in Malaya could be.

He had seen something of this in Singapore during the battalion's fortnight stay on the island. He had gone into the city to look around a bit, and had run into old friends of his, a Captain Narang and his wife (people who came in thirty-nine had been able to bring their families). He had had meals at their place,

> *and thought I must return their hospitality. Some of my British friends had taken me to the swimming club, which I had joined as a temporary member. So I said to Captain and Mrs. Narang, "come and have dinner with me at the swimming club." "What do you mean, the swimming club?" they said. "We can't have dinner with you there. Non-Europeans aren't allowed." "Don't be silly," I told them, "I'm a member." "You can't be," they said. "But I am," I said, and showed them my membership card. "There must be a mistake," they said. So I checked. They were right.*

In Kelantan things were, if anything, worse. The civil servants behaved *like little tin gods.* The planters were more friendly. *They used to invite us to their houses.* But they were sticky about Indians joining the Club. "*How can we take Indian officers as members,*" they said, "*when we don't take senior Malays?*"

For Indian officers in the service of the Raj, love of country and pride in regiment did not connect, could not be linked (though elsewhere in the world the juxtaposition was held to be perfectly natural, was indeed taken for granted). And Prem, who strikes one at that period as a young man devoted to his profession and thoroughly enjoying it, had not challenged the separation. Not yet, at least.

In Peshawar, with the 5/10th, he and a brother officer had sometimes worn white dinner jackets made of khadi. And he had not hesitated to visit openly the house of Dr. Khan Saheb, brother of Abdul Ghaffar Khan, the "Frontier Gandhi," and an old friend of the family. Both actions may have raised a few eyebrows, may even have generated comment. But *by this time,* Prem remarked to me, *most British officers, at least the enlightened ones, knew that you could not suppress the nationalism of the younger Indian officers,* and so no one had said anything to him. These, however, had been no more than gestures. Now, in Kalentan, far from India and facing the prospect of real fighting (for which, not politics, he had trained), Prem began to feel that things were not as they should be in the very routine of army life. And he began to act upon that feeling. Four episodes stick in his memory. Two have to do with messing.

The Baluch was a class company regiment. In the 2nd Battalion A and D companies were composed of Punjabi Muslims, B Company of Pathans, C Company (Prem's own) of Dogras. (Pathans are the Pushtu-speaking Muslim people who live on both sides of the present Pakistan-Afghan border. Dogras come from the hill country about Jammu, between the Punjab and Kashmir, and are overwhelmingly Hindu.) Each company had its own mess. The officers, however, ate together. So did the jemadars, the subadars, and the subadar-majors—but in two mess halls, one for the Muslims, one for the Hindus. Now, when the 2/10th reached Kelantan, the battalion camp at Pasir Puteh was still under construction. Messing arrangements had yet to be settled. In conversation one evening with the colonel, the subadar-major, and his own Dogra subadar, Prem suggested that the VCOs eat in one room, at separate tables if they wished, and use the other (to which they would still be entitled) for recreation. Colonel Frith was taken aback. *"Prem,"* he said, *"I hope you're not trying to rush things."* All turned on the Dogra VCOs, outnumbered by Muslims three to one. Would they accept the experiment? Prem's subadar was sure they would, and they did; the business was arranged. It was the first time in the Baluch Regiment, Prem believes, that VCOs messed together in a garrison situation. Though he does not say so, perhaps even then he wondered why ordinary jawans could not do the same.

Almost a year later, on the occasion of the Hindu festival of Dasehra, he tried again. It was at Bachok. The Dogra VCOs of C Company invited him to dinner. Prem accepted, on one condition. B Company was camped close by. Its officers messed with C Company's. Prem said he would come if the Pathan VCOs of B Company were invited too, and asked to sit at the same table. *"Look,"* he said to his Dogras, *"you are prepared to sit at table with me and eat with me. Yet in some ways I'm worse than those Muslims, because I eat beef and they don't."* So they agreed. *The Muslim VCOs, the Dogra VCOs, and I all sat at the same table.* Telling this tale more than forty years after the event, Prem is at pains to explain why it is worth telling. Because it illustrates *the unnatural barriers which had been built up in the Indian Army to keep Hindus and Muslims apart. It probably wasn't done with any evil intention. After 1857 the British were so scared of hurting the religious feelings of the men that they went far out of their way to respect those feelings. "If you want to eat separately,"* they said, *"we'll have separate messes." But if the men were given a little encouragement, they were willing to eat together.* Prem knew, for he had given that encouragement and they had.

Breaking down the barriers that separated whites from Asians was a different business, requiring much more than encouragement, inviting less charitable assumptions about intent.

At Peshawar, Prem had devised a modest but effective stratagem for teaching manners to English officers' wives who deliberately left the club pool whenever an Indian officer took a dip. *I collected my chaps, and we got beer and lashings of sandwiches and lay along the edge. When an English girl went in, we went in. And when she got out, we got out. So after a while she got tired of all this going in and getting out, and there was no more problem.* Now, in Kelantan, he was more direct. There came a moment when the battalion band was invited to play at the Club. Prem heard about it, went to Colonel Frith, and said, *"Sir, it won't play, there are three of us contributing towards its maintenance who cannot join that club."* Even five years earlier no Indian officer, surely, would have spoken in that way.

Or if he had, his colonel would not have replied, as Prem's to the best of his recollection replied, *"quite right, it won't play."*

At Bachok there was an actual collision. The men were constructing a multiple wire fence along the beach. Gaps had to be left so that the battalion's Bren gun carriers, and the local fishermen too, could get down to the water. Prem saw to it that no gap fell in front of the Club's branch building. The predictable consequence was a summons, one afternoon, from a very angry assistant adviser to the Sultan of Kelantan. *There was the Britisher, drinking tea. He didn't have the courtesy even to ask me to sit down and have a cup.* "What do you mean?" he shouted. "I come here to spend a weekend, and I have to walk miles to get to the beach!" Prem must have a gap cut. But Prem refused, and Headquarters did more than back him up: it threatened to put the entire beach off limits to civilians.

There was the Britisher, drinking tea.

Lakshmi too uses the term, for example in the tale of the boy who shot Delahaye, and we wonder why it sounds archaic yet at the same time natural—until we remember that "Britisher," with its implied baggage of exasperation and contempt, is exactly what we Americans called the British when we, too, were fighting for our independence. Prem laughs when he spits the word out. It is unlikely he felt quite so jaunty at the time, or that he allowed it to show if he did.

It may be, too, that these stories have improved with the telling. It may be that his colonel took a little more talking to in language a little less peremptory, and that omitting the gap at the beach had reasons beyond a simple desire to needle the Club. Nevertheless the stories are clearly about things that actually happened. And they suggest that Prem is a more than ordinary young officer, with a manner more than ordinarily compelling. We have only his word for it that he is one of Colonel Frith's favorites. The war diary's terse entries tell us that at the very least he is singled out for special duties and responsibilities. "Battalion flank guard exercise: Captain Sahgal commands the battalion," one reads. He is the only Hindu among the three or four Indian officers, and for a time the only ICO. Indeed, the 2/10th, like all battalions in the ballooning Indian Army, is so short of officers it entrusts companies to subadars (two command A and D companies when the Japanese attack), and when it receives any, almost invariably discovers they are emergency commissioned. Prem is a valuable commodity. He can afford to push a little here, shove a little there. We may take the stories as evidence that this is exactly what he does.[2]

But of course it all means very little at the moment, in the context of what is about to happen. There is the wire to be strung. There are concrete pillboxes to be built and manned, one every thousand yards—which is too far apart for mutual support (below Melawi the pillboxes are dummy). There are mines to be laid, light and medium machine guns and the few mortars to be sited, telephone wire to be run. The 2/ 10th has been given two 18-pounder guns, which it puts right down on the beach and mans itself, and in October it receives a third. A rifle battalion is some 850 men, in four companies plus headquarters. But one of the four will be kept in reserve (for the 2/10th it is D Company), and this means that the companies actually on the beach must be spread very thin. From Bachok around to the river's mouths the three forward companies of the 3/17th Dogra must each cover three miles. At Bachok Prem's company is responsible for five. "Grossly under-manned and under-gunned" is how the official history will put it years after the event,[3] and even at the time men know that if Key fails to give prompt artillery support and bring his two reserve battalions up quickly, the Japanese cannot be prevented from penetrating wherever they choose to land.

Everyone expects a landing. The old hands do not think it will come before February or March, when the northeast monsoon rains will be largely over. It comes much sooner, very early on the morning of Monday, the 8th of December, 1941.

The assault, by a part of one Japanese division brought by sea all the way from Hainan, went in shortly after midnight on the beaches nearest Kota Bharu. It was timed to coincide with the strike at Pearl Harbor, thousands of miles away. And since that was a matter of planes and ships only, Kota Bharu became the first land battle of the Pacific War.

At the start things did not go easily for the attackers. A heavy swell capsized a number of landing craft. Hudsons from Kota Bharu airfield hit three of the transports, eventually sinking one, and so disrupted the off-loading that many Japanese did not reach the beaches until long after dawn. There the Dogras fought stubbornly, while elements of

Key's reserve came forward to counterattack. But over ground soaking from recent rains and laced by creeks they made little progress, and by late afternoon it was clear the beaches were lost. At the airfield a rumor that the Japanese were approaching demoralized the Australian ground crew, which packed up and fled. That night Key, afraid of landings further down the coast, and aware that his left was threatened by a column from Thailand, ordered a general withdrawal to a position covering Kota Bharu town. Successive withdrawals over the next ten days brought his brigade all the way back to Kuala Krai. There, as all three airfields were in Japanese hands, he was authorized to break contact and get away south along the railroad.

At Bachok, on the Monday, nothing happened. But the battalion camp at Pasir Puteh was set on fire by incendiary bombs. Half the huts were destroyed, with all the quartermaster stores and the men's spare kits. That evening the three beach companies began withdrawing inland. D Company went north to help cover the retreat.

Up to now, Prem remembers, *our men had been very confident. "The Japanese, they're such little chaps,"* they said, *"they can't see, they can't fight, we'll kill them like flies."* Then the reaction set in. For several days panic was in the air. A reserve battalion, the 4/19th Hyderabad, hurried up from the south by rail and put into position at dusk, mistook the 2/10th for the enemy, and there was wild firing by friend upon friend. Not until the men had actually fought a little did their confidence return.

It rained a great deal. The country was open, rice paddy mostly with occasional groves of coconut, crisscrossed with waterways. The villages were built on stilts. There came a moment—it was probably on December 12, for on this and the following day the 2/10th acted as rear guard to the brigade—when Prem took a platoon to clear the Japanese out of a village. It was not easy. The Japanese were dug in beneath the huts. Prem's platoon havildar was killed, the battalion's first casualty. But the village was cleared. Next day Prem was holding another village in a clump of trees when the Japanese attacked across an open field. *They came in a mass. The light and medium machine guns made them drop in the paddy. Then the mortars got them.* And the war diary entry, which records this little skirmish, ends with "withdrawal effected without difficulty." After this the men lost their nervousness. Japanese planes made movement by day difficult. When the brigade finally reached Kuala Krai and entrained, leaving some of its transport behind, it was weaker by several hundred dead, wounded, or missing. But it remained an effective fighting unit. It had experienced nothing like the catastrophe that overcame the 11th Indian Division on Malaya's west coast.

There the failure to anticipate the Japanese landing on the Kra Isthmus was followed by the astonishing action at Jitra, where a handful of Japanese battalions with tanks drove three brigades from a prepared defensive position in a day and a half, in the process cutting one of the brigades to pieces. Jitra crippled the 11th. After Slim River, four weeks later and two hundred miles further south, the division practically ceased to exist.

There was nothing subtle or mysterious about the tactics of the Japanese. The popular notion that they beat the British by taking to the jungle is the reverse of the truth. On the western coastal plain there was little jungle. But there were roads, and it was precisely because the Japanese sent tanks and infantry headlong down these roads, or down any track that offered, and went around by the flanks only when checked, that they moved so quickly. If no one applied the term "blitz" to their performance, it was only because the word seemed so exclusively German. Had the 2/10th Baluch been part of the 11th Division, it too would almost certainly have been overwhelmed and scattered in the first six weeks of the campaign—and Prem, if he survived, have had a different tale to tell. Chance, however, put the 2/10th not on the west coast, where the main Japanese blow fell, but on the east.

So we fought holding actions all the way back to Kuala Krai, and then were brought south by train. Weeks passed. Kuala Lumpur was abandoned. The British withdrew into northern Johore. Its defense became the responsibility of Westforce, a union of Indian and Australian units under an Australian, Bennett. For a time it looked as if Westforce might stem the Japanese advance. The Australians were fresh and full of confidence. Two new brigades, the 45th Indian and the 53rd British, had arrived. On the 14th of January an ambush on a considerable scale killed a great many Japanese on the trunk road west of Gemas. Mechanics were assembling Hurricanes that had reached Singapore by sea. They were expected to recover control of the air.

The Japanese, however, proved as irresistible as before. With their right, moving often in light craft along the coast, they enveloped and destroyed the inexperienced 45th and 53rd. With their left they pressed relentlessly down the trunk road. There the 8th Indian Brigade shared the defense with the 22nd Indian and some Australians. Within hours of the successful Gemas ambush it was clear the retreat would have to continue. At Batu Anam, in northwest Johore, remnants of the 11th Division passed through Prem's battalion—unfit for further fighting, a dispiriting sight. Nevertheless from Batu Anam to the tip of Malaya it is more than one hundred miles, and the peninsula narrows. *We were told that across this narrow waist defense lines were being built, that fresh troops were arriving, that eventually we'd get behind them, be rested, and then counterattack.*

Meanwhile the 8th and the 22nd, leapfrogging southward, protected Westforce's flank.

Movement away from the road was very difficult. The Japanese did it, but in most cases by the time they got around our flanks we were falling back again. It was almost like a drill. We'd fight the whole day and then retreat at night—go back seven or eight miles, pick up a feature where some kind of antitank defense could be put up, high ground perhaps, or a nullah or stream. But the most maddening part of it was that you never got a night's rest. I slept for days with my steel helmet as a pillow.

They passed through burning Segamat. Brigadier Key, well thought of and promoted, left to rebuild the 11th Division, and for a time the brigade was commanded by a certain Lay, *mad Brigadier Lay. All he did in the evening was get drunk. He wouldn't give an order,* and was with difficulty persuaded to let others do it for him. At Labis, where the road and the railroad passed over the river, Japanese tanks reached the road bridge before it could be destroyed. Artillery fire caught the lead tank as it was crossing. The rest turned and made for the railroad line, where Prem survived shelling at very close range and blew the bridge in their faces. He had plenty of machine guns and mortars, and adequate artillery support, but there were no tanks at all, and the Hurricanes were not much in evidence.

C Company took casualties, of course. They were replaced by men straight from India who had no idea what to do and had to be looked after. Because of the casualties the companies were now quite jumbled. Prem was commanding Pathans and Dogras.

> *I remember one incident. I always told my men, "when you get to a new position, dig. And when you dig, throw the earth behind you, then throw the dirt in front of you, because that way you won't be in silhouette." This I used to din into them and din into them.*
>
> *Now one day I had these Dogras and Pathans together. The Japanese had come through our position, we were in a hell of a mixup, when a very young Pathan recruit ran up to me crying, "Sahib! Sahib!"*
>
> *"What's the matter?" I asked.*
>
> *"Sahib, when I joined you told me that when you stop in a place you must dig. And when you dig, you must throw the earth behind you, and then throw the dirt in front of you."*
>
> *"Yes," I said, "that's what I told you."*
>
> *"Sahib, when I got to this place I took my shovel and began digging. And first I threw the earth behind me, and then I threw it in front of me."*
>
> *"Yes," I said, "but what are you so excited about?"*
>
> *"Sahib, there I was sitting in my hole, I had dug it the way you told me, and the bastard jumped right in!"*
>
> *"Who jumped in?" I said.*
>
> *"Sahib, I had dug my hole the way you told me, the way you taught me, and the bastard, the son of a whore, jumped right in! This is my hole, I told him. But he wouldn't listen. So I bayoneted him."*
>
> *My God, I thought, he's gone and murdered a Dogra. I had visions of him being court-martialed. "For Heaven's sake," I said, "tell me who was it jumped in?"*
>
> *"A Japanese," he said.*

An ECO of the usual sort would not have had the Urdu to understand the man, particularly as he spoke with a strong Pushtu accent. Indeed, an emergency commissioned Englishman would not even have been approached.

At Rengam, halfway between Labis and Johore Bharu, there came a moment when the company, pressed hard and low on ammunition, found itself quite alone. Prem climbed a tree, looked about, discovered no one, and made haste to get his men moving. Hurrying close behind, he tripped, fell, saw a Japanese coming at him with a bayonet, and just managed to shoot the fellow with the revolver he carried in his right hand. Later, to his relief, he bumped into a party of Sikhs—who, however, would not believe his shouted Punjabi and fired, so that he was obliged to take his men in another direction, through nearly impassable marsh. Eventually he struck a track, followed it, heard noises, took cover, and watched as scores of Japanese went by on bicycles. It struck him they could be slipping between his own brigade and the 22nd. But when he brought his company safely back to battalion that evening, no one paid much attention.

The battalion was astride the railroad. Next morning Prem sent a patrol along the line to reconnoiter. It returned with the news that the Japanese occupied a small bridge a mile away. At this moment General Barstow, commanding the 9th Indian Division, came up with two staff officers. Determined to make contact with the 22nd Brigade, he ignored all warnings and pushed on in a trolley. Only the two staff officers stumbled back. They had been fired upon, Barstow was missing, and a company sent to find him and dislodge the Japanese could do neither. It withdrew, and as it withdrew the Japanese came with it. There was a moment of hand-to-hand fighting. A Japanese officer with a sword came at Prem *in a curious half-sitting position, like a Cossack dancing.* Then the battalion broke free. But the affair had been a disaster. C Company was down from two hundred men to hardly fifty, and had to be merged with B, Prem commanding both. The 22nd, its escape route cut, blundered off through the jungle to death or surrender. The 8th fought no more engagements of importance. There was hardly room for any. On the evening of January 30, Prem's battalion withdrew to Singapore in trucks. Next morning the pipers of the Argylls played the last of the defeated army across the Causeway with "A Hundred Pipers" (though there were only two), a section was blown, and Singapore prepared for a siege.

On Sunday, December 7, the tide was wrong for swimming, so Lakshmi and "K" played tennis instead. Unni was not with them. Like other civilian technicians he had been called to his post on the sighting of a Japanese fleet off the tip of Indochina. The newscasts, however, made this out to be normal maneuvers, and the arrival of the *Repulse* and the *Prince of Wales* a few days before had reassured people. *I remember we had really strenuous tennis.* Lakshmi came home tired, had dinner, and went to bed.

About three in the morning she and Padmini were awakened by a thud, thud, thud, and the sound of sirens. They went out on the veranda. The street lights were on. A Chinese air-raid warden who lived nearby was rushing off, and they asked what was happening. Just a practice, he replied. At first light, however, their Chinese amah, who had had Sunday off in the city, came and told them the bombs had been real. They turned on the radio. *For a long time all we heard was the song "Keep the Home Fires Burning" over and over, as if it was some sort of code. Then at last the news that the Japanese had attacked Singapore and Pearl Harbor, and that war had come.*

"K" arrived for breakfast as usual, and they talked things over. They must move. Civilians close to the island's shore had been warned they would have to evacuate, and Katong, where Kutty and Padmini had their house—near Geylang on the east side of the city—was directly on the water. Fortunately one of K. P. K.'s daughters lived in Paya Lebar, about two miles to the north. She had agreed that if war came she would join her father and let Kutty and his family have her house. So with the Morris and a hastily hired truck they shifted that very day to Paya Lebar. Lakshmi and "K" kept their Geylang clinic. They were active members of the Medical Auxiliary Service, with first-aid haversacks and steel helmets. At her first-aid post Lakshmi gave short lectures on midwifery to ambulance men.

On the 10th Japanese aircraft caught and sank the *Repulse* and the *Prince of Wales.* Lakshmi was of two minds about the news. Though she was glad to see the British shaken, she did not particularly want the Japanese to win. There was nothing ambivalent, however, about her feelings when Penang, well up the west coast and therefore indefensible, was evacuated. First came the rumors. Then Singapore was full of the evacuees. *The color of these was pure white.* The British had brought out their own.

She noticed, too, that there was very little on the radio about her countrymen. Not that she had much love for the Indian Army. *I felt that anyone who joined it was a mercenary.* It annoyed her, however, that the British recruited so largely from the so-called martial races of the north. In Kerala this was *rather a sore point, because the Nairs of Kerala, from whom*

I come, consider themselves a martial race too, and in the old days used to form the armies of the local rulers. In all our houses we have these spears and shields and blunderbusses. What particularly bothered her now was that, though much of the force defending Malaya was Indian, Britishers got all the attention. *When the Australians went into action in Johore, they were splashed across the front pages as the saviors of Malaya.* The Indians received no such treatment. It was rumored that some of them were surrendering readily, were behaving as if they thought the Japanese would win—were behaving as if they actually wished them to.

For several weeks the war receded. Another of K. P. K.'s daughters became seriously ill, and Unni, who left his post to be with her, was very nearly court-martialed *for thinking his sister's life more important than Britain's war.* In January, Japanese bombers began coming over *regular as clockwork. The naval base, the airfields, the dock area, all received their daily loads. Occasionally civilians were hurt and we had some work to do.* Lakshmi was surprised and put off by the coolness of the Chinese. They began clearing debris and salvaging belongings even before the "all clear" had sounded. No one bothered about the wounded and the dying, it was only property that mattered.

More evacuees arrived, government servants mostly, *whites, confident as usual that whatever happened their skins would be preserved.* The war was so close they no longer felt safe even in Singapore. *Now began the stampede. We knew Singapore was going to fall because the whole calculation was wrong.* The British had supposed the Japanese would attack from the east, *those wretched guns were facing only east—and the Japanese didn't come from there at all. Everybody knew this.* So there was panic, and people made desperate efforts to leave. By spending hundreds of dollars, a cousin of Lakshmi's wrangled passage for himself and his family. *I tried to send Padmini and the children with him, but she refused to go without us.* Lakshmi herself was determined to stay. Being able-bodied and a doctor, "K" would not be allowed out. So they all remained. Early in February the war came right to their doorstep.

From Changi, on the eastern tip of the island, along the Johore Strait to the swamps and tidal inlets of its western end, it is fifty miles. Percival had some one hundred thousand men, more than he had begun the campaign with, and more than twice what the Japanese could bring to an assault—though Percival did not know this. Many, however, were line-of-supply troops. Many were new arrivals, raw, and quite unfit after weeks at sea (one British division had only just landed). Most were tired, dispirited, and confused by the constant shuffling and amalgamation of units. So Percival chose to commit almost the whole of his fighting force to a static defense at the water's edge.

The 8th Indian Brigade, of which the 2/10th was still a part, was one of the few units in reserve. It was bivouacked east of the main road that runs from the Causeway to the city, near the naval base which, useless now and abandoned, burned under clouds of oily smoke. If the Japanese succeeded in crossing in the vicinity of the base, the brigade would have the job of pushing them back into the water. Meanwhile it waited.

Several miles to the south and east, Lakshmi and "K" waited too. Though Padmini was nervous, so nervous Kutty did not dare leave the house, *we were in fact enjoying the excitement. So far we hadn't dug a trench. We depended on the dining table reinforced by mattresses.* But when shelling began in earnest on February 5, six days after the 2/10th reached the island, they thought better of it and dug one.

On the afternoon of Sunday, February 8, the shelling intensified and spread. Lakshmi and "K" were at a movie. They went home, got Padmini and the children into the trench, and continued on to their aid post just north of the Paya Lebar bazaar. Prem was in the city, at the Raffles Hotel east of the padang (that piece of open ground for public use that in India is called a maidan). He had been given the day off; had taken a vehicle to the Raffles, rented a room, and treated himself to a hot bath and a few drinks. But he didn't like the atmosphere. *People knew the end was coming and tried to be gay.* So he started back (at one point shelling drove him into a ditch), reached his company, went to sleep, and perhaps because of the bath and the drinks did not wake until morning.

By then it was known that the Japanese were crossing to the west of the Causeway. By mid-morning that Monday the defending Australian brigade had practically ceased to exist. Other crossings followed Tuesday, the Japanese foothold spread, the 2/10th was ordered to counterattack. *We did, and reached the beaches. But because the*

Australians were being pushed back, we had to fall back too. The country was rubber plantations, Chinese villages, here and there modern buildings, all heavily populated and mixed up. And nobody quite knew what was happening.

At Neesoon, due north of the reservoirs that supply Singapore, the battalion was engaged by Japanese tanks and managed to knock out two. Later it was ordered to relieve an Australian unit. Before it could do so the Australians, perhaps unnerved by the rumor that English units were evacuating and leaving them in the lurch, abandoned their position. Repeatedly the 2/10th tried to recover it. Battalion casualties that Wednesday were among the heaviest in the campaign. Prem almost joined them. As he carried a wounded subadar to safety, the poor fellow, slung over his shoulder, took a bullet through the head. That night the battalion withdrew still further east and south, to the neighborhood of Paya Lebar. It could hardly withdraw much farther. From Paya Lebar it is only four or five miles down the Serangoon Road to the padang and the center of the city.

Next day, Thursday the 12th, there was a lull. The 2/10th was not in contact with the enemy. Prem was settling his men in a Chinese cemetery just south of the Paya Lebar bazaar when an Indian civilian came up and said he had a family, where should he go? *"Go east,"* Prem told him. *"If the Japanese come, it will be from the other side"* (which was indeed the case, the main assault had struck the British left). Prem offered him a truck from several he had orders to destroy. The man declined. As he was leaving he told Prem there was a doctor on the other side of the bazaar. *"A lady doctor. Please help her. Otherwise she'll get caught in the fighting."* Prem walked to the north end of the bazaar. He did not find the lady doctor. Her name, the man had said, was Lakshmi.

Lakshmi and "K" had spent most of their waking hours at the aid post, which held British refugees from the mainland as well as Singapore casualties. On this same day Moncer, the Englishman in charge, *a nice man, decent, absolutely without color prejudice, came to us practically in tears and said, "I've got very sad news. It's only a question of time before the whole thing is over. I've instructions to move British women and children to Government House. As for the rest of you, I can only ask you to go back to your homes and hope for the best."* Having thus, however reluctantly, separated whites from Asians in unconscious anticipation of what would happen on a much larger scale five days later, Moncer added that Lakshmi and "K" might help themselves to any medical stores they wished. So the next day, Friday, they went back to the aid post, collected what they could (Chinese were already stripping the place), and set off for the Paya Lebar house in their Morris.

> We were driving down this main road. To reach our house you turn left at a junction into a little side lane. When we were close to this junction, a group of Malays stopped our car and said, "Japanese, Japanese, get out and run for your lives!" There was a large drain by the side of the road. We got into it and waited. While we were sitting there, the Japanese came.
>
> After all the stories we'd heard about them, how they'd overrun Malaya, the atrocities, what their attitude was, I was afraid. But seeing them was a bit of an anticlimax. The Indian Army! My impression of it was of men smartly turned out, marching in step. But these people had bits of leaves and grass stuck in their helmets. They looked tired. Many of them had yellow skins, probably from malaria. They wore black canvas shoes, like sneakers but with a cleft by the big toe, and they shuffled along like . . . [laugh] like the devil with his webbed feet. Their weapons looked as if they'd come from some secondhand dealer. They didn't look like a conquering army at all.

Some of them stopped and set up a machine gun. They called Lakshmi and "K" over and listened while the two tried to explain that they were Indian. Later they took the gun down and carried it away. It struck Lakshmi that these men did not know what was going to happen next, which was reassuring, because it was what she felt herself. Nevertheless she wished she and "K" were not wearing their khaki Medical Auxiliary uniforms. As soon as they dared, they went to a house close by that belonged to Indians they knew. There Lakshmi borrowed a sari, "K" a shirt and *sarong*. By this time it was dusk. They spent the night in the house.

Saturday morning was very quiet, Prem remembers.

> Nothing was happening. I was sitting talking to my chaps when suddenly an orderly came up and said, "Leigh Sahib sends you his salaam." Now Bertie Leigh was commanding the company in front of me. I thought he wanted something. So I picked up my equipment, didn't even put it on properly, and walked along the ditch to where his company was. Suddenly I saw half a dozen Japanese. The battalion was half young recruits, you

know, and before they knew what was happening the Japanese had crept in. Leigh had tried to warn me, but I had got the message wrong. Here I was, about to be evacuated, and I had walked into this!

Headquarters hoped to get a few particularly valuable Indian officers out to India. Prem had been told he was on the list.

There was no question of making a run for it, there were Japanese all around. One said something sharp, something that sounded like *"Australian-ka"?* Prem was too surprised and furious to do anything but shout back. His hands were tied, his equipment taken, and he was led away. A little later along came the rest of his men, led by the English lieutenant who was his second in command. Someone had gone to the young man and told him to collect the company and bring it up the same *nullah* along which Prem had so blithely walked.

I was sitting under a tree with my hands tied in front of me. They took this young British officer, put him under another tree, and tied his hands too. A Japanese noncommissioned officer came up, worked the bolt of his rifle, and shook his head, meaning a bullet was too good for me. Then he took out his sword. I looked around and saw that they made this young Britisher kneel and chopped off his head. Next it would be my turn.

There was a Japanese soldier sitting beside me. He looked at my identity disc—in the Indian Army it is worn on the wrist, in the Japanese Army on the belt—then pointed to it and said something like "kore ka?" I made a motion towards his disc and said, "sama, sama," meaning "the same." Now, the first thing on your disc is your name. Most Japanese soldiers know Roman letters, and this soldier started spelling my name: Prem Kumar Sahgal.

"Kore ka?" he said.

"Nama," replied Prem.

Methodically the soldier spelled out the next line on the disc and asked what it meant. *"Religion,"* said Prem. *"You Buddhist, Shinto. I Hindu."*

"Oh!" said the soldier with sudden interest. *"Indoka? Ganjika?"*

"Indoka," replied Prem. *"No Ganjika,"* he added, not quite understanding.

The Japanese gave him a tremendous wallop on the head. With his tied hands Prem returned the blow as best he could. Then the Japanese stuck out his thumb in the universal gesture of Number One, and announced, *"Nippon, Tojo, hun! Indo, Ganji, hun!"*

Suddenly Prem understood what he meant. *"Gandhi family friend,"* he said eagerly. *"Ganji friend,"* repeated the soldier, and ran off and fetched an officer. *"You Indian?"* the officer asked. *"Don't I look Indian?"* Prem replied. To the Japanese he did not. When an interpreter was brought, however, and Prem explained who he was and that he did not know Gandhi personally but his father did, his captors were persuaded. *"Why did you go and kill my poor second in command?"* Prem asked. *"We kill all English and Australian officers,"* he understood them to reply. But Indians were friends.

> *They took me along to their colonel. He was sitting eating an omelette, a bottle of cognac on the table. I was introduced, and after a bit he said, "have a drink." I picked up a glass and poured one that big, and drank it. And then, for the first time, it struck me just what had happened. Until that moment I'd been paralyzed.*

On this same Saturday morning, Lakshmi and "K" left the house in which they had taken shelter and returned to the road junction. There was no sign of the Japanese. Their Morris was just as they had left it, so they got in and drove to the Paya Lebar house. Kutty and Padmini were relieved to see them. With the children they all settled into the trench. It seemed the only safe thing to do. A man in a house opposite, who would not take shelter, had been killed by shell fragments a few days before. They spent the night in the trench.

On Sunday morning, February 15, Japanese soldiers appeared, commandeered the Morris, indicated by signs that there would be fighting soon, and made everybody in the neighborhood move into the woods. Lakshmi barely had time to grab a feeding bottle for Padmini's baby. In the woods there was a clearing, a small field really. All afternoon they remained in that clearing. They could hear no fighting, not even in the distance. There were Japanese sentries about, but toward dusk they disappeared. Then, shortly after dark, K. P. K. came and said it was all over. Singapore had surrendered. But it would be best to stay where they were until dawn.

At dawn they left the clearing and returned to the house. Looters were already at work, rooms had been ransacked and food and clothing taken. With difficulty Lakshmi and "K" prevented two Chinese boys from dragging off a large bag of rice.

CHAPTER 4

FARRER PARK

Kate Caffrey's *Out in the Midday Sun* is a vivid account of how Malaya fell, one of the best I've seen, based largely on the recollections of men who fought in that miserable campaign. There is something odd, however, about the names. You notice a Braddon and a Brereton, a James, a Morrison, a Russell-Roberts. The units are the Bedfordshires and the Cambridgeshires, the Royal Norfolks, the 18th Australian Division. You come across "Painter's men"—it is only when you look closely that you realize these are actually the Sikhs and Garhwalis of the 22nd Indian Brigade, whom Caffrey prefers to call after their British commander. Indeed, all through the fighting Indians *as Indians* rarely appear. And when the fighting is over, when Singapore has surrendered and Caffrey starts to tell us what happened to the survivors, they become utterly invisible.

In her account of the campaign we do meet a few Indian units. It will please any veteran of the 2/10th Baluch, and also startle him since the regiment had long ceased to recruit from that part of the subcontinent, to read that "heavy fighting went on . . . around the village of Nee Soon, the Imperial Guards hammering away at a regiment from Baluchistan that gave a good account of itself in spite of being faced by tanks. . . ."[1] The fighting over, however, units and men alike quite disappear. "The British and Australian troops," Caffrey writes, "were given until five in the evening of February 7—forty-four and a half hours from the official cease-fire—to assemble in the Changi area." Changi being at the eastern tip of the island, the men would have over a dozen miles to walk. So on that Tuesday, which Caffrey says dawned clear and hot, "the long, long column set off, headed by at least four files of brigadiers and full colonels, with here and there a lorry on which some soldiers hitched a ride for part of the way." What she does not say is that many of these brigadiers and colonels had commanded Indians. (There were more Indians in Percival's army than British and Australians combined.) Key, for example, whom Prem thought so well of, and whom Caffrey describes as "a short, thick-set, hearty man with a round face" and a very determined manner—Key must have been in those files, and Key had commanded the 8th Indian Brigade, and later the 11th Indian Division. But none of Key's jawans were in the long, long column. None of his VCOs and ICOs were in it either. Prem himself, had he surrendered with the others instead of being tricked into captivity a day early, would not have trudged off behind Key. Virtually no Indian did.

This was not because they did not wish to. The Japanese gave them no choice. Already Prem had discovered, when his English second in command was beheaded and he was not, that the Japanese intended something special for their Indian prisoners. In fact, the process of distinguishing Indians from the British and the Australians had begun early in the Malayan campaign. It had begun with a Sikh captain of much personal and political restiveness named Mohan Singh.

❧

Japanese tanks had shattered Mohan Singh's 1/14th Punjab Battalion at Jitra, on the west side of the peninsula, early in the fighting. After a day spent wandering in jungle and swamp, and several days hiding while the fighting moved farther and farther away, Mohan Singh was in a frame of mind to listen (it owed something to his longstanding dissatisfaction with the way the Army had treated him) when by chance he was picked up by the Japanese Army *kikan*, or agency, charged with making friendly contact with Indians. A certain Pritam Singh, expatriate Sikh and founder in Bangkok several years before of an Indian Independence League, did the talking. But the driving force in this *Fujiwara Kikan* (sensibly, the Japanese called these agencies after the men who led them) was Fujiwara himself.

By all accounts Major Fujiwara Iwaichi was a remarkable man. Young, newly promoted, hardly two months on his assignment, with no Hindustani, little English, and supported by only a tiny staff, he had nevertheless already managed to set up a joint *Kikan*-Indian Independence League office at Alor Star, near Jitra, and to collect several hundred Indian stragglers. He had the confidence of Pritam Singh and the other Indians from Bangkok, though he had met them only in October. More surprising, he believed in the overtures he was instructed to make with a sincerity not to be doubted. (Years later he was to refer to himself as the Lawrence of the Indian National Army.) Japan must capture the hearts of the Indians, a thing she had signally failed to do with the Chinese. Japan must help them obtain their freedom. And she must do so for the reason that it was right to do so, not simply to advantage Nippon.[2]

The fighting had left Alor Star behind, there was a good deal of looting, Fujiwara lacked the means to stop it—and turned to Mohan Singh. Mohan Singh assembled a few score fellow Indians and did the job. The two hit it off well (they were both thirty-three), and in a short while Mohan Singh was organizing Indians all over northern Malaya. At the end of December, after meeting the Japanese commanding general and receiving assurances that Fujiwara spoke for more than himself, Mohan Singh agreed to raise an army to fight alongside the Japanese. Though it might eventually draw upon Indian civilians, for the time being it must be recruited from captured Indian soldiers. A headquarters was established and volunteers called for. As they came forward they were issued rifles, given arm bands bearing the letter F, and sent south to collect more of their kind.

Of all this Lakshmi had some inkling. *At the aid post our position became very awkward, because some of these Britishers said, "oh, we've been let down by the Indian troops, they've gone over to the Japanese."* But she did not really believe it. As for Prem, he was quite unaware of the rumor. Much later, it is true, he allowed himself to wonder whether the message that had brought him up the fatal *nullah* into the arms of the Japanese had not been the work of Fujiwara Volunteers. If it had, it had worked only because it concealed a ruse. Units that avoided being trapped or broken and retained their confidence and fighting spirit, as Prem's had, offered few stragglers and therefore few prospective recruits for Mohan Singh's roving parties. And so long as the fighting continued, the men in such units had little time or inclination to question the politics of the war, or to ask themselves what India and Indians should do.

With the fall of Singapore, however, things changed. Prem was identified as an Indian, which saved his life. He was separated from the British officers of his battalion. His captors of the Imperial Guards Division kept him with them, though more as a guest than as a prisoner. And when, after several days, he grew restless and asked to rejoin his battalion, they gave him a vehicle and let him go find it himself.

It was while he was the guest of the Guards Division that the Farrer Park meeting took place, the meeting that more than any other single act set the Indians in Malaya on the road to active war against Britain-in-India.

❧

Singapore surrendered on Sunday, February 15. Next morning the 1/14th and 5/14th Punjab, amalgamated as one battalion because of the losses suffered at Jitra and Slim River, piled their arms near Bidadari, a mile or so south of Paya Lebar. In the evening an order was received— a British order—that all Indians were to march the following day to Farrer Park, a sports ground a few miles away. That meant jawans, noncommissioned officers, VCOs, ICOs, the lot. The 14th Punjab had no British other ranks or NCOs. But it did have British officers—and they were not covered by this order, they had their own. It directed them not southwest to Farrer Park but east to Changi.

To Shah Nawaz, a captain in the 1/14th, this was disturbing. Shah Nawaz came from a large family in Rawalpindi, close to the Northwest Frontier; a Muslim family, but one conscious of Rajput origins; an old military family of the sort that generation after generation had sent its sons to be jemadars and subadars and subadar-majors in the Indian Army. Shah Nawaz's father had served for thirty years. Shah Nawaz himself was later to say that not one of his able-bodied male relatives had failed to wear the King-Emperor's uniform in one World War or the other. Indianization permitted Shah Nawaz to lift himself above the VCO level. In 1933 he entered Dehra Dun. Though three years Prem's senior (he was the 58th Indian cadet to receive a commission, Prem the 226th), circumstances kept him at the regimental depot long after Prem had gone overseas. Asked for at last by his British battalion commander, he reached Singapore at the end of January in time to join the amalgamated battalion on the island's north shore and withdraw with it to Bidadari. The experience galled him. "To have brought me to Singapore so late in the fight, only to be ordered to lay down my arms and surrender unconditionally, I considered to be extremely unjust to myself and to my sense of honour as a soldier." But what bothered Shah Nawaz now was the order to proceed to Farrer Park. For "according to the laws of civilized warfare, all captured officers, whether Indian or British, are kept together, and separate from rank and file," and this the order proposed not to do.[3]

Another officer of the 1/14th, Lieutenant Gurbaksh Singh Dhillon, was similarly bothered. Dhillon, too, came from a military family, a Sikh family of Lahore. His father was a veterinary surgeon at a cavalry remount depot, one brother was a jemadar in the Service Corps, another was an army clerk. Dhillon himself was marked for medicine. Failing the entrance examination to medical college, however, and with the cloud of family disappointment heavy about his head, he enlisted in the army as an ordinary recruit. By this time he had a wife. Married life on a sepoy's pay (he himself uses the term sepoy) was difficult. Dhillon was overeducated for the men he rubbed shoulders with, and over-qualified for the tasks he was set. For a time he thought of quitting. But his wife's encouragement, and his own determination and exuberance, drove him instead to search out every possible avenue of training and advancement, with a commission his goal.

Inclined from his youth to imagine slights and fancy himself insulted, his path upward was by his own account marked by scuffles. Nevertheless he rose, qualified for the two-year course at Kitchener College, and went on to the Military Academy at Dehra Dun. Emerging in 1940 number 336 on the ICO list, at a time when the war had put a stop to the practice of placing graduates temporarily with a British battalion, he was posted to the 1/14th Punjab at Lahore "in the very lines where I had stayed as a Sepoy."[4] When the battalion went south to Secunderabad, he went with it.

His recollections of his first months as an officer, however, read very differently from Prem's. At Lahore he was refused admission to the swimming club. Of Secunderabad he remembers not polo (he did not play), not mess nights (he was probably ill at ease), but how some senior British officers ignored him socially. "When I told my feelings to some of my brother officers," he adds after making this brief but bitter observation, "I was surprised to learn many more stories of discrimination." In March 1941 the 1/14th sailed for Malaya. As he went aboard, Dhillon exchanged angry words with an English sergeant-major of the embarkation staff. "The result was the C.O. did not talk to me throughout the voyage." In Malaya, where the battalion was quartered first at Ipoh, later at Sungei Patani, there was further unpleasantness: when the Indian officers tried to introduce Indian food into the mess; when they protested emergency-commissioned tea planters being given companies over their heads. Like Mohan Singh—a fellow Sikh, and in the same battalion, who had also worked his way up from the ranks—Dhillon carried with him a considerable baggage of resentment. A load he was temperamentally unable to lighten by riding with these Britishers, drinking with them, compelling them by the sheer force of his assurance (as Prem could) to amend their British ways.

Shortly after the battalion reached Malaya, the adjutant, an early Dehra Dun graduate named Zaman Kiani, fell ill. Temporarily, Dhillon took his place. Later he was sent back to India to do a signals course. Leave followed. He rejoined the 1/14th a few days before the Japanese attack. At Jitra his experiences were much like Mohan Singh's, but turned out differently, for with others he managed to escape down the coast by boat and rejoin what remained of the battalion. That, however, was for him the end of the fighting. He fell sick and went into hospital in Singapore, where characteristically he noted and protested the habit of refusing Indian troops access to British canteens. Though he was discharged before the final battle began, he had not managed to rejoin his battalion when the surrender came.

So when, on the morning of Tuesday, February 17, the combined 1/14th and 5/14th paraded under Zaman Kiani and marched off without their British officers to Farrer Park, Shah Nawaz marched with them. Dhillon marched with a unit to which he had been temporarily attached. Prem did not go at all. Of the three men who not quite four years later would be brought to trial in Delhi on a charge of treason, of the three defendants in the first Red Fort trial, two would remember (because they were there) the symbolic act by which the bond binding Percival's Indians to the King-Emperor's service was severed.

๛

Not that the guilt or innocence of Prem Sahgal, Dhillon, and Shah Nawaz would necessarily turn on the issue of allegiance. In the concluding address that old Bhulabhai Desai, chief counsel for the defense, delivered in late 1945 at the court-martial of these three, the point was early made that allegiance was not the issue. "Here is a case in which I venture to say—and the evidence supports it—that it is not at all a case of what you might call three individuals waging war against the king."[5] It was not a case of personal allegiance at all. "I quite agree," Bhulabhai continued, "that if ten persons in a village declare war on Britain, they are rebels," and may be dealt with individually. But here was another matter. Here was a provisional government and an army. Sahgal, Dhillon, and Shah Nawaz were members of that army. It was not they who were on trial, it was that army, the Indian National Army. More exactly, what was on trial was the right of the Indian National Army to wage war for the liberation of India.

Of course those who waged a war of liberation, Bhulabhai admitted, began that war still bound by the previous allegiance, "the *prima facie* allegiance if I may so call it." And this allegiance could not wholly disappear until the war was won and liberation achieved— which, in this case, had not occurred. But neither had it occurred in the case of the American South, whose soldiers had nevertheless not been charged with breach of allegiance and put on trial for their lives. Win or lose, a war for the liberation of a people, if properly declared and conducted, gave to men fighting that war the rights and immunities of belligerents. Bhulabhai would demonstrate this with examples drawn from international law and history. And he proceeded to do so, in parts of an address that lasted ten hours and consumed two days.

Had not these rights and immunities passed, at England's insistence no less, to the South American rebels of Bolivar's day? to the Greeks for whom Byron died? to Garibaldi and The Thousand? In the European conflict just ended, fleeing remnants of Dutchmen, Poles, and Yugoslavs had taken refuge in England and constructed governments in exile there, governments possessing "not an inch of territory they could call their own. . . . And the fact that they were deprived of their territory temporarily, or the fact that the Indians were deprived of their territories for a hundred and fifty years, makes not the slightest difference to the point that we are submitting to the Court." Belligerent rights had been successfully demanded for the one and could not reasonably be denied the other. Even the fragmented and frequently furtive French Resistance had qualified. Indeed, "if the Maquis," Bhulabhai pointed out, "were entitled to all the privileges and immunities of a fighting force," as Eisenhower himself had warned the Germans they were, "I cannot see how you can fail to accord a similar treatment to the Indian National Army." Allegiance was irrelevant. It was for the court simply to determine whether there had been "a de facto political organization sufficient in numbers, sufficient in character, and sufficient in resources to constitute itself capable of declaring and making war with an organized army." If the court found that such there had been, Sahgal, Dhillon, and Shah Nawaz must go free.

Bhulabhai knew, however, that the prosecution would not agree with him. Bhulabhai knew that the seven officers of the court, three Indians and four Englishmen, were not going to dismiss from their minds all considerations of loyalty. They were not going to rule inadmissible the question, were these three renegades? For the principal charge against the three was treason.

To be exact, they were charged with waging war against the King-Emperor contrary to Section 121 of the Indian Penal Code. But that in common parlance was treason, it being understood by every English-man that to set oneself against king and country was a traitorous act. The good subject was loyal to king and country both. It was a common, an undivided, allegiance.

Suppose, however, that king and country did not coincide, so that a person's allegiance, if he was not to be utterly faithless, must desert the one and attach only to the other. Such cases existed. From his historical stock Bhulabhai chose a celebrated one. It was the case of America. Bhulabhai had already borrowed the Civil War to demon-strate that even a rebellion that fails confers belligerent rights. Now, to seven officers perhaps a little tired of history anyway and certainly not eager to receive further instruction from the far side of the Atlantic, he proceeded to recite the Declaration of Independence, from the self-evident truths and inalienable rights of the opening paragraphs to the colonists' solemn repudiation of allegiance to the British crown at the close. 1776, he submitted, was "a classical instance of a case where the choice between allegiance to the King and allegiance to the country was presented to the world, and men of honour chose allegiance to their own country." And who were these men of honor? The same Americans whose descendants were now the friends and allies of England, "and if I may say so, their warmest and greatest supporters in the task of saving civilization. You could not have a stronger instance than that."

It was at Philadelphia, in 1776, that the Americans resolved the dilemma of their divided allegiance. At Farrer Park, on the 17th of February, 1942, the Indians of the Indian Army in Malaya did the same—or discovered that willy nilly it was being resolved for them. What happened was this.

On that Tuesday morning the combined 1/14th and 5/14th paraded at Bidadari. The British commanding officer shook hands with Kiani and the other Indian officers, remarking (Shah Nawaz remembers him saying) "I suppose this is the parting of the ways." The battalion moved off. Across the island, in all the places where the fighting and the surrender had deposited them, battalions, companies, and smaller packets of the defeated did the same.

Captain R. M. Arshad of the 5/2nd Punjab remembers that his battalion, reaching Farrer Park shortly after nine o'clock, found a considerable number of men already there. By noon the ground was thick with uniforms. Had every Indian soldier alive in Malaya that day answered to the roll, an observer might have counted some 55,000 men. As it was, though there were jawans on the island who did not receive the order, and jawans on the mainland to whom it was not sent, perhaps 40,000 had collected on the great open space that in better days had been used for horse racing when, early in the afternoon, word went around to assemble before the stadium building on one side of the park.

Officers (there were not many of these, less than 250) came to the front. The men stood behind, grouped some say not by units but by classes, Dogras here, Punjabi Muslims there. On the second floor of the stadium building there was a sort of balcony on which loudspeakers and a microphone had been set up. A number of Japanese and Indians were on this balcony. Some of the Indians wore white arm bands bearing in red the letter F.

"When the parade was ready," continues Arshad, "a British officer—later I learned his name was Colonel Hunt from Malaya Command Headquarters—came in front of the microphone, brought us to attention, and addressed us."[6] Exactly what Hunt said is uncertain. Though he survived the war, he was in England on medical leave when the Red Fort trials began, and so was not asked.[7] Arshad first testified that he told the Indians, "from now on you belong to the Japanese Army," and would have to obey its orders. Later, under cross-examination, he decided that he had said no more than that they were all prisoners of war, and that he was turning them over to the Japanese. But whatever Hunt said he said briefly, in a simple, almost perfunctory manner, with no indication that he was bothered or uncomfortable. "After that," remembers Subadar-Major Baboo Ram of the 1/14th, who was near the front with the other VCOs, "he handed over certain papers to Major Fujiwara, a Japanese officer." (As each unit arrived that morning it had given its strength in writing to Hunt. These, presumably, were the papers.) "Then he saluted him and went back. And after that Major Fujiwara came to the microphone and made a speech in the Japanese language which was translated into English and then re-translated into Hindustani."[8] Fujiwara said a number of things with great and obvious sincerity. He ended by announcing that he was turning the officers and men over to Mohan Singh. Then Mohan Singh came to the microphone and made a speech too. So each handed over to the next, not as one speaker making way for another speaker, but as one command surrendering men to another command.

Much later, in the chorus of anger and embarrassment that rose among Englishmen on the subject of the INA, no one was heard to suggest that Percival should have refused to let himself and his colleagues be separated from their brothers in arms, the Indian officers. No one was heard to suggest that Hunt, on coming to the microphone that February afternoon, should have declined to announce what he was instructed to announce, or should at least have told the men that he spoke because compelled to, and with a heavy heart. At the Red Fort no one charged Hunt with anything (of course the British were not in the dock). No one even asked, of the affair, what had those who sent him intended?

Yet it is perfectly clear that the purpose in addressing those thousands of officers and men just two days after the fall of Singapore cannot have been simply to tell them that the battle was lost and that all of them, British and Indians together, were now prisoners of the Japanese. They knew that well enough. There had to be another purpose. And the purpose that was perceived, conveyed not just by the words "and I hand you over to the Japanese authorities" but by the arrangements that had gone before, and particularly by the separating without protest of the British officers and other ranks—the purpose perceived by these men whose discipline and loyalty Malaya Command had no reason to doubt, and who had fought bravely some of them the full length of the peninsula, was the deliberate, formal, one might almost say ceremonial, abdication of a responsibility. In good times, in victorious times, the two races of the Indian Army (to use the traditional term) were bound to each other in "a matter of honour." Now times were bad. So the British were backing out.

"I had a feeling of being completely helpless, of being handed over like cattle by the British to the Japs and by the Japs to Mohan Singh." That was how Shah Nawaz later remembered it. Dhillon, too, felt "like one deserted."[9] Yet at this very moment these men, so recently defeated, so thoroughly abandoned, so far from home, were being offered (by the speakers who followed Hunt) the means of reversing that defeat, of overcoming that abandonment, even of returning to India. Speaking slowly because what he said had to be translated first into English and then into Hindustani, Fujiwara welcomed the soldiers, by this time seated on the ground. They were, he said, to consider themselves not prisoners but friends. In Malaya the British had been thoroughly trounced. In Burma they soon would be. Through her victories, Japan was creating for the peoples of East Asia a co-prosperity sphere based on amity and equality. That sphere would not be secure without an independent India on its western flank. So Japan wished India to be free. To that end she was cooperating in the formation of an army that should liberate her, an army he hoped all would join. And Mohan Singh, following Fujiwara to the microphone, put the new loyalty, the fresh allegiance, squarely to his listeners. "We are forming an Indian National Army that will fight to free India. Are you all prepared to join the Indian National Army?" Were they? As Baboo Ram remembers it, "the audience lifted up their arms, threw their turbans in the air, and showed great pleasure."[10]

Just how great the pleasure, and by how many experienced, it is impossible to tell. Dhillon reports "a feeling of hope and joy by all of us present," and Fujiwara himself says that Mohan Singh's short speech left some men weeping. He spoke in Hindustani, so that almost everybody understood him instantly. And he was an effective speaker. Lakshmi, who of course was not present, remembers of the time she first heard him, months later, how impressed she was. *He had an emotional way of talking. He seemed convinced he had taken the right step, he didn't have any doubts of any kind.* At Farrer Park that certainty of tone and manner was directed at men who were beginning to realize that in this part of the world the Raj was finished, and that acquiescence in Japanese wishes was probably their only choice.

For that the British might some day return to Singapore did not seem remotely possible—or particularly desirable, either.

We in the West are so used to regarding the Second World War as a critical contest for the possession of civilized society's body and soul; a contest nearly lost by mismanagement, kept alive by England's stubborn refusal to capitulate, and at last won when America and Russia met in the center of Europe—we in the West are so used to looking at the war in this way, that its Asian dimension never rises in our eyes above the level of a sideshow, an enormous and shameless irrelevance. Germany began the conflict. It would be over, and the world safe again, when Germany was smashed. Meanwhile Japan's entry, like Italy's earlier but on a much larger and more dangerous scale, was an act of the grossest opportunism, a monstrous and unforgivable diversion, for which she would be duly punished when the work of saving civilization in Europe was done.

That is the way we view the war now, that is the way we of the North Atlantic community looked at it then. And seeing it thus gave to military events east of Suez a decidedly lower level of significance than attached to events west of it. Even the most chilling disasters in the Pacific theater, even Pearl Harbor, Singapore, and Bataan, struck us as inconclusive. Thrown out of this place or that by the Japanese, we all of us, like MacArthur, knew that we should return. When the real business of the war, the European business, was finished, we should come back to Asia. And then everything would be as it had been before. Or if there had to be changes, as for example in India where some form of independence would have to be arranged, it would be seen that the war had nothing to do with it. Japanese victories had nothing to do with it. They were an interruption, a damned nuisance of an interruption, which far from initiating or accelerating those changes had actually prevented us from getting on with them.

Things, however, did not look this way to Asians. Perhaps Bhulabhai Desai meant it when he complimented the British and their "supporters" the Americans for undertaking "the task of saving civilization," but he was speaking after the war had ended, from Delhi which the Japanese had never occupied, and to a British court he was determined to sway. Indians at the time cannot have thought the task urgent, or Britain the indispensable agent. Whose civilization, anyway, were the British trying to save?

East of Calcutta the Japanese did not appear as usurpers of lands, lands to which the British, French, Dutch, and Americans must triumphantly return when more pressing business elsewhere had been attended to. The Japanese were fellow Asians, with as much right to those lands as westerners had. They offered their fellow Asians, if not equality of status, at least a secure and honorable place in an ordered hierarchy of Asian peoples. As for triumphant return, it was one thing for an Englishman with the Battle of Britain behind him, or an American from a continent that had never been invaded and never could be, to believe in its inevitability. It was quite another for someone on the spot—for an Indian or Malay, say, observing from Singapore's waterfront one April morning a great fleet of battleships and aircraft carriers lying in the roads, the same battleships and carriers that had delivered the crushing blow at Pearl Harbor four months before, and that had given Japan mastery of the waves from Hawaii all the way to the Indian Ocean.

Never much interested in Europe's war except, perhaps, as it might advance a military man's professional career. Accustomed to seeing, where Britain was concerned, not gallant little England of Dunkirk and the white cliffs of Dover but the great, unbending Empire of the Gateway, the Viceroy's Palace, and the Jallianwala Bagh. Confronted, suddenly, with the swift and complete collapse of the eastern portion of that empire and its replacement by a new imperial power both Asian and irresistible. And then invited, with apparent warmth and sincerity, to join in a march westward that should expel the British, obtain *purna swaraj* for Mother India, and (no small point) bring themselves home—how could officers and men fail to be swept away by such a prospect? An army for an independent India, a true Indian Army, was offered that afternoon at Farrer Park. What is surprising is that, even so, there were some who had doubts and held back.

CHAPTER 5

The Beginning of the INA

Even Mohan Singh admits this. Admits that while most of the men shouted for joy when he had finished speaking, there were some, particularly among the officers, who remained silent; who sat "downcast and indifferent."[1] Shah Nawaz was one.

Shah Nawaz, as I have said, came from a family that had served the Raj for generations. His father and his father's father had been of that class of veteran subadars and subadar-majors who, when asked to speak at this village gathering or that, closed their remarks with the ritual *Sarkar-e-Bartania ki chhatri hamare sir par hamesha qayam rahe* (may the umbrella of the British government remain over our heads forever). He was, moreover, by nature loyal. Lakshmi says of him (he has only recently died) that *once he gives his loyalty, he never wavers.* Eventually he would withdraw that loyalty. For the moment, however, chilled though he was by Hunt's words and behavior, he could not. "The very idea of joining hands with our former enemies and fighting against our own kith and kin was fantastic. . . . Not only did I make up my mind to keep out of the I.N.A. As the head of a famous military tribe, I felt it my duty to warn all others, especially the men I commanded."[2] When, therefore, the combined 1/14th and 5/14th left Farrer Park, Shah Nawaz marching with it turned over in his mind not how to help this enterprise of Mohan Singh's but how to hinder it. And Prem, locating his outfit with the help of the vehicle the Japanese had given him, and learning that he might join or not as he thought best, was inclined to choose the second course too.

For the time being they were all still prisoners of war. But as the Japanese hoped to engage their active cooperation, and hadn't the men to impound them properly in any case, they were allowed to govern themselves. Two headquarters were formed. One, Mohan Singh's, was given the lofty title of "Supreme Command" and received handsome quarters at Mount Pleasant, a suburb on the northern edge of the city. The other was the prisoner-of-war headquarters at Neesoon, the largest of the POW camps (it was there that Prem found his men). There was another large camp at Bidadari, and smaller ones at Tyersall and Buller to the west, at Seletar on the island's northeast coast, at Kranji near the Causeway, and later at one or two other places. Zaman Kiani was made responsible for the Neesoon camp, with Shah Nawaz his second in command. To Lt. Colonel Niranjan Singh Gill, the Sikh officer who had done the English-to-Hindustani translations at Farrer Park, went the overall direction of the prisoners of war. Prem became a staff officer, in charge of the administrative branch, which meant that among other things he concerned himself with medical matters. It was not a trifling responsibility.

For the camps were overcrowded, fifty men using facilities meant for ten, and the confusion and demoralization of the surrender hung over them still. A. C. Chatterji, the senior Indian medical officer and now Gill's director of medical services, found when he took his hospital unit into Neesoon that drinking water was drawn from drains and shallow pits, men fouled the hillsides, flies were everywhere, and dysentery threatened. Together he and Shah Nawaz had wells and trench latrines dug, and put in electricity. But obtaining medical supplies for the sick and wounded was another matter. The British had carried the lion's share with them to Changi. So Prem took the vehicle the Japanese had given him, went foraging with his number two man, a south Indian by the name of John Somasundaram, and in this way met Lakshmi. Somasundaram's family had known Lakshmi's well, in Madras. As Lakshmi tells it, *one afternoon he and Prem came in an army lorry, and John introduced Prem and said, "we've come from our camp and we have this transport here, we want medicines badly."* She and "K" let the two have some of the medical stores they had salvaged from Moncer's aid post. Lakshmi added a huge tin of jam.

At first Lakshmi paid little attention to the opportunities that circumstances were thrusting upon the Indians. Through K. P. K. Menon she knew what was going on. And she was excited by what she heard about the freedom army. But for the moment she and "K" had other things on their minds. The Japanese were encouraging doctors to return to their work. *We went back to our house in Katong. It was in a bad state, and we had to reopen our dispensary, so we were very, very busy.* There was another reason, too, for keeping to herself. She found it difficult to suppress her dislike of the Japanese.

There was no particular reason for this. The Indians of Singapore were not treated as the Chinese were. They, *poor things*, were rounded up in thousands, herded into open spaces (one was the clearing where Lakshmi and her neighbors had spent the night), and held without food, water, or shade while male suspects (to be a schoolteacher was automatically to condemn yourself) were weeded out and led away. To prison, sometimes. More often to be machine-gunned, or roped in batches and dumped in the open sea. This Lakshmi and her sort escaped. *We were very well treated. Our car was returned, with many thanks. As doctors we were given an extra ration of petrol.* Soldiers made much of Padmini's children and heaped her with tinned milk.

But day-to-day relations with the Japanese were soured by their refusal to use English, which Lakshmi attributed to their hatred of westerners, though fear of ridicule was more probably the cause. And it was impossible to ignore the *Kempeitai*, the Japanese military police. For the first few months they were posted at all important crossroads, and if the bow you made as you passed did not satisfy them you were recalled, slapped hard across the face, and made to bow again. Lakshmi noticed that the smarter the appearance of the passerby, the more probable this treatment. Like everybody else she took to wearing casual dress.

Gradually, however, the Indians learned to deal with the new imperial power. They did so through the medium of their local Indian Independence League. Everywhere in Southeast Asia where Indians lived these leagues, sometimes adapted from an Indian Association (Japanese victories making it no longer necessary to dissemble), were beginning to appear. The Japanese encouraged this. In Malaya the leagues so multiplied that one might have expected some Malayan Indian, K. P. K. perhaps, or the Penang barrister Nedyam Raghavan, to emerge as the recognized leader of the overseas Indian independence movement. But it was not from Penang or Singapore that the leadership came. It came from Tokyo. This was not because there were many Indians in Tokyo. There were very few. It was because Tokyo was the seat of the Japanese imperial government, and therefore the place where Rash Behari Bose lived.

✒

Just as England in the nineteenth century had received the Karl Marxes and Giuseppe Mazzinis of continental Europe, so Japan more recently had been the refuge of Asian revolutionaries. Rash Behari Bose was a Bengali of that pre–World World War I generation which, infuriated by the partition of Bengal, turned to terrorism long before Bhagat Singh and his fellows took the tactic up. Suspected of complicity in the attempt on Lord Hardinge's life (in 1912 a bomb was thrown at the Viceroy as he entered Delhi on the back of an elephant), Rash Behari went underground, and after a time took shelter in Japan. When the British traced him there and tried to have him extradited, he put himself under the protection of those ardent Japanese patriots— "double patriots" they came to be called—who were, with increasing success, pushing Nippon into a course at once revolutionary, authoritarian, and expansionist. Bose became proficient in Japanese, married a Japanese, was naturalized as a Japanese. In the end he sent a son to serve and die in the Japanese Army. The identification grew so close that it was hard for Indians who worked with him to be sure he was one of *them*. But when the Pacific war began, and the double patriots came into their own, this identification enabled him to seize command of the overseas Indian independence movement.

Even before the war began, he had tried to interest the Japanese military in the cause of Indian independence. No doubt the military would have had a certain interest in it anyway. It would have seen in it opportunities to weaken Britain. So the *Fujiwara Kikan* would have existed, and General Tojo (the Prime Minister) would have made his Diet speeches urging India to rise, whether or not Rash Behari had been at hand.

But he *was* at hand. His persistence in Indian revolutionary activity was known. When, therefore, General Staff Headquarters took stock of what Fujiwara had been doing, found it promising, and cast around for ways of expanding the work, it turned to Rash Behari Bose. He advised it to go ahead with Mohan Singh's army, attaching it, however, to a political organization that would speak for Indians all over

Southeast Asia—an organization he, naturally, would direct. In due course an invitation went out, over his name but through Japanese military channels, for a conference at Tokyo. And early in March a score or so of persons met at the home of S. C. Goho, a Singapore lawyer and chairman of the Singapore Indian Independence League, to consider the invitation.

A photograph of the group survives. Fujiwara is there, with his interpreter Lieutenant Kunizuka and another *F-Kikan* man. He stands between Pritam Singh, soon to be killed in a plane crash, and the much taller and turbanned Gill. To the left are Mohan Singh and K. P. K. Menon. To the right are Goho, in white shirt and shorts and what looks like a Congress cap, and Zaman Kiani, tallest of the lot, in the khaki shirt and broad khaki shorts of the Indian Army. It is a mixture in roles as well as in dress, civilians mingling with Japanese and with men from both the fledgling INA and the POW camps. Raghavan, who had been president of the prewar Central Indian Association, presided over the discussions. It was decided to accept Rash Behari's invitation. A delegation with Raghavan at its head was appointed to go to Tokyo. Toward the end of March it left.

But the delegates, in particular Raghavan, had no intention of putting themselves unreservedly at Rash Behari's service. They did not wholly trust him. He had lived too long among the Japanese, was too much at ease with certain officers under whose patronage the conference (held at a Tokyo hotel) visibly proceeded. So the conference decided nothing. In April the delegates returned to Singapore, bringing Rash Behari with them. There he was invited to chair a public meeting. At this meeting the formation of an All-Malayan Indian Independence League was announced, with Raghavan at its head and K. P. K. and Goho on the governing board. As for the other matters raised—the body to which the regional leagues would report, the Council of Action that would be that body's executive arm, the relations between the Council and INA on one side and the Japanese on the other—these took the form of proposals only. And proposals they would remain until they were voted upon by a larger and more representative group than the Tokyo assembly, meeting elsewhere than on Japanese soil.

Lakshmi paid her Singapore dollar and joined the League. She found it difficult, however, to translate her enthusiasm into day-to-day activity. The higher councils of the League were a male preserve. Except for K. P. K. nobody was interested in giving women real work to do. In spite of its name, the *Azad Bharat Sabha* (translated literally this becomes the Free India Association) did not seem to her to be seriously in the business of securing India's independence. It was popular enough. In four months its membership topped one hundred thousand. Belonging to it was useful. *You got a membership card written in English as well as in Japanese. It had little Japanese stamps on it, rations were issued through it,* and when you came to a barrier and had to show your papers you produced it—it identified you as an Indian, which saved you much trouble. Lakshmi had to admit, too, that the League did try to relieve the misery of the plantation laborers who had been thrown out of work. But what had all this to do with freedom for India?

If Lakshmi felt a bit put off by the League, Prem was not sure he wanted anything to do with the freedom army. He had not been present at Farrer Park. Though he had met Mohan Singh, it had been only casually, at Penang during a spell of leave before the Malayan campaign. He had no opportunity now to talk privately to him. Nor did he desire one. The early period of INA activity, when Indian stragglers were being invited to turn against the British, had been no more than a rumor to the 2/10th Baluch—an unpleasant rumor. *There had been nothing like that with us on the east coast. We came back intact, we came back fighting. When we reached the Neesoon camp we quite looked down on Mohan Singh and his group as people who couldn't fight, who had no liver for fighting.* Gill he knew much better, and liked. He was on Gill's staff. And he had plenty to do.

I told you one of our main difficulties was milk for our patients. We started badgering the Japanese—at that time there were hardly any cattle in Malaya, most of the milk was powdered or tinned, and of course it was in extremely short supply. We kept badgering the Japanese. And at last they said, "all right, we'll make arrangements." So one morning we got a message they wanted the senior Indian officers to come to an enclosure just outside Bidadari Camp, a wire enclosure built by the British as a prisoner-of-war cage.

There we found fifty bulls. Lt. Kunizuka of the Fujiwara Kikan was there, and I said to him, "what is this?" "Sahgal-san," he said, "Imperial Japanese Army going to present fifty cows to India side, milk for their patients." "Where are the cows?" I said. "Here are the cows," he said. "Those aren't cows," I said, "they're bulls." "What is the difference?" he said. "Those are he-cows," I said. "He-cows no give milk?" "No," I said, "he-cows no give milk." "Not even a little?" "Not even a little."

So we went through the ceremony, Japanese coming and standing opposite, terrific bowing, fifty cows presented on behalf of the Imperial Japanese Army, Mohan Singh bowing back, very grave. And after the Japanese left, we opened the gate and let the bulls go.

In Japan milk and butter were almost unknown. Quite possibly Kunizuka and his fellow officers had never seen a cow in all their lives. Prem noticed that Japanese soldiers who came across tins of ghee (clarified butter) used the precious stuff to grease their boots. Just as exasperating was the childish language you had to employ with all but the trained interpreters. With the Chinese or the Malays you could speak in simple English because they had grown up under British rule and had some facility in it. To the Japanese you spoke in pidgin or risked not being understood.

Nor could the Japanese be made to see that a jawan's diet could not be composed of rice alone. A jawan required dal, for the preparation of which you had to have certain spices. But *when we drew rations for our troops, so many kilograms of rice, so much of dal, so much of turmeric and coriander, the Japanese would say, "this is too much for us, today you take all dal." Then another time they would give all curry powder. We tried to explain that you don't eat curry powder. It was no use.*

In April, when the delegates returned from Tokyo, Prem had a long talk with Gill. Gill was not happy. He did not trust the Japanese. He wanted the follow-up conference at Bangkok that had been agreed upon. But Mohan Singh did not share Gill's misgivings and had no intention of waiting for a conference. Convening a group of officers (Prem was one) at Bidadari, he told them that Japanese intentions and good faith were clear enough to permit an immediate start.

So a set of resolutions, the Bidadari Resolutions, were framed. Short, uncomplicated, they announced that Indians stood united above all differences of caste, community, or religion. Independence was every Indian's birthright. An Indian National Army would be raised to fight for it. There was nothing in the resolutions about how that fight was to be coordinated with the Japanese, nothing about the Japanese at all. The resolutions *did* allow—Prem believes it was he who insisted upon this—that the army would go into action only when the Congress and the people of India asked it to, but as no one knew how party and people were to give an unmistakable signal, Mohan Singh cannot have felt this would much tie his hands.

Acting with his usual dispatch, Mohan Singh had the Bidadari Resolutions circulated, then accompanied Fujiwara on a tour of the mainland POW camps to explain them to the men. On May 9 recruiting began. But first Mohan Singh had POW headquarters dissolved and its staff transferred to his own.

This struck Prem as reasonable. Gill's office had become superfluous. Prem did not make the move himself, however, for Gill's suspicions reinforced his own. Besides, though recruiting was proceeding busily enough, there were no further plans, nothing to indicate what kind of force would result. *The whole thing looked phony to me. I had no wish to join a phantom army.* Efforts were being made to identify units from which volunteers might be expected, hold them at Neesoon and Bidadari, and send the others elsewhere. Prem's 2/10th Baluch was not a likely prospect. So it was marched to Tengah airfield, in the west central part of the island. Prem joined it there.

I was quite happy at Tengah. Our boys were working. (The Japanese wanted the runways extended and underground operations rooms dug.) *We used to get as wages 20 Straits cents a day.* Prudently managed that bought two bottles of beer a week, which Prem saved for the weekend, fortifying the first half-bottle with rectified spirits from the hospital and taking the rest as it came. A couple of times a month he got a pass to town, and sometimes it was possible to slip away without one. So Prem began to see a good deal of Lakshmi, usually with John Somasundaram. They talked a good deal. Often their conversation turned to the question, what should they do about the INA?

Lakshmi knew what *she* would do. She would join. She could see, however, that Prem held back. This was partly, she believes, because at bottom his hostility toward the Japanese was stronger than her own. *I didn't particularly like them but I wasn't as anti-Japanese as he was.* It was also because he was afraid they meant to make stooges of men like himself, and this he would not have. If there was to be an Indian force it must be an independent allied army, not Nippon's instrument. Because she liked and respected Prem, understood his reservations, and anyway could discern no place for women in Mohan Singh's army, she did not press her opinion. He for his part pursued the issue less with her than with his fellow officers, among whom Arshad was one.

Arshad had been at Government College and Dehra Dun with Prem, had fought through the Malayan campaign, and had marched to Farrer Park. Now he was attached to Mohan Singh's headquarters, not because he was a convinced INA man, but because his good friend and fellow Muslim, Inayat Kiani, a cousin of Zaman Kiani and confidant of Mohan Singh, had asked for him. Prem visited Arshad frequently at his Mount Pleasant bungalow. There they talked about whether to join, going round and round the question, until at last, setting an evening aside for the purpose, they and two or three others met and examined the business methodically, item by item, point by point. "We discussed all the pros and cons," Arshad testified at Prem's trial, "and we unanimously decided that under the circumstances we all owed our allegiance to our country"—meaning India, Arshad made it plain.

꧁꧂

Of the chief of these circumstances they were reminded by Mount Pleasant itself. The Indian National Army was not simply a notion in Mohan Singh's head. It was an established fact, with a headquarters and men. But it was only half-formed. Many jawans had not made up their minds about it. Even more officers held back. If officers, senior officers in particular, did not come forward soon, bringing their men with them, "some people would join and some would not," Arshad continued.[3] "And the Japanese would take advantage of that and enrol people amongst the prisoners of war who would be willing to do any service for them." But if senior officers entered, "and organized the INA as a regular army, and fought the Japanese on every point regarding the army," the Japanese would not be able to do this. They would not be able to turn the prisoners into bond servants.

Then there was the civil population to consider. What the Japanese were doing to the local Chinese was well known. If, now, the prisoners of war refused to join Mohan Singh's force, might not local Indians be exposed to the same brutal treatment? And there were Indians in Burma. They, too, needed help and protection. Grim stories were reaching Singapore about their plight.

For the British had been as thoroughly defeated in Burma as they had been in Malaya, Rangoon bombed on the 23rd of December and abandoned on March 8, with the difference that as Burma is not surrounded by water, the defenders might hope to escape. With great difficulty, leaving most of their equipment behind, many did. The last British column crossed the Chindwin River and disappeared into the mountains that separate Burma from Assam just as the monsoon began. With them went tens of thousands of Indian civilians—went, or attempted to go. For in the rush to get away it became apparent, as it had been apparent at Penang during the Malayan campaign, that food, transport, help of every sort, were reserved for the British. And after the British, for the Anglo-Indians (or Eurasians). Very little was arranged for the Indians. What was arranged, came late.

Indeed, afraid of losing Rangoon's dock labor while there was still a chance of holding the city, the British for a time actually compelled Indian coolies to stay. "The Burma Government issued orders," writes Hugh Tinker, "that no adult Indian should be allowed to depart on any ship as a deck passenger." (At the time Tinker was a young man with an Indian Army unit which, when the rains began, was set the almost impossible task of trucking refugees out over the Tamu-Manipur road.) "All except middle class Indians habitually travelled as deck passengers," continues Tinker, "so this sealed off the exit for all but the wealthy Indians."[4] And though this and other restraints were eventually lifted, leaving Indians of all classes free to escape if they could, tens of thousands died trying, uncounted numbers of others got part way and stuck, and the condition of those who made it was so bad, and contrasted so sharply with the state of mind and body of evacuated Englishmen and Anglo-Indians, poor as that was, that sharp questions were asked in Delhi and London, questions that no one could adequately answer.

Though none of this was known in Singapore, it was suspected. Even more worrisome was the probably condition of the Indians who remained in Burma. Anti-Indian feeling there, fanned by a communal

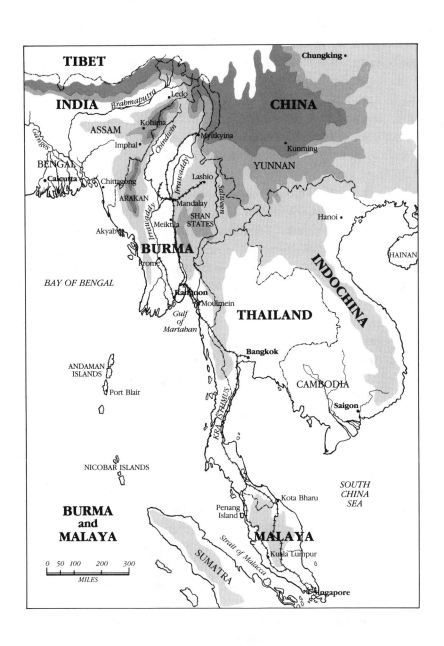

TIBET

INDIA

Brahmaputra

•Ledo

CHINA

Chungking •

ASSAM

•Kohima

Myitkyina

Chindwin

Imphal•

•Kunming

YUNNAN

BENGAL

•Calcutta

Chittagong•

Ganges

Lashio•

ARAKAN

Irrawaddy

Mandalay•

Salween

Hanoi •

HAINAN

Akyab•

Meiktila•

SHAN
STATES

BURMA

Prome•

INDOCHINA

BAY OF BENGAL

Rangoon•

•Moulmein

*Gulf
of
Martaban*

THAILAND

ANDAMAN
ISLANDS

•Port Blair

Bangkok•

CAMBODIA

Saigon•

KRA ISTHMUS

NICOBAR ISLANDS

SOUTH
CHINA
SEA

Kota Bharu•

Penang
Island

BURMA
and
MALAYA

MALAYA

Strait of Malacca

Kuala Lumpur•

0 50 100   200   300

SUMATRA

•Singapore

MILES

system of representation that gave Indians reserved seats in the legislature, was notorious and longstanding. In 1930, several hundred Indians had lost their lives when gangs of Burmese incensed over a labor dispute ran amok in Rangoon. Eight years later thousands died in anti-Indian riots that spread this time throughout Burma. The collapse of the Raj could easily bring such violence into the open again. As the Japanese might be too preoccupied or too little interested to control it, the sooner an Indian armed force reached Burma the better.

And beyond lay India. Might not an armed force push right on? It would have to move, of course, in concert with the Japanese, and *even at that stage,* Prem remembers, *we weren't certain the Japanese were going to win the war.* But they did not have to win the war. They had only to go a little further. That, it was now apparent, they could do. *We had talked with Japanese officers, we had heard about Japanese operations, and we realized that it was a very small force that had captured Malaya.* It was the same in Burma. *We had people who had been in Burma and come back, and they told us that in Burma also there were very few Japanese troops.* There too, Prem believed, a handful had defeated a multitude. As for the army that barred the way to India, if the reinforcements that had reached Singapore toward the end said anything, they announced that the Indian Army had ceased to be a fighting force. No unit that had received a draft of those raw recruits could be in doubt about that.

In fact, British India in the spring of 1942 *was* indefensible. It had already sent more than three hundred thousand of its best men overseas, principally to the Middle East, but also to Burma and Malaya, and in Malaya all, of course, had been lost. With them had gone the best of the matériel. For much of this, England was the only source of supply. The Mediterranean being closed, it had to come round the Cape. And as merchant shipping losses to U-boats were more severe in 1942 than they had ever been, and India must anyway take a back seat to the Middle East (where on the north African coast a British army was being forced back toward the Nile), it was a question whether fresh Indian troops, if they could be raised, were going to have much in the way of arms and equipment to fight with.

In India itself, moreover, there was an enormous physical reorientation to be accomplished. The Indian Army had always been positioned on the Northwest Frontier, because that was the traditional route into the subcontinent. All the strategic roads, railroads, airfields, and administrative installations were there. They had now to be reproduced in West Bengal, more than a thousand miles away. There was a further difficulty. To get from West Bengal to the Burmese frontier was a formidable undertaking. No roads reached the Brahmaputra. Everything, even vehicles, had to approach by broad-gauge rail. Everything had then to be ferried across the river (there were no bridges), and continue by meter-gauge rail or by the few second-class roads of East Bengal, across ground cut by innumerable watercourses, rife with malaria, and drenched by monsoon rains. Archibald Wavell, Commander-in-Chief India, with three incomplete divisions in his newly created Eastern Army, estimated that if he could find a spare brigade, it could not be moved to the prospective front in less than seven weeks.

Early in March, on the very day Rangoon was abandoned, Wavell had given the Chiefs of Staff his forecast. Upper Burma would fall, he had predicted, and when it fell the Japanese would push on at once into India. (Until 1937 Burma had been *part* of India.) The peril would be extreme unless he was given certain reinforcements which, he knew, the Chiefs intended for Ceylon. He was overruled. The reinforcements went to Ceylon. But there, early in April, the British suffered a blow that appeared to put India's entire east coast at risk. With some difficulty the British had assembled a fleet off the island. It was surprised by Japanese carriers, the very same carriers that had attacked Pearl Harbor, and in a series of engagements lost heavily while inflicting very little damage in return. Meanwhile, other Japanese warships, moving close against the mainland, sank a score of merchant vessels in the space of a few hours. Bombs fell on the port of Vishakhapatnam. Madras panicked. Tens of thousands fled into the interior. For a time it was seriously supposed the Japanese meant to land.

In fact they had no such intention. Their carriers passed back into the China Sea and did not return, then or later. The British, however, could not foresee this. They withdrew their warships to the east coast of Africa. Madras, Vishakhapatnam, Calcutta were closed to merchant shipping; only Karachi and Bombay remained to handle India's entire seaborne trade. The Japanese were left in undisputed possession of the Bay of Bengal. They were free to supply their Burma army by the sea route to Rangoon. It seemed entirely likely that when they had completed the conquest of upper Burma, they would move upon India not simply across the mountains but up the coast as well. And if they did, it was entirely possible they would break into the subcontinent to take Assam, east Bengal, even Calcutta.

For Wavell and the British the prospect was alarming. But for Mohan Singh and the enthusiasts about him, it was just the opposite. If the Japanese could be persuaded to make the INA a part of their invading force, armed Indians whom the British would be powerless to evict would soon stand on India's soil—and the Raj must topple. First, however, that army had to be raised and organized. For this men were needed; men were desperately needed; men must be induced to come forward. If men had doubts or harbored reservations, these would have to be settled later, it could not be done now. So Mohan Singh pushed ahead with his recruiting drive. He was impatient. He encouraged his subordinates to be impatient. And this had consequences, consequences that threatened the Indian National Army's good name.

~𝕏~

In theory every man was free to join or not as he thought best. In practice there were pressures—especially from the officers, to whom naturally the jawans listened. Prem's own unit consisted, as we know, of Dogras, Pathans, and Punjabi Muslims. Now Punjabi Muslims, explains Prem, *were traditionally loyal to the British, and political consciousness among them was nil*, so Mohan Singh's appeals had little effect upon them. And because they would not join, the Dogras and the Pathans would not either. *They had this strong feeling of being together*, Prem continues. *The Dogras wanted to join, the Pathans wanted to join, but they did not want to leave their Punjabi Muslim brothers.* Prem did not try to make them. Not all officers similarly abstained.

Some did as Shah Nawaz at first did, and worked circumspectly to keep their men out. Others tried to persuade them to join, or bluntly ordered them to, with mixed results. And a few, no one denies it, went further: to threats and positive ill-treatment.

A year or so later, when the British were wrestling with the problem of what to tell India about the renegade army, these threats and this ill-treatment were darkly alluded to. And when at last Burma and Malaya had been recovered, and a few of the actual renegades stood before courts-martial at the Red Fort in Delhi, the threats and the ill-treatment were more than alluded to. They were laid out in detail.

The Indian National Army, it was said, had been peopled not merely with the simple-minded and the duped but with sepoys forced to enlist. There had been a concentration camp (for Americans the very term is sinister) to which men who flaunted their loyalty to the Raj or tried to dissuade others from joining were sent. There their lives were deliberately made miserable. "No food was given to them for days"—I am quoting Sir Naushirwan P. Engineer, Advocate-General of India and chief counsel for the prosecution in the first Red Fort trial[5]—"and such food as was given was extremely bad. No medical aid was given at all. They were made to lie down on the ground and [were] beaten with a stick about five feet long and two inches thick." This man was forced to move cow dung. That man was put in a cage hardly longer than himself. Brutality or the threat of it was so widespread and persistent that no one could remain true to the King-Emperor without fear.

Yet the instances of ill-treatment actually pointed to do not strike one as the stuff of which "gross atrocities" are made. Engineer, whose phrase this is, states baldly that "the only alternative to joining the I.N.A. was starvation and torture."[6] The prosecution in the third trial avers that the concentration camp first referred to by Engineer was "in fact a torture camp established for the express purpose of torturing those who refused to join the I.N.A."[7] You will search in vain through Engineer's opening address, however, and through his closing address, too, for convincing substantiation of the charge. At one point he seems to say no more than that gravel was mixed in a man's rice, at another that an officer waiting for his food was obliged to fall in with ordinary jawans. In his summing up the Advocate-General remarks that in the concentration camp "men were beaten, badly fed, made to carry earth slung on bamboo poles and forced to salute the I.N.A. sentries."[8] He says nothing about treatment that was worse. Indeed, though Bhulabhai Desai asked for evidence of the horrors broadly hinted at—"by all means," he told the court, "let those who commit torture be brought before this or any other tribunal"[9]—in the whole of the trials no explicit accusations of this nature ever surfaced.

This was partly because Bhulabhai himself did not permit it. Early in the first trial a certain K. P. Dhargalkar took the stand prepared to tell how he had been tortured in the spring of 1942—and was cut short. Dhargalkar had reached Malaya with the 3rd Cavalry shortly before the Japanese struck. He had fought through the campaign and been taken prisoner when Singapore fell. Then a curious thing occurred. Dhargalkar was a King's commissioned officer (KCO), that is to say a Sandhurst man, of what we would call the class of 1931. Like many Indian graduates of Sandhurst, he was thoroughly Anglicized. His friends called him "Drag," and an Indian newspaperman covering the trials noticed that he spoke "with a carefully-cultivated English accent."[10] So Anglicized in fact was he, so British in manner and even in consciousness, that when two days after the Singapore surrender the British marched off to Changi, he marched blithely with them. The association did not survive anyone's scrutiny except his own. Next day "Drag" was ordered to rejoin his countrymen in the Neesoon camp. But from the first he preached loyalty to the regiment and to the Raj, with the consequence that he was arrested, moved to another camp, and in March sent to Thailand with a batch of his own men to labor for the Japanese. There, too, he continued to be difficult. At last the Japanese, thoroughly annoyed, took him and a fellow 3rd Cavalry officer named Hari Badhwar and put them in a cage. A cage seven feet by six by five, partially underground. In that cage they remained, apprehensive, acutely uncomfortable, and fed only boiled rice (so that they came down with beriberi), for eighty-eight days.

That, at least, was Dhargalkar's story, and Badhwar's too. In the light of what we know about the Japanese it sounds plausible enough. But though such treatment qualifies as torture, it was not torture at the hands of fellow Indians. Indians did not administer it. (Neither Dhargalkar, nor Badhwar, nor any of the Englishmen who made heroes of these two, ever alleged that Indians had.) Indeed, it is hard to believe that Indians were even pleased. Shah Nawaz maintains that it was Mohan Singh himself who got the two officers released and sent back to Singapore.

So when Dhargalkar took the stand, began his tale, and reached the point at which the Japanese took him out of the Thai camp and prepared to teach him a lesson, Bhulabhai objected. "If he has got

grievances against the Japanese," he told the court, "this is not the place."[11] The court agreed. Everybody knew of the cage because for weeks all Delhi had been hearing the story. But in court Dhargalkar was allowed to say nothing about it—with the consequence that he had only his subsequent Singapore treatment to complain of, and of that the worst he could say was that he had been kept in a tent infested with white ants. He had not even been beaten, though he had, he said, seen blows administered to others.

There was, however, *one* allegation of honest-to-God torture by Indians. It was made by the man actually (or so he said) tortured, a Muslim officer named Durrani. The allegation was pressed hard, and in official British quarters came to be accepted as proved. The story goes like this.

❧

Mahmood Khan Durrani was a captain in the Bahawalpur Infantry, a very tall man of almost no military training whom the ruler of that ridiculous princely state (it is described with devastating effect in Prakash Tandon's *Punjabi Century*) had recruited because of his height. Durrani reached Malaya before the Japanese attacked, was taken prisoner at some point during the campaign, joined the INA, and after a time managed to talk himself into the task of training agents for dispatch to India, where they were to raise fellow Muslims against the British.

No sooner had the first batch of agents been landed by submarine, however, than they gave themselves up. This made both the Japanese and the Indians suspicious. In June, 1944, Durrani was arrested and questioned. But as he refused to admit that he had planned or encouraged the defection, in fact refused to say anything at all, nothing further was done to him, and he remained in safe though uncomfortable detention until the end of the war.

Then the British, recovering Malaya, picked him up along with many others—and suddenly Durrani found his voice. He had, it seemed, a tale to tell, a tale of severe and prolonged maltreatment at the hands of the INA. All along he had meant his agents to defect. He had, in fact, taught them how to do so. When they did defect, and he was arrested, he had kept a resolute silence though deprived of sleep, beaten

into insensibility, put to the notorious finger pressers and the even more dreadful water treatment (bits of Old China these, so that you could imagine the Japanese and their stooges the INA using them). He had endured all this, though it had permanently enfeebled him. He had never faltered. He had remained true to his salt.

But Prem, who at the time of the alleged torture was in Burma a thousand miles away, does not believe the story. He is contemptuous of Durrani, remembering him as *a tall, well-built chap, but not much of a soldier.* (The Bahawalpur Infantry had proved so inferior that midway through the Malayan campaign part of it was converted into a labor battalion.) Prem does not believe Durrani. In particular he does not believe that Cyril John Stracey, the Anglo-Indian who ran the Adjutant-General's branch at Singapore INA Headquarters, would have permitted torture in the interrogation of suspects. And today's reader, dipping into Durrani's book-length personal account, has his doubts too.

For what emerges from a reading is not Durrani the brave and the constant, as Durrani would wish to appear, but Durrani the manipulator and malingerer, a six-foot-four crybaby with a pathological hatred of Hindus and Sikhs. The very length and elaborateness of the account prompts disbelief. As Durrani tells it, he spent the last few weeks before the British landed, recording in the greatest possible detail the dreadful things his INA jailers had done to him. He had, after all, joined the traitor army. For that he would have to answer unless he could prove that he had tried to subvert it from within. The proof would be the physical abuse he had undergone. There might be no other. As he scribbled, then, did he embroider here, enlarge there, and at last add whole pieces to his stock of wrongs and injuries? It *is* an impressive pile.

He was certainly believed. A year and a half after the British recovered Durrani's person, the Viceroy pinned the George Cross (a considerable decoration) on his tunic. The Viceroy must have had grounds. Hugh Toye certainly thinks he did. In the biography of Bose he published some thirty years ago, Colonel Toye unhesitatingly credits Durrani with the principal elements of his tale. Durrani, Toye believes, was a loyal servant of the Raj who withstood with great fortitude interrogation that moved toward physical torture and at last embraced it, finger pressers, water treatment, and all. And though it was the

Japanese who made the arrest, senior INA officers did the questioning and directed the treatment—did so, indeed, with the tacit encouragement of their commander in chief. "Bose did not specifically sanction torture," Toye writes, "but . . . he cannot escape responsibility for what happened to Captain Durrani."[12]

Moreover, it was not Durrani's memoir that convinced Toye. In the early autumn of 1945, Toye—as will appear—was one of a handful of British intelligence officers in recently recovered Malaya whose job it was to question such men as Durrani. (Hugh Toye is the "Toy" whom Durrani gratefully remembers for food and sympathy when he was feeling at his lowest.) It is inconceivable that Toye and his colleagues did not try to confirm Durrani's story; inconceivable that they did not look for witnesses to the alleged brutality, and for the brutes themselves. Stracey was suspected of being their chief—Stracey who, with his fair complexion and excellent connections (one brother with the forest service, another with the police, a third in the ICS), must have puzzled and eventually infuriated his captors. And Stracey, too, was in the bag. It *has* to be because Toye collected evidence independent of what Durrani told him, that he is so certain Durrani's tale is true.[13]

Why, then, Stracey and Durrani remained at Singapore throughout the autumn of 1945 is a puzzle. Long before Christmas the authorities in New Delhi were searching hard for instances of brutality (of this, more in a later chapter)—serious, provable instances. They knew what Durrani had risked for them, if indeed he was the hero he made himself out to be, because the defecting agents would long ago have told them. Here was a torture case, a case of *torture*, with victim and torturer comfortably in hand. Yet they were not brought back to India until early 1946, by which time a decision to drop all further trials was imminent—and it was too late.

Perhaps no one touched Durrani. It is an assumption that allows one to believe, nevertheless, that Bose was wild with anger at the man. And on the other hand, perhaps Stracey or others did abuse him physically, but escaped trial because of a hitch of some sort, crossed signals, general weariness, muddle. Yet even if Hugh Toye is right, even if Durrani's experiences do indeed constitute "the heroic personal story" his publisher avers them to have been,[14] his case has nothing to do with how men entered the Indian National Army. For Durrani was tortured, if tortured he was, not for refusing to enlist. He was tortured for suborning men who had.

נ

We are left, then, with the petty deprivations, the deliberately demeaning fatigues (it demeans a VCO to make him carry cow dung for a garden plot), the putting into cages—though I suspect, here, some confusion between the cage of traditional Chinese criminal justice and the prisoner-of-war "cage" of modern military practice. We are left, above all, with the beatings.

There is no question that in the concentration camp—close by Bidadari there was one, a few bamboo huts surrounded by barbed wire—beatings were frequent. Prem says that Abdul Rashid, the Pathan in charge, used to order them himself. When Rashid was put in the dock for this offense at the fourth Red Fort trial, and drew a sentence of seven years' transportation, Prem protested. But this was not because he thought the charge false. *He did ill-treat people. He had them beaten up. He had a sweeper named Nimbu, funny name for a sweeper, who used to do the beating.* (A nimbu is a lime. Nimbu was the accused in the sixth trial.) Then there were Singhara Singh and Fateh Khan, the one a Sikh subadar and the other a Muslim jemadar. Prem remembers them with particular distaste. They were big men, Singhara in particular was huge, *but they were cowards, very impressive build and no guts at all. You know, a person who is a coward is often a bully.*

For the most part beatings were given for plain indiscipline, something it was almost impossible to make the prosecution in the trials see. Due partly to the shortage of officers, partly to the men's perception that Farrer Park had severed normal military bonds, there was a good deal of this indiscipline. Sometimes it took a light turn. Uniforms were beginning to wear out, patching was necessary; cloth would have been best, but canvas would do. So a Japanese quartermaster who pitched a supply tent one evening, planning to fill it next morning, might find nothing but tent pegs when he returned at dawn. Aviation fuel fetched good money on the Singapore black market. At the airfields it was stockpiled in fifty-gallon drums. One day Prem and a fellow officer from the 2/10th Baluch, K. P. "Thimmy" Thimayya, learned that forty drums were missing from an airfield the jawans had access to, and had some difficulty persuading the Japanese that their own guards were doing the pilfering—because in point of fact they *weren't*. But there were also men who refused to obey their officers. There were men who crept out at night, stole pigs or the rare bullock, brought them back to camp, and slaughtered them there. Between Hindus and Muslims this meant violence sooner or later. For such men a concentration camp, or what the American Army calls a stockade, was a perfectly appropriate response.

Yet other jawans were consigned to this concentration camp, and sometimes beaten, simply because of their known or suspected hostility to the INA. And the men who did this went further. Visiting Kranji one August day to enlist if they could Punjabi Muslims of the 7/22nd Mountain Regiment, or at least arrest those who were thought to be holding the rest back, Singhara Singh and Fateh Khan became abusive, passed from abuse to threats, and, when their threats were thrown back at them with interest, called for a volley from the armed guards they had brought with them. The volley wounded several Punjabi Muslims, and so inflamed the rest that within moments the two were running for their lives under cover of further and now fatal firing, leaving one of the guards dead of a blow to the head. It was the same at Bidadari. There, in September, INA recruiters tried to enlist the sweepers, water carriers, and other followers of the 2/9th Gurkha Regiment. When these fellows said they did not want to leave the regiment, the recruiters became angry, beat them, and made as if to beat several of the Gurkhas too, which brought the rest to their feet. Alarmed, the recruiters fired into the air; then, as the little men came on in earnest, flinging their *chappals*, aimed low. Had their attackers been people of the plains they might have behaved otherwise, for leather *chappals* are not a fearsome thing. But the sandals the Gurkhas wear are made of wood. Flung hard and true, they can be as lethal as brickbats. So the recruiters, terrified, shot to kill, and gravely wounded eight.

Of course in every body of men there may lurk bullies. They will come into the open, however, only when they think it safe. So it remains to be asked why, in the Indian National Army of 1942—the first INA as it is sometimes called—they thought it was.

Probably Mohan Singh's personal limitations had something to do with it. Give Mohan Singh an audience and an occasion, and he could be persuasive, even moving, as many of his listeners at Farrer Park had discovered and as Lakshmi admits. At such a moment he might carry an army. But that moment gone, he was only himself again: a young man with no political experience let alone stature, a man with no compensating military reputation (he had, after all, *not* fought the length of the peninsula), a man to whom half a dozen other officers were senior—J. K. Bhonsle, for example, a Sandhurst graduate in his middle thirties; and Gill, a KCO of an even older class. A man, too, from a community celebrated for its courage and energy, but liable to brashness. Thinking about Mohan Singh, Lakshmi remembers that *the moment you saw him you felt, oh well, he's just another junior officer. I like Sikhs, but somehow you felt Mohan Singh wasn't big enough for the movement.* Perhaps Rash Behari Bose didn't think he was big enough either, for after a while he arranged to have him made a general, with insignia of star, crossed swords, and bar; as if his authority needed reinforcement.

On one side of him were the civilians, Rash Behari and the rest, speaking or claiming to speak for all Indians east of Bengal. For in Bangkok, during June, the promised conference had at last been held. A single, all-embracing Indian Independence League had been formally constituted. At its head was a Council of Action. Beneath the Council was a Committee of Representatives from the dozen Indian "territories," each territory sending representatives in proportion to its Indian population (thus Burma 21, Malaya 14, Thailand 6, and so on). Below the Committee were the territorial and local branches. It was an impressive structure. It was also, in design at least, a powerful structure. And the army was to be subordinate to it. Though Mohan Singh and another officer named Gilani had seats on the Council of Action, K. P. K. and Raghavan had seats too, while Rash Behari occupied the chair. If push came to shove, the civilians would triumph.

The prospect annoyed Mohan Singh. He did not want these fellows looking daily over his shoulder. As long as Rash Behari remained in Bangkok, they didn't. Yet Mohan Singh did not rest easy. The possibility of interference from the civilian side remained. Perhaps it was to compensate for this that he surrounded himself with notoriously compliant officers, of whom Gilani was one. Perhaps this helps explain, too, why he gave bullyboys like Singhara free reign.

On Mohan Singh's other side, meanwhile, were the Japanese. They were less sympathetic and helpful than they had been. Fujiwara, a victim of his own success, no longer served as chief go-between. His place had been taken by Colonel Iwakuro Hideo. The *Iwakuro Kikan* was much larger than the *Fujiwara Kikan*. It opened offices in Rangoon, Penang, Saigon, and Hong Kong; it numbered some 250 officers and men, a figure that would eventually double. But the close rapport Fujiwara had had with Mohan Singh was not repeated.

Like Fujiwara, Iwakuro had a good deal of freedom. Unlike Fujiwara, he did not use it to encourage a true Indian army. It was clear to him, as it might have been to a less enthusiastic Fujiwara, that Imperial General Headquarters had no plan for an immediate campaign against India, and therefore no real use for an INA. What General Headquarters *did* want was to keep the British in India off balance. This might be accomplished by a careful program of infiltration, subversion, and sabotage. The program suited Iwakuro exactly. Though he had commanded a regiment in the Malayan campaign, his professional experience had been principally in intelligence and special missions. So he bent his best efforts to the training of Indians for such work, and paid only as much attention to the building of the INA as was necessary to keep Mohan Singh happy.

At the same time Iwakuro did not shelter the Indians from Japanese commanders who, needing men for this and that, saw in these idle fellows a ready source of labor. To be fair, the *F-Kikan* had not managed to shelter them either. Most of the Indians did not mind reasonable fatigues. In Prem's account of the digging at Tengah airfield there is no suggestion that he or anyone else in the 2/10th thought they were being ill-used. It was another matter, however, when the Japanese tried to make auxiliaries of the POWs. A few weeks after Farrer Park, Mohan Singh was asked to send guards to replace the Japanese at Changi. Dhillon was put in charge. Prem, who knew him slightly from Dehra Dun (where Dhillon had been his junior), remembers Dhillon cheerfully telling everyone that the *firangi* were glad to have Indians patrolling their wire. This Prem doubted. As for Shah Nawaz, he did not like the business at all. Guard duty had nothing to do with freeing India. Besides, he did not care to see Indians employed in the deliberate humiliation of Englishmen.

By this time Shah Nawaz had joined. He had turned in his name not long after Dhillon, reasoning that Mohan Singh was going to go ahead and build his army anyway, and that officers could best serve their men by staying with them and preventing Japanese ill-treatment. "If we were unable to do this," he wrote later, "then we would try and wreck the INA from within."[15] But almost at once he had had a falling out with Mohan Singh, because the latter picked only yes-men to accompany him to the Bangkok Conference. As a consequence he had been shipped off to Kuala Lumpur.

At Kuala Lumpur there was more of this Changi business. Unable or unwilling to distinguish between Indians who had volunteered for the reputed "national" army and Indians who had not, the Japanese announced plans to use them all in one capacity or another, and grew threatening when the nonvolunteers refused. At Seremban they sited machine guns around the POW camp. Persuading them to back down was not easy. For three months Shah Nawaz hurried from place to place heading off further such confrontations, at the cost of being humiliated daily by junior Japanese officers. Meanwhile, other Indians were being shipped much greater distances—to Thailand, for example, where large numbers were put to work on the railroad the Japanese were constructing from Bangkok up the Khwae Noi River (the "lesser Kwai") and over Three Pagodas Pass to Thanbyuzayat, close to Moulmein. No one could protect men on the Death Railway, as it came to be called, or in New Guinea, or beyond. And as the months and years passed, and the Japanese tide ceased to rise, turned, and began to wash back, many were left stranded in these faraway places, and many sickened there and died.

None of this could Mohan Singh have foreseen. Neither could the Indians to whom he issued his appeal—or was it, in its way, a threat? Jaghri Ram, an illiterate laborer from Jullundur who became a nursing orderly in the Malayan campaign, and much later a nursing orderly again in Prem's regiment, joined the INA because, he says, he and others "were given very hard fatigues by the Japanese in connection with the loading of coal at the ports."[16] Would he have joined had he been extending the runway at Tengah with Prem's men? What was Mohan Singh to do when the Japanese demanded bodies for coal here, roads and runways there?

The fact was that Mohan Singh was not in a good position to protect the prisoners of war. Perhaps his only chance of sheltering them lay in bringing them into the INA. Perhaps he was right to look the other way when overzealous VCOs bullied reluctant jawans, right even when they provoked a Kranji or a Bidadari. As for the positive inducements to join—foot drill in place of coal heaving, decent food and quarters, a weekend pass with a few dollars in the pocket—these were certainly offered. But why should they not have been? "The truth," wrote Zaman Kiani years later (and he had been there), "was that almost all who had been left in Malaya felt disgusted with the British, who were considered responsible for their plight. The main consideration for the Indian POW after the fall of Singapore was to keep away from any more fighting," do nothing that would prompt the authorities at home to stop his family's monthly allotment, and survive. "Patriotism in the sense of loyalty to the British did not figure in the decision of joining or not joining."[17] Not for most.

⚜

For some, however, and they were officers mostly, the decision *did* hang on the issue of loyalty, not loyalty to the British but loyalty to India. What would India do if the army Mohan Singh was forming should approach her border? How would Indians take it?

Everyone knew that when, in the late summer of 1939, England went to war in distant Europe, Congress party had deliberately withheld its support. Everyone knew that at the same time many Congressmen, Gandhi and Nehru among them, had expressed their moral sympathy for England, and had tendered the same to Russia when she became involved. It was plain that Indian opinion favored the Chinese in their resistance of many years to the Japanese Army. Yet here was Mohan Singh proposing to enter India arm in arm with these same Japanese.

The Bidadari Resolutions of April had stipulated, and at Bangkok in June the stipulation had been repeated, that the INA should go into action only when the Congress and the Indian people asked it to. Just how the invitation was to be extended, and if extended how recognized, were questions for which, of course, there were no satisfactory answers. Nevertheless the matter could not be avoided. Suppose, then, a successful joint crossing into Assam and Bengal. How would India respond?

As Shah Nawaz later put it, "we were not sure whether, when we arrived in India accompanied by the Japanese, the people would welcome us or spit in our faces."[18] That doubt was removed by the gathering force of the Quit India movement.

CHAPTER 6

"QUIT INDIA!"

"I am engaged here," the Viceroy of India wired the Prime Minister on the last day of August 1942, "in meeting by far the most serious rebellion since that of 1857."[1]

The actions to which Lord Linlithgow assigned this grave and ominous label, and which he compared so confidently to the frightening convulsion of eighty-five years before, were then barely into their fourth week. And if they constituted a rebellion, it was a rebellion of a most unusual sort. For it had not been hatched, nor was it led, by known persons whom the state must now attempt to capture and jail. The rebellion had no leaders. The acts of civil disobedience and violence that distinguished it were the work of faceless, nameless, ordinary Indians. They were first reported after the British, in a lightning move, arrested the men and women these ordinary Indians expected to follow. The rebellion would not be crushed when these men and women were put behind bars because it had begun when they were.

On the 8th of August the All-India Congress Committee, meeting in Bombay, had declared that if the British did not immediately surrender power in India, the Congress would embark on a mass struggle to compel them to. The reaction had been instantaneous. Early on the morning of August 9, Congress leaders right across India were plucked from their beds. Within days all were securely in prison. By this preemptive strike, planned weeks before, the Government of India meant to scotch the rising before it could begin, and in the process crush the Congress—perhaps once and for all. Yet the business had not worked out that way. For here, on the 31st of the month, was Linlithgow confessing to Churchill that what he faced was nearly as serious as the Mutiny had been.

He did so, it was true, with the particular purpose of alarming the Prime Minister over a proposed visit to India by Wendell Willkie, the recently defeated Republican candidate for the American presidency. Linlithgow distrusted "peripatetic Americans." He thought their zeal for telling Englishmen how to run India scandalously greater than their understanding of the problems there. Willkie would certainly poke around. He might even ask to see Gandhi. Churchill must head him off (which apparently he did, for Willkie skipped the subcontinent entirely and wrote *One World* from other material). So the language of the telegram had to be somber, a good deal more somber than the daily reports Linlithgow sent to Amery at the India Office. Nevertheless the reference to 1857 was apt. Three years into the war, with the Japanese at her gates, India was rising in revolution, and it was Gandhi, now incommunicado in the Aga Khan's palace outside Poona, who had given the signal.

～✕～

Revolution was no stranger to the Indian independence movement. A dozen years earlier Gandhi, with his march to the sea at Dandi, had deliberately and publicly performed a revolutionary act. But the mass withdrawal of obedience that this act was intended to provoke, and for a time did provoke, had been selective. Gandhi had picked the salt monopoly because it touched every Indian, and because to deny to the poor what every creature needs, and the sea freely offers, flew in the face of humanity and natural rightness. Gandhi, moreover, had performed this revolutionary act himself. He had walked the 240 miles to Dandi, stooped (on the 6th of April, 1930), and personally picked up the symbolic handful of salt. He had not asked others to do it for him. In that long process of self-discovery to which he had in a manner set India, the moment had not yet arrived when he could step aside and expect Indians to apply *satyagraha*, hold fast to the truth, on their own.

There was another respect in which the revolutionary movement that Gandhi had created, and which he unquestionably led, was less advanced in 1930 than it would be twelve years later. In 1930 Gandhi was still willing to talk to the British.

This was not because he was responsible in the sense intended when Englishmen applied that word to Indians. To an Englishman, even a quite liberal Englishman, a responsible Indian was an Indian who understood that his country could not be granted independence until she had been brought forward, carefully prepared, suitably schooled—until, in a word, she was ready. And she would not be ready when she approximated, say, England in 1066, England in the time of Queen Elizabeth, England in Cromwell's day. She would be ready when she behaved as England behaved now. The judges of her readiness, moreover, would not be Indians. They would be Englishmen, the very Englishmen who had prepared her. Only they could estimate when it would be safe and prudent to let her have her head.

This was the reasoning. And from this reasoning there sprang a consequence. The consequence was that, treated in this way, your "responsible" Indian might never leave the dependent stage. He might forever resemble (as Francis Hutchins puts it in *India's Revolution*) "a middle-aged infant perpetually straining for signs that an oft-deferred recognition of maturity may eventually be granted by kindly but still sceptical parents."[2]

Gandhi was not such a one as this. Gandhi was in no danger of straining for signs. Gandhi did not ask when Indians would be ready for independence. Gandhi asked *when will the British be?* Just as he looked for Indians to direct their gaze inward and discover their true selves, so he looked for a transformation, a change of heart, in India's occupiers. They were to recognize that they had no business being in India. They were to recognize that they had never *had* any business being in India. When that realization came, they would be allowed to depart with dignity, perhaps even with honor. They would (it is Hutchins again) be "permitted to withdraw to compose their memoirs."[3]

When that realization came? More likely, *if*. Gandhi hoped for a change of heart in the occupiers, encouraged a change of heart in the occupiers, sometimes acted as though he believed it was occurring. It does not follow that he expected one.

The promise, made late in the First World War, that India would in due course achieve self-governing status within the Empire, had received statutory expression in a Government of India Act of 1919 so modest and limited that politically minded Indians were embittered. "They had expected," Philip Mason writes, "a sudden recognition of their nationhood, an instantaneous partnership. They had been offered instead the position of an articled clerk, which might in the course of a life-time or so lead to partnership if they were good."[4] What little confidence they still retained in British intentions was destroyed later that same year by the massacre at Amritsar, the horror of the act (almost four hundred killed by rifle fire directed for ten minutes against men, women, and children trapped in the walled space of the Jallianwala Bagh) lying as much in the arguments advanced to condone it as in the act itself. But Gandhi had not on this account refused further dealings with the Raj. He possessed, and knew that he possessed, a remarkable capacity for touching the humanity of individual Englishmen. And though he did not plot his course with this useful capacity in mind, he can hardly have failed to notice that close encounters with Englishmen often brought great political advantage. Perhaps this is why, soon after his release from the long imprisonment which had followed his walk to the sea, he went to Delhi and closeted himself with the Viceroy. (It was now that Churchill permitted himself the remark about the nauseous little fakir "striding half-naked up the steps of the viceregal palace.") The result was the Delhi Pact, which called off civil disobedience with very little to show.

In hindsight the pact has this to be said for it: that it raised the Mahatma to the level of a recognized political adversary (which is what made Churchill furious). But at the time, as I have earlier remarked, it dismayed Pandit Nehru and a large part of the Congress leadership. It bothers historians too. Some detect, in Gandhi's abrupt abandonment of his campaign, disturbing signs that Indian businessmen, fearful of strikes, countrywide refusal to pay land taxes and rent, and other actions subversive of property generally, had reached him and made him listen. Perhaps, however, Nehru's dismay and the historians' suspicion are beside the point. Eight private conversations with Lord Irwin did not, so far as anyone can tell, translate into a change of heart. Irwin was due to go home, and went. His replacement embarked on a campaign of frank political repression. Congress party was declared illegal, and the declaration enforced. The proscription left young Prem Sahgal, had he been eager to follow politics, with no politics to follow. It put Nehru behind bars for the fifth time; it put Subhas Chandra Bose, the Bengali whom Lakshmi had watched drill volunteers at Calcutta, behind bars for the seventh. And it made it difficult for

Gandhi to go on hoping for, let alone expecting, anything of the British.

It was at this point that Gandhi turned to other matters. It was in 1932, and in the years immediately after, that he compelled (by fasting) the withdrawal of separate electorates for the depressed classes. It was then that he began calling untouchables *harijans* (children of God), "a term that has passed into India's vocabulary," observes Geoffrey Ashe, "though it has not always been popular with the Children themselves."[5] It was then that he left Ahmedabad for Wardha in remote central India, moving later to the nearby village of Sevagram, even resigning from the Congress, so that he might devote himself to village uplift. Meanwhile the Congress, its proscription lifted when the government thought the lifting safe, began once more to function, and to debate whether to take advantage of the India Act just passed. For there had been movement in England even while things stood still in India.

This India Act, the Act of 1935, replaced provincial ministries responsible to legislatures for some of the functions of government, with ministries responsible for all. Thus the measure in its liberal aspect. But the Act also had a calculating side, a Tory side, though this did not prevent Churchill from heatedly opposing it. The calculation was this.

If the Congress could not be entirely suppressed (public opinion in England would not allow it), and if sending individual members to jail simply encouraged Indians to see Congressmen as the representatives of all against the Raj (exactly what Congressmen claimed they were), then it was that much more necessary to encourage and support those Indian communities that had so far shown a reluctance—a proper reluctance, most Englishmen would say—to let the Congress speak for them. It was that much more necessary to encourage and support them as a counterweight against the Party. This the India Act of 1935 set out to do.

In parts of India there had for some time been separate electorates for Muslims, arranged less out of calculation (it is only fair to observe) than from a sense of what India was and what India was not. Now, by a Communal Award announced in London in 1932, the arrangement was extended to other communities and to all the provinces. In each provincial legislature, seats in proportion to their strength were set aside for Muslims, easily the largest group; for Indian Christians, Europeans, and others; in the Punjab for the Sikhs. For these seats only members of the designated community could stand. In the elections to them only members of the designated community could vote. Thus constitutionally entrenched, the calculation ran, these communities should be able to survive as political alternatives to the Congress even in provinces—Madras and the Central Provinces, for example—where their numbers were small. In Bengal, the Punjab, and Sind, where Muslims were particularly numerous, they should quite crowd the Congress out.

This design was not lost upon the Congress, which further objected to the Act because, while abolishing divided responsibility in the provinces, it retained it at the federal level (what Indians call the Center). The Act, however, did make it possible for ambitious Congressmen to take power and exercise it, not in New Delhi to be sure, but in the provincial capitals. The prospect was attractive, so attractive that most of the leadership neither accepted nor rejected the Communal Award upon which the Act rested, but looked only to the elections that must follow. Gandhi not actively resisting (though technically no longer a member, he was in practice once again first among equals in the councils of the Party), Congressmen campaigned, won majorities or pluralities in more than half the provinces, beat Nehru's objections aside, and formed ministries.

The ministries functioned. To the chagrin of those British for whom the point of the experiment had been less to confer responsibility upon Congress politicians than to prove that they were incapable of it, the Party showed that it could govern. The result was an enormous increase in Congress visibility. Membership swelled. White Congress caps were everywhere. Except for the Muslims, who at last grew alarmed and turned from their provincial groupings to Muhammad Ali Jinnah's Muslim League, the communities the British had hoped to turn against the Congress failed to establish themselves politically. For Congressmen, it is true, this was not all gain. Once perceived as specially selected members of a disciplined army with a lofty national goal, they were beginning to look now like mere party men avid for the loaves and fishes of office. Yet there was no doubting the fundamental change. The British were withdrawing to the Center. There they continued to command finance, external relations, defense. Beyond the Center's range, however, in day-to-day affairs across large parts of India, British Raj was giving way to Congress Raj. Even law and order, because a provincial matter, was ceasing to be Britain's business.

This was the situation when, in the late summer of 1939, Germany attacked Poland and the Second World War began.

~*~

Such views as the Congress held on world affairs were largely shaped by Pandit Nehru, and Nehru's mind and heart had always been with those who resisted fascism—something new in Europe but thoroughly familiar to Indians, fascism and imperialism being (in his opinion) twins. In the early summer of 1938, just before the Spanish Loyalists' last, gallant, vain offensive across the Ebro, Nehru had paid a visit to Barcelona and been profoundly moved by the atmosphere there. In London two months later he had watched in misery and disgust as Chamberlain gave Czechoslovakia away. Now he made it clear that in this European war, just beginning, his sympathy and the sympathy of the Congress lay with Poland and with the countries that came to Poland's support.

Sympathy did not mean participation, however. If India was to join the struggle it could only be as a free nation, her government acting as her people desired. Yet how far from free Indians actually were, how little war and peace were matters the Britisher bothered even to discuss with them, Linlithgow had already made plain. Within hours of England's formal entry into the war, this tall, long-faced, Scots aristocrat, whom Nehru once described as "heavy of body and slow of mind, solid as a rock and with almost a rock's lack of awareness,"[6] had proclaimed India at war too. From a purely constitutional point of view this was perfectly proper. Was it necessary, however, to move so abruptly? Was it necessary to advertise, by the very language of the proclamation (which said that hostilities had broken out between the King-Emperor and Germany but did not mention India), how utterly invisible the subcontinent was at moments of imperial crisis? Australia and New Zealand went to war on the advice of ministers. Canada and South Africa waited for Parliament to confirm the action. For years and years India had been told she was approaching the dominion status of these four. Now this—war declared not by, but *for*, her.

What happened next might have happened anyway. Even to Congressmen the party appeared, in its preoccupation with provincial office holding, to be losing its esprit. Now that the war was on, the Center seemed certain to resume, as a hurried addition to the 1935 Act empowered it to resume, many of the powers recently handed to the provinces. These were reasons enough for what Congress proceeded to do. They paled before the manner of India's entry into the war.

As Nehru put it several years later from his prison quarters in Ahmadnagar Fort, "one man, and he a foreigner and a representative of a hated system, could plunge four hundred millions of human beings into war without the slightest reference to them."[7] Linlithgow published his declaration on the 3rd of September, 1939. Eleven days later the Congress demanded to know what were Britain's war aims with respect to India (they must include independence), and what immediate steps toward their fulfillment the Viceroy intended. Weeks passed, weeks during which Congressmen wondered what they should do if the Viceroy met them halfway. They need not have worried. Linlithgow's response made no reference to independence, soon or ever. For the better prosecution of the war he would appoint an advisory committee on which the Congress should be represented. At war's end there would be, if Indians wished it, some modest modification of the 1935 Act. That was all. On the 22nd of October the Congress instructed its provincial prime ministers to resign. Led by Rajagopalachari in Madras, they complied.

Linlithgow's reaction to these resignations mingled annoyance with relief. He had come out to India with excellent intentions, determined to make the new India Act (which coincided with his appointment) work. But from the beginning he had found Congress party difficult. And he had suspected that it was Gandhi who made it so, a suspicion these resignations now confirmed. Anyone could see that though the All-India Congress Committee (AICC) had met earlier in the month, it was the Working Committee, the fifteen men and women of the so-called High Command, that had ordered the ministries to step down. Anyone could see that it had issued the order from Wardha, where it had consulted the Mahatma.

Another thing annoyed the Viceroy. Congress party purported to embody the nation, to represent all the classes and communities of

India, to be in fact the Indian *National* Congress. But this was absurd. Every Englishman knew that without Britain's imperial presence, India would be no more than a geographical expression. Unity was Britain's greatest gift to the subcontinent. It could not be Gandhi's gift as well. It was presumptuous of the Congress to pretend that in the matter of India's relations with the Raj it spoke for everyone, even those who on election day had voted for the Liberals or the Hindu Mahasabha or the Muslim League. And when the Congress announced that it alone could take delivery of independence, that only it could lead India to freedom, you listened to no less than a "candid declaration of totalitarianism."[8]

All the greater, then, was Linlithgow's relief that the Congress had removed itself from the political scene, and by doing so had freed the Government of India to get on with the real business of the hour. That business was war. It was the Viceroy's duty to harness India to the prosecution of the war. And Linlithgow, turning happily to the work, for the remainder of his unusually long viceregal term made everything else subordinate to it. Somewhat later, on the occasion of one of Gandhi's fasts, he was asked by a visiting American what would be the consequences if the Mahatma died. "Six months unpleasantness steadily declining in volume," he replied, after which India would be "far more reliable as a base for operations" than she had been before.[9] That was the limit of his concern for India's future. "I am not a bit fussed about the post-war period," he remarked confidentially to the India Office.[10] It was the here-and-now of Britain's military effort, and the subcontinent's part in it, that occupied his thoughts.

But not exclusively. Though the Congress, by resigning from office, had left the political arena, it was still capable of great mischief. It would continue to be capable of great mischief as long as its membership and its machinery remained intact. Here, however, the war itself came to Linlithgow's rescue. War brought renewed vigor, or at least the appearance of renewed vigor, to the Empire. War stiffened every Englishman's back. War attracted to England's side those Indians (and there were some) who saw for what cause she fought in Europe, thought the cause noble, and wished India to be a part. And if these developments strengthened Linlithgow's position, how much more was it improved when, in the spring of 1940, Churchill succeeded Chamberlain as Prime Minister.

For the man thus belatedly rewarded for warning his countrymen so long and so insistently about the German peril, was the same man who had repeatedly cautioned them about the "Hindoo priesthood machine"—by which Churchill meant Gandhi and the Congress. So far as India was concerned, Churchill had not changed since the evening when, dropping off to sleep at the end of his third day in India (it was 1896, and he was a very young officer with the 4th Hussars), he had allowed his thoughts to rest briefly but happily upon Britain's role in the subcontinent, "her high mission to rule these primitive but agreeable races for their welfare and our own."[11] Then and since he had entertained the most rigid Tory notions about India's society, believing unhesitatingly that only a few of her communities were naturally martial, and that the "Hindoos" were not among them. Though in May 1940, when he replaced Chamberlain, his famous "I have not become the King's First Minister in order to preside over the liquidation of the British Empire" lay more than two years in the future, it might have been uttered at any time.[12] It was how Churchill felt. And by it he meant the Indian subcontinent. Let England lose that jewel in the crown and she ceased to be imperial. She ceased to be even a great power.

With such a man in charge, the Viceroy could be confident that Whitehall would not make difficulties should he choose to have done with politics-as-usual and meet Congress obstruction with a crushing blow. Even before 10 Downing Street changed hands, there had been discussions about how and under what circumstances that blow might be delivered. Now, in the summer of 1940, a Revolutionary Movement Ordinance (Linlithgow paid Congress the compliment of considering it revolutionary) was drafted and quietly circulated. Should the Congress, by some clearly provocative act, make clear its intention to bring the normal processes of the Raj to a stop, the ordinance would be used to arrest its leaders and seize its offices and funds. Civil servants suspected of sympathy with it would be dismissed. Colleges and other hotbeds of Congress activity would be closed. And these measures would have more than temporary suppression as their object. "There must be countless Indians," a manifesto drafted for the coming occasion ran, "who will feel that, whatever the future may hold in store, India can now best fulfill her destiny and her due place among the nations of the world only after the total extinction of the political party which, at this vital juncture, has seen fit to betray them."[13] The Congress was not to be simply checked. It was to be smashed.

Many months and much maneuvering passed, however, before the provocation was offered and the blow fell. For the Congress itself was divided. Radical Congressmen, in particular Jayaprakash Narayan's Congress Socialists and the men who followed Subhas Chandra Bose, wanted to offer mass resistance to the Raj and its imperialist war, and offer it at once. Nehru was of much the same opinion, though he belonged to neither of these groups and felt impelled, as they did not, to express his sympathy for the European democracies. On the other hand Sardar Vallabhbhai Patel, Bhulabhai Desai, Rajagopalachari, and like conservatives wished to wait, to bargain, to offer active participation in the war effort in exchange for an immediate though limited advance towards *swaraj*. At particular moments these conservatives, Gandhi now objecting now abstaining, prevailed in the counsels of the party. Approaches were attempted. Churchill's government, the Prime Minister's private convictions notwithstanding, was driven in the same direction, partly because it included Attlee and other Labour ministers, partly because it was aware that England needed India more than India needed England. So London, too, made overtures, and there was intermittent dialogue. But nothing came of it.

Always the British put the winning of the war ahead of the winning of India. Always they saw India in terms of communities naturally divided against themselves, with the Congress speaking not for the whole but only for a part. Britain had to remain, that was their unchanging view. Nothing else was possible as long as Indians could not agree on what should take Britain's place. It did not occur to them that *India* should take Britain's place, in such a form, and with such a degree of prior agreement, as it would be for Indians alone to say.

While the approaches and overtures pursued their sometimes active, sometimes perfunctory, way; while the Government of India prepared for a decisive counterstroke, in the meantime giving what aid and encouragement it could to any who opposed the Congress; the Congress itself, tugged this way and that, yet in the end more willing than it had been for years to let Gandhi set the course—the Congress moved toward revolution.

✦

Not that Gandhi was in any hurry. He considered the great majority of his countrymen morally unprepared for nonviolent resistance, and told them so. He thought (and here many Congressmen agreed with him) that the political situation was not yet ripe. In March 1940, at its annual session, the Congress had formally resolved upon a campaign of civil disobedience. It was to start, however, only when Gandhi said it should. Gandhi did not give the word until a particular overture from London, the so-called August Offer, had by its emptiness damped the negotiating ardor of the conservatives. What Gandhi then asked India to offer was selective *satyagraha*.

Beginning with Vinoba Bhave (then known chiefly for his devotion to hand spinning) but passing rapidly to Nehru, Abul Kalam Azad, and other leading Congress figures, Gandhi asked individuals by name to declare publicly that it was wrong to help the British with their war. Since such declarations could conceivably suborn soldiers and munitions workers, the government was bound to react, and did. Across the United Provinces Nehru had been making speeches so inflammatory that New Delhi believed he pushed Gandhi, not the other way around. Now, even before he could offer the brief ritual statement the Mahatma asked for, he was arrested and sentenced to four years imprisonment. Lesser Congressmen followed. Eventually any four-anna member who wished was authorized to make the declaration—and by the autumn of 1941 more than twenty thousand men and women had been jailed. Then Gandhi, who kept tight control, allowed the movement to subside. The Government of India responded by releasing the prisoners. It was disappointed that it had not been given the chance to crush the Congress. Spread as they were over nearly a year, even these individual acts of defiance were not sufficient provocation. It supposed, however, that Gandhi was capable of nothing further. In this it was mistaken.

For Gandhi had simply been testing. The outbreak of the war and the stiffening of the British position had made plain to him, too, the futility of politics-as-usual. The campaign of limited civil disobedience just concluded had shown that Congressmen, including very ordinary Congressmen indeed, were capable of offering *satyagraha* without his presence. The British had been given a gentle, a hardly more than symbolic, push. They had met it with condescending unconcern. It was time to shake them seriously.

The decision to do so, or at least the sign that the Congress was moving in that direction, coincided with Japan's entry into the war at the end of 1941, but was independent of it. The jailed *satyagrahis* were released on December 4, four days before the landing on the beaches of Kelantan. Gandhi declined to be grateful. Nehru's message to his jailers, as he walked through the prison gates at Dehra Dun, was "leave." Nevertheless the fall of Singapore and Rangoon, the British fleet withdrawal from Ceylon, the prospect of a Japanese invasion of India, affected relations between the Congress and the Raj profoundly. It sharpened the dispute between them. It hastened the confrontation that each, for different reasons, had been edging toward, and made that confrontation more bitter. Many Englishmen, even during the dark summer of 1940 when Germany threatened England from across the Channel, had been able to countenance a certain Indian reluctance to pull their full weight in the European war. But how could any Englishman (and how could responsible Indians) feel anything but shock, anger, and dismay when that reluctance extended to the defense of India itself? As for the Congress, it had always argued that Indians, like everybody else, fought well only when they fought by choice. Choice presupposed, however, freedom. With the war on India's doorstep, it was more than ever necessary that England let India go.

Gandhi, of course, was not interested in what would make Indians fight. He did not believe in fighting. Not many Congressmen, however, were pacifists—indeed, what particularly infuriated Nehru about the British was that they had, by their ineptitude, actually prevented Indians from joining in the struggle against the Nazis. Besides, *ahimsa* (nonviolence) was not the limit of Gandhi's advice. It was only the summit of it.

"Gandhi ordinarily supplied a hierarchy of recommendations," Hutchins writes, "starting with what he considered ideally preferable, and ending up with what he considered better than nothing." And a little later: "nonviolence, violence, and cowardice formed a hierarchy, and Gandhi had no qualms about making a positive recommendation that violence should be used by a man who was capable of choosing only between violence and cowardice."[14] With respect to the Japanese, India was in the position of this man. Though the imperfect nonviolence she had so far attained was able, through its cumulative effect, to make some impression upon the British, it would not halt the Japanese. Only the "non-violence of the strong"[15] could do so, and this India did not possess. So, just as it was right for a woman to use her nails and teeth upon the man who tried to rape her, and right for the Poles to fight the Germans, it would be right for Indians to resist the Japanese. In such situations the only practicable alternative was abject surrender.

But sanctioning resistance cut both ways. Until the British loosed their grip on India, they were in the position of the would-be ravisher, of the Germans overrunning Poland, or of the Japanese were they to come up the coast to Chittagong. In 1939, at the beginning of the war in Europe, Gandhi had extended his moral support to Britain. Now he withdrew it. Englishmen supposed that in this hour of peril, with the Japanese at the door, Gandhi would call off or at least mute his assault upon the Raj. Had he not supported the British in the Boer War, and in the First World War too? Gandhi did just the opposite. This was partly because, after so much time and so many disappointments, he no longer expected much of them. It was also because this war actually touched India. Imminent invasion by Nippon was a reminder of earlier conquest by Britain. Prospective occupation from one quarter forced India to notice that she was occupied from another. Between the Japanese and the British, was there really much to choose?

What the Japanese had done in China was not, it was true, encouraging. They might try to take India by the neck—and "if a man holds me by the neck and wants to drown me, may I not struggle to free myself directly?"[16] But if it was possible the Japanese would try to take India by the neck, it was a *fact* that the British had done so. Should they now, while holding India with one hand, manage to drive the Japanese off with the other, what then? Would they turn and release their grip? Gandhi did not think they would. "If they will not trust you now"—Gandhi is referring to the proposal that a truly Indian government take charge of India's defense—"there is no warrant for supposing they will after victory. They will then ask you with greater force than now to produce the unity which cannot be produced whilst they are here."[17] It would be the same dreary business all over again, the British declining to withdraw from an India they pronounced divided while their very presence kept her so.

There was only one way out of the tangle. Britain must let India go. (In the dark days just before Bataan fell, President Quezon had asked America to do the same for the Philippines.) If Britain complied, she could, if she wished, go on fighting from Indian soil. By freeing India, she would demonstrate that she fought not to keep the subcontinent but for some other, better reason. If she did not comply, the Indian people would rise.

For a moment early in 1942 it looked as if so drastic a step might still be avoided. America, in the war at last, was attractive for her freshness, her vigor, and her apparent innocence of empire. Ravaged China had long invited sympathy. Russia fought for her life. Circumstances made all three the allies of England. Certain Congressmen began to hope that, late as it was, something could be arranged that would make India an ally too, and bring themselves back into office. London, too, was anxious to negotiate. Sir Stafford Cripps reached Delhi with a proposal. There were meetings, memoranda, all the paraphernalia of impending agreement; the trimmers in the Congress, it appeared, were going to have their way. But they did not. The Cripps Offer left Linlithgow's powers intact, and so was rejected. It was now the end of March 1942.

Early the next month came the air raid on Vishakhapatnam and the panic in Madras. Far to the east the Burma Road was cut and Mandalay evacuated. In Russia the Germans laid siege to Stalingrad and neared the Caucasus. In North Africa they stood on the borders of Egypt. Not since the summer of 1940 had England's situation appeared so bleak.

Gandhi, however, had made up his mind. There was a time when he had been unwilling to make trouble for the British in the moment of their distress. There was a time when he had been unwilling to move until his fellow countrymen were ready for nonviolent struggle. He was unwilling no longer. "I feel that if I continue to wait, I might have to wait till doomsday."[18] Nehru, upset by the Mahatma's apparent indifference to the prospect of Japanese invasion, still resisted. But Gandhi repeated his offer. Let England continue fighting from free India's soil. And at last Nehru yielded, persuaded that a successful defense of India meant nothing if India remained in Britain's grasp. Of what use was Allied victory when one's own country remained in bondage? "If India perishes . . . it does not do me any good if other nations survive."[19]

Late in April the All-India Congress Committee (AICC), without specifying the day and the hour, called on Britain to let India go. Right through the hot weather Gandhi repeated the message in press interviews and articles, explaining at length his reasons. Early in July the Working Committee went a step further. British rule must not simply end, it must end immediately. If it did not, the draft resolution ran, Congress would launch a national struggle which the Mahatma would lead. The struggle would be nonviolent, but "if people do not understand it and there is violence, how can I stop it?"[20] Enough of the testing and preparing that had consumed so many years. Indians must do what they must do. Gandhi would not stand in their way.

Misgivings over the hardening of the Congress line were already widespread in India and abroad. With the publication of the "Quit India" resolution (a journalist invented the phrase), they became dismay. Sir Tej Bahadur Sapru, speaking for the Liberals (a party with distinguished leaders but little electoral support), appealed to Gandhi not to gamble the lives and safety of four hundred million Indians upon Japanese restraint. Jinnah called the business an obvious attempt "to coerce the British Government to surrender to a Congress Raj."[21] The American press was as outraged as the English, Labour MPs as incredulous as the Tories. In the Congress, Rajagopalachari resigned.

Gandhi, however, was unmoved. "There is no room left for negotiations," he told newspapermen who wondered whether the British might not attempt some. "Either they recognize independence or they don't."[22] On the 7th of August, the AICC met in Bombay as scheduled to consider the July resolution. "We shall get our freedom by fighting," Gandhi told the 250 members present. "It cannot fall from the skies."[23] On the afternoon of the 8th, before thousands of onlookers on the Gowalia Tank Maidan, the resolution was moved by Nehru. That evening it went to the vote. Only a dozen no's were recorded. Early the next morning the government struck.

_S&._

For this was the provocation Linlithgow had hoped to see. Gandhi and the Congress leaders were about to launch "open rebellion" (the Mahatma's own words), and they were about to launch it at a moment of great military peril for India. They had given ample warning of their intentions, named the date, and collected themselves obligingly at a designated place. All the authorities had to do was coordinate a roundup and lay on a train. Early on the 9th of August, 1942, the arrests were duly made. Later that morning the train steamed out of Bombay's Victoria Terminus. It carried the Mahatma, Nehru, and most of the other members of the Working Committee—so easy was it to lay hands on the Congress High Command.

But the government did not stop at this. All over India the police descended upon Congressmen wherever they happened to be. In the United Provinces, where the party was unusually strong, more than five hundred were arrested on the very first day. Provincial Congress Committees were banned, party bank accounts were sealed, party offices were occupied and their files seized, rifled, or trashed. As a functioning organization the Congress, it was Linlithgow's intention, must cease to exist.

A few of its leading figures were not at once arrested, or managed somehow to avoid the police. Asaf Ali was on the government's list. His wife Aruna was not. She came to Victoria Terminus anyway, to see her husband off, and as the train started to move, told Congress President Azad (who was aboard of course) not to worry about her. "I shall find something to do," she said[24]—which was true, for, quietly disappearing when a warrant for her arrest was at last issued, she led an active underground life under an alias right through the war. There were others like her. And as they were helped by an informal network of sympathetic and well-placed Indians, their existence was often far from furtive. They moved about. They met and talked. But there was very little coordination, no central direction. "Anyone with an idea was encouraged to try it out. If a student—or a professor—arrived to spend the night with a suitcase full of explosives, his host would wish him well even if he personally abstained from his violent schemes."[25] And at this point in his study of India in revolution, Hutchins gives us the story of Radhe Shyam Sharma, professor of chemistry at Benares Hindu University, who reacted to the Quit India resolution and the government's counterstroke by doing what he could with what lay to hand.

When news of the arrests of August 9 reached Benares, Sharma and a colleague called for a general protest. The gates of the university were closed, the university training corps declared itself the army of free

India; students marched into the city and raised the Congress flag. Ten days later British troops entered the campus and drove the students out. With a bounty of five thousand rupees on his head, Sharma slipped quietly away and walked the seventy miles to Allahabad disguised as a sadhu. From Allahabad he reached his native Gwalior, and there applied his considerable scientific skills and even greater ingenuity to the wholesale manufacture of bombs and other explosives, until at last in late December he was caught. Perhaps Sharma had at some point paid his four anna membership fee and joined the Congress. Hutchins does not say and may not know, though he has personally interviewed the man. The point of his tale is that, party member or no, Sharma did what he did not because the party told him to, and certainly not because he had an assigned role in an insurrection carefully plotted in advance; but because this was what it occurred to him to do when he learned that Gandhi and the others had been swept into the government's net, and realized that the struggle for freedom would have to be undertaken by ordinary people like himself if it was to be undertaken at all.

All across India people undertook it. Schools and colleges closed. Much of the nationalist press stopped publishing (in Calcutta only two of the sixteen daily newspapers continued to appear), partly out of protest, partly because editors did not care to be told what they might print. In many places *hartal* (total suspension of work) was declared. Strikes and the deliberate destruction of materials and machinery seriously affected the production of coal, cement, bricks, leather goods, parachute silk, cigarettes. The Madras mills that produced half the armed services' requirements of khaki cloth shut, the Tata iron and steel works at Jamshedpur shut; in Ahmedabad, where owners and workers alike were strongly Congress, the cotton mills stood idle for three and a half months, which left cotton thread in such short supply it was a question whether the manufacture of army uniforms could continue.

There were marches, demonstrations, riots. The riots were particularly severe in Bombay, where students took to the streets and the police repeatedly fired. But the government was prepared for this. It lost control of no big city except Patna, in Bihar, and there only briefly. What it was *not* prepared for were the scale and intensity of the attacks made outside the cities on the links that held British India together.

The government expected mass ticketless travel on the railroads and such nonviolent disruptions as the uncoupling of cars, the pulling of emergency cords, wholesale lying down across the tracks. What it got was much worse: the burning of station buildings, the smashing of signals, the tearing up of whole lengths of track. In Bihar, the eastern part of the United Provinces, and northern Madras Province, the destruction was so widespread and persistent that for weeks rail communication between Calcutta and the rest of India ceased. Ian Stephens, editor of the Calcutta *Statesman*—being British, it continued to appear with armed sentries at the gate—was quite unable to reach Delhi, where the paper also published, until mid-September, and even then "trains only got across at unpredictable hours and in convoy, a memorable and absurd sight peering out of the window . . . while we snaked round a double curve."[26]

Telegraph wires were cut or the poles pulled over, government seed stores looted, post offices wrecked. Not all the acts of anger and defiance were the work of the moment, unrehearsed and unpremeditated. An "All-India Congress Committee Office," staffed by lesser Congress figures using assumed names, operated secretly in Bombay. A clandestine radio station broadcast from the same city for months before it was betrayed and silenced. Underground literature gave advice on how to organize guerrilla bands and derail trains. For some time bomb explosions occurred almost daily in the countryside around Bombay, and so professional were the perpetrators that few were caught. Acts of this sort encouraged the government in the opinion, which it was anxious to confirm, that the rebellion had been planned in advance, and that it would have been even more widespread had not the Congress leadership, by a timely stroke, been put away.

But there was no grand plan. All that Gandhi had intended was mass *satyagraha*, for which the selective campaign of the previous year had been a preparation and a test. As for the course it was to take, as usual with the Mahatma that must hang upon events. Efforts were made to uncover something more concerted and conspiratorial. Churchill, ever resourceful, thought he spied Tokyo's hand in the business, asked the India Office for a note not to exceed three pages "on Mr. Gandhi's intrigues with Japan," and was assured in two lines that there had been none.[27] In the end no detailed program for the dislocation of government by the methods actually employed was unearthed. None could be. None existed. What had moved the AICC to vote Gandhi's resolution was not a plan or timetable but a determination, a determination that had spread (Gandhi sensed this better than most Congress leaders) clear through the ranks of the party. A determination that was felt by large numbers of other Indians as well. A determination to do whatever had to be done to get the British out of India—now, instantly, never mind the cost. And never mind how.

"Karenge ya marenge," Gandhi had said. We shall do or we shall die. Or more simply "karo ya maro," do or die; which, Gyanendra Pandey tells us on the evidence of surviving participants, was frequently converted into "karo ya *maaro*," achieve or kill.[28] There were certainly many Indians (as Gandhi knew, deplored, but could not help) who wanted to defeat the British with the militant tactics of a Bhagat Singh. The Congress Socialists in particular saw, now, their chance. Their leader, Jayaprakash Narayan, broke out of jail and waged guerrilla war for months before he was caught and caged again. All across northern India (where, incidentally, Hindi makes the pun on dying possible) the nonviolent tactics of the Mahatma coexisted uneasily with, or collapsed before, the violent instincts of individuals and mobs.

Very few Englishmen lost their lives, so few that in the narratives the same unfortunates crop up again and again: two RAF officers, for example, dragged from a train near Patna and hacked to death. More disconcerting was the government's relative powerlessness in the face of the popular upheaval. In some places hundreds turned out in broad daylight to topple signal towers, dismantle bridges, dig up embankments; and the military, when it discovered what was going on, could do no more than machine-gun the wreckers from the air and later burn the nearest village. There were more British troops in India than there had been for years, and Indian troops in even greater numbers, so that at the height of the rebellion fifty-seven battalions or their equivalent were employed—perhaps forty thousand men. But they could not be everywhere. In Bihar and the United Provinces, in parts of Bengal and Orissa, in the Central Provinces and Bombay, the British were in real danger of losing the countryside. Paul Greenough relates how assaults on four of the six *thanas* (police headquarters) in the Tamluk Subdivision of Midnapur District, delivered simultaneously over the course of

two days, so thoroughly broke the government's control over 150 square miles of flat and accessible land at Calcutta's very door, that the police officer who was sent with a detachment of British troops to recover the area had to move by boat along the Hooghly (the roads had been thoroughly breached), and approached Tamluk "like an explorer going into an unknown land."[29].

✾

It was, indeed, an unknown land. For what this police officer faced as he groped his way through the district, though he did not suspect it and would have denied it if he had, was a new India. Not the India of innumerable self-sufficient village republics, with no Englishman in sight and no Englishman needed, that Gandhi saw with his mind's eye. What he encountered was an India that for the first time was more than the sum of its parts. This India had not shown itself in 1857, though there have always been people who will tell you that it had. It showed itself now, in a wave of purposeful action that swept the subcontinent, some of it organized, some of it spontaneous, some of it nonviolent, much of it not. With the Quit India rebellion of 1942, the Indian nation was at last emerging.[30] Was there some perception, in Linlithgow's somber wire, that this was occurring and could not be reversed?

Moreover the Viceroy deceived himself, and Churchill too, when he added—as he did in his telegrams to London—that censorship happily concealed the gravity and extent of the rebellion. What precisely was going on, which railroad lines were out and which districts lost or unaccounted for, was hidden well enough. But the rebellion itself could not be, because the government itself had announced its coming and trumpeted its outbreak. For weeks New Delhi had warned the world that Congress meant to plunge the country into confusion and chaos. When on the 9th of August Linlithgow's people arrested Gandhi and the others, they justified the act by describing in the most lurid terms the orgy of burning, looting, and general destruction that was going to be avoided by this masterful stroke. Had the stroke been successful, and the rebellion been nipped in the bud, there would, indeed, have been no orgy to report, and therefore no censorship needed. But censorship descended instantly— so serious trouble was inferred. Censorship can never conceal everything anyway, for though you may muffle a Bombay riot, you cannot silence it, and if the great Delhi–Calcutta express trains cease running, someone is sure to notice.

The fact of the convulsion, then, became known quickly enough inside India. It became known as quickly outside, for the same reason, and for the additional one that while the British preferred to keep their Indian subjects ignorant of the wreckings and riots, lest they imitate them, this did not apply to Englishmen or Americans. *They* might as well learn how dreadfully Gandhi and the Congress were behaving. So Germany and Japan discovered what was happening from the English and American radio, and beamed the news right back. "Nine large stations batter at India every night," a BBC man reported.[31] From Tokyo the English-language *Bangkok Chronicle*, too, got word of what was going on. "India Demands Independence Now" ran its headline of August 3, four days before the AICC gathered in Bombay. On the 10th it reported the passage of the Quit India resolution and the spiriting away of the entire Congress High Command, on the 13th "strikes, riots spreading to all provinces." It was the *Chronicle's* opinion that Congress had put India in a state of open war with Britain. "Casualties Mount in India's Battle for Freedom" its headline of the 15th read.[32]

At Singapore the news was the same. Lakshmi remembers a mass rally, Mohan Singh speaking, much general excitement. "Make no mistake," Gandhi had warned the Japanese, "you will be sadly disillusioned if you believe that you will receive a willing welcome from India."[33] But no one heeded or perhaps even heard the caution. What mattered to listeners in Singapore was the welcome that *Indians* might expect.

It had been stipulated that the Indian National Army do nothing until the Congress and the Indian people asked it to. With the news of the August rising, that stipulation was met—and in a week or two (he does not remember the precise date), Prem joined. There was nothing formal about it, *no question of taking an oath or anything. I never went to anyone and volunteered.* Bhonsle, the Sandhurst man put briefly in command of Garhwalis, had for a time presided over the administrative and quartermaster branches of the prisoner-of-war headquarters at Neesoon. Prem had worked for him there, and they had become friends. When Bhonsle moved to INA Headquarters he had asked Prem

to come with him, and in July Prem, though technically still a POW, had done so. Now Bhonsle was to command the Hindustan Field Force. He wanted Prem with him. His staff must consist of bona fide INA men. So he sounded Prem out, learned he was at last willing, sent his name to be printed in the official military gazette, and that was that.

WAITING FOR A LEADER

The table of organization of the Indian National Army called for twelve infantry battalions, each approximately 650 strong, grouped in four regiments of roughly 2,000. Add signals, motor transport, and supplementary arms and services, and you had some 10,000 men—a division if you like. But Gill, who had drawn up the table, and Zaman Kiani, who had to implement it, were not thinking in terms of divisions, at least not yet.

From the Garhwal Rifles, the 3/17th Dogras, and the combined 1/14th and 5/14th Punjab, enough men had come forward (or came forward now) to make up, with additional volunteers, the first of these four regiments: Bhonsle's Hindustan Field Force. They did not bring with them, however, their Garhwali, Dogra, and Punjabi designations. That would have been to invoke a loyalty the Indian National Army existed explicitly to sever. The regiment's three battalions were simply numbered. As for the other regiments, they were given a name quite unknown to the old Indian Army. They were called "guerrilla" regiments, not so much from a sense (which would have been mistaken) that the Japanese in the recent campaign had triumphed by avoiding set-piece assaults, as from the feeling that, given the arms they had, and particularly the terrain they would have to traverse, guerrilla tactics would yield the best results.

There could be no question of moving against India by sea, no question of landing, say, on the beaches of Orissa or Madras. Even if India seethed with revolution, a dozen battalions lightly armed and put ashore where roads and railroads permitted the British to concentrate, could do very little unless accompanied by a sizable Japanese force with guns and armor. But landing Japanese guns and armor in the middle of India might easily alienate and anger Indians. Besides, there was no reason to suppose that the Japanese would agree to such an enterprise even if they could collect the force, provide the necessary air cover, and transport it *and* the INA across the Bay of Bengal. A sea approach was out. India would have to be entered by land.

The land approach, however, across the India-Burma border, was roadless and without a railroad; mountainous, heavily forested, much cut up by watercourses; and everywhere almost impassable during the monsoon, which in this part of the world comes once a year but is extremely heavy. An army that attempted it with a normal complement of transport, armor, and heavy weapons would have great difficulty getting through, and if obliged to fight, with what that cost in fuel and ammunition, might not get through at all. So a force that travelled light should actually have an advantage. In Malaya the Japanese, operating on an extremely slender margin of food, fuel, and ammunition, and combining bold thrusts with an instant readiness to break off and go around by the flank, had beaten British forces greatly superior to them in numbers and in some respects better armed. It would be a good idea to imitate the Japanese.

It would be a good idea to learn to travel light, carrying the kind of rations the Japanese carried—*not* the kind, Prem observed to me one day, that the 2/10th Baluch had been supplied with during the Malayan campaign. *We had so many different kinds of food to carry, rice, wheat, dal, vegetables. Each Japanese soldier carried fifteen days' rations on him: rice in cotton socks, and powdered fish. He boiled the rice and sprinkled the powder on it, that's how he did it. But we had to set up field kitchens and cook. And if that wasn't possible, all the men got was tea and chappaties.*

No, these guerrilla regiments would have to learn to travel light. Since the ground on the Indian side of the India-Burma frontier was if anything worse than on the Burmese side, this would be as essential for the descent as for the approach. And then, when the more open parts of Bengal and Assam were reached, and the British tried to use their armor and heavy weapons, they would discover that the jawans of the freedom army had made contact with the people of India, and that all India was rising at the signal.

That was the whole point of the guerrilla regiment: avoid positional warfare and formal assaults of any sort, *go deep behind the British lines, and persuade the men in the Indian Army to come over.*

> *You remember that earlier I said we were not certain the Japanese were going to win the war, and that our strategy depended upon a revolution in India. Our strategy was to build up units that would go and fight on Indian territory, persuade the British Indian troops to come over, and then touch off a revolution. We were confident that once there was a revolution in the country, the combined forces of the revolutionaries and the INA would drive the British out. Then, even if the British won the war, they would not be able to come back.*

Of course this could not be done without Japanese assistance. The army had to be moved to Burma and supported there. Though guerrilla tactics would serve it well, unless it was a good deal larger than twelve battalions it would not be able to break across the frontier on its own—it would need Japanese help. But once in India it would need help less and less, for with every mile it advanced it would be joined by Indians, among them sepoys bringing their weapons, so that as it moved deeper it would actually grow in size.

This, at least, was the hope and the prospect. To make it happen the table of organization called for the addition of special units in part modeled on the Japanese Army. An Intelligence Group, to gather front-line intelligence. A Special Service Group, to penetrate the British lines and induce sepoys to desert. A Reinforcement Group, to collect these deserters as they arrived and prepare them for service with the freedom army. Until that army reached the front, however, the Reinforcement Group would act as a depot for the unfit and for men who as yet could find no place. Of these last there were a great many. The list of volunteers had lengthened, and was about to lengthen again. Kiani had many more than he could use.

Except officers—there were not enough officers, because the battalions from which the volunteers came had been largely British led, and the British had been separated out. There remained, of course, the VCOs. They could be offered full officer status. This was one of the things that had attracted Baboo Ram. But given their age and their background, only so much could be expected of VCOs. It was not from them, it was from a score of Indian commissioned lieutenants and captains, and a handful of King's commissioned majors and lieutenant colonels, that men must be found to fill the staff positions and command the battalions and regiments of Gill's scheme.

By moving men up a step while at the same time grading command appointments a rank below Indian Army practice, so that battalions went to majors and brigades to lieutenant colonels, this could be done. In the medical service, where Indianization had gone far, the old ranks already met the new requirements, and some volunteers did not advance at all. In the fighting arms, however, there were clearly not going to be enough officers. Somehow they had to be found and trained. Meanwhile, those available were given the lowest rank, then immediately lifted to the level dictated by their individual circumstances. Thus Special Order No. 1 announced the gazetting "to the rank of 2/Lieut. in the I.N.A. with effect from 1st September" of Prem, Dhillon, and Shah Nawaz.[1] Ten days later all three were gazetted captains, and within six weeks the first two were majors and Shah Nawaz a lieutenant colonel—so swiftly in this instant army could a man rise. At the same time the real work began.

"I was posted to the 1st Infantry Battalion, Hind Field Force," Baboo Ram later testified. This was at Bidadari. "After a few days we received machine guns, mortars, pistols, and rifles." All were familiar to Baboo Ram because they were Indian Army issue. Familiar, too, was the uniform, which everyone continued to wear. To it was added an arm band embroidered with the Congress flag and the letters INA. On the center of the arm band was a chocolate star upon a red background, a device later abandoned because it could be mistaken for the Japanese rising sun. "Captain Sahgal was Adjutant," Baboo Ram continued. "He was wearing the I.N.A. badges."[2] As a prosecution witness, Baboo Ram's chief function was to establish that by September 1942 Prem was irreversibly embarked on a thoroughly renegade course.

Equally renegade were the men of the guerrilla regiments, named Gandhi, Azad, and Nehru after the Congress big three. (Azad, which means free, was the pen name Abul Kalam had adopted as a young man to indicate that he was no longer tied to his inherited beliefs.) They began their training at Neesoon. And so a force took shape, a force whose outward look quite belied its purpose.

Outwardly it was almost indistinguishable from the army of British India. There were some small adaptations: the arm band just mentioned, the insignia of rank, the salute (the British Army style, palm out with forearm level, gave way to something more like that of the Japanese, the Americans, and the Royal Navy). Though the army continued to conduct its written business in English, it drilled in Hindustani. It had no British officers, of course, and therefore no VCOs. Otherwise it was the Indian Army, the old prewar Indian Army, dressed and armed in the old manner—as it was obliged to be.

For it had only the stock remaining at surrender to draw upon. It could neither replenish what it had, nor replace it with things fresh and new. In one way only might it have changed. It might have set about acquiring Japanese clothing, Japanese arms, Japanese equipment, and so have gradually become indistinguishable (except in face and build and the little mannerisms that separate one people from another) from the army of Nippon. It might have gone this route. It chose not to. And the Japanese, partly because they would have felt odd clothing and arming men they had so recently defeated, partly because they did not have much to spare, honored the choice. Unchanged, then, to the eye, the force seemed as if petrified, frozen in time, a living antique. When later the men in it met British Indian troops again, they were surprised to discover that these fellows wore not khaki like themselves but jungle green.

Inwardly, however, the Indian National Army was not frozen at all. Early in October, when training had been going on for hardly more than a month (but of course the men were veterans and knew their drill), there was a grand review on the padang. Thousands of men in files of three, motionless, rifles at present arms, filled the enormous grassy stretch—then, at the command, formed columns and executed a march past. It was an impressive sight. Everything about it suggested the normal ceremonial of the Indian Army under the Raj. But the suggestion was deceptive. This was October 2, the Mahatma's birthday. Neither Raj nor Army had ever honored that day. And the man who took the salute was not some British general but a Sikh officer carried in the latest fat, red volume of the Indian Army List as a captain. Day and man confounded the appearance of the scene. What these men were about promised no comfort for Britain and her empire.

So the freedom force prepared, and for two or three months everything prospered, so that looking ahead to 1943 a person might easily imagine the twelve battalions moved to Burma, poised on its northern border, ready to descend into India and join hands with fellow Indians in the final struggle for independence. It did not work out that way. When 1942 ended the twelve battalions were still in Malaya. Their commander was under arrest; the Indian National Army had formally ceased to exist. How and why this happened makes a complicated tale in which Prem was very little involved, and Lakshmi not at all. The chief actor was Mohan Singh.

It is difficult to know what to make of Mohan Singh. His actions and his memoirs suggest a man of great vigor, impetuous, persuasive, loyal, genuinely patriotic. At the same time a man with more than the usual allowance of self-estimation and esteem; a man accustomed to blowing his own horn, though he does it so guilelessly it is easy to forgive him. Of the Bangkok Conference in June he recollects that the first day was entirely taken up by himself. "I was heard with rapt attention for seven and a half hours in pin drop silence."[3] Yet it is apparent from other sources that Rash Behari Bose, three other Indians, a Thai, and a Japanese also spoke. And if at first we are surprised to hear him charged with making all INA men swear to be loyal to him personally, when in fact the oath simply binds a man to fight for India's freedom in the army he commands, in the end we may agree that his critics have a point. For Mohan Singh believes that the men are *his* men, the army *his* army, and that he may do with them as he pleases.

At least he knows, in the autumn of 1942, exactly what he *wants* to do. He wants to send the twelve battalions and the special groups to Burma. He wants to raise a second division from the remaining volunteers, and a third from those prisoners of war who have not volunteered—he is sure they can be persuaded. He wants to tap the large resident population of Indian civilians in Malaya and Burma (this has been Fujiwara's ambition from the start), and build from it a patriotic army of a quarter of a million. He believes all this can be done quickly.

The Japanese demur. They tell him that the twelve battalions will require four months' training. "I challenged that the whole work could be completed in one week," he remembers. After Gandhi's birthday parade he is gleeful. He has won his bet; the Japanese seem "highly pleased and greatly impressed."[4] But they make no move to ship the twelve battalions or raise more.

In fact it was going to take a good deal longer than Mohan Singh supposed to get the twelve ready. *The men had been in prisoner-of-war camps*, Prem recalls. *They were not in good condition. They had to be trained.* That meant individual exercises, then training by platoons, companies, and (with the responsibilities of new and inexperienced officers particularly in mind) still larger units. Arms and equipment made difficulties too. "Rifles were old and rusty and had no oil bottles or pull-throughs," begins one account.[5] Spare parts for the machine guns were in short supply, and the Japanese issued a Dutch model along with the British Bren and Lewis—which compounded the parts problem, and practically guaranteed that in the confusion of fighting some guns would get the wrong ammunition. All this was not wholly the fault of the Japanese. Collecting and caring for British weapons had not been one of their campaign priorities. But the campaign was over now, and the spoils substantial. If the Bren and Lewis guns in their possession numbered several thousand, why issue the Dutch model at all? Why offer a handful of artillery pieces from a stock of approximately three hundred; why find, for the armored vehicles battalion that Gill had designed, just thirteen Bren gun carriers and fourteen armored cars (these in such a precarious state as to be useful only for parades) when there were actually scores?

The Japanese might have replied that Mohan Singh and his fellows entertained grossly inflated visions of the future. For Burma, which was central to their dreams, the Japanese had originally intended nothing more than the occupation of enough territory to cut the road to China and keep Thailand quiet. It was true that in the excitement of the assault they had gone some distance past Mandalay. They had even talked of a limited offensive into Assam. It was only for a moment. American successes in the southwest Pacific alarmed them. 15th Army settled down well short of the Indian border.

Southern Army, to which the 15th belonged, had moved its headquarters to Singapore—renamed Shonan (Brilliant South). It was under orders to raise volunteer forces from among the local inhabitants, including Indians but not, of course, Chinese. It did little, however. It was losing staff to the divisions that Tokyo felt obliged to keep in Manchuria, facing the Russians. It had few actual Japanese troops. The presence of thousands of ex–Indian Army men clamoring for weapons made it nervous. So in this business of Mohan Singh and the freedom army it felt no sense of urgency. It did not rush to answer and accommodate the resolutions voted at the Bangkok Conference in June.

Some of these resolutions had to do with how the Indian Independence League and its military arm should be put together. More, however, concerned free India's relations with the Japanese. On this matter there had been no disagreement among the Indians. Impatient Mohan Singh had been as determined as cautious Goho, K. P. K. Menon, and Raghavan that the Japanese commit themselves clearly and unequivocally before collaboration went any further. They must recognize free India's sovereignty. They must bind themselves to respect its territorial integrity. They must promise to release all Indian prisoners of war to the Indian National Army, and accord it the status of an allied army. They must help that army with loans, and not ask it to march for any purpose other than the liberation of the motherland. But it was the first—the explicit, public recognition of India as an independent nation, and of themselves as that nation's representatives and guardians—that the delegates at Bangkok had shown themselves most determined to have. Four months had passed, and still they did not have it.

They had expected it in August, when the Quit India rebellion broke out. They had expected it in September, when the INA formally began. They had certainly looked for it, Prem remembers, on the occasion of the Gandhi birthday parade. And always it had not come.

This was not altogether the fault of Fujiwara's successor. Iwakuro had sent the Bangkok Resolutions on to Tokyo quickly enough. He did not, however, press his government to issue the asked-for declaration. He was older than Fujiwara, more experienced, more calculating, and at the same time less clear in his mind. "I've met the man," Joyce Lebra says, "and know well how he can obfuscate."[6] Lacking Fujiwara's enthusiasm for Indian independence, quite cold in fact to anything Indians thought or felt, Iwakuro told Tokyo only what Tokyo was prepared to hear, and this was *not* that these ex–Indian Army men and these Indian civilians had to be treated as if they spoke for India. None, after all, actually stood on Indian soil. Very few had moved as close, even, as Burma. The most they could reasonably expect was some encouragement. They might be reminded, for example, that Prime Minister Tojo wished India free and had told the Diet so. They ought to be happy with morsels like this, and not suppose that Tokyo's withholding of the declaration of recognition carried any sinister implication. The result was that by November of 1942, Mohan Singh was much troubled in his mind.

Signs of Japanese duplicity appeared. For some time the Indian Independence League had been permitted to use the broadcasting facilities of Radio Shonan. Lakshmi had been one of the first to go on the air. *One day some bright guy discovered that I had come from India comparatively recently and that my family was well known, that my mother was a member of the Congress, and knew Gandhiji, and Pandit Nehru, and everybody.* So she had been asked to talk. She remembers quite well what she said. *I used my own name, Lakshmi Swaminadhan.* (To south Indians she was, in the manner usual in that part of India, S. Lakshmi.) *I said if any member of my family or any friend is listening, I would like my mother and my brothers told that I am quite safe.* Then she described what was happening in Singapore, and in a second broadcast a fortnight later talked about the League and its plans for the future. K. P. K. managed these broadcasts. Under a promise of complete freedom to do as he thought best, he had assembled a staff (Lakshmi's cousin Kutty was a member) and begun writing scripts. Now he found that the Japanese did not live up to their promise. They altered his scripts. They meddled with his people.

The Penang branch of the *Kikan* was busy setting up schools to train intelligence agents—men who would slip into India, gather information, encourage Quit India rebels, and make mischief generally. There were a number of these schools, one composed exclusively of Muslims, another preparing wireless operators, and so forth, and among them was one that Raghavan directed. Raghavan took great pains with his curriculum. To lessons in how to tap telephones, forge documents, and make explosives he added serious political and cultural instruction. He was determined that his young men enter India as informed citizens. He was determined that they do so only when they were fully and truly ready. But the *Kikan* marched to a different drummer. It wanted spies and saboteurs, not citizens, and it meant to send them off, ready or not, the moment the situation demanded. One day Raghavan discovered that a score of his best students had abruptly sailed for India aboard a Japanese submarine. Furious, he closed his school. Annoyed in their turn, the Japanese placed him under house arrest.

It was in Burma, however, that the Japanese were most difficult. Perhaps this was because in Burma, by the summer of 1942, they had already burned their fingers on an independence army. There Fujiwara's equivalent, a Colonel Suzuki, whose alias (he could not afford to be recognized) was "Minami," had begun work early. The *Minami Kikan* preceded the *Fujiwara Kikan* by over half a year. Its director was a dozen years older, just as enthusiastic for independence movements (Lawrence of Arabia was on his lips too),[7] and more willing than Fujiwara to bypass or defy his superiors if he felt himself obstructed. Such was Suzuki's vigor that when the Japanese Army entered Burma early in 1942, the *Minami Kikan* had at its command several hundred armed Thais of Burmese origin, and more than a score of young Burmese nationals whom the Japanese had trained on the island of Hainan—the Thirty Comrades, as they came to be called. These formed the nucleus of the Burma Independence Army (BIA). And soon the Japanese were beginning to wish it did not exist.

For as the Thirty Comrades and their fellows moved deeper into Burma, they aroused furious public excitement. Young men flocked to them, partly out of the passion to be rid of the foreigner that lies close to the surface in all Burmese, partly because joining offered possibilities for settling old scores against Indians, Karens, and other non-Burmese, and gave license for general freebooting. Before long the BIA was tens of thousands strong, and all the more hotheaded because it thought it was the army of independent Burma—a notion the enthusiasm and impatience of the *Kikan's* chief encouraged it to entertain. Already the Japanese high command was of two minds about Burmese independence. Tempers rose. There were clashes with the *Kempeitai*. By the time the British had been driven over the mountains, 15th Army was thoroughly fed up with the Burma Independence Army and with the *Minami Kikan* too. In July it dissolved both. Suzuki was sent home. The BIA, renamed the Burma Defence Army and weeded until it was only a few thousand strong, was committed to a rigorous program of training. It was in this context, in an atmosphere of extreme Japanese annoyance, that the Indian independence movement in Burma began its work.

As elsewhere east of Calcutta, local Indian associations had been formed the moment the British left. They showed great promise. In Burma, Indians numbered more than half a million even after the exodus of early 1942, and as the Chinese were few, these Indians held the heights of trade and finance. It was the Chettiar moneylender who carried the Burmese rice farmer from harvest to harvest—one reason, of course, for the widespread popular dislike of his kind. To numbers and wealth add the presence of Indian soldiers taken prisoner during the campaign (though there were not many of these), and it was inevitable that the Indian Independence League and the Indian National Army should take root and flourish. It would have happened even if Burma had not been the obvious stepping stone to India.

Because it was the stepping stone, the Japanese were impatient to put Indians to the practical tasks of intelligence gathering, subversion, and sabotage. Through the *Iwakuro Kikan*, which had an office in Rangoon, spy schools were set up, and in their management and the disposal of their graduates the Japanese behaved just as they had behaved at Penang. When Indians objected, they were accused of being in British pay. At a party given to honor the members of the League's Burma Territorial Committee, some Japanese blithely sang a song that had their armies parading in Melbourne, their generals taking the salute in New York, "my grandfather . . . catching fish in the Ganges."[8] And at last a dispute over the disposition of evacuee property brought matters to a head, in a manner that thoroughly alienated Indians not just in Rangoon but everywhere.

Indians fleeing Rangoon with the British had left behind property that the League wanted to put to the service of the freedom movement. One of the Bangkok Resolutions asked the Japanese to make this property available. Nothing, however, had been done. So at last, in October 1942, a meeting was convened to thrash the matter out, Indians of the Burma Territorial Committee on one side, staff of the *Iwakuro Kikan* on the other. And what the Indians heard they did not like at all.

The Japanese, it seemed, did not feel bound by the Resolutions. If they allowed the League to use the abandoned property, it would be for purposes determined by themselves. Law and custom alike assigned the spoils of war to the victors. The Indians were not victors, they were not even partners; more like paupers they were, or puppets—yes, puppets was the word! "We do not want you to be puppets. But if we do, what is the harm in being puppets, why is *puppet* bad?"

When the Indians persisted, the Japanese officer who had made these remarks turned to a colleague and in his own language, which one Indian quite understood, remarked that you could not contest a point with these people. "The Indian way of arguing amounts to indulging in useless feats of hairsplitting," he said.[9] That did it. Puppets! Hairsplitters! Accounts of the scene quickly reached the Indians in Bangkok and Singapore, and stuck in their craw.

Their anger and resentment was complicated by the differences of opinion that existed among themselves. The Japanese, anxious to get at least some of the INA men out of Malaya, had asked Mohan Singh to provide several hundred for shipment to Burma. Mohan Singh had complied. But he had not consulted the Council of Action—which, it is only fair to note, rarely met. And he was promising now, though with no particular eagerness, to provide several hundred more. This annoyed K. P. K., Raghavan (who was at liberty again), and the others. They felt that Mohan Singh exceeded his powers. They also felt, and here they and Mohan Singh pursued parallel trains of thought, that, given the lengthening history of Japanese delay, interference, and insults, it would be foolish to cooperate further unless the Bangkok Resolutions were immediately accepted, and full and open recognition accorded to both the Army and the League. By this time Rash Behari Bose had come down to Singapore. He did not share, or perhaps even understand, the anger and resentment. Gilani, however, was as usual passive. K. P. K. and Raghavan, the two civilian members of the Council, pressed their case. The result was that at the end of November Iwakuro received a Council memorandum whose softness of tone did not conceal the fact that a real crisis was at hand.

Iwakuro tried to face the Indians down. The puppet business, he told them, had been misrepresented in translation. If the INA was to be militarily successful, its existence must be kept secret until it struck.

How could the League insist upon full recognition and the trappings of sovereignty when it was a government only in embryo? "You cannot make arrangements with a child in mother's womb."[10]

The Indians, however, were not to be silenced. Their country had risen. If the League and the Army were not immediately and publicly acknowledged, they would forfeit all confidence at home and their usefulness would be at an end. Tokyo had to make a declaration. Iwakuro must inform his government that this was absolutely necessary. "We know that Imperial Rescripts are issued only in exceptional cases. But the case of India affects one fifth of the people of the world."[11]

And as the talks went on, Mohan Singh's back stiffened. Eager as he was to move his army to Burma, he was not happy at the way the Japanese called for immediate drafts. Now he was determined that not another man should sail until the declaration was made. Iwakuro tried every trick and argument. He called in Fujiwara, and that honest advocate of Indian independence pleaded with his old comrade not to wreck the common enterprise. He pleaded in vain. Mohan Singh's suspicions were aroused. They grew sharper when he learned that the Japanese were resuming control of all POWs not actually serving in his units—which meant that many would be sent to distant labor camps. When early in December the Japanese arrested Gill, his suspicions turned to anger.

Gill was just back from Burma, where he had arranged the dispatch to India of certain infiltration parties. The officer leading one of these parties had defected, which threatened all the others, and the Japanese suspected Gill of having encouraged the fellow. It was a fact that Gill was of two minds about the INA. If the Japanese only suspected it, Mohan Singh knew. But he and Gill were fellow Sikhs. They had promised to stand together. They had sworn a solemn oath to this effect. It was from a room next to Mohan Singh's that the Japanese took Gill away very early on the morning of December 8. Mohan Singh was furious.

So furious that by that evening every member of the Council except Rash Behari had resigned. Some had been preparing to anyway. Gill's arrest persuaded the rest. In Mohan Singh's view the Council was now defunct, the link between league and army broken, the men of the INA unreservedly what he had always felt them to be: "pledged to me and me alone by name."[12] Though ships were waiting in the harbor, for the moment no jawans would embark. The Japanese must first give the Indian National Army the formal recognition it deserved. They must let any prisoner of war join who wished to do so. And they must treat directly with himself. There could be no more going through the League and its elderly and compromised civilian leader.

Not unnaturally Rash Behari did not see matters this way. He did not consider the Council of Action dead, civilian control of the INA abrogated, or himself a creature of the Japanese. For three weeks he tried to bring Mohan Singh to heel. If Mohan Singh had stood alone, he might have succeeded. Most of the officers, however, closed ranks behind their commander. They, too, resented having offered Nippon so much in effort and enthusiasm, only to be treated with so little openness and respect. They encouraged Mohan Singh to dig in, and dig in he did. The loyalty, impetuosity, and vigor that had always been his principal virtues were concentrated now upon the supreme task of holding firm against the Japanese. Not for a moment did he waver. He could not, he would not, budge.

But neither, of course, could he prevail. For if Rash Behari was no match for him, the *Kikan* was. Midway through December, Mohan Singh quietly circulated an order calling for the instant dissolution of the INA should what he feared occur. On the 29th it did. He was summoned to Iwakuro's bungalow and told the conditions under which alone he would be allowed to continue in his command. When he refused them, he was handed a letter of dismissal signed by Rash Behari. That was not all. Even Fujiwara could not have persuaded the *Kikan* to let such a man revert to simple prisoner-of-war status. The Japanese took him into custody. They put him in a seafront bungalow. Later they moved him to an island in Johore Strait, later still to Sumatra. On Sumatra he remained for the rest of the war, treated decently enough but kept carefully away from the men he had stirred and the movement he had begun. For Mohan Singh everything was over. And as his last order was obeyed, it looked as if everything was over for the Indian National Army too.

It wasn't. Too much had happened, at Farrer Park on that distant February day and since, for the freedom force to be abandoned simply because its commander declared it so. *Who was he to dissolve us?* Prem remembers thinking. *A man cannot start a movement of that magnitude and then just call it off*, was Lakshmi's view.

Slowly the INA revived. With Mohan Singh gone and the other civilians on the sidelines, Rash Behari Bose had the field to himself. Encouraged by Iwakuro, he went from camp to camp talking with the officers, exhorting the men, until gradually most of them came around. Dhillon rejoined and was assigned to Kiani's headquarters. Prem went to a new Military Bureau as military secretary. Shah Nawaz was put in charge of the operations branch. Rash Behari took steps to tie the revived army securely to the Indian Independence League, whose headquarters he brought down from Bangkok. Through Bhonsle at the Military Bureau he gave instructions to Kiani, who resumed command of the troops.

So the army was in being once more. From India it could hear the roar of the Quit India uprising, muted a little as the old year ended, louder again in the new (on the 10th of February, 1943, Gandhi, in prison but no longer incommunicado, began a twenty-one-day fast). From Europe the news was less encouraging. The Germans had surrendered at Stalingrad and the Allies had landed in North Africa. But nothing imperiled the Japanese hold on Southeast Asia. The prospects for a joint descent on Assam and Bengal when Indians and Japanese were ready, seemed as bright as ever. And still, something was wrong.

It was not just that the revived force was smaller than it had been. (In spite of Rash Behari's efforts, scores of officers and several thousand men declined to rejoin. As they were now unprotected, the Japanese took many and shipped them off to distant places. In this way Baboo Ram, whom we last encountered training with the Hind Field Force, reached New Guinea but managed to survive.) It was not this. It was not even that the Bangkok Resolutions remained unacknowledged, and that the Japanese continued to treat the Indians more like clients than allies. It was something else.

What the Indians needed, soldiers and civilians alike, was a man who could grasp the enterprise with both hands and carry it forward—

with Japanese help if possible, without it if necessary. Mohan Singh had tried. He had begun the business, urging it along with an almost desperate haste, and he had failed. Failed because he was young, because he was brash, because he had little military and no political experience; because he lacked those qualities of weight and substance and genuine assurance that compel respect. Now Rash Behari was trying. He had survived the December crisis, had more than survived it, and now concentrated in his person every power that the head of a revolutionary movement could desire. But to have survived was not enough.

A certain K. R. Palta, who met him in Rangoon in September of 1942, was struck by the extent to which this "wrinkled old man" lived still in the world of the Bengal bomb throwers of thirty years before. Rash Behari was apparently quite satisfied with Mohan Singh's battalions, though Palta thought them a token force, and quite content to leave the real work of liberating India to the Japanese. Three months later Palta and his friends were arrested by those same Japanese, who connected them with Gill, and Rash Behari did nothing to obtain their release. In his published recollections of the period Palta does not reproach him on this account.[13] He acknowledges the old patriot's many services, not least his resurrection of the army after the December crisis. But it is not Rash Behari he is proud to have served, it is another Bose. And though, in the early months of 1943, he was not, perhaps, consciously waiting for the arrival of this other Bose, a great many Indians in Rangoon, Bangkok, and Singapore were. They had been waiting for over a year.

Mohan Singh himself had asked the Japanese to arrange this man's passage almost from the moment he met Fujiwara. The same request had been put by the delegation that went to Tokyo; it was the subject of one of the Bangkok Resolutions; in the December crisis the Japanese failure to act upon the request had been one of the things that drove Mohan Singh to take the position he took. And when Shah Nawaz explored with Iwakuro the terms and conditions under which he and others might rejoin the freedom army, "I told him that there was only one man outside India who could start a real I.N.A."[14] This man, this other Bose, was Subhas Chandra.

CHAPTER 8

SUBHAS CHANDRA BOSE

Subhas Chandra Bose was born on the 23rd of January, 1897, in Cuttack, some two hundred miles southwest of Calcutta. Today Cuttack is a principal city in the state of Orissa. In the 1890s, however, Orissa did not have a separate identity. It was part of Bengal. And Subhas Chandra's parents did not speak Oriya. They were Bengalis. His father, from a village so close to Calcutta's southern edge that it has since been swallowed by that awesome metropolis, had moved to Cuttack because in a provincial town a lawyer had a better chance of getting ahead professionally.

Subhas Chandra's parents, moreover, were not ordinary Bengalis. They were Bengalis of breeding and status, people of gentility, "as we say in Bengali *Bhadra Lok*—a class based equally on occupation and on birth," remarks Bose's contemporary Nirad Chaudhuri in a tone of some contentment, he being of that class himself.[1]

Bhadralok were high-caste Hindus. They were comfortable with English institutions, and thoroughly at home in the English language. They had to be. They earned their living in the schools, courts, and offices of the Raj, and brought up their sons to do the same. The gentility they took such pride in, and that barred them from engaging in manual labor (so that though they invested in land and drew income from land, they were never themselves cultivators)—this gentility was in some measure patterned on the English model. Indeed, the word *bhadralok* (it is not a traditional Bengali term) was probably contrived in imitation of the English "gentlefolk."[2] Young *bhadralok* set great store by their accomplishments in English, cultivated manners that matched the best in English manners, and took pains that others should treat them as the gentlemen they knew themselves to be. In this respect Subhas Chandra was very much one of his kind.

For out of the recollections of him that others have left, and from the meager account he has given of himself, one obtains a picture of a young man, and later of a man in young middle age, who is serious in his manner, careful in his speech and dress, courteous to others, and determined that they shall be courteous to him. Dilip Kumar Roy, a close friend of his undergraduate and later days, remembers with admiration how neatly Subhas kept his Cambridge rooms, books and papers out of sight, nothing left lying about. Remembers that his coat was never frayed, his trousers never baggy, "his ward-robe never in dearth of clean stiff collars and gorgeous ties." Dilip himself found western dress tiresome, and in the privacy of his quarters in Fitzwilliam Hall wore a *dhoti*, until Subhas surprised him in it and asked him not to, "no, not even behind closed shutters." If Dilip, forgetting his surroundings, talked loudly and gesticulated, Subhas would order him to lower his voice. "And don't for God's sake fling your hands about like lassos."[3]

Of course in conducting himself so, and insisting that others do the same (his prohibitions extended to drink, and especially to women, "no playing with fire if you please"), Bose had the English of Cambridge, not the English of Calcutta, in mind. He was determined that Indians up at the varsity not give their country a bad name. This Dilip rather resented. Must he go out of his way to impress the Britisher?

Privately, Dilip rather suspected that his friend suffered from a sense of inferiority. But Subhas Chandra, he admitted, possessed great intensity of purpose—"one-pointed ardour" is his phrase.[4] Others have commented on the young man's gravity, his powers of self-discipline, the determination with which he set about getting up the nine subjects that would be tested on the Indian Civil Service examination while simultaneously reading for a tripos. Harindranath Chattopadhyaya, the same who met Lakshmi at Gilchrist Gardens when she was a girl, happened to be at Cambridge when Bose came up and always remembered how quiet and reserved he was. "His lips," he later wrote, "were always set in silence." But it was not the silence of vacuousness. His eyes, when you caught them, "seemed to look through the wall of the room into distance, into the future, into the very heart of India."[5] If you ignore the triteness of the image, what the poet seems to be saying is that this strange young man knew to an unusual degree what he was about. Indeed, that is the impression Subhas Chandra in his Cambridge days leaves. He is very busy. He cannot be bothered courting fellow Indian students who think him priggish, as some do. And he cannot be bothered proving anything to the English.

In fact he has discovered that he rather admires them, and in two letters to his friend Hementa Kumar Sarkar explains why.[6] The English are precise, methodical, and energetic, he writes. (It is Christmas, there has been snow as there sometimes is in Cambridge, perhaps it is the climate that makes them so). They are optimists. "We think more of the sorrows of life, they think more of the happy and bright things of life." They have common sense, and apply it (the compliment is a touch grudging) in the pursuit of national self-interest. And they treat their university students well. A Cambridge undergraduate, Bose has found, can buy books on credit at the bookshops. A Calcutta undergraduate, he remembers bitterly, cannot. Altogether there is a good deal to be said for these English. And then, inserted with no apparent relevance into the catalogue of their virtues, comes a line that is much quoted and often made to bear a greater burden of interpretation than it can sustain. "Nothing makes me happier than to be served by the whites and to watch them clean my shoes."

Presumably these "whites" were the college gyps, middle-aged men of a particular class who made the beds, swept the rooms, and emptied the chamber pots of Cambridge undergraduates. In Calcutta Subhas had not been so served. Calcutta colleges were not residential; students were scattered across the city in homes and hostels. What delighted Subhas with his Fitzwilliam Hall experience, and led him, I think, to write this startling sentence, was not that whites were abasing themselves before him, an Indian. One may be sure he did not actually *watch* his servant. Why should he? There was nothing of interest to the viewer, and nothing degrading to the doer, in a servant cleaning shoes. What pleased Subhas was that among their other virtues the English, in England, were prepared to treat him as they treated their own university undergraduates—were prepared, that is, to treat him as a gentleman. When people on a train questioned him (it occurred often enough, England was not accustomed to Indians), he had only to reply that he was up at the university, and "the attitude of the questioner would change at once. He would become friendly—or shall I say more respectful? This was my personal experience."[7] It had not been his experience in Calcutta.

Particularly after the outbreak of the First World War, which followed close upon Subhas Chandra's entry into Presidency College, Calcutta University (he matriculated during the monsoon of 1913 at the normal Indian age of sixteen), there had been frequent incidents between Englishmen and Indians in the part of the city through which he had to pass every day. Riding the trams, Englishmen would sometimes put their feet up on seats occupied by Indians. "On the streets the same thing happened. Britishers expected Indians to make way for them, and if the latter did not do so they were pushed aside by force or had their ears boxed."[8] Whereas an Indian undergraduate entering the compartment of a London train could expect at worst a certain coolness, and at best friendly curiosity, even a High Court judge boarding at the Howrah Station for Patna or Lucknow might discover that, first-class ticket or no, the British he thought to sit among proposed to throw him bodily out. Such indignities, offered to others or to himself, made Bose angry. At some point early in his life he decided that he would not permit them.

The tale is told—it is an indication of how much this decision became a part of Bose's public character—that when, at the age of twenty-seven, he became Chief Executive Officer of Calcutta (which meant he ran the city), his Chief Engineer, an Englishman named Coates, who had been around a long time and thought he knew how to handle Indians, regularly lit cigarettes in Bose's presence, a thing no well-brought-up young Bengali will do in the presence of his father even today. At last Bose inquired, smiling but firm, "is it proper, Mr. Coates, to smoke before a superior officer?" Coates extinguished his cigarette. An equally pointed query some days later put an end to his habit of doing business with Subhas Chandra seated on a table, legs dangling.[9]

There are other such tales. One concerns an encounter in the 1920s with a police officer named Ellison who, as he prepared to stop Bose from entering Dacca (where Bose meant to investigate police excesses), addressed him as Subhas. Bose made the man use Subhas Babu. But the incident that has caught everyone's attention, partly because Bose himself made so much of it, occurred at Presidency College early in 1916. This was the Oaten affair.

～❀～

Edward Oaten was an Englishman who at the age of twenty-five had come out to Calcutta to teach. Young Indian Educational Service men of his sort were rarely distinguished scholars in prospect (Oaten with a Cambridge First was something of an exception), yet they had from the moment of their appointment an advantage over their Indian colleagues of the Provincial Educational Service: they automatically became heads of departments. At Presidency College Oaten taught history—Europe's, not India's, it need hardly be observed. He taught in English, like everybody else. He lived among his fellow countrymen, perhaps in the part of Calcutta Subhas passed through daily. And in the brief memoir of the affair that he wrote when he was nearly ninety, he says that he did not see much of his students outside college hours.

Sometimes he talked to them on the cricket field. Sometimes he took a sherbet with them. He attended one pupil's wedding. With another he corresponded, in Bengali be it noted, and was delighted to discover, fifty years later, that the fellow still kept his letters.

He was never close to them, however. They were a courteous lot. They stood up when he entered a room. "In my historical seminar the senior students wrote excellent papers and joined in the discussion of them afterwards."[10] One imagines that the topics included the Long Parliament of 1642 and Burke's views on the French Revolution. But when Oaten looked out over the sea of polite faces that greeted him daily in the lecture hall, he could, he remembers, "deduce nothing as to what was passing through their minds politically speaking." He noticed only that in 1915 there came a change in the college atmosphere, a perceptible slackening in manners and discipline—expressed, to his particular annoyance, in the way the students behaved in the corridors.

Verandas really, these corridors ran (they still do) at every level around the courtyard of the U-shaped college building, and were the means of access to the lecture halls. Between bells they were supposed to be empty, because "owing to the heat one had to lecture with open doors, and movement along the corridor drowned one's voice and led to the premature end of the lecture." On the 10th of January, 1916, however, the usual schedule having been upset by a prize-giving ceremony, a number of students passed along the veranda outside Oaten's room during the noon class hour, chattering noisily, and disturbed him so much (Calcutta can be nippy in January, but perhaps Oaten kept his door open anyway) that he stopped his lecture and ordered them away. A short while later, still before the bell, an Indian colleague named Ghosh dismissed a class close by and followed it along the same veranda. Thoroughly annoyed now, Oaten rushed out, recognized Ghosh, allowed him to continue, but insisted that his students return to their room. When some of them hesitated, he gave two or three a shove.

In the aftermath H. R. James, the college principal, was at some pains to remind his countrymen that it was unwise to touch an Indian student's person. No doubt it was. Presidency College students, however, were used to more than an occasional shove. They were used to verbal abuse. They were accustomed to being reproached, scolded, belittled, sneered at. And this was something James could not very well caution his staff against because from time to time he treated them so himself.

James seems to have been in many respects a decent fellow. Hemendranath Das Gupta, a contemporary of Bose and one of his biographers, says that the Principal "used to take boys to restaurants and at times gave them lessons on various outside matters including the sport of Boxing."[11] But the new political consciousness of the under-graduates, dimly perceived through the veil of their polite reserve, made James edgy. By the time the war began he was telling them that, while it was all very well to make much of their Bengaliness, "one thing that patriotism in Bengal should not do is to direct the national spirit into an attitude of hostility to British rule." That would be worse than ungrateful. It would be "patricidal."[12]

In speaking so, James must have had in mind, may almost have been quoting, Sir John Strachey, dead now eight years but still tremendously influential. The lectures Strachey had delivered at Cambridge in 1884, after retiring from a lifetime of administrative work in India, had recently been reprinted for the third time. They were known, directly or by hearsay, to every Englishman, Irishman, and Scot who served the Raj. Strachey had been in British terms a liberal.

He had followed with the greatest sympathy Italy's struggle against Austria and the Papacy, and had in fact spent a part of his retirement in that country—indeed, it was said of him that the one regret of his life had been his inability to serve the cause of Italian independence as a volunteer under Garibaldi. Of India, however, he had pronounced (and in reissues of *India: Its Administration & Progress* continually repeated) that nothing by that name existed. "This is the first and most essential fact about India that can be learned."[13] And as there was not, and never had been, an India "possessing according to European ideas any sort of unity physical, political, social, or religious; no Indian nation, no people of India," it followed that the British had never offended against India's consciousness of self. There was no consciousness of self to offend against. "No national sentiment has been wounded," there being none to wound.

Of course the British had given the subcontinent railroads and the telegraph, roads and canals, courts, police, public services of every kind, "the whole paraphernalia of a great civilized administration"—to which, Sir John might have added, he had contributed measurably himself. But none of this could ever make of India a nation. "However long may be the duration of our dominion, however powerful may be the centralising attraction of our government, . . . no such issue can follow."

"It is conceivable," Strachey had continued, "that national sympathies may arise in particular Indian countries." It was impossible, however, for a patriotic spirit to bind Indians as a whole, impossible that "the men of Bombay, the Punjab, Bengal, and Madras should ever feel they belong to one great Indian nation." Not the least of the reasons why this was so was that "the manlier races" such as the Sikhs and the Pathans would never allow themselves to be governed from Calcutta. Indeed, if the British were to lose their grip, if the "unspeakable blessing of the *pax britannica*" were to be withdrawn, Bengalis might easily find themselves ruled from Amritsar or from Peshawar—and by no means gently either. To men like James, Strachey's lesson was clear. Bengali pride, Bengali consciousness of self, would flower only so long as Bengalis accepted Englishmen *in loco parentis*. This was why signs of undergraduate hostility towards the Raj were so troubling.

So James warned the young men of Presidency College off the path that leads to patricide. Oaten and the others, however, did more. They practiced upon their students a species of denigration that was far harder to bear than the Principal's political cautions. And this, too, had been taught them by an Englishman of a previous generation. What they were transmitting, though perhaps not conscious whence it came, was the frame of mind (and with it some of the juicier aspersions) of Macaulay's famous Education Minute of 1835.

___

In the fourth decade of the nineteenth century, twenty years before the Sepoy Rebellion, there had occurred a sharp struggle in the upper circles of the Raj over the direction Indian higher education ought to take. Should Indian students be invited, as was presently the case, to explore their own cultural inheritance in their own tongues? To study Indian law, literature, and religion through the languages in which these had developed? Or should they be directed to turn their backs upon that inheritance, and address instead the world of western thought?

Arguing for the status quo were the so-called Orientalists, Englishmen who took a scholarly (some would say antiquarian) delight in Indian learning and Indian speech. Arrayed against them were those who believed that the culture of the subcontinent was fundamentally backward and obscurantist; who believed that waiting for western ideas to penetrate and leaven it, as the Orientalists urged, was a prescription for procrastination, delay, and eventual failure; who believed that it would be better to abandon the old culture and start afresh. The Orientalists were well established. In Calcutta they occupied all the important education posts. Their opponents, however, could turn for support to evangelical and utilitarian opinion in England, which at this moment was extremely powerful. It happened, moreover, that Lord William Bentinck, the Governor-General, inclined toward their party. In 1835, as the struggle approached a decision, Thomas Babington Macaulay, a young essayist and Member of Parliament with the celebrated *History of England* still ahead of him, arrived in Calcutta as Law Member of Bentinck's Council, threw himself into the business, induced the already half-persuaded Bentinck to act, and composed for

him the manifesto, the famous Minute, that announced the defeat of
the Orientalists and the triumph of the Anglicists.

Anglicists because the practical matter on which the controversy
turned was language. As long as the first task of indigenous scholars was
to rediscover cultural roots, Indians had to have a solid grasp of the
classical Indian languages. If, however, they turned to western science,
thought, and learning, then obviously they would have to work in
English. So the question was, should the colleges that the government
was prepared to support, continue teaching Arabic and Sanskrit, or
should they switch to English? Bentinck's decision, for which Macaulay's
Education Minute provided the rationale, was that they should switch.
"The great object of the British Government," Bentinck declared in
words written for him by Macaulay, "ought to be the promotion of
European literature and science among the natives of India."[14] That
meant putting India to school in the English language, if not all Indians
(though there were enthusiasts who thought this practicable), at least
the Indian elite. This the Government of India prepared to do.

It was a major change of direction. And it was one that did not take
place in isolation, but was part of a general shift in the way the British
regarded India. There had been a time when Englishmen were
genuinely anxious to learn an Indian language, to adapt themselves to
Indian habits and practices, to discover something about Indian life.
This, of course, had been partly a matter of necessity. Ways of ruling
enormous numbers of Indians had to be devised, and it had seemed
only prudent to the men involved that they should get to know, and in
some degree understand, these Indians—including Indian women,
since (no small point) these were the only women they had access to.

By the fourth decade of the nineteenth century, however, arrivals
from the United Kingdom looked at things differently. They were
bursting with their generation's special self-confidence. They were
beginning to bring their own women with them. What they expected
now was not that they should adjust to their exotic surroundings, but
that their surroundings should adjust to them. They would not learn to
think and live like Indians. Indians, at least educated Indians, must learn
to think and live as they did.

The new attitude had its virtues. There was something to be said
for it, and something *was* said for it—even by Indians. A man more

passionately Indian than Ram Mohan Roy it would be hard to find. Yet Roy was an ardent advocate of English schooling. Had he not died (in England) two years before Macaulay wrote his Minute, he would have applauded its sentiments. The distinguished historian K. M. Panikkar, writing shortly after independence, credits "the Macaulayan system" with producing a "like-mindedness in politics" that was essential to the development of national feeling. "Except for a hundred years of uniform education through the English language," he says, India would today remain as fragmented as Europe.[15] Besides, Macaulay or no Macaulay, there existed among Indians—among the Bengal *bhadralok* particularly, but among the Hindu gentry of south India as well—an enthusiasm for European literature and science that antedated the Minute by years. This enthusiasm was fired in part by the realization that there were jobs to be had for those who knew the Englishman's tongue. And as the Government of India, for reasons of economy, was inviting Indians into the lower judicial and administrative posts of the Raj, Calcutta and Madras would have pressed for higher education in English even if Macaulay had made no case for it.

Nevertheless the change, with what it implied about past Indian accomplishments, was wounding to Indian self-esteem. It was made more so by Macaulay's rhetoric, which (as John Clive puts it) "had not been calculated to soothe."[16] It was one thing for an Orientalist to admit that West outstripped East in many areas of intellectual endeavor. It was another for an Anglicist to announce that a single shelf of European books matched the entire literature of India and the Arab world. Parts of the Minute were rhetorically so powerful they could not help but survive in the collective memory long after the rest of the document, which contained a good deal of common sense, had been forgotten. Would any reasonable man, Macaulay had asked, wish his sons to be exposed to medical doctrines that would embarrass a blacksmith, to astronomical propositions that would make a schoolgirl laugh? Should public money be put to the teaching of "History abounding with kings thirty feet high and reigns thirty thousand years long—and Geography made up of seas of treacle and oceans of butter?"[17] This last was a reference to the ancient, popular belief in continents separated from each other by bands of liquid that passed from salt water through treacle, wine, ghee, and curds, to water that was fresh and pure. No doubt such a mental picture had once been a real obstacle to the growth of an empirical geography. Was it an obstacle still?

Macaulay had written as if it were. And even at Presidency College, Calcutta's (and therefore India's) premier institution of higher learning, the British faculty *taught* as if it were. The consequence was that, perhaps without being fully conscious of what they were doing, the Oatens and the Jameses turned upon their students a steady drumfire of cultural disparagement.

"Evidence has been given us," reported a Committee of Enquiry set up after the Oaten affair, that on one occasion "a professor of the College" told assembled students that "as the mission of Alexander the Great was to hellenise the barbarian people with whom he came into contact, the mission of the English here was to civilize the Indians." The professor in question was Oaten. "We also have evidence to the effect that a young European professor asked certain students why they were howling like wild beasts; another asked . . . why they were chattering like monkeys; while a third is reported to have enquired of his students why they had behaved like coolies." Only four such instances had been brought to their attention in the past four years, continued the committee (three Englishmen and two Indians). "But reports of these have spread and have not been forgotten."[18]

Indeed they had not. The Indian press made sure that they weren't. But it is also likely that Oaten and his fellows put rhetorical questions of this sort far more often than the committee knew, and that young *bhadralok*, forced to listen, thought them outrageously invidious. So they were coolies, monkeys, hyenas? Benighted Asiatics? (That Oaten had used "barbarian" in its literal Greek sense of "non-Hellenic" was probably lost upon his hearers.) It was this, I think, that turned the business of January 10—an irritated professor shoving a few students— into more than a passing unpleasantness, and led to the really serious incident a month later.

The students whom Oaten had pushed went at once to Principal James to lodge a complaint. With them went Bose, for several were of the third year, as he was, and on the consultative committee the Principal had arranged, he spoke for the third year. Besides, Bose may have been among those shoved. To Oaten, James wrote privately (by this time Presidency had almost one thousand students and a staff of sixty), suggesting that he try to make peace with the grievants. To the grievants themselves, however, he said nothing conciliatory—with the consequence that "we were naturally not satisfied, and the next day there was a general strike of all the students." Bose, whose words these are, helped organize it. It lasted two days, was generally observed, and ended with Oaten expressing qualified regret for what he had done. But a five-rupee fine levied on the strikers was not remitted. And when, on the first day of resumed classes, some of the strikers tried to attend Oaten's lecture, he barred their way, alleging that they had been disloyal to him personally. So the bitterness continued.

On the 15th of February, Oaten was again disturbed by noise on the veranda, and again rushed out. This time, however, he did more than shout. He grabbed a boy, by the arm perhaps, by the scruff of the neck the boy alleged, and dragged him away. In an instant, word of what had happened was all over the college. Though this boy (whose name also was Bose) was a first-year student, and so not directly Subhas Chandra's responsibility, Subhas was determined to do something for him. But what was he to do?

It was no use asking Oaten to apologize. He would certainly refuse. Besides, the indignity he had inflicted this time cried out for more than an apology. "Constitutional protests like strikes would simply provoke disciplinary measures, and appeals to the Principal would be futile. Some students therefore decided," Bose wrote some years later, "to take the law into their own hands."[19] And though he does not say so, it is highly probable that among those students was himself.

It may even have been he who concerted the little act of retribution that followed. Dilip Roy, recollecting "the ominously grim face of Subhash," was sure he had.[20] Two hours after the scuffle, Oaten went down to the college notice board to post a notice. There a dozen students surprised him, knocked him to the ground, and fled. It was over in seconds, Oaten was not hurt only bruised and shaken, but nothing like this had ever happened—and all Calcutta rocked with the news. The college was closed. The Committee of Enquiry I have mentioned was appointed. A college servant identified Subhas as one of the attackers. Already he had a reputation as a troublemaker. The nature of the assault, Oaten surrounded and mobbed, outraged Europeans and even disturbed some of Bose's friends. How unsporting to take a man from the rear. (Probably no Englishman failed to notice, at least with one corner of his mind, that poor Oaten had gone down to post a *cricket* notice.) How curious that young, well-educated Bengalis did not see the shamelessness of the act. Or, since they *were* Bengalis, how much to be expected!

Yet it is difficult to see how these angry and embittered young men could have served Oaten as they believed he must be served in any other way. English boys did not like being pushed or grabbed by the scruff of the neck. They were not, however, outraged by physical violence. To be caned by a master was part of public school life, and in the Royal Navy, as late as the Second World War, midshipmen regularly caught beatings. But the caning or the beating took place between prospective equals. The public school master had once been a public school boy. The midshipman would in due course become a lieutenant. Whereas a Presidency College student could never become an Oaten—nor did he wish to. ☞

Were these students supposed to abide by the Englishman's sporting ethic? If one side of that coin tells a man not to hit his enemy from behind, the other tells him to offer a challenge face to face, then fight with fists or other manly weapons—and how on earth was an Indian to manage that? Was he to take lessons in boxing (perhaps from Principal James), in the epée or the quarterstaff, then confront Oaten in his blessed lecture hall one fine morning and have the business out? Let any undergraduate attempt such a thing and he would not simply be humiliated all over again, by Oaten laughing and turning away (for Oaten would certainly refuse the challenge). If he persisted and actually struck a blow, be would instantly be charged with assault and battery and pursued with the full force of the law. No, if you wanted physical satisfaction from an Englishman, and these young *bhadralok* did, there was only one way to obtain it, the way of surprise and speed and anonymity. Gang up, jump the fellow, and run. Only in that way could he neither refuse to fight, nor single you out and ruin you after the assault was over.

Refuse to fight, decline to accept you as an adversary, laugh you away, or if you persist, isolate and destroy you—too often the predicament not just of schoolboys but of entire independence movements, minorities, women almost everywhere.

There was no way in which Subhas Chandra could compel the Oatens and the Jameses to behave towards the students of Presidency College as gentlemen behave towards gentlemen. But he did not in consequence stand helplessly by. The matter cannot be proved, there is no independent testimony to tell us exactly who set up the ambush, but it was hardly spontaneous, and Bose was certainly involved. Questioned, he denied being present at the notice board. Asked whether he had nevertheless planned the assault, "I won't tell if I am guilty or not guilty," Hemendranath Das Gupta has him say.[21] Had he then acknowledged the shamelessness of the act and lapsed into silence, he might have been let off. But he would not. Instead he used the opportunity, he later wrote, "to narrate seriatim the misdeeds of the Britishers in Presidency College."[22] In short he challenged the legitimacy of the questions put to him, and by implication the legitimacy of his questioners. And so he and one other student were expelled.

It was no light matter. He could not remain in Calcutta. His older brothers, aware that students about the city were being arrested, hurried him back to Cuttack. To Hemanta he wrote that while he did not expect to be permanently rusticated (he uses the English expression), he felt shaken and hardly knew how he would survive. In fact it was a year and a half before he was readmitted to the university, and then it was not to Presidency College.

I said earlier that Bose made a great deal of this business. So in time he did, in the process perhaps tailoring a little his recollection of things done and said so that the whole served his purpose. In 1937 he told Emilie Schenkl, the Austrian woman who was his secretary (and would later be his wife), that he had gradually come to realize "the inner significance of the tragic events of 1916. My Principal had expelled me, but he had made my future career. I had established a precedent for myself from which I could not easily depart in future."

Exactly what that precedent was does not emerge from the succeeding lines, which, concluding this chapter of his hurriedly written autobiography, convey only woolly generalities about courage, initiative, and duty fulfilled, about the "foretaste of leadership" the incident had granted him and the "martyrdom" this would probably involve.[23] But I think the drift is clear. What others might consider undue sensitivity (the Committee of Enquiry had remarked upon "a spirit of excessive touchiness amongst students of the rising generation"[24]), Bose was determined to make a constant of his behavior. Henceforth he would insist that the British, in all matters large and small, treat him and his with dignity and respect. No matter how promising the opportunity he might forfeit, no matter how high the cost, in future he would not touch his cap to them.

Nor to the Japanese. He was as unwilling, much later, to jump to their instructions or allow them to manipulate his people, as he was unwilling to be bullied by an Oaten or a James. But this did not make Subhas Chandra anti-Japanese. Nor did the Oaten affair turn him against the British. It did not put at the center of his life a passionate desire to do Englishmen in. It is surprising that some people should apparently believe that it did.

Hugh Toye inclines in that direction. In his biography of Bose, Colonel Toye has it that young Subhas came out of the Oaten affair believing himself "a victim of racial prejudice, struck down for protesting against an insult to his Motherland." He did not forget the injury, continues Toye. "He brooded over it with all the vehemence of his nineteen years," adding other examples of racial prejudice, until at last "racial hatred ate into his soul." And it is Toye's view that although this "racial complex" moderated as Bose grew older, it never went away. "To show himself superior to the white-faced foreigner," to so manage affairs that India as a whole should show itself superior, became the object of his life, his mission, his (and here Toye borrows Dilip Roy's adjective) "one-pointed aim."[25]

One may agree with Toye, and with Dilip Roy too, that Bose was unusually single-minded. And Dilip himself has Subhas announce at one point in his Fitzwilliam Hall stay that Indian students up at the varsity must "prove it home" to the English "that we are their superiors," a conversational remark reconstructed like the others long after it was uttered, and one from which very little can safely be inferred—any young man set down in a foreign place might say such a thing.[26] But that Bose developed a racial complex; that he was eaten with racial hatred, and that this was what drove him; seems to me not so much wrong as an unwitting inversion of what actually went on between Oaten and the students, and between Englishmen and Indians at any number of places and on any number of occasions.

For it was the *Englishman* of that day who felt race, thought race, and used the word often and publicly. It was the Englishman who, encountering an Indian or an Egyptian or a Zulu, and observing that he differed, attributed the difference not to circumstance but to blood, not to culture or community but to race. It was race Strachey had in mind when he addressed himself to the question, should Indians be admitted by competitive written examination to the higher levels of the public service. (Already they filled the lower levels, in Strachey's opinion entirely properly.) It was race Strachey had in mind when he observed that in the Englishman's case the most important part of this examination had already been sat and passed for him, "by his forefathers, who, as we have a right to assume, have transmitted to him not only their physical courage, but the powers of independent judgment, the decision of character, the habits of thought, and generally those qualities that are necessary for the government of men, and which have given us our empire. The stock-in-trade with which Englishmen start in life," he continued, "is not that of Bengalis."[27] The one was born with imperial talents and instincts. The other was not.

It is hard to believe that the Jameses and the Oatens did not share this attitude. If they had not read Strachey they had certainly read Kipling, or had listened to Curzon, the Viceroy from whose lips issued on every possible occasion news of his countrymen's God-given capacity for the evenhanded administration of distant places. What is more, not being themselves members of the Indian Civil Service, the elite corps that Strachey and Curzon had specifically in mind (and that Lloyd George would style the "steel frame" of the Raj just when it was ceasing to be)—not being themselves prospective proconsuls or even military men, but only middle class English schoolmasters brought out to India to play an imperial part, the Jameses and the Oatens had almost certainly discovered that to their sense of racial separateness were joined other feelings. Disturbing feelings. Feelings of anxiety, irritation, and resentment. Resentment that the obvious superiority of their race, the British race, was not conceded by the people among whom they moved.

Simply existing in India was no easy matter. There was the food. There was the climate. There were the natives themselves. "Our complexion, religion, language, and habits," observed Rabindranath Tagore a few weeks after the Oaten affair, "are most annoyingly different from theirs." Exactly so. Indians were different, annoyingly different, and they were apparently quite content to remain different. If James and Oaten read the piece in which Tagore made this observation (it appeared in a Calcutta journal and was addressed directly to what had just happened in Presidency College[28]), they discovered that though the poet had some sympathy for them in this "land of exile," he was entirely with the students in their Bengali assertiveness and their Bengali pride. For Englishmen, therefore, liking Indians was not easy. Especially in periods of loneliness or general malaise, when India's foreignness grew almost unbearable and the heat was at its worst, it was easier to take the other direction, and quite possible in moments of extreme exasperation to pass from dislike to open animosity. One cannot, of course, be certain. But when Oaten burst shouting on to that veranda and confronted those chattering students, among whom we may suppose was Bose, it was surely the Englishman who moved with the fury of "racial hatred"—*not* the Indian.

That Bose himself did not hate the British is further suggested by the kind words he has for the "rough Scotsman" with a heart of gold who taught him infantry drill; for two successive superintendents of Mandalay prison, where he spent some time (as will appear); for Lord Irwin (in his opinion few viceroys exhibited "such a friendly attitude towards the Indian people"); and even for Principal James ("I must say in fairness to him that he was very popular with the students for protecting them against police persecution on several occasions").[29] There are no kind words for Oaten. But I do not think Subhas hated him. Oaten simply made him angry. From that anger came the determination I have mentioned, the determination that made him extinguish the cigarette of Chief Engineer Coates and compel Additional Superintendent of Police Ellison to address him as he ought to be addressed. In that determination Bose set his course.

It was at first, however, a course outwardly not very different from that which would be pursued by any Bengali gentleman's son.

CHAPTER 9

CONGRESS REBEL

A course not very different from that pursued *by any babu's son*, you might once have written. For babu *means* gentleman.

"Properly a term of respect attached to a name, like *Master* or *Mr.*" Employed particularly in Bengal, explains *Hobson-Jobson*, Yule and Burnell's glossary of Anglo-Indian words and phrases (called "Hobson-Jobson" because this is how the repeated wailing of "Ya Hasan! Ya Hosain!" during the Muslim festival of Muharram sounds to English ears). It was because Bose did not propose to let Ellison address him familiarly, that he insisted on "Subhas Babu."

But long before the Ellison incident, long even before Henry Yule and A. C. Burnell put *Hobson-Jobson* together, *babu* had acquired a derogatory twist on western lips. "It is often used," continues *Hobson-Jobson*, "with a slight savour of disparagement, as characterizing a superficially cultivated but too often effeminate Bengali." The big Webster unabridged dictionary, admitting first that the word signifies "a Hindu gentleman," adds that it means as well "a native clerk who writes English; often applied disparagingly to any native, esp. a Bengali, having more or less education in English." Now Janaki Nath Bose, Subhas Chandra's father, was never a clerk. Nor does "more or less" adequately describe his attainments in that language.

A true Bengali gentleman like Janaki Nath expected his sons, in Subhas Chandra's own youthful words, to "grow up to be judges, magistrates, barristers, or high-placed officials"[1] working alongside if not actually for the British. Civil employment with or close to the Raj had for years been the preferred occupation of Bengali gentlemen. Indeed, the *bhadralok* filled posts all across north India. It was because they dragged in their train so many Indians of a lower level of education and competence than themselves, that the British began to apply *babu* to any Indian who wrote English—and eventually to any Indian who behaved as if he thought he could.

But it was not for clerical jobs that Janaki's sons were trained. The road to *their* intended positions led through long and rigorous schooling, especially schooling in the English-language colleges that Macaulay's Minute had encouraged. And if a Janaki Nath wished his sons to reach the very top, that schooling was capped by time spent in England, at a university or one of the Inns of Court. Sarat Chandra, the second Bose son, was called to the bar from Lincoln's Inn in 1914. Satish Chandra, the eldest, took his dinners for the same purpose while Subhas attended Cambridge. It was, therefore, not at all out of the ordinary that Subhas was sent as a boy to the best schools in Cuttack; and quite expected that he place head of the list (in fact he placed second) in the matriculation examination for Calcutta University, and that he enter its oldest and most prestigious college.

Expulsion midway through the third year was a blow. To the Cuttack household, moreover, it came as a complete surprise. Janaki Nath had been a public "pleader" or prosecutor, had accepted nomination to the Bengal Legislative Council, and bore the title Rai Bahadur, an honor the Raj conferred on its most loyal and distinguished servants. His wife had no interest in the British and spoke not a word of their language. In his autobiography, Subhas Chandra says that the partition of Bengal (which occurred when he was eight), the first bomb throwing, and the beginning of the organized boycott of foreign cloth, were hardly mentioned at home. "Politics was tabooed in our house." He himself was so undeveloped politically that at the age of fourteen he went without a qualm to watch the new King-Emperor, George V, pay a state visit to Calcutta, and returned home "in an enthusiastic frame of mind."[2] Expelled he had been, however, and for a political reason.

His parents, to his surprise, made no fuss. His father did not even question him. In the summer of his first college year Subhas had gone off on a pilgrimage to the holy places of upper India with no more notice to them than a postcard, so perhaps they were used to independent behavior. He was the sixth son and ninth child, had never been made much of, and was later to write how he envied "those children who were lucky enough to be on friendly terms with their parents"[3] (as Prem, though this meant nothing to Bose, had been). But it was made clear to him that he must resume his studies, and that it must be at Calcutta University. So after a time he ventured back to the city, and with the help of his older brother Sarat (who was starting a law practice) obtained admission to Scottish Church College. He meant to read, as before, for the Honours B.A. in Philosophy. He had lost a year and a half.

Before resuming his studies, however, he did something as indicative of his future course as the Oaten affair had been. He set about proving that, though a Bengali and a gentleman, he was not what the British supposed all babus to be. He was not a milksop.

⟡

In the political narrative he dictated in Vienna in 1934 and published under the title *The Indian Struggle*, Bose blamed Macaulay for launching this particular libel. "The trouble began with Macaulay," he wrote. "When he was out in India as a member of the Government, Macaulay wrote a scathing denunciation of the Bengalees and called them a race of cowards."[4] Indeed, Macaulay had done just that, though it was after his return to England, and in a piece whose purpose was to demonstrate not that the people of Bengal were sheep but that Warren Hastings had been something of a wolf.

Warren Hastings had been British India's first governor-general. It was one of the articles of impeachment brought against him when he returned to England in 1785 that, in his efforts to bring order and a sense of responsibility out of the anarchy and self-seeking of Company rule, he had pursued with shameless vindictiveness a certain "Nuncomar" (Nanda Kumar)—had pursued him because the fellow sided to dangerous effect with Hastings's enemies on the Council.

Hastings had caused Nuncomar to be charged with forgery. He had caused him to be speedily convicted and as speedily hanged. Nuncomar was a Bengali Brahmin. He had gone to his unexpected and, in the Indian view, wholly undeserved death with calmness and dignity. But there was no doubt in Macaulay's mind, and certainly none in Hastings's, that the talents that had brought him such power and influence, and made it necessary for Hastings to put him out of the way, were the talents of a schemer and an intriguer, not those of an honest man. And in the course of hammering home this point, Macaulay had allowed himself a paragraph about the people of Bengal; a paragraph intended to make Nuncomar intelligible to English readers of his generation (he wrote in 1841); a paragraph composed, however, in such a manner that it passed beyond this particular Bengali to a characterization of Bengalis in general, Bengalis as a whole, Bengalis for all time.

"The physical organization of the Bengalee is feeble even to effeminacy," begins the part most frequently quoted. "He lives in a constant vapor bath. His pursuits are sedentary, his limbs delicate, his movements languid. During many ages he has been trampled upon by men of bolder and more hardy breeds." Alas, the treatment has not stiffened his backbone. Rather has it taught him "those arts which are the natural defence of the weak." Taught him so thoroughly and so well that those arts have become "more familiar to this subtle race than to the Ionian of the time of Juvenal, or to the Jew of the dark ages. What the horns are to the buffalo, what the paw is to the tiger, what the sting is to the bee, . . . deceit is to the Bengalee." And Macaulay, with Nuncomar in mind but quite prepared to let his audience assume that Bengal contains any number of such fellows, feasts his reader upon the ignoble tactics and devices, the "smooth excuses, elaborate tissues of circumstantial falsehood, chicanery, perjury, forgery," and more, that are "the weapons, offensive and defensive, of the people of the Lower Ganges."[5]

It was to these lines that Bose referred. The paragraph complete (it ends with an admiring reference to "the steady step and even pulse" with which the unfortunate Nuncomar mounted the scaffold), Macaulay continues with his arresting tale of a governor-general whose greatness was flawed only by hardness of heart. But after a time nobody read any further. Through the power of the prose and the enormous reputation of the author, these lines, passed forward generation after generation, fastened upon the Bengali the reputation of being on the one hand shifty, on the other hand effeminate. It was a reputation that, once acquired, was not easily shed.

Rudyard Kipling encouraged it.

Indians did not grow up on Kipling. Why should they? But by the time Bose was a Cuttack schoolboy, hardly an Englishman who read can have failed to read *Kim*. Hardly an Englishman can have failed to be familiar with the "hulking, obese Babu" of the patent-leather shoes and the blue and white umbrella, who goes out to meet two spying Russians in the foothills of the Himalayas, and in due course, with Kim's help, after one of the Russians has struck the lama, manages to lift from them eight months' worth of maps and papers. In those hills Hurree Babu proves his courage and his powers of endurance in the service of the Raj. It is as if, for a moment, Kipling had in mind the real Bengali secret agent, Sarat Chandra Das, who reached Lhasa in 1881 twenty years before *Kim* was published, and whose account of that exploit appeared one year later. But when the adventure is over and lama, boy, and babu have returned to the plains, Hurree becomes his old self again, "with new patent-leather shoes, in highest condition of fat." As fearful as ever. "I tell you I am fearful man."

The effect upon today's reader is mixed. How great indeed, Lurgan Sahib has earlier remarked to Kim, must be a business that "brazens the heart" of a Bengali. There is nothing mixed, however, about the impression left by "The Head of the District," which Kipling wrote five years earlier. In that tale the Bengali Grish Chunder Dé is sent, by a viceroy who should have known better, to administer a district on the Northwest Frontier. There he is panicked by the belted, bearded men of the marauding Khusru Kheyl (a thing to be expected, Kipling explains in Macaulayan language, of one "born in a hothouse, of stock bred in a hothouse, and fearing physical pain as some men fear sin"). From the moment of his appearance in the district to the end of the grisly tale, he lives in a state of funk, the very type and model of the gold-spectacled, liver-hearted Calcutta clerk. A *babu*. Bose did not wish to be taken for such as this.

For though he felt obliged to insist that Additional Superintendent of Police Ellison address him by that term, it carried for him a painful freight of implied weakness. "God has given us a pair of legs, but we are unable to walk 40/45 miles because we are *Babus*," he complained in an early letter to his mother. We cannot bear the heat, we are frightened of the cold, we neglect our bodies and surrender physical labor to our servants—"because we are *Babus*."[6]

Perhaps most Bengalis of his generation felt as Subhas did, asked themselves what had become of their manhood, lived with what two

close students of the phenomenon have termed "the fear of cowardice."[7]

It was not just that the Raj deprived so many Indians of the
opportunity to exercise the martial arts. It was worse than that. Indians
were beginning to believe that timidity and passivity were natural to
their character. Gandhi himself had once remarked that "the Hindus as
a rule are notoriously weak."[8] It was worst for the *bhadralok*, for high-
caste Bengalis, because it was they who staffed the offices of the Raj,
they who were led to cultivate the skills and temperament of the pen
and the ledger, they who were obliged "to nurse compliance, with its
female implications, as a condition of success."[9] Bengalis, above all
others, feared that what the British said in the matter of manliness
might be true. "Bengal is the only country in the world," ran the most
recent edition of Strachey's much-thumbed lectures, first reproducing
Macaulay's lines about the effeminate "Bengalee" and his "constant
vapor bath"—"Bengal is the only country in the world where you can
find a great population among whom personal cowardice is looked
upon as in no way disgraceful." This was not simply Strachey's personal
opinion. "The Bengalis," he wrote, "have themselves no shame or
scruple in declaring it to be a fact."[10]

From this humiliating self-estimate Gandhi escaped by substituting
for the Englishman's courage, which begins with self-assertion and
proceeds to physical mastery, the courage which begins with self-
control and proceeds to the nonviolent affirmation of truth. Imitating
the English, Gandhi believed, would simply produce imitation Englishmen. Better far to call up, from the depths of India's own spiritual
experience, instruments the occupier could neither match nor indefinitely resist. *Satyagraha* was one. *Ahimsa* was another. Skillfully applied,
they had the power to disconcert, discomfit, and in the end paralyze
the Raj. And in the process India would obtain more than freedom.
She would regain her soul.

Yet to put tactics so lofty to a use so mundane struck Englishmen
then, and has never ceased to strike some Englishmen (and some
Indians) since, as an unlikely and probably fraudulent pairing of two
irreconcilables, saintliness and guile. Either Gandhi was a holy man or
he was a politician. He could not be both, at least not at one and the
same time. With Bose, however, the difficulty was not that saintliness in

politics skirts deceit. The difficulty was that he had no taste for the first half of the equation.

Dilip Roy was sure that his old friend and Cambridge companion would eventually perceive his true calling to be, like Dilip's own, the path of the sage. In 1928 Dilip went to Pondicherry to sit at the feet of Aurobindo Ghose. Aurobindo was a Bengali of an older generation. In the first decade of the century he had made himself the darling of the Calcutta revolutionaries. Then, suddenly, he had turned his back on armed insurrection, slipped away to this French enclave hundreds of miles to the south, and opened an *ashram*. "Come with me to Pondicherry," Dilip pleaded.[11] Bose refused.

In his youth Subhas had taken up meditation and the practice of yoga. Discovering at age fifteen the writings of Vivekananda, he had been driven by the social teachings of the swami to take an interest in the poor and homeless. Once he spent part of a vacation nursing villagers who were stricken with cholera—spent part, not all, for midway an uncle found him and made him drop the dangerous work.

But service of this sort did not content him. He was not the "mystic in essence of his being" that Dilip supposed him to be.[12] He was an activist, "an activist with a religious side" suggests Leonard Gordon, his most recent (and ablest) biographer. Bright and determined enough to do well in examinations and win scholarships, he nevertheless thought little of those who did. "Good boys" he called them in his prison notebooks, with the hearts of eunuchs and the habits of sheep.[13] His contemporary, Nirad Chaudhuri, once boasted that *he* had "picked up the gauntlet thrown down by the English" by mastering their language.[14] The boast would have made Subhas Chandra smile. He did not prepare himself, as Chaudhuri did, to write about the arts of war. (For some years Chaudhuri made a living as a military commentator.) He prepared himself to *use* them.

While in Calcutta trying to reenter the university (this in 1917), he volunteered for a regiment that the British, forgetting their estimate of the "martial" qualities of Bengalis, were raising in that quarter. He failed the eye test. Once admitted to Scottish Church College, however, he could join the university's Territorial unit—its physical requirements were lower—and did. It was a curious lot that turned out on the Maidan for drill, some in *dhotis*, many like himself wearing spectacles. The Englishmen who took them in hand were sure they would never make soldiers. In fact they mastered in a morning what ordinary jawans could not master in three. At one point they were trucked out of Calcutta and put under canvas near a rifle range. "When one day our camp was washed away by rain and wind, and the next there was continuous firing from dawn until 4:30 in the afternoon, we felt as if we were in field service."[15] Years later Bose was surprised to remember how much fun it had been. But it had been more than fun. It had lifted a doubt, an anxiety, about his manliness. And one little experience had given him an intimation, as it were, of the future.

The regulars who ran the training came from Fort William, the enormous star-shaped mass in the center of the Maidan that housed military headquarters for the province. Fort William was off limits to Indian civilians. To Indians in uniform, however, it was not. One day Subhas and his unit marched into the place on an errand of some sort, and Subhas had "a queer feeling." It was "as if we were taking possession of something to which we had an inherent right but of which we had been unjustly deprived."[16] He did not add, as he recorded the recollection, that this was a feeling all Indians deserved to have, should have, must make it their business to have. Yet it was surely on his mind.

This little trial of arms completed Subhas Chandra's preparations for life—or almost did. One step remained.

In the summer of 1919 Subhas took his B.A., as usual placing high. Somewhat at loose ends, toying with the notion of doing a second degree, he was suddenly summoned by Janaki Nath and asked whether he wished to enter the Indian Civil Service. The question put him in a quandary. Applying for the ICS meant going to England, for the examination was as yet only offered there—besides, if an Indian was to have a chance against Englishmen, he had to prepare himself at an English university. Subhas was not keen to commit himself to the service of the Raj. On the other hand he very much wanted an English degree, and this was his chance; there might never be another. He was confident he would not do well on the civil service examination, and so would not actually have to join. But suppose he scored high in spite of himself, and was selected? His father gave him no time to think, the university term was about to begin, he must decide. In September he sailed.

At Cambridge, as we have seen, he obtained admission to Fitzwilliam Hall, and prepared to read simultaneously for the Mental and Moral Sciences Tripos and the civil service examination. Though his Indian B.A. automatically shortened his university stay, he was permitted two years in which to complete the tripos. The civil service exam, however, he must take at the end of one year, or breach the age limit. In July 1920 he sat for it, paper after paper, as sure as ever of failure though he had worked hard, and when the ordeal was over, let his mind turn to other things. August passed, and part of September. One day he learned that he had placed fourth. Six places were available. He was in.

Family correspondence of the most agitated sort followed. His father wanted him to take up the appointment. The Civil Service Board assumed that he would. But there was never a real likelihood of Subhas becoming one of "the heaven-born," as the term went. In February he wrote to C. R. Das, a well-known Bengali barrister whom he had met briefly five years before. Das, he knew, had just thrown up law for politics. Could he be of use to him? Das replied, promising "plenty of congenial work for me when I return."[17] In April Subhas resigned from the Service. Asked repeatedly to reconsider, he refused. Two months later he sat for the tripos, collected his degree (uncharacteristically he placed in the Third Class), and sailed for India. On the 16th of July, 1921, he stepped ashore at Bombay.

"A nice flat income with a good pension in after life," he had written his brother Sarat, of his prospects if he joined. First a subdivisional officer; later, if he was conscientious and rocked no boats, a district magistrate or collector. "Given talents, with a servile spirit one may even aspire to be the Chief Secretary to a provincial Government."[18] The thought had sickened him.

Some months before sending in his resignation he had happened upon printed India Office instructions to probationers like himself, instructions about the care of horses (of course a district officer rode). They implied that in India a syce (groom) ate the same food as his horse. Subhas had gone straight to the ICS representative at Cambridge, compelled his attention to the ridiculous statement, and made him promise that it would be amended. Thus far in his twenty-four years, such things had been the limit of his reach. Now they would no longer be.

❧

This is not the place to lay out in detail Bose's career over the next two decades. It began well, and passed from triumph to triumph, so that by the time he was thirty-five he stood in the very front rank of Indian politics. It was a career, however, that after a time faltered. Circumstances and issues put Subhas at odds with many in the Congress, and pitted him against the Mahatma, until at last he was forced quite out of the main current of the independence movement, and might have drifted indefinitely in some eddy, had not the war allowed him to summon once more the instincts and inclinations of his youth, collect a fresh following, and set out upon a new and truly revolutionary course.

When he stepped ashore at Bombay, he obtained a brief interview with Gandhi, which he later remembered as pleasant enough but fundamentally unsatisfactory: the Mahatma could not explain how his tactics were going to shift the British. It was not with Gandhi, however, that Subhas Chandra meant to take service. It was with Das. In Calcutta, Das immediately put his new assistant to work.

It was the time of Gandhi's first great noncooperation movement, of the public burning of foreign fabrics that Prem remembers from his Jullundur childhood, of strikes and paralyzing city-wide *hartals*. Subhas wrote articles for the nationalist press. He became principal of a National College that was to draw Bengali youth away from the establishment schools. (It didn't. The *bhadralok* were reluctant to sacrifice their sons' careers). He led volunteers in the picketing of cloth shops, and helped shut Calcutta down the day the Prince of Wales began his Indian tour.

But when the Mahatma, dismayed by outbreaks of violence, and in particular by the lynching of twenty-two policemen at a place called Chauri Chaura, suddenly called noncooperation off, Das and his group saw their opportunity and took a new tack. In place of withdrawal, they proposed penetration. Let patriots grapple with the machinery of the Raj, seizing what they could, bringing the rest to a standstill by calculated obstruction. "Council entry" this was called. Gandhi was reluctant to endorse the tactic. He would not, however, throw his weight against it. So Das and Motilal Nehru (Jawaharlal's father) organized within the Congress a new party, the Swaraj party. In Bengal, in the 1923 elections, the Swarajists not only took a bloc of seats in the Legislative Council, they captured the Calcutta Municipal Corporation as well, and made Das mayor. Das appointed Bose as Chief Executive Officer. That meant he ran the city.

To the work he brought enthusiasm, vigor, and his own particular brand of assertiveness (it was now that the little business of Coates and the cigarette occurred). Municipal employees were clothed in khadi. Municipal departments were enjoined to buy Indian pipe and Indian light bulbs. Money was found for schools, dispensaries, a municipal gazette. And Muslims were given preference in the filling of corporation jobs—it was the price Das was willing to pay to bring that community into a common alliance, and the Bengal Pact (which arranged it) was signed by Bose himself.

In 1926 Subhas won election to the Legislative Council. In 1927 he became President of the Bengal Provincial Congress Committee. A year later he organized and drilled the Volunteers at the Calcutta annual session of the Congress (Lakshmi slipped out to watch), and attached to a Gandhi motion an amendment so challenging and popular (it called for independence rather than dominion status) that the Mahatma defeated it only by exerting his full political weight. In 1929 he presided again over the BPCC, and took his turn at the head of the All-India Trade Union Congress. In 1930 he became Mayor of Calcutta. He was known now far outside Bengal. "The round cherub face, the horn-rimmed glasses, the Gandhi cap which covered the encroaching baldness of his forehead but revealed hair at the back,"[19] were familiar all across India. Yet of Bengal itself he was not safely the master.

In the early twenties Das had pulled his fellow *bhadralok* together and added to them enough Muslims—this was crucial, for though poorer and less well educated, they outnumbered Hindus in the province—to form a united front against the Raj. But in 1925 Das suddenly died. With his death the front unravelled. Hindu extremists attacked it, the British worked to undermine it; Bose was very young, and in any case shut away for some time in a Burmese prison, as will appear. An older man whom Gandhi pushed in Das's place lacked Das's commitment to communal harmony and let the Muslim connection languish. In 1926 serious Muslim-Hindu riots broke out in Calcutta. More followed, with much arson and bloodshed, and the Bengal Pact was finished. Meanwhile jealousies and quarrels poisoned the provincial Congress party. Men embraced each other one day, parted company the next. Elections to party office and to seats in the Calcutta Corporation and the provincial legislature became occasions for furious public disputes. And to this unhappy talent for factional politics (Nirad Chaudhuri once remarked that Bengalis are positive virtuosi of factiousness) was joined an inability to recognize that in the Indian independence movement, Bengal no longer led the way.

It was in Bengal that the Raj had begun. It was there that the British had first passed beyond trading and politics to revenue raising and direct governance, it was from Bengal that these practices had spread. So that when you looked at a map of the subcontinent, you discovered Bengal at the base of what was easily the largest block of British red. (Princely India was always given another color.) There it was, a great crimson swathe stretching without interruption from the mouth of the Ganges to Delhi, Amritsar, Rawalpindi, and beyond.

That Bengal had allowed this—the great crimson swathe—to happen was in the true patriot's view, of course, shameful. It required atonement. But Bengal had paid, and more than paid, the debt. Long before 1900 she had shown India the way in matters of almost every sort. Though Calcutta was the Englishman's capital, it was also the place where nationalist consciousness was most advanced and political activism most intense. Over the first thirty years of its existence the Indian National Congress had drawn a third of its presidents from Bengal. The *Swadeshi* movement—*swadeshi* means "own country," it teaches you to turn your back on foreign fabrics and wear native cloth—had been a Bengali inspiration. Indeed, when anyone remarked (as someone was always certain to remark) that what Bengal thought today, India would think tomorrow, that person stopped, in *bhadralok* opinion, a good deal short of the truth. Bengalis did more than think. Bengalis acted.

Bengali pride in Bengali accomplishment had been accompanied, however, by a tendency to regard Bengal not simply as a guide and model for the rest of India but as India in prospect—as India itself. This did not sit well with people from other regions, particularly in the 1920s and 1930s when Bengal's chief city was ceasing to be unchallengeably India's first. Calcutta was still a great commercial center. It was still the light of India's intellectual life. In politics, however, it was sinking to the level of a provincial capital.

A British maneuver was the immediate cause. In 1912 the Government of India left Calcutta for new quarters rising, with redundant grandeur of design and scale, just outside Delhi. New Delhi thus replaced Calcutta as the nerve center of the Raj. Another development, meanwhile, was costing Calcutta its preeminence in national politics. Until the First World War the various parts of India had each had their own political groupings, operating independently. Congress party, to a degree, operated regionally too. In the 1920s, however, this pattern changed. The Congress, its base substantially broadened now that anyone with four annas (the fourth part of a rupee) could join, was given fresh authority at the top. More and more it spoke and acted—*claimed* to speak and act, successive viceroys would have protested—not for the parts and regions of the subcontinent, but for India as a whole. At just the moment, then, that Bengal lost its natural political advantage, Congressmen of ambition discovered that it was necessary, as it had not been necessary before, to carve out for themselves positions in a national structure.

This Das managed to do. In 1922 he was elected President of the Congress. But he was the last of the Bengali presidents. For the next several years no one from Bengal except Bengali-born Sarojini Naidu reached the top. Now men and women from elsewhere in India pushed Bengali Congressmen aside. Now others filled the All-India Congress Committee and occupied most of the fifteen places on the Working Committee—the High Command. And year after year the most important figure in that High Command, no matter that often he was technically without a seat, was not a Bengali Brahmin but a Gujarati Bania. A little man from the shopkeeping community of the remote Kathiawar Peninsula. A man whose name translated "grocer." A man quite without *bhadralok* cultivation and style who, nevertheless, had by artless ingenuity and implacable humility achieved a command of the Indian political scene that neither Das nor any other Bengali could match. Where the Mahatma was, *there* you found activity. What Gandhi did, *that* India noticed.

๑๕

In one respect only did Bengal lead India still, and that was in the use of revolutionary violence. In violent acts not even the Punjab was Bengal's equal. It was probably this Subhas Chandra had in mind when, looking ahead (in *The Indian Struggle*) to the opening of the great civil disobedience movement of 1930, he promised his readers that they would shortly find Bengal once more "the political storm-centre of India."[20]

In April 1930, two weeks after Gandhi reached the sea at Dandi and picked up the handful of salt, armed men stormed the armory at Chittagong in the easternmost part of Bengal, cut the telegraph lines, proclaimed a provisional government, and though soon driven out, carried with them enough captured rifles and ammunition to wage guerrilla war for months. It was an isolated act. Not until 1942 were assaults on this scale repeated. But individual attacks were something else again.

All over Bengal daring young men (and sometimes daring young women) lay in wait for Englishmen at their clubs, bungalows, and offices, hunted them down on the roads, shot at them or threw bombs. The authorities reacted with police sweeps, house searches accompanied by much smashing of property, and indiscriminate arrests. (It was while he was investigating police response to the attempted murder of Dacca's district magistrate that Bose had his little set-to with Ellison in the matter of how he should be addressed.) These attacks were not numerous. Actual killings in any one year could be counted on the fingers of one hand. But open violence directed at their persons shocked and dismayed Europeans. In Bengal the business had been going on intermittently for a long time. And from the beginning of his career, Bose was implicated.

For Subhas, if he did not applaud attempts on British lives, did not apologize for them either—and did not distance himself from those who made them. In 1924 a student named Gopinath Saha set out to assassinate Sir Charles Tegart, Calcutta's commissioner of police. Tegart was in the habit of wearing mufti, which made him look like an ordinary English businessman. One day Saha spotted what he took to be Tegart walking along Chowringhee Road, came close, drew a pistol, and shot the man dead. Instantly collared, he discovered that he had made a mistake. It was not the commissioner he had killed, but a certain Ernest Day. While European Calcutta trembled with indignation and alarm, Saha expressed regret. Regret, however, only for the mistake.

Das agreed. Day's death was a pity, he remarked, but willingness to sacrifice one's life for a cause must be commended. And Subhas Chandra, visiting the jail where they hanged Saha, openly helped take possession of Saha's effects. If their behavior encouraged terrorist acts, Das and Bose seemed to be saying, that could not be helped. It was the least the *bhadralok* could do for their own, the least they could do for persons who, though perhaps misguided (Das's term), risked much and died bravely, not like the spineless babus Englishmen supposed all Bengalis to be.

It is quite certain that Bose was no stranger to people like Saha. Men who committed assaults and served their terms he positively welcomed upon their release. Their support was indispensable to his brand of Congress politics. He might try, it was true, to wean them from the bomb before they threw one. If he failed, however, he would not let on that he had tried. It was the Oaten affair all over again. Had he terrorist connections? He refused to say.

But silence, of course, only redoubled suspicion. And as the years went by and attacks on Englishmen continued, the Bengal government watched Subhas's every move, and used every excuse to put him behind bars. His first stretch, earned in 1921 by his efforts to shut Calcutta down during the Prince of Wales's visit, he actually welcomed. Prison, after all, was the freedom fighter's accolade. As he was led away to Calcutta's Alipore Central Jail he inquired jauntily (and with a curious verb), "Only six months? Have I then robbed a fowl?"[21] Later it was different. In twenty years Bose went to prison ten times, often for much more than six months, often under conditions far less agreeable. Most nationalist leaders of his generation spent time in jail, of course. Many put the time to good use. Gandhi read and rested. Nehru wrote books. But detention was wearing, particularly when you did not know when you were going to get out. It was hard on a man's family. Worst of all, it made political activity difficult—as it was intended it should. For Bose it made political activity, in the end, impossible.

In 1924 the authorities picked him up for the second time. Hard evidence of his complicity in the Tegart business or anything else they did not have. No matter. Without charge, hearing, or trial he was shipped off to Mandalay, where the great Maharashtrian patriot Bal Gangadhar Tilak had spent six years for encouraging (it was alleged) the assassination of the hated plague commissioner of Poona.

Men of Tilak's stamp the British often confined at a distance, out of reach of family and friends. After the 1857 rebellion it was to Burma that they brought the last Mogul emperor to live out the pitiful remnant of his life. It complimented Bose, therefore, that he was deemed too dangerous for incarceration in India. But Tilak had been given a trial, and with it a determinate sentence. For Bose nothing was fixed. It was perhaps this that depressed him so and made him ill—this, and the prison itself, built of wood, with slatted walls like a zoo, so that the inmates looked to passersby "like animals prowling about behind the bars."[22] It was from Mandalay Jail that he ran successfully for the Bengal Legislative Council. (His brother Sarat managed his campaign, ran also, and was elected too.) But when he began to experience continual fever and loss of weight, he was moved from Mandalay to Rangoon. Later he was returned to Calcutta. By June 1927 he was free.

But not for long. Over the next several years he was jailed several times. He missed the independence declaration of January 1930 at Lahore because he was in prison for organizing a public protest against police brutalities. Released after seven months, Mayor of Calcutta now, he celebrated 1931's Independence Day by leading a huge procession across the Maidan to the Ochterlony Monument, where he was lathi-charged by the police, beaten about the head, and after a quick trial—there was no lack of evidence for Tegart had forbidden the business—sent to jail again. Increasingly he seemed committed to the public encouragement of terrorist acts. Only days after Bhagat Singh was hanged for attempting. by tossing bombs in the Central Legislative Assembly, to make the deaf hear, Subhas appealed to the Sikhs of the Punjab to produce more men like him, men who might teach Indians to submerge their communal differences in a common love of country.

Hundreds were needed, he said. "Thousands!" reported the Calcutta *Statesman*, too horrified to bother about the zeros. This wretched Bengali asks for "thousands of Bhagat Singhs . . . who will shoot down officials in circumstances in which they have not a chance of defending themselves." To drive home the point it assembled and printed a little list of Englishmen who had met death in this dreadful way.[23]

By now the Government of India was as convinced as the Government of Bengal that Bose was too dangerous to be left at large. So at last, early in 1932, on the eve of the abortive resumption of civil disobedience, he was arrested and put away for a really substantial period, a period that almost matched Tilak's six-year stretch a quarter of a century before. Not behind bars, however. Bose was sick when they took him, he grew sicker, tuberculosis was suspected. It became apparent he might die if not properly treated. Only a Swiss or German sanitorium could provide proper treatment.

Early in 1933 he was placed on board a ship bound for Europe. When it reached the open ocean, they said, he could consider himself free. But his passport, though good for the Continent, was not (he was given to understand) good for England, and it was made clear to him that he would not be allowed to return to India.

✖

Subhas went first to Vienna. He liked it, made friends, and used the city as a base for such travels as his health and pocketbook permitted— Sarat, in jail himself for the first time, had lost his income from the bar and could no longer support his younger brother, but friends and other family members came through. In Geneva, Warsaw, Prague, Belgrade, Budapest, Istanbul, and elsewhere Bose put India's case to everyone who would listen, and discovered that he was better known in Europe than any other Indian except Nehru and the Mahatma. In Berlin, Hitler was busy burying the Weimar Republic and would not see him. Rome was more receptive. Bose had several talks with Mussolini. London he did not try to visit. He thought his passport was not valid for England, though in fact he could not have been kept away.

In the summer of 1934 he began work on his political narrative, *The Indian Struggle*, against a London publisher's advance of fifty pounds. Late in November, the manuscript complete, he received word that his father was dying and caught a Dutch plane for Calcutta (which in those days meant daylight hops with nightly stopovers). At Karachi he was told his father was dead. Police met him at the Calcutta airport, took him to the family house, confined him there for the several weeks of the cremation and other ceremonies, and then put him on board ship for Europe once more.

The Indian Struggle appeared, and was well received—except in India where, being banned, it was not received at all. In April 1935 months of diagnosis came to a fruition of sorts: Bose's gallbladder was removed by a Viennese surgeon. This made him feel better, though it turned out he was not yet out of the woods. Others were sicker than he. In a German sanitorium Nehru's wife, Kamala, lay dying of tuberculosis, the disease Subhas had been afraid he might have. When the end was near, Jawaharlal, his latest detention suspended for the purpose, hurried from India to be with her. Bose paid a brief consolatory visit.

Perhaps he envied him even in his bereavement. He himself had no wife, and none in prospect. Though making no public commitment to celibacy, he had let people (particularly Sarat) suppose that he would never marry. Without money, property, or livelihood, it was difficult to imagine how he could.

Many of his contemporaries in politics depended upon others, of course, for their support. Even Nehru by this time was in such straits that the Birla family offered to make him a monthly allowance (Nehru declined). Nehru, however, had a profession. He had followed his father into the law, had practiced for several years though without enthusiasm, and it was while practicing that he had married Kamala. Several more years had passed. Indira, their only child, was four and Jawaharlal thirty-two when he was jailed for the first time. That was in December 1921. In the same month Subhas Chandra went to jail for the first time too. For both it was a sign that life-as-usual was over. But Bose, seven years younger than Nehru and only five months out of Cambridge, was embarked upon no profession. He had just thrown up his ICS appointment. So it would have been difficult for his father to arrange anything even had Bose wished him to. With each year the possibility of marriage grew more remote.

Remaining single did not mean that Subhas was without normal human feelings. His relations with Sarat, which went far beyond political and financial support, suggest quite the contrary. In the late twenties Subhas lived with Sarat just around the corner from the main family house at 38/2 Elgin Road, and Sarat had a wife and many children. In these Subhas delighted. Leonard Gordon gives us a charming picture of the younger brother romping through the house with his nephews and nieces, playing hide-and-seek with them up and down the stairs (he occupied the top floor), listening to them; helping Biva, their mother, nurse them through their illnesses. "They teased him, hit him, confided in him," he writes on the basis of what he has been told (he knows the family well), "and every one of the children of the new Bose generation has only the tenderest feelings for the uncle they knew when they were young."[24] With adults Subhas was reserved and purposeful. In the company of these children and their mother he became warm and loving, even a little dependent. This was his true nature, Lakshmi believes. To be deprived of the opportunity of expressing it cannot have been easy to bear.

It was made less bearable by exile. Nehru would not have taken an enforced foreign residence so hard, particularly residence in England, where he had lived longer than Bose, and from which he brought attachments and values that never left him. "Throughout his life," his biographer Sarvepalli Gopal writes, "Britain was a country with which Jawaharlal identified extensively in the personal sense."[25] No one will ever say anything like that of Subhas Chandra. Reflecting years later about the two men, Dilip Roy remarks that, while Jawaharlal never felt completely comfortable in India, Subhas never felt at home anywhere else. In Vienna, thousands of miles from his family and his place of birth, he must have been doubly lonely.

Lonely and ineffectual. For the one accomplishment of his European stay, his flirtation with fascism, did India little service and his own reputation no good. Bose, of course, had not gone abroad in order to study how best to dislodge the Raj at home. Placed in Europe against his will, he nevertheless looked about for possible instruction. Circumstances put him in contact with Italy and Germany. What was going on there was new, and in many ways inviting (something we tend now to forget). Is it surprising that he drew, from what he saw, lessons that reinforced what personal experience had previously suggested?

In Italy and Germany he saw, or thought he saw, purposeful collective action. Both countries seemed to know where they were going. (France under the Third Republic did not.) In Italy and Germany he saw, or thought he saw, a mechanism capable of generating that purposeful action, for each had a single party, and the leader of that party was also the chief of state. Mussolini and Hitler spoke the language of command—and, it might be added, wore its uniform. The orders they gave directed action of the hand, not of the heart or head; armed action; action that was revolutionary too, for Hitler in particular smashed and overturned before he built. And there was one more thing. The European democracies upon which their revolutionary ardor beat were sustained by the very nation Indian patriots wished to see humbled and expelled. As the 1930s advanced, and the European powers aligned themselves for a resumption of the 1914 war, it became clear that Mussolini, Hitler, and whoever should lead India's freedom struggle, had an enemy in common. That enemy was Britain.

So Bose looked keenly at what the fascists were doing, and gave Mussolini and Hitler a place among those men of action, alive or dead, upon whom any Indian leader might wish to model himself. This is plain from a number of passages in *The Indian Struggle*. At one point Bose wonders whether Das might not have become, had he lived, the Lenin, Mussolini, or Hitler of India. At another he compares Gandhi's march to the sea with Mussolini's march on Rome. At still another, reflecting upon the Mahatma's return from the second London Round Table Conference in late 1931, he asks why Gandhi has nothing to show for his twelve weeks? And gives the answer: instead of speaking to the English "in the language of Dictator Stalin, or Il Duce Mussolini or Fuehrer Hitler," he approaches them in his usual witty, self-deprecatory manner, which may charm Labour MPs and George Bernard Shaw but has no effect on Whitehall. With Whitehall he should have been cold and peremptory, and "John Bull would have understood and would have bowed his head in respect."[26] At least the Mahatma on his way home stops in Rome to chat with the Italian leader. Bose is pleased. His only regret is that Gandhi does not talk longer with "a man who really counts in the politics of modern Europe."[27]

Nehru on *his* way home after Kamala's death barely avoided a similar encounter. On the pretext that condolences were in order, Mussolini proposed a meeting at Rome's airport, where the Indian was changing planes. Tactfully, Nehru declined. Subhas Chandra would have leapt at the chance. Does he fancy himself, Nehru noted in his diary, India's future dictator?

In the frustration and futility of his European exile, perhaps Bose did. Mussolini, in particular, attracted him. But in those days, before the Ethiopian adventure and the Spanish Civil War, Mussolini attracted lots of people. American tourists, who told their friends that Il Duce made the trains run on time. Winston Churchill, who wrote Clementine that Italy "gives the impression of discipline, order, smiling faces. A happy strict school—no talking among the pupils."[28] The dark face of Italian fascism was not then so apparent, nor the incompetence.

Germany Bose saw less of. But Nazi racial policy did not escape him. "When I first visited Germany," he wrote some years later, "I had hopes that the new German nation which had risen to consciousness of its strength and self-respect would instinctively feel a deep sympathy for other nations struggling in the same direction."[29] He had not entertained those hopes for long. Asian visitors, he had discovered, received lectures on the innate superiority of Aryans. Indian students were laughed at or abused because of the color of their skin. Nazi bigwigs made no effort to restrain the ugliness. They knew very little about the Indian independence movement. And they were openly contemptuous of the one Indian political figure even they could hardly miss. They were openly contemptuous of Gandhi.

Of course Subhas Chandra was contemptuous of Gandhi too. But he was contemptuous for a different reason, and only, so to speak, with a part of himself. The other part acknowledged Gandhi's political genius and moral force. It was with this other part that he began a chapter of *The Indian Struggle* devoted entirely to the Mahatma.

How wonderfully attuned Gandhi is to the mass of the Indian people, he wrote. How consonant "his vegetarian diet, his goat's milk, his day of silence every week, his habit of squatting on the floor instead of sitting on a chair." Wherever he goes, "even the poorest of the poor feels that he is a product of the Indian soil—bone of his bone, flesh of his flesh." With what assurance and skill has he taken Congress Party and built it from a debating society, "a talking body," into a national organization that reaches into every village and speaks for India as no one and nothing else can.[30]

But it is many years since he began this work. Is *swaraj* closer, Britain's grip less? (As Bose wrote, in the early autumn of 1934, Congress was emerging from a proscription so effective that for several years it had been unable to hold annual sessions.) Real independence remains as distant as ever. And Gandhi himself has abandoned politics; he has quit the Congress, and devotes himself entirely to introspection, the relief of *harijans*, and village life.

Bose did not write, though he may well have thought, that there was something a bit theatrical about this latest posture. The hours at the hand-held *charkha* or spinning wheel, for example. The insistence upon travelling third class. Though Subhas took, as every good Congressman had to take, his turn at the *charkha*, his heart was never in it. And of the elaborate simplicity of Gandhi's domestic arrangements he may have observed sotto voce what Sarojini Naidu once remarked aloud: that it cost a good deal of money to keep the Mahatma in poverty.

He must have felt, too, with Tagore and other educated Bengalis, that to reduce life to the level of the village as Gandhi asked you to, was to abandon shamelessly the vigor, variety, and richness of Indian culture. He did not say this, however. What he did say was that the Mahatma's recurring withdrawals were having a devastating effect. For these withdrawals did more than leave the mass of Indians leaderless. They were often accompanied by the abandonment, at the Mahatma's command, of some longstanding, collective, political effort, some mass movement which the Mahatma himself had begun. Or, if not its abandonment, then its redirection to purely social ends. Gandhi's genius for conceiving and launching bold political strokes it was impossible to doubt. But when, in the full flush of a campaign, with spirits high and the enemy about to break, the Mahatma suddenly gave the order to cease fire, stack arms, and begin (as it were) digging wells for village drinking water; when that happened, and it had happened with both the noncooperation and the civil disobedience movements, what were you to think—what *could* you think? Save that Gandhi was "utterly blind to and oblivious of objective realities."[31] That Gandhi had taken leave of his senses. That Gandhi was a fool.

In the early 1920s, it was true, this behavior had made sense. Armed revolution then was impossible; nothing further was to be expected from constitutional reform; so raising, without fully releasing, the political consciousness of ordinary Indians was all that any responsible man could attempt. But now things were different. Successive mass actions, particularly the last, the aborted civil disobedience movement, had lifted *swaraj* to the level of a familiar, almost palpable, notion. Ordinary Indians had become politically aware. The problem was how to transform that awareness into action. For this Gandhi was not prepared.

About his own people Gandhi could be marvelously perceptive. But he did not grasp the character of his opponents. He imagined that the British were troubled by Indian honesty, softened by Indian humanity, embarrassed by Indian humility. He supposed that they cleared their minds and hearts by the same process of self-examination and self-recognition to which he set himself. They felt none of these things, and did none of these things. They stood, unmoving, where they were. And, since they retained both the tools of power and the will to use them, neither the purity of the Mahatma's character nor the size of his following would prevail against them.

What was required was a pointed and discriminating advance, conducted by a small, disciplined body, inviting if possible assistance from outside. For, if the friend of my friend is my friend, is not the enemy of my enemy my ally? An advance undisturbed, too, by moralizing. (One reason the Mahatma had failed was that he tried to be simultaneously Britain's foe and humanity's tutor.) An advance, above all, that used not the weapon of passive resistance, for passive resistance can never eject a determined foreign occupier, but the weapon of active revolution. An advance, then, that never pausing except for brief tactical advantage, pressed steadily on until it had obtained, by force of arms if necessary, India's freedom.

The Irish had taken this route. Early in 1936 Subhas Chandra went to Dublin, met Eamon De Valera and the other Free State heroes, and took heart from what he saw. Then he sailed for India, determined to reenter politics.

ஜ

Not that the authorities told him he could, or that Gandhi was inclined to step aside. They didn't, and Gandhi wasn't. The moment Bose landed, he was arrested. As for Gandhi, Bose himself had predicted that though he would retreat from time to time into village uplift and village repose, his hand would always remain firmly on the machinery of the Congress. "One thing is certain," he had written. "The Mahatma will not play second fiddle to anyone."[32]

Nehru was another matter. "You cannot submit to indefinite exile," Nehru had written when Subhas told him he was going to return to India.[33] In April 1936, when Jawaharlal became President of the Congress for the second time, he named Subhas to the Working Committee. Of course Subhas could not sit. When, predictably, he fell ill, he was taken out of prison and put into Sarat's house, in the hills near Darjeeling. There he was allowed to see family but denied all political visitors. No other Congress leaders of importance were still treated in this way. Not until March 1937 was he told he might talk to whom he pleased and travel as he chose—for the first time in more than five years.

By then Nehru was well into a third presidential term, and elections to the provincial legislatures under the 1935 Act were over. Nehru had wanted to use these elections to return members who, by refusing ministerial appointment, would wreck the Act from the inside—exactly Bose's ambition. Among Congressmen, however, the desire for office was intense. Nehru was brushed aside. Congress ministries took office in half a dozen provinces. Meanwhile Subhas, still far from well, rested in the hills. The hot weather passed. The rains came and went. A meeting of the All-India Congress Committee was arranged for Calcutta. Subhas came down for it. And then a curious thing happened. Gandhi asked him to be the next president.

Exactly why he did this we do not know. Perhaps he thought to "chain the rebel with responsibility," as Mihir Bose puts it.[34] Perhaps he wanted to throw a bone to Bengal; perhaps he simply felt that Bose, after all these years, deserved the office. Prison and exile had certainly not cost Bose his popularity. There had been an enormous outcry, and that not only in Calcutta, when on landing a year and a half before he had been whisked straightway to jail.

Pending the formality of election at the next AICC meeting, Subhas made a quick trip to Europe. In Vienna he found Emilie Schenkl, the secretary who had helped him with *The Indian Struggle*, took her with him to the health resort of Bad Gastein, and there in less than two weeks wrote his autobiography. Manuscript in hand he went next to London, which he had not seen for sixteen years, and from which no attempt was made to bar him. There he met with the Indian community and leading Labour politicians, and was received well enough. But Gandhi and Nehru were better known and had excited more attention. As for the manuscript, though Nehru's own autobiography, *Toward Freedom*, had appeared quite recently, was selling well, and left people decidedly curious about Indian politics, *An Indian Pilgrim* had to wait ten years for a publisher—perhaps, of course, because it is not as good a book.

In India, however, Bose was the center of attention. At the annual Congress session in February 1938, he delivered the presidential address. In it he paid generous tribute to the Mahatma, and pledged Congress to *satyagraha* (which, he said, included "active resistance . . . of a non-violent character").[35] Perhaps for this reason Gandhi, though he must have known something of Bose's state of mind, gave him little trouble; while Nehru, in Europe again (it was now that he made his bittersweet visit to Barcelona and watched Chamberlain abandon Czechoslovakia), gave him no trouble at all. At the end of the year, however, an unexpected storm blew up. Bose wanted a second presidential term. Nehru, after all, had just had his third. But Gandhi, encouraged by Congressmen of the so-called Old Guard, and thinking perhaps that he had done enough for the Bengali, declined to recommend him. A conservative of no great prominence was found to take his place. To everyone's astonishment Bose declared his candidacy anyway, campaigned vigorously, and won by 205 votes in a total AICC count of not quite 3,000.

It was only the beginning of the struggle, for Gandhi was determined to overturn the choice, and being Gandhi set about it in his own way. He did not tell Bose that his majority was narrow (it was), that it would probably disappear (it did), and that he should therefore step down (he knew Subhas wouldn't). He told Bose that since he had won "a decisive victory," he must name his own Working Committee and take complete charge. I have lost, he said. I admit defeat. And he advised like-minded Congressmen to do the same—but with a twist. It would be wrong, he said, to obstruct the reelected president. They need not, however, actively help and assist. Let them rather step to one side. Better still, if they could bring themselves to do so, let them quit the Congress altogether. Those who resigned would, by that act, show the country where the true Congress majority lay, who the genuinely "Congress-minded" were.[36]

It was, Francis Hutchins observes, the tactic of a Solomon. When Solomon offered to divide the baby between the two women, his purpose was to discover, through renunciation, who the real mother was. Now Gandhi was asking true Congressmen to discover *themselves* by leaving the party. The difficulty, of course, was that it was Gandhi who asked them. The difficulty was that it made truth and obedience to the Mahatma one.

In this Gandhi was of that type of boarding school headmaster who mingles great moral authority with the natural despotism of his position. In such a school the most independent boys will often wonder, perhaps years later, why they suspected and resented the man so much yet did exactly as he asked. A part of Subhas Chandra suspected and resented the Mahatma. The other part sat to school with him. All India did. "I do not know what sort of opinion Mahatmaji has of myself," Bose said shortly after Gandhi made his move. Whatever it was, however, he would always be attentive to the Mahatma's wishes. For "it will be a tragic thing for me if I succeed in winning the confidence of other people but fail to win the confidence of India's greatest man."[37]

But winning the Mahatma's confidence at this late date required of Subhas Chandra (it is Leonard Gordon's image) that he submit to having his eyes opened as every spoilt and willful child eventually must. This, of course, he would not do, with the result that the Working Committee, remembering the Mahatma's advice, resigned—twelve in one group, Nehru characteristically by himself (though this did not lessen Bose's bitterness). Only Sarat and Subhas remained. At the annual Congress session that followed, Bose discovered that his position had eroded further. The Old Guard, with Gandhi's obvious consent, demanded that he appoint to the now empty Working Committee only persons agreeable to the Mahatma. In the critical times ahead, their resolution declared, Gandhi must lead the Congress and the country. The resolution carried.

This was at Tripuri, early in March 1939. (Bose was down with an unexplained and crippling fever. Sarat had to read the presidential address for him.) But Tripuri did not end the matter. The resolution bound the president to appoint a Working Committee to Gandhi's liking. Blandly the Mahatma pretended otherwise. Let Bose choose his own people and set his own program. If they and it prevailed, Congressmen loyal to himself (Gandhi did not describe them in these terms, but that is what he meant) would make no difficulties. "They will help you where they can, they will abstain where they cannot." But if the numbers were on the other side, a problem would arise. Honest men "may not suppress themselves if they are clearly in the majority."[38] Something would have to be done, and Bose knew what that something was.

For six weeks the duel was waged by telegram and letter, Gandhi shrewdly keeping his distance. Subhas did not want to give up the presidency. He suggested this, he advanced that, he proposed the other. Deftly the Mahatma turned every offer aside—while Bose's support dwindled. At last Bose capitulated. On the 29th of April he resigned.

And still it was not over. Bose announced the formation of a Forward Bloc to fight Gandhi's policies from inside the Congress. This was impertinent. Worse was his apparent intention to resume civil disobedience at will. The AICC declared this impermissible. Bose replied by organizing public protests against dictation of any sort. It was a breach of party discipline, a breach so blatant the Working Committee could not ignore it. In August 1939 Bose was removed from the presidency of the Bengal Provincial Congress Committee and pronounced ineligible to sit on Congress committees for three years. Technically this was simply a suspension. Bose believed, and said, that he had been expelled.

~ ❧ ~

Not silenced, however. On the 3rd of September, 1939, as he addressed a crowd on the beach at Madras, someone told him that war had broken out in Europe. He was elated. England preoccupied meant opportunity for India. And as 1939 passed into 1940, and England preoccupied became England in peril, his elation grew. Word came that France had fallen. "I remember how Subhas' face lit up with joy," an acquaintance remembers. "He hugged some of us and danced round the room like a merry schoolboy."[39] But if he was pleased (like Lakshmi) to see the western imperialists *taste the bitter fruit of defeat*, he was also impatient (as Lakshmi in distant Singapore with "K" and her practice was not) to see India take advantage of it.

His Forward Bloc, however, though it operated like a proper party with a journal and its own all-India conferences, could not act for the nation. Even in Bengal, where indignation over his treatment ran high and the now elderly Tagore supported him stoutly, Bose did not enjoy universal support. He had never been good at political work. "A superb public organiser but a poor private intriguer" is how Mihir Bose puts it.[40] In a straight political fight Gandhi had beaten him. Now only Gandhi was in a position to seize the opportunity the war provided, and Gandhi was not ready—Quit India was still two years away.

Bose bit his lip. It was time, it was past time, to offer active resistance to the Raj. Instead the Mahatma prescribed personal preparation at the *charkha* (we are to "spin our way to Swaraj," Bose bitterly observed).[41] In March 1940, three weeks before the Germans invaded France, Subhas had called on his Forward Bloc to begin civil disobedience on its own. In April, on the twenty-first anniversary of the Amritsar Massacre, civil disobedience had begun. It was scattered and fragmentary; Bose's coalition, such as it was, was coming apart; but even so the authorities began picking people up. For a time they left Bose alone. When, however, he announced a public demonstration to demand the removal of the monument to the Black Hole of Calcutta— few Indians believed that the dreadful event it was supposed to commemorate had ever actually occurred—the Bengal government moved. On the 2nd of July Bose was jailed, as it transpired for the last time.

This time not his health but his patience failed. Given the circumstances, it was clear he could accomplish nothing by remaining where he was. India was a dead end. He must get out and join Britain's enemies abroad. But how?

Through the rainy season and the autumn he tried, with no success and in mounting exasperation, to pry open his prison door. Late in November he abandoned legal tactics and, plucking an arrow from Gandhi's quiver, told his jailers that henceforth he would eat nothing and drink only water. Anxious lest he take sick and die on their hands, they released him to the family house on Elgin Road, where from police posts outside he could be watched. The watch, however, was ineffectual. Very early on the morning of January 17, 1941, Subhas slipped out of Calcutta by car, Sarat's son Sisir at the wheel, and drove north. That night, at a small country railroad station, he boarded the Kalka Mail for Delhi. Ten days later he was in Kabul. Two months later still he was in Berlin. But Berlin was a dead end too.

It is true that after an initial period of suspicion and reserve, he was treated as a person of some importance. He met Ribbentrop. He met Goebbels. He was given a house, a car, and a generous personal allowance, allowed to open a Free India Center, and provided with facilities for broadcasting to India. Best of all, he obtained access to Indians taken prisoner in North Africa. Turning upon them the full force of his personality, he persuaded several thousand to join an Indian Legion that, when the moment came, would be the spearhead for a thrust into India.

The moment, however, did not come, and Subhas soon saw that it never would. If Germany and Japan had concerted their strategies, if the first had struck hard for Suez and the Persian Gulf while the second, after crippling the United States at Pearl Harbor, had moved seriously into the Indian Ocean, they might have joined hands in the Arabian Sea and given Bose the opportunity to raise India against the crumbling Raj. But they did not. It is a question whether, after the first bold lunges and stupefying gains, either had a strategy to concert.

India was so very far away. For Hitler, moreover, Britain's rule on the subcontinent was the model for what Germans might do in Russia. For the moment he was quite content to leave to the British the governance of lesser peoples overseas, provided they left him alone in Europe. Repeatedly Subhas tried to get Berlin to accord him some sort of public recognition, or at least to declare that India should be free. Always he was told that this must wait until German forces had advanced far enough to make a declaration plausible. And, of course, after El Alamein and Stalingrad it was clear this could not be.

Long before that, however, in the spring of 1942, Bose had made up his mind to try the other side of the world. (It was now that he met Hitler for the first and last time, and received the cigarette case the Granada documentary mentions.) Months passed. The Quit India rebellion broke out, filling him with the wildest joy that his country was stirring, the deepest despair that he was not there to participate. The Germans were not sure they could pass him safely across the enormous distance. The Japanese were not sure they wanted him at all. At last, on the 8th of February, 1943, Bose and one carefully chosen companion, a young man named Abid Hasan, left Kiel in a German submarine. Late in April, off Madagascar in rough seas, they were hauled drenched and half drowned aboard a Japanese submarine sent to meet them. On the 6th of May they stepped ashore at Sabang, on We Island, just off the north tip of Sumatra.

Bose left behind three thousand Indian men in Wehrmacht uniforms whose future would be halfhearted participation in the manning of the Atlantic Wall and then a British prisoner-of-war cage— three thousand men, and a wife and child. (Emilie Schenkl had begun living with him almost from the moment he reached Europe. They had married secretly; she had born him a daughter; Anita was five months old when he sailed.) He brought with him enormous intensity of purpose, the "one-pointed ardour" Dilip had noticed, and twenty-five years of preparation for the task at hand. A short time earlier Shah Nawaz had told Colonel Iwakuro that there was only one man outside India who could start a real Indian National Army. This man was about to arrive.

A Fresh Start

It was Yellappa who arranged to have Lakshmi present when Bose reached Singapore.

Yellappa was a barrister from the south Indian state of Coorg who had come to Malaya before the war to work for a firm of English solicitors. He had no interest in politics and disliked the Japanese, a dislike Lakshmi says he never lost. But he had recently begun to devote a good deal of time to the Indian Independence League, and was now chairman of its Singapore branch. Lakshmi knew and respected Yellappa. When the League at last opened a women's section, and he asked her to join, she agreed. So she did a little broadcasting again, a little writing (a piece on Gandhi's wife, a piece on the Congress leader Sarojini Naidu), a little relief work among the refugees from upcountry.

Not that this occupied her much. She and "K" had opened a second clinic, in the center of the city, and she was very busy with the usual obstetrics and gynecology, some pediatrics, some general practice. On Sundays she and her cousin Padmini kept open house for Indian officers. Prem and John Somasundaram came regularly. Sometimes on a Saturday evening they went together to one of the little restaurants that had sprung up in Singapore since the surrender. She had been glad when Prem and John joined the INA. She looked now for signs that it would amount to something—and could find very few. The army had ceased to grow. There was no more talk of Burma. So she stuck to her own work. It was out of curiosity only that she accepted Yellappa's invitation to meet Bose's plane.

It was supposed to land on the morning of Thursday, July 1, at Kallang Airfield just east of the city. Lakshmi duly went there with Yellappa and others, but no plane arrived. Next morning they went

again. Again no plane, and when, towards ten o'clock, some of the
Japanese quietly left, the Indians began to wonder what was up. About
noon, however, word came that for security reasons the flight had been
diverted to another field. The occupants would be brought to Kallang
by road. After a time a line of cars drove up to the tarmac, and out of
the first stepped Bose.

The moment ought to have been dramatic. Here was the man the
Indians of Malaya had been looking for, longing for, expecting—for
more than a year. At last they had a leader. But almost no one was
present. It was raining. Bose inspected a Japanese guard of honor, then
walked over to Yellappa, Lakshmi, and the others and shook hands. He
was obviously tired, said little, and in a short while got back into his car.
Lakshmi was left with *a sort of flat feeling*. When Prem dropped by that
evening, she told him so. That was Friday. On Sunday, however, there
was a public meeting at which Bose appeared again, and she began to
change her mind.

The meeting was held in the movie theater of the Cathay Building.
The place was jammed with League members, and on the platform sat
the two men bearing the name Bose. Rash Behari was the first to
speak. He looked weary and ill, and his talk (delivered in English) was
brief. Nevertheless Lakshmi, who had come with Padmini and Kutty,
was moved. Here was the old Bengali singing his swan song, turning his
league and his army over to the younger man with dignity and evident
sincerity. Several others took the microphone. Then it was Subhas
Chandra's turn.

He was wearing the same cream-colored silk suit he had worn at
the airfield. But his tiredness had left him and he spoke with an electric
vigor, using simple and direct Hindustani, pausing only for the
translation into Tamil. Exactly what he said is immaterial. What
Lakshmi gives us does not correspond with what we have from other
sources. He was to make so many speeches in the next few days, and
follow these with so many during the next two years, that their
contents must inevitably have run together in the minds of his listeners.
But everyone agrees he took the hall by storm. By the time he finished,
the man he was supplanting was practically forgotten. And on the next
day, Monday the 5th, he spoke with even greater effect. This time his
hearers were the men of the Indian National Army, men who had never

really accepted Rash Behari because he was a civilian and a Bengali. They might decline to accept him too, not in his political capacity but as a soldier. And a soldier he was determined to be.

The scene was the padang, where these same men had paraded for Gandhi's birthday the previous October. A wooden platform had been laid across the City Hall steps, and on it Subhas stood. Gone was the cream-colored suit, in its place military garb of the most complete and formal kind. If you visit, today, the Bose family house and examine the uniform Lakshmi saw him wear as he drilled Congress Volunteers so many years ago, you may agree with Lakshmi's mother that the outfit, with its braid, aiguillettes, and heavy Sam Browne belt, is a little overdone. What he wore now seemed a bit much too, in this climate especially: breeches, glistening top boots, tunic buttoned up to the chin. Nevertheless on this July day, and over the months that followed, it worked. No one thought his dress—in public he wore no other, never again appeared in civilian clothes—vain or theatrical. The uniform expressed the man. The man was authentic. And a moment came that Monday morning, Lakshmi tucked away in a corner with the other women remembers it clearly, when the men whom Bose was addressing felt this authenticity so strongly that they were compelled to rise and respond.

They were seated in ranks upon the grass of the great open space, their backs to the sea, listening as Bose told them it was time to deal the British a crushing blow. Gandhi had paved the way. Gandhi had made Indians conscious of their bondage. Armed struggle was the necessary step now, and it was they who must undertake it. Subhas was telling them this, and giving them slogans: "*Chalo Delhi*" (on to Delhi), and "*Jai Hind*" (victory for India, though "up India" catches better the liveliness of the phrase). But these arguments and these slogans, he was saying, mean nothing as long as they remain only things in my mouth. Do *you* feel them, are they part of you, yours as much as they are mine? And as he said this, the entire mass came to its feet. *It was spontaneous. It was absolutely fantastic. They didn't get any word of command, they just stood up and put their rifles in the air—you could see a forest of rifles.* Standing thus, brandishing their rifles, they roared their assent.

This was only Monday. The public functions were by no means over. There was another speech and march past on Tuesday, this time for the Japanese Prime Minister, General Tojo, and on Friday an enormous rally at which Bose spoke again. It, too, was held on the padang. We know little about it. Indeed, there is much about this exuberant period that is uncertain. It is a pity. We should like to have a sharp and detailed picture of these July days, days so important to the participants that they were celebrated the following year and the year after, with appropriate ceremonies. Even the picture we have has a tendency to crumble.

For example, there is the description, in Mihir Bose's biography, of the march past I have just mentioned, the one on Tuesday the 6th. It began, Bose writes, with an act of annoying clumsiness. In front of the reviewing stand "the leading tank, flying the Indian flag, got entangled with some wires across the road, crashed and was run over by another tank."[1] Now this is absurd. A tank does not *run over* another tank. Bose obviously writes in a hurry, and the wise reader, if he notices the slip, will forgive him and hurry after. Still, *something* happened, an accident far less sensational but at the same time more credible. It was not the tank that fell and was mangled. It was the flag. "The Indian flag hoisted on the first tank got caught between some wires across the road and crashed down, to be run over by the tank." Thus M. Sivaram, in his published recollections—from which Mihir Bose almost certainly took his tale.[2]

If Sivaram's account is more credible, however, it is not wholly so. He gives us a flag to be run over, and that we can believe. He gives us a tank to do the business, and that, too, is plausible. But did it happen? A tank? *Tanks* with the Indian National Army? Percival's defeated force had had none. It is unlikely that Japan's Southern Army offered the Indians its own, and inconceivable that Subhas Chandra allowed Japanese of any sort, even drivers, into his parading columns. So the unhappy flag must have been carried by an armored car or a Bren gun carrier. Photos published at the time show armored cars, three abreast, passing the reviewing stand. And Prem, who was on the stand, remembers that an officer on one of the lead cars held a flag above his head, and that overhead wires wrenched it from his hands. But experienced newspapermen do not mistake armored cars for tanks. Sivaram was an experienced newspaperman.

This is the dismaying part. Sivaram was writing for a Bangkok daily, and had been for years, when the Japanese struck. From the internal evidence of his book it is apparent that he was in Singapore doing publicity work for the League when Bose reached the island. He writes of Bose's doings as if he had watched them with his own eyes. But he cannot have seen tanks at the Tojo review. And it is almost certain that he did not see what he tells us he saw when Subhas reached Kallang Airfield the previous Friday, one day later than expected, in the rain, and with the Japanese worried about security (they seem to have been afraid some Chinese might take a shot at their guest). Sivaram did not see a huge crowd waving and cheering. He did not see Bose fix his gaze long and keenly upon the honor guard. He did not see Japanese officers bow almost to the ground. He could not have seen these things. Yet he writes as if he had.

From 1943 onward, there is a lot of this dressing up, armored cars turned into tanks, skirmishes translated into battles, chance standoffs metamorphosed into splendid victories. There is much inflation of numbers and a good deal of plain, unadulterated puffery. It has given hostile critics of Bose and the Indian National Army a field day. It probably confirms many doubters in their doubts. And though some of it arguably was necessary, some of it certainly was not.

❦

It was necessary to persuade the Japanese that the Bangkok Resolutions of the previous year could no longer be ignored. It was necessary to persuade them that the Indian overseas community must be treated as an equal partner and ally. Subhas went about the business not by pleading, scolding, or threatening to sit on his hands until the Japanese came around. He went about it by acting as if they already had. It was the tactic of a Charles de Gaulle. Subhas behaved not as he was but as he wished to be, and he demanded of his fellow Indians that they do the same.

Of course, behaving thus was not just a matter of striking poses. There had to be substance. For this reason Bose had not come directly to Singapore. From Sabang, where the Japanese submarine landed him, he had flown incognito to Tokyo. There he spent the second half of May and all of June laying the groundwork for the performance that was to follow. It was not easy. For four weeks, Tojo, who remembered the troubles of the previous December only too well and thought

Indians tiresome, avoided seeing him. Bose had to be content with Japanese of lesser rank. These, however, he systematically cultivated, talking to them in groups through an interpreter, making sure they knew who he was and what he had accomplished, so that Tojo, when he made inquiries downward as he was bound to do, would not draw a blank. At last a meeting took place. The Prime Minister was much impressed. Indeed, Joyce Lebra, who has read the Japanese sources, believes he was more than impressed, he was enthralled. There was a second meeting. Subhas attended a special session of the Diet at which Tojo affirmed Nippon's determination to help India free herself. His incognito was lifted, he held a press conference, he broadcast to India. And when at last he set off for Singapore, he carried with him not only the assurance of active Japanese support, but the knowledge that the *kikan* through which that support would be extended was to be headed not by Iwakuro but by an officer more in tune with his aims.

What Bose had established, then, before ever he set foot among his own people, was the rough sketch for his scenario: overseas India marching with the assistance of the Japanese to the liberation of India-at-home. He had now to fill in that sketch. For this it was perhaps inevitable that he should encourage, even float, some of the pufferies I mention.

An army must have a commander. None of the officers at his disposal, not Bhonsle or Zaman Kiani, and certainly not a medical man like Chatterji, had the stature or the experience to fill a commander's shoes. He would have to do the job himself. Accordingly, Supreme Commander (he did not make Mohan Singh's mistake of assuming a specific rank) he declared himself to be.

But an army, if it is to be more than a band of freebooters or a collection of condottieri, must also have a government, a government in whose service and at whose direction it fights. This government will be the government of the nation. It will normally be found on the soil of the nation. In India's case, unfortunately, the nation's soil was occupied by foreigners. (It was to dislodge these foreigners that an Indian *national* army had been formed.) Nevertheless the desperate venture about to be undertaken would be without legitimacy, and even without purpose, were there no government for the army to obey. Therefore one must be formed, a government in exile, as it were. In due course one was. Bose announced the formation of the *Arzi Hukumat-e-Azad Hind*, the Provisional Government of Free India.

I say in due course because it was easier to think about these things (and Bose, Abid Hasan tells us, did a great deal of thinking on the two submarine voyages) than it was to carry them through. If Kiani and the others had limited military experience, Subhas Chandra had none beyond those few weeks with the university cadet corps, a few days drilling Volunteers at the Calcutta session of the Congress, and what little he had acquired with the Legion in Germany. Getting a Chinese tailor to run up a uniform was no problem, it could be done overnight and was. Obtaining the confidence of the professionals was another matter. In the event, Bose accomplished it swiftly. He met the senior officers, Prem among them, on his first full day in Singapore. He stood with them on the reviewing stand two days later, with the consequence Lakshmi has described. He assumed personal command of the *Azad Hind Fauj*—the "Free India Army" or Indian National Army—four weeks later still. Zaman Kiani went off to command the battalions now designated as the 1st Division. There is no reason to suppose that he or anyone else thought the supersession presumptuous.

No doubt there were officers who wanted to leave things as they were. Ambition, patriotism, loyalty (it could cut either way), a repugnance for the barbed wire of the POW cage, a predilection for the fleshpots of Singapore such as they were, and a dozen other circumstances among which the chief was probably what a man's immediate fellows did—these tugged some men into the freedom army and kept others out. Among the joiners there were surely a number who were content with garrison life and did not want to be disturbed. But even they may have wondered how long it would be before the Japanese grew tired of their inactivity and shipped them off to New Guinea or worse. As for the rest, the committed ones, they had been idle long enough. They were happy to see Bose arrive because they believed he had the will and the clout to get things moving.

Many of these he overwhelmed at once by the sheer force of his personality. We may discount the stories that grew up around Subhas Chandra, some of them contrived or encouraged by his own staff, and yet believe that with certain people he had exactly this effect. Others took their measure of the man by getting to know him in a working situation. Prem was such a one. He was well situated for this, for he kept the post of military secretary that he had held since the beginning of the year, and this meant that when the Supreme Commander was in or about Headquarters, he saw him two or three times a day, and frequently spent the evening with him. So Prem came to know Subhas well. In the process he developed a respect for him that was perhaps not as passionate as Lakshmi's but certainly as deep.

Subhas, he noted, was quick to pick up what he needed for intelligent talk about arms, equipment, training, supply. He was meticulous. Prem remembers driving with him one day to a place where he was to give a speech in Hindustani, being pumped as they drove for the correct Urdu expression for this and that, and discovering when the speech was delivered that Bose used them all. But Prem's memory works best through the device of the story. There are two about Bose and his relations with his officers that demand to be told. The first is a drinking story, vintage Prem Sahgal, and it goes like this.

It happened that in the course of a New Year's Eve dinner party one of the guests, a German military attaché, turned to Prem and asked "what do you people say when you drink to each other?" Prem did not know what to reply. Under the circumstances "cheers" would hardly do. But suddenly the word *chakta* popped into his head. *Chakta* is Punjabi for "put up." Instructors on the rifle range shout *chakta* when the men are firing low and must raise their sights. At Dehra Dun the cadets had made *chakta* something of a war cry, and Prem seized on it now. "We say *chakta*," he told the German. Together they drank.

Some weeks later, at an official banquet, the same German found himself opposite the Supreme Commander, caught his eye, raised his glass, and bellowed *chakta*. Now Bose, Prem says, had no taste for alcohol. He would toast if he had to, however. Without a moment's hesitation he, too, raised his glass and cried *chakta*. They must have exchanged chaktas two or three times, Prem believes. But later, Bose came to Prem and said, "Major Sahib, I do not understand this chakta. I never heard it in Germany. Where did the fellow pick it up?" So Prem told him. *And he said, "next time you decide to commit India to something, will you please consult me first."*

The second story has to do with a moment very early in Prem's service under Subhas. Because the Indian National Army inherited no senior officers from the Indian Army, all having of course been British, it had been necessary, as we have seen, to move King's commissioned and Indian commissioned officers up, and let jemadars, subadars, and subadar-majors of the discontinued VCO class take their place. Now it was easy enough, by using the date of the first commission, to keep such men in step with each other. But civilian volunteers and officers from the States Forces (the little armies of the princely states) were another matter. None of the first and few of the second had been through the Military Academy, yet many were of an age, or had experience such, that they could not be consigned to junior ranks. So a committee chaired by a medical officer named A. D. Loganadhan had drawn up guidelines for fixing the relative seniority of special cases. It was Prem's job as military secretary to apply these guidelines. It was his job to recommend who should be what, and have the appointments published in the official military gazette.

Soon after Subhas Chandra settled in as Supreme Commander, Prem prepared to submit for his approval a forthcoming issue of this gazette. It was to be his first official encounter with Bose—and he was worried, for Chatterji did not like his recommendations. A. C. Chatterji came from the Indian Medical Service. He was a doctor by training, an administrator and political operator by inclination, and a civilian at heart. He had not questioned Loganadhan's guidelines, but neither did he put much stock in them. When a civilian volunteer for one of the administrative branches of the INA came to him saying that he had been such and such in an accounts department somewhere, and ought to have a higher rank than he was offered, he listened, then went and badgered Prem. Chatterji outranked Prem. He had more to say about League affairs than any other single person. He was a Bengali, like Subhas Chandra. And Prem was pretty sure he had already been to Subhas with his complaints.

So Prem wrote out his resignation and put it in his pocket. "*If the gazette is not accepted as I have written it,*" he told Lakshmi (by now she, too, had an office in the headquarters building), "*I am resigning as military secretary—though not from the army, of course.*" Then he went in. But he need not have worried. Bose asked him to explain the principles by which appointments and promotions were made. Then he asked him if he was satisfied that the items in the forthcoming gazette adhered to those principles. *I said I was. And he just signed. He didn't even look at it. Lakshmi was waiting outside, her office was very close by. When I came out, she said, "what happened?" And I said, "thik!"* Which is Hindustani for "okay."

Is it unreasonable to infer from these stories that Subhas was relaxed in his relations with his officers, and knew how to leave them to get on with their work? He did not abandon all details to subordinates. Lakshmi says that when a diplomatic dinner was scheduled he always reviewed the menu, and often decided who should sit where. S. A. Ayer describes his practice of descending upon this camp or that "when the soldiers were about to sit down on the floor in parallel rows, back to back, for their dinner. He would walk straight to the kitchen, see for himself what had been cooked and in what hygienic or unhygienic conditions, then go on to the dining hall and quietly sit on the ground in the middle of one of the rows and ask to be served along with the men."[3] But even in the West, officers are enjoined to keep an eye upon the mess hall. And it is possible that in a society such as the Indian, in which food and the taking of food carry values and offer connotations that they do not have with us, this act of sharing and attention held an importance not apparent upon its surface.

In any case, Bose was far from a busybody, and not at all the sort of person whose amour propre compels him to pretend to a competence he lacks. It was one thing to worry about the jawans' diet. It would have been another had he tried to direct them in the field. Somewhere there is a picture of him standing deep in thought, in uniform as usual but with a steel helmet upon his head. He has a map in his hand. The implication is unmistakable. The Supreme Commander is making his dispositions for the battle that is about to begin. In fact he never did any such thing. His officers are unanimous that he left operations entirely to them. What he *did* do was much more important. He gave to his army the authority and purpose that come from being the arm of a legitimate government with a recognized man at its head.

That he waited until almost the end of October to announce this government was a sign of the difficulties, the chief of which was that it would be pointless to proclaim such a government—it would be downright damaging—if nobody was willing to take it seriously.

Enthralled though Tojo may have been, the Prime Minister had not actually advised such an extraordinary step. Bose had induced him to include Singapore in a trip to Manila. It was this that had brought him to the reviewing stand on July 6. But it would take more than a parade to extract formal Japanese recognition of an Indian government in exile. Besides, there were the hostility of Southern Army and the misgivings of the *Kikan* to overcome. So Bose bided his time, meanwhile behaving as a recognized national leader should behave.

Burma's independence, promised early in the year, was about to be granted. Ba Maw was to be the new country's head of state. Ba Maw had visited Singapore while Tojo was there. He had met Bose and invited him to Rangoon for the independence ceremonies. Bose went, first spending several days in Bangkok. From Rangoon he returned to Bangkok, from Bangkok he flew to Saigon. He had left Singapore on July 25, and did not get back until the evening of August 11. Everywhere he went, on this and subsequent trips (for in September he was in Rangoon again, and later in the year visited Manila, Shanghai, Nanking, and of course Tokyo), he closeted himself with the principal Indian businessmen and League people, and met the local heads of state, the high-ranking Japanese officers, the diplomatic representatives of Germany and Italy. Everywhere he gave dinners and had dinners tendered to him, held press conferences, delivered public speeches, spoke over the radio in Hindustani, Bengali, English, German even. It was a formidable, it was an exhausting, performance.

And it was successful. "In political showmanship and the tactics of mass appeal," writes Sivaram, "Subhas Chandra Bose was a genius and an accomplished expert. Driving up to address mammoth meetings, standing upright in a huge open car, acknowledging the cheers of jubilant crowds lined up along the streets—Subhas was leadership personified."[4] Since it was Sivaram's job to publicize Bose's doings, to have the crowds cheer in the wire service filings even if they were silent in the flesh, and since Sivaram is the fellow who makes tanks out of armored cars, we may take this with a touch of salt. But we cannot altogether dismiss it. Ba Maw was so struck by the Indian leader that in his memoirs he gave him an entire chapter.

So Subhas Chandra moved about Southeast Asia behaving and looking like the national leader he believed himself to be—and

Japanese reluctance melted. Early in October he was informed that if he set up a government, Tokyo would recognize it. On the 21st, once more in the movie hall of the Cathay Building before an audience that filled every seat and spilled into the street outside, the *Arzi Hukumat-e-Azad Hind* was proclaimed. Two days later the Japanese recognized it. Three days later it declared war on Great Britain, and (a little gratuitously) on the United States. A Provisional Government of Free India was now in place. But the *Arzi Hukumat* faced another difficulty: an absence of men of stature to serve beneath the head of state.

It was an astonishing spectacle. Here was a politician of the first rank, sometime mayor of Calcutta, leader of a formidable Congress bloc, twice president of Congress Party itself; a man who for a quarter century had rubbed shoulders with his country's major political figures. Yet this man was obliged to be his own prime minister, his own minister for war, his own minister for foreign affairs; and to consign the three remaining ministries in his modest cabinet to an army doctor, a journalist, and a female obstetrician not yet thirty years of age.

The fact was that Bose, in spite of the love and adoration that surrounded and warmed him, was very much alone, and his enterprise, whose object was nothing less than the overthrow of the Raj, precarious. Japan and eight other governments had recognized his *Arzi Hukumat* or shortly would, among them Germany and Fascist Italy (by this time there were two Italies, one on either side). But most of these, Mussolini's Italy included, were puppets, or at best clients, of Germany or Japan. With none, not even with Japan, was Bose able to exchange diplomatic representatives. Besides, even the puppets possessed some territory. The Provisional Government of Free India had not one square inch.

This had been a problem for De Gaulle and the Free French too. They had solved it by winning over, or forcibly seizing, pieces of overseas France—to begin with, two islands off Newfoundland's coast. In the Bay of Bengal, midway between Rangoon and the northern tip of Sumatra, there are two groups of islands, the Andamans and the Nicobars, which for some time had been part of British India. To Port Blair, their chief town, went Subhas Chandra at the end of 1943, meaning to raise his tricolor as the Free French had raised theirs over St. Pierre and Miquelon. There was a difference, however. When De

Gaulle made his move, foreigners did not occupy these islands. The Free French had landed among Frenchmen. And they had arrived in their own warships, modest but unmistakable symbols of a budding sovereign power. Bose had no warships, no ships of any kind, not even a seagoing junk. He came to Port Blair in a Japanese bomber and at their invitation—the Japanese had occupied the island groups early in 1942, and used them to control the eastern side of the Bay of Bengal. The difference was enormous. Nippon's navy might allow Bose a ceremony or two. It would never let Port Blair go.

So Bose ran up his flag, had himself photographed gazing thoughtfully at the prison where freedom fighters were once incarcerated (the British had used Port Blair as a penal colony), and flew back to the mainland. Later he sent A. D. Loganadhan with a staff of five to set up a civil administration—as he had been assured he might. Tokyo's declared intention of surrendering the islands remained, however, just that: a declaration of intent. The Japanese would not give Loganadhan police powers, and without them he could do nothing. After seven months of ineffectuality he was, to his own great relief, allowed to come home.

Unable to rest his government upon territory, even a fragment of territory, Bose was all the more determined to rest it upon people. The *Arzi Hukumat*, he early warned his audiences, was not simply an intimation of what might someday be. It was a reality, existing in the here and now, and like every government it expected certain things of its citizens. In theory these citizens included Indians everywhere, all four hundred million of them. The Provisional Government, Subhas Chandra was fond of saying, is entitled to the allegiance of every Indian. In practice Bose meant the Indians living east of the subcontinent, the Indians of Burma, Malaya and other places in Southeast Asia. Of course he had no means of compelling their service. To announce that a Bangkok seller of sweets, for example, was now a citizen of India would accomplish nothing so long as the Thais considered him a subject of their king. Nor could the Provisional Government legislate a change of status for the sweets seller. It was powerless to legislate anything, powerless even to enforce a law. Yet it was essential that the Indians of Bangkok and elsewhere behave like citizens, at least with their pocketbooks. Otherwise the *Arzi Hukumat*, unable to incur bills because it could not pay them, would be reduced to mere playacting, and might better have not been formed at all.

The army, in particular, was going to be expensive. Bose was perfectly willing to let the Japanese support the men already in it. They were former POWs; Nippon was responsible for them anyway. But for the civilians he meant to recruit and train, he was determined that his own government should pay. And he already foresaw that in Malaya, and even more in Burma, there would be a hundred deficiencies in the army's maintenance and supply that he would have to meet by buying in the open market. The League had for some time been raising money. Bose did not scrap the machinery for doing this. He did not scrap the League itself (he had been President since early July). He embraced it, enlarged it, and used it for many of the things he wished his Provisional Government to do. So the League did not so much run parallel to the government as *become* the government for certain purposes. Of these, raising money was the chief.

It was the duty of every adult Indian male to join a local branch. There had been twelve of these in Malaya at the time of the Bangkok Conference. Now new ones were added by the score (it was the same in Thailand, though on a far smaller scale, and later in Burma too). Singapore's branch was the largest. Yellappa chaired it, and it had over 60,000 members. Kuala Lumpur came next with 30,000. At Penang there were 20,000, at Alor Star 10,000. By June 1944 even small and remote Kota Bharu had 1,535 members, and little Gemas 38.

Through his local League branch every Indian was expected to contribute generously and regularly. To help get him in the habit, Bose went on tour. Arriving at a place, he would assemble the resident Indians, speak to them as only he could speak—and when their enthusiasm reached the proper pitch, the real work began. Men offered notes and coin. Women surrendered bangles, brooches, jewelry of every kind. Perhaps the string of flowers with which Bose had been garlanded only a half hour before went up for auction, and fetched from some unusually susceptible head of household a princely sum. If the well-to-do held back, and Bose sometimes suspected that they did, he allowed severity and even a touch of menace to enter his voice. Do not suppose, he cautioned his listeners, that your wealth and possessions are yours to do with as you please. Like your very lives, they belong now to India, which is at war and in peril. If you attempt to withhold them you may find that you have chosen to join the English, for whom there is only one place left: the prison cell. Give freely, he admonished. And encouraged by this judicious combination of exhortation and threat, the givers gave. Then Bose would climb into his car and drive away, motorcycle outriders ahead of him, staff behind, the tricolor of Free India snapping proudly from the hood. By the end of 1943 the League was raising from its seventy or so branches in Malaya almost two million local dollars a month.

It was to manage this fund-raising mechanism that Subhas made Chatterji his Minister of Finance. The journalist in the cabinet was the S. A. Ayer already mentioned, a Reuters man of great experience (he had reported the trial that sent Gandhi to prison in 1922) who happened to be in Bangkok when the Pacific war began. Much as he needed money, Bose needed publicity more, and looked for it from his Minister of Publicity and Propaganda, which Ayer became. But his third appointment was the most interesting and unexpected. Bose asked Lakshmi to be the minister responsible for women's affairs. And he asked her to raise a regiment of women to fight beside the men.

The regiment, Lakshmi believes, was entirely Bose's notion. He was a great student of revolutionary history. Joan of Arc was one of his heroes, Rani Lakshmibai of Jhansi another—this amazing young woman who during the Sepoy Rebellion led her men against the British at Jhansi, at Kalpi, at Gwalior, and was killed at last fighting in male dress as an ordinary *sowar* or cavalry soldier. Indian women, Bose had always felt, should take their rightful place in public life. But Lakshmi does not know exactly how or whence the idea for the regiment came.

Abid Hasan says that Subhas talked about it during the two submarine voyages. Certainly he had made up his mind before he reached Singapore, for he broached the business at the mass rally on the padang July 9, when he had been in the city only a week. At that rally he called for the total mobilization of all Indians in Burma, Malaya, and beyond. A freedom force made up only of ex-Indian Army men would not do. The British would sneer, saying that the men had joined only to escape the POW cage. He must have a truly national army; every able-bodied civilian must volunteer. And there must be a place in that army for women. He meant to have a regiment of death-defying women. It would be called, after the heroine of 1857, the Rani of Jhansi Regiment.

How much of a general impression this announcement made it is hard to say. For Lakshmi, however, it was *an absolute bombshell.* She lay awake most of the night wondering how such a regiment could be raised and who could be found to lead it; and in the morning, discovered that Yellappa shared her excitement. He called her to his office. Would she help him pursue the idea? She would. They talked a little. At last they decided to hold a women's rally on Monday and have Bose speak. Why not surprise him, too, with a guard of honor composed entirely of women? Lakshmi undertook the work.

Sunday morning she spent trying, with the help of Mrs. Chidambaram, chairman of the Women's Section of the League, to put a group together. Upper-class women of her own sort were few (many had left Singapore before the Japanese attack), and girls from a more modest background were often reluctant, or had parents who were. But by noon Lakshmi had twenty willing volunteers. That afternoon they began to drill.

Yellappa got INA Headquarters to provide rifles and two havildars. Experienced ex–Indian Army men, the two went about their work with never a hint of the astonishment they must have felt. There was no time to devise uniforms. The women wore saris, wrapping the shoulder part tightly, and tucking the loose end into the waist as any woman doing manual work will do. The rifle was the standard British three-nought-three, a heavy weapon for a woman. *They drilled us for three hours that afternoon, and again for three hours the next morning, by which time our arms were ready to fall out of their sockets.* Nevertheless on Monday afternoon, when Bose appeared at the building in which the rally was to be held, they were ready for him, came smartly to attention, and presented arms. At the rally he talked at length about his hopes for the regiment, speaking as usual in Hindustani. Most of the women were south Indian and could barely understand him. But when a man volunteered to translate, Lakshmi objected. Women should speak for women, she said—and did the job herself.

Early on Tuesday, John Thivy came to see her. Thivy was an old friend. His family and Lakshmi's had known each other well in Madras. Like her father and her older brother, he had been called to the bar in London, and was practicing law at Ipoh when the Japanese struck. After a time he joined the League, became chairman of the Ipoh branch, and eventually succeeded Raghavan as director of the All-Malayan territorial association. Thivy's errand was simple. Bose required someone to take his women's regiment in hand. Thivy and Yellappa had suggested Lakshmi, and now Thivy had come to see if he could persuade her to consider the assignment. Lakshmi gave him no time for artful advocacy. Of course she would. Thivy made arrangements for her to see Bose that very evening.

She went to his official residence east of the city, a handsome building set among roses and yellow cannas in grounds that stretched down to a beach of white sand. Every day scores of people visited the place, some on business with the leader, many just to be blessed by the sight of him (have *darshan* of him, as the Indian expression goes). For Lakshmi, however, Subhas had set several hours aside. It was for this reason that he had asked her to come in the evening, when his real day's work began.

He was aware who she was, and not simply from the guard of honor or what Thivy and Yellappa had said. Her father's name was familiar and he had met her mother, south Indian support for his Forward Bloc having brought him on several occasions to Madras. Besides, there cannot have been in all of Singapore another young Indian woman quite as active and visible. A Japanese civilian high in the administration of the city remembers watching "beautiful, talented, well-educated Dr. Lakshmi" walk along Stamford Road one day with a young Japanese woman of his acquaintance; remembers that it was she who commanded "the Ranee of Jhansi Regiment," and laments that at the end of the war "this flower of Indian independence disappeared forever"[5]—though nothing of the sort occurred. In a sense she and Bose were not strangers at all. Nevertheless, the time they spent together that evening left an indelible mark on her. The understanding they reached quite changed her life.

He was charming. I was very, very impressed. I don't think I have ever been so impressed by another person as I was by him. He asked me whether I would be willing to take up the job he had in mind. "What I am asking of you is not a small thing," he said. "Just now we are in Singapore. But don't think I want to have this women's regiment simply as a showpiece. After training you people I intend to send you to Burma. You'll have to fight in the jungles of Burma. And it won't be easy there, because the Allied forces are gathering strength. So think it over very carefully. I want you to be absolutely sure this is something you want to do."

Lakshmi told him that she did not need to think it over. Ever since she had heard him speak in the Cathay Building she had felt ready to do whatever he asked. When should she start?

"*Tomorrow*," Bose replied.

He had an office ready. Her first task would be to recruit. So she went back to the clinic and told "K". *He took it very badly. He was convinced that after this we were finished*, that she would be so occupied with her work that she wouldn't have time for anything else. *And that's what happened.*

Next morning a staff car took her to her office at INA Headquarters in Chancery Lane, Abid Hasan helped her get settled, and she went to work.

❦

First she visited the women who had formed Monday's honor guard. Fifteen signed up on the spot. The other five had small children and could not join. For though the Japanese civilian I have just mentioned paints a touching picture of young volunteers breast feeding their babies during intervals in foot drill, in actuality new mothers were not accepted—even Padmini was turned away. Wives, however, were welcome. It sometimes happened that in the enthusiasm of the moment a couple enlisted together, she in the Rani of Jhansi Regiment, he in a regular unit. So gradually the list of recruits lengthened. By the following Monday they numbered fifty, and training began on a piece of vacant ground.

Borrowed instructors drilled the women for a few hours each afternoon, in groups of fifteen, their commander drilling with them when she could. It was a makeshift arrangement, however, workable

only while numbers were small and each girl went to her own home
for the night. What Lakshmi needed was a proper camp, and this it was
not easy to find. For her undertaking did not sit well with the Japanese
military. It offended their sense of what women should be—submissive,
walking modestly behind their men. They were clearly not going to
hand Lakshmi a building unless Bose pushed them, and in late July
Bose was away. When he returned he sent Lakshmi to the mainland to
recruit, and went recruiting there himself—to great effect, as Janaki
Davar discovered.

Janaki Davar lived in Kuala Lumpur. Her father was a man of some
consequence there. He had come to Malaya from south India in 1911,
worked for a time in a law office, and was now the owner of a dairy
farm. Janaki first learned about the Rani of Jhansi Regiment by reading
his English-language newspaper. She read that[6]

the Indian National Army was going to have women. A regiment
of women. Naturally I was curious, and wanted to know more.
Then one day I heard that Subhas Chandra Bose was coming to
Kuala Lumpur and would speak on the padang. I was keen to go.
But I knew my mother would forbid me. So I said nothing, just
told the cook, made him promise to cover for me, got out my
bicycle, and went.

At the padang I left my bicycle in a ditch and walked to the
platform where Bose was speaking. There was a large crowd about
this platform. Bose spoke in Hindustani and also in English. He
spoke in such a way that we all listened and were very attentive.
He said that we must work for India's freedom. He said that
women should fight for India's freedom, that a regiment was being
formed for us. And as he spoke, the feeling grew in me that I must
join.

When he had finished speaking, he asked people to come
forward and offer money, jewelry, anything they had, to the
freedom cause. So I went up, took off the earrings I was wearing,
and put them into his hand. There was a cameraman there. He took
a picture of me doing this. Then I got on my bicycle and went
home. But when I reached home I was very nervous because I
could pretend I had lost one earring but I couldn't pretend I had
lost two. So although I had not had any supper, I did not sit with
my brothers and sisters but went right to bed.

Next morning I saw my father reading his paper. On the front page was a picture of me giving my earrings to Subhas Chandra. I didn't know what to do. I was sure he had seen the picture. After a while he put the paper on a shelf. But my older sister, Papathy, came along, saw the paper, took it, and next thing she was calling to my mother, "come see what Janaki has done." My mother came and she was very, very angry. She wanted to hit me. But my father said, "don't hit her, what's done is done."

I thought perhaps my father would help me, because he was a very broad-minded man, so when I heard that Captain Lakshmi was coming to Kuala Lumpur too, I went to him and said, "can we have her to tea?" You see, my father and the head of the Indian Independence League in the town were good friends. And of course it was at League headquarters that Captain Lakshmi would be. So he said he would ask her, and she came, and he was terribly impressed.

I had got hold of an application form for the regiment, and filled it out, and after my father had met Captain Lakshmi I asked him to sign it; I had to have a parent's signature; and he signed it. Before he could change his mind I turned it in at the League. After several weeks, instructions came to go down to Singapore.

By then there was a whole group of us. My family was very well known in Kuala Lumpur, and if I was allowed to go others would be allowed to go too, though I was only seventeen. Papathy also joined. We went by train, and at Singapore lorries met us and took us to the camp. There were already girls there. The first night I cried because I wasn't used to being treated the way we were treated. Especially the food. You stood in line and it was dished out to you in a milk tin with the top cut off. There were no proper mess kits yet. I wasn't used to that. In our house we had servants. But Captain Lakshmi was very understanding. She told us we would feel better after a while, and we did.

The camp to which Janaki and her sister were brought was a building off Bras Basah Road, halfway between the Cathay Building and the Raffles Hotel. It was a building the Japanese could not make difficulties about because they had turned it over to the League. Once a club for Australian servicemen, more recently a temporary hospital for refugees, it was filthy and had been stripped of everything movable, even windows and doors. But Yellappa collected money from his Chettiar clients, persuaded one to act as a general contractor, and in no time a Chinese crew working double shifts had put the place in condition to receive the first group of "Ranis" from upcountry, a group that preceded Janaki's.

Lakshmi joined them. *We all huddled in one room and slept on the floor. The kitchens weren't ready, so food was brought in from one of the INA camps. We had a tailor working right there. As each recruit arrived she was measured, and by the evening her uniform was ready.* The recruits wore laceless chukka boots, blouses, long trousers for training, and jodhpurs for parades.

October came. On the 21st of the month Bose announced his provisional government, and Lakshmi took her place for the official photograph. She was in uniform like the others (even Ayer and the civilian advisers wore khaki), and had put on a captain's insignia of rank. For she had been commissioned a few days previously. "*Prem,*" she told me once, "*took good care that I was always one rank lower than himself.*"

On the 22nd her regimental camp formally opened. There is a picture of Subhas Chandra inspecting the guard of honor on this occasion, each recruit at attention with her rifle, its bayonet fixed, vertical at her side. Lakshmi walks at the Supreme Commander's right. Her face is serious. A mass of black hair pushes defiantly from beneath the regulation INA forage cap. The Cathay Building is visible in the background, perhaps a quarter of a mile away. At the time there were, she believes, a little over 100 on her roster, though in his address that afternoon Bose used the figure 156.

Serious training started behind high plank fencing, for Lakshmi did not want her women laughed at or ogled—as they sometimes were, Janaki remembers a little bitterly. Lakshmi did, however, let Japanese journalists inside to watch. Unlike the military they were interested, even sympathetic. Before long Japanese magazines were carrying articles about the "Indian Women's Regiment," and photographs too. A time would come when one of these would save Lakshmi's life.

The day began at six with P.T. In the morning there was infantry drill, in the afternoon classes. Illiterate recruits got reading lessons. Potential officers (from the beginning Janaki was one) listened to lectures on tactics and how to read maps. Later they would be sent to the army's regular Officers Training School. A nursing detachment was organized. It consisted partly of volunteers, partly of women who were physically not fully fit. The nursing trainees worked in the hospital at Bidadari, but did their foot drill too. For the regulars there were periodic visits to the rifle range. And once a week the entire regiment set off in the cool of dusk for a route march that lasted three or four hours, and that accustomed large parts of Singapore to the sight of young Indian women preparing with evident seriousness for work no one who knew them in their ordinary sheltered state would have thought them capable of.

Except when cabinet duties called her away, Lakshmi drilled and studied, marched and shot (*I was a very poor shot*), right alongside her recruits. She was with Prem a good deal still. He came often to her office, and helped find instructors and equipment for her training program. But leisurely Sundays at home, with friends dropping by for a chat and food, were no more. Lakshmi lived now at the Bras Basah camp and saw Padmini and Kutty rarely. As for K. P. K. Menon, she gradually ceased to see him at all.

Since his resignation from the Council of Action the previous December, K. P. K. had refused to have anything to do with the Indian National Army. Bose's arrival simply hardened his opinion. The Bengali, he felt, let hatred of British rule blind him to Japan's real purpose. "You substitute Japanese domination for British domination, isn't it?" he later remarked. "Well, I would any day prefer the British."[7] Lakshmi asked Bose to talk to him, but K. P. K. would have none of it. Day by day his abuse of the Japanese, the INA, and the Supreme Commander grew louder and harsher, until at last the Japanese lost patience and put him behind bars. Lakshmi never saw him again. But she was too occupied with her work to miss her old friend and mentor much. The twenty-four hours in the day, the seven days in the week, were hardly enough now for all she had to do.

CHAPTER II

"And They Were All My Brothers"

"Let the slogan of the three million Indians in East Asia be total mobilization for total war," Bose had announced. "Out of this total mobilization I expect at least three lakhs of soldiers . . . ."[1]

His figures were not to be taken literally. There were three million only if you included the Indians of Fiji, South Africa, and the Caribbean, all overseas Indians without a doubt but quite unable to reach Singapore. To expect 300,000 men (a lakh is one hundred thousand) was fantasy. If, however, Bose added 30,000 civilian recruits to the jawans taken prisoner by the Japanese, he would have more than enough for the three divisions that had been Mohan Singh's dream. Enough, perhaps, for four or five.

Recruiting began within weeks of his arrival. The love of India, the determination to set her free, that Subhas managed to excite in young women like Janaki Davar, he planted also in young men. And if the women, in spite of their enthusiasm, responded only in driblets to what was for them an extraordinary invitation, and for their families a frankly shocking one, the men came forward in a flood. Up and down Malaya Indian Independence League branches became recruiting offices. In Singapore the rush to volunteer was so great that men scuffled for a place in line. Long before the year was out the two training camps, at Seletar on the island and Kuala Lumpur on the mainland, had all the men they needed for the six months' training program.

An Officers Training School, begun in Mohan Singh's day under Shah Nawaz but soon abandoned, was revived under Habib-ur-Rahman (like Shah Nawaz a Muslim Rajput from the 1/14th Punjab) at Bahu Pahat on Johore's west coast. There were not nearly enough noncommissioned officers for the jawans who would soon be emerging from the camps, so a special NCO school was opened in Singapore itself. Arms remained in short supply. Captured British stocks, after still another year of unsystematic storage or plain abandonment, did not have much to offer. But of other things there was, thanks to the League, enough. The League bought boots in Bangkok. It bought cloth wherever it could find it and had it made up into uniforms. It arranged for the manufacture of haversacks, mess tins, and water bottles. It found medicines and mosquito nets; it published newspapers in English, Hindustani, Tamil, and Malayalam; it even ran the training camps—all Headquarters had to do was appoint instructors and draw up training schedules. There was almost nothing it did not undertake, which made the indefatigable Chatterji, who was its General Secretary as well as the Provisional Government's Minister of Finance, almost as important a figure as Bose himself.

Indeed, some people suspected Chatterji of presuming that in the fullness of time *his* establishment, not the Provisional Government, would set up shop in Delhi. But Bose remained master of the situation. In no respect was this more apparent than in the vigor and authority with which he moved to make the freedom army truly national.

❧

The Indian Army, of course, was not really national at all. It recruited from certain carefully selected communities, drew most of its officers— and all its high-ranking ones—from a community (the British) that was not even Indian, and nourished the caste and religious differences of the men it did admit by paying careful attention to who ate what with whom. With a war on, some of these peculiarities became less noticeable. Prem, it will be remembered, had cracked the social barrier at the Peshawar club pool, though not at the Kalentan Club. He had persuaded Pathan and Dogra VCOs to sit down together at table. The enormous wartime increase in numbers, moreover, had been paid for by expanding beyond recognition the roster of communities deemed capable of producing fighting men. Indeed, to fill the technical branches it had become necessary to solicit men who were not "martial" at all—just educated. So the Indian Army of 1942 and 1943 was a bit more like a national army than it used to be. Yet it remained at bottom a professional establishment, a mercenary force, the sum of its regiments and not the sum of its men. It had its colors and its emblems. It made much of its traditions and its ceremonies. It appealed to the heart. But no one could say that what held it together, and gave it purpose, was its sense of being the nation in arms.

From the beginning the *Azad Hind Fauj* set out to be different. Deprived of its British officers by the surgical stroke that sent them all to Changi two days after the surrender, it became at that instant wholly Indian in composition—this was the first step. Because it existed to fight India's war of independence, not the Empire's war of survival, it was from the moment of its formation wholly Indian in purpose—this was the second. It did not practice selective recruitment because it had only the prisoners of war to recruit from, and beyond them only those Indians who happened to be living in Malaya. As for differences of caste and community and religion, now that the British were gone who remained to preserve and cultivate such divisive things?

The answer, alas, was that the British had not invented the divisiveness. They had only adapted themselves to it, and in some degree used it. Though in the INA camps and stations the British were conspicuous now by their absence, the differences—and some of the adaptations and games—remained. A nomenclature that had once told you that a unit consisted of Garhwalis or had been raised in the Punjab, might be replaced now by one that honored Gandhi or Nehru or Hindustan in general. Yet the men still came in groups, from designated communities. And often, as Prem points out with respect to his Dogras, Pathans, and Punjabi Muslims, and as certain recruiters discovered when they tried to bully the 2/9th Gurkhas, the decision whether to join the *Azad Hind Fauj* was made not by individuals at all but by these groups. So the class characteristics of the old army lingered in the new. One may hazard the guess that a Jat jemadar who became a lieutenant under Mohan Singh was given, if possible, a platoon of Jats. Certainly there is nothing to suggest that such assignments were deliberately avoided.

One may also hazard the guess that the men of Mohan Singh's INA still entertained the notion that though they would be fighting for Indians everywhere, for India in all its parts and provinces, it was right and proper that *they* do the fighting—they, the martial ones, the born soldiers of the north. The taxonomy the British had found, perfected, and fastened upon the subcontinent, the habit of classifying communities by their assumed martial propensity or lack thereof, could not be thrown off in a day. Of course, as long as the *Azad Hind Fauj* drew only from the prisoner-of-war pool, there was no problem. POWs were ex–Indian Army men, which made them by definition born fighters. What would happen, however, when the freedom army began taking civilians, the overwhelming majority of whom, being south Indian, were by the same definition *not* fighters? Though Madras had provided sappers and miners (in American parlance engineers) for the defense of Malaya, there had been no Madras rifle battalions in Percival's army. There had been none anywhere in the Indian Army.

Under Mohan Singh some things had changed. There was a national flag to march beneath, the green, white, and saffron tricolor (green for Muslims, saffron for Hindus, white for everyone else) that had been raised for the first time at the Lahore Congress session fourteen years before, and on innumerable occasions by all sorts of daring people (it was illegal) since. There was, in Hindustani, a common language of instruction and command. And a start had been made with common messing, not just for the officers (Dehra Dun had always had this) but for the men. But beneath the flag, the common language, and the common messing old identities threatened trouble. Sikhs, for example, stuck with Sikhs. Muslims stuck with Muslims. Potentially this last was the most dangerous identity of the lot.

It was dangerous because, in India, Muslim self-identification had already reached the point where it challenged the possibility of a nation one and indivisible. Muslim officers of the Indian Army were as little encouraged to think or talk politics as Prem had been. They were well aware, however, that though there were many Muslims in Congress Party (in the North-West Frontier Province Muslims *were* the party); though the current Congress President, Azad, was not just a Muslim but a maulana or Muslim scholar; Congress as a whole, taking leaders and members together, was Hindu. They were aware that some Congressmen believed that an independent India should be Hindu too. They were aware that Jinnah, the leader of the Muslim League, was not simply suspicious that a Congress India would be a Hindu India, with cow slaughter prohibited and wedding bands blaring impudently outside every mosque—Jinnah was convinced that it would. And they were aware, finally, that as between themselves and the Hindus, the British preference for themselves was plain.

So the Muslim officers in the POW camps had examined their position and charted their course with a cautiousness beyond that of other communities and groups. It was apparent from the story Shah Nawaz tells. He was hostile to the first INA. At Neesoon, in late February of 1942, he organized "a bloc of officers approximately 20 in number" to resist Mohan Singh. "These officers were mainly Muslims and the intention was to keep the bulk of the Muslim rank and file out of the I.N.A."[2] By May, however, it was clear that Mohan Singh was going to have his army. Resistance was useless. Officers who attempted any would be separated from their men. So Shah Nawaz decided, as we have seen, to join. He would be better able to protect his Muslims, he calculated, if he was a member—protect them not simply from the Japanese, but from ill-treatment at the hands of other Indians.

Shah Nawaz did another, curious thing. "I called a meeting of all Muslim officers in the mosque."[3] (This being at Neesoon, the largest of the camps, he presumably collected quite a number.) To these officers he again announced his decision to join, hinting at the reasons, but urging them not to follow his example unless genuinely persuaded. Will you promise, he asked, not to let yourselves be coerced? Together they made the promise, and sealed it with a Koranic affirmation.

Why the meeting in the mosque? I put the question to Prem as I was talking to him about the Red Fort trials, for at those trials some of the Muslim defendants argued that they, too, had joined the *Azad Hind Fauj* because they feared for their men. Was this general among Muslim officers? I asked. Had any Hindus felt the need to form *their* people into blocs? To which Prem replied, a little testily I thought, that it was something *they might have done.*

"But did not do," I muttered under my breath. For I think that Shah Nawaz, a loyal VCO's son, a devout Muslim, but in those days, as he says himself, "politically almost uneducated"[4]—I think Shah Nawaz was fearful of something that did not bother others. That did not even occur to Lakshmi, for example. Lakshmi's dismissal of Mohan Singh expressed her disappointment, not her suspicion. *Somehow,* she had said, *you felt Mohan Singh wasn't big enough.* With Shah Nawaz it was otherwise. Shah Nawaz was afraid Mohan Singh might be big enough all right. He was afraid Mohan Singh might be big enough to harm the Muslims. For a Sikh, if he had the power and authority, was bound sooner or later to raise his hand against Muslims. And if the Hindus went with him, the Muslims wouldn't stand a chance. Call this venture an Indian *national* army? In Shah Nawaz's opinion Muslims would be well advised to keep up their guard.

But no voyage can prosper if the ship's company are continually posting sentinels against each other, and this Mohan Singh—given who and what he was—was probably incapable of preventing. If, then, he had succeeded in surmounting his difficulties with Rash Behari and the Japanese, if he had managed to thread the December shoals with his hand still upon the tiller, his vessel might well have gone dead in the water anyway. It might have stuck motionless in Singapore, training a little, parading a little, meanwhile losing little by little its best men, the willing assigned to those intelligence and sabotage forays across the Burma-India border that were Nippon's real interest, the unwilling sent to labor camps elsewhere in Nippon's contracting empire. Until at last the British, returning, stumbled upon the remnants and caged the lot. In that case the Indian National Army would be more than half-forgotten today. It would deserve to be.

Bose saved it from this. Bose compelled Shah Nawaz and the others—or almost all the others, for an honest K. P. K. Menon and a half crazed Mahmood Khan Durrani he could not touch—to submerge their differences, of community and religion and political affiliation, in the common pursuit of what to any cool and calculating eye must have appeared a will'-o'-the-wisp: freedom by force of arms, independence by direct assault. And perhaps only Bose could have done it. Without Subhas Chandra, Prem once said to me, *we would have been nothing.*

❧

There was such charm and determination to the man.

Shah Nawaz felt it. "It will not be wrong," he told the court at the opening of his trial, "to say that I was hypnotized by his personality and his speeches. . . . For the first time in my life I saw India through the eyes of an Indian."[5] So devoted to Bose did Shah Nawaz become that after a time S. A. Ayer began to think he saw Bose-like qualities in the fellow, qualities acquired presumably by a sort of spiritual osmosis.

Of course Ayer was inclined to hyperbole. It was an inclination his job as the Supreme Commander's principal public relations man did nothing to rein in. Much later he credited Bose with combining in his person "the qualities of Akbar, Shivaji, and Vivekananda,"[6] which is a little like saying that Charles de Gaulle was Joan of Arc, Louis XIV, and Victor Hugo all rolled into one. If, however, Ayer simply meant that Shah Nawaz gave himself heart and soul to the cause of India's freedom, the expression makes sense. No other officer seems to have matched Shah Nawaz's complete surrender to Subhas Chandra's influence, but many approached it.

Bose did more than exercise his powers of persuasion. He made a deliberate effort to have Muslims around him, and to place them well. His single companion on the submarine voyage from Europe had been Abid Hasan. The commander of his 1st Division was Zaman Kiani. Determined to have at least one unit ready for action before the year's end, he stripped the three guerrilla regiments of their best men to form a fourth and gave it to Shah Nawaz. Lakshmi remembers that some Hindus were upset by this apparent partiality. She remembers, too, his explanation. "*We are in the majority. We can afford to be magnanimous. The time will come when they will think of themselves as Indians, not as Muslims, but at this stage we should try to avoid any little thing that might hurt their feelings.*" It was the spirit of the Bengal Pact of many years before.

Among the things that might hurt a Muslim's feelings was the *charkha* or spinning wheel, superimposed upon the tricolor flag, and signifying Gandhi, Congress Party, and the arts of peace. To take the *charkha*'s place Bose turned to an image of an entirely different sort, to a representation of a fierce and noble beast traditionally associated with Tipu Sultan, the Muslim hero of certain late eighteenth century wars against the British. For fifteen years Tipu had struggled to prevent the extension of British rule in south India. He had failed. The British had been too numerous, and reliable Indian allies too few. When in the summer of 1799 he fell fighting in the ruins of hotly defended Seringapatam, the victors had discovered in one relatively undamaged apartment "a rude automaton of a tiger killing and about to devour a British soldier." Inside the mechanism was "a kind of organ turned by a handle" that produced notes "intended to represent the growls of the tiger and the moans of the dying victim."[7] The tiger had been Tipu's emblem. "Tiger of Mysore" he had been styled. Bose had tried the emblem out when he was in Germany. Now he resolved to make a springing tiger the symbol of his movement.

Then there was the matter of the national anthem. On October 21, at the proclaiming of the Provisional Government, the crowd sang *Bande Mataram* as crowds had been singing it for years. The words are those of the enormously popular writer Bankim Chandra Chatterji, who in 1882 introduced the poem that contains them into his most successful historical novel. *Anandamath* is the story of a band of sannyasis or ascetics in rebellion against the British. The place is Bankim's own Bengal. The time is the early 1770s. It is a period when the British, in the form of the East India Company, are shamelessly plundering the province. The sannyasis set out to do something about it. From their lair deep in the jungle they mount a series of raids upon Company revenue columns. The work is bloody and dangerous. To sustain themselves they invoke the Mother—the mother goddess, consort of Siva; but also Mother India, *Bharat Mata*. It is with the words *bande mataram*, "I bow to thee, Mother," that the poem of some sixty lines begins.

Such a poem and such a song (for *Bande Mataram* was soon put to music), set in so inspiring a tale, would seem hardly likely to disquiet Muslims. Is not India their motherland too, and the ruthlessness and greed of Company men as hateful to them as to the Hindus? But a female deity—indeed, deities in general—have no place in Islam. Worse, though the British are plundering Bengal, they do so with the acquiescence and even connivance of the Muslim Nawab (a thing quite accurate historically, in this matter the novel reflects fact). By the end of the novel, moreover, it is clear that Muslims are to have no part in the regeneration of Bengal. The Bengal that was once happy, was a Hindu Bengal. The Bengal that is to be, will be Hindu too. Bankim, it appears, cannot conceive of Hindu-Muslim brotherhood.

For a time this passed unnoticed. *Anandamath* was a novel, *Bande Mataram* lay buried in it, the political message could be ignored—and was. In 1905, however, Curzon announced the partition of Bengal. Hindus and Muslims alike protested the scheme. Neither had been consulted. (Characteristically Curzon consulted no one.) But where the Muslims of Bengal eventually acquiesced, and in time even discovered advantages to partition, the indignation of the Hindus did not abate. They reread Bankim's novel, unearthed its verses, and sang them in the protest meetings that swept the province.

The song was proscribed. It was sung all the same. The opening words became, in fact, a revolutionary cry. (In the comic book version of *Anandamath* that you may pick up from almost any Indian book stall, *bande mataram* is what the sannyasis yell when they charge the Company's sepoys.) Then, in 1911, partition was reversed. Gradually Bankim's novel was forgotten again. But *Bande Mataram* survived. Even Muslims sang it, though at the height of the antipartition fury it had been turned upon them and their newly created Muslim League. By the 1920s it was known and sung all over India. Most Muslims, nevertheless, were not comfortable with it. In the thirties their discomfort turned to active dislike. And though the Congress, over the objections of most Bengalis, stripped it of all but its first two stanzas (they were the least provocative), by 1938 Jinnah was denouncing its use in any shape or form.

The problem was known in Singapore. In the spring of 1943 there had been a meeting at Yellappa's bungalow to consider complaints about both the *charkha* and *Bande Mataram*. After some discussion it had been decided to drop the one, and to excuse Muslims from singing the other until Bose could arrive and settle the matter. Lakshmi hoped he would settle it by selecting Tagore's *Jana Gana Mana*, which had been heard at Congress sessions as early as 1911 and is India's national anthem today. At a women's meeting not long after his arrival, she arranged to have it sung. Bose was much interested. "*This is a truly representative national song*," she recollects him saying. And in one respect it is, for it invokes by name all the parts of the Indian subcontinent, and so perhaps compares to *Bande Mataram* with its Bengali focus as *America The Beautiful* compares to the verses about the fort at the head of Chesapeake Bay. "*But the words are really Bengali or Sanskritized Hindi*," Bose added. "*They're not Hindustani.*" So the verses as they stood would not do. For Bose was determined to have a truly national language.

≈

English did not answer, of course, nor Subhas Chandra's own Bengali, nor Hindi, though on the subcontinent far more people spoke Hindi or the tongues closely related to it than spoke any other language.

The trouble with Hindi was that south Indians did not use it. North Indians associated it in its written form with Hindus, though they did not make the foreigner's mistake of supposing that a Hindu was simply someone who used Hindi, and that Hindi was the language of all Hindus. If north Indian Muslims were not to be alienated, Hindi in the Devanagari script was out.

Urdu, which north Indian Muslims would naturally prefer, did not qualify either. It had its own script, so that while Hindi speakers could speak and understand it well enough, they generally could not read or write it. Besides, like Hindi it meant nothing to southerners.

Mohan Singh's INA, obliged to settle on something (for soldiers do not drill in silence), had settled on Hindustani. In a way this was curious. Hindustani was not really a language. It could not be studied, at least not formally; schools did not teach it, no university offered a degree in its literature. It had developed as the spoken language of the people in and about Delhi, the language of the market and the bazaar at that imperial seat, becoming by extension the common speech of the Mogul Empire all across the north. Hindustani mingled Urdu with Hindi, though leaning more to the first than to the second. Or, if you wished, Hindustani *was* Urdu and Hindustani *was* Hindi. "We must define Urdu as the Persianized Hindostani of educated Muslims, while Hindi is the Sanskritized Hindostani of educated Hindus," a veteran Indian civil servant observed at the turn of the century.[8] This was what Hindustani was held to be before people began to examine and regularize it, Muslims deliberately searching for its Arabic and Persian roots, Hindus turning in the same spirit to Sanskrit, both in the process tearing it apart.

Today, after a century of effort, the purists have made so much progress that it is only at the lowest level of everyday conversation that Hindi and Urdu still meet—and educated people no longer admit to using "Hindustani" at all. In the 1940s, however, it was still a recognized tongue, neutral as between Muslims and Hindus, with the added advantage that, having no script of its own, one could be chosen without regard to past usage. In 1938, at the Haripura session of the

Congress, Bose had urged just that. He had pronounced the distinction between Urdu and Hindi "an artificial one." For India "the most natural lingua franca would be a mixture of the two, such as is spoken in daily life in large portions of the country." And though the scripts particular to each need not be abandoned let alone proscribed, the opportunity to adopt a new script for the mixture ought not to be lost.

For this he proposed to go outside the subcontinent. "I confess," he had continued, "that there was a time when I felt that it would be anti-national to adopt a foreign script." A visit to Turkey during his European exile changed his mind. There in the late twenties Arabic gave way to Roman. The shift was not popular. It proceeded at Ataturk's command. But in a country with so many illiterates, so many people who recognized no script whatever until they were taught one, it had proved comparatively easy to effect. It would be easy in India too, and for the same reason. "Some of our countrymen will gape with horror," Bose told the Haripura delegates.[9] Nevertheless he begged them to move toward romanized Hindustani for India at large. Now this was again his choice.

There was one drawback. Since Urdu and Hindi meant little or nothing to south Indians, Hindustani meant nothing too. That was why instant translation was so often necessary, not at meetings like the one at Farrer Park, which only the men of the old Indian Army had attended, but at functions to which men and women of Malaya's Indian community came. That community was very largely Tamil speaking. Many of Lakshmi's recruits knew no other language (some were illiterate even in it). They would have to be taught the new, and common, tongue. This disadvantage aside, Hindustani was the best possible choice. And Bose took care that the Hindustani taught was not a bastard Hindi but contained a full complement of Urdu words. That is why he pumped Prem for correct Urdu expressions, and why the INA watchwords—unity, faith, sacrifice—were rendered as they were. In Hindi they would be *ekta, viswas, balidan,* and these did appear on the badges the Indian Independence League devised for its civilian members. But on Prem's cap badge, a little brass thing with the letters "INA" and a tiny map of India, the words across the bottom read *ittefaq, itmad,* and *kurbani.*

That also is why Bose, on hearing Lakshmi's women sing *Jana Gana Mana*, was interested but insisted that the words be rendered in true Hindustani. This was done. A free translation was commissioned. The result, beginning *Subh Sukh Chain*, took *Bande Mataram*'s place.[10]

❦

Not all divergences and differences could be settled by a change of symbol or a choice of song. The men of the *Azad Hind Fauj* took their water and their tea from common containers, and were served from a common cookhouse, but there could be no question of asking the Hindus to eat beef or the Muslims pork, or of obliging either to sit shoulder to shoulder with anyone engaged in so offensive a practice. Neither beef nor pork entered the kitchen. The men, squatting in rows as Ayer describes them, were given their rice, their dal, and their vegetables. Then those who wished received a helping of mutton. That was the limit of possible accommodation.

What Bose hoped to do was lift the nation's business above such considerations, above religion and its divisiveness. In this he was quite unlike the Mahatma, Lakshmi believes. Gandhi brought religion *into* things. He used religious sanctions to compel political action, a habit that continues, she says, to this day. *In the INA, she once told me, we never observed any sort of religious rite as such. But here, now, every time they launch a steamer they have a puja.* In her Rani of Jhansi Regiment religious holidays were celebrated with a mutual exchange of hospitality. On Diwali, a Hindu festival, the Muslims arranged something and invited the Hindu women to be their guests. When the Muslim Id (*Id al Fitr*, the feast of the breaking of the month-long fast of Ramadan) came around, the Hindus returned the courtesy. At Christmas there were carols. Though there were very few Indian Christians in the regiment, and no Anglo-Indians at all, some of the women had excellent voices and it seemed too good an opportunity to miss.

It was the same in the regular INA. There were even reciprocal visits to places of worship, Hindus entering the mosque on the occasion of Id, later paying visits with fellow Muslim officers to the Sikh gurdwara. But the most dramatic exchange involved the Chettiar temple and Subhas Chandra himself. It happened that the trustees of the temple, asked to contribute money to the freedom struggle, had

told the League (which of course did the asking) that they would give handsomely if Bose himself came to the temple at Dasehra time and gave a little talk. Bose had declined. Religion and matters of state do not mix, he had observed. Besides, the temple was notorious for excluding not only persons who were not Hindus, but persons from certain castes who were. The trustees, however, had persisted. And at last Bose had agreed. But he would bring with him, he insisted, officers and men of his own choosing.

His choice was deliberately provocative. Hindus of all sorts went with him, Muslims of course, Sikhs—there were even a few Christians. Abid Hasan, arriving late with the Supreme Commander, found the temple "filled to capacity with the uniforms of the I.N.A. officers and men, the black caps of the south Indian Muslims glaringly evident. At the entrance some priests met us and reverently led the way, and we found ourselves before the holy of holies. When Netaji stepped into the sanctuary, I held back, but the priests behind me gently but resolutely pushed me in." Hasan had never performed a puja, "but I did what Netaji did, submitting the offerings already prepared for us, and being blessed in turn by a tilak on the forehead put there, with a reverent smile on his face, by the high priest himself."[11]

Hasan adds that as they left "Netaji wiped the tilak from his forehead." Perhaps he did. But what Chatterji particularly remembers is that after tea and light refreshments in another part of the temple, Subhas Chandra rose and spoke. Not about the pressing need for money, though that was what had brought him to the temple. About what the movement stood for. There is an old Indian saying that goes, "On the way to Delhi I met many men, and they were all my brothers." Bose did not recite it in the temple that day. But he could have, for brotherhood across all barriers was his message. Chatterji says that when he finished his listeners were filled with love and respect for one another, and "there was a glow in the faces of all."[12]

Dasehra falls in October. On the 9th of December a special committee on national integration (Lakshmi was a member) brought to a full meeting of Bose's cabinet its recommendations—common messing, romanized Hindustani, *Jai Hind* and *Chalo Delhi*, the new anthem, the springing tiger, the tricolor without the *charkha*—and these recommendations were accepted. The committee might also have made it its business to recommend, for the man who led the movement, a form of address adequate to his position and the regard in which he was held. It did not. It did not need to. A candidate was already in widespread use.

Abid Hasan had brought it with him from Europe, where it had been conceived with the German and Italian models in mind. Ayer and Sivaram had done their best to popularize it. But it would probably have taken hold anyway, it supplied so well what many were looking for. *Neta* means "leader." Whether it further translates "*the* leader" is moot and in the end unanswerable, there being no articles as such in Hindi. What is not arguable is the force of the syllable *ji*. It softens what it is appended to or what it precedes, so that where *nahin* alone is as abrupt as our "no," *ji-nahin* has the effect of our longer "no, thank you." How, then, are we to translate *Netaji*, how express the mingled affection and respect that *ji* contributes? Perhaps it is wisest simply to employ the term. And since *Netaji* is what Prem, Lakshmi, and virtually all their surviving comrades use when they refer to Subhas Chandra Bose, for the remainder of this book *Netaji* it will frequently be.

Shah Nawaz's guerrilla regiment, known to its men as "Subhas Brigade" though Netaji was not pleased with the attention, trained hard at Taiping in northern Malaya and left for Burma in several parties between the 9th and 24th of November. The three original regiments, which together with Subhas Brigade made up the 1st Division, prepared to follow. They began by rail. There was no direct link to Burma, however; the Death Railway, though pronounced complete, had barely begun to function. So a large part of the enormous distance—as the crow flies it is twelve hundred miles from Singapore to Rangoon—had to be covered by truck, coastal vessel, and on foot.

Some units detrained at Chum Pon on the east side of the Kra Isthmus, marched west over the hills to the Bay of Bengal near Mergui, were carried by ship as far as Tavoy, and then walked or were trucked to Ye, eighty-five miles below Moulmein, where the railroad resumed. Others were put on coastal craft much farther south. Sivaram accompanied one unit on board a Japanese freighter at Butterworth, opposite Penang. She carried Japanese as well as Indians, was so crowded he

thought himself privileged to find a place to sleep on deck, and for privies offered packing cases lashed outside the rail. But he was lucky. His freighter carried him straight to Rangoon, and did so in six days. For those travelling overland six *weeks* was a more likely sentence, at the end of which many were so weakened by exhaustion or sickness that it was another six before they were fit again.

December passed. Two days after Christmas, Lakshmi and her women put on a variety show for Netaji and some of the departing troops to which she contributed a dramatic sketch she called "Freedom Or Death." Did the title and the theme reflect Gandhi's *karo ya maro*—do or die—of Quit India seventeen months before? Until the very eve of that rising the Mahatma's prescription for independence had ruled a freedom army out. Now one was in being, preparing to burst into the subcontinent, and Gandhi by inference had given it his blessing.

On New Year's day Lakshmi spent several hours with Prem, fresh from the party at which he had committed four hundred million Indians to *chakta*, the Punjabi rifle instructor's shout. Next day she received orders to prepare for her own departure. A Rani of Jhansi camp had been opened at Rangoon and she was needed. She travelled by plane. Bangkok was the intermediate stop. Arriving on January 5 with other senior INA officers, she was startled when the young Thai foreign office secretary who met them gave her a deep and solemn bow. In fact she was so startled she very nearly giggled. Formalities of this sort always touched her funny bone, but someone nudged her, and with an effort she managed a passable salute.

She had lunch with Netaji, just in from the Andamans. A. D. Loganadhan, who had come up on the plane with her, would soon be off to his exasperating assignment on those islands. She called on the Thai prime minister's wife. Then on the 7th a Japanese bomber took her, Netaji, and several other members of the *Arzi Hukumat* on to Rangoon, a little more than two hours' flying time away. Shah Nawaz came in with the bulk of Subhas Brigade. Prem arrived with INA Headquarters, the running of which was added now to his duties as military secretary. Lakshmi paid a visit to the wife of the Burmese head of state. "The First Lady of Burma, H.E. Daw Khin Ma Ma Maw, and the First Lady of Azad Hind, Dr. S. Lakshmi," a press account began, and there were pictures of Lakshmi in an uncharacteristically rumpled khaki uniform shaking hands with a slim and elegant woman. Account and pictures appeared in *Greater Asia*, Rangoon's Japanese-sponsored English language newspaper.[13] From now on *Greater Asia* would do its best, though for want of newsprint it published only three times a week, to make its readers aware that the government and army of a nation aspiring to be free, had been welcomed to the hospitable soil of Burma.

CHAPTER 12

HIGH HOPES IN BURMA

Rangoon, some thirty miles from the sea on the eastern side of the many mouths of the Irrawaddy, lies at the base of a U whose bottom and left arm are formed by the Rangoon River, its right by Pazandaung Creek. A railroad running down one arm and out the other describes a lesser U within the larger, and in 1944 the city proper was confined to the strip of ground between the bottom of one U and the bottom of the other, between the railroad and the river; a strip perhaps a mile and a half long and three-quarters of a mile deep, with streets laid out in a regular grid. Eden Street. Dalhousie Street. Dufferin Street. Strand Road. Most have Burmese names now. By early 1944 British and American bombing was beginning to knock the area about a good deal. It was a poor place to settle.

So a day or two after his arrival Prem went reconnoitering north of the railroad line, where the city proper gave way to partially open country. There, on a lane with the improbably grand name of Jamal Avenue, just beyond Royal Lake and due east of the spectacular gold spire of the Shwe Dagon pagoda, he came across several houses that belonged to the Zeyawadi Sugar Factory. Zeyawadi is a place near Toungoo, about 150 miles north of Rangoon. Late in the previous century fifteen thousand acres of land there had been leased to an Indian entrepreneur who wished to raise cane and manufacture sugar. The enterprise prospered. By the time the war began, Zeyawadi had the largest sugar factory in Burma. When the Japanese arrived they commandeered it, and with it the factory's Rangoon office at No. 11 Jamal Avenue as well as several other buildings in the vicinity. These, in the spirit of the Bangkok Resolutions (though that piece of paper had never formally been affirmed), they now turned over to the INA.

Prem made No. 11 into a billet for himself and Headquarters staff. Headquarters proper went into No. 9, a bungalow (as large houses in this part of the world are often called) on a rise close by. Netaji was already settled west of the pagoda, in a house left vacant when its occupant, a retired Indian Medical Service officer, evacuated to India. As for the troops, they were in huts or under canvas further north, some at a place called Myang, some clear out by Mingaladon airfield a dozen miles from the city. Lakshmi's Rani of Jhansi women occupied a two-story bungalow in a large compound at Thingangyone, also at some distance. (Later they moved to Kamayut, much closer in.) Already there were more than fifty recruits. Obtaining more ought to be easy, for in spite of the exodus of almost two years before, Rangoon was still very much an Indian city.

Before the war over half its population had been Indian. Even now, Lakshmi discovered, in the shops and bazaars Hindustani was practically all you heard. And though most Rangoon Indians were dressmakers, engine drivers, clerks, coolies, or factory hands, a fair number were men of property. They had built the city. They filled the professions, owned the places of business, occupied the better homes. It was from among their daughters that Lakshmi obtained many of her finest cadets. The fathers, too, would be indispensable to Bose and his army. For, just as in Malaya, the enterprise would have to support itself; and only the Indian business community, commanding as it did the greater part of whatever stocks of goods and commodities the Japanese had not bought up or seized, could make this possible. Nor was it a trivial matter. By 1944 shortages of tobacco, matches, paper, salt, soap, medicines, machinery and hardware of every sort, were severe—and the shortage of cloth desperate.

In normal times Burma obtained these things half from India, the rest largely from England. The war, of course, had cut those suppliers off, but this did not disturb the Japanese. Conquest would make the whole of East and Southeast Asia their exclusive market. "So optimistic were the small businessmen of Osaka," writes Dorothy Guyot, "that they compiled a directory for Burma offering every type of goods from toothpaste to cement."[1] Hardly had it been printed, however, when shipping cement there, toothpaste, anything at all, became distinctly problematic. The Japanese navy had driven Britain's fleet out of the Bay of Bengal. From the Andaman and Nicobar Islands it patrolled the eastern reaches of those waters. It could not, however, clear the skies of planes launched from airfields in Bengal, or guarantee unconvoyed merchantmen against submarine attack. Naturally the British attempted both. As the months advanced they were more and more successful. At last the Japanese stopped sending anything to Rangoon by water except, as one Burmese lightly put it, "arms, ammunition, *sake*, and comfort women."[2]

So Burma was left with the Death Railway, winding 250 miles from Bangkok over the jungle-covered hills to Moulmein. In its middle portion, however, this triumph of improvisation and slave labor climbed grades so steep and crossed bridges so rickety that trains carried nothing like a normal tonnage and did well, one British POW remembers, to average eight miles an hour. Before long bombs were dropping on it, too. So not much went into its freight cars except war materiel and gasoline (the British, as they left, had blown up Burma's single refinery and wrecked the oil fields), while in Rangoon everything, even sugar, kerosene, and cooking oil, grew harder and harder to find. Nevertheless *some* stocks remained. They were mostly in the hands of Rangoon's Indian businessmen. And these Bose knew well how to tap. "Money and materials flowed into the Azad Hind Headquarters," wrote Ayer years later, "in an unending stream."[3]

Perhaps *unending* overstated the case. Indians, too, suffered from the shortages. As prices leapt upward, encouraged by the Japanese practice of printing money to finance military purchases, many grew reluctant to give and some refused to give at all. At the beginning, however, the response was generous; so generous that Yellappa was able to set up, in a bungalow just off Jamal Avenue, an Azad Hind Bank. Capitalized at several million rupees, it quickly became the preferred bank of deposit for the Indian community, and paymaster to Netaji's government and army.

Free Burma had nothing to equal this. But then, in few respects was Free Burma a match for *Azad Hind*. Proclaimed on the 1st of August, 1943, at a ceremony Bose attended, Free Burma bore all the marks of a full-fledged concern. It had an anthem. It had a flag, a dancing peacock upon a tricolor of yellow, green, and red. It had a head of state, Ba Maw, with the splendid if somewhat intimidating title of *Naing Gan Daw Adipadi*. And beneath the *Adipadi* there was a complete roster of ministers—no gaps in Ba Maw's list, nor did he wear several ministerial hats as Subhas Chandra was obliged to do. Nevertheless there was something missing, a lack of substance, an apparent absence of purpose, which was particularly noticeable when you set Free Burma next to Azad Hind in the city that housed them both. There, on their own home ground, the ministers of an independent and sovereign state of twenty-five million people, spread across an area the size of Texas, had less to do, and less to do it with, than a handful of men (and one woman) who were temporary visitors to the place, and who justified their presence by claiming to speak for a country hundreds of miles distant on whose soil not one of them had set foot for years.

Nowhere was the disparity greater than between the army of the visitors and the army of the hosts.

In the heady days of early 1942, when Aung San and his Burma Independence Army marched side by side with the Japanese, that army had been fully as large as Bose's present force, which now counted perhaps eleven thousand men in or en route to Burma, and in Malaya another twenty thousand training or waiting to be trained. The BIA, however, had not been large for long. Its mushroom-like growth, its freebooting ways, above all the openness with which it put Burma's interests ahead of Japan's, had surprised, nettled, and at last so thoroughly exasperated the Japanese that in July 1942 (it will be remembered) they cut the force back and renamed it the Burma Defence Army. It was the Burma Defence Army, three thousand men somewhat augmented by recruiting and still commanded by Aung San, that became, with August's independence, the Burma *National* Army.

But the Burma National Army grew slowly. With independence apparently secure, few men were eager to enlist. And the BNA had another and more serious problem. Its cadre, its most senior officers even, were almost without exception greenhorns. Very few had any prewar military experience. Aung San, now a major general (as well as Minister of Defence in Ba Maw's cabinet), had not so much as handled a rifle until the Japanese took him and the rest of the Thirty Comrades in hand. There had been no opportunity to acquire military experience, for the reason that British Burma had never possessed the equivalent of the Indian Army. It was, in fact, the *Indian* Army that had always defended and policed the place.

A few battalions, it is true, had eventually been raised in Burma itself. Their men, however, were not Burmese, as the people who speak the Burmese language and compose the majority community in Burma may for convenience sake be called. The Burmese, the British believed, were by nature rebellious. Arming them only made them more so. It was wiser to recruit Karens, who had preceded them on the lower Shan plateau, were not Buddhists as the Burmese were (many Karens were in fact Baptists), and did not get along with them. It was wiser to make sepoys of other minority peoples from the hills. And this the British did, with the consequence that on the eve of the Second World War Britain's Burma garrison consisted of a few battalions raised from these non-Burmese, and a few on loan from India. It was a force, observes John Furnivall with obvious disapproval (Furnivall was that rare bird, a colonial civil servant with genuine sympathy for the nationalist aspirations of the people he governed), "entirely distinct from the people, an instrument for the maintenance of internal security rather than for defence against aggression."[4] A force in which it was impossible for Burmese to learn the use of arms.

And now that Burma was free, the British rule of thumb—do not enlist Burmese, enlist others—had been simply and neatly reversed. Though one Karen with a Sandhurst commission was invited, and eventually enough Karen volunteers absorbed to form one under-strength battalion, in general the Burma National Army took no Karens; took no Shans, Kachins, or other such peoples; even Indians born and raised in Burma need not apply. A Burmese army for Burmese it must be. The consequence was that it had no core of veterans upon which to build, no Prem Sahgal to train it, no Shah Nawaz to model itself on. It had only the Japanese. And as the Japanese were more than willing to accept the assignment, Aung San's men went to school with Nippon as the men of the Indian National Army never were asked to do.

They wore Japanese uniforms, carried Japanese rifles, and drilled Japanese-style under the eye of NCOs who, if a trainee did not carry out an order smartly enough, slapped him hard across the face. Discipline was harsh, the Japanese holding with the general run of foreign opinion that Burmese men were intelligent and good-humored enough, but would do anything to avoid hard physical labor. Officer cadets (a military academy had been set up near the airfield) were required "to practice Zen, sitting erect in straight lines, so that they might acquire the spirit of Nippon."[5] And when the first class graduated, the top cadets were sent for further military education all the way to Japan.

When the second graduated, again the best went off. Aung San was ambitious. He wanted artillery, tanks, planes, the full panoply of arms and services, for which Japanese training ought to prepare his men. But though the Japanese took ten cadets for flight instruction, they had no intention of supplying the BNA with aircraft, or even with heavy weapons (they had none to spare). When Aung San's battalions completed their basic training, the Japanese did not group them in brigades or regiments. They scattered them at random. This was not because they distrusted Aung San, though they should have. It was because they did not consider his force, in spite of its training, a proper army, did not expect it to become a proper army, and in any case saw nothing particular for it to do.

The treatment was resented. In matters military the Burmese played second fiddle to nobody. They were a martial people. "Before she clashed with the British," observed U Tin Tut, the first Burmese to enter the Indian Civil Service, "Burma was herself an Empire."[6] The Burmese had, in fact, a talent for overrunning places.

As late as the middle of the eighteenth century, when the British were just beginning their effective conquest of India, the Burmese laid siege to the Thai capital at Ayudhaya, took it, and sacked it so thoroughly that when, later, the Thai set out to rebuild the place, they did so not on the original site but at Bangkok, forty miles away. At the start of the nineteenth century, by which time British command of the subcontinent had been established beyond reversal, the Burmese were making such successful forays to their north and west that it looked as if they actually meant to challenge the white man. Indeed, what precipitated the first of the Anglo-Burmese Wars, the war that broke out in 1824, was a well-founded British suspicion that if the Burmese were not checked, and checked promptly, they would soon invade Assam.

Nevertheless the Burmese were defeated. In the two wars that followed (the third and last occurred in 1885) they were defeated again, quite easily, and the whole of Burma annexed to British India. It was a terrible experience. And to people of U Tin Tut's generation, it was a living experience. In 1942, when Tin Tut wrote—from the Indian hill station of Simla where the Government of Burma had settled after escaping from Rangoon—men and women not much older than he remembered the lightning British advance up the Irrawaddy of fifty-seven years before (the third war was over in days), just as elderly Englishmen today remember the abdication of Edward VIII and elderly Americans the crash of the *Hindenburg*. Burmese raised in Mandalay perhaps even recalled the arrival of those battalions of red-coated giants, and watched again with the mind's eye as King Thibaw, "a tiny dignified figure, helpless, humiliated, and pale, riding on a common cart," was hustled away to exile and death on the coast below Bombay.[7]

"A Burmese child," Tin Tut continued, "is brought up on Burmese history and traditions which have as their background the ancient glories of the past, and it is with a shock that he realizes in his adolescence that he is a member of a subject race." Aung San was not much more than half Tin Tut's age when these lines were written. But it is reasonable to suppose that he, too, was brought up in this way and experienced this shock, perhaps when he went off to university, perhaps much earlier when he learned that his mother's uncle had died fighting the British.

Because for over a year Aung San and his Burma National Army lived side by side, and in apparent unity of purpose, with Bose and the Indian National Army, only to turn suddenly and execute an astonishing volte-face. Because this volte-face, shrewdly timed and artfully executed, made Aung San the hero of his country's independence movement. Because, finally, this behavior, with all that it implied, oddly left no mark upon Aung San's reputation, not even with the British, while Bose and his people have always labored under the reputation of being opportunists, unprincipled seizers of the main chance—for these reasons, and particularly the last, it is worth pausing for a moment to look more closely at this interesting young man, and at the Burmese who, like him, called themselves Thakins.

Thakin—it means lord, prince, master—is what the British in Burma were addressed by and expected to be addressed by, as in India they expected to be called *sahib*, and as schoolmasters everywhere expect to be called *sir*.

Exactly when certain Burmese of an irreverent turn of mind began to address each other thus is uncertain. Furnivall, teaching at the time at Rangoon University, remembers a freelance writer and student organizer named Ba Thoung coming into his office one morning in 1930 to announce that in future he must be addressed as Thakin Ba Thoung. Furnivall remembers laughing. But Ba Thoung and others persisted. The term, half mocking and half assertive, took. It became the sign and symbol of the young revolutionary patriot. It identified him. It identified his party. It even became part of his name. (This was made easy by Burma's way with names. Most Burmese have one or at most two, and though in middle age these are usually prefixed by the half-respectful, half-affectionate U or Daw, the package remains wonderfully, sometimes stupefyingly, short. For example Daw Khin Kyi, Aung San's wife. Or U Nu, of whom more shortly.) If Indian nationalists had done the same, we would speak now not of the Congress party but of the Sahib party, and glance with interest at each new biography of Sahib Jawaharlal Nehru as it appeared. But Indian nationalists did not do this. The tactic was peculiar to their cousins over the water.

Aung San probably met his first Thakin when he entered Rangoon University. This was in 1932. The university was young, and very British. "All the senior administrative and academic positions," writes the Burmese historian Maung Htin Aung, "were held by Englishmen, who as civil servants assumed an attitude of superiority over the students. All the wardens of the dormitories were English, and the sight of professors and their guests dining and dancing on the campus irked the students. In history classes the English professors belittled the achievements of the Burmese kings and tried to impress upon the students their view that the Burmese were indeed fortunate to be under British rule."[8]

Surely Furnivall did not stoop to such a thing. But he may have shared a determination common in young places, a determination to "keep up standards." High standards meant frequent academic failure. Half the students flunked by the end of the second year. With these somber odds in mind, the dutiful sons of ambitious parents committed themselves to the step-by-step accumulation, in accordance with the syllabus laid down for their particular course (Aung San read literature, modern history, and political science), of the things young Englishmen in England studied, things conveyed in English. At intervals they reproduced those things in three-hour examinations, again of course in English, examinations upon which alone their successful progress depended. Little of the material interested them or carried much meaning. Mastering the material, however, was the path to advancement, as it was in India. By it a few might hope to pass, as Tin Tut had, into the civil service.

Even the dutiful, however, were less than enthusiastic for this regimen. And there were rebels who, from the beginning, could not bear the overwhelming Britishness of the business, and expressed their resentment by wearing homespun and being ostentatiously crude. It was from university students of this sort that the first Thakins came. After a time they formed the Dobama Asi-ayone or "We the Burmese Association," opened an office, and began to behave like a party. Meanwhile Aung San, though still reading for his B.A., was developing talents and staking out positions that would take him to the front rank of politics as swiftly as Bose, and at an even tenderer age.

Two young men seemingly more dissimilar it would be hard to find. Bose was a cultivated person, born into a cultivated family. Aung San was neither. He came from the town of Natmauk, forty miles south of Mount Popa. His parents were respectable but without pretensions to more than small-town status. At Natmauk he might have remained all his life had not a streak of determination, private and inexplicable, taken him first to school at Yenangyaung, where English was taught, then to Rangoon University. At the university he lived in a style that Subhas Chandra would never have permitted himself.

"His room was always a mess," a friend wrote years later. "His bed was always unmade; the mosquito net hung lazily; and when he climbed into bed he would just draw it down, and that would be that."

He was careless of his dress. "Once he had put on a shirt or a *longyi*," a skirt-like garment much like the Malayan *sarong* and the south Indian *lungi*, "he would not take it off for days, . . . and we would have to literally force him to take a bath." He was careless of people, too. Abrupt. Unresponsive. If friends met him in a hallway or on the street, likely as not he would pass without a sign of recognition. But then one day—or perhaps one night, for he habitually worked at night, in this he *did* resemble Bose—he would suddenly drop in on them and talk. Talk on and on with growing animation, gesturing wildly, edging closer and closer to his listeners, until at last Bo Let Ya, whose recollections these are, would feel obliged to remind him of the priest "who did likewise in his preaching and eventually pushed his disciple into the well."[9]

Women were not necessarily put off by this behavior. Down with a fever shortly after the dissolution of the Burma Independence Army in mid-1942, Aung San fell in love with his nurse, courted her from his hospital bed, married her the moment he was able, and lived quietly with her right through the war, taking great delight in the children she bore him, obviously much upset when one died at birth.

Men, too, discovered humanity and simplicity beneath his now prickly, now inscrutable, exterior. An aide remembers the march north up the west bank of the Irrawaddy in April of this same 1942. "General Aung San's paraphernalia of office," writes the aide, "were simple. He had an American army binocular [*sic*] and an American style helmet made of pressed cardboard"—this must have been a helmet liner—"and one rather handsome Japanese officer's sword. He had few clothes; he had a Japanese-style green bush shirt and cotton breeches and some vests, towels," and a cotton *longyi*.[10] What he did not have on, he carried in a small bundle.

There is a photograph of him on this march north. He wears the bush shirt, open at the neck, and looks past the camera with a grave expression which, however, seems neither portentous nor put on for the occasion. He is short, small, boyish. A westerner might fix his age at twenty, though actually he is twenty-seven. He does not look like an important military or political figure, nor is there anything to suggest that he wishes he did. He could be anybody. Yet there is about him something intense and authoritative that would prevent you from dismissing him even if you did not know who he was. He certainly was not dismissed, by the Burmese or by the British either, during the Rangoon University strike of 1936. It was, in fact, Aung San who precipitated the strike.

The strike had its origin in the Student Union, a body part club and part debating society in the English manner, at whose meetings all the great issues of the day—Japan's designs on China, Mussolini's tweaking of the British lion's tail in the matter of Ethiopia, the prospects for true self-government in India and Burma—were raised, argued, and carried to a vote. Aung San was a member, and often on his feet. Three years back his maiden speech, delivered in stilted English, had provoked the sort of laughter that stops the ordinary person dead. But Aung San had refused to be silenced. In determination and one-pointedness he was fully Subhas Chandra's equal. He continued speaking, finished his speech, and in the years since made himself an effective orator, in English as well as in Burmese. Now, early in 1936, on the eve of the annual examinations, he had to decide whether as editor of *Oway*, the Union's journal, he would protect the identity of a student whose unsigned attack on the university bursar he had just printed.

The bursar was unpopular. He was also, which is interesting, Burmese. A graduate student named Nu (later he became U Nu) who happened to be the Union's president, had already criticized him savagely for one thing and another. The *Oway* piece, however, raised tempers more sharply because it did more than criticize. It slandered. The bursar, it declared, was no better than a hound on the loose. Women should beware of his deceptively avuncular attentions, men kick him back to the hell in which he had been whelped. And the piece was unsigned. Though the university authorities had already discovered who had written it, they called Aung San in and told him he must give them the name.

"They said," Aung San confided to a fellow student who twenty years later reproduced the conversation for a Rangoon weekly, "that they would not take action against me if only I would give them confirmation of what they already knew. My reply, of course, was that journalistic etiquette prevented me from revealing the identity of the author. I walked out from the room after saying that."[11]

One is reminded of young Subhas Chandra Bose leaving Principal James's office exactly twenty years earlier after refusing to say whether he had been one of the party that jumped Oaten at the notice board. Bose, of course, did more. He used the opportunity (or so he later believed) to rehearse the other grievances he and his classmates harbored. Aung San apparently kept silent, though his standing charge against the university was much what Subhas Chandra's had been: a course of study infused with the Britisher's conviction of his cultural superiority, and enforced through mechanisms the British alone controlled. But the outcome was the same. Bose had been sent down. So, now, was Aung San.

His expulsion followed Nu's, for the older man's public attack upon the bursar had not been forgotten. Nu, however, was reading law and would be allowed to sit for his examinations. Aung San, still in the B.A. course, would not. It was when word of Aung San's predicament got out that the university exploded. If the editor of the student journal was to be barred from the examination halls, no one else would enter either—there would be a general strike. Positioning themselves at the Shwe Dagon pagoda not far away, the students set about bringing the university to a standstill. It was bad enough that they managed, by blocking roads and building entrances, to force postponement of the scheduled examinations. When student representatives visited more than thirty high schools outside Rangoon and closed them too, the authorities gave way. Nu and Aung San were reinstated. The postponed examinations were held in June.

The strike set Aung San irreversibly upon a political career. Eighteen months later he followed Nu into the Dobama Asi-ayone. He became, that is, a Thakin. By this time normal political activity was possible, for the Burma Act of 1935, which took effect in 1937, had (besides separating Burma from India) provided for a prime minister responsible to a legislature. Ba Maw, a politician of some experience, was then prime minister. As his own party was small, he governed through a coalition. When his coalition fell apart, as coalitions will, he accepted the Thakins' invitation and formed one with them. It was called the Freedom Bloc. The name was not fortuitous. Rangoon followed Indian politics closely, the year was 1939, Bose and his Forward Bloc were on everybody's lips.

But whereas the Forward Bloc was an association of like-minded people, the Freedom Bloc was in many ways a union of opposites. Ba

Maw was in his forties. Most of the Thakins were half that age. Ba Maw was a past master of party tricks and maneuvers. The Thakins were novices, and couldn't care less. Ba Maw had studied in Europe and been admitted to the English bar. Most Thakins had never set foot outside Burma. Above all, Ba Maw as he grew older became more and more the actor, a man who strove less for ends than for effects; a man, too, who welcomed admirers above followers, and followers above colleagues—whereas the Thakins, though there were sharp divisions and disagreements among them, were nothing if not a band of equals, and did not believe that politics and revolution were simply a variety of theater art.

So the alliance was from the beginning at risk. It survived, nevertheless, perhaps because, in spite of his airs and manners, Ba Maw was as anxious as the Thakins to get the British out of Burma, perhaps because the leaders were arrested before the contradictions could tear the bloc apart. In the spring of 1940 several Thakins, Nu among them, were put in jail. In August, at the close of a political rally during which he declared that it was immaterial whether England or Germany won the war, Ba Maw followed them there. The same month Aung San left Rangoon on a freighter. As the general secretary of the Dobama Asiayone he was already under suspicion, and had in fact already been jailed briefly. He saw no profit in waiting to be jailed again. "The time had come to strike," he wrote later, "and I slipped out of the country— to Amoy in China—to search for contacts and aid in Burma's struggle for freedom."[12]

Like Bose, Aung San proposed to make England's peril his country's opportunity, and England's enemy his country's friend. India itself was one obvious prospect. Early in 1940 he had led a delegation to the Ramgarh session of the Indian National Congress, only to find that he could obtain nothing in that quarter beyond verbal encouragement. Japan was another matter. Japan moved to anticipate his overtures. Two months before Aung San boarded the freighter, Colonel Suzuki, the officer assigned to raise Burma against the Europeans, arrived in Rangoon. It was Suzuki who arranged to have Aung San met when he reached Amoy.

From that moment the Japanese connection crowded all other possibilities out. Early in 1941 Aung San slipped back to Rangoon.

There he set about recruiting Thakins for a Japanese-sponsored freedom force. As fast as the Japanese military attaché could arrange passage, off went the volunteers, until by April more than two dozen, Aung San among them, were training on the island of Hainan off China's south coast. In the autumn of 1941 they moved to Bangkok. On the 7th of December the Pacific war began. When the Japanese invaded Burma, the Thirty Comrades with Suzuki and Aung San at their head led the nucleus of the Burma Independence Army across the Thai-Burmese frontier.

In the tumult and excitement that followed, with young Burmese flocking to the freedom army and the British in full flight, Aung San might have proclaimed his country's independence. He did not. Perhaps he was unable to grasp what was happening. Perhaps, as he later said, he did not wish to act without some sort of constitutional authority. Ba Maw, meanwhile, escaped from his upcountry prison and hurried south. The Japanese were glad to see him. He was, after all, better known than any Thakin. In due course they put him at the head of a provisional government, leaving Aung San to command the stripped-down army. It was Ba Maw who on the 1st of August, 1943, became Free Burma's first head of state.

ﷺ

Ba Maw did not turn his back upon the Thakins. Thakin Nu became his foreign minister, Aung San handled defense, others held ministerial posts. But his relations with these young men were strained. Their very youthfulness irritated him. He preferred older and more polished types, of that class whose western dress and English speech had once provoked the jeering cry "dog collar, dog tongue." They for their part found his grandness of manner—taking the oath of office in royal language, announcing a general pardon for criminals such as ascending monarchs announce—unnecessary and repugnant. People had long remarked that on public occasions the *Adipadi* was given to extended flights of rhetoric, delivered as often as not in English. Prem believes that he was actually more at home in that language than he was in Burmese. For how long could the country endure a leader whose behavior was so lofty, whose contact with reality so slight?

The reality was that, independence or no, Burma's affairs remained very much Tokyo's business, as by the terms of a secret treaty they were supposed to be. The Japanese Army continued to run the railroads and river boats. It went right on conscripting labor for bridge and road repair, it went right on commandeering bullocks to haul its wagons (a serious matter, since without bullocks the peasants could not plow). Though the trappings of administration had passed to Ba Maw and his people, the workings remained with Nippon.

Once only did Ba Maw attempt something of substance. Late in 1942 he offered to provide labor for the building of the western portion of the Death Railway. Calling for volunteers, using compulsion when word of the working conditions seeped back and dried up the supply, his unhappy district officers managed to enroll tens of thousands of men and women in what began officially as the *chway tat* (Sweat Army), but became—the Burmese love puns, and this was a natural if macabre one—the *thway tat* (Death Army). Perhaps half of these recruits actually reached the rail line. Perhaps a quarter died. It was a disaster, and thereafter the *Adipadi* was content to let form substitute for content. "All the pieces were present for the game of government," Guyot observes. "The cabinet and the head of state deliberated and promulgated laws, the secretariat prepared an annual budget, and the district officials manned their posts."[13] But it was just that, a game, a going through the motions.

What was the use of annual budgets when tax revenues had shrunk to ten percent of their prewar value? And what were ministers to fill their days with—Foreign Minister Nu, for example? Nu had an office, secretaries, messengers, the lot. "If you wanted one of these secretaries," he remembered later, all you had to do was "tinkle the little bell on the office table. In comes the messenger and you tell him to call the secretary. The secretary enters and you explain what you want." Perhaps you want to send a telegram. To whom? Not to a foreign service officer. Burma has none. Probably to a government that is as much a client of the Axis as Burma herself. And to what purpose, this telegram? Perhaps to offer congratulations on the occasion of some absolutely inconsequential event. "We noted down in a calendar the national days of every country and the birthdays of statesmen and that kind of thing,"

Nu's recollection continues. It was for these that the wires went out. And they were numerous, "so numerous that before long the Foreign Office came to be known as the Telegraph Office."[14] After a while Nu left the tiresome business entirely to his secretaries. After a further while he asked to be relieved of his post.

The other ministers cannot have been much busier. Suppose one with something to communicate to Mandalay. It could go only by post (the Japanese monopolized the telephone system), and by 1944 the normal two-day delivery between Rangoon and Mandalay had stretched to two weeks—by 1945 it would stretch to four. What should he write it on? Paper was in such short supply that some ministries inscribed orders on the backs of old telegraph forms. For road transport only a few hundred trucks remained in Burmese hands, most of them in advanced stages of improvisation, cannibalization, and decay. You might encounter a Ford engine on a Chevrolet chassis behind a Dodge radiator grille, running on rice spirits, its crankcase filled with a mixture of peanut and old engine oil, its tires bound with wire. "These mongrel derelicts," remarked the Burmese who gave us the bit about *sake* and comfort women reaching Rangoon by sea, "would clank and rattle their way through the potholes of the main road, lurching, groaning, creaking, clanging . . . ."[15] Sometimes, "like obstinate beasts," they refused to move at all. Then the passengers, dozens "hanging from the fenders to the roof," got down. The driver unpacked his tools and his collection of worn or improvised parts, took a fortifying swig from a fuel can (the better grade of rice spirits, at eighteen rupees a gallon, was distilled twice and kicked like a mule), and went to work. An hour passed. The passengers collected, put their shoulders to the tail gate, and pushed. "A couple of explosions," a lurch forward, everybody scrambled aboard, and off they went—unless, of course, an Allied plane had spotted them and came down to strafe. As with all aspects of Burmese life, there was always the war to consider.

Always the war.

In one respect it had been good for Burma. It had swept the Raj away, and put in its place a framework of sovereignty which, with time and luck, the Burmese might fill out. But it had been destructive. As they retreated up the Irrawaddy, the British had torched and blown far more effectively than they had managed to do in Malaya. It had isolated

Burma. Neither toothpaste nor cement reached the country now, from Osaka or any other place. Above all, it was not finished, it was not even winding down. To judge by the Japanese merchant vessels that did not reach Rangoon, and the Allied bombers that did, the war resembled not a short, sharp summer shower, but one of those thunderstorms that, coming up unexpectedly in the middle of the afternoon, sends you running for cover; after a time seems, from the more distant flashes and diminishing growls, to be passing; then suddenly announces, with a darkening sky and a rush of rain, that it is with you again and means to hold you housebound right through the evening. So it was with the war, thought to be over, now blustering once more. It was this second round that set the Burmese and the Indians upon separate paths.

Previously the British had been the enemy, for Aung San's people as much as for Netaji's. And since they still occupied the Indian subcontinent, for the Indians the British still were. It was *they* who must be made to leave.

To the Burmese, however, matters were no longer so clear. Leaving aside the obvious hollowness of independence Japanese-style, there was a great deal to resent in the people who currently held the country. The unthinking intensity with which they went about replacing English not with Burmese but with their own language. Their habitual recourse to physical violence. "It is difficult for the Burmese people," wrote a Burmese woman who passed the war years in Rangoon, "to see any culture in the habit of face slapping. The lowest menial will suffer his entire wages to be cut rather than suffer to have any hand laid on him for punishment."[16] Their shameless vulgarity, bathing naked at village wells, lifting a girl's skirt to see whether she had the required cholera inoculation marks on her buttocks. When the Burmese asked themselves who were their occupiers now, they could hardly help admitting that it was the Japanese.

But as time went by it became equally difficult not to see that those previous occupiers the British, no less resented in their day, showed signs of wishing to return. At some point they would probably make the attempt. If they did, what should the patriot do, caught as he would be between two sets of foreigners, between the British and the Japanese? Surely the only hope was to play one against the other, as before. But how did this rid you of both?

It was a dilemma, but one from which, if the business was carefully managed, there might be an escape. Much later, when the war was over and independence safely in sight, Aung San maintained that he had seen as early as the summer of 1942 what that escape might be. Perhaps he had. He was certainly toying with a course of action by the summer of 1943. He had certainly shared his thoughts with others, and effectively committed himself, by the start of the following year.

These others were Thakins like himself, but Thakins who had Marxist leanings, and belonged (as Aung San himself once had) to Burma's little Communist Party. Hitler's invasion of Russia in the early summer of 1941 had obliged them, as it obliged good Party members everywhere, to perform an ideological somersault and come down on the Allied side. This accomplished, they pushed Aung San in a direction he was for other reasons already inclined to take. They were in contact, these Thakins, with Force 136, the Southeast Asia arm of Special Operations Executive, Britain's wartime undercover agency. It was the business of Force 136 to find, arm, and direct underground groups against the Japanese. With its help Thakins slipped back and forth between Burma and India, feeding the Indian government with rumors of growing disaffection at home, doing what they could to make the rumors fact. Some of the rumors were wild. One held that Aung San's state of mind worried the Japanese so much they wouldn't let him near his men except at parades, and even that "presents some difficulties, as from being a very temperate young man he is now almost continuously drunk. . . ."[17] The rumors' drift was accurate enough. Aung San's disaffection was real though his tippling was not. By early 1944 New Delhi knew that if the reconquest of Burma were seriously undertaken, the Burma National Army would at some moment hand the Japanese a surprise.

Ba Maw had some sense of what was going on. With Thakins all about him, he could hardly fail to. But though some Burmese now called him not *Adipadi* but *Mati-tati,* meaning "neither one thing or the other," and thought him a likely prey to any breeze that blew, in this matter he steered a straight and resolutely neutral course. He would not aid those who plotted against his friends the Japanese. Neither would he betray them. The Indians, too, suspected that something was up. Prem remembers Aung San coming to see the Supreme Commander

one evening early in 1944; remembers the two closeted together for
several hours; remembers feeling, as Aung San left, that all was not
right. Later he decided that Aung San had as good as told Netaji that he
would eventually change sides.

In a way this was too bad. Bose liked the Burmese. He remembered them from his stay in Mandalay Jail. "They are exceedingly
warm-hearted, frank, and jovial in their temperament," he had written,
adding that if they had a fault, "it is their extreme naivete and"—here
he misjudged them—"[the] absence of all feeling against foreigners."[18]
Lakshmi liked their women (the men she could do without), they were
so cheerful, hardworking, and efficient. But she could not forget, nor
could others, what she had heard about the riots of a few years back in
which so many Indians had been killed. So a reserve, a coolness almost,
lay between hosts and guests, between Burmese and Indians. The
formalities were observed. There were conversations at staff level.
Pictures appeared of Burmese and Indian officers bending earnestly
over maps and papers, and Ba Maw, who liked to make speeches, seized
every opportunity to hail "the new Asiatic unity in action." Nevertheless, there was no disguising the fact that the two armies followed
different paths.

The one was small, going nowhere, and outwardly intent upon
nothing. All that even Ba Maw could say of it was that in the event of
renewed fighting, it would ever be found "zealously protecting the vital
rear. . . ." The other was large, going somewhere, and unmistakably
intent upon something: in Ba Maw's words again, "the liberation of its
motherland."[19] And if in fact appearances were deceptive; if Aung San
and his men were even then plotting a great patriotic stroke of their
own; why, though Netaji perhaps knew what was coming, his officers
only half suspected, and had neither time nor inclination to worry their
heads about it. So busy were they with preparations for pushing across
the border into India and raising there a second, and this time
irresistible, Quit India rebellion.

<hr />

Among the preparations for the push was the establishing of good
relations with the Japanese, who of course would be very much part of
the enterprise. These relations were to be conducted through an agency

or *kikan* no longer denoted, as Fujiwara's had been, by its chief, but called instead *hikari*. The word was promising. *Hikari* translates "light from the east". The chief's rank was high, suggesting serious official recognition. Nevertheless, the proper rapport did not come easily, for Burma Area Army was reluctant to treat a few thousand Indians as an equal allied force.

There was nothing new about such reluctance. In Malaya, Bose had faced and only partly overcome it. Now, with the prospect of actually entering India, came a fresh worry. Suppose the Japanese behaved as though they owned the subcontinent? Shah Nawaz had been so conscious of this possibility that before bringing his men up from Malaya he had lectured them on the subject; lectured them to such effect that two years later, at the trial in which he stood charged with being no better than Nippon's creature, a veteran of the Subhas Brigade, one Dilasa Khan, was able to reproduce, uninvited and with a touching eloquence, the gist of what he had said.

> When we reach India [Shah Nawaz warned them] we shall meet Indian men and women. And those among the latter who are elders to us, we should consider them as our mothers; and those who are younger, we should consider them as our daughters and sisters. And if anybody will not obey these instructions, he will be shot dead. And if and when India is freed, and the Japanese who are now helping us try to subdue us, we shall fight them. He also said that even now, if a Japanese gives you one slap, you should give him three in return; because our Government is parallel to the Japanese Government, and we are in no way subservient to them. And that when we reach India, if we notice any Japanese maltreating an Indian lady, he should first be warned by word of mouth not to do so, but if he continues to do so, we are at liberty to use force and even shoot him in order to prevent it. Because the fight which we are making now is for the freedom and well-being of India, and not for the benefit of the Japanese.[20]

Thus Shah Nawaz to his men. But some matters could not be settled by a simple exhortation of this kind.

Should the Indian National Army march as one independent body, or let itself be broken into small parties attached to the Japanese? When the allies stood upon Indian soil, with whom should the administration of the liberated territory lie? If the Indians were to operate under Japanese direction, as must probably be the case, should they be subject to Japanese military law? What about saluting? Though a senior would expect a junior to initiate the courtesy, between officers of equal rank should it be, as the Japanese argued, the Indian who saluted first?

To these questions Bose brought not only serious prior thought—Abid Hasan says that during the voyage from Germany he had reviewed every possible difficulty—but the confidence, assertiveness, and attention to protocol that years before, in Calcutta, had forced Chief Engineer Coates to extinguish his cigarette and slip quietly off the office table. Particularly the attention to protocol. Prem remembers that when Lt. General Kawabe Masakazu, commanding Burma Area Army, reached Rangoon and asked Netaji to dine, Netaji declined. *"He hasn't called on me,"* he said, *"and until he calls on me, I will not attend his dinner party."*

But Bose did more than anticipate the reality of equal treatment by insisting on its form. He went over the *Hikari Kikan*'s head to the commanding generals in the area—to Kawabe; to Kawabe's subordinate, Lt. General Mutaguchi Renya of 15th Army; to Kawabe's superior, Field Marshal Terauchi Hisaichi of Southern Army. And he brandished his Tokyo connections, made the previous June and reinforced in November. If in the course of some prolonged and heated discussion the *Kikan* intimated that it might be compelled to consult Tokyo (which would undoubtedly rule its way), Bose would offer to test the proposition. Go right ahead, he would say. I for my part will cable Army Chief of Staff Sugiyama, get in touch with Foreign Minister Shigemitsu, have a word with Tojo himself. And he would mean it. Perhaps he actually did cable. More likely the threat was enough. *I saw some of the correspondence of these people with him*, Prem says, *and one felt that they held him in tremendously high esteem.*

The result was that Bose pretty well had his way. It was agreed that, special groups aside, the *Azad Hind Fauj* would operate in formations of never less than battalion size. It was agreed that liberated territory would be handed over to its civil arm, the *Azad Hind Dal.* (This "Free India Organization," as it is perhaps best translated, was supposed to give liberated Assam, Bengal, and beyond temporary civil administration. A school to train personnel for it had been opened in Singapore. As, however, there was no time to wait for its graduates, volunteers were hastily recruited right in Rangoon.) Kawabe was not so easily shifted in the matter of military law. All the local armies allied with Nippon, he pointed out, the Nanking army, the Thai army, the Burma National Army, accepted Japanese military law. But Bose found the prospect intolerable. It meant surrendering uniformed Indians to the tender mercies of the *Kempeitai*. The INA had its own Army Act and its own military police. These must suffice. And in the end Kawabe gave way. He even agreed that when Japanese and Indian officers of equal rank met, neither would wait, they would salute together.

But patience—Ayer says that if the Japanese came prepared for a two-hour conference, Bose was ready to sit for three—a commanding presence, and friends in high places, could not move the *Hikari Kikan* in matters of supply. Only through the *Kikan* had the INA access to Japanese dumps and godowns. And getting the *Kikan* to approve requisitions took a good deal of arguing.

Sometimes an argument had its light side—as when the Japanese supposed the Indians to be demanding comfort girls by the hundreds when all they actually wanted was a supply of those individual sewing kits known in British military parlance as "housewives." Other encounters were less amusing. *You see*, explains Prem, *they had nothing laid down who the liaison should be with. You used to go to the Hikari Kikan and somebody would appear, maybe Kitabe, maybe somebody else.* (Colonel Kitabe was of that breed of Japanese officer, found particularly in the Manchurian Army, who subordinated everyone and everything to Nippon's interests and cared not a fig who knew it. At INA Headquarters they called him "Pustak", a simple pun, *kitab* and *pustak* both mean book. But there was little affection in it.) *Then they'd listen to you and say they'd think about it. But never a commitment. And I used to think, for God's sake tell me whether you're going to do it or not.*

Perhaps the *Kikan*, too, sometimes swore softly to itself. Months before Prem reached Rangoon, British intelligence picked up a little Japanese handbook that made no bones about the trouble to be expected when dealing with Indians. Not that it began in this vein. Its purpose (in the words of the intelligence translation) was to tell Japanese soldiers how they should "feel and act" when they encoun-

Second Arakan Debacle Imminent," screamed *Greater Asia*
ry 8. "General Offensive In Arakan Heightens," it announced
ly on the 10th. Over the days that followed the curious
reader who paid his 20 cents and bought the paper
that the enemy was being forced inexorably into the jaws of
p." And then one evening, as Prem sat talking with Netaji in
me Commander's bungalow, several Japanese staff officers
and told them that what the Rangoon reader had been led to
is indeed the case. The trap had closed on two divisions.
he 5th Indian, was commanded by a man named Briggs.
embered him well. *Don't be too confident,* he warned the
Ie's from my regiment, I know the kind of chap he is. Old Briggs
t. And presently Briggs did. To be exact, he refused to move
all force got astride his line of communication, and at the
days smashed the roadblock it had planted. But Messervy's
Division, five miles away on the east side of the Mayu
was not so lucky. Parts of it, with division headquarters, a
mulation of stores, and Messervy himself, were trapped in an
an a mile square and besieged there. And though the siege
a after an epic struggle known to aficionados of the Burma
s the Battle of the Administrative Box, even the British did
consider their victory decisive. While the Japanese, though
ed, were content to have drawn British attention (and men)
igh country west of the Chindwin where they planned to
r really serious blow.
-March, Rangoon's attention shifted there. On the 14th
carried word of heavy fighting at Fort White and Tiddim.
later it reported an assault by "a vanguard of the Indian
rmy in close collaboration with a Nippon unit" upon a
ition east of Tongzang. Two days later still it announced the
gzang. And on March 23, under the headline "Victorious
ional Army Enters India," there was a long account, with
f a press conference at which Subhas Chandra Bose,
ly uniformed, behind him senior members of his govern-
taff (Prem among them, Lakshmi of course not), declared
ad Hind Fauj stood at last upon Indian soil.

tered the "Indian National Army." Acknowledge these Indians to be
"not by any means a fifth column of the Japanese Army," the handbook
advised, nor a convenient source of coolie labor, but men "fighting for
the independence of their motherland, fighting our common enemy
with a common purpose"—true allies, in a word. That was the lesson.
But a caution accompanied it. "Years of oppression, deceit, and
exploitation at the hands of the British" have given Indians qualities of
mind and patterns of behavior that make them "very difficult to
handle." It would be well to recognize this at the start. And shortly the
handbook ceased to give instruction in the virtues of Nippon's Indian
allies and became a catalogue of their failings.[21]

Their touchiness. Do not strike an Indian. "One blow will destroy
years of kindness, and the ear will not incline our way a second time."
Their readiness to entertain suspicions. "Do not tell lies. They have
extremely good memories. They remember who said what, and when,
and where, and having labored under British lies for so many years are
extremely shrewd at discerning them." Their inability to accept
disappointment in even the littlest thing. "For instance, they think they
are entitled to a fixed ration of all kinds, and if owing to difficulties of
supply we ourselves do not get a meal but supply them theirs, they will
not be happy if it is not full scale. Rather will they insist on their right
to the amount deficient."

And when this happens, "anger is futile. It is equally futile to think
that they will be grateful for any trouble we may take to look after
them. If we do them a kindness, they will not think of it as a kindness.
They are quite fixed in this line of thought."

Did the staff of the *Kikan's* Rangoon office keep a copy of this
handbook handy, for comfort when a round was over, for courage
when a round was about to begin? Prem noticed that often they came
out fighting, and eventually adopted the tactic himself. *I'd think of some
trouble between our men and theirs, where theirs were to blame. I'd draw their
attention to it, start talking about it, do my damnest to put them in the wrong.
And then, when they'd softened a little, I'd turn around and say, "what about
a couple of wireless sets, what about kerosene for the cook stoves, what about
this, what about that?" And it worked.* Well, sometimes.

There were all sorts of deficiencies. Much of the rifle ammunition
had lain in the open for months. Prem remembers corroded .303

rounds spilling out of disintegrating boxes. A field ration was needed. With the help of a Burmese woman who had professional training in nutrition, he and Lakshmi set about devising a mixture of powdered fish, tamarind, pepper, salt, and dal for sprinkling on boiled rice. But they did not have the time or the means for producing it in quantity, so it could not be issued to the troops. Clothing, too, was a problem. Even at Burma's latitude, men who expect to live and fight at five or six thousand feet must have woolens. Bose's jawans had none. Even their blankets were miserable cotton things. The renegade army, remarked a British intelligence report in a tone of some astonishment, "marched blithely into the Imphal campaign wearing K.D. [khaki drill] shorts."[22]

But none of this bothered Prem, Shah Nawaz, or anyone else. For if the men of the INA were ill supplied with this and utterly without the other, they were nevertheless, thanks to what they had brought with them from Malaya, what the *Hikari Kikan* had provided, and what Rangoon's Indian community had dug up, a good deal better off than their opposite numbers in Aung San's command. Besides, they didn't need much. The *Azad Hind Fauj* was a guerrilla force. It would travel fast and light, and when it reached India help itself from what the men called, with a smile, "the Churchill supply."

So Shah Nawaz and the three battalions of Subhas Brigade (as the 1st Guerrilla Regiment was usually called) got ready to leave. On the 3rd of February they passed in review and stood at ease while Bose spoke. They were the vanguard of a great and desperate enterprise, he told them, an enterprise that would end when they stood before the Red Fort and free India's flag flew over the Viceregal Palace. Bose spoke for some time. When he had finished, Lakshmi saw Shah Nawaz come up and salute. *He was very emotional,* she relates. *The tears were streaming down his cheeks. He told Netaji he was going, and that his only hope was that he would be victorious or die on the field of battle..* Then the battalions moved off to board troop trains, at a suburban station because bombing had knocked Rangoon's main station out. The march to Delhi had begun.

In Rangoon, as the three battalions of the 2nd (Gandhi) Regiment started to arrive from Malaya—with the 3rd (Azad) and the 4th (Nehru), these three regiments would make up Zaman Kiani's 1st

Division—All India Radio brought wife, had died in the Poona prison to been confined since 1942. Bose wa Lakshmi explained to me, *there might cal about it. But everyone loved Kasturbh to him, but she used to tell us, "you can an* next broadcast to India was made witl too. For the first time she did not ha went directly on the air.

Early in March she flew to Singap *on the floor, looking down through some did not mind the position, it must h Japanese with their long swords clanking swords.* It was ten weeks since she h training camp, and she was pleased to fighting unit, another hundred in the under way to send the first party to B and file, fifteen nurses. The eight, Jar receive their commissions at a passin month. Meanwhile Lakshmi collecte necessaries. From Burma came rum crossed the border—but not in the Ara that the great Japanese offensive had b

A year earlier the British, inching had been given a severe drubbing in t swamp, tidal creeks, and knife-edge however, rebuilt their forces, and pr Christmas they were once more astrid sea on one side, the Mayu River on dagger towards Akyab at the Mayu expectation that they could be surpris or forced at the very least to use up al Japanese division, moving rapidly but s and the terrain, sliced into their flanl Brigade paraded for departure.

Success was swift, and in Rangoon language press made it as swiftly publi

Offensi on Febr more s Rangoc discover a "steel the Su walked believe, On Prem r Japanese *will slip* when a end of 7th Inc Peninsu large ac area les was bro campaig not at 1 disappc from th deliver In *Greater* Two d. Nation. British fall of Indian picture immac ment a that th

Just where his men had crossed he did not say. Possibly he did not know. Lacking proper signals equipment of their own, INA units communicated with Rangoon through the Japanese—who transmitted what and as they pleased.

A few days later, however, two Japanese Army press corps men filed a story that seemed to fix the place. The two had accompanied a column of Japanese and Indian troops that marched for days across hills and valleys, dark blue mountains in the distance, until at last they came upon "an open line running from south to north," a line passing through thick stands of teak. At one place stood a white pole "pointing to the sky against the sparkling stars." This was the frontier. The sight was moving. "Is there anyone," wrote the press corps men, "who would not be moved when they see the Indian soil for the first time?" Looking about, they could discover no sign of the enemy, nothing "except a torn Union Jack stained with mud," and some cigarettes "wrapped not with tin foil but paper." Apparently the British had decamped in a hurry. Cigarettes wrapped in paper meant that they were short of tin, "a vital material for war." And as they continued their tale, the two Japanese remarked that all this had taken place west of the Kabaw Valley, on the approaches to "the Manipur basin."[23]

✣

The Manipur basin, then a pleasant spread of villages set among plantain, bamboo, and rice paddy on a plain perhaps forty miles long and twenty miles wide, lies just west of Burma's border with India at the point where the Chin Hills give way to the more northerly Naga Hills. The basin itself is several thousand feet above sea level. As the ground around, however, rises a good deal higher, and in the rainy season particularly is very difficult to cross, the Manipuris kept—and still keep—much to themselves.

In 1944 rough tracks, which the British had tried to make passable for motor vehicles, led west from Imphal, the basin's chief town, to Silchar and lower Assam; south through Tongzang, Tiddim, and Fort White to Kalewa on the Chindwin; southeast through Tamu to the Kabaw Valley; and north to Kohima, beyond which lies the upper valley of the Brahmaputra and the meter gauge rail line. When in 1942 the

British withdrew from Burma (if fled is not the better word), it was along these tracks, particularly the Tamu-Manipur track, they largely moved. Once into the mountains, however, they went no farther. They held on to Imphal, and to the basin about it. Now, early in 1944, they were under attack there.

And as March passed into April it seemed to Indians in Rangoon that the attack must be succeeding. Day after day the news filtering down from the north was good, names of places approached, names of places taken, and as the ring closed about the Manipur basin, other names recited not once but again and again. For there were several British divisions inside the ring. Trapped, they fought bitterly—that was why certain names were so often repeated. "Desperate Resistance Being Shattered," cried *Greater Asia.* "Preparations to Storm Imphal Completed," it added. "Confusion in Enemy's Camp." Then, breathlessly, as if the composer had been unable to finish his thought, "Last Stronghold Now Only A Stone's Throw." From Malaya, where he was obliged as *Azad Hind*'s regional director of publicity to keep tabs on what his Japanese opposites were doing, Sivaram discovered that all across East Asia, in Bangkok, Manila, Shanghai, Tokyo, newspapers trumpeted the same exhilarating messages.

On occasion something of a purveyor himself, Sivaram had rather an eye for hype. About this time he spotted a photograph purporting to show soldiers of the Indian National Army entering a Manipur village carrying a large portrait of Bose. The picture appeared in several newspapers published by the Indian Independence League. Singapore readers promptly protested that the scene wasn't a Manipur village at all, but a lane in the Bukit Timah area of their city. Quietly Sivaram made inquiries at the local office of the *Hikari Kikan.* There had been a mix-up, the *Kikan* said. The photograph should not have appeared. It and others like it "were meant for distribution in territories other than Singapore and Malaya."[24]

One suspects Sivaram was not happy with this explanation. Still, most of what the news managers were producing seemed solid enough. He could check it against what All India Radio and the BBC were saying. They said that Britain's forces faced a serious test at Imphal. They made no reference to *Indians*, they talked only of the Japanese, but that could be explained. It was the censor's hand. Neither Delhi tered the "Indian National Army." Acknowledge these Indians to be "not by any means a fifth column of the Japanese Army," the handbook advised, nor a convenient source of coolie labor, but men "fighting for the independence of their motherland, fighting our common enemy with a common purpose"—true allies, in a word. That was the lesson. But a caution accompanied it. "Years of oppression, deceit, and exploitation at the hands of the British" have given Indians qualities of mind and patterns of behavior that make them "very difficult to handle." It would be well to recognize this at the start. And shortly the handbook ceased to give instruction in the virtues of Nippon's Indian allies and became a catalogue of their failings.[21]

Their touchiness. Do not strike an Indian. "One blow will destroy years of kindness, and the ear will not incline our way a second time." Their readiness to entertain suspicions. "Do not tell lies. They have extremely good memories. They remember who said what, and when, and where, and having labored under British lies for so many years are extremely shrewd at discerning them." Their inability to accept disappointment in even the littlest thing. "For instance, they think they are entitled to a fixed ration of all kinds, and if owing to difficulties of supply we ourselves do not get a meal but supply them theirs, they will not be happy if it is not full scale. Rather will they insist on their right to the amount deficient."

And when this happens, "anger is futile. It is equally futile to think that they will be grateful for any trouble we may take to look after them. If we do them a kindness, they will not think of it as a kindness. They are quite fixed in this line of thought."

Did the staff of the *Kikan's* Rangoon office keep a copy of this handbook handy, for comfort when a round was over, for courage when a round was about to begin? Prem noticed that often they came out fighting, and eventually adopted the tactic himself. *I'd think of some trouble between our men and theirs, where theirs were to blame. I'd draw their attention to it, start talking about it, do my damnest to put them in the wrong. And then, when they'd softened a little, I'd turn around and say, "what about a couple of wireless sets, what about kerosene for the cook stoves, what about this, what about that?" And it worked.* Well, sometimes.

There were all sorts of deficiencies. Much of the rifle ammunition had lain in the open for months. Prem remembers corroded .303

rounds spilling out of disintegrating boxes. A field ration was needed. With the help of a Burmese woman who had professional training in nutrition, he and Lakshmi set about devising a mixture of powdered fish, tamarind, pepper, salt, and dal for sprinkling on boiled rice. But they did not have the time or the means for producing it in quantity, so it could not be issued to the troops. Clothing, too, was a problem. Even at Burma's latitude, men who expect to live and fight at five or six thousand feet must have woolens. Bose's jawans had none. Even their blankets were miserable cotton things. The renegade army, remarked a British intelligence report in a tone of some astonishment, "marched blithely into the Imphal campaign wearing K.D. [khaki drill] shorts."[22]

But none of this bothered Prem, Shah Nawaz, or anyone else. For if the men of the INA were ill supplied with this and utterly without the other, they were nevertheless, thanks to what they had brought with them from Malaya, what the *Hikari Kikan* had provided, and what Rangoon's Indian community had dug up, a good deal better off than their opposite numbers in Aung San's command. Besides, they didn't need much. The *Azad Hind Fauj* was a guerrilla force. It would travel fast and light, and when it reached India help itself from what the men called, with a smile, "the Churchill supply."

So Shah Nawaz and the three battalions of Subhas Brigade (as the 1st Guerrilla Regiment was usually called) got ready to leave. On the 3rd of February they passed in review and stood at ease while Bose spoke. They were the vanguard of a great and desperate enterprise, he told them, an enterprise that would end when they stood before the Red Fort and free India's flag flew over the Viceregal Palace. Bose spoke for some time. When he had finished, Lakshmi saw Shah Nawaz come up and salute. *He was very emotional,* she relates. *The tears were streaming down his cheeks. He told Netaji he was going, and that his only hope was that he would be victorious or die on the field of battle.*. Then the battalions moved off to board troop trains, at a suburban station because bombing had knocked Rangoon's main station out. The march to Delhi had begun.

⸺

In Rangoon, as the three battalions of the 2nd (Gandhi) Regiment started to arrive from Malaya—with the 3rd (Azad) and the 4th (Nehru), these three regiments would make up Zaman Kiani's 1st

Division—All India Radio brought word that Kasturbhai, Gandhi's wife, had died in the Poona prison to which she and the Mahatma had been confined since 1942. Bose was upset. *If it had been Gandhiji,* Lakshmi explained to me, *there might have been something, well, hypocritical about it. But everyone loved Kasturbhai. You know, she could not stand up to him, but she used to tell us, "you can and you must."* So Subhas Chandra's next broadcast to India was made with unusual feeling. Lakshmi spoke too. For the first time she did not have to pass her text by Ayer, she went directly on the air.

Early in March she flew to Singapore in a Japanese bomber. *You sat on the floor, looking down through some sort of thick glass,* and though she did not mind the position, *it must have been very uncomfortable for the Japanese with their long swords clanking all over the place. They always wore swords.* It was ten weeks since she had last seen her Rani of Jhansi training camp, and she was pleased to find four hundred women in the fighting unit, another hundred in the nursing wing, and preparations under way to send the first party to Burma: eight officers, eighty rank and file, fifteen nurses. The eight, Janaki Davar among them, would receive their commissions at a passing-out parade at the end of the month. Meanwhile Lakshmi collected clothing, footware, and other necessaries. From Burma came rumors that the freedom army had crossed the border—but not in the Arakan, though it was in the Arakan that the great Japanese offensive had begun.

A year earlier the British, inching down the coast from Chittagong, had been given a severe drubbing in that miserable country all jungle, swamp, tidal creeks, and knife-edge ridges. They had recovered, however, rebuilt their forces, and prepared for a fresh advance. By Christmas they were once more astride the Mayu Peninsula which, the sea on one side, the Mayu River on the other, points south like a dagger towards Akyab at the Mayu's mouth. And it was in the expectation that they could be surprised and destroyed a second time, or forced at the very least to use up all their reserves, that parts of one Japanese division, moving rapidly but stealthily under cover of darkness and the terrain, sliced into their flank only a few days after Subhas Brigade paraded for departure.

Success was swift, and in Rangoon the Japanese-sponsored English language press made it as swiftly public. "Nippon Forces Launch Bold

Offensive, Second Arakan Debacle Imminent," screamed *Greater Asia* on February 8. "General Offensive In Arakan Heightens," it announced more softly on the 10th. Over the days that followed the curious Rangoon reader who paid his 20 cents and bought the paper discovered that the enemy was being forced inexorably into the jaws of a "steel trap." And then one evening, as Prem sat talking with Netaji in the Supreme Commander's bungalow, several Japanese staff officers walked in and told them that what the Rangoon reader had been led to believe, was indeed the case. The trap had closed on two divisions.

One, the 5th Indian, was commanded by a man named Briggs. Prem remembered him well. *Don't be too confident,* he warned the Japanese. *He's from my regiment, I know the kind of chap he is. Old Briggs will slip out.* And presently Briggs did. To be exact, he refused to move when a small force got astride his line of communication, and at the end of two days smashed the roadblock it had planted. But Messervy's 7th Indian Division, five miles away on the east side of the Mayu Peninsula, was not so lucky. Parts of it, with division headquarters, a large accumulation of stores, and Messervy himself, were trapped in an area less than a mile square and besieged there. And though the siege was broken after an epic struggle known to aficionados of the Burma campaign as the Battle of the Administrative Box, even the British did not at first consider their victory decisive. While the Japanese, though disappointed, were content to have drawn British attention (and men) from the high country west of the Chindwin where they planned to deliver their really serious blow.

In mid-March, Rangoon's attention shifted there. On the 14th *Greater Asia* carried word of heavy fighting at Fort White and Tiddim. Two days later it reported an assault by "a vanguard of the Indian National Army in close collaboration with a Nippon unit" upon a British position east of Tongzang. Two days later still it announced the fall of Tongzang. And on March 23, under the headline "Victorious Indian National Army Enters India," there was a long account, with pictures, of a press conference at which Subhas Chandra Bose, immaculately uniformed, behind him senior members of his govern-ment and staff (Prem among them, Lakshmi of course not), declared that the *Azad Hind Fauj* stood at last upon Indian soil.

Just where his men had crossed he did not say. Possibly he did not know. Lacking proper signals equipment of their own, INA units communicated with Rangoon through the Japanese—who transmitted what and as they pleased.

A few days later, however, two Japanese Army press corps men filed a story that seemed to fix the place. The two had accompanied a column of Japanese and Indian troops that marched for days across hills and valleys, dark blue mountains in the distance, until at last they came upon "an open line running from south to north," a line passing through thick stands of teak. At one place stood a white pole "pointing to the sky against the sparkling stars." This was the frontier. The sight was moving. "Is there anyone," wrote the press corps men, "who would not be moved when they see the Indian soil for the first time?" Looking about, they could discover no sign of the enemy, nothing "except a torn Union Jack stained with mud," and some cigarettes "wrapped not with tin foil but paper." Apparently the British had decamped in a hurry. Cigarettes wrapped in paper meant that they were short of tin, "a vital material for war." And as they continued their tale, the two Japanese remarked that all this had taken place west of the Kabaw Valley, on the approaches to "the Manipur basin."[23]

❧

The Manipur basin, then a pleasant spread of villages set among plantain, bamboo, and rice paddy on a plain perhaps forty miles long and twenty miles wide, lies just west of Burma's border with India at the point where the Chin Hills give way to the more northerly Naga Hills. The basin itself is several thousand feet above sea level. As the ground around, however, rises a good deal higher, and in the rainy season particularly is very difficult to cross, the Manipuris kept—and still keep—much to themselves.

In 1944 rough tracks, which the British had tried to make passable for motor vehicles, led west from Imphal, the basin's chief town, to Silchar and lower Assam; south through Tongzang, Tiddim, and Fort White to Kalewa on the Chindwin; southeast through Tamu to the Kabaw Valley; and north to Kohima, beyond which lies the upper valley of the Brahmaputra and the meter gauge rail line. When in 1942 the

British withdrew from Burma (if fled is not the better word), it was along these tracks, particularly the Tamu-Manipur track, they largely moved. Once into the mountains, however, they went no farther. They held on to Imphal, and to the basin about it. Now, early in 1944, they were under attack there.

And as March passed into April it seemed to Indians in Rangoon that the attack must be succeeding. Day after day the news filtering down from the north was good, names of places approached, names of places taken, and as the ring closed about the Manipur basin, other names recited not once but again and again. For there were several British divisions inside the ring. Trapped, they fought bitterly—that was why certain names were so often repeated. "Desperate Resistance Being Shattered," cried *Greater Asia*. "Preparations to Storm Imphal Completed," it added. "Confusion in Enemy's Camp." Then, breathlessly, as if the composer had been unable to finish his thought, "Last Stronghold Now Only A Stone's Throw." From Malaya, where he was obliged as *Azad Hind*'s regional director of publicity to keep tabs on what his Japanese opposites were doing, Sivaram discovered that all across East Asia, in Bangkok, Manila, Shanghai, Tokyo, newspapers trumpeted the same exhilarating messages.

On occasion something of a purveyor himself, Sivaram had rather an eye for hype. About this time he spotted a photograph purporting to show soldiers of the Indian National Army entering a Manipur village carrying a large portrait of Bose. The picture appeared in several newspapers published by the Indian Independence League. Singapore readers promptly protested that the scene wasn't a Manipur village at all, but a lane in the Bukit Timah area of their city. Quietly Sivaram made inquiries at the local office of the *Hikari Kikan*. There had been a mix-up, the *Kikan* said. The photograph should not have appeared. It and others like it "were meant for distribution in territories other than Singapore and Malaya."[24]

One suspects Sivaram was not happy with this explanation. Still, most of what the news managers were producing seemed solid enough. He could check it against what All India Radio and the BBC were saying. They said that Britain's forces faced a serious test at Imphal. They made no reference to *Indians*, they talked only of the Japanese, but that could be explained. It was the censor's hand. Neither Delhi

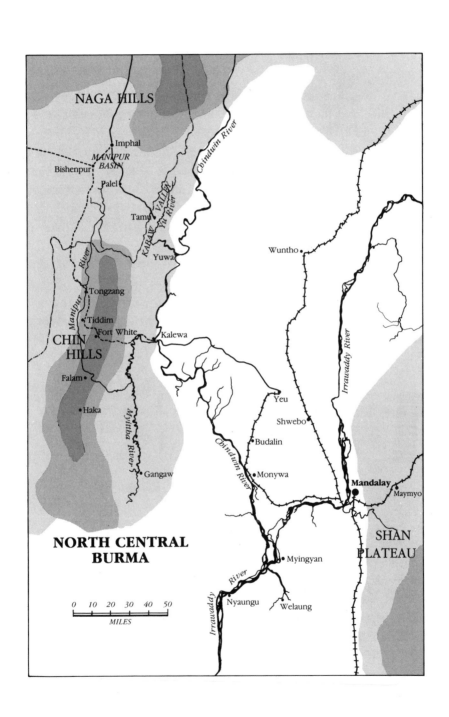

NAGA HILLS

• Imphal
MANIPUR
BASIN
Bishenpur•
Palel•

Chindwin River

Tamu•
KABAW VALLEY
Yu River

Yuwa•

• Wuntho

Manipur River

•Tongzang

•Tiddim
•Fort White   •Kalewa

CHIN
HILLS

Falam•

Myittha River

• Yeu

Shwebo•

Irrawaddy River

•Haka

Chindwin River

•Budalin

•Monywa   **Mandalay**   Maymyo•

• Gangaw

**NORTH CENTRAL
BURMA**

SHAN
PLATEAU

0 10 20 30 40 50
MILES

Irrawaddy River

Nyaungu•   • Myingyan

• Welaung

nor London were about to admit that there was a truly Indian army in the field, though there *was*—as every reader of *Greater Asia* knew.

West of the Chindwin as in the Arakan, that paper told him, Indians and Japanese ate, marched, and shouted "Jai Hind" and "Banzai" together. So Sivaram let himself be carried away on a wave of confidence and hope. "Imphal was the rage," he remembers. "At the rear headquarters of the League we made the most elaborate preparations to celebrate its fall. Military parades, mass rallies, special radio programs, theatrical performances. . . ." Suddenly it was easy to raise money, persuade Tamil rubber tappers to enlist, do all sorts of things. One Singapore resident who was *not* Indian, and so did not share in the general euphoria, remarked that overnight Indian patriots had become as thick on the ground "as mushrooms."[25]

In Rangoon the excitement was surely as great, though Lakshmi, who flew in from Singapore on April 6, does not remember it. She was busy making arrangements for the Rani of Jhansi contingent that was about to arrive. She was busy, too, preparing for a move north. Netaji proposed to establish his advanced headquarters at Maymyo. He had flown there the day before Lakshmi arrived. As soon as she could, she was to join him.

Maymyo, named after a Colonel May (*myo* means town) whose regiment had once been stationed in the vicinity, was a delightful spot on the edge of the Shan plateau a little distance east of Mandalay. Four thousand feet of altitude perceptibly tempers Maymyo's summer heat, at its worst in April and May before the rains begin, and it was for this reason that in British days the governor regularly summered there. Of course the place was a long way from where the Japanese and Indian forces were fighting. But Mutaguchi, whose headquarters had been in the town for nearly a year, did not mind. He had planned his offensive, he had sent his divisions forward, he saw no need to manage operations day by day. "My officers do everything," Hugh Toye has him say to visitors who catch him in his garden. "I just tend my roses."[26]

Even had he been in touch with his field commanders, Bose could not have told them what to do. He had no training for such work, nor talent either, and he knew it. Besides, operational control of INA battalions lay not with *Azad Hind Fauj* Headquarters but with the Japanese. Nevertheless, it made good sense to be at Maymyo. Mutaguchi was there. From Maymyo some sort of contact with the jawans was at least imaginable. And Maymyo being, after all, much closer to Imphal than Rangoon was, from Maymyo it should be possible to move to the Manipur basin without delay when the time came. This was important. The whole point of the offensive, as Free India saw it, was to put an army and a provisional government on Indian soil—and put them there soon. So one week after Bose flew off to Maymyo, Lakshmi followed by car, taking with her half a dozen women from the regiment and several INA officers.

Because air activity this far south was still limited, and potholes made night driving dangerous, they traveled by day. The trip took five days. The first night they stopped at Zeyawadi, where the sugar mill is. Later they stayed in villages, picking Indian ones, villages that had been granted two or three generations back to soldiers of the conquering Indian Army, for in those days men whose terms of enlistment expired while they were in distant places had sometimes been taken care of in this way. The villagers were happy to see Indian uniforms. *During the British retreat they had suffered a great deal at the hands of the Burmese.* This, Lakshmi believes, was because the Burmese envied them. *Compared to the Burmese, you see, these Indians were prosperous. They were much more hard working. A lot of them had married Burmese women.* In Lakshmi's book this was a good thing. *I particularly remember a great big Pathan known as Sardar Langua*, the headman of Langua, *who had eight or ten wives, and hordes of children. I've never seen so many children, all ages and sizes.* Several of his daughters were young women now, the sardar told her, and ought to join the Rani of Jhansi Regiment. *But they did not agree.*

A number of Ranis recruited and trained in Burma had preceded Lakshmi to Maymyo, and she found them there, housed on a large piece of open ground. Prem flew in, took up quarters with Netaji in a house once used by Ba Maw, and was served strawberries and cream—the first he had had in years. Lakshmi was introduced to Mutaguchi. *He was very confident, and quite relaxed. He thought that everything was going according to plan. We thought so too. At that stage we had no reason to think otherwise.* On the 21st of April there was a public meeting at which the monthly anniversary of the proclamation of the Provisional Government was celebrated. Maymyo had an air raid, with little damage and no casualties.

On the 30th of April the officers put on a variety show for men about to leave for the front, and Prem and several other officers offered to sing. It was an odd choice, Lakshmi thought, since none had any talent in that department. *They all started off in different keys.* The next evening Lakshmi and her girls prepared a special meal for the departing jawans. The officers played hosts. Netaji himself served chappaties and dal. By sundown the meal was over, the men went off to their camp, the moon came up. And with the moon came the bombers. *We barely had time to reach the air raid shelter. One of the girls had gone to bed early with a headache. I remembered this after we were all settled, and just managed to drag her in before the bombs fell.* One struck very close, blocking the entrance, and when the debris had been cleared away and the girls crept out, they saw that their building had been reduced to matchwood. No one was hurt. But they had lost their rifles, and all of their clothing except what they stood up in.

They moved to another building, standing among trees and therefore not so inviting a target. Small Dutch rifles were issued in place of the .303s. Cloth being terribly short, there could be no question of working up uniforms on the previous model. Jodhpurs were out. INA issue, suitably altered, would have to do. A certain seriousness crept into daily life. Blackout regulations were drawn up and enforced, sentries doubled as air raid wardens, and it became the rule that if the siren sounded, you jammed all your clothing into your rucksack and took it with you to the shelter. Meanwhile military training went on as usual, two or three hours of it a day, with occasional route marches and tactical exercises thrown in. When Imphal fell, as much of the regiment as had come up to Maymyo must be ready to move there. And Imphal would fall any day.

So May advanced. Prem went back to Rangoon, where the army's functioning headquarters remained, and where he had work to do. Bose followed. Ayer, who had moved into Netaji's bungalow to keep an eye on the contents, was startled one day to find its true occupant back. Mutaguchi, too, moved—to a place just beyond the Chindwin. But Lakshmi remained at Maymyo. The news that reached her there was muffled and uncertain. There was fierce fighting all around the Manipur basin, fighting in which brave jawans participated, and still the British held out.

Early in June black clouds built up over the town. The campaign, everybody knew, was to have been fought and won before the rains began, yet in the mountains to the north and west the monsoon had arrived and must by now be heavy. And a feeling grew that all was not as it should be. The freedom army, launched with such high hopes, no longer moved forward. It faltered, there had been a check somewhere, a check of some sort. Of course this check was bound to be temporary. It would be overcome, and when it was the march to Delhi would resume. Nevertheless, the delay was disquieting. Only later, a good deal later, did people perceive that what had happened at Imphal was not a check at all, but a disaster.

CHAPTER 13

DISASTER AT IMPHAL

There is something ironic about the Imphal campaign. To Shah Nawaz and his battalions climbing the Chin Hills, to Prem pushing papers in Rangoon though he would much prefer a field command, to Lakshmi wondering when she will receive word to collect her women and go forward once more with Netaji, to Netaji himself—what is happening in and about Imphal is of enormous importance. Bursting into India, after all, is what the Indian National Army is all about, its raison d'être, the excuse for its existence. It can only be done at the Burma-India border. No other place offers an approach. If it is to be done—and it is already late, quite possibly too late—it must be done at once. But while the Indians are filled with a sense of urgency, and are committed to the enterprise heart and soul, they are too few in number, and too weak in arms, to much affect the outcome let alone do the job themselves. Whereas the Japanese and the British, whose big battalions will decide the matter, are unconcerned, indifferent even. Serious fighting in Burma has never been central to *their* purposes. Neither had intended much for this part of the world. Both would have preferred to make their major effort somewhere else.

For the Japanese, Burma lay at the outer edge of the projected new order, India beyond it. The Burmese were expected to take their place in a hierarchy of peoples at whose summit stood Nippon. The Indians were not. Stunning victories early in the war had, it is true, encouraged the Japanese to suppose that their Greater East Asia Co-Prosperity Sphere might extend farther than they had originally thought. But the battles of the Coral Sea and Midway, and the subsequent sea and land actions in the Solomons and New Guinea, had forced Imperial General Headquarters to recalculate Japan's prospects. By early 1943 it was clear that she had overreached herself. She would prevail only if she withdrew a little, hunkered down like the porcupine, and let her enemies bloody themselves to exhaustion upon her quills. So a defensive perimeter was sketched, a line that in the west included Burma but touched no part of India except the Andaman and Nicobar Islands.

It did not follow that this line was never to be breached. Though plans to follow the 1942 conquest of Burma with a quick thrust into India had not passed beyond the point of studies at the level of staff (Mutaguchi, then commanding a division, objecting that a border crossing was impossible given the absence of roads), neither had they been abandoned—only shelved. They came off the shelf quickly enough when it became apparent that the Allies were preparing the very same operation in reverse; were getting ready, that is, to cross the Burmese frontier themselves.

Looked at one way, this was odd. For the British had never meant to take Burma by direct assault. They wanted, of course, to erase the shame of their expulsion. That meant reoccupying the country. But it need not be done at once, and it certainly need not be done by land. Better to return to this part of the world as, many years earlier, they had first approached it—over the water. Churchill in particular was determined to avoid ground campaigns. "You will utilize to the full the advantages of seapower," he instructed Mountbatten when, in August of 1943, he made that sailor (Lord Louis was then a Vice-Admiral) Supreme Allied Commander of the newly created South-East Asia Command. "You will proceed to form . . . a Combined Striking Force or Circus which will be available as the foundation of whatever amphibious descent is eventually chosen."[1] *Circus* suggested something sent quickly and with decisive effect, like the special fighter squadrons in the First World War, to particular places. The Prime Minister's inventive mind was rich with notions of what these might be.

The northern tip of Sumatra was one, Singapore another, and beyond these the Prime Minister looked to amphibious operations in the Dutch East Indies, a linkup with the Australians, a respectable part in the final Allied assault upon the Japanese homeland. Set against these exciting possibilities, which were the eastern equivalent of his notorious preference for striking at the Germans through the "soft underbelly" of Italy and Greece, a long, slow slog over the rain-forested mountains into Burma was of no interest. What, after all, could it accomplish? Burma is a dead end, leading as unmistakably nowhere as it is possible for ground not actually an island to do. So Churchill wanted no part of such an exercise. And he would probably have carried his commanders with him, if he and they had not had to come to terms with America's obstinate concern for the Chinese.

America's self-appointed role as guardian of that immense mass of disinherited humanity went back many years. Pearl Harbor simply reinforced it. China, Americans felt, was much more than one friend among many. China was their most appealing and deserving ally. When, shortly after the United States entered the war, President Roosevelt reviewed for the benefit of Congress the peoples they were fighting beside, he received the loudest and most spontaneous applause when he mentioned not the Russians, not the British, but the Chinese. And Americans had great confidence in what the Chinese, with a little help, could do.

Already, Americans believed, their armies tied down large numbers of Japanese. Soon they would tie down a great many more; soon Americans bombers flying from Chinese bases would drive Japanese shipping from the sea lanes along China's coast, and strike Japan itself. For this work, however, the Chinese would need arms, aviation fuel, supplies and materiel of all sorts. Ways would have to be found to move these things to them. And this meant doing something about Burma. For ever since the moment, late in 1938, when the Japanese simultaneously seized Canton on China's south coast and Hankow up the Yangtze, Chiang Kaishek and his people had been confined to the interior of their enormous country. Their only link to the outside world had lain through Burma.

That link was the famous Burma Road, a nine-foot-wide unpaved track scratched laboriously out of the steep rain-soaked hillsides along the China-Burma border. For three years, weather permitting, supplies reached China by freighter to Rangoon, railroad car through Mandalay to Lashio, truck beyond. Then early in 1942 the Japanese took Rangoon, Mandalay, Lashio, and Myitkyina in upper Burma, actions that did not so much sever the Burma Road as swallow its lower half— and China was wholly cut off.

Of course cargo could be flown in direct from India, and was. But to airlift things over "the Hump," as pilots termed the tumble of peaks where India, Burma, and China meet, was a miserably expensive and inefficient business, a gallon of gas burned for every gallon landed; and the Americans who did it—and possessed in the DC-3 or C-47, which the British called the Dakota, the only aircraft capable of doing it— were from the beginning not happy with the arrangement. They wanted another ground link. Chiang wanted one too. Without it, he warned, China would collapse. (Chiang was always threatening collapse.) A new road was conceivable if you struck off from Ledo, high up in Assam, and pushed south and east to a point on the old road beyond Japan's reach. So work began, almost before the old road closed. And soon the completion of the Ledo Road became virtually an obsession with the Americans of the China-Burma-India theater, and with Joseph Stilwell their chief.

Stilwell had been sent to Burma early in 1942 to command the Chinese divisions which Chiang was reluctantly contributing to its defense. No more than the British, however, could he and his Chinese save Burma. They too were beaten, Stilwell barely getting out on foot. (It was the presence of these Chinese that permits one to say that in Burma, as in Malaya, the Japanese prevailed with an absolute inferiority in numbers.) But Stilwell was determined to go back, and to take the Chinese, some of whom he managed to fly to India for rest and retraining, with him. This personal determination was one of the things that eventually compelled the British to make an over-the-border recovery of Burma the centerpiece of their war against Japan.

"Vinegar Joe" had no use for Chiang. "Peanut" he called him— first employed as a code name, the epithet fitted the Generalissimo so perfectly that Stilwell used it all the time. He was equally contemptuous of the British. In military matters they lived, it seemed to him, in a world of make-believe where men always did their best, nobody floundered, and defeat was touched with as much nobility as victory. Stilwell could discover nothing noble in Burma's loss. The Allies had taken a hell of a licking there, that was the way he looked at it (that was also the language he used), and what they had to do now was pick themselves up, go back, and hand the Japanese some of the same. Signs of reluctance he took for gutlessness, the sort of gutlessness that had

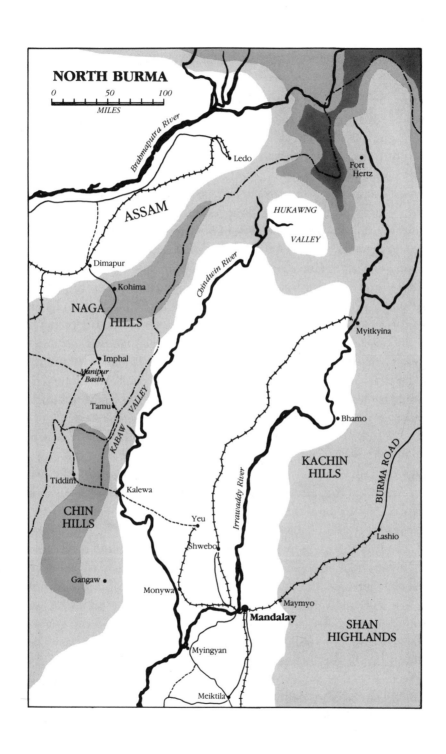

NORTH BURMA

0   50   100
MILES

Brahmaputra River

Ledo

Fort
Hertz

ASSAM

HUKAWNG

VALLEY

Chindwin River

Dimapur

Kohima

NAGA

HILLS

Myitkyina

Imphal

*Manipur
Basin*

Tamu

KABAW VALLEY

Bhamo

BURMA ROAD

KACHIN
HILLS

Tiddim

Kalewa

CHIN
HILLS

Yeu

Lashio

Shwebo

Irrawaddy River

Gangaw

Monywa

Maymyo

Mandalay

SHAN
HIGHLANDS

Myingyan

Meiktila

brought Singapore to premature surrender. (Like many Americans, Stilwell believed that Percival's defense of Malaya did not bear comparison with MacArthur's defense of the Philippines.) Was it possible the British meant to let Americans do all the fighting in the war against Japan? Only an honest effort to recover at least the northern part of Burma, and so make road contact with China secure, would lay that suspicion to rest.

If Britain had continued to dominate the alliance, as in 1942 she clearly did, she might have shrugged such suspicions off. By 1943, however, she had passed the peak of her capacity to mobilize men and resources; whereas the United States, with very much more to draw upon, was just beginning to discover what it could do. The result was that at the Allied conferences held periodically about the North Atlantic's rim, conferences at which Roosevelt, Churchill, and their staffs struggled to agree upon strategy for the months ahead, there was a perceptible shift of weight and influence between the two partners. A shift particularly observable in the allocation of landing craft, equipment no one even two or three years earlier could have predicted would be of such crucial importance—but without which Mountbatten was quite incapable of doing what the Prime Minister asked.

Of landing craft there were never enough. And the British, who produced few, had nothing to offer in exchange, not even the cargo-carrying Dakota, which of course they did not produce either. (Early in the war they had made a deliberate decision not to build transport aircraft but to buy them from the Americans. Though later they changed their minds, few were ever built.) Anxious as Churchill was to avoid a land campaign in Southeast Asia, he was even more determined to preserve an independent British strategy in the Mediterranean. When, therefore, the Americans pushed hard for a cross-Channel assault on Fortress Europe—never mind the casualties, and the post-war consequences should the Balkans be abandoned to the Russians—it was over the Mediterranean that he tried to hold his ground, and over Burma that he was inclined to bend. Even so there might have been no movement in Mountbatten's theater, nothing by sea for lack of amphibious capacity, nothing across the border either, had not Wingate and his Chindits given Churchill an opportunity to buy the Americans off on the cheap.

Prem, seated at the right, with instructors and other students at the Animal Transport Course, Peshawar, 1940.

Facing page, top

Subhas Chandra Bose, standing second
from the right, with the Calcutta University
Territorials.

Facing page, bottom

Bose reviews the Indian National Army
on the padang at Singapore, July 1943.

Bose presiding at the 1938 annual session of Congress Party. Gandhi is seated to his
right, Nehru stands on his left.

Bose and the principal figures in his army and provisional government, probably late 1943. Lakshmi stands to his immediate left.

Mount Popa

Lakshmi parading at the head of her Rani of Jhansi Regiment.

Netaji Subhas Chandra Bose

The three defendants in the first Red Fort trial shortly after their release—from left to right Shah Nawaz, Dhillon, and Prem. The man behind salutes Indian Army style while they salute INA style.

Netaji inspecting a guard of honor at the opening of the Rani of Jhansi Regiment training camp off Bras Basah Road in Singapore, 22 October 1943. Lakshmi walks on his right.

Defense Counsel at the Red Fort trial, first day. In the front row, from left to right: Dalip Singh, Nehru, Sapru, Bhulabhai Desai, Asaf Ali, Katju

Janaki Davar in her INA 1st lieutenant's uniform.

Orde Wingate was a career army officer (and distant relation of Lawrence of Arabia) of unorthodox views and disconcerting intensity of mind who, happening to be posted in Palestine when the Arabs rebelled, taught the Zionists to meet attacks on their settlements with raids even more savage, and in the process developed a taste for irregular warfare. In 1941 Wingate led native levies against the Italians in Ethiopia. Then he was brought to Burma. There, though the British were being hustled out of the place, he saw enough to convince first himself, then his superiors, that Long Range Penetration Groups directed by radio and supplied entirely by air could play havoc with an enemy's rear if used boldly and sent deep.

Wingate was given the men, some of them British and some Gurkha. He was given facilities for special training. He contrived a name—take *chinthe*, the mythical creature with the head and wings of an eagle and the body and hind quarters of a lion that guards Burmese pagodas, get it wrong when first you hear it (as Louis Allen believes Wingate did), and you have *chindit*. In February 1943 Wingate left Imphal with several thousand Chindits, passed through the Zibyu Hills (then the limit of the Japanese advance), cut the Mandalay-Myitkyina railroad, crossed the Irrawaddy, prowled murderously beyond it for several weeks, and when at last he withdrew, left behind him three accomplishments of lasting importance.

Serious harm to the Japanese was not one. The damage the Chindits inflicted on the enemy was superficial, and did not match the damage the Chindits inflicted on themselves (few who got out were ever of much use again). But the news of their exploits, coming at a moment when defeat in the first Arakan campaign seemed to say that nothing in this theater was ever going to go right, gave British spirits (Churchill's not least) an enormous lift and went far to restore Britain's credibility with the Americans. After Chindit One the Chindits could do no wrong. At Allied strategy conferences they became Churchill's favorite card. Once played, however, the card stayed on the table. And as the announced purpose of long range penetration was to throw the enemy off balance and give regular forces a chance, by late 1943 the British found themselves drawn willy-nilly towards border crossings that were much more than raids.

Moreover, it wasn't only landing craft they needed from the Americans. Long range penetration makes heavy demands on air transport, the whole point being to supply, reinforce, and even dispatch your roving columns by air. Later, regular forces collecting at the border would discover that they needed air transport too, lots of it. But this meant asking for Dakotas. And Dakotas the Americans, as anyone could see, were going to part with reluctantly, or refuse to part with at all, until and unless the Ledo Road was built. No road, no Dakotas. So the consequence of giving Wingate his head was that the British had to move seriously in Burma, or face not only American irritation right round the globe, but the withholding in Burma itself of the means of doing anything at all in that theater. Churchill could instruct Mountbatten to look seaward and plan amphibious descents. Mountbatten had to clear north Burma first.

For the purpose he had a man every bit as determined to whip the Japanese as Stilwell, and for the same reason. William Slim, commander of the recently formed 14th Army, had led two infantry divisions and an armored brigade during the 1942 retreat from Burma. He too had been defeated there. Now, thanks to an ambitious program of training and re-equipment, Mountbatten had in Slim's new force a formidable instrument for the reconquest of the area. But he had something else, something he might have preferred to do without. He had an enemy prepared to anticipate him by striking first.

That was Wingate's third accomplishment. The speed and apparent ease with which he had pierced their lines, startled and alarmed the Japanese. It also gave Mutaguchi, who by now commanded their 15th Army, a notion. Mutaguchi had fought the British in Malaya, and despised them. Whatever they could do, he could do better. If this Chindit exercise meant that a regular Allied offensive was in the making, it must be met and thrown off balance by a prior Japanese blow. A blow that he and his three divisions—all that 15th Army consisted of, Japanese army organization did not know the corps—were well placed to deliver.

Once delivered, moreover, why should the blow not carry past Imphal, over the mountains, down into Assam? That would give Subhas Chandra Bose the opportunity to raise India against the British. If the rising succeeded, Britain east of Suez would cease to exist and Japan's western flank be utterly secure. In 1937 Mutaguchi had commanded a regiment at the Marco Polo Bridge. There, near Peking, had occurred the incident that gave Japan her excuse to begin the conquest of China. "If I push into India now, by my own efforts, and can exercise a decisive influence on the Great East Asia War, I, who was the remote cause of the outbreak of this war, will have justified myself in the eyes of our nation."[2] Or so Mutaguchi said to himself.

He did not tell higher headquarters this. All Headquarters expected of the offensive, which it duly authorized, was that it catch the British off guard, scatter their forces, and by occupying the bases they had built and stocked along the border, particularly around Imphal, deter them from attempting anything serious against Burma. To this end Kawabe, of Burma Area Army, was promised seven divisions, eventually raised to eight. Two would watch Stilwell and his reorganized Chinese in the far north. Three would cover the Arakan and the coast below. In the Arakan a prior strike could be expected to destroy or at least pin down the British there, while sucking in reserves—which indeed it did. And in the center Mutaguchi's three divisions would deliver the decisive blow. If the operation began early in March, it should be over by mid-April. That would allow time to consolidate positions on the far side of the Manipur basin before the rains came; time even to push on, as Mutaguchi privately intended, into the valley of the Brahmaputra.

It was in this way, by this chain of events and this play of circumstances, that the battle began which gave the Indian National Army its opportunity—and dragged it to disaster.

✆

At first the offensive, which began on March 8, went just as it was supposed to go. Elements of Mutaguchi's 33rd Division, curling around the flanks of the British some distance down the track that led due south out of the Manipur basin to Tongzang, Tiddim, and beyond, came within an ace of trapping the 17th Indian Division. And though the 17th managed to extricate itself, Mutaguchi did not mind. It would be his, with the others, at Imphal. "*I got big net, I catch big fish,*" Prem remembers the general saying. Further north, where the rest of Mutaguchi's 33rd together with the 15th and 31st Divisions were strung out in line, a dozen columns moving (as Slim later put it) "like the probing fingers of an extended hand"[3] attacked with desperate ferocity such British parties as blocked their way, or brushed past and hurried westward. At the very end of March one of these columns cut the Imphal–Kohima road. Early in April another column approached Kohima itself, having covered, writes Louis Allen, "about 160 miles, across the grain of the country, over endless ridges reaching to 8,000 feet or more above sea-level, in twenty days, . . . an epic march by any standards."[4]

Kohima, the peacetime headquarters of a British deputy commissioner, was little more than a village. It had great strategic value, however, for it lay at the point where the road from upper Assam into the Manipur basin climbs to forty-five hundred feet and turns south for Imphal. This was the road over which most of Slim's men and stores had to come. If the Japanese took Kohima, they denied Slim the road and at the same time threatened Dimapur and the rail line to Ledo. So both sides fought desperately for the place. The British, however, were caught off balance by the speed and scale of the Japanese attack. Shortly they found themselves squeezed into an area so small that a day's action might turn upon defending a bungalow here, disputing a tennis court there. Away to the south, meanwhile, other Japanese cut the Silchar track, Imphal's last lifeline, and drew their ring so tightly about the Manipur basin that at Nungshigum, on the basin's northeast rim, the Japanese looked down on the streets of Imphal itself. No wonder to Mutaguchi, dallying in his Maymyo rose garden, victory seemed within reach.

What upset his calculation was, oddly enough, *not* Chindit Two. Early in March, just as Mutaguchi's divisions began crossing the Chindwin, Wingate flew nine thousand men into the Hukawng Valley 150 miles to the northeast, established strongpoints complete with artillery and airstrips, and prepared to deny the entire area to the Japanese. The operation grew. Before it was over, more than sixteen thousand men had been committed to it. (Among them were the several thousand members of 5307 Composite Unit Provisional, otherwise known as Merrill's Marauders, the only American infantry force to serve anywhere on the mainland of Asia during the war.) Wingate himself was killed early in the business, attempting to fly out of Imphal in a rainstorm. But Chindit Two went on without him, long range penetration on the most massive scale, unmistakably threatening the Japanese 15th Army's rear. Surely it ought to have given Mutaguchi pause.

It didn't. For one thing, it wasn't directed at 15th Army at all, but at the two Japanese divisions that prevented Stilwell and his Chinese from bringing the new Burma Road down from Ledo, and of this Mutaguchi was soon aware. For another, it stripped Slim of men he could have used to face 15th Army (and simultaneously threw many of them away: Chindit casualties from disease and exhaustion alone were appalling). Had *half* Wingate's twenty-one battalions been in a position to meet the Japanese columns—the "probing fingers" of Slim's figure of speech—as they pushed toward the Imphal–Kohima road, Mutaguchi would never have managed to draw, let alone tighten, a ring around the Manipur basin. In any case that old soldier was not a bit bothered when he learned what Wingate and his people were up to. "How are they going to supply the men they've dropped?" Louis Allen has him ask. "While they're scuttling around . . . I'll be into Imphal and cut the line to Ledo." (He meant the rail line.) "They'll simply wither on the vine."[5]

What did confound him was, first, the strength of the army he was attacking. Even without the battalions Wingate had siphoned off, the British greatly outnumbered him. They had three divisions at Imphal alone. They had tanks (one of Mutaguchi's columns had tanks too, but only a few), more guns than he could possibly manhandle or pack in, and much surer access to fuel and ammunition. Above all they had command of the air, and with it an airlift. Their commitment to a ground campaign in north Burma, which Chindit Two of course advertised, guaranteed them this. Dakotas and the much larger Commandos, some already with British markings, others borrowed (after a brief telegraphic tussle) from the Americans, carried Briggs's 5th Division and part of Messervy's 7th directly to Imphal, kept them supplied there, and brought thousands of sick and wounded out. At the height of the aerial effort, which went on for months, the daily tonnage lifted was more than twice what the German Sixth Army had received when it was cut off near the Volga eighteen months earlier. "Air supply, made possible by borrowed resources," writes Raymond Callahan, "turned Imphal-Kohima into a Stalingrad in reverse. . . ."[6]

And like the Germans, though with less reason—the Germans, being the besieged not the besiegers, had had very little choice—the

Japanese refused to see what was happening. "The whole ethos of the Imperial Army," continues Callahan, "reinforced by Mutaguchi's personality, forbade breaking off the offensive." Though Mutaguchi's 31st Division almost took Kohima, which would have locked away for good the only road of consequence into beleaguered Imphal, it could not quite turn the key in the lock. The British hung on until a brigade, followed by elements of an entire fresh division, forced its way up from Dimapur and relieved the desperate garrison. This was twenty days into April, and Mutaguchi's 31st Division never regained the initiative. It had had to approach Kohima over terrain impossible for normal transport. It had made a virtue of necessity, and brought with it food and ammunition for only three weeks. Surprise and élan, it had assured itself, would carry the day. They hadn't. Now it was stranded, out at the end of an enormously long and difficult line of supply. The 31st should have been withdrawn. It was ordered, instead, to cling to the high ground around the devastated village and prevent the British, at all costs, from pushing on to Imphal.

For at Imphal, way to the south, Mutaguchi still tightened the ring about the Manipur basin. His 15th Division astride the Kohima road would have trouble doing its bit if the British came down on its rear. But it was not from the Kohima side that Mutaguchi meant to exert the greatest pressure. He would exert it from the southeast, up the Tamu road. It was more than a track now. Obligingly, the British had greatly improved it. And it was short: from Tamu on the west slope of the Kabaw Valley nine miles to Sibong, from Sibong to Shenam Saddle another nine, from Shenam to Palel five. At Palel, where there was an airfield (one of the basin's precious few), Imphal lay only twenty-five level miles away. So from the middle of March right through April, May, and June a portion of 33 Division known as Yamamoto Force struggled to climb the Tamu road.

It could not do so directly, as Mutaguchi discovered when the tanks he sent charging straight up (it was here that he used the few he had) were shelled and stopped. Yamamoto Force would move forward only if it first penetrated the tumbled ground on either side. This, using more artillery than any Japanese unit elsewhere on the battlefield possessed, it set out to do. The going was slow. Slim's men were well aware of the danger, and resisted stubbornly. For every hill seized and

not relinquished, or from the outset found impregnable, there were several that changed hands at least once, and some that changed hands again and again. Nowhere save at Kohima was the fighting more prolonged and furious.

It was to the general vicinity of the Tamu road that the INA's four guerrilla regiments were directed, as each in turn gained Rangoon, collected itself, and pushed off on the last lap of the fifteen hundred mile voyage from training camp to action. Eleven battalions hurried to cross the Chindwin and position themselves for the push into India when Imphal should fall. Only one went somewhere else.

This was the 1st Battalion of Subhas Brigade. Bose had been anxious to have at least a part of his especially armed and prepared guerrilla regiment participate in the diversionary attack he apparently knew would precede the main Japanese thrust at Imphal. So on the 3rd of February the 1st Battalion had entrained not for the north, as the 2nd and 3rd Battalions had done, but for the west. It had left Rangoon by the rail line for Prome. From Prome it had marched eighty miles across the Arakan Yoma (*yoma*, literally backbone, signifies a range of hills) to Taungup, on the Bay of Bengal. From Taungup it had moved in small craft up the coast towards Akyab, expecting to take part in the Arakan campaign.

All this took weeks, however. The Battle of the Administrative Box had been fought and lost before February was over; it was March now; it is unlikely the Japanese would have wished to use so lightly armed and inexperienced a battalion in a direct assault upon a British position anyway. So when it reached a point just below Akyab, the battalion was sent due north up the Kaladan River. By the middle of the month it was approaching Kyauktaw, thirty miles east of the Mayu Peninsula. There it expected to stay. But operations against a black West African division which the British had sent overland to the upper valley of the Kaladan went better than expected, and drew the battalion farther and farther up. Until at last, in May, it crossed the Burma–India border one hundred miles north of Akyab, occupied a little place called Mowdok, and stopped.

Meanwhile Shah Nawaz and the 2nd and 3rd Battalions had left Rangoon by the rail line to Mandalay, detrained at Yeu, been trucked to the Chindwin at Kalewa, and after crossing had marched up the Myittha River valley to the edge of the Chin Hills below Tiddim and Fort White. There, at the very end of March, the 2nd Battalion had been told off to shield Mutaguchi on the south from a force of Chin irregulars led by British officers that was known to be operating in the area.

The assignment troubled Shah Nawaz. Fujiwara, then attached to Headquarters 33rd Division, describes meeting this "small-statured colonel with a gentle but handsome face" (they had not seen each other since Malaya), who at once began protesting that he and his regiment were not being given the combat role they had been led to expect.[7] Fujiwara tried to persuade him this was not so. He had the important task of making the British imagine that Mutaguchi's real objective was Chittagong. But Shah Nawaz would not be persuaded. He knew that the high ground to the west was virtually impassable. The British would never suppose themselves seriously threatened there. He also knew, however—for Netaji had warned him—that the Japanese meant to test the *Azad Hind Fauj* in the persons of himself and his men. Swallowing his annoyance, he moved quickly to get the battalion out to Falam and Haka.

Falam, at an altitude of six thousand feet, lay fifty walking miles south-southwest of the brigade's base in the Myittha River valley. Haka was higher still, and thirty-five miles farther. The men had to carry everything on their backs, so Shah Nawaz set up relay points at eight-mile intervals, put most of the 2nd Battalion to moving rations between them, and sent a company into Falam to relieve the Japanese. When sufficient stocks had accumulated there, he sent a second company to Haka, and went with it to look around. Nights at this altitude were cold, and the men, lacking woolens, lit fires to keep from freezing. Medicines were in short supply. "Twenty-five percent of my men have malaria," Shah Nawaz wrote Bose. "We are without tea, sugar, and vegetables. Many men are barefoot. There is no soap." Relations with the Japanese were "fairly satisfactory," but saluting was still a sore point. "Our soldiers definitely resent saluting Japanese officers when their soldiers do not salute ours."[8]

From Falam and Haka patrols went hunting for Chins. Shah Nawaz remembers one that reached a point forty miles west of Falam, set a trap for a British officer notorious for his guerrilla skills, and though the trap failed, returned with twenty-five prisoners. Towards the middle of May an attack was mounted on Klang Klang, a hilltop fortress protected by sheer cliffs, from which the British were thought to be directing their operations. Shah Nawaz's Japanese advisors warned him it could not be taken without artillery or air support, but he went ahead anyhow, directing the reconnaissance himself, turning the actual assault over to his brigade adjutant, Mahboob Ahmed. "Boobie," as he was called, took a handful of men by night up a slope so steep the British never thought of watching it, burst in, scattered the garrison after a brief fire fight, and signaled Haka that he was master not only of Klang Klang but of quantities of butter, jam, and other canned foods.

Meanwhile the 3rd Battalion, sent first to the Fort White–Tongzang area in the expectation that it would join in the general rush when the 17th Indian Division surrendered, discovered (when the 17th broke free instead) that it had nothing to do. Whereupon the Japanese, presuming on the good nature or innocence of its commander, set it to repairing roads. Mahboob Ahmed found it doing this at the end of March. "Boobie returned from Kennedy Peak," Shah Nawaz wrote in his diary. "His report is distressing. The Japanese are using the I.N.A. crack regiment as labourers. . . . I wonder what is going to be the outcome of all this one-sided co-prosperity."[9] Angrily, he ordered the battalion back to base.

There it stayed until the middle of May, when the Japanese conceived the curious notion that Subhas Brigade might be usefully employed at Kohima. Hopeful that he was going to be given serious work at last, Shah Nawaz started at once with the 3rd Battalion and the unengaged portion of the 2nd, moving right across the rear of the Japanese with some help from their motor transport and more from his men's own feet. It was a grueling journey, made worse by the first heavy rains, and when Shah Nawaz reached Ukhrul he learned that 31 Division was already withdrawing from its impossible position—against orders, it turned out. "Role of the Div. has been changed," he noted in his diary. "They are now going to participate in fight for Imphal." Staff officers, "very courteous" types, asked him what he wanted to do, and "of course my choice is attack Imphal."[10]

But by this time the Japanese were so exhausted, and so short of everything, that to incorporate Shah Nawaz's little force into their last attempt struck them as utterly impracticable. So in the end none of Shah Nawaz's battalions, in spite of being specially picked, took a direct part in the great enterprise for which Netaji had maneuvered so long and worked so hard, the plunge forward, Indians and Japanese together, that was to have carried an army and a government of *Azad Hind* across India's border. None participated because, Shah Nawaz darkly suspected, the Japanese wanted it that way.

The 2nd (or Gandhi) Regiment also found itself playing a marginal role—though it, at least, was posted not in the wings but along the axis of 15th Army's attempted advance. With Zaman Kiani's cousin Inayat in command, it left Rangoon in the middle of March, detrained at Yeu like Subhas Brigade's two battalions, crossed the Chindwin at Kalewa, and turned north for Tamu. And as the lead battalion approached that place (it was late April now), Zaman learned that a column of Yamamoto Force was close to the airfield at Palel. If Inayat was quick about it, his battalion might join the Japanese in a raid upon the place.

The men were tired. Bullock carts had yet to bring up the machine guns. But a number of Japanese officers, among them Fujiwara (who was on the lookout for his old friends), urged him on. Only a force that traveled light would get to Palel in time. So Inayat picked three hundred men, put a major at their head, and sent them off with a blanket, a rifle, and fifty rounds apiece. A Japanese officer who happened to pass the party near Sibong always remembered the sight of these men, "wild with enthusiasm as they walked on Indian soil, holding their rifles aloft and yelling *Jai Hind! Chalo Delhi!*"[11] Palel airfield was covered by fortified posts. It was Kiani's understanding that the Japanese would go in from the east while his men attacked from the south. So difficult was the country, however, that the officer commanding took two nights to reach his jumping-off place. When he began his final approach on the evening of May 2, the Japanese (so far as anyone knows) had already made their move.

That was not all. Several miles short of his objective, while the men were still in extended order, talking, some with lighted cigarettes in their mouths, he had the bad luck to run into a detachment of Gurkhas well dug in and concealed. Their fire, delivered at the last moment, sent

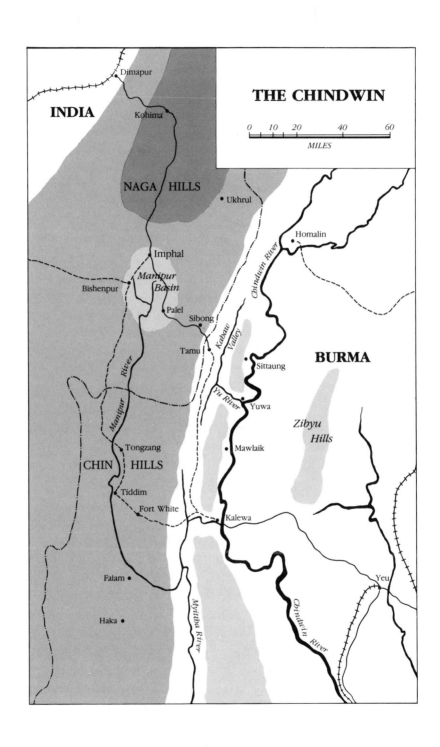

THE CHINDWIN

0   10   20   40   60

MILES

INDIA

Dimapur

Kohima

NAGA HILLS

Ukhrul

Homalin

Imphal

Manipur
Basin

Bishenpur

Palel

Sibong

Tamu

Kabaw Valley

Chindwin River

BURMA

Sittaung

Yu River

Yuwa

Zibyu
Hills

Manipur River

Tongzang

Mawlaik

CHIN HILLS

Tiddim

Fort White

Kalewa

Falam

Myittha River

Chindwin River

Yeu

Haka

his lead platoon flying. And though the men rallied and in the course of the night made several determined attacks, at dawn he had to withdraw leaving dead, wounded, and prisoners behind. It was not the end of the affair. Kiani brought up reinforcements and prepared to renew the assault. But the British were on the alert now. They sent in more infantry, called up guns, delivered air strikes at tree-top level. After two days of this Kiani prudently withdrew. He had suffered over two hundred casualties. Palel, the British estimated, had been "a dismal failure." The Japanese were not likely to employ the regiment again "as a fighting force."[12]

Indeed it took no further part in attacks up the Tamu road. When the last of its battalions came up, it was sent deep into the rough country to the south with instructions to cover Yamamoto Force's left flank. The Azad Regiment, which did not arrive until the end of May—finding no motor transport at Yeu, it had been forced to cover the more than one hundred miles to the Kabaw Valley on foot—was given a similar assignment on the right. As for the 4th or Nehru Regiment, it left Malaya so much later than the other three that it never reached the Chindwin at all. This, then, was how the twelve INA battalions were arranged at the beginning of June: one high up in the Arakan's Kaladan Valley, two split between the Chin and Naga Hills, six near but not on the Tamu road, three still en route. In all, before attrition and losses, not far short of nine thousand men. It cannot be said that they contributed much to Mutaguchi's offensive punch.

✦

Yet these men do not deserve the derogatory comments they routinely receive in popular accounts of the Burma war and in the memoirs of serving British officers. Slim, writing a dozen years later, says of the Palel affair that the Indian survivors, "disguised as local inhabitants and as our sepoys" (Slim seems to have forgotten why the INA wore Indian Army clothing), could be observed for days "wandering about the country without object or cohesion." As for the Gandhi Regiment, "what was left of it the Japanese in disgust used mainly as porters."[13] This is untrue. For one thing, it is explicitly contradicted by a brother officer, Lieutenant General Sir Francis Tuker. In Tuker's memoirs, which appeared six years earlier, there is an account of the regiment in action *weeks* after Slim has it reduced to coolie work.

Not that Tuker compliments Inayat Kiani's men on their fighting qualities. The tale he tells has quite the opposite intention. This, he begins, is "the story of a single Mahratta battalion cheerfully and with little loss putting paid to a whole brigade of the I.N.A., the Gandhi Brigade." The time is June 1944, the place somewhere off the Tamu road. Ordered to divert Japanese attention from a planned encircling movement, a brigadier sends the 4th Mahrattas against a hill the traitors occupy. When one company is held up by small-arms fire, brigade lays down a "short but sharp artillery concentration." The effect is astonishing. The hill is rushed. Those who fail to escape "by running away" are killed (they include a company commander). "About five prisoners" are taken. Then Gandhi Headquarters itself is overrun, this time without a fight (it too has been shelled), and the next line of hills falls as well.[14]

The story is hardly convincing. (Nor is it firsthand. At the time Tuker was serving in North Africa.) Would an encounter so filled with panic end with just *five* prisoners in the bag? But an action of some sort involving Kiani and his men certainly took place. For Hugh Toye, who at war's end was in a position to talk to Kiani and some of his men (and may have done so), tells a roughly similar tale.[15]

He tells it of July, not June. The "Gandhi Regiment" has shrunk from 2,500 or so to 750. The hilltop the Mahrattas attack is held "by fewer than fifty men." And though the Mahrattas do indeed push some distance further, the force facing them does not disintegrate but maintains a "precarious hold" on the ground it is supposed to cover, until Indians and Japanese alike begin a general withdrawal. Differ though they do, Tuker and Toye both declare Field Marshal Sir William Slim to be mistaken.

So does British intelligence. Of late June it reports "guerilla actions . . . south of the road Palel–Tamu by No. 2 Guerilla Regiment [the Gandhi Brigade], whose morale a month ago was reported to be low." A raiding party "about 60 strong" attacks a position and is repulsed. Another ambushes a British patrol. Still another attacks a roadblock. "Our troops say that they fought well but did not dislodge our block; their casualties were estimated at 25."[16] There are reports of similar activity by the Azad Regiment north of the road.

I wish we had the story direct from the INA side. If the *Azad Hind Fauj* had won its Burma campaign, if it had simply come home as one body, some of the survivors might have sat down one day and written what they could remember about the days up the Kaladan Valley and astride the Chin Hills. It did not happen. Personal accounts are few and far between. The only person who reached the far side of the Chindwin *and* wrote about it in a systematic way was Shah Nawaz, and what he wrote is often far from plausible.

Shah Nawaz would have us believe that inferior equipment, grossly inadequate supplies, Nippon's reluctance to use its Indian ally to best advantage, and "sheer bad luck," prevented Netaji's men and the Japanese jointly—he insists it would have been jointly—from taking Imphal. "While the I.N.A. was on the offensive," he writes, "there was not a single occasion on which our forces were defeated on the battlefield, and there was never an occasion when the enemy despite overwhelming superiority in men and material was able to capture any post held by the I.N.A."[17] It is impossible to believe this. It is difficult, too, to credit some of the scenes of individual prowess which punctuate Shah Nawaz's narrative, scenes in which jawans express themselves in faultlessly heroic language.

Neither is it certain, however, that when the Mahrattas were sent charging up Tuker's hill, they went about it "cheerfully." Military reportage has its conventions, which vary of course with the culture. And there is an equal discrepancy, though for a different reason, between what survivors of the Indian National Army have to say about changing sides, and what the British remember.

⁕

For the Indians, persuading fellow countrymen to quit the service of the King-Emperor was not simply one object among many. It had the highest priority. How else could the *Azad Hind Fauj*, so small, so lightly armed, hope to reach Delhi and raise the tricolor flag? For the British, however, the compulsion was quite the other way around. Of course Slim did not need Netaji's jawans to swell his ranks. He did, however, have to be certain of those he had. The magnificent confidence trick that made possible the Indian Army, indeed the Raj itself, turned on the unthinking reliability of the sepoy. And without the sepoy, Slim was nothing—for Indians made up the bulk of 14th Army, particularly in the fighting arms.

Slim, then, had to be certain. From the moment 14th Army was created, he had made morale something to be worked at quite as much as health and supply. He was confident, now, that the work had gone well, that the sepoy was safe. But the corollary of absolute confidence was the assumption that if the sepoy *did* desert, it was because he was tricked into doing so. And that assumption, carried back in time, let one suppose that the men taken prisoner when Malaya fell, the men who joined the renegade army before ever it reached Burma, had been tricked too—tricked, or coerced. Let these men see an opportunity to return to their old allegiance, and they would seize it: like stray sheep they would return. The more 14th Army pressed on, the more homecomings there would be.

So the impression left by such mention of the Indian National Army as manages to surface in most of the pieces written about the Burma war, is an impression of men with no heart for battle, men who will lay down their arms as soon as they can. Their allies and masters the Japanese are made of sterner stuff. When defeat stares *them* in the face, as it does at Kohima and Imphal, they do not waver, they fight to the death. But the Indians, "after a token struggle," watch for "the most opportune moment to slip across to the nearest British or Indian unit" (I am quoting from a popular account).[18] And as we read snatches like this, we see with the mind's eye men in the khaki of the prewar Indian Army, unarmed, bedraggled, moving in no sort of formation but with obvious purpose, moving to meet their old comrades and turn themselves in. That is the picture. But the picture is not accurate.

Some INA men *did* defect. When Shah Nawaz writes that in June "the Second-in-Command of Gandhi Brigade, being unable to face the hardships of the battle any longer, deserted to the British side,"[19] he admits (it being inconceivable that only one man found the going unbearable) that others did the same. In fact the Major Garwal in question was by British count the *fourth* INA officer with a Dehra Dun commission to turn himself in since the beginning of the year. Men from the ranks went over in far greater numbers.

But surrenders were never the flood the British assumed they would be. "In spite of Japanese reversals on the Arakan front," observed an intelligence summing up in the autumn of 1944, "our expectations that large numbers of the I.N.A. would desert were not realized." It was the same about the Manipur basin. In late July, intelligence reported that of the original 1,900 or so men in the Gandhi Brigade only 650 were still present for duty. But that was not because the rest had deserted. "Up to 30 June only 116 had surrendered or been captured." The rest were sick, and sickness was not confined to the Gandhi.

In one battalion of the Azad Brigade, this July report went on, "a daily strength return at the end of June showed that of approximately 600 men hardly more than 300 were present; 250 were sick in the back areas; 12 had deserted; 3 had committed suicide; and 3 were casualties." Of course it wasn't all that easy to surrender. It couldn't be done at all unless you were reasonably close to a British position, and there was always the chance you'd be shot by mistake. But whatever the reason, mass desertion did not occur. "Only some 700 of the I.N.A. have come into our hands since the end of February," the autumn summing up continued.[20] And of these 700 how many, one wonders, were men who deliberately set out to surrender and how many were men who, exhausted, wounded, straggling, or lost, saw that they were going to fall into the hands of the British anyway, and decided to act as if it had always been their dearest wish?

In this they had every encouragement. From the air the British showered INA units (when they could find them) with leaflets inviting men to come over, and with safe-conduct passes to make the coming safe. On a smaller scale the INA did the same. A British officer with a Gurkha battalion picked up a number of INA leaflets. "*Bahadur Hindustani sipahio,*" one begins. "Fearless Indian soldier, the ruthless British have sent you to fight your Asian brothers. Do you wish to remain their slaves? An army of free India is here, here in Burma, preparing to march on Delhi. Come join us! Death, death to the English!" Some of the leaflets carry illustrations. A bearded, turbanned Sikh clutches a rifle and looks fiercely into the distance. An elephant, the tricolor painted on its side, tosses with its trunk a startled and helpless John Bull. Many tell men how to turn themselves in. "Wave something white, point your rifles at the ground," they advise.[21]

It is doubtful these leaflets accomplished much. Because the INA had no means of dropping them behind the British lines, they could only be picked up by men going forward—and a man going forward is not commonly disposed to show the white flag. Something may have been achieved during periods of no movement by Bose's men identifying posts without British officers, creeping close, and appealing to the occupants in their own tongue. But the most promising times were early in the campaign, when the advancing Japanese were accompanied by parties from the Bahadur Group (as the Special Service Group had been renamed).

The job of these Bahadurs—*bahadur*, I repeat, translates "fearless"—was to penetrate British lines, make contact with sepoys, and persuade them, whole bodies of them if possible, to come over. Long before any of the guerrilla regiments had reached the front, these Bahadurs were active. There were several hundred in the Arakan, and more along the Chindwin. The INA border crossing at the place where a white pole pointed to sparkling stars was almost certainly the work of a Bahadur party, characteristically accompanying or accompanied by Japanese. So were the other encounters that filled *Greater Asia* and thrilled Rangoon's Indian community during February and March. It *had* to be the case, for at this time not even Subhas Brigade was far enough forward to be actually in touch with the enemy. And these Bahadurs had some success.

How much it is difficult to say. A year earlier, in the Arakan, sepoys had been induced to desert in some number (of this, more in a later chapter). As the Bahadurs were more numerous and better trained than their equivalents of that period, hopes for them were high. Yet they cannot have brought over sepoys in anything like the quantity suggested in a late February issue of *Greater Asia*. "A long and continuous stream of British Indian troops wends its way daily to an Indian National Army Camp somewhere on the southern Burma-India border," *Greater Asia* announces beneath a picture of men advancing in apparently endless file down a tree-bordered lane. The photographer is Japanese. Date and adjacent material make this the Arakan. But the scene has been posed. The photograph is a fake. For though the men are Indians right enough, their uniforms are khaki in color—leftover khaki. By 1944 true British Indian troops are wearing jungle green.

Just to the left, however, on the front page of this same February 29 issue, is a story quite as questionable under the caption "Azad Hind Army Continues to Advance." On a day not specified but recent, the story reads, "a unit of the Indian National Army waving their impressive tri-colour flag captured a highland a few kilometers east of Buthidaung, and has succeeded in winning over a unit of British Indian troops. . . ." Is this, too, a fabrication? Evidently not. For some months later intelligence informs New Delhi that at roughly the time indicated a troop of dismounted Gwalior Lancers (an Indian States Forces outfit) led by Jemadar Gajendra Singh was surprised not far from Buthidaung, east of the Mayu Peninsula, by "propagandists" of an Indian National Army "Bahadur Group." Taking refuge on a hill, the lancers prepare to defend themselves. But no attack is delivered. Instead the group's commander, one Misra formerly of the 5/17th Dogras, talks the troop into surrendering. The twenty-five men are taken to the rear and drafted into the traitor army. Gajendra Singh becomes an INA 2nd Lieutenant.[22]

And it is not an isolated case. In the weeks following, intelligence continues, Misra obtains access to a hundred or so sepoys taken prisoner in the Arakan by the Japanese. Most of them volunteer for the INA and are sent to Rangoon. And when Mutaguchi begins his Imphal offensive several hundred miles to the east and north, where other Bahadur Groups are waiting to do as Misra has done, the phenomenon recurs.

So on the testimony of the British themselves, going over was not something to be expected only of Subhas Chandra Bose's people. It was a two-way street. And if the first Japanese successes had been followed by still greater ones, successes that carried them and their Indian allies over jungle and mountain clear down into Assam, defections by Slim's sepoys might have grown from a trickle to a flood, and destroyed 14th Army—as Bose was convinced they could. It did not happen. For a time Misra and the other Bahadur Group commanders were the toast of Rangoon. By May or June they were forgotten. By then there was precious little opportunity to approach dismounted lancers or anybody else in circumstances that could make an invitation to desert persuasive. The fighting was going badly for the Japanese. And the Indian National Army was less than ever at the center of that fighting.

Shah Nawaz came to believe this was because the Japanese did not trust him and his fellows. "They had found out through their liaison officers that the I.N.A. would not accept Japanese domination in any way," that it would fight to prevent Nippon from replacing Britain in India. So they had set about capturing Imphal on their own, not asking their allies for assistance. "In fact, I am right in saying that they let us down badly, and had it not been for their betrayal of the I.N.A., the history of the Imphal campaign might have been a different one."[23]

Yet it is difficult to see how Bose's battalions, given what they were and how armed and equipped, could have written the Imphal story differently even had there been complete trust and confidence between the allies. Take the "crack" 1st Battalion of Subhas Brigade—courtesy, as so often in these matters, of British intelligence:

> The battalion is composed of Sikhs, Jats and Dogras, all ex-prisoners of war. It possesses no signal equipment, bicycles, or motorcycles, and only one 3-ton ration lorry. Each platoon has a mule cart which is manhandled by six men. These carts carry ammunition and officers' kits. There are no stretchers, and there is a great shortage of bandages and iodine. Only half the battalion possess field dressings, the majority of these are the original British issue. Each company [there were five in the battalion] has six anti-tank rifles, six Bren light machine guns, and six Vickers machine guns. The senior representative of the Bahadur Group has a stock of British hand grenades which he issues to men going forward on duty. Some NCOs and men in the battalion carry grenades. . . . Number 2 and 3 Battalions are said to be similarly equipped and organized.[24]

A force like this, without mortars or field radios to name just two deficiencies (the INA had mortars but not at battalion level), was quite incapable of meeting on anything like equal terms a unit from 14th Army, particularly when that unit had artillery and air support—as it generally had. So for the work the Japanese had cut out for themselves along the Mayu Peninsula, about the Manipur basin, at Kohima and half a dozen other places, the Indian battalions were not of much use, as Shah Nawaz in his calmer moments was quite ready to admit. But then, they weren't supposed to be. The understanding, Zaman Kiani wrote years later, "was that the Japanese, possessing heavier weapons, should first break the outer defences of India, and then allow the I.N.A. 1st Division to pass through and spread out for Guerilla operations . . . in Assam and Bengal." That was how the business was to have gone.

Bose, it is true, had wanted his jawans to move at the very tip of the Japanese advance. But he had wanted them there, Kiani believes, "for sentimental and historical reasons. It was not in reality a practical proposition"[25]—as indeed it wasn't, though Shah Nawaz sometimes talked as if it were. It was up to the Japanese to take Imphal. When they failed to do this in the first six weeks, they should have called the campaign off. Instead they turned it into an endurance contest, a slugging match, into which the Indians unwisely let themselves be drawn. Sustained fighting even on the battlefield's margin, where the Japanese prudently arranged that they should be, was more than Bose's men could handle. They weren't expecting it, they weren't trained for it, they hadn't the means. The result was that the help they gave was a good deal less than might have been expected from their numbers. The Japanese noticed this; and some, forgetting that at one time no one had expected the Indians to take any part in a direct assault upon Imphal, dropped caustic remarks about their performance there.

So did Slim and Tuker, of course, and others from the British side. But intelligence, pausing that September to marshal the information it had collected, decided that the traitor army's performance could not properly be judged unless placed "against the evidence that the Japanese did not originally intend using the I.N.A. as a fighting force prior to the capture of Imphal. It may be argued, therefore, that it is the Japanese Army which failed the I.N.A. It was the failure of the former to attain its objectives that prevented the latter being used in the role for which it was designed. . . ."[26]

Shah Nawaz could not have agreed more. By late June of 1944, however, the INA's problem was not how to protect its reputation but how to survive.

ॐ

Surviving in the Chin and Naga hills meant coping with perils the least of which were those that catch the imagination the quickest, that leap most vividly from the printed page. The common cobra. The common cobra's cousin the hamadryad or king cobra, twice as large and frankly aggressive. The deadly little dust-colored krait. Scorpions—the big black ones were bad enough, the small grey ones were worse. Leeches lying in wait in stream beds or dropping from trees. They spotted their prey, it was believed, "by earth vibrations," that is by sensing the tramp of approaching feet, and "the chances of escaping them," continued a Government of India *Burma Handbook* in a sweetly matter-of-fact tone, "are few."

Flies that sucked blood. Flies that stung like bees. Flies from whose bite, if untended, there could develop the dreaded Naga sore—it begins, wrote an Englishman as he described refugees struggling to reach Assam in 1942, "as a small blister, usually on the leg or foot, in a place where there is not much flesh. It develops rapidly for four or five days and then stops. By this time it may be five inches in diameter and half an inch deep, destroying all the upper layers of skin and often the tendons and muscles as well. Though it often has a clean appearance when washed, the under part frequently stinks to high heaven from the pus which rapidly accumulates in the cavity." Pus on which maggots fed. Maggots swarmed in every wound, and the sight could be unnerving. "On one occasion," continued the Englishman, "kerosene oil was poured into a hole in a small boy's head, and three hundred and fifty half-inch maggots, of four different species, were removed."[27]

The less spectacular dangers were in the mass more damaging. Louis Allen tells a tale of "a hundred men of the Devon Regiment" who, near Shenam Saddle on the rim of the Manipur basin, came across "an attractive camp site where green bamboo was growing afresh after being cut. But the hill was infested with the mite that carries scrub typhus. Seventy of the hundred were infected, and fifteen died."[28] Presumably this would not have happened had the Devons picked another hill. Malaria, however, prevailed across large stretches of ground that could not be avoided, the Myittha and Kabaw valleys for example, and for men who had to traverse them the *Handbook's* injunction to keep mosquito nets in good repair and "properly tucked in" would have been about as useful as some of its other Health Notes. "Wear a well-fitting topee while the sun is up," ran one of these. "Do not drink alcohol before the sun sets," cautioned another.[29]

Everybody suffered at one time or another from diarrhea. Many contracted dysentery. The amoebic variety often killed quickly. For most, however, dysentery was a slow, miserable, wasting business that made bloody bowels a man's daily companion, like the flies, the head lice, and the rain. By the end of the third week in May, the monsoon had well and truly settled in. It did not rain all the time. There were intervals of brightness. But mist or cloud often blanketed the ground, and the rain, when it came, was heavy and relentless. Foxholes filled with water. Cooking fires went out and could not be relit. Clothes, bedding, and equipment rotted. So did feet. Trying to get from one place to another, a man slipped and slithered with every step he took, or sank to his ankles in mud. And because movement was so difficult, very little moved—with serious consequences.

Supply was the Achilles' heel of the Indian National Army anyway. Two motor transport companies raised in Singapore from civilian volunteers operated between the railhead at Yeu and Kalewa on the Chindwin River. For this and other responsibilities they had several dozen trucks. These, however, were "mongrel derelicts" of the sort described earlier, often laid up for repair or want of parts. And as the fighting regiments had only a handful of their own (Subhas Brigade possessed exactly *three*), the 1st Division was hard put to keep arms, ammunition, and rations moving to the Chindwin, and quite unable to move men too unless the Japanese helped. That was why the Azad Regiment, arriving late, had to walk.

Beyond Kalewa, rations, stores, and ammunition went by hand cart, bullock cart, or pack mule. Once in the hills they were carried on men's backs. Keeping the stuff moving through these conduits, each narrower than the last, was difficult enough even in the dry weather. When torrential downpours turned the trails to streams or washed them away, it became impossible. There could be no question of living off the country. It offered nothing, no game, no fruit, no edible roots. If rations failed, the men went hungry. What the average daily ration on either side of the Tamu road was in June is unknown, but it was unquestionably low. Abid Hasan says that near the end of the month food simply stopped arriving. "By that time," he explains, "rations meant to us only a handful of rice or atta [wheat flour]."[30] It was then

that Major Garwal, Inayat's second in command, went over to the British, and Hasan, who took his place, believes it was despair born of hunger that made him do so.

Had each battalion been taken out of the line from time to time, the Naga sores, the malaria, and the dysentery, the numbing fatigue and the grinding hunger, would not have had such a disastrous cumulative effect. Slim's battalions, after all, though much better fed, faced the same perils and discomforts yet did not waste away in anything like the same degree. But British and Indian Army units (except for those serving with Chindit Two) were relieved at reasonable intervals. Slim's air transport capacity was such that he could, if he wished, lift an entire division out of Imphal to rest and refit. His sick and wounded were flown out too, treated before they were past recovery, and in surprising numbers sent right back into the battle. No such arrangements were possible for Bose's men, or for Mutaguchi's either. Once over the Chindwin and into the hills, they stayed. By late June many had been in those hills for upward of three months.

On the 22nd of that month British troops coming down from Kohima met British troops pushing up from Imphal, and broke the ring about the Manipur basin. Mutaguchi knew then that he was beaten. But several weeks passed before his superiors could bring themselves to sanction a general withdrawal. And as the British, meanwhile, were doing their best to slice 15 and 31 Divisions into fragments and cut the fragments off, Yamamoto Force had to hold where it was to give these divisions (or what was left of them) time to reach the Chindwin. Not until mid-July did it begin a fighting retreat down the Tamu road. Parts of Azad Regiment evidently stayed with it. British intelligence reports aggressive Indian patrolling on the Force's right flank as late as July 13. By then, however, most of the 1st INA Division was on the move. (Fujiwara had arranged to have it start two days before Yamamoto Force. "This was the only thing I could do for my comrades as a token of friendship."[31]) The men Shah Nawaz had brought back from the abortive move toward Kohima were already at Tamu.

It was a division in name only; in strength it was hardly more than a regiment, each regiment the size of a battalion (early in July Inayat Kiani reorganized the Gandhi Regiment as such); so the men to be extricated were not, after all, numerous. But the want of food, medicines, and transport that had contributed so much to their wasting away, made getting them out slow and difficult. Instructed to bring his column (2nd and 3rd Battalions less the men left at Falam and Haka) down the Yu River to the Chindwin, Shah Nawaz was at first comparatively hopeful. From Tamu to Ahlow, where the Yu leaves the Kabaw Valley and turns east towards the Chindwin, the sick had bullock carts to ride in. At Ahlow, he was promised, they would be transferred to river boats; at Teraun, twenty-five miles further down, there would be boats for all. But when Shah Nawaz reached Ahlow, he found the river in flood and not a boat in sight.

He waited. Eventually a few boatmen appeared. With their help he got his men to the far bank and on the track to Teraun. Meanwhile his rations had dwindled to nothing. "Four Garhwalis have died of starvation," he wrote in his diary. The *Hikari Kikan* "seem NOT to take the least notice. . . . I do not know what is the idea behind this deliberate starvation of my men."[32] Foraging was out of the question, the Japanese had picked the villages clean, so there was nothing to do but set off on foot carrying the helpless. At Teraun Shah Nawaz found a depot the Japanese had overlooked, with salt and enough rice to last a week. But again there were no boats. The local boatmen, it turned out, never attempted the rapids (of which there were many) while the Yu was in flood. Once again the men marched, and this time Shah Nawaz did not ask them to assist their fellows—they could not have done it. The sick were left behind.

Fujiwara, who walked out too but in another area, has left a description of these evacuating columns.

> Japanese and I.N.A. officers and men, skinny and half-naked, staggered along with the help of canes. Many of us walked on bare feet smeared with mud and blood, and our faces were ashen, swollen with malnutrition and scaly because of skin disease. Along the edge of the jungle on both sides of the road, the bodies of fallen soldiers lay in an endless line. Many of them had already decomposed because of the humidity, and the torrential rain had bleached their bones white. Others were turning into skeletons with maggots eating away their flesh, and still others lay dying, with their vacant eyes staring into space. . . . There was no means of

transporting the sick because every soldier was half sick and could hardly take care of himself. There was nothing to offer but an encouraging word. Sick persons unable to walk but with some strength left, committed suicide lest they be a burden on their fellow soldiers. A number of them, completely drained of energy, were drowned in a muddy river. Bodies of I.N.A. soldiers who died near a river were tossed into the water by their comrades according to Hindu rituals. It was painful to watch.[33]

At Kuwa, where the Yu meets the wider and more kindly Chindwin, there were boats at last; at Kalewa, fifty miles to the south, food, medical care of a sort, and trucks. So the survivors went off, in packets (for the trucks were not many), some to camps hastily thrown together to receive them, others to INA hospitals—at Monywa ninety miles down the Chindwin, and Maymyo another ninety miles further east. Shah Nawaz does not say how many men were with him when he reached Kalewa. But of the four hundred sick he was obliged to leave at Teraun he writes that it was September before the last of them had been brought out, and adds that by then death had halved their number.

No doubt the Gandhi and Azad regiments had similar experiences, though no one has recorded them. Most of the men who survived the Imphal campaign stuck together and kept discipline. It may have been the only way. But there were many who, though also in groups and in reasonable order, never made it. The officer of Gurkhas who picked up those INA surrender leaflets remembers stumbling, east of the Chindwin in late 1944, upon abandoned *bashas* or native huts in one of which were skeletons, "skeletons with long hair"—the mortal remains, he believes, of Sikhs who had dropped out and died during the retreat.[34] For a long time people on both sides of the Chindwin must have come across such scenes.

Meanwhile there were questions to be faced by the men who did return, of which the first and chief was how did matters stand with the freedom army? What were its prospects, what was its state? Reaching Mandalay in September with brother officers of the Gandhi Regiment, asked the question by Netaji himself, Abid Hasan fell back upon what he had heard a Japanese say late in the battle for Imphal. How were things going, an INA officer had asked this man. By then the Japanese attack was obviously faltering. "To tell you frankly," the Japanese had replied, "the situation is slightly"—he had paused—"the situation is slightly not so very good."[35]

The situation now was slightly not so very good, and Bose knew it.

CHAPTER 14

"Blood! Blood! Blood!"

He had not, however, known it for long. Right into July Subhas Chandra had supposed that the Imphal offensive, though behind schedule, was going well and would in the end succeed. Had he troubled to look himself, had he motored to Kalewa and climbed the Tamu road, he might have discovered otherwise. He did not. Probably the Japanese would have put obstacles in his path had he tried. Meanwhile his own headquarters was as much in the dark as he.

It was partly a matter of the Rangoon scene. The wave of enthusiasm and hope that had lifted the Malayan Indian community (and with it Sivaram) in February and March, had swept Burma too. It was in Japan's interest to see that the wave did not subside. And though Indian staff officers dismissed, or at least ignored, propaganda representations that were transparently false—such as a widely distributed photograph of twenty-five pounders "with a crack artillery unit of the Indian National Army at the front," a photograph actually taken in Malaya where these relics of the British defeat remained—though Indian staff officers knew these for what they were, they did not try to swim against the current of Japanese news releases. Why should they? Cassandras do not win campaigns. Besides, the Imphal campaign *had* opened well. What became of it later was concealed far longer than anyone would have expected by the difficulties people encountered when they tried to discover what, exactly, was going on across the Chindwin.

"At present," Prem wrote Zaman Kiani on June 16 from his office at No. 9 Jamal Avenue, "communications between our Hqs. and the front line units are most inadequate. We have started a weekly courier service between Rangoon and Mandalay." From Mandalay onward radio transmission ought to be possible. But the INA had neither sets nor operators, and would have to ask the Japanese to do the transmitting. Meanwhile "everyone here has been most thrilled to read about the bold action of Unit No. 24. . . . Please convey my heartiest congratulations to Col. I. J. Kiani, Pritam Singh, and the others who took part in it."[1] This "bold action" was the Palel affair of early May cast in its most favorable light. Kiani had made it the centerpiece of an operations report dated 15 May, a report that did not, however, reach Jamal Avenue until the 4th of June. So when Prem sat down to congratulate Inayat and Pritam Singh on their accomplishments, he was reacting to something that had happened a full six weeks before. Had his chief asked him at any point up to the middle of June how the Gandhi Regiment was doing, he would have been bound to reply that it was doing fine.

And as it happened, over most of June Bose wasn't in Rangoon to ask. Made restless by inactivity, impatient to get on with the kind of business for which he was by temperament and experience particularly suited, and that he knew he alone could do, Bose had flown off to Malaya to see what was going on in the training camps and the League branches there, and if necessary (but it was always necessary) shake things up. Returning to Rangoon towards the end of the month, he plunged at once into more of the same.

Some time earlier he had widened his administrative base by persuading a number of leading Malayan Indians (among them Raghavan) to come to Rangoon and join his official family, and by creating new ministries for Revenue and Supply. Now he added a Minister of Manpower, and prepared to split the cabinet into three groups. One was to keep an eye on Burma and Malaya, where the Army and the League were based. One was to look after the frontier regions, especially the Manipur basin, that were in the process of being liberated. The third was to concern itself with "enemy-occupied Indian territory, where the revolution has to be worked up and into which our Army will have to penetrate."[2] By this Subhas Chandra meant not a part of India but *all* of it. A subcommittee of his cabinet was to form plans for the civil administration not just of Assam and Bengal but of the whole subcontinent. It was an assignment having about it, one is inclined to say, an atmosphere of wishful thinking, of castles built in air.

But perhaps that is to misunderstand Subhas Chandra. Always he behaved, and asked Indians to behave, not as he and they were at the moment but as he and they meant to be one day. Always he moved to meet the future with an anticipation, an assertion, a posture (his critics regularly accuse him of striking poses), because he believed—it was also his experience—that in this manner the future might not simply be brought forward. It could actually be determined and shaped.

His battalions off and away, he had like Mutaguchi (though for a different reason) left their daily direction to his officers. But while they fought, he could not, like Mutaguchi, retire to tend his roses. He had work to do. He must prepare the ground for the freedom army's triumph, prepare it in every detail (already the details included freshly printed *Azad Hind* rupee notes and *Azad Hind* stamps). And the more that triumph eluded him, the harder he must work, not to compensate for tardiness or possible failure, not to take his mind off the fighting at the front, but because the effort of will that hard work requires could of itself effect that triumph, that desired end. He would *will* his way to Delhi. (In his confidence in the supremacy of will over matter Bose much resembled, of course, the Japanese.) It was in this frame of mind, and with this purpose, that early in July he led the Rangoon Indian community in a celebration of the freedom movement's achievements over the past year.

On the face of it these achievements were considerable—an army tripled in size, a government created to complement and direct it, both moved to Burma, both poised on India's frontier—and for seven days the Indians of Rangoon did them honor. The Army paraded. The Rani of Jhansi Regiment staged a mock battle. There were concerts, films, sports events; Yellappa, the chief organizer, produced events of every kind. No doubt some were larger and better attended in the planning than they were in the execution. No doubt some, too, were cut short or quite washed away by downpours arranged not by the program committee but by the time of year. From all accounts, however, Netaji Week was a great success. Netaji himself spoke, and it was clear that he had lost none of his power to capture and delight a crowd. Only when you review some of his language—"we did not expect an early victory"—"though of late our progress has not been spectacular, we have nevertheless been pushing on"[3]—do you wonder whether he was not beginning to feel uneasy about happenings to the north.

But if he was uneasy, it was nevertheless impossible for him to admit, perhaps even to himself, that the offensive had failed. What he *could* do, and did, was urge the Japanese to attack, and again attack. Indeed, he put so much pressure on Burma Area Army Headquarters, right there in Rangoon, that in an interesting reversal of roles it was Mutaguchi the enthusiast who first recommended abandoning the Imphal venture, and Kawabe who said, no, you must have one more go. So July went by. And Bose, one ear cocked for news from the front, labored as hard as ever to enlarge and solidify Free India's rear.

Observing that there was room on the Zeyawadi sugar estate for more than his INA training camp, he persuaded the Japanese to let the Indian manager transfer the entire fifteen thousand acres to his Provisional Government, and set about adding a hospital, a convalescent home, and a poultry farm—all under the tricolor flag. Money being more than ever wanted, given the sharply rising cost of everything the army needed, he canvassed personally for the League, touring the branches, making speeches, distributing medals to willing givers and black looks to the unwilling; and when a merchant named Habib exuberantly pledged the whole of his personal property, incorporated his name into a maxim and used it everywhere. "Take a dose of Habeeb mixture," he told wealthy but reluctant prospects, meaning they would be well advised to part with everything they had.[4]

On August 1 the Burmese Government celebrated its first anniversary with a rally and a march past by a battalion of the Burma National Army. Though there was not the slightest indication that Aung San's men were preparing to engage the British, Ba Maw assured the marchers that future generations would ever remember them for their gallant part in "the 4th Anglo-Burmese War."[5] By now, however, it was clear even in Rangoon that the fighting beyond the Chindwin did not go well. Exactly when Bose discovered that Mutaguchi's divisions were retreating is uncertain. Prem believes it was toward the middle of July. It could have been as late as August 12, the day Tokyo first publicly admitted that Japanese units had "shortened their line of operations in the vicinity of the Indo-Burma border."[6] In any case, Bose was ready.

Two days after Tokyo's admission he told the men of the *Azad Hind Fauj*, in a Special Order of the Day, that though they had met and defeated an enemy "numerically superior and better equipped," the fruits of victory had been snatched from them by bad weather. "All preparations had been completed and the stage had been set for the final assault on Imphal when torrential rains overtook us, and to carry Imphal by an assault was rendered a tactical impossibility." It would continue to be impossible as long as the rains went on. So it would be wise to withdraw to "a more favourable defensive position," rest there, and attack again when the weather improved. Final victory was certain. "May the souls of those heroes who have fallen in this campaign inspire us to still nobler deeds of heroism and bravery in the next phase of India's War of Liberation. Jai Hind!"[7]

To blame the failure on the monsoon was not unreasonable, though some might remember that in May, when the rains began, press releases had made much of the trouble rain was going to give the British. To suggest, however, that the sick and the exhausted who dragged themselves down to the Chindwin were executing a carefully measured withdrawal, was hogwash. Prem knew it. At Headquarters he listened to their desperate appeals for help.

It was no use forwarding those appeals to the *Hikari Kikan*. "Ever since the Japanese have decided to go on the defensive," he wrote Zaman Kiani in the middle of August, "I feel a change in their attitude, which I find it very difficult to explain. . . ." They turned their backs on the simplest attempt at cooperation. When they were offered a steam launch to help evacuate the men Shah Nawaz had left at Teraun, "even that they did not agree to."[8] Headquarters would have to manage on its own. So Prem found, bought, and arranged the sewing of enough cloth to cover, at least, Kiani's bedraggled, half-naked men. He opened a shop to make boots for their feet. As proper materials were unobtainable, the bootmakers used rubber for the soles and canvas for the tops. He collected six broken-down trucks, got them running, and sent them north with medical supplies. Rangoon's Indian community did its best to help. But no amount of scrounging or improvising could fully make good the survivors' deficiencies in clothing and equipment, or restore them to good health. That they might be asked to turn when the rains ceased and climb again into the hills, was inconceivable.

Nor did Bose hew long to the line he had taken. In September he left Rangoon and went north to discover for himself the extent of the disaster. At Yeu he watched as men from the decimated battalions were brought in by truck. At Mandalay he conferred with senior officers and members of his cabinet. It was now that Abid Hasan, asked what he thought of the situation, replied with the Japanese officer's "slightly not so very good." It was now that Bose was fed stories of the *Hikari Kikan's* miserable performance in the matter of supply, and of gross mistreatment of jawans by the Japanese. The most disturbing was Shah Nawaz's tale of ten men from his 2nd Battalion seized on suspicion of spying for the British, tied to trees, bayoneted, and left hanging till they died.

Lakshmi, who came down from Maymyo, recalls that Subhas was *in very good spirits. He told us that the tide of war had turned. But that shouldn't worry us, the revolutionary movement in India was still strong. He put all his faith in that.* Did she mean, I asked her, that he expected a fresh attempt soon to break into India? No, she said. *Netaji told us frankly that an offensive was no longer a possibility. He gave us the full picture, about all the reinforcements the British had, how MacArthur's island-to-island strategy was succeeding, that a second front had been opened in Europe. But he still had hopes of a revolution in India. So he was determined that we should continue.* If this left her wondering quite how, where, and with what the struggle should continue, it may be less because she failed to understand him than because he did not know himself.

Late in the month he went to Maymyo, reoccupied his old quarters, and visited the INA hospital. Lakshmi had ordered the Rani of Jhansi nurses up from Rangoon to work in it, but there were only enough of them to scrub for operations and do other such specialized tasks. Temperature taking, sponge baths, and the like fell upon untrained Indian women, and as the hospital filled, these were stretched to the limit. Shah Nawaz came across a girl of sixteen who was caring for eighty-five dysentery cases—an astonishing burden, since persons with that disease cannot help fouling themselves and their bedding over and over and over. Battle casualties were few, perhaps because the lightly wounded had recovered and the seriously wounded had died long before they could be got to Maymyo, but there was a good deal of malaria. The hill strain was virulent. If accompanied by dysentery, it very often killed. Lakshmi found that she knew many of the officers.

Their condition appalled her. Mahboob Ahmed, when they brought him in, was so weak he could barely stand.

What went through Subhas Chandra's mind as he walked the wards and observed the human wreckage cast up by the disaster, it is impossible to say. Shah Nawaz, who was often with him, overheard him talking one day to a beriberi patient. Bending over the man, Bose asked when was he going to get well. "Netaji," came the reply through grotesquely swollen lips, "I will be absolutely fit the day you give us orders to advance again."[9] The words sound contrived, and no doubt were—by the soldier himself, who in spite of his discomfort surely knew how to rise to an occasion. Yet Shah Nawaz believed there was genuine feeling behind both the question and the answer. Indeed, it is impossible to read what people have written about Bose who knew him well, and not conclude that in situations like this, at a bedside, in a mess hall, chatting with aides over tea and cigarettes (he smoked prodigiously), all grandness of manner, all posturing, dropped away. He directed great natural warmth upon those with whom he was engaged, and they returned it. At such moments men and women loved him.

Lakshmi herself had a private moment with her leader, also at Maymyo but weeks earlier, sometime in August perhaps—she remembers heavy rain. A private moment of a sort, however, that told her less that he was warm (which she did not doubt) than that he was vulnerable. It happened in the following way.

Bose had gone back to his old practice of asking a few officers in nightly for dinner and conversation. Lakshmi often came. One evening, just as dinner was ending and the group had settled down to talk, the other officers were suddenly called away. Lakshmi remained. Her hospital lay at some distance, she could not leave until a vehicle was found; an aide went to look for one. And it was then, at that point in the day when he was usually at his most relaxed and communicative, that Netaji turned to her and said: *"I have done something that I don't know whether people in India will be able to understand."* He meant his secret European marriage.

It was not just that Emilie was a foreigner. It was also that though he had made no formal commitment to celibacy, he had allowed people to suppose that he would never marry, that India should be his bride. Emilie, however, had wanted marriage. She had been his friend and

companion from the time of his first visit to Vienna. She had helped
him learn German by reading the daily paper to him, translating the
difficult bits as she went along. She had worked with him on *The Indian
Struggle*, she had seen him through his gallbladder operation; she had
helped him again as he wrote *An Indian Pilgrim*. How could he refuse
her? But the secret was bound to come out some day. "*Do you think
people in India will understand?*"

Lakshmi was sure that they would. "*If you had just had an affair with
her and left her stranded,*" but it wasn't like that at all. "*You haven't done
anything wrong. Besides, your stature is so great that a thing like this. . . .*"
Her recollection of the conversation dies at this point. She may have
been silent a moment, he may have said nothing, and that would be
that. Later she wondered why he had confided in her. (At the time no
one else in the army except Abid Hasan knew that he was married.) He
hadn't seemed himself. *Somehow I could feel that he was under great strain.*
Perhaps he was facing for the first time the fact that the Imphal failure
was irretrievable, that the next year could only bring defeat, and that
defeat meant—for himself— flight, capture, or death. Perhaps this was
why he had wanted to talk to a woman. But Lakshmi did not question
him and there was no further opportunity for private conversation. We
shall never know.

⁂

In October Subhas returned to Rangoon, stayed two weeks, then left
Burma altogether. The cold season was half over before Rangoon saw
him again.

He went first to Japan. For reasons unconnected with Imphal, Tojo
had resigned. His successor was anxious to meet the Indian leader.
Leaving a Muslim officer named Aziz Ahmed in charge, bringing
Chatterji, Habib-ur-Rahman, and Zaman Kiani along, Bose set off. In
Tokyo, where Foreign Minister Shigemitsu gave him one sort of
welcome and American B–29s another, he pressed hard for better
relations between the partners. The *Hikari Kikan* had been a disappointment. Its powers ought to be reduced. At the highest level
Nippon and the *Arzi Hukumat-e-Azad Hind* should treat with each
other in the manner usual between sovereign powers—through ambas-
sadors. Though the Japanese supply dumps would, he hoped, continue

to furnish staples like rice and dal, for the many other things his jawans needed the *Azad Hind Fauj*'s own "Q" branch would make itself responsible, helped by a monthly rupee subsidy from the Japanese. Only military liaison should remain with the *Kikan*. And even here Netaji's expectation was that Indian and Japanese battalions placed side by side would communicate directly, through interpreters.

To all this, and more, the Japanese agreed. There was, after all, little in these arrangements to alarm them. December was almost over before they got around to appointing an envoy to the Provisional Government, and it was March before the man set off. How little Tokyo expected of him was suggested by his previous assignment: Minister to Bulgaria just as the Russians took Sofia. And as he reached Rangoon without proper ambassadorial credentials, Bose refused to receive him.

There was a similar hollowness to the other concessions won. Let the Indians, indeed, undertake more of their own supply. In Burma what was there left to supply anybody with? Why object when the Supreme Commander demanded that the authorized strength of his freedom force rise by tens of thousands? As the men who survived the Imphal campaign had brought a part only of their arms back with them, and the men who perished none, the question now was not how many men might shoulder rifles in the coming year, but how many rifles could be found for men to shoulder.

Subhas Chandra, however, did not perceive how little he was actually getting, or if he did, gave no sign that he was disappointed or annoyed. It was time to celebrate the first anniversary of the Greater East Asia Conference of Nations whose inauguration he had attended the previous November. During the seven days of ceremonies he took his customarily commanding place among the leaders of Japan's half-allied, half-client states. Then he stayed on, renewing old acquaintances, addressing public meetings—at one, Joyce Lebra says, he talked without pause for two hours in a voice so powerful that people unable to get into the jammed auditorium heard him clearly as they stood outside. He spoke, too, over Radio Tokyo, to his overseas listeners in the several languages at his command. As much as ever, though air raids made plain how badly the war was going in the Pacific, he retained his vision of an India independent not at some undefined and distant date but in the foreseeable future.

And when, at the end of November, he shifted from Tokyo to Malaya, stopping en route at Shanghai and Saigon, from Singapore making quick trips to Bangkok and Sumatra, that vision remained the staple of what he had to say. By this time the flow of civilian volunteers had dwindled to the point where new recruits at the Seletar and Kuala Lumpur training camps barely outnumbered men shedding their uniforms and slipping away. The freedom movement's income, too, was drying up. The League pleaded. The League threatened. Indians grossly in default were reported to the Japanese, who arrested some. And still each month's take, upon which both army and provisional government depended, was less than it had been the month before. Yet when Bose at last reached Rangoon, on the 10th of January after an eleven weeks' absence, he sounded—or tried to sound—as confident as ever.

At a press conference held the day after his arrival, he reminded the assembled newsmen that the war had proceeded by stages. The first stage had been marked by spectacular German and Japanese successes. In the second the initiative had passed to Britain and America; the tide had flowed the other way. Now the third stage was approaching. Free India's allies, forced back to the borders of their homelands, are turning. (Though Bose did not elaborate, no doubt he had in mind the surprise German attack in the Ardennes of three weeks before, and the much wider Japanese "Ichi-Go" offensive in south central China—an offensive that had overrun half a dozen provinces and knocked out the airfields the Ledo Road was supposed to support.) The Anglo-Americans are overextended, he said. Their losses at sea and in the sky have been enormous, and cannot easily be replaced. In any case, it is not material power that will decide this conflict, but spiritual force—in which they are notoriously deficient. The third stage will be decisive. In it we Indians must play our rightful part. The struggle will be hard, harder than last year's, for in Burma the enemy's strength is more than it was and grows greater daily. But Imphal has taught us something precious. Imphal has taught us that we can defeat the British. Had the rains not intervened, we should by now have occupied the Manipur basin and be descending into the plains. Imphal has given us the knowledge and the certainty that in the fight for independence, which Indians at home will join as soon as they receive the call, we shall ultimately prevail. It is in this spirit of confidence that we enter the new year.

These were the terms in which Bose put the freedom army's prospects. This was the frame of mind he attempted to convey. But he said other things as well, things which implied that confidence was not what he felt himself. He said that his staff was organizing suicide squads on the model of the Japanese kamikaze. And he repeated an earlier suggestion: the freedom army, he said, must have a new war cry. He had introduced the new cry at a rally in October. Now he recited it again, and in the days that followed asked audiences to accustom themselves to it. The cry was simple. It was the Hindustani word *khun*, repeated. At one time the men of the Indian National Army had chanted that they were on the march to Delhi. Now they were to cry for blood.

The blood Subhas wanted was not British blood, though an Englishman who chanced to overhear the shouting might well have supposed it was. It was Indian blood Netaji wanted, and he asked for it because the old slogan did not fit the situation in which he and his men now found themselves. It was true that in the most general sense they still marched. The war continued. It had not stopped. But Bose knew, and in his oblique way said, that in the months ahead, during what was left of the dry season, the fighting season, his men were *not* going to climb the Chin and Naga hills again with Delhi the goal. They hadn't the arms, the numbers, or the strength. Even the Kabaw and Myittha valleys were beyond them. How, then, were they to occupy themselves? Where should they station themselves? What should they do?

His answer was that they should anticipate India's freedom by paying freedom's price right where they were, in Burma—with their bodies. For freedom, like all things high and difficult, carries a price. The price of freedom is the observed willingness of men to fight and die for it. The price of freedom, in a word, is blood. And blood it was in the power of these young men to offer. The British no longer waited in the high country. They were coming down the Tamu road, they were crossing the Chindwin, already they approached the Irrawaddy. When the *Azad Hind Fauj* marched out this time, the most it could realistically hope to do was bar, for a while, their way. *Tum mujhe khun do, main tumhen azadi dunga.* Give me blood, and I will give you freedom. Die for your country, that through your death your country may live. As 1945 opened, this was all Bose had to offer.

🙦

Subhas Brigade, or what was left of it, had spent the early autumn at Budalin, south of Yeu. The Azad had been billeted at Chaungu, still further south, the Gandhi (reduced to one battalion) at Mandalay. In November all three were ordered to Pyinmana, 150 miles below Mandalay on the main road and rail line to Rangoon. There, in a camp much closer to the freedom army's chief source of supply, these skeleton regiments would, it was hoped, recover something like their former strength.

They went by rail, a difficult and dangerous business requiring weeks, for by this time British tactical aircraft from airstrips in the Manipur basin and the Kabaw Valley were hitting bridges and rolling stock as far south as Meiktila. Nothing moved by day. At first light troop trains stopped, if possible in cuttings; the precious engines were run into pens made of woven bamboo filled with rocks; the men scattered and slept. The 4th (Nehru) Regiment did not accompany the other three. It had been brought as far as Mandalay, but too late to take part in the Imphal campaign. Now it moved southwest, to Myingyan, where the Chindwin joins the Irrawaddy. Untouched by battle or the wasting effects of the rain-sodden hills, it was expected to be everything the three other guerrilla regiments were not.

It had troubles of its own, however. Mutiny was the worst. The mutineers were south Indians, Tamils mostly, rubber tappers and coolies from the plantations and docks of Malaya caught up in Netaji's first great recruiting drive, and they had mutinied because they could not bear the way they were treated by their officers. The problem went back to the Malayan training camps—to the moment when the instructors, all drawn of course from the "martial races" of north India, had discovered to their surprise that they were being asked to make jawans out of men on the average four inches shorter, thirty pounds lighter, and several shades darker than themselves. Out of men unable to understand the simplest order given in Hindustani, the warrior's tongue; men who by the standards of the old Indian Army might become sweepers, but never soldiers.

The instructors' surprise had turned to exasperation, their exasperation to contempt, and this had stirred in the recruits a smoldering resentment that passed at last to insubordination and covert acts of violence. At one point Bose himself rushed to Seletar to try to defuse the tension. Because he was south Indian, John Somasundaram was asked to take command of the Kuala Lumpur camp, where he stayed until the end of the war. But the tension did not go away. It infected the Nehru Regiment, perhaps because the Nehru had more civilian recruits than the other guerrilla regiments. And at last it produced the mutiny. At Mandalay, in September, six hundred men suddenly refused to obey their officers. The mutineers were placed under arrest. Steps were taken to bring them to trial. But Bose refused his consent. He understood better than most what had been driving the men. Would you be willing to take the mutineers back? he asked when, on the 26th of October, just before leaving for Tokyo, he offered the regiment to Gurbaksh Singh Dhillon.

At the time the Imphal campaign opened, Dhillon was serving with the 5th Guerrilla Regiment, which had been formed later than the other four and was still training at Ipoh. Impetuous by nature, quick to anger (and quick to apologize when apologies were due), he quarreled one day with the regiment's commander, let the quarrel continue, and was transferred to the 1st Infantry Regiment at Jitra. The 1st Infantry was Bhonsle's Hindustan Field Force under a new man and name. It was the oldest regiment in the INA, with the heaviest weapons. One would have expected it to move to Burma ahead of all the others. Bose, however, chose to make it the nucleus of his 2nd Division, which—largely because it contained so many civilian re- cruits—could not be ready when the 1st was. So the 1st Infantry did not start for the front until May 1944, the men by the overland route used by Subhas Brigade five months before, the heavy weapons by sea. Somewhere between Victoria Point and Mergui the ship carrying the heavy weapons was torpedoed. When the regiment collected at Rangoon in September, it was judged unfit to proceed farther until it could be reequipped.

Dhillon considered it unready anyway. At Jitra he had been appalled by the leisurely pace at which it trained. He wanted no part of it, and shortly after reaching Rangoon got himself transferred to 2nd Division Headquarters, just in from Malaya too. But again he had a row with a senior officer. This time he asked to be removed from staff altogether. Might he have a field assignment? So Aziz Ahmed, who commanded the 2nd Division, sent him to Bose, who had never met him but took to him at once. They had several private conversations, very warm, very frank (if we may accept Dhillon's reconstruction of them), and Netaji offered him the Nehru Regiment, mutiny and all. Dhillon accepted. He agreed, also, to take back the mutineers. Three weeks later he was at Myingyan.

He found his three battalions scattered outside the town, and felt at once an atmosphere of slackness. Afraid of being spotted from the air and strafed, the men had shed their uniforms and walked about in Burmese dress. They seldom paraded, never drilled, and the digging of trenches and antitank traps—it was the Nehru's task to make Myingyan defensible—went on only during the hours of darkness, which in practice meant on nights without a moon. Dhillon moved at once to change all this. He ordered the wearing of the uniform, always and by all ranks. He told his company commanders to set a part of each day aside for foot and weapons drill. He insisted that drills, and digging too, go forward by day as well as by night. That was not all. Possessing as he did an unusual capacity for personal contact, he made it his practice to recognize his officers by name, even to the most junior. He invited his jawans to come to him with their problems, grievances, fears—he would be as a father to them. But he deceived himself if he supposed that he could whip the regiment into shape by sheer bustle and warmth. The rot had gone too deep, how deep he discovered when one of his battalion commanders was caught selling rations to the Burmese and had to be sent back to Rangoon.

There Prem, also, had tired of staff work, and with more cause. Though he was far from being the most senior among the twenty or so KCOs and ICOs who were now officers in the *Azad Hind Fauj*, he had seen more action than any of them. He had been in the Malayan campaign from its beginning, and fought the full length of the peninsula. Yet here he sat, his field experience wasted, cutting orders, arranging troop movements, grappling with the *Hikari Kikan*—and, which was worse, sniped at because of it. For there were people who believed that he liked the life on Jamal Avenue, enjoyed his ready access to the Supreme Commander, traded on it, and never meant to give it up. Soon they would be saying so openly. *I knew it was coming.* So he made up his mind, though he was sure the war was lost, to leave

Headquarters and get into the field. When Bose returned to Rangoon in October, he asked for a regiment. Bose promised him one.

He went up to Yeu for a spell. There he ran into Thakur Singh, second in command of Subhas Brigade. It was early one morning; Thakur had just arrived; Prem's work was done, and Thakur insisted that they have a few drinks together. *So we went to a village where they were brewing the local brew, and sat next to the still, and drank the whole day.* That night they drove to Maymyo. During the drive *Thakur Singh got into a very violent mood. He wanted to murder every Japanese we met on the way*—"*they let us down,*" *he said.* By the time they reached Maymyo, Prem had a terrible pain in the small of the back, *and my liver was that size. I went to the hospital, and Lakshmi had one look at me and said, "what have you been up to?"*

It had long been understood between them that when the war was over, when her Tata Airlines pilot gave her a divorce, *if* they both survived—they would marry. Meanwhile they saw as much as possible of each other, in those patches of time when they happened to be in the same place. There had been one such patch at Rangoon in April, between Lakshmi's return from Singapore and her departure for Maymyo. Prem had had a staff car and they had spent afternoons together. And there were evenings at Maymyo, on the occasions (including this one) when Prem could manage for reasons genuine or contrived to stop there. As long as he attended on the Supreme Commander, he could at least keep track of Lakshmi, for Headquarters was always in touch with the big INA hospitals. Once he went into the field, however, communication of any sort would be difficult and an exchange of letters impossible. He was about to go into the field now.

Early in December he returned to Rangoon, emptied his desk at No. 9 Jamal Avenue—Mahboob Ahmed, back on his feet, was to be military secretary—vacated his billet, and drove out to Mingaladon Camp. There, on the 10th of the month, he took command of the regiment that Netaji had promised him: the 5th Guerrilla Regiment, two thousand strong and just in from Malaya. Its commander was angry at being superseded, but Prem, who knew him well (they had been at Dehra Dun together), smoothed his ruffled feathers and saw him off to a staff job. Then he set about getting a grip on his new command.

He would have to redirect his thinking. Gone was the prospect of climbing the jungle-covered hills on the flanks of a Japanese column, slipping down the far slopes to the plains below, melting into the villages, raising the countryside against the British occupier. The *Azad Hind Fauj* would fight now not on the Brahmaputra but on the Irrawaddy. And its posture would be defensive. It was time, therefore, to abandon the designation "guerrilla"—and abandoned it was. The 5th Guerrilla Regiment, reinforced by several hundred officers and men from the luckless 1st Infantry and the civilian training center in Rangoon, became the 2nd Infantry Regiment. Providing it with appropriate arms, transport, signals equipment, and the like, was another matter, however. A few things Prem managed to lay his hands on. "Went to the range in the morning and fired the new mortar," he noted in his diary one January evening. "It is a very accurate weapon."[10] But there was very little ammunition for it; very little, too, in the way of heavy machine guns, field telephones, and much else. Prem's influence at Headquarters guaranteed that he would get whatever was available. That was all that could be said.

I trained them very hard. Mingaladon Camp was a beautiful camp, relatively safe from air attack because close to the airfield, which still held fighters; and there, over the next six or seven weeks, Prem put the men through a series of field exercises, platoon level first, company next, then battalion and regiment. He also talked to the men, in small groups, explaining to them what they were doing and what they might expect. By now they, too, knew that Imphal, and beyond it India, were quite beyond reach. They, too, knew they were going to remain right where they were, there in Burma—perhaps die in Burma. What for?

In one respect it was easier to give these men an answer than it would have been had they been jawans in one of the older guerrilla regiments. The men in those were almost all ex–Indian Army, which is to say they came from India and had families there. Telling *them* that they were not, after all, going to march across the border, would have been construed as an invitation to watch for an opportune moment, then give themselves up. For if the *Azad Hind Fauj* was never to enter India, how could a man hope to reach home again? Only through the POW cage. It would be his only way.

But half the men in Prem's regiment were not ex–Indian Army at all. They were civilian recruits, south Indians mostly. They had grown up in Malaya, Malaya was where their families were; India did not call to them. And it was the same with the junior officers. All the platoon and many of the company commanders were civilians who had been trained in Habib-ur-Rahman's Officers Training School. (The rest were former VCOs. The only person in·the regiment besides Prem who had held the King-Emperor's commission was Major Negi, the second in command, and he had been emergency commissioned.) Prem did not tell these men that the war was lost and that it remained only for them to give their blood so that India might some day be free. Nor did he talk about suicide squads (none were ever actually formed). He talked about what Japan was doing. Japan's strategy, he told them, was to withdraw into a circle, a circle so carefully prepared and fortified that the British and the Americans could never break into it. The edge of the circle passed through Burma. It ran along the Irrawaddy. We are going to defend a segment of it, he told his jawans. We are going to show the world that we are a real army, not stooges of the Japanese. This was what Prem remembers saying as he went from platoon to platoon. *And I think I succeeded in convincing them that this was the truth.*

On the 14th of January, four days after his return from his East Asian tour, Bose spoke to a great rally at Rangoon's city hall. "*Khun! Khun! Khun aur Khun!*" he cried to the Indians assembled. Eager bidders pledged princely sums for the privilege of bearing off the garlands draped about his shoulders. On the same day the British crossed the Irrawaddy forty miles north of Mandalay. The information did not make its way into the pages of *Greater Asia*. But Rash Behari Bose's death, in Tokyo after a long illness, did; so did word that he had been posthumously awarded the Second Class Order of the Rising Sun with Double Rays; so did the news that in Europe the Russians had broken into Upper Silesia. At Mingaladon Camp, while Japanese officers watched, Prem led his new command through a final exercise involving all three battalions.

On the 26th the regiment paraded preparatory to departure. Netaji spoke. Though he began (as the regimental adjutant later remembered it) with ritual observations about crushing Allied losses and the inexorably turning tide, the burden of his remarks was decidedly more somber. "I do not wish to paint a rosy picture to you," he said. "We are not so well equipped with arms, equipment and manpower as our enemies are. You will have to face hunger, thirst, other hardships and even death when you go to the front," and some of you may falter— may even be tempted to dishonor yourselves and your comrades by deserting to the other side. It happened last year. It must not happen again. "This time I do not want that a single man should go over to the enemy. . . ."[11] The unsure and the fearful were to report to their officers so that arrangements could be made to leave them behind. Then the Supreme Commander led the men and spectators in shouts of Blood! Blood! Blood! There were cries of *Chalo Delhi* too. But when, several days later, the regimental advance party departed, no one can have seriously supposed that Delhi was the goal.

Indeed, on the 29th of January Dhillon received orders to move the Nehru Regiment in quite the opposite direction—to Nyaungu, thirty-five miles down the river. Setting off with a small party that very evening, Dhillon reached the new position, reconnoitered both banks, returned to Myingyan, and got his three battalions away at dusk on February 4. Meanwhile Prem's 2nd Infantry Regiment was moving up to Prome by road, a company at a time as transport became available. Prem himself remained in Rangoon. At a little ceremony Bose pinned major general's badges on Zaman Kiani. Shah Nawaz too would soon become a major general (the INA did not have brigadiers). Prem had been a lieutenant colonel for quite a while.

The last of his companies was trucked away and he was on the point of following when Allied bombers struck the INA hospital at Myang, a few miles outside the city, and left scores of men and women dead or injured—among them Aziz Ahmed, with concussion of the brain. Someone would have to take Aziz's place, at least temporarily, at 2 Division. Bose turned to Prem. When, therefore, Prem started north in a staff car, he was wearing two hats—commander of the 2nd Infantry Regiment, and commander of the division of which it was a part. Before leaving he paid the usual courtesy call upon the army's commander in chief. It did not occur to him that he would never see Netaji Subhas Chandra Bose again.

He set off on a Tuesday. Very early the next day, Wednesday the 14th of February, 1945, several hundred men of Slim's South Lancashire Regiment, 7th Indian Division, came down to the right bank of the Irrawaddy opposite Nyaungu, climbed into boats, and pushed off for the far shore. The last act in the British reconquest of Burma had begun. The great drive that would, after one serious interruption, carry 14th Army to the outskirts of Rangoon was under way. At that moment Prem Kumar Sahgal was forty miles out of Rangoon on the road to Prome. Gurbaksh Singh Dhillon was in his regimental headquarters just south of Nyaungu. Shah Nawaz Khan was with the three skeleton guerrilla regiments at Pyinmana.

Sahgal, Dhillon, Shah Nawaz.

Nine months later, at the Red Fort in Delhi, these three would be put on trial for offenses that, if proved, could shut them away from their families, from life itself, for the rest of their days. But it was now, close to the Irrawaddy and still very early in the year, that they came together and set out together on the road that led them to that peril. There was nothing predetermined about this. Each might have continued to have only a nodding acquaintance with the other. Each might have followed a separate, and a safer, path. Circumstances, however, and the character of each, drew them down a common course. So that, looking back, one can see why the British, casting about in the moment of their apparent triumph for renegade figures to whom they could instantly apply the salutary treatment of a public trial, did not have far to look. Sahgal, Dhillon, and Shah Nawaz were the obvious candidates. They'd asked for it, as the expression goes. And the place where they asked for it was Mount Popa.

CHAPTER 15

MOUNT POPA

At roughly the point in Burma's great central valley where the Irrawaddy bends sharply west, receives the Chindwin, then turns again for the Bay of Bengal, there is a stretch of country perhaps 150 miles from north to south and rather less from east to west which, because it lies in the shadow of the Chin Hills, receives only twenty to forty inches of rain during the monsoon season—one third of what Rangoon can expect, one fifth of what will fall upon the Arakan coast.

Burma geographers call this the Dry Belt. In its southern portions particularly, the dryness is very apparent. Stunted trees, prickly bushes, cactus and clumps of dry bamboo, dot a plain whose surface in some places is largely sand and gravel. Stream beds wind everywhere, empty most of the year. Villages are small, patches of cultivation infrequent, the landscape utterly without interest—except where Mount Popa, sixty miles from the Chin Hills on one side, sixty miles from the first heave of the Shan Highlands on the other, lifts its massive head. Popa rises gently. Partway up there are trees, higher still grass broken by blocks of lava. At the top, some four thousand feet above the surrounding country, the climber stands on the lip of a volcanic crater a mile in diameter. Below, green jungle mantles the crater's floor.

During the monsoon Popa's height attracts rainfall much above the Dry Belt's average, so that streams begin high upon its slopes (one feeds the lake, forty miles to the east, on which Meiktila stands), and things grow that will not grow on the plain. Dhillon remembers groves of mangoes, guavas, jack fruit. In early British days dacoits made the place their refuge. So did the wild pig; so does the hamadryad, with whom (they say) girls specially trained for the purpose dance—*but I never met a girl*, Prem once remarked to me, *and I never met a cobra*. Mount Popa is, in fact, an oasis. At the height of the dry season the springs on its western side are the only reliable source of water for miles around. But it was not the water that brought Prem Sahgal, Dhillon, and Shah Nawaz there in the third week of February 1945. It was the British thrust, passing just to the north.

In the aftermath of Imphal the Japanese had for a moment considered abandoning Burma altogether. The moment had passed. With difficulty men and weapons had been brought in. And though some of these were subsequently recalled, it remained Japan's intention to hold Burma on the line of the Irrawaddy. When, moreover, the British crossed that river north of Mandalay in mid-January, and crossed again south of it a few weeks later, Burma Area Army Headquarters took it for a certainty that Mandalay was the region where the principal British blow would fall, and disposed its forces accordingly. But Slim had another plan.

That he could devise and execute it was indicative of how little the strategic considerations of two years before affected operations now. Britain had not wished to retake Burma by overland assault. It had not wished to retake Burma at all except, as it were, in passing. It had preferred amphibious operations directed at Singapore and beyond. An army had been sent into north Burma only because the Americans, determined to reopen a road to China, had made it plain that the transport and landing craft necessary for amphibious operations would not be forthcoming until north Burma was cleared.

Cleared it had been. The Stilwell Road, as it was officially called, was open. The first convoy left Ledo on the 12th of January, 1945, and rolled into Kunming on February 4. But the road no longer mattered. Undone at last by Peanut's hot resentment and his own acerbic manner, Vinegar Joe had been ordered back to the States. Since B–29s would never reach Tokyo now from Chinese airfields (the Japanese had overrun them), but *could* from the Pacific islands the Americans had seized, China's usefulness in the war against Japan was not what it had once promised to be. (The current American worry was that the Japanese "Ichi-go" campaign on the Chinese mainland would continue until China ceased to be in the war at all.) Even the road itself did not live up to expectations. During the half year between its opening and the end of the fighting, the total tonnage trucked did not exceed what the airlift had handled in a month.

So the reestablishment of ground contact with China no longer drove relations between Britain and the United States. One might have expected the British to revert, at this point, to their original strategy— and do nothing further in Burma. One might have expected them to wait for the day when, the war in Europe finished, they could shift their full weight eastward and send ships, planes, and men to take part in the grand Pacific offensive the Americans had launched, the offensive that was to end with the invasion of the Japanese homeland itself.

The war in Europe, however, once thought likely to be over before Christmas, had continued into the new year. It continued still. And even if it were to end at once, Britain's declining strength would never permit her to contribute in any significant way to operations against Japan—these, by contrast, were moving faster than anyone had foreseen. Britain might send forces to fight alongside the Americans. They scarcely would be noticed.

This did not deter the British Chiefs of Staff. If only for professional reasons, they wanted men from all branches of the armed services to take part in the Pacific fighting. Churchill, however, feared the political consequences if everywhere east of Calcutta Britain played second fiddle to America. Reestablishing Britain's presence in that part of the world, which he was determined to do, turned upon erasing the shame of her defeats. That would occur only when British forces overcame Japanese forces somewhere, alone and unassisted. Burma was a likely place. Britain had an army there (the Americans did not), an army that had already met the Japanese and stopped them. In Burma a convincing, independent British victory appeared possible. Indeed, Burma might be the only place in Asia where it was.

Slim, then, was instructed to press on across the Chindwin. Or perhaps we should say he was suffered to, for Sir William (he had been knighted in a little ceremony at Imphal) had already made up his mind. He meant to repay the Japanese, in kind and with interest, for what they had done to him in 1942. His men shared that determination. Mountbatten, too, was coming around to the opinion that a victorious campaign in Burma, though leading nowhere (Burma was as always a dead end), was worth having. 14th Army, it seemed, was not to be denied.

Permission to press on did not, however, solve Sir William's problems. He hoped to catch and destroy the Japanese on the Shwebo plain west of the the Irrawaddy. But Lieutenant General Kimura Hyotaro, Kawabe's replacement at Burma Area Army, shrewdly declined to fight where the British could so conveniently deploy their armor. He withdrew across the river. 14th Army might follow, of course. The obvious route to Rangoon ran through Mandalay down the east side of Burma's great central valley. But it was long. Taking it meant meeting Kimura's divisions head on. Then there was the monsoon to consider. If 14th Army attempted to fight the full length of the valley, by June, when the rains were certain to have begun, it would advance at no better than a crawl. By July, mired in mud, it might cease to advance at all.

Slim had no intention of permitting this. Slim looked for a maneuver that, by placing a force across the Japanese line of retreat, would provoke a decisive battle well short of Rangoon and allow his columns to get there ahead of the monsoon. 14th Army had two corps. Slim instructed the 33rd to follow the Japanese across the Irrawaddy, and press them hard, so that they would suppose him primarily interested in Mandalay. Meanwhile 4 Corps, Frank Messervy commanding—the same Messervy who had led a division at the Battle of the Administrative Box—was to slip south through the hills on the west side of the central valley, cross the Irrawaddy below Myingyan, and make a dash for Meiktila and Thazi. There, on the main rail line and highway seventy miles below Mandalay, lay the administrative center, the dumps, depots, and airfields, that supported the Japanese to the north. From there lines of communication and supply fanned out "like the extended fingers of a hand whose wrist was Meiktila. Crush that wrist, no blood would flow through the fingers, the whole hand would be paralyzed. . . ."[1] The Japanese would disintegrate. Then Messervy, at the signal, would turn for Rangoon not three hundred miles away. If he adopted the tactic the Japanese had used with such devastating effect in Malaya three years before—never mind flanks or rear, plunge straight down the best available road—he should just reach the city before the rains began.

That was Sir William's plan. Success hung partly upon air transport, needed to keep 4 Corps in fuel and ammunition not only as it approached Meiktila but afterwards, when it cut loose for Rangoon. South-East Asia Command would protest, of course, that air transport on the scale required was not to be had. Slim meant to pay this protest no heed. Once 14th Army was well and truly launched, Mountbatten would discover that he *must* find the Dakotas—and he would find them, of this Slim was sure. What concerned Sir William more was what Messervy had to do.

Messervy had to get down to the Irrawaddy below Myingyan, which meant taking an entire corps (two divisions and a brigade of tanks) two hundred miles over a fair-weather track—a track he must improve to receive not just trucks but tank transporters with their much greater length and weight. He had to do this undiscovered. And he had to do it promptly. The move, from Kalewa up the Myittha River valley to Gangaw and beyond, then southeast to the Irrawaddy at Nyaungu, began in the middle of January. It consumed a month, just what Slim had allowed. And though the advance party met stiff resistance from Japanese rearguards, Burma Area Army remained ignorant of the formidable column that followed, perhaps because Messervy maintained radio silence while a dummy headquarters at Tamu transmitted misleading messages, perhaps because British fighters kept Japanese planes from spotting the clouds of red dust thrown up by vehicles and men. When, therefore, the South Lancashires of 7th Indian Division came down to the Irrawaddy opposite Nyaungu very early on the morning of February 14, the Japanese, though not surprised to find the enemy testing the river line, had no idea of his ultimate purpose. Nor any inkling of the weight of the blow that was about to fall.

At Nyaungu the Irrawaddy, elsewhere more than a mile wide and in some places much wider still, narrows a good deal. It was partly for this reason, and partly because from Nyaungu tracks negotiable by motor vehicles led east toward Meiktila, that Messervy had chosen this spot. But Nyaungu possessed another advantage Messervy knew nothing about. At Nyaungu the extreme left of the Japanese 15th Army (no longer commanded by Mutaguchi, he had long since been called

home) touched the extreme right of the 28th. Guarding the whole
length of the river was an impossibility. Neither army felt responsible
for this stretch. It fell to the Indians. The official British history of this
theater avers, without elaboration, that "the defence of the Pagan-
Nyaungu area had been left mainly to the *I.N.A.*" And in his personal
account of the campaign, Slim identifies the unit. It was, he says, "the
2nd Indian National Army Division"—with numbers, he adds, "variously reported as between five and ten thousand."[2]

That, however, is to mistake a part for the whole. When the 7th
Indian Division reached the river, only the Nehru Regiment occupied
the left bank. Its strength cannot have exceeded fifteen hundred men (it
may have been less). For though Dhillon had readmitted many of the
mutineers, he had discarded others he thought unreliable or medically
unfit; with the consequence that Hari Ram's 7th Battalion (for some
reason the three battalions were numbered 7, 8, and 9), which was
strung out along the bluff east of Nyaungu town, had some four
hundred men only. Chandar Bhan's 9th, at Pagan four miles down the
river, had perhaps five hundred. The 8th, held in reserve, had the same.
Besides rifles, the regiment possessed three light mortars with twenty
rounds apiece, and four machine guns. (There had been eight but
Dhillon had abandoned the less serviceable, first cannibalizing them for
parts.) A pitiful force, pitifully armed. No wonder the men were
dispirited and nervous, as Dhillon says they were.

Nevertheless for a while they held. The long haul down from
Kalewa had damaged some of the South Lancashires' boats, which had
to be repaired, and many of the outboard motors would not start, so it
was full daylight before the crossing began. Because of sandbanks—one
masked Nyaungu town itself, which was why a crossing there was not
attempted—the boats had to follow a diagonal course, making this
(writes Slim with more than a hint of satisfaction) "the longest opposed
river crossing attempted in any theatre of the Second World War."[3] And
Hari Ram was ready. He was not being shelled. Messervy's artillery had
not registered the evening before lest it give the show away. When the
boats were still some distance out, his machine guns dug in at the
water's edge (Dhillon had given him all four) opened fire to good
effect. A number of boats were holed, others capsized in the confusion,
the rest turned back. At Pagan, to the southwest, a smaller diversionary

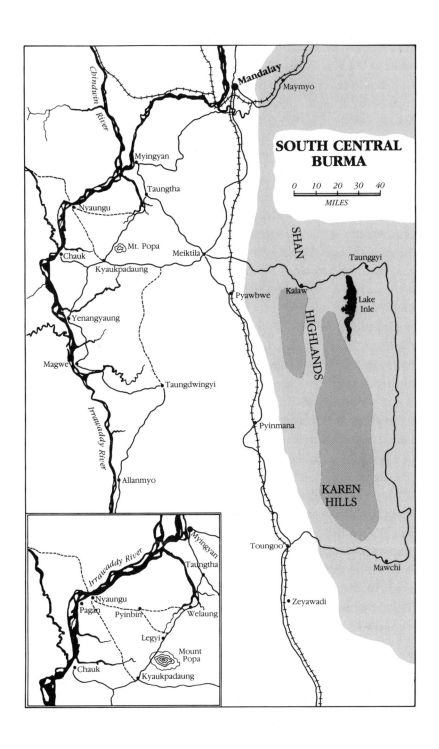

SOUTH CENTRAL
BURMA

0 10 20 30 40
MILES

Chindwin River

Mandalay
Maymyo

Myingyan

Taungtha

Nyaungu

Mt. Popa
Chauk
Kyaukpadaung
Meiktila

Pyawbwe

SHAN

Kalaw
Taunggyi

Lake
Inle

HIGHLANDS

Yenangyaung

Magwe

Taungdwingyi

Irrawaddy River

Pyinmana

Allanmyo

KAREN
HILLS

Toungoo

Mawchi

Zeyawadi

Irrawaddy River

Myingyan

Taungtha

Nyaungu
Pagan
Pyinbin
Welaung

Legyi

Mount
Popa
Chauk
Kyaukpadaung

crossing by part of a Sikh battalion was stopped by rifle fire. For a moment Dhillon's men supposed the day was theirs.

They were mistaken. The British were not so easily dissuaded. Before long several companies of a Punjabi battalion were afloat and making for Nyaungu behind a curtain of fire laid down by 25-pounders and the guns of the tank brigade, while tactical aircraft from a "cab rank" overhead raked bluff and beach. Dhillon, meanwhile, had been awakened by the noise of battle. He had left his command post in the little village of Tetthe, where his reserve battalion was stationed, and hurried forward, visiting Chandar Bhan at Pagan first, reaching Hari Ram in time to see the overturned boats of the British drifting away. There, with Hari Ram, he ought to have remained, communicating with his other battalions by runner.

But neither temperament nor battle experience (he had little of the latter, just a few days at Jitra during the Malayan campaign) inclined Dhillon to stay long in one place. He *had* to be on the move. So at the rumor of fighting further east, where he understood a Japanese detachment to be, off he went, found what he was looking for—some South Lancashires had slipped across the river during the night, and the Japanese were trying to dislodge them—and was trapped for a time in the crossfire. When at last he started back, he was met by word of a disaster. The British had come ashore at Hari Ram's position. Hari Ram himself had raised the white flag. More than a hundred men had surrendered with him. The rest had fled.

Hurrying to his reserve battalion at Tetthe, Dhillon discovered that the demoralizing news had preceded him there. He ordered the battalion forward. It would not to budge. "What will you gain by getting the remaining men killed?" the commander objected. "For God's sake have mercy upon us and allow us to surrender."[4] Exhausted, distraught, feverish with what may have been an attack of appendicitis, Dhillon by his own account was close to collapse. All that saved him, he believes, was an intercession from on high.

For when, in his desperation, he raised his head and bellowed for help, his shout was heard—by Govind Singh, tenth Sikh guru and founder of the Sikh military brotherhood. "There, just above the trees in the sky, was the Guru, wearing the Golden Crest on his turban, with his Quiver slung over a shoulder and the Golden Hawk perched on his hand." To this saintly specter Dhillon promptly unburdened himself. He was, he admitted, clean shaven, which a good Sikh ought never to be. But did he on that account deserve the disgrace and obloquy that would be heaped upon him if he failed his Netaji? "Grant me courage, O Guru, grant it before it is too late."[5] And courage was granted. Suddenly Dhillon was his own self again. Observing a jawan fastening a white cloth to a stick, he rushed over and tore the shameful object from the fellow's hand.

Yet he did not try to hold Tetthe, much less return to the river. Men with no will to fight, he let leave. The rest he had dig in against the random mortar fire that was beginning to fall. Late that night he ordered them, too, away—to Mount Popa, which in daylight was clearly visible to the southeast. Lingering behind to try to get in touch with Chandar Bhan, he did not set off himself until the evening of the 15th. Another day and night passed before he reached Popa. There he found Chandar Bhan, and jawans from all three of his battalions. Hundreds of men, however, were missing. Some were dead, some had surrendered, the rest had fled. A regiment that had once numbered almost two thousand could muster now not four hundred. Many of these had lost their rifles, their personal equipment, and (which was worse) their self-respect. "They wander about and give away my position," Prem noted in his diary.[6] Prem, too, had arrived.

He had left Rangoon on the morning of February 13 and spent the next day at the headquarters of 28th Army, some distance up the Prome road, talking to staff officers. Three days later he had paused at Yenangyaung, on the Irrawaddy fifty miles below Nyaungu, to see Yamamoto Tsunoru, the man who during the Imphal campaign had led Yamamoto Force against the Manipur basin. Yamamoto commanded the 72nd Independent Mixed Brigade now. He also directed Kanjo Force, a much smaller composite of two infantry battalions and a handful of guns. From Yamamoto, Prem learned that in the campaigning ahead his regiment and Kanjo Force, Kanjo *Butai* as the Japanese called it, would work hand in glove.

28th Army, to which the 72nd IMB and Kanjo *Butai* belonged, was responsible for southern Burma, and for the Arakan as well. There, early in the year, greatly superior British forces had obliged the Japanese to abandon Akyab and the offshore islands of Ramree and Cheduba. From these places, and particularly the last two (which lie on a level with Prome and Toungoo), British tactical aircraft would have no difficulty ranging down Burma's central valley as far as Rangoon itself. That was bad news. But at the moment 28th Army paid little attention to the Arakan. It was preoccupied by what was going on along the Irrawaddy.

It did not, of course, expect that in the great British offensive everyone knew was coming, the main blow would fall this far south. It took seriously, however, its responsibility for the left flank of the Irrawaddy line, which in the lower reaches of the river included both banks, and close by the Yenangyaung oilfields. Forty miles from Yenangyaung rose Mount Popa. Holding Popa would not of itself secure the Irrawaddy. But it would help. And given what these Indians could and could not do; given, also, their leader's insistence that they have separate, independent battlefield assignments; it made sense to have them hold it. "Got the news that my role is going to be defence of Popa Hill," Prem had written in his diary five days before leaving Rangoon.[7] When he learned, at Yenangyaung on the 17th, that the British had crossed the Irrawaddy a short distance to the north, the news did nothing to alter his plans. Yamamoto simply asked him to hurry.

He reached Mount Popa early on the morning of February 18, accompanied by a few men from his own regiment and a few from 2 Division Headquarters. But this did not mean that the division itself had come up. The 1st Infantry had not yet left Rangoon. Most of Prem's own 2nd was still making its way from Prome on foot. As for the Nehru, Prem could observe for himself its sorry, wasted state. For all practical purposes the division was a head without a body.

For the moment Prem did not let this bother him. Popa was a pleasant place. Most of the villagers had cleared out, but gardens and orchards well watered from springs above were there to be enjoyed. At the top of a rise he came across a shed containing a great many little Buddhas (perhaps it had once sheltered priests), and this he took for himself. The spot was lovely. No sound of fighting broke the silence, no sound at all. It was there, on the morning of February 22, that Shah Nawaz and Mahboob Ahmed found him.

They came at Netaji's request—indeed, the Supreme Commander had meant to visit Popa himself. Anxious to see how his units were faring, he had left Rangoon by the Mandalay road shortly after Prem's departure, taking with him Mahboob, a Japanese liaison officer, and two or three others. At Pyinmana, where Shah Nawaz was waiting, he had inspected the three regiments that comprised the 1st Division, and had decided that the men (few in number, some still very weak, many lacking rifles) were in no shape to fight. So he had moved on, and Shah Nawaz went with him. As no one knew when, or *if*, Aziz Ahmed would recover from his head injury, Bose proposed to give Shah Nawaz the 2nd Division, and to do so at Mount Popa, where he presumed divisional headquarters to be.

But to get to Popa from the Mandalay road one had to pass through Meiktila, and as the party approached the town, Bose learned that the British had crossed the Irrawaddy, scattered Dhillon's regiment, and were coming his way. He could, of course, reach the mountain by the metalled road to Kyaukpadaung. Once there, however, he might be cut off. Best not to risk it, his officers advised. So Bose turned east to Kalaw, where he had a hospital to inspect, and sent Shah Nawaz and Mahboob in his stead, carrying with them several bottles of whisky— a present from Netaji to the man who had served him so long as military secretary, and whom Mahboob had just replaced. None of the bottles reached Prem's lips. *Boobie like a silly ass left them in his truck, unattended, a mile out of my position, and by the time I got there they'd been pinched.* Prem was glad to see his visitors anyway. "Spent the day explaining the current situation to Col. S. N," he wrote in his diary. "He seems to be a decent sort."[8] A few days later Mahboob and Shah Nawaz were back in Meiktila. Netaji too had returned. But it was a question whether even Meiktila was safe now, so rapidly did the British draw near.

Though Bose and his people did not know it, the approaching force was not the 7th Indian Division, which had crossed at Nyaungu first, but the 17th, which had followed later with the tank brigade. Armored cars and Sherman tanks leading, infantry in trucks and half-tracks behind, a column had set off for Meiktila expecting to be supplied and even reinforced by air. Its course lay east to clear Mount Popa, then southeast down the Myingyan–Meiktila road. The going was comparatively easy. For this was good tank country, the Japanese had little to throw in a tank's way, and what they had was improvised. At one place they tried to stop the Shermans by lacing the ground across which they must move with man-sized holes, each occupied by an infantryman with a 250-pound aerial bomb between his knees, and instructions to strike the nose cap smartly when a tank was overhead. A British officer swept this human minefield by coolly walking from hole to hole shooting each poor wretch in the head. By the 25th of February, the day Bose and his little party met again in a field outside Meiktila, the column was not far from Mahling. And Mahling was only twenty miles away.

Early the next morning their Japanese liaison officer hurried up with this alarming information. For a time Bose tried to stick to his original plan. He should have pushed on to Mount Popa long ago, he protested. Nothing was going to stop him now. "England has not produced the bomb that can kill Subhas Chandra Bose."[9] But Shah Nawaz told him bluntly he was mad. Twenty miles meant nothing to tanks, they might burst in at any moment. And when it became evident that the Kyaukpadaung road had been cut, which made Popa unattainable, and that even the route south would not be secure for long, he gave up and allowed his anxious subordinates to bundle him into the one staff car. Off they went, the liaison officer on the running board, Bose's personal physician next to the driver, Shah Nawaz and Bose in the back, everyone armed, cheerful, and ready to crash through anything that tried to block their way—even Bose had a loaded tommy gun across his lap. Near Yindaw, twelve miles out on the Rangoon road, low-flying planes forced them to turn into the brush and hide. That night Shah Nawaz picked up a second vehicle and doubled back to collect the rest of the party. The others went on.

At Pyinmana Subhas Chandra assembled the more fit and resolute of the 1st Division men, gave them what arms there were, and put Thakur Singh in command. When the British arrived—he was sure they were coming—"X" Regiment (as he called it) would march out to fight, and he would march and die with it: it would be the freedom army's last hurrah. But Shah Nawaz, catching up with him two days later, persuaded him that to give battle at Pyinmana was not an immediate option. The British were not coming down the road, not at the moment at least. It would be better if the two of them went on to Rangoon. There Netaji could resume general direction of the enterprise. He, meanwhile, would set off for Mount Popa and the 2nd Division by way of Prome and Yenangyaung. Though Meiktila's fall was a blow, all was not lost, he assured his chief.

When Bose reached Rangoon, however, he was met with news so unexpected, so shocking, that for a time he believed that all, indeed, *was* lost.

☙

The news was this. At Mount Popa, a week or so earlier, five officers had gone out on an evening exercise of some sort and failed to return. The hours passed, anxiety turned to suspicion, at dawn suspicion hardened into certainty. And when, several days later, British planes dropped surrender leaflets bearing the signature of one of the five, certainty was confirmed as fact. Calmly, by prearrangement, without an excuse of any kind (for there had been no fighting), four majors and a lieutenant had picked up and walked over to the British.

It was Prem who forwarded this bombshell, and Prem was angry. In his diary he calls the five "swine." But Prem was to a degree prepared. His own men knew, because he had taken care to tell them, that he wanted no cowards with him, no one unwilling to fight. These five, however, were not his men. They were staff officers from Division Headquarters (one *ran* the operation) who, with only Dhillon's remnant of a regiment in place, and Popa quiet, had had very little to do. No doubt that was part of the trouble. Well, he would see that their behavior did not spread. "From now on I am going to be absolutely ruthless. I have already replaced one battalion commander. I have issued orders that anyone making a suspicious movement is to be shot. I wish Shah Nawaz could come back and take charge of his Division. . . ."[10] This would leave Prem free to devote his attention to his own regiment as, company by company, it arrived.

Shah Nawaz, too, took the desertions in stride. When he left Rangoon by the Prome road on March 7, as it happened never to return, five replacements for the traitors went with him. At Bose's express request he had chosen them himself. He knew they would remain steady, as indeed all five did. The Popa business annoyed him—

"a very sad affair," he calls it in *his* diary[11]—but he wasn't shaken by it. Bose was.

It was one thing for a battalion commander (Bose knew all about Hari Ram) to raise the white flag just as he and his men were on the point of being overwhelmed. It was quite another for an entire division headquarters to go over, in circumstances such that panic could not explain it and premeditation could. No doubt the shameful business was already a topic of conversation in every Rangoon household, an invitation to laughter in every Japanese mess. That was bad enough. Worse was the damage it might do to the freedom movement itself.

It was not that cowards and deserters could rob a commander of victory. Of course they could. But such a consideration meant nothing to Subhas Chandra now that victory was utterly out of reach. What was important, now, was that the men of the Indian National Army remain constant, stick to their posts, and go on fighting. Behaving thus, they announced to the world that though they might perish, others would take their place, others and still others, until India received at last her due. This was what mattered. This was why the freedom army must not lay down its arms. But deserting to the enemy made a mockery of such a posture. Indeed, mass defection at the level of division staff threatened to turn what was left of the *Azad Hind Fauj* into just such a masquerade as K. P. K. Menon and others had always said it was. So the news from Mount Popa left Subhas badly shaken.

For a week he brooded, shut away in his bungalow and in great pain from a thigh muscle torn somehow doing his daily exercises. Then he rose, assembled every uniformed man and woman in and about Rangoon, and addressed them—perhaps not for four hours, as S. A. Ayer remembers, but certainly at length.[12] The year before, he told his listeners, the liver-hearted behavior of a handful had marred the heroic achievements of the many. This year was to have been different. He had looked forward this year to "an unsullied record." Alas, it had been as before. "The recent treachery of five officers of the Headquarters of the 2nd Division has come as an eye-opener to us, that all is not well within our ranks, and that . . . cowardice and treachery have yet to be wiped out." He was determined to wipe them out now. Men who did not want to fight would have one week to declare themselves and quit the army. Those who shrank from admitting such a thing, yet were suspect, would be sent packing anyway. In the *Azad Hind Fauj* thus cleansed, future instances of base behavior would be dealt with summarily—and not just by courts-martial. Henceforth it would be the duty of the lowliest jawan to arrest any man who played the coward, shoot him if he tried to desert, and do so no matter what his rank.

There was more. The constancy of the army must be shielded from cowards and traitors by a "moral bulwark" of hatred and contempt, and this bulwark could not be left to grow of itself. There wasn't time. It would have to be cultivated. So Subhas Chandra set the INA camps and stations in and about Rangoon to competing with each other in the fashioning of indignant poems, angry plays, effigies of the detested five in wood or straw or clay. And on an appointed day the poems were read, the plays staged, the effigies paraded and jeered. Ayer was among the judges. Subhas distributed the prizes. The whole business was a huge success, Ayer says, particularly the plays. "Netaji had triumphed as usual. All the camps worked night and day to knock off the trophy for the best anti-traitors' drama. The morale of the entire army shot up high."

Perhaps in Rangoon it did. Or perhaps we are listening to a man who has not lost the habits of mind of a minister of publicity and propaganda. We do not know what Subhas thought. It is unlikely he shared Ayer's euphoria. A part of him believed that politics, and war too, are theater. The other part was realist, and the reality was that the men and women with him in Rangoon (Ayer estimates their number at over five thousand, a possible figure if the 1st Infantry Regiment had not yet departed) were not in a position to put a two-weeks' course in cowardice avoidance to much practical use. They were too far from the field of battle. So, also, was their leader.

He had been close to it, briefly, outside Meiktila, and for a time it had looked as if the fighting might follow him down the Rangoon road. But Shah Nawaz had been right. The British were fully occupied elsewhere. "Powerful Nippon Units Pushing Enemy," *Greater Asia* announced on the 20th of March. "Foe's Mobile Forces Virtually Surrounded." This was true. The 17th Indian Division and the tank brigade had taken Meiktila in a matter of days. Japanese resistance had ended at dusk on the 3rd of March. Slim had his wrist. The extended fingers of the hand ought now to shrivel and grow limp. But the 17th Division and the tanks had seized Meiktila by cutting loose from the rest of 4 Corps, and this had allowed the Japanese to close behind them—which gave Kimura an opportunity, an opportunity that might well be his last. He would surround the flying column at Meiktila. He would surround it and destroy it there.

Way to the north the Irrawaddy barrier had already crumbled. The 19th Indian Division of Slim's 33rd Corps had broken out of its bridgehead forty miles above Mandalay, moved south, and before March was a week old, stood on the city's edge. Mandalay did not fall at once. The Japanese garrison, holed up in Fort Dufferin behind a moat two hundred feet wide, held out until March 20. Meanwhile, however, while one brigade of the 19th pushed into the hills and seized Maymyo, the two other divisions of 33 Corps, the 20th Indian and the 2nd British, crossed the Irrawaddy below Mandalay and ranged south and east, playing havoc with Japanese communications and rear areas.

Kimura let them. His attention was riveted now on the ground Messervy's flying column had just traversed. Yamamoto's 72nd IMB he sent north along both banks of the Irrawaddy, with orders to reoccupy Nyaungu as well as the places on the west bank from which Messervy's men had begun their crossing. Kanjo *Butai* and the INA battalions at Mount Popa were to command, by vigorous patrolling, the country to Nyaungu's east. The garrison at Myingyan would deny the British a landing place for the supplies and equipment they were sending down the Chindwin on river craft. But the greater part of what battalions and brigades Kimura could collect, he sent against Meiktila itself. This was the heart of his plan. If Meiktila could be retaken and Messervy's column smashed, Slim would have nothing in place to send south. When the rains came he would find himself well short of Rangoon. After that, anything could happen.

The battalions and brigades Kimura had in mind were scattered all over the map, woefully understrength, constrained by Slim's command of the air to move only by night, and not easily communicated with. Nevertheless their commanders received their orders somehow, made for Meiktila, and as they arrived took their units piecemeal into the attack. Their chief objective was the airfield east of the town. If the British lost that, reinforcements and supplies would have to be dropped by parachute. Right through March the remarkable scratch assault went on. For four weeks, while Messervy's men clung desperately to town and airfield, Slim waited to learn whether his bold stroke—the secret column down the west side of the central valley, the surprise river crossing, the lunge eastward—was going to succeed. His purpose had been to force a decisive battle well short of Rangoon. He had it now, though not in quite the form intended. And while the battle raged, there was no further movement south. For almost the whole of March the war, as it were, stood still.

Bose, meanwhile, made no further effort to visit his jawans in the field. His path and theirs diverged. He remained in Rangoon, trying with exhortations, games, and every trick at his command to pump life into the rear. They, the fighting men, were at Popa three hundred miles away. At Mount Popa, where nobody bothered with poems, plays, or effigies in straw or anything else, the Indian National Army fought its last engagements and made its last stand.

⁂

For a time Prem and Dhillon did little. They had little to do anything with. Dhillon busied himself trying to round up the men who had fled Nyaungu. It wasn't easy. Some had run for miles. Others had gone to ground and chose to remain there. In the end he collected enough to bring the Nehru's strength to perhaps seven hundred. One battalion of Prem's 2nd Infantry Regiment was almost as large, but it would be some time before Prem had assembled all three.

My regiment was arriving by driblets. I didn't want the British to discover how weak we were. So I ordered very active patrolling. Dhillon did the same. He had the recent debacle to get over. And he had just been promoted lieutenant colonel—there was that to live up to, and a letter from the Supreme Commander praising him for his bravery and expressing unbounded confidence in his men. As much as Prem, but for slightly different reasons, he was eager to engage the enemy.

Patrolling brought almost at once a small but spectacular success. One evening, as Prem entertained the commander of Kanjo *Butai* at dinner, word came that his men had surprised a hostile party a few miles away, killed two British soldiers, and captured a field radio and two jeeps. It was a rare haul. Happily Prem appropriated one of the jeeps for his own use. Shah Nawaz should have the other when he returned.

Other skirmishes followed. As the days passed and their strength grew (the last company of Prem's 3rd battalion reported on March 20), patrols pushed farther and farther out. Dhillon had his base near Kyaukpadaung. From there the men of the Nehru ranged northwest toward Taungzin. Prem's battalions, positioned in an arc about Popaywa (a village on high ground astride the Kyaukpadaung–Taungtha road just west of Mount Popa itself), roamed an area bounded roughly by Mount Popa, Pyinbin, and Welaung. Between them Dhillon and Prem worked a considerable spread of country, in shape a box perhaps twenty miles on a side, with Mount Popa in its lower right-hand corner. They did so with not quite three thousand men.

But their opponents, too, were thin upon the ground. From the Nyaungu bridgehead the British sent roving columns "to seek out and destroy" (in the words of the official history)[13] across the same four hundred square miles the Indians patrolled. Not that they wished to make this space their own. Their intent was to reopen ground communication with embattled Meiktila—and the route to Meiktila passed well north of Popa, not through it. The Japanese, for their part, were trying to block that route by retaking Nyaungu, where it began. This, too, meant movement well west of Popa, not through it. Neither side wished to occupy the box. That would be a waste of men and resources. But neither could quite ignore it for fear that the other, discovering it was open, should push swiftly through and come down upon a flank. A month earlier, before Messervy's surprise crossing at Nyaungu, the 2nd INA Division;s assignment had been simply "defence of Popa Hill." It was wider and more precise now: to keep Kimura's men from being flanked in this manner, and to compel the British to take seriously the possibility that it might happen to them.

The tactics this required were guerrilla tactics, the tactics of slip in, strike, and withdraw (so that the 2nd Infantry Regiment might, after all, have kept its "guerrilla" designation), and these were the tactics Prem practiced. Dhillon was less skillful, or perhaps less lucky. Near Taungzin one day a company of his let itself be trapped in the open by light tanks, armored cars, and infantry in trucks, tried vainly to break out with the bayonet, and lost several score men dead or captured. That was how the British moved, in motorized columns—and by day. As they ruled the skies, why not? It was wise to steer clear of these columns. It was comparatively easy, too, if you had Mount Popa at your back, for the sharp spurs and gullies of its lower slopes were proof against tracked as well as wheeled vehicles, and there was always water. Dhillon's beat was farther from Popa than was Prem's. That was a disadvantage. But Dhillon was also prone to heroics. When the publicity people at Rangoon heard about the Taungzin disaster, they transformed it into a sort of latter-day Charge of the Light Brigade, and Dhillon was pleased. Privately, Prem may have wondered whether courage was an adequate substitute for judgment.

My patrols went out fifteen, twenty miles. I told them, go seek the enemy. But don't get caught. Attack, and come back. My chaps were mobile, they could be out for days on their own. The only thing was, they had to go from water point to water point, because they could carry only so much water with them. As daylight reconnaissance was hazardous, the patrols depended on the local Burmese for intelligence. They paid for it in rice, which Prem had stockpiled. He had men who spoke Burmese and passed for Burmese, and these he sent (dressed in *longyis*) into the villages, where they sat and listened and watched.

Successive diary entries for mid-March suggest what Prem's larger raids were like.[14] "I have made up my mind to move out tonight with two companies of Banta Singh's battalion and attack the enemy," he writes on a Wednesday. Pyinbin and its vicinity are the objective. The British appear to be withdrawing there, and Kanjo *Butai* is on the move. The two companies set off from Popaywa toward midnight and reach Setsetyo at dawn. "Marching through the sand very hard indeed. Bullock carts carrying water could not reach us, nor could my car and the motorcycle. Had to buy water locally." It is nine miles as the crow flies, but the men have surely had to cover more.

At Setsetyo Thursday morning Prem makes contact with a Japanese company commander who seems to know how the British are disposed—and decides to attack that night. The two companies move off after dark and reach Myene, halfway between Setsetyo and Pyinbin, toward midnight. "Attacked from the left flank with one company under 2nd Lt. Jogindar Singh and made a feint from the right flank with one platoon under Amar Chand. Two sections of the Japanese accompanied J. S." They meet no resistance, the British positions are empty, but Amar Chand bumps into a patrol and there is a short fire fight. "Casualties enemy about 8 to 10 killed. Our side one killed and one missing." It is early Friday now. That evening Prem and his men retrace their steps to Setsetyo, and by sunrise Saturday have reached Popaywa again.

So the days pass. Casualties are few, food adequate. From the fruit of the bel tree, which grows on Mount Popa and is known for its medicinal properties, the men make a brew that is good for the stomach as well as pleasant to drink. It is time to select candidates for the next Officers Training School class. From a small pile of books he has pinched from a Rangoon club, Prem picks one about Stonewall Jackson and starts to read. The Confederate general is a familiar figure. His tactics were part of the curriculum at Dehra Dun. "Our milk goat died this morning, so from now on we shall be in milkless coffee."[15] That is too bad. But at least there is coffee. Decidedly, things are not as they had been for the men who climbed the Tamu road or stumbled down the Yu.

Almost it looks as if this routine may continue indefinitely. It can't, of course. Appearances notwithstanding, the war in central Burma will not stand still forever. There is something else, too, something more urgent. Desertions have not ceased with the infamous five.

For this Prem, as I have said, was to a degree prepared. At Rangoon, and again at Popa, he had told his men that if they had no stomach for fighting they would be permitted to withdraw. If you wish to join the British, he had said, I will arrange to send you in a group. But do it at once. "I do not want that men should desert in driblets afterwards."[16]

The day after the infamous five went over, however, a signals officer was brought before Prem charged with refusing to take out a fighting patrol—and Prem was not nearly so complaisant. "I had to sentence an officer to death this morning," he wrote in his diary. "What a pity, it is such a waste of human life."[17] In the event the man was not shot. Prem remitted his sentence (if, indeed, it was ever formally pronounced) because he confessed his offense and did not grovel. It was otherwise with four ordinary jawans.

These disappeared on February 28, the same evening as the five. Unlike them, they were caught and brought back. They belonged to

Dhillon's 8th Battalion, the reserve battalion that had refused to fight the day of the debacle. Perhaps Dhillon wanted to make an example of them. For when they were shot—not in the open, that would have invited air observation and attack, but in a large *nullah* or ditch on Mount Popa's flank—Dhillon took care to have men of the 7th, Hari Ram's battalion, brought to the *nullah* to watch. And he came himself, picked the men to do the shooting, and gave the order to shoot. But first Prem, as acting division commander (Shah Nawaz had not returned yet), had to pass sentence of death on the four. And though Prem did not watch the miserable business, the poor wretches called up one by one, dying without ceremony, begging for their lives, there is nothing to suggest that he hesitated.

We know a great deal about these four jawans from Dhillon's 8th. We know a great deal about Muhammad Hussain, shot three weeks later because he, too, meant to desert. Muhammad Hussain had tried to suborn men in Prem's 1st Battalion. This was detected. Several were put under arrest. And one, nursing orderly Jaghri Ram, who had enlisted in the freedom army in 1942 (the reader may remember) in order to be rid of loading coal for the Japanese—Jaghri Ram was actually compelled to join the firing squad. Khazin Shah, the battalion commander, ordered him forward. When Jaghri pleaded that he could bandage a man but did not know how to fire a rifle, Khazin Shah told Lt. Aya Singh to take one, put it to Jaghri's shoulder, and curl Jaghri's finger around the trigger. "There were three of us, one Sikh, one Tamil and myself," Jaghri Ram later said. "Muhammad Hussain was blindfolded by Aya Singh. He was made to sit on the ground with his back against a tree stump and his hands were tied behind his back. Aya Singh ordered me to fire, and we all three fired. Muhammad Hussain died there."[18]

We know a great deal about these summary executions, perhaps more than we care to know, because eight months later, during the first Red Fort trial, Sir Naushirwan P. Engineer, chief counsel for the prosecution, devoted two whole days to them. The Prosecution Section of the Adjutant General's Branch had sent him six witnesses, all men who had served at Mount Popa under Dhillon or Prem—one was Jaghri Ram. With the testimony of these six, Sir Naushirwan proposed to establish that Hussain and the four jawans from Dhillon's regiment had actually been shot. They had died when and how the witnesses said they had. That was all Engineer meant to do.

Six witnesses examined and cross-examined over the course of two days simply to establish that five men had died? Surely Engineer intended to widen the inquiry, demonstrate that the four jawans had never deserted, or show that extenuating circumstances made death by firing squad excessive if they had. But he didn't. For in his view—and it was the court's view too—the Indian National Army, lacking as it did any standing in law or jurisprudence, had no business attempting a court martial at all. It was by definition incapable of putting anyone on trial for anything. The proceedings against the five had been plain illegal. And if five men had died because of them, there was only one word for what had happened. That word was murder.

So on the charge sheets at the first Red Fort trial, Dhillon stood accused of murdering Hari Singh, Duli Chand, Daryao Singh, and Dharam Singh because, it was alleged, he had had them shot in a *nullah* at the base of Mount Popa towards dusk on the 6th of March. Prem Sahgal stood accused of abetment of murder because he had awarded the sentences. For doing likewise in the matter of Muhammad Hussain, Shah Nawaz stood accused of the same. All the court needed to convict the three defendants was proof the five had died.

But Prem, Dhillon, and Shah Nawaz denied, of course, that they had. Since any other defense was obviously going to be dismissed out of hand, what else could they do? Besides, no one cares to be branded a murderer, it has an ugly sound. So all three protested that no one had been shot. The four jawans "were found guilty and were sentenced to death," Prem told the court. And "the fact of the sentence having been passed was, of course, used for its propaganda value in order to deter others. . . ."[19] That was all. Quietly, without fanfare, the four had been let off with a warning. As for Muhammad Hussain, he wasn't hauled up until the very end of March, Prem explained; when, before anything beyond charging him could be arranged, his battalion almost ceased to exist and further proceedings became impossible. No one was shot. Not one of the five paid the penalty that might properly (for they did not concede Engineer's premise) have been exacted.

This was untrue. The five *did* die. Only defense counsel's keen legal eye playing upon gaps and inconsistencies in the testimony of the six prosecution witnesses kept the court in doubt. But for the moment that is neither here nor there. What needs relating now is how these desertions, a trickle in March (for there *were* others who went over), swelled in April to a freshet, and then to a flood.[20] And *why* they did so—this is the curious thing—at a time when parts of Prem's 2nd Infantry Regiment were fighting a larger and more hotly contested engagement than the Indian National Army had so far seen in this war, or would in fact see again.

❧

On the evening of Thursday, March 29, the day Jaghri Ram's reluctant trigger finger helped send Muhammad Hussain to his death, Prem Sahgal took his jeep and a truck up the Kyaukpadaung–Welaung road. Some distance behind marched Khazin Shah with the whole of the 1st Battalion, and Major Bagri leading one company of the 3rd. Once again Pyinbin was to be raided, this time on a generous scale. Elements of Kanjo *Butai* already in position at Setsetyo were to strike, with artillery support, from the south. Some of Prem's men were to do the same from Kabyu, on the southeast, while the rest pushed on toward Welaung. Prem had planned to put all three battalions to this work, but Shah Nawaz, once more commanding the division (he had returned), had thought this risky and scaled Prem's contribution back. The attack was to go in on the night of Friday the 30th. Thursday night's movement would simply bring the 1st Battalion to Seiktein, its jumping-off place. And as there were thought to be Japanese there, Prem, motoring forward to reconnoiter, moved with less than his usual caution. That was a mistake.

For as he approached Seiktein, out of the night came a burst of small-arms fire. Supposing his party mistaken for a British patrol, Prem asked his liaison officer to shout something in Japanese. The firing redoubled; the air was thick with bullets. Prem's jeep still ran, it could probably be turned and driven, but with no way of telling in the dark how the ground lay, where were the holes and the patches of soft sand, the truck was almost certain to get stuck. The only thing to do was ditch both and try to get away on foot.

Several miles back Shah Nawaz heard the firing, and wondered. When an officer appeared and told him that there had been an ambush, and that the colonel sahib was missing, he hurried forward, not at all sure he would see his regimental commander again. Out of the dark came Prem, angry but unharmed. He had brought his party safely out. When Khazin Shah's battalion came up, Prem sent the leading company on to the spot where, he estimated, the ambush had occurred. Don't stop to deploy, he told the men, rush the place, use the element of surprise. The stratagem succeeded. Both vehicles were recovered and, though riddled, could be driven off. Prem's map case, however, was missing. So was his personal diary.

The diary's loss had consequences that did not make themselves felt for months. It was otherwise with the map case. In it were copies of the operations orders for the raid on Pyinbin, and this, together with the boldness of the ambush, suggested that it would be prudent to delay. So Khazin Shah turned the 1st Battalion around and took it back to Legyi. Bagri, meanwhile, had reached Kabyu. There, Friday morning, his company and a Japanese company to his right were attacked in broad daylight by a considerable British force. The attack was held. But it was beginning to look as if the whole Pyinbin venture, due to start in earnest that evening, had better be abandoned. And when, toward dusk, British aircraft spotted and destroyed Kanjo *Butai's* carefully husbanded handful of guns, it was.

Not a moment too soon. For though Shah Nawaz and Prem did not realize it yet, the war no longer stood still. Kimura's bold throw had put the British on the defensive from Meiktila to the Irrawaddy and beyond. But it had not unhinged, it had only interrupted, 14th Army's progress south. Along the Irrawaddy Yamamoto's 72nd Independent Mixed Brigade never came within twenty miles of Nyaungu, though it gave the British some anxious moments west of the river. At Myingyan the Japanese did better. March was three weeks old before Slim's 7th Indian Division finally drove them out of the place. But at Meiktila itself, where Kimura's men *must* prevail if this last, best chance was to succeed, the British clung so obstinately to the town, and to the airfield too (though for a time Dakotas could not land because of the shelling), that by the middle of the fourth week in March it was clear they could not be dislodged. On the 28th the Japanese bowed to the inevitable and broke off their assault. Already Slim had issued his final instructions for the advance on Rangoon.

Sunday afternoon, April 1, Hill 1395 sent word that there
t from Welaung—trucks carrying stores and men, motor-
an armored car. At dusk it remained unclear whether
o come down the Kyaukpadaung road or turn west at
yinbin. So Prem sent two patrols out, one toward Seiktein
anded by Abdullah Khan, the man who had nabbed the
the field radio four weeks before), the other in a more
tion. At four in the morning Abdullah came back with
nificance to report. The other patrol did not return.

ay men and vehicles were again seen some distance to the
noon aircraft bombed and machine-gunned Legyi
it on fire. There was some shelling, aimless but harassing.
Prem was forced to use his machine guns to drive away
ned to be scouting his position. Night fell. The missing
ap. At the same time Prem learned that Yasin Khan, who
irected the machine gun fire but actually handled a gun,
d away, taking with him several other officers, NCOs,
is the night wore on, despondency settled like a blanket
efenders. Surely the British knew their strength and how
osed. What chance had they of withstanding an assault?
hazin Shah was in such a state of nerves that Prem had
ommand of the battalion.

Tuesday the 3rd, the British at last moved in earnest.
re was much distant coming and going, reported first by
d up later by Prem's field glasses. But this time a sizable
rectly down the road, and Prem braced for an attack. It
the front, however, but from the flanks and was
shelling, which forced everyone to keep their heads
ome parts of the perimeter it took the defenders by
arty broke into Prem's rear and surprised men cooking
ter. Another moved clear behind the battalion and got
to Kyaukpadaung. To his left Prem was in contact with
ich gave him some security. But his right was in the air.
right that the attacks came that broke into his rear
the road. And as the afternoon wore on, it looked as if
d at any moment overwhelm his defenses and pour into

His 4th Corps, which had begun the 1945 campaign by stealing
down the west side of the great central valley, was to continue down
the east side, the 17th and 5th Indian Divisions leapfrogging as they
went (the 5th had reached Meiktila during March). The 19th Indian
Division, fresh from its capture of Mandalay, was to cover the rear and
left flank. Meanwhile the 33rd Corps was to follow the Irrawaddy. But
as the Irrawadddy, below Mandalay, bends to the west to receive the
Chindwin before it turns south again, this put the 33rd on the west side
of the valley. The two corps were trading places.

Some units did as the 19th did. Transferred from 33 to 4 Corps, it
did not have to move at all. But a certain amount of shifting was
unavoidable, and this Slim put to a calculated use. Across the great
swathe of ground where for the past month Kimura's men had made
their supreme effort, there remained "many scattered but sometimes
strong parties of Japanese" who either hung on "with dull ferocity" or
tried to flee south. "I took advantage of the regrouping necessary for
the advance on Rangoon," Slim later wrote, "to comb this area, whose
roads and railways were essential to us, by what I called a 'Union Jack'
manoeuvre." As anyone who has ever tried to draw that most
perplexing flag will readily understand, "this entailed passing strong
columns diagonally through it."[21] One of these diagonal thrusts was
entrusted to the 5th Brigade of the 2nd British Division.

The division was on the point of leaving Burma. Given the
difficulties 14th Army would have before the rains began, in particular
with respect to supply, it made sense to shed British divisions, even
British battalions that were part of Indian divisions. They consumed far
more daily tonnage than comparable Indian units required. And the
rising pressure inside England to bring home men with long overseas
service made keeping them up to strength impossible. So the 2nd
Division was to go. Two of its brigades, the 4th and 6th, made a few
sweeps along the Irrawaddy bend and prepared to fly out. The 5th,
however, was given a more substantial assignment further south. It was
directed to make a diagonal thrust down the Taungtha–Kyaukpadaung
road. It would leave Burma when Kyaukpadaung had been reached.

About this assignment there is a touch of the gratuitous. If the 7th
Indian Division, now part of 33 Corps, really could not (as the official
history implies) take Chauk unless Kyaukpadaung to its east had first

been secured, why advance along a road that brushed Mount Popa? Why take a route on which the enemy, perceived as consisting chiefly of determined Japanese, was sure to make good defensive use of the terrain? Why not approach Kyaukpadaung across the excellent tank country to the west, why not approach from Nyaungu and Pyinbin? As long as the Japanese stood on a defensive line that included Popa, the mountain was valuable as an observation tower, natural fortress, and anchor. Let the line be broken, however, and Popa was nothing. Why bother with it, then? Why not avoid it and let its defenders wither on the vine?

Unreasonable or not, 5th Brigade's instructions were to go straight past Mount Popa. The order went out. The brigade began to move. The ambush in which Prem lost his map case and diary was the work, it is a fair guess, of an advance patrol of its attached 2nd Reconnaissance Regiment. Behind came the brigade proper, accompanied by 25-pounders of the Royal Artillery's 10th Field Regiment and a squadron of Carabinier medium tanks, with Hurricanes and Thunderbolts giving air support. Though in numbers of men no larger than Prem's regiment, 5th Brigade because of its mobility and fire power was altogether out of Prem's class. It was a force against which he had little hope of standing, a force he should never have had to face. But face it he must, for it had set a course that would take it to Welaung, to Legyi, through Popaywa itself.

Perhaps this was just as well. Perhaps it was just as well, too, that 5 Brigade was composed not of fellow Indians but of British. For if Slim's thinking had been different and his instructions otherwise, the crowning action of the war in Burma—14th Army's final dash for Rangoon—would have left Prem and his men untouched. And how, in that case, could they have fulfilled Netaji's injunction to pay freedom's price by barring, at least briefly, the Britishers' advance?

Legyi, to which Khazin Shah and his men withdrew after the ambush, *is like a saucer, with high ground on all sides. And absolutely bare. No trees, nothing.* There was a village, which gave the place its name, but it cannot have been a large village, for the ground was barren and rocky, so rocky that when Prem's machine gun crews began preparing the pits for these

indispensable weapons, they fo
three or four feet.

Nevertheless it was mor
why Prem had ordered the
morning. The low hills arour
Prem made it his habit to w
approached. Up to a point he
what part of the saucer they
by runner. He had help in thi
on Hill 1395, six miles to t
Welaung. It could report Br
Headquarters, which then al
that he had some sense of
came in sight.

Moreover, though Legyi
gradually does that mountai
made difficulties even at th
Difficulties even for tanks if
have been. This was crucia
ground was, if the men du
they could take a good de
and the British infantry ca
*where we were, one section ad
machine gunners had only
their eyes. I had mortars too.*
up with a mortar company
*little ammunition. My main s
light machine guns.* Neither
have been of much use a
antitank mines, of which
tanks were frequently spo

Saturday passed witho
Nawaz noted, "Popa hea
hit."[22] By now everyone
this scale. Because of the
shed at the top of the ris

Then on
was moveme
cycles, tanks
these meant
Seiktein for
(it was comn
two jeeps an
westerly dire
nothing of si

On Mon
north. Towar
village, setting
Late in the da
men who see
patrol turned
had not only
had just slipp
and men. And
upon Legyi's
they were disp
Before dawn
to take direct

Next day,
Once again the
Hill 1395, pick
force moved d
came not fro
accompanied
down. Along
surprise. One
and carrying w
astride the roa
Kanjo *Butai*, w
It was from th
echelon and cu
the British wou
the saucer.

What saved him, in part, was the enemy's tactical behavior. They delivered their attacks *in penny packets. If they had made a concerted attack on my position, they would have overrun it. But they kept on putting one attack here, one attack there. Probably they weren't quite certain what our strength was, probably these were probing attacks. Once I sent a company, under Kanwal Singh, into a counterattack with the supporting fire of only one light machine gun, and because the British weren't expecting anything, it drove them off and reoccupied the position.*

But there was more to the business than British irresolution. There were the likes of Kanwal Singh, leading a counterattack. And there was Prem, who knew when and where to order one—Prem, who had far more command experience than any of his battalion commanders (in the Indian Army all three had been subadars). What we are working with here is Prem's account of the action, his formal report to 2nd INA Division Headquarters, date 6 April, introduced as evidence during his trial, and available because when the British captured or stumbled upon that headquarters they found it, recognized it for what it was, and laid it carefully aside. It is long and detailed, this battle report, proceeding day by day and sometimes hour by hour. It is the only account we have. But I have been able to supplement it with what Prem told me one evening as we bent over the Surveyor General of India's quarter-inch topographical map of central Burma spread out on the floor of the bungalow he and Lakshmi occupied in Kanpur's Civil Lines.

That evening Prem relived for my benefit the action at Legyi, pointing out Hill 1395 and the spot from which he could see the British coming, explaining where he had placed his companies, one here, another there, his medium machine guns sighted to fire over the men's heads, the light machine guns with their flat trajectory in position on the flanks, *all dug in and scattered so the British couldn't see us at all.* Prem took me through those several days of anxiety, excitement, and boredom. (The expression "fighting all day" is meaningless, he explained. Fighting never lasts long. *In between there are periods when nothing happens and you don't know what to do with yourself.*) We read the battle report line by line.[23] And as we read, I had the feeling that on this climactic Tuesday, though he could not be everywhere at once, and certainly did not always know what was going on (it was hours before he learned what had happened to his rear echelon), he had been very much on top of things—and had, besides, thoroughly enjoyed himself.

So he sent Kanwal Singh and his company into a successful counterattack. It was not part of the 1st Battalion, it was the company from Bagri's 3rd, and this day it served Prem well. By moving it where needed, by plugging gaps with whatever else he could find (so that sometimes a platoon was sent to do a company's work), by binding the Japanese on his left to cover that flank and so allow him to concentrate on the right, Prem survived until nightfall, at which point the situation actually improved. At nine-thirty word reached his command post that his rear area had been cleared and that jawans were once again astride the road south.

If we could stop here, we should be able to say that this engagement, which receives little attention in the British and even less in the Indian official histories, but is known to the INA as the Battle of Legyi,[24] was an unqualified success. One lightly armed battalion reinforced by part of another and supported on one flank by some Japanese, but utterly without artillery or air support, had faced and held a brigade. Indeed, we might expect to read that it did the same the next day and the day after. Instead, there is only the terse statement that at five o'clock on Wednesday morning "withdrawal was commenced and carried out without any casualties." Prem was leaving Legyi, not because his 1st Battalion was beaten or even badly battle worn, but because it had almost ceased to exist.

The leakage began with the disappearance, Sunday night, of the battalion's mortar officer. Twenty-four hours later Yasin Khan deserted, taking several more officers and a dozen men. It was not until Tuesday night, however, *after* the hardest of the fighting was over, that the hemorrhaging set in for fair. At seven that evening Prem, hearing at last that the British had broken into his rear echelon, ordered C Company to drive them out, and was astonished to learn from Khazin Shah that C Company couldn't—two of its three platoons together with the mortar section had gone over. From other companies Prem collected a force to do the job. But at nine-thirty, along with the news that this force had been successful, word came that Khazin Shah himself, the whole of battalion headquarters, and one platoon of A Company under Abdullah Khan had decamped. After that the floodgates opened. By midnight all five of the battalion's company commanders and some two hundred men were gone. The remainder, Prem's battle report continues, "could not be trusted." Prem might still count on the one company from Bagri's battalion, though it was exhausted, and toward morning Major Negi arrived with a second company and an additional section of machine guns. But he could hardly expect to hold the saucer with these.

Turning the miserable business over in his mind two days later (his conclusions form a note attached to his battle report), Prem thought to himself that the deserters had not been cowards. Quite the contrary, many of the officers who slipped away, usually taking their men with them (that was half the difficulty), had been conspicuously brave under fire. Abdullah Khan and Yasin Khan had not hesitated to expose themselves as they moved about directing their men. When the battalion fought, it had fought well.

But let there be a lull, above all let night fall—a man's spirits are rarely at their best then—and there came a hopelessness that affected the officers particularly. Hopelessness not just for the hour and the day, but for all the days ahead. "They are in their own minds convinced that the Anglo-Americans are going to win the war and it is futile to carry on the struggle," Prem noted. Probably the surrender leaflets generated by the infamous five had had some effect. And if Indian Army veterans deserted in greater numbers than civilian recruits, that was only to be expected. For those leaflets promised Aya Singh, even lowly Jaghri Ram (both disappeared now), a homecoming. They offered no such prospect to men from Malaya.

There was some consolation in these reflections. But at the time, very early on Wednesday, Prem could not close his eyes to what this mass desertion meant. From the commander of the Japanese company on his left he learned that a battalion was coming to relieve him. Very well, he would pull what was left of his force back the instant the first Japanese appeared. It was done. The men were out and moving before dawn broke, leaving the Japanese to take over. At Popa, Prem rested and reorganized his three battalions, reforming them into two. But by now the Japanese line had crumbled everywhere. On April 8 a Japanese liaison officer told Shah Nawaz there must be a general withdrawal. On the 10th Shah Nawaz issued the necessary orders (that day bombing caught the INA field hospital near Kyaukpadaung, killing four score men and wounding thirty). Next day what was left of the 2nd Division began to move.

🪷

How Dhillon and Prem's men got clear of Mount Popa and struggled south would make a story in itself. From the beginning the possibility of stopping somewhere to turn and fight was slim. Transport now was entirely by bullock cart, in darkness only (for even carts were likely to be strafed), and this meant that Slim's columns, moving by day in tracked or wheeled vehicles along metalled roads, would inevitably outstrip the Indians and cut them off unless the Japanese threw up roadblocks and brought those columns to a halt.

For a moment it looked as if they might. At Pyawbwe, a little below Meiktila, 14th Army was held up for days by the determined resistance of three skeleton Japanese divisions. But resistance ended on April 11th, just as Shah Nawaz and his two regiments were quitting Popa. That very morning Slim stationed himself by the roadside as Messervy's corps began its dash for Rangoon, three hundred miles to go with three weeks of dry weather sure to do it in, the vehicles stirring up great clouds of dust between the trees so that the column seemed to be plunging "into a thunderous yellow tunnel, first the tanks, infantry all over them, then trucks filled with men, then more tanks, going fast, nose to tail, guns, more trucks, more guns—British, Sikhs, Gurkhas, Madrassis, Pathans. . . . The old Indian Army going down to the attack, for the last time in history." And John Masters the novelist, whose words these are, who was then a lieutenant colonel of Gurkhas serving as G–1 of the 19th Indian Division, and who stood that morning not far from 14th Army's commander—Masters remembers that "twenty races, a dozen religions, a score of languages" went by as he and Sir William watched.

"When my great-great-grandfather first went to India," he writes, "there had been as many nations"—a dozen, perhaps a score. Now there was one. "And he and I and a few thousand others, over two and a half centuries, sometimes with intent, sometimes unwittingly, sometimes in miraculous sympathy, sometimes in brutal folly, had made it." Whether his forebears should ever have set foot on the "ramshackle subcontinent" was a question Masters would not attempt to answer, though he was quite certain that if they hadn't, the French or the Russians would have. "I only know that I saw, beside the road outside Pyawbwe, what *we* had made."[25] Where once there had been twenty races, a dozen religions, a score of languages, he saw now one Indian Army—the nation incarnate.

Of course there were those not far away—sixty miles west with a touch of north, to be exact—who, if asked, might have protested that this was nonsense. It was idle to try to pass Slim's men off as the nation in arms. Which, after all, was more truly *India's* army, the Goliath barreling down the Rangoon road or their own bedraggled, fugitive force? But they were not asked; and anyway Prem, who would have been the chief of those protesting, was much too busy trying to get his men across the Kyaukpadaung–Meiktila road before the British, who had just taken Kyaukpadaung, cut them off.

He got them across shortly after midnight on the 13th, all except for one platoon from Bagri's 3rd Battalion left too long on the Legyi–Popaywa road and trapped there. (Invited to surrender, the Gurkha ex–havildar who commanded this platoon sent back a scribbled "Gentlemen, I do not come," and fought on until he was killed.) But they had to abandon their motor transport. It was now that they turned entirely to bullock carts. And Prem himself was confined to one, for, rushing about in the dark to collect his men and get them moving, he had tripped and sprained an ankle so badly he could not walk.

Below the road Shah Nawaz, Dhillon, and the few hundred survivors from the Nehru Brigade turned toward the Irrawaddy at Magwe, as the Japanese directed them to do. Prem led his much larger remnant due south towards Natmauk, keeping the road and railroad, which the British were sure to be using, well to his left. It was barren country, the ground so broken that even the bullock carts sometimes had trouble, the villages few. *We moved from village to village, hiding in them during the day because a village was the only place that gave cover. When we came near one, I would send men ahead with instructions to pretend they were looking for the Indian Army. And if they were told, yes, the Indian Army is here, we would avoid that place.*

His ankle gave him trouble until Banta Singh, commanding the 2nd Battalion, sent him a man expert in such things, *a huge tough chap who sat next to me and took the bandage off and began feeling it very, very gently. We were chatting. Suddenly he said, "look up, Saheb, plane." So I looked up. And as I looked up, he gave my foot a twist. The most terrible pain went through it. I thought I would die. But soon afterwards it felt much better.* Just the same Prem was happy to pick up a horse.

West of but on a line with Natmauk he met a Japanese officer who told him that the British had taken Yenangyaung, with its oil fields, and were approaching Magwe. No defense line was possible, the officer said, even as far south as Taungdwingyi. He had best head for Prome. Up to this point Prem had kept Banta Singh's battalion and Bagri's together. Now he split them. So many men in one spot invited discovery. He went ahead with Banta Singh. Bagri followed, keeping on a parallel track. They were heading south by west now, with the Taungdwingyi– Allanmyo road on their left. From time to time the sound of guns reached them from the Irrawaddy, drawing near on their right.

Then one night Prem lost Bagri. It happened in this way. There were British behind, quite possibly looking for him. More appeared to be approaching on his left. So he turned a little more toward the west and sent Bagri word to do the same. Bagri did not respond. *To this day I don't know whether he got the message,* for Prem never saw the battalion or its commander again. Later he learned—from the British, who also gave him the story of the Gurkha ex-havildar—that in the darkness and confusion Bagri had turned *east,* been spotted in open country, and died with many of his men desperately trying to beat off armored vehicles with rifles and hand grenades.

Prem pushed on with Banta Singh's 2nd Battalion, regimental headquarters, and what was left of the division's field hospital. Scouting a route was becoming more and more difficult, the men were so tired; during the night marches they often fell asleep on their feet. Allanmyo was his goal now. If he could reach it before the British on the road did, he might be able to break through and continue downriver to Prome. But the road, too, led to Allanmyo, so the farther he went, the closer it came. Almost unconsciously he edged right, toward the river. As the crow flies he had marched well over eighty miles since leaving Mount Popa, and of course he and his men were not crows.

At dawn on April 26 he reached the Irrawaddy a little above Allanmyo, sent a patrol downstream, and discovered that the British had

His 4th Corps, which had begun the 1945 campaign by stealing down the west side of the great central valley, was to continue down the east side, the 17th and 5th Indian Divisions leapfrogging as they went (the 5th had reached Meiktila during March). The 19th Indian Division, fresh from its capture of Mandalay, was to cover the rear and left flank. Meanwhile the 33rd Corps was to follow the Irrawaddy. But as the Irrawadddy, below Mandalay, bends to the west to receive the Chindwin before it turns south again, this put the 33rd on the west side of the valley. The two corps were trading places.

Some units did as the 19th did. Transferred from 33 to 4 Corps, it did not have to move at all. But a certain amount of shifting was unavoidable, and this Slim put to a calculated use. Across the great swathe of ground where for the past month Kimura's men had made their supreme effort, there remained "many scattered but sometimes strong parties of Japanese" who either hung on "with dull ferocity" or tried to flee south. "I took advantage of the regrouping necessary for the advance on Rangoon," Slim later wrote, "to comb this area, whose roads and railways were essential to us, by what I called a 'Union Jack' manoeuvre." As anyone who has ever tried to draw that most perplexing flag will readily understand, "this entailed passing strong columns diagonally through it."[21] One of these diagonal thrusts was entrusted to the 5th Brigade of the 2nd British Division.

The division was on the point of leaving Burma. Given the difficulties 14th Army would have before the rains began, in particular with respect to supply, it made sense to shed British divisions, even British battalions that were part of Indian divisions. They consumed far more daily tonnage than comparable Indian units required. And the rising pressure inside England to bring home men with long overseas service made keeping them up to strength impossible. So the 2nd Division was to go. Two of its brigades, the 4th and 6th, made a few sweeps along the Irrawaddy bend and prepared to fly out. The 5th, however, was given a more substantial assignment further south. It was directed to make a diagonal thrust down the Taungtha–Kyaukpadaung road. It would leave Burma when Kyaukpadaung had been reached.

About this assignment there is a touch of the gratuitous. If the 7th Indian Division, now part of 33 Corps, really could not (as the official history implies) take Chauk unless Kyaukpadaung to its east had first been secured, why advance along a road that brushed Mount Popa? Why take a route on which the enemy, perceived as consisting chiefly of determined Japanese, was sure to make good defensive use of the terrain? Why not approach Kyaukpadaung across the excellent tank country to the west, why not approach from Nyaungu and Pyinbin? As long as the Japanese stood on a defensive line that included Popa, the mountain was valuable as an observation tower, natural fortress, and anchor. Let the line be broken, however, and Popa was nothing. Why bother with it, then? Why not avoid it and let its defenders wither on the vine?

Unreasonable or not, 5th Brigade's instructions were to go straight past Mount Popa. The order went out. The brigade began to move. The ambush in which Prem lost his map case and diary was the work, it is a fair guess, of an advance patrol of its attached 2nd Reconnaissance Regiment. Behind came the brigade proper, accompanied by 25-pounders of the Royal Artillery's 10th Field Regiment and a squadron of Carabinier medium tanks, with Hurricanes and Thunderbolts giving air support. Though in numbers of men no larger than Prem's regiment, 5th Brigade because of its mobility and fire power was altogether out of Prem's class. It was a force against which he had little hope of standing, a force he should never have had to face. But face it he must, for it had set a course that would take it to Welaung, to Legyi, through Popaywa itself.

Perhaps this was just as well. Perhaps it was just as well, too, that 5 Brigade was composed not of fellow Indians but of British. For if Slim's thinking had been different and his instructions otherwise, the crowning action of the war in Burma—14th Army's final dash for Rangoon—would have left Prem and his men untouched. And how, in that case, could they have fulfilled Netaji's injunction to pay freedom's price by barring, at least briefly, the Britishers' advance?

※

Legyi, to which Khazin Shah and his men withdrew after the ambush, *is like a saucer, with high ground on all sides. And absolutely bare. No trees, nothing.* There was a village, which gave the place its name, but it cannot have been a large village, for the ground was barren and rocky, so rocky that when Prem's machine gun crews began preparing the pits for these indispensable weapons, they found they could not dig down more than three or four feet.

Nevertheless it was more than ordinarily defensible, which was why Prem had ordered the 1st Battalion there early on the Friday morning. The low hills around gave excellent observation. From one Prem made it his habit to watch through field glasses as the British approached. Up to a point he could see what they were about, estimate what part of the saucer they were heading for, and warn his companies by runner. He had help in this respect from a Japanese patrol concealed on Hill 1395, six miles to the northeast overlooking the road from Welaung. It could report British movements by radio to Kanjo *Butai* Headquarters, which then alerted Prem over a field telephone line, so that he had some sense of what was going on long before anything came in sight.

Moreover, though Legyi is some five miles from Popa's summit, so gradually does that mountain rise that the spurs and gullies of its slopes made difficulties even at that distance for vehicles that left the road. Difficulties even for tanks if timidly handled, as the Carabiniers seem to have been. This was crucial. Prem could accept shelling. Hard as the ground was, if the men dug in only a little, and kept well spread out, they could take a good deal of shelling. And when the shelling lifted and the British infantry came on, *moving from cover to cover, not certain where we were, one section advancing while the other gave it covering fire,* his machine gunners had only to wait *until we could almost see the whites of their eyes. I had mortars too.* At Rangoon the regiment had been beefed up with a mortar company. *But I didn't use them much because I had very little ammunition. My main strength was in my medium machine guns and my light machine guns.* Neither mortars nor machine guns, however, would have been of much use against tanks, nor could Prem depend upon antitank mines, of which he had a few. So it was fortunate that though tanks were frequently spotted, they were never seriously used.

Saturday passed without incident. At his division headquarters Shah Nawaz noted, "Popa heavily bombed and machine-gunned. Supplies hit."[22] By now everyone was used to air raids, though perhaps not on this scale. Because of them Prem had long since abandoned his little shed at the top of the rise.

Then on Sunday afternoon, April 1, Hill 1395 sent word that there was movement from Welaung—trucks carrying stores and men, motorcycles, tanks, an armored car. At dusk it remained unclear whether these meant to come down the Kyaukpadaung road or turn west at Seiktein for Pyinbin. So Prem sent two patrols out, one toward Seiktein (it was commanded by Abdullah Khan, the man who had nabbed the two jeeps and the field radio four weeks before), the other in a more westerly direction. At four in the morning Abdullah came back with nothing of significance to report. The other patrol did not return.

On Monday men and vehicles were again seen some distance to the north. Toward noon aircraft bombed and machine-gunned Legyi village, setting it on fire. There was some shelling, aimless but harassing. Late in the day Prem was forced to use his machine guns to drive away men who seemed to be scouting his position. Night fell. The missing patrol turned up. At the same time Prem learned that Yasin Khan, who had not only directed the machine gun fire but actually handled a gun, had just slipped away, taking with him several other officers, NCOs, and men. And as the night wore on, despondency settled like a blanket upon Legyi's defenders. Surely the British knew their strength and how they were disposed. What chance had they of withstanding an assault? Before dawn Khazin Shah was in such a state of nerves that Prem had to take direct command of the battalion.

Next day, Tuesday the 3rd, the British at last moved in earnest. Once again there was much distant coming and going, reported first by Hill 1395, picked up later by Prem's field glasses. But this time a sizable force moved directly down the road, and Prem braced for an attack. It came not from the front, however, but from the flanks and was accompanied by shelling, which forced everyone to keep their heads down. Along some parts of the perimeter it took the defenders by surprise. One party broke into Prem's rear and surprised men cooking and carrying water. Another moved clear behind the battalion and got astride the road to Kyaukpadaung. To his left Prem was in contact with Kanjo *Butai*, which gave him some security. But his right was in the air. It was from the right that the attacks came that broke into his rear echelon and cut the road. And as the afternoon wore on, it looked as if the British would at any moment overwhelm his defenses and pour into the saucer.

What saved him, in part, was the enemy's tactical behavior. They delivered their attacks *in penny packets. If they had made a concerted attack on my position, they would have overrun it. But they kept on putting one attack here, one attack there. Probably they weren't quite certain what our strength was, probably these were probing attacks. Once I sent a company, under Kanwal Singh, into a counterattack with the supporting fire of only one light machine gun, and because the British weren't expecting anything, it drove them off and reoccupied the position.*

But there was more to the business than British irresolution. There were the likes of Kanwal Singh, leading a counterattack. And there was Prem, who knew when and where to order one—Prem, who had far more command experience than any of his battalion commanders (in the Indian Army all three had been subadars). What we are working with here is Prem's account of the action, his formal report to 2nd INA Division Headquarters, date 6 April, introduced as evidence during his trial, and available because when the British captured or stumbled upon that headquarters they found it, recognized it for what it was, and laid it carefully aside. It is long and detailed, this battle report, proceeding day by day and sometimes hour by hour. It is the only account we have. But I have been able to supplement it with what Prem told me one evening as we bent over the Surveyor General of India's quarter-inch topographical map of central Burma spread out on the floor of the bungalow he and Lakshmi occupied in Kanpur's Civil Lines.

That evening Prem relived for my benefit the action at Legyi, pointing out Hill 1395 and the spot from which he could see the British coming, explaining where he had placed his companies, one here, another there, his medium machine guns sighted to fire over the men's heads, the light machine guns with their flat trajectory in position on the flanks, *all dug in and scattered so the British couldn't see us at all.* Prem took me through those several days of anxiety, excitement, and boredom. (The expression "fighting all day" is meaningless, he explained. Fighting never lasts long. *In between there are periods when nothing happens and you don't know what to do with yourself.*) We read the battle report line by line.[23] And as we read, I had the feeling that on this climactic Tuesday, though he could not be everywhere at once, and certainly did not always know what was going on (it was hours before he learned what had happened to his rear echelon), he had been very much on top of things—and had, besides, thoroughly enjoyed himself.

So he sent Kanwal Singh and his company into a successful counterattack. It was not part of the 1st Battalion, it was the company from Bagri's 3rd, and this day it served Prem well. By moving it where needed, by plugging gaps with whatever else he could find (so that sometimes a platoon was sent to do a company's work), by binding the Japanese on his left to cover that flank and so allow him to concentrate on the right, Prem survived until nightfall, at which point the situation actually improved. At nine-thirty word reached his command post that his rear area had been cleared and that jawans were once again astride the road south.

If we could stop here, we should be able to say that this engagement, which receives little attention in the British and even less in the Indian official histories, but is known to the INA as the Battle of Legyi,[24] was an unqualified success. One lightly armed battalion reinforced by part of another and supported on one flank by some Japanese, but utterly without artillery or air support, had faced and held a brigade. Indeed, we might expect to read that it did the same the next day and the day after. Instead, there is only the terse statement that at five o'clock on Wednesday morning "withdrawal was commenced and carried out without any casualties." Prem was leaving Legyi, not because his 1st Battalion was beaten or even badly battle worn, but because it had almost ceased to exist.

The leakage began with the disappearance, Sunday night, of the battalion's mortar officer. Twenty-four hours later Yasin Khan deserted, taking several more officers and a dozen men. It was not until Tuesday night, however, *after* the hardest of the fighting was over, that the hemorrhaging set in for fair. At seven that evening Prem, hearing at last that the British had broken into his rear echelon, ordered C Company to drive them out, and was astonished to learn from Khazin Shah that C Company couldn't—two of its three platoons together with the mortar section had gone over. From other companies Prem collected a force to do the job. But at nine-thirty, along with the news that this force had been successful, word came that Khazin Shah himself, the whole of battalion headquarters, and one platoon of A Company under Abdullah Khan had decamped. After that the floodgates opened. By midnight all five of the battalion's company commanders and some two hundred men were gone. The remainder, Prem's battle report continues, "could not be trusted." Prem might still count on the one company from Bagri's battalion, though it was exhausted, and toward morning Major Negi arrived with a second company and an additional section of machine guns. But he could hardly expect to hold the saucer with these.

Turning the miserable business over in his mind two days later (his conclusions form a note attached to his battle report), Prem thought to himself that the deserters had not been cowards. Quite the contrary, many of the officers who slipped away, usually taking their men with them (that was half the difficulty), had been conspicuously brave under fire. Abdullah Khan and Yasin Khan had not hesitated to expose themselves as they moved about directing their men. When the battalion fought, it had fought well.

But let there be a lull, above all let night fall—a man's spirits are rarely at their best then—and there came a hopelessness that affected the officers particularly. Hopelessness not just for the hour and the day, but for all the days ahead. "They are in their own minds convinced that the Anglo-Americans are going to win the war and it is futile to carry on the struggle," Prem noted. Probably the surrender leaflets generated by the infamous five had had some effect. And if Indian Army veterans deserted in greater numbers than civilian recruits, that was only to be expected. For those leaflets promised Aya Singh, even lowly Jaghri Ram (both disappeared now), a homecoming. They offered no such prospect to men from Malaya.

There was some consolation in these reflections. But at the time, very early on Wednesday, Prem could not close his eyes to what this mass desertion meant. From the commander of the Japanese company on his left he learned that a battalion was coming to relieve him. Very well, he would pull what was left of his force back the instant the first Japanese appeared. It was done. The men were out and moving before dawn broke, leaving the Japanese to take over. At Popa, Prem rested and reorganized his three battalions, reforming them into two. But by now the Japanese line had crumbled everywhere. On April 8 a Japanese liaison officer told Shah Nawaz there must be a general withdrawal. On the 10th Shah Nawaz issued the necessary orders (that day bombing caught the INA field hospital near Kyaukpadaung, killing four score men and wounding thirty). Next day what was left of the 2nd Division began to move.

卋

How Dhillon and Prem's men got clear of Mount Popa and struggled south would make a story in itself. From the beginning the possibility of stopping somewhere to turn and fight was slim. Transport now was entirely by bullock cart, in darkness only (for even carts were likely to be strafed), and this meant that Slim's columns, moving by day in tracked or wheeled vehicles along metalled roads, would inevitably outstrip the Indians and cut them off unless the Japanese threw up roadblocks and brought those columns to a halt.

For a moment it looked as if they might. At Pyawbwe, a little below Meiktila, 14th Army was held up for days by the determined resistance of three skeleton Japanese divisions. But resistance ended on April 11th, just as Shah Nawaz and his two regiments were quitting Popa. That very morning Slim stationed himself by the roadside as Messervy's corps began its dash for Rangoon, three hundred miles to go with three weeks of dry weather sure to do it in, the vehicles stirring up great clouds of dust between the trees so that the column seemed to be plunging "into a thunderous yellow tunnel, first the tanks, infantry all over them, then trucks filled with men, then more tanks, going fast, nose to tail, guns, more trucks, more guns—British, Sikhs, Gurkhas, Madrassis, Pathans. . . . The old Indian Army going down to the attack, for the last time in history." And John Masters the novelist, whose words these are, who was then a lieutenant colonel of Gurkhas serving as G–1 of the 19th Indian Division, and who stood that morning not far from 14th Army's commander—Masters remembers that "twenty races, a dozen religions, a score of languages" went by as he and Sir William watched.

"When my great-great-grandfather first went to India," he writes, "there had been as many nations"—a dozen, perhaps a score. Now there was one. "And he and I and a few thousand others, over two and a half centuries, sometimes with intent, sometimes unwittingly, sometimes in miraculous sympathy, sometimes in brutal folly, had made it." Whether his forebears should ever have set foot on the "ramshackle subcontinent" was a question Masters would not attempt to answer, though he was quite certain that if they hadn't, the French or the Russians would have. "I only know that I saw, beside the road outside Pyawbwe, what *we* had made."[25] Where once there had been twenty races, a dozen religions, a score of languages, he saw now one Indian Army—the nation incarnate.

Of course there were those not far away—sixty miles west with a touch of north, to be exact—who, if asked, might have protested that this was nonsense. It was idle to try to pass Slim's men off as the nation in arms. Which, after all, was more truly *India's* army, the Goliath barreling down the Rangoon road or their own bedraggled, fugitive force? But they were not asked; and anyway Prem, who would have been the chief of those protesting, was much too busy trying to get his men across the Kyaukpadaung–Meiktila road before the British, who had just taken Kyaukpadaung, cut them off.

He got them across shortly after midnight on the 13th, all except for one platoon from Bagri's 3rd Battalion left too long on the Legyi–Popaywa road and trapped there. (Invited to surrender, the Gurkha ex–havildar who commanded this platoon sent back a scribbled "Gentle-men, I do not come," and fought on until he was killed.) But they had to abandon their motor transport. It was now that they turned entirely to bullock carts. And Prem himself was confined to one, for, rushing about in the dark to collect his men and get them moving, he had tripped and sprained an ankle so badly he could not walk.

Below the road Shah Nawaz, Dhillon, and the few hundred survivors from the Nehru Brigade turned toward the Irrawaddy at Magwe, as the Japanese directed them to do. Prem led his much larger remnant due south towards Natmauk, keeping the road and railroad, which the British were sure to be using, well to his left. It was barren country, the ground so broken that even the bullock carts sometimes had trouble, the villages few. *We moved from village to village, hiding in them during the day because a village was the only place that gave cover. When we came near one, I would send men ahead with instructions to pretend they were looking for the Indian Army. And if they were told, yes, the Indian Army is here, we would avoid that place.*

His ankle gave him trouble until Banta Singh, commanding the 2nd Battalion, sent him a man expert in such things, *a huge tough chap who sat next to me and took the bandage off and began feeling it very, very gently. We were chatting. Suddenly he said, "look up, Saheb, plane." So I looked up. And as I looked up, he gave my foot a twist. The most terrible pain went through it. I thought I would die. But soon afterwards it felt much better.* Just the same Prem was happy to pick up a horse.

West of but on a line with Natmauk he met a Japanese officer who told him that the British had taken Yenangyaung, with its oil fields, and were approaching Magwe. No defense line was possible, the officer said, even as far south as Taungdwingyi. He had best head for Prome. Up to this point Prem had kept Banta Singh's battalion and Bagri's together. Now he split them. So many men in one spot invited discovery. He went ahead with Banta Singh. Bagri followed, keeping on a parallel track. They were heading south by west now, with the Taungdwingyi–Allanmyo road on their left. From time to time the sound of guns reached them from the Irrawaddy, drawing near on their right.

Then one night Prem lost Bagri. It happened in this way. There were British behind, quite possibly looking for him. More appeared to be approaching on his left. So he turned a little more toward the west and sent Bagri word to do the same. Bagri did not respond. *To this day I don't know whether he got the message,* for Prem never saw the battalion or its commander again. Later he learned—from the British, who also gave him the story of the Gurkha ex-havildar—that in the darkness and confusion Bagri had turned *east*, been spotted in open country, and died with many of his men desperately trying to beat off armored vehicles with rifles and hand grenades.

Prem pushed on with Banta Singh's 2nd Battalion, regimental headquarters, and what was left of the division's field hospital. Scouting a route was becoming more and more difficult, the men were so tired; during the night marches they often fell asleep on their feet. Allanmyo was his goal now. If he could reach it before the British on the road did, he might be able to break through and continue downriver to Prome. But the road, too, led to Allanmyo, so the farther he went, the closer it came. Almost unconsciously he edged right, toward the river. As the crow flies he had marched well over eighty miles since leaving Mount Popa, and of course he and his men were not crows.

At dawn on April 26 he reached the Irrawaddy a little above Allanmyo, sent a patrol downstream, and discovered that the British had preceded him. So that evening he took his men upriver, to a little village called Magyigan that from the lay of the land looked as if it could be defended, and nexr morning brought his officers together for a council of war. To break through at Allanmyo was out of the question, they hadn't the strength. They might cross the river. But once across, where would they go? If they split into groups, some at least would probably get away. That was a viable option. Surrender was another. Going civilian—some of his south Indians suggested this, they would put on *longyis*—was a third. And as they weighed the alternatives, they heard shots.

> *My outposts had opened fire at an approaching Gurkha battalion. Then aircraft began flying low over the village. So the villagers came to me and said, "if you stay and fight, they will bomb this village and set fire to it. Don't fight." I had to make a decision. The bulk of my men were going to surrender in any case. Those who wanted to turn civilian were already beginning to. For the sake of the few of us who wanted to try to break out, was I to risk burning this village? So I said, "all right, we'll surrender."*

Under a white flag, Banta Singh was sent with a note to this effect. Presently he returned with a British captain. Not all of Prem's men knew what was going on and somebody dropped a mortar shell on the Gurkhas. With difficulty Prem smothered what might have turned into a nasty little fire fight. Later the Gurkhas' commander, a lieutenant colonel named Kitson, came up. They talked. Prem told Kitson that he and his men wished to surrender—as proper prisoners of war (the note was explicit about that). Kitson was civil but noncommittal. He could not accept their surrender instantly, he said. "*I've got no rations to give you. I've got no means of feeding you.*" So both sides remained where they were until the next day.

The next day was Saturday the 28th of April. There was no surrender ceremony, nor could Prem parade his men and say farewell. On Sunday he was taken, alone except for his personal orderly, to brigade headquarters on the north side of Allanmyo. Kitson noticed that his prisoner was lame and provided a jeep. On Monday he was moved to division headquarters south of the town. It was the 20th Indian Division, part of 33 Corps, that had caught him.

There his escort turned him over to a major. The major was sitting under a tree. He was *not* eating an omelette, as the Japanese colonel had been during Prem's first time around in the surrender business, nor did he offer Prem cognac. He did ask him to sit down. So Prem sat. He noticed that the major was doing a *Times of India* crossword puzzle. Evidently he was having trouble with it, for after a time he turned to Prem and said, *"come, old chap, do you know anything about these things?"* *"Not much,"* Prem replied, *"but I'll help."* So Prem moved closer and they sat together under the tree doing the crossword puzzle.

CHAPTER 16

THE LEADER LOST

Two weeks later almost to the day, Aung San reached the west bank of the Irrawaddy at Allanmyo, crossed, and flew on to 14th Army Headquarters in a British plane—but not as a prisoner like Prem, far from it. As the leader of the Burmese resistance, or what the British were beginning to call the Anti-Fascist Organization or AFO. The purpose of Aung San's visit was to meet Slim. It was Slim who had provided the safe conduct as well as the plane. Aung San meant to use the occasion to review with Sir William, as one commander reviews matters with another, how the military arm of the AFO, the seven battalions of the Burma National Army, could best help speed Burma's liberation.[1]

Right the length of Japanese occupation those battalions had done nothing to dislodge the occupiers. They had not taken to the hills as Tito's Partisans and the French Maquis had done, they had not prowled the great central valley blowing bridges, cutting telegraph lines, making mischief in other ways. They had done none of the things that a Resistance normally does. They had continued to wear Japan's uniform; they had gone on behaving as Japan's friend; until, at the very end of March, they sprang suddenly to life.

Not, however, with a head-on attack upon the Japanese. Lacking heavy weapons just as the INA did, they knew they would have to operate, guerrilla fashion, on the fringes of serious action. Certainly they could not confront the enemy in Rangoon itself. And as Rangoon was where most of the battalions happened to be, Aung San had first to extricate them and get them safely away. He managed this by pretending, with magnificent impudence, that they were leaving not to fight the Japanese but to help them. He went further. He arranged for his men a grand ceremonial sendoff.

On March 17, the day Prem and his men returned from their raid toward Pyinbin, the thing was staged—Burma's army, impatient to show what it could do, departing at last to join its imperial ally in the struggle to recover Meiktila. "Unforgettable scenes," reported *Greater Asia*. On this day "crack forces of the Burmese Army commenced their victorious march to the battlefield, holding aloft the tricolour peacock flag." The public farewell took place in the shadow of the Shwe Dagon pagoda. Aung San said a few words. Kimura sent a warm congratulatory message. "Comrades," cried Ba Maw, as breezy and effusive as ever though he may have suspected what was going on, "today is the day when we are about to clear up old scores against the white-faced English." And while a Japanese military band played the Burmese national anthem, several thousand young men with Japanese tunics on their backs and Japanese rifles on their shoulders passed in review and disappeared from the city, bound presumably for the front hundreds of miles to the north.[2]

Ten days later "bandit gangs disguised as soldiers" attacked Japanese posts near Pegu, only forty miles away. A week went by, and these bandits became (in the words of *Greater Asia*) "soldiers of the Burmese Army led by shallow-thinking officers." Another week, and the *Adipadi* announced that he was taking personal command of that army. It was to return at once to Rangoon. But Ba Maw cannot have expected to be obeyed, for he coupled the order with a warning that any village harboring "mutineers" would be attacked from the air. And he did not mention Aung San.

Aung San had not, in fact, left Rangoon at once. He had stayed behind, possibly to tie up loose administrative ends, more probably to see to the safety of his wife and children. One of his officers remembers a farewell luncheon given by Kimura himself. There stood the Bogyoke—the term, which loosely translates "general," like Netaji mingles affection with respect—"grim-faced, tight-lipped, in his seaweed green uniform and shiny top boots, with his sword hanging by his side and a Japanese peakcap perched on his head."[3] Perhaps, speculates Kya Doe, he was thinking that in a day or two, when Khin Kyi and the little ones were securely in hiding, it would be time for him to slip away. Perhaps he was thinking that Kimura must know what he planned, perhaps he was inwardly daring Kimura to do something about it. What Kimura thought we do not know. Both Joyce Lebra and Louis Allen believe that the Japanese had for some time been expecting a defection on a large scale. Both believe that they hesitated to act upon this feeling, for fear that disbanding a BNA unit and arresting its officers might push the rest into the arms of the British. Better to trust, or at least appear to. Besides, in Rangoon there was a problem of numbers. On the day of the farewell Kimura may have realized that the marching men were up to no good, and simultaneously realized that he did not have enough troops in the city to confront and disarm them.

So the great defection of 27 March went off without a hitch, at least as far as shaking loose from the Japanese was concerned. Getting the British to recognize these marching men for what they held themselves to be, was something else again.

Of course the Government of India had known for over a year that at a moment of Aung San's choosing the Burma National Army would change sides. But New Delhi, though it welcomed the prospect, did not mean to recognize that force as the army of an independent Burma, or the AFO as Burma's legitimate government in prospect. Its views on Burma's constitutional future, established early in 1943 by Linlithgow himself, were otherwise. "I should have thought," the Viceroy had written Whitehall in response to a query on the subject, "that Crown Colony Status was the best that Burma was entitled to, or to look for, for many years to come; and that this was the right moment to prick the bubble of Burma's vanity and to make it clear that this was the basis on which their country was going to be run for them."[4] And at the hill station of Simla, where Sir Reginald Dorman-Smith, Governor of Burma, presided over a government in exile, the feeling that at war's end the Burmese must expect to have their country "run for them" was even stronger—though for a slightly different reason.

Sir Reginald's attitude was not, like Linlithgow's, coolly dismissive. Sir Reginald was acutely, almost miserably, conscious that his countrymen had twice let the Burmese down: by failing to defend them from the Japanese, and by destroying the country as they withdrew. No redress was possible for the first. It should, however, be possible to repair the second. As soon as the Japanese had been expelled, civil government must go in and rebuild towns, roads, bridges, irrigation works, rice mills, oil wells, the lot. But exactly because this was what the Raj must do, it could not surrender political control. The physical reconstruction of the country, if nothing else, demanded a period—Dorman-Smith estimated it at five to seven years—of direct British rule.

Meanwhile Aung San made him nervous. Sir Reginald knew as much as New Delhi knew (Force 136, the Southeast Asia arm of Britain's wartime undercover agency, kept him posted), and in a telegram to Whitehall late in 1944 agreed that a resistance movement that was brought into the open might help 14th Army. "I hope it will." But the political implications disturbed him. If Aung San's battalions acquitted themselves well, the AFO would probably demand full self-government for Burma the moment the war was over. It might even try to set up a provisional government. The attempt would not easily be thwarted. "Resistance movements," observed Sir Reginald gloomily, "seem to be quite capable of continuing to resist if things do not go precisely as they wish." So the AFO had best be kept on a tight rein. Thakins, in particular, must be treated with caution. (The AFO was not wholly Thakin, he knew, but Aung San and most of the leaders were.) "They should be told quite bluntly that they are the most suspect political group in our eyes, and that they must work their passage."[5]

Work their passage. The phrase suited to a T those old hands from the Indian Civil Service who had served with Dorman-Smith at Simla for the past several years. Many of them were being sent now—under the name Civil Affairs Section—to Burma to give the colony, as 14th Army recovered it mile by mile, a temporary military administration. (Though called Civil Affairs, they went in uniform and carried army rank.) And as they used the phrase, these Civil Affairs Section officers saw with the mind's eye Aung San. Pushy, importunate young Aung San. Aung San must be forced to secure his place by patient attention to duty over a considerable stretch of time. Aung San must be made to work his passage. And if he refused? There was a word, *quisling*, for the sort of person he would, by refusing, show himself to be. Vidkun Quisling was the scoundrelly Norwegian politician who, in 1940, had invited the Germans to enter and seize Norway. Hadn't Aung San welcomed, in fact accompanied, the Japanese as they invaded Burma? Indeed this, perhaps, was what Aung San *really* was, a quisling—and the men he commanded the Burma Traitor Army. It was a designation sometimes used by British intelligence itself.

Force 136, however, thought differently. Force 136 had made contact with these Thakins. Force 136 wanted Aung San and his battalions to do for the war in the great central valley what Karen irregulars were poised to do for it in the hills. Force 136 did not care if legitimizing Aung San and his battalions disturbed old Burma hands, or alienated moderate Burmese who might otherwise cooperate with a reconstituted Government of Burma. It was not the Force's business to worry about such things. Its business was to win the war. So when Colin MacKenzie, the Force's chief, discovered that letting Major General C. F. B. Pearce (commanding Civil Affairs Section) in on his plans only stirred misgivings in the Section, he became secretive. He stopped telling Pearce anything—and went ahead with what he was doing.

But Pearce eventually found out, of course. There was a row. And as many military men shared Civil Affairs' repugnance for quislings and left-leaning Thakins, while at the same time MacKenzie was determined not to have his preparations for behind-the-lines risings ruined, the row was not easily settled. It boiled right up to the top. There, at Mountbatten's elegant headquarters in the lovely Ceylonese hill town of Kandy, the Supremo settled it himself. The decision he arrived at, the instructions he issued, constituted what Hugh Tinker has called "arguably the most important British policy commitment made in Burma's reconquest and decolonisation."[6] Mountbatten decided to support anti-Japanese risings no matter what form they took. And he instructed Sir Oliver Leese, his C-in-C Allied Land Forces (and Slim's immediate superior), to rescind an order that prohibited giving arms to the resisters.

This was in February 1945. Though the Burma National Army did not depend upon the arms that Force 136 proposed to parachute drop—it had already been armed by the Japanese—the lifting of the order had the effect of recognizing it not simply as a legitimate military representative of the Burmese people, but as *the* representative. It had no rivals. The guerrilla bands that Force 136 had organized along Burma's eastern hills were Karen, not Burmese. Aung San, too, had no rivals. There was no De Gaulle or anyone approaching him among the politicians and civil servants with Dorman-Smith at Simla. Ba Maw had lost everyone's respect. There was only Aung San. By recognizing him and his battalions on the eve of Burma's liberation, Mountbatten guaranteed the young man a preeminent position in Burmese politics, and positioned him to become the arbiter of Burma's future. One has to wonder why he did.

He had operational reasons. A properly timed BNA rising might make the difference between 14th Army reaching or not reaching Rangoon before the rains began. Aung San's men could be invaluable, too, in the mopping up to follow. But Mountbatten took a more than military view of operational necessity. Politics entered into his calculation, as it might with a different twist have entered into the calculations of his subordinates had he allowed it to. ("I reserve political decisions to myself," he warned Leese[7].) Without fixed opinions, he approached problems in a matter-of-fact manner—"a pragmatist in all things," his biographer Philip Zeigler calls him, with "egalitarian instincts" and a "generalized belief in progress."[8] At Kandy he looked ahead to what lay beyond victory just as anxiously as Slim did, but arrived at a different conclusion. It would be wise, he saw, to grant in advance those things that would have to be conceded later anyhow. And it would be wise to do so generously.

That many Burmese genuinely wanted to help throw the Japanese out, Mountbatten did not doubt. Of course there was always the problem of timing. You wanted to rise soon enough to establish that you were not Britain's lackey, not so early that you were crushed. This, in his view, the BNA had managed to do, for there was evidence that the March 27 rising had been planned *before* his February decision. It was true that the Thakins were in many ways unappealing. It was true that recognizing them was bound to give offense to those Burmese, and they existed, for whom Simla spoke. "But it must be remembered," he observed just before the rising, "that the more respectable elements have been inactive, while the elements who are about to undertake this action comprise the active, politically conscious and organised elements in the country—those in fact," he added a little tartly, "who are in a position to give trouble or not to give it depending on our present decision."

It was true, also, that for the past three years the Thakins, Aung San among them, had openly and unashamedly joined hands with the Japanese. But this had to be viewed in the context of 1942. In that year the British had been chased out of Burma. Their pursuers, by extraordinary military successes elsewhere in Southeast Asia as well as in Burma, had shown that they could remain as long as they chose. Even as they fled, the British had refused to tell the Burmese when they might expect their freedom. Was it surprising, then, that many Burmese, left at the mercy of the Japanese, should have agreed to collaborate in return for independence? Indeed, continued Mountbatten almost as if he had Farrer Park and the Indian prisoners of war in mind, "this must at the time have seemed the only step they could reasonably take."

Nevertheless the Burmese now recognized that they had made a mistake. The events of March 27 gave clear evidence of this. And though it might be said that they were rising "for their own ends, and not for love of us, I think it would be unrealistic on our part to suppose that the people of any nation engage in war except in their own interests." The world was watching. "In America particularly, they will want to see how the British handle the native population in the first British territory to be liberated from enemy occupation." If the British refused to let the Burmese take part in their own freedom struggle, there would be repercussions in the United States, and in England too. There would be a storm. Was he to follow a policy "which might lead us into a position where we were obliged to suppress this movement by force?" Suppression could take time, tie down tens of battalions, and put at risk the prompt recovery of Malaya and an early end to the Pacific war. So it would be much better to welcome Aung San and his fellows as allies. When in due course they became national heroes, "as all those who fight the Japanese occupying forces are bound to become," at least they would be seen to have been national heroes *with* us—not against us.

Thus Mountbatten's reasoning.[9] To anyone conscious of what he would do later as India's last viceroy, it appears shrewd, large-minded, and uncannily anticipatory. At the time, however, it was met with a reserve bordering on open hostility. Most Civil Affairs Section officers believed implicitly that the Burma National Army had by the sheer act of putting on Japanese uniforms declared itself a traitor force. Besides, hadn't Aung San its leader committed an additional, specific, criminal offense? In 1942, during the British flight, had he not had a village headman killed for persistently urging his villagers to remain loyal to the Raj? Had he not bayoneted the fellow to death himself?

There was substance to this allegation. Aung San admitted the death, but not for the reason advanced. The headman, he eventually explained, had been terrorizing his villagers over matters that had nothing to do with loyalty to the Raj. As law and order had broken down with the departure of the British, and as he, Aung San, had happened to pass through the village, he had felt obliged to try, sentence, and execute the fellow. But neither at the time nor later did Civil Affairs Section accept Aung San's story. It wanted the criminal charge pursued, and moved to see that it was. The consequence was that early in May, just as Aung San was preparing to meet Slim, Leese's headquarters were formally advised that Aung San's record "demands he be treated as a war criminal and placed under arrest pending trial." Leese hesitated. Alerted by wire, Mountbatten telegraphed a furious "on NO account will Aung San be placed under arrest,"[10]—and took steps to get rid of Pearce. But efforts to check or reverse Pearce's policy did not cease with his removal.

That they eventually failed was due partly to the Supreme Allied Commander's panache, royal connections, and unassailable political position as Churchill's choice for the post, partly to the support he received from officers in the field. On the 15th of May, Slim informed Leese that he and his two corps commanders were delighted by what these Burmese had accomplished, "cutting off stragglers, ambushing parties of Japanese, carrying out acts of sabotage, and above all giving the forward units and formations a great deal of valuable information." They were not driven, he was sure, by some suddenly rediscovered loyalty to the Raj let alone any affection for the British. "The young Burman of today," he believed, "regards us merely as a lesser evil than the Japanese. His real ambition is to be quit of all foreign rule," to which end he will use force if he sees the opportunity. Therefore it would be prudent to disband the BNA as soon as the war was over, replacing it with an army directly under British control. Meanwhile there was plenty for it to do. Rangoon had fallen, but tens of thousands of Japanese stranded between the Irrawaddy and the Sittang were trying to break out to Thailand. They must be hunted down and killed. It was just the sort of work at which Aung San and his men should excel. To help them he proposed to supply clothing and rations, arms and ammunition, and to meet Aung San's payroll at the Indian Army scale.[11]

And so the curious partnership prospered. Aung San, chasing Japanese west of the Irrawaddy, left that work, crossed the river at Allanmyo, and on May 16 flew to Meiktila. His arrival, Slim later wrote, "dressed in the near Japanese uniform of a Major-General, complete with sword," startled one or two staff officers who had not been forewarned. At first the visitor took rather a high line, demanding "the status of an Allied and not subordinate commander." His intelligence, however, his excellent English, his good humor, above all the frankness of his manner, quite captivated Slim. Aung San freely admitted that the uniform was his by choice. He had hoped that the Japanese would give real independence to Burma. When he found they would not, and were tightening their grip, he had decided to turn to the British. Then this exchange:

> *Slim:* "Go on, Aung San. You only come to us because you see we are winning!"
>
> *Aung San:* "It wouldn't be much good coming to you if you weren't."

Reconstructing this conversation a decade later, Slim introduced it into his personal account of the war with evident pleasure.[12]

What Aung San thought of the meeting we can only guess. On the 15th of June, in pouring rain, the Bogyoke once again marched his battalions through Rangoon, this time beneath the proper resistance flag: solid red with a white star in the upper left-hand corner—and no peacock. The marchers formed a part, a very small part, of Mountbatten's victory parade, though they received much more than a small portion of the applause. *Greater Asia* said nothing. It had printed its last issue on the 21st of April, under the headline "Stunning Blows Dealt to Enemy Off Okinawa," and had then shut down like everything else Japanese-sponsored in the city. But if it had reported the event, it would have told its readers that the British had a new name for the Burma National Army. They called it the Patriotic Burmese Forces.

Perhaps this allowed the British to imagine that there was little divergence between themselves and it. Patriotism is such a comfortable word. Rarely does a patriot give half the trouble a nationalist can. Besides, the sentiment could be that of any loyal subject of the King-Emperor. From the beginning Mountbatten had instructed his public relations people to represent the Burmese resistance as "an example of patriotic resistance within the British Empire," not resistance *to*.[13]

But there was no deflecting the independence movement now. Aung San's army was disbanded. As he declined, however, a commission in the force that took its place, he was free to take part in politics. An association of Burma National Army men who, like him, refused to put on the new uniform, gave him a private army to use at will against political opponents—and against the British too, should they prove difficult.

For a year it seemed they might. Civil administration returned, depriving Mountbatten of his direct authority, bringing Dorman-Smith back. Dorman-Smith kept Aung San at arm's length while he attempted a modified version of his let-us-rebuild-first scenario. Aung San, however, held all the cards. He was the hero of the hour. Practically all Burmese of consequence were attached to the Anti-Fascist People's Freedom League, which he led. From a distance Mountbatten pressed Dorman-Smith hard, persuading London not to let him arrest Aung San on the old murder charge, winning Attlee (by this time prime minister) to his general view. In August 1946 Dorman-Smith stepped down. Weeks later a police strike that escalated into a general stoppage confronted the new governor with the reality Mountbatten had attempted to anticipate. There were almost no British troops left in Burma. Indian troops were few, and New Delhi had served notice they were not to be used to suppress civil disorder. Burma's official army was unreliable. Aung San's private army was ready.

From that moment complete independence for Burma was never in doubt. Agreed to by Attlee when Aung San visited London early in 1947, it arrived the following January—in double strength, for Burma, unlike Britain's other colonial possessions, also left the Commonwealth. Thakin Nu conducted the final negotiations. Aung San was dead, assassinated along with half his cabinet by gunmen in the service of a disgruntled prewar political rival. But no one doubted then, or has doubted since, that independence was his doing more than it was any other man's. He remains what he was perceived to be, the father of his country.

It is otherwise with Subhas Chandra Bose.

In 1945 the monsoon came to lower Burma in late April, two weeks earlier than usual, and was soon heavy. Slim, flying down to Pegu on the 1st of May to see for himself how 4 Corps was doing, remembers downpours lasting hours. Even tracked vehicles were finding they had to keep to the main road, and the road itself, with many bridges blown and the approaches to their temporary replacements often washed away, was not easily navigated. "The troops slipped, splashed, and skidded forward," Slim writes,[14] covering the ground so slowly that when on the 6th Messervy's leading battalion was still two dozen miles short of Rangoon, it met elements of another corps coming up from the city. An amphibious assault arranged, at Slim's suggestion, in case 14th Army lost the race against the weather, had gone in at the mouth of the Rangoon River on May 2, and reached Rangoon the following day without fighting. The Japanese had evacuated the place more than a week before. Ba Maw went with them. So did Subhas Chandra.

He had been for some time out of touch with his units to the north. He made no effort now to take with him the four to five thousand INA men in and about Rangoon. Some were sick, many lacked arms or were rear-echelon types, and there was very little transport. Nor did he consider staying himself to make a last stand of the sort he had contemplated at Pyinmana two months earlier. Bose was a brave man. There are enough stories of his coolness in the face of danger—erect and motionless on the reviewing platform during a Mingaladon parade one October afternoon, for example, though British planes are overhead and an ack-ack splinter has killed a soldier just yards away—to silence doubters. But the war was not over. In Malaya and elsewhere it would go on. Who could tell what turn it might take? Besides, even if it led to the utter defeat of the country with which circumstances had obliged the freedom movement to ally itself, that movement would survive and triumph only if—that this was

Bose's train of thought is speculation but nothing else suggests itself—only if the army and he proved to be constant and true. That meant continuing to fight on Japan's side.[15]

There could be no question of attempting an Aung San maneuver. It would never have worked. One has only to imagine Subhas Chandra flying to Meiktila for a private chat with Slim to see that, similarities notwithstanding, the Indian National Army and the Burma National Army were worlds apart in British eyes.

So Bose picked up and left. With him went senior officers of the *Azad Hind Fauj*, among them Bhonsle, Chatterji, and Zaman Kiani—all major generals now, for there had been a rash of promotions, these three plus Shah Nawaz and Loganadhan to major general (the INA did not know the brigadier), Prem and Dhillon to full colonel, others to other ranks. With him went several hundred men of Subhas Brigade's 1st Battalion, back from distant Arakan in relatively good health and spirits, whom he was reluctant to lose. With him, finally, went those civilian members of the *Arzi Hukumat* (Thivy was one) who belonged to Malaya, and the hundred or so Rani of Jhansi women who came from there too. The Burma-born Ranis he thanked and sent home.

The men of Subhas Brigade moved off at once on foot. Half the Ranis got away by train. For Janaki Davar and the other half the Japanese, much occupied with their own departure, arranged nothing—until Bose made it plain he would not leave until arrangements were made. Reluctantly they rounded up a few staff cars and trucks. On April 24 Bose toured the camps, said goodbye to the men who were staying behind, gave final instructions to Loganadhan (left in charge with Arshad and Mahboob Ahmed to assist him), and at dusk led a little convoy up the Pegu road. "It was a moonlit night," Ayer remembers. "The Japanese had started evacuation the previous day. They were vacating bungalows and burning papers all over the city."[16] No doubt there had been a good deal of smoke along Jamal Avenue too, though Ayer does not say so, for it was now that the records accumulated during the freedom movement's stay in Burma were torched or otherwise destroyed.[17]

The Pegu road was crowded with men and vehicles struggling to get around the top of the Gulf of Martaban before 14th Army took Pegu and cut the route. At the Waw–Sittang canal, and again at the

Sittang River itself, there was a terrible crush at the ferries (the bridges were out) and much confusion, made worse by the darkness: the crossings had to be made at night. Fortunately the Japanese, Ayer says, gave Netaji's people priority, perhaps because they were accompanied by Lieutenant General Isoda Saburo, who commanded the *Hikari Kikan*, and by Ambassador Hachiya, the improperly credentialed envoy from Japan, who just six weeks after reaching Rangoon was desperately trying to leave. They gained the far bank of the Sittang and comparative safety with only one casualty, Chatterji's aide-de-camp mortally wounded in a strafing run. But scarcely a vehicle got across.

"From now on we march on foot," Janaki wrote in her diary.[18] "Going is very heavy, we are night birds, we do all our marching at night and rest during the day. My girls are wonderful, each one of them is carrying her own pack," and a rifle as well, for there were "plenty of enemy guerilla troops in the area [Janaki probably meant Aung San's men], and we must be prepared to fight." Bose, too, carried his own pack. (Ba Maw, traveling the same road at the same time, by his own account never walked a step.) After several days he began to limp. So one morning Janaki got him to take off his top boots, and was shocked to discover that his feet were "a mass of blisters." Appealed to, Isoda produced trucks. Ayer, whose feet were blistered too, gratefully climbed into one. Chatterji did the same. Bose refused. Janaki heard him say, with some anger, that if he left his people and motored ahead, they were sure to be shouldered aside at the ferries. Janaki could see that Isoda was disappointed. "Poor devils, they hate walking. But they have to when Netaji is."

Eighty miles and six days after leaving the Sittang they crossed the wide mouth of the Salween and reached Moulmein, western terminus of the Death Railway, which in spite of persistent Allied air attacks still ran. Ba Maw and his little party had already come to rest in the little town of Mudon close by. There, under the peacock flag, they waited quietly for the British to arrive. Some passed the hours constructing out of wood a little monument to two years of Burmese independence. U Nu improved his mind. "I spent my whole time reading books that I borrowed from the Moulmein Library."[19] Bose, however, was all impatience. The rail line to Bangkok was at hand. As soon as he could he sent Janaki and her women on.

"We are allotted a few goods wagons and are packed in like sardines," she wrote. "Anyhow, it is better than marching in mud. Our train left Moulmein late at night." At one in the morning it came to a dead halt. A bridge was down, hit by American bombers. "They are a terrible nuisance. It is with the sheer weight of metal that they are winning this war." The women detrained, put their packs in bullock carts ("it is such a relief, my shoulders are aching"), and set off on foot into the blackness. Next morning, as they prepared to settle into hiding near a station, they saw the Japanese break up a train that had just arrived and scatter the cars along the track so that they would appear to be damaged. A bamboo shelter took the engine. At dusk the cars were reassembled, they climbed aboard, and the train went on.

In this way Bose, his senior officers, the several hundred men from Subhas Brigade, and Janaki Davar with five score Rani of Jhansi women reached Bangkok, not all together but within a few days of each other, the last party safely in by the middle of May. There they were joined by five or six hundred men of "X" Regiment, whom Thakur Singh had led east from Pyinmana into the Shan Highlands, south down the Salween, and so to Moulmein and the railroad. But that was all. In the course of the past year and a half some sixteen thousand men had entered Burma under the tricolor flag. Sixteen thousand men and a hundred women. Less than a tenth of that number got out.

When and how the rest—those who were not already dead or prisoners—passed into British hands, or simply disappeared, it is not easy to determine. The 1st Infantry Regiment, which had left Rangoon not long before Prem began withdrawing from Mount Popa, was in or about Magwe, sixty miles north of Allanmyo, when on the afternoon of April 19 tanks and Bren gun carriers burst into the town. "No organized opposition could be put up," Shah Nawaz wrote in his diary.[20] Headquarters and one battalion surrendered instantly. The other two were rounded up within days. As for the 1st *Division*—Subhas, Gandhi, and Azad Regiments, less of course Thakur Singh's "X"—it had quit Pyinmana for the Zeyawadi sugar estate in March. It was at Zeyawadi, together with an INA hospital holding several hundred patients and over a thousand convalescents, when Messervy's 4 Corps overran the place (no resistance was offered) on April 23. But of lesser units, perhaps because British intelligence thought it unnecessary to identify them, there is little or nothing to say.

One of the freedom army's two motor transport companies surrendered near Meiktila. What became of the other? What was the fate of the INA gunners (five companies had been formed) who manned Japanese antiaircraft guns at Moulmein and elsewhere? Among the six men who eventually testified that the deserters whom Prem, Dhillon, and Shah Nawaz were accused of murdering had indeed been shot, was a certain Allah Ditta. In March, there in the shadow of Mount Popa, Ditta had been placed under arrest on suspicion of planning to desert himself. Early in April, with everything falling apart, he and sixteen other delinquents had been ordered south to Rangoon under guard. They walked, of course. And of course they never made it. "We reached Magwe. On April 19 the British attacked and the sentries guarding us ran away."[21] So Ditta turned himself in. No doubt the others did the same. But what happened to the sentries?

Perhaps they, too, found someone to surrender to, though if they were recruited in Malaya and so did not come from India as Ditta did, they would have lacked Ditta's motive. Perhaps they got away and were picked up later. Perhaps they shed their uniforms and melted into a local Indian community somewhere in Burma. Perhaps they managed to escape the country altogether, perhaps they even reached home and family a thousand miles to the south. There were hundreds like these, scattered on both sides of the Irrawaddy by the defeat and disintegration of the *Azad Hind Fauj*. Some of them surface anonymously in the British Weekly Intelligence Summaries, six INA men taken here, a dozen there, on such and such dates. And some are simply missing, gone without a trace.

Shah Nawaz and Dhillon were not among these. When the British burst into Magwe, they and the couple of hundred men with them had just reached that place, and they did *not* surrender. They slipped out of the town, crossed the river, and worked their way down the right bank, heading for Rangoon. Near Prome they changed their minds. "Learned all our parties are making for Moulmein," Shah Nawaz noted. "Japs say Toungoo is still in their hands [it wasn't] and that route to Thailand is still open." Returning to the Irrawaddy's left bank, they pushed east by south into the Pegu Yoma, moving as usual by night. Progress was slow.

"May 4. Spent the day in a small hut. Rained all day. The Japanese have left us completely in the lurch, they are running themselves and are not bothering about us." Morale sank, and with it discipline. On the 7th one of Dhillon's men took a shot at him, "but luckily missed. He was put away." Repeatedly alarms of one sort or another obliged them to alter direction or double back. On the 13th, despairing of ever reaching the Sittang, Shah Nawaz gave any who wished, permission to turn themselves in. The majority did. He and Dhillon pressed on with those who did not.

"May 14. There are also many Japanese who are trapped in this forest. All the inhabitants are very pro-British. Our strength now is only 49." Two nights later they were surprised and fired upon at very close range, saw their Burmese guide fall, and went to ground in the bush. Knowing they would be hunted hard when morning came, they were up and out at first light "but found all routes blocked." At six that evening they surrendered to a patrol from the 2/1st Punjab, 5th Indian Division, the same division that had thundered south past Slim and John Masters as they stood beside the road at Pyawbwe five weeks before. It was the 17th of May. The place where they were taken was a few miles west of Pegu.

ᴥᴥᴥ

Bose remained in Bangkok for nearly a month, making sure Thakur Singh's men were properly billeted and fed, sending deputies to shake down the local Indian businessmen (as always, money had to be raised), mulling over what Germany's surrender meant. News of the surrender met him when he reached the city. It surprised him, he confessed to his radio listeners. Now Nippon fought alone. But let no one despair. "You know very well that I have been always of the opinion that if Germany collapsed, it would be a signal for the outbreak of an acute conflict between the Soviets and the Anglo-Americans."

That conflict was at hand. Beneath the facade of Allied unity the struggle had already begun. It could not be otherwise, for Russia, as the world's leading socialist power, was the natural enemy of imperialism. (This was naive of Netaji, but Roosevelt too tended to absolve Stalin of imperialist ambitions.) Now that Hitler was dead and the Soviet Union's territorial integrity restored, she *must* break with the imperialist powers, and she would. But this gave the freedom movement a particular opportunity. "The fundamental principle of our foreign policy," Bose reminded his listeners, "has been and will be: Britain's enemy is India's friend." In the months ahead he and his government would maneuver in such a way that Britain's newly revealed (and deadly) enemy *became*, indeed, India's friend.

This was how Subhas Chandra talked, perhaps in his treasured late evening conversaziones, certainly in his Bangkok radio broadcasts.[22] But it was only talk. He did not actually try to place himself, his army, and his provisional government, in alliance with the Soviet Union. He did not even scout the ground.[23] Saigon would have been a good place to start, Shanghai better, Tokyo better still. Bose was a great traveler, and flying to these places, though sometimes interrupted by American air action (which could close a key airfield for days), still possible. But he did not go north. Instead he went south, to Singapore. There he prepared to deal with the bad news from India; for in India, the shortwave told him, political activity was occurring of a sort that threatened everything his freedom struggle had so far achieved.

In May of the previous year the Government of India, afraid that Gandhi might die on their hands—he was anemic, suffered from hookworm and amoebic dysentery, and had periodic bouts of very high blood pressure—had at last released the old man from his place of detention in the Aga Khan's palace at Poona. His health somewhat improved, his freedom of action restored, his inclination to move things by a direct personal approach to the top stirring in him once more, the Mahatma had tried to see Wavell, who was no longer Commander-in-Chief but Viceroy in Linlithgow's place. Together they might break the numbing constitutional deadlock. But Wavell would not see him. And though Jinnah had at least been willing to talk, Gandhi had discovered that with respect to the things that separated *them*, the leader of the Muslim League was not to be shifted either.

Nevertheless, Bose had been alarmed. And now the Mahatma was at it again. On the 14th of June, 1945, Wavell announced over All-India Radio the imminent convening at Simla of a conference to consider the formation of a new Viceroy's Executive Council, a council that should in some way (perhaps simply by existing) move India closer to "full self-government." Among the persons to be invited to this conference were Gandhi and Jinnah, of course—but also Azad, Nehru, Patel, and their Congress brothers. Orders had been given for the immediate release of Working Committee members still in detention. At Simla, Gandhi would have about him the entire High Command.

The news cannot have taken Subhas Chandra altogether by surprise. He knew that the Tory freeze on serious constitutional reform in India was over, the ice breaking up. On May 18, nine days after the formal end of the war in Europe, Churchill had suggested that his coalition government continue until Japan fell. Labour had refused. Piqued, Churchill had resigned, formed a caretaker government in which Attlee ceased to be Deputy Prime Minister, and called a general election for July, the first in ten years. But whether he won or lost, things could not remain as before in Britain's distant jewel in the crown. The fact that the caretaker government had authorized Wavell to free the Congress leadership and call the Simla conference, made this perfectly plain.

Bose knew, then, that there was movement once more on the constitutional front. He could not know that it was Wavell who had pushed it, that the conference was the Viceroy's idea. Bose supposed Gandhi to be the prime mover. The thought filled him with anger and dismay. The very language troubled him. To move India toward "full self-government"—why would the Viceroy call a conference on such a matter unless he wished to make it crystal clear that attaining even *that* halfway station depended on prior agreement among all the Indians concerned? Always agreement first, always agreement before action, always the Britisher telling Indians "we cannot take steps, even small steps, towards departing this property, until you have settled its future disposition fairly, amicably, and completely among yourselves." Was not this the prescription for foot dragging and delay that Quit India, by rearranging the priorities to read "independence first, agreement *after*," had thought to clear from the shelf?

If the Congress party leadership attended the conference, it would soon discover what Wavell's real motives were. Indeed, Gandhi probably recognized them already—so ran Netaji's train of thought—and in some configuration of weakness, saintliness, and guile did not care. But why should *he*, who had raised an army, formed a Government of Free India to direct it, and led both in a bitter struggle against the Raj—why should he let this old man and the contemptible clique about him squander the freedom movement's moral gains in a cowardly accommodation to Lord Wavell's schemes. In the Viceroy's broadcast, he noticed, nothing had been said about releasing the hundreds of Congress workers still languishing in jail. On the 15th of June, when prison gates at selected places opened, only the Working Committee had gone free. Well, he would appeal over its head to the party rank and file. He would appeal beyond the party to India at large. The "compromise mongers" must be stopped dead. In radio address after radio address, still not attacking Gandhi by name, he pressed the message home.

And Sivaram, the publicity professional and occasional purveyor of hype, was horrified. Horrified by what seemed to him an utter lack of taste and balance. Netaji's courage, sense of purpose, and determination to remain true to the Japanese he acknowledged. "But I just could not understand the thinking behind the challenge he was flinging daily at the leaders of Indian nationalism."[24] If only Subhas, instead of discharging his anguish nightly on the air waves, would accept that his gamble—for it was a gamble—had failed. But Subhas, apparently, could not. After a time Sivaram withdrew to Phuket Island, on the west side of the Isthmus of Kra, and waited quietly for the British to arrive.

One has the feeling that during June and July, senior lieutenants of the Supreme Commander on both the civil and military side were behaving just as Sivaram behaved: withdrawing, waiting, preparing themselves for what must come. Not too uncomfortable about it either, indeed quite comfortable in one sense of that word, for life in Bangkok, Singapore, or Kuala Lumpur could still be rather pleasant. Sivaram is probably right when he says that Indians in Malaya no longer believed the British could be thrown out of India by force, and so welcomed the Wavell proposal. He is probably right, too, when he says that in the INA's 3rd Division, most of whose junior officers and nearly all of whose men were local volunteers, there was very little readiness to resist the inevitable British landing on Malaya's beaches. But Bose could be neither accepting nor idle. He called for the second annual celebration of Netaji Week, and presided over the usual complement of sports events, concerts, and parades. On the waterfront edge of the padang, only a hundred yards from where massed ranks had once risen and acclaimed him with *a forest of rifles*, he laid the cornerstone of a memorial to the *Azad Hind Fauj*. He toured training schools and camps. He was at Seremban, 150 miles northwest of Singapore, visiting one of these camps, when on the evening of August 10, four days after the atom bomb dropped on Hiroshima, Inayat Kiani phoned to say that Russia had entered the Pacific war.

⚜

The news, followed thirty-six hours later by the rumor that Japan wished to surrender, and five days later by the announcement that she had, called out the best in Netaji. No use worrying now about what was going on in India. There were things to be taken care of, and decisions to be made, right where he was. Ayer says that he was all energy and good cheer, "cracking jokes" with his staff, up to all hours, busy all the time. Should the Provisional Government declare war on Russia because Russia had declared war on Japan? No, the rest of the world might wonder if "the next things these fellows will do is declare war on Mars." What instructions should be sent to League branches, what orders issued to the 3rd Division, one of whose regiments Netaji now addressed at Seremban itself. There were the several hundred Rani of Jhansi women at the Bras Basah Road camp to be sent home to their families. There were the forty-five cadets in Japan to be recovered somehow.[25]

On the 12th Bose drove down to Singapore, in armed convoy because the INA's active partnership with the Japanese had increasingly exposed it to attacks by Chinese guerrillas. There he continued to dictate instructions and confer with staff. On the 14th he had a tooth pulled, and in the evening watched the Rani of Jhansi Regiment stage a three-act play about the Rani herself. Several thousand officers and men sat spellbound through the performance, Ayer says, then rose and sang the *Subh Sukh Chain*—which Netaji would never hear again. Ayer might have added that if the Rani spoke her last lines correctly, the men and women of the audience listened to an exhortation that could have been uttered by Netaji himself. "Don't rest," the actress pleaded as she prepared to die. "Don't rest till you have made India independent. This is my last order to you all."[26]

Up to this point whether the Supreme Commander should try to get away or not had been matter for discussion only, some arguing one way and some the other. By the 15th, however, when Japan's formal surrender was announced, and no one could say how much longer Japanese aircraft would be able to fly, a decision could be put off no longer. So that evening Ayer and others sat down with Netaji on the verandah of his seaside bungalow to examine the question. And it was not long, Ayer says, before Netaji was persuaded he must leave.

What persuaded him Ayer does not say. As so often over the years in Malaya and Burma, not a piece of paper survives to throw light on the question, no diary entry—did Subhas Chandra even *keep* a diary?- no scribbled notes from that evening on the verandah, no letters in which he or others explain how he arrived at the decision to quit Singapore, and why. Perhaps he kept his own counsel. He frequently did. But it is reasonable to assume that he brought to the decision two familiar aspects of his character.

One was a determination to remain faithful as long as possible to any course of action once embraced. The other was a resolve never to humble himself before the British. Of the two, the second was perhaps the more deeply ingrained. Bose must have known that his ministers and officers would surrender if they had to. They would let themselves be caged—they wouldn't like it but they would allow it. *He* could not. He was Chief of State (it was no pose). The chief of state of a sovereign power must be treated in a certain way.

It was a lesson he had set out to administer to the Japanese, and on the whole he had succeeded. But if the British found him when they landed, would *they* treat him as a chief of state, even in defeat, should be treated? They would not. They would treat him very differently. The prospect must have appalled him. To be captured by some pup of a Britisher with pips on his shoulders and a swagger stick in his hand, to be abused, penned, charged, tried—no doubt he saw it all. And it was more than painful to think about, it was unbearable.

So the decision was made. Early on the 16th Bose met his senior people for the last time, asked Zaman Kiani to take charge in Singapore, tapped Ayer, Abid Hassan, Habib-ur-Rahman, and two others to go with him, and in mid-morning flew off to Bangkok. At Bangkok, where a startled Bhonsle arranged a place to stay, numbers of

INA officers, League officials, and Indian merchants caught wind of his presence and hurried to see him, so that he sat up half the night holding court—and in the morning flew on to Saigon, this time accompanied by General Isoda and Ambassador Hachiya. But at Saigon he hit a snag.

He was not running away. He moved with an assurance and vigor that suggested the midnight departure from Calcutta four and a half years before. That, too, had looked like flight, though in fact Bose had simply decided that he would have to pursue his enterprise in a different part of the world, and in a radically different way. He had had a purpose then. He had a purpose now. It was to make contact with the Russians pushing down through Manchuria, not to position his army and his government with them—there was nothing left of either—but to position himself. A long, varied, successful public career had taught him that he possessed the power to command the attention of public men. Knowing what he knew about the estrangement of Great Britain from the Soviet Union, he was confident, I think, that he could persuade the Russians to give him a place from which he might resume, in due course, the struggle against the Raj. But first he had to reach them. For that he needed Japanese approval or at least Japanese consent—and, of course, an aircraft. At Saigon on Friday the 17th it looked for a moment as if he might obtain neither.

For when he landed he discovered that there was no plane, nothing to carry him and his party up the China coast. Simply getting beyond Saigon was going to be difficult. It was mid-morning. What happened next is unclear. Ayer believes that Netaji asked Isoda and Hachiya to fly at once to Terauchi's Southern Army Headquarters at Dalat, the French summer capital an hour away, and plead for transport. Some have it that they actually *saw* Terauchi, who wired Tokyo for instructions and was told to fend the Indian off. The difficulty here is that Bose almost certainly reached Saigon on that Friday morning, and certainly left that afternoon, which does not give much time for consulting Tokyo or even Dalat. Probably Isoda did not fly to Dalat at all. He was committed to helping Bose. He almost certainly knew where Bose wanted to go because Bose had told his long-time Japanese translator that he *had* to reach the Russians, and it is unlikely the translator kept it to himself. Probably Isoda set about arranging what he could right in Saigon.

Meanwhile, Bose let himself be driven into the city. The streets were deserted. Many houses had their windows shuttered. Wild rumors circulated about what the French, when they returned, would do to Indians who had allied themselves with the Japanese. At the home of a League member Bose shaved, bathed, and went to sleep. In less than an hour, however, he was awakened with word that a plane was warming up at the airfield. It had a place for him. Would he come, at once.

He wouldn't. Instead he asked questions. Where was this plane going? Why was there no room for his staff? Isoda and several other Japanese appeared, and Bose and they withdrew into a private room. It is possible that Isoda produced, at this point, a complete scenario: a plane bound for the Manchurian port city of Dairen bears an army officer named Shidei whose task will be to negotiate the surrender of Japan's Kwantung Army, and who will therefore be in a position to introduce Subhas Chandra to high-ranking Russians. It is possible that Isoda had put together such a script. But when Bose emerged from the conference he did not behave, in Ayer's recollection, like someone for whom everything is settled and clear. He behaved like someone clutching at straws. Shidei, it turned out later, was indeed bound for Dairen on the assignment just mentioned, but it is unlikely Isoda knew it. What Isoda *did* know was that he had found one seat, northbound, for his Indian. Probably Bose recognized that at this moment of great tension and confusion for the Japanese—they were as anxious to get away from Saigon as he was—to be offered a seat on a plane bound in the right direction was all he could expect. Very well, he would ask for *two* seats. He asked. The harried Isoda agreed. There was a rush for the airport.

There, while the exasperated Japanese held the plane until certain pieces of baggage could arrive, Subhas was introduced to Shidei, and perhaps discovered that he was traveling with the person best placed to put him in touch with the Russians. At last the baggage came. There were quick handshakes, warm *Jai Hinds*. Habib-ur-Rahman, named to occupy the second seat (though one might have expected Subhas to choose his old submarine companion Abid Hasan), followed his chief into the plane, a twin-engine bomber of the type known as a Sally. The cabin door closed. Ayer hurried to stand so that he could catch a last glimpse of his leader. He did not spot him. The plane moved off. The five Indians who were left behind drove away "thoroughly depressed," Ayer writes, "and on the verge of tears."[27] They did not, however, despair of seeing their Netaji again, for they had hopes of following in a day or two. This had been Bose's hope too. But even the next day would have been too late.

As it was then nearly evening, the pilot decided to land at Tourane (now Da Nang), spend the night, and attempt the over water flight to Formosa next day. Leonard Gordon, whose account I largely follow, says that at Tourane the crew lightened the plane by removing the machine guns and some of the baggage. At five the next morning, Saturday the 18th of August, the plane with its crew of four, its six Japanese passengers, and the two Indians, took off again, climbed to twelve thousand feet, and headed for Taipei, nearly a thousand miles away. The flight, which lasted six to seven hours, was uneventful. At Taipei, while the crew refueled and checked the engines (the port one ran a little rough), the passengers ate lunch in a tent. They boarded again about two-thirty in the afternoon.

Bomber or no, the twelve men plus the remaining baggage and a full load of fuel were almost more than the Sally, which was old and tired, could manage. Nearly out of runway when at last it lifted into the air, it climbed steeply, both engines laboring, and at less than a hundred feet lost the port propeller, which tore loose with a noise like a backfire. A wing dropped. The plane dove, struck the ground, and broke in two. Shidei, pilot, and copilot died instantly. Habib-ur-Rahman was knocked unconscious, but came to and tried to lead Bose out the back. Baggage blocked their way so they turned and made for the front, which by now was on fire. Habib reached the ground safely. Gasoline, however, had soaked Bose's uniform, the uniform caught, and by the time he struggled free he was a living torch. Habib tried to beat the flames out with his hands. Bose seemed unable to help himself. Habib noticed that his face was battered and cut.

Men came in trucks and carried the survivors to an army hospital. There Japanese doctors did what they could for Subhas Chandra, who was obviously the most seriously injured. He had third-degree burns over most of his body. They knew, and he knew, that he could not live.

For several hours he was conscious and quite clear in the head, though in terrible pain. Then he sank into a coma. Habib, who was lying in the same room with burns on hands and arms, told Ayer later that Netaji spoke to him before he died. "Habib," Ayer's rendering goes,[28] "I have fought all my life for my country's freedom. I am dying for my country's freedom. Go and tell my countrymen to continue the fight," for though freedom has not triumphed, its time is near. The Japanese doctor who dressed his burns and was with him to the end remembers no such deathbed statement. It is possible that Bose spoke to Habib while they lay together by the burning Sally, waiting for help. It is possible Bose never spoke at all. But we can agree with Leonard Gordon that these were the words he would have wished to say, and would have prepared himself to say, had he known that by some miracle he would be granted, in his last extremity, command of his head and his voice.

He died between nine and ten that evening. It was still Saturday the 18th.

❧

In Singapore Cyril John Stracey, the Anglo-Indian who ran the Adjutant-General's branch at INA Headquarters, had been working hard to complete the memorial to the freedom army whose corner-stone Bose had laid on July 8. Stracey had designed it himself: a rectangular shaft perhaps eight feet across and some twenty-five feet high, bearing in large block letters the words *ittefaq*, *itmad*, and *kurbani*—unity, faith, sacrifice. He had hired a contractor and was supervising the work. Just when it was finished is not clear. What is certain is that when the unbelievable news of Netaji's death reached Singapore, a service was held at this memorial. A photograph shows it banked with flowers, Zaman Kiani and Stracey stiffly at attention in the foreground. Then on the 5th of September the first British troops landed. The memorial was instantly noticed. On the 8th sappers appeared, placed charges, and blew it to bits.

So the leader was dead. Anyone watching the dust of that explosion drift across the padang must have believed that the army was dead too. But there were people who were determined that this should not be the end of the matter. Among them was Lakshmi.

CHAPTER 17

LET INDIA LEARN

To go back a little.

When Bose returned to Rangoon after his trip north in September 1944, the trip he made to find out what had happened at Imphal, the Rani of Jhansi women at Maymyo were ordered to Rangoon too—and went, protesting bitterly. Lakshmi, however, did not accompany them. Netaji agreed that she and a few from the nursing wing should stay and devote themselves to Maymyo's INA hospital. As air raids were daily occurrences now, it was moved to an inconspicuous spot outside the town.

October and November passed. By December few patients were still arriving, and the hospital began to discharge those it had. Early in January 1945 it closed. Lakshmi went down to Mandalay and joined a motor convoy heading south. The convoy moved only at night. There were frequent stops at bombed bridges. *When you came to one you had to get down, whoever you were, and help rebuild it—carry dirt on your head, or bricks or whatever, and throw it here, throw it there.* Zeyawadi with its sugar factory was the goal. *Lots of INA men had collected there, and part of my Rani of Jhansi Regiment.* And it, too, had a hospital.

We reached Zeyawadi on January 17, and on the 23rd we were attacked from the air. It was Netaji's birthday. A plane came in low and dropped a bomb right through the boiler of the sugar factory. There was a big explosion. As soon as we could, we rushed in. It was terrible. The poor wretched men working in the boiler room had had molasses, burning hot molasses, thrown all over them; the molasses stuck; and though we did our best to clean them up, it was impossible. For more than half, all we could do was give very large doses of morphia and let them die in peace.

Lakshmi learned that a new hospital was to be opened at Kalaw, in the hills east of Meiktila. So she volunteered, though it meant retracing her steps, and reached Kalaw at the end of January. There she found several well-educated Burmese who had made the place their refuge early in the war. One, a barrister, invited her to stay with him and his family, and as the hospital buildings (huts really) were only just beginning to go up, she did. It was very pleasant. The fighting seemed far away. But on the 22nd of February Netaji appeared. He had come north to put Shah Nawaz in command of the 2nd Division, only to discover, as we have seen, that if he tried to reach Mount Popa from Meiktila he risked being cut off. So he had contented himself with Kalaw.

During his two days there he and Lakshmi talked a good deal. About the fighting—it was only a matter of time, he said, before the British reoccupied Burma. About the future of the INA. *Netaji wanted India to know that a freedom army had been raised. He wanted India to know what it had accomplished, he wanted somehow to convey this message—it preoccupied him.* Then he returned to Meiktila. But just before he went, he asked Lakshmi whether she wouldn't like to go down to Rangoon with him. No, she said, she would rather stay where she was and be useful. So Bose left without her. She never saw him again.

The day after his departure they heard the thud, thud, thud of bombs off to the west. Presently Yellappa, who had looked in once to inspect the hospital construction, appeared with word that the British were very close to Meiktila. Netaji had barely managed to escape, he said. They must think of leaving too. But this was easier said than done. The first batch of patients had only just arrived, many were stretcher cases and mustn't be moved, they couldn't simply be abandoned. Then there was the question of transport and route. They couldn't hope to get out through Meiktila, not now. They would have to go east through Taunggyi, then south through the Shan Hills, using bullock carts (trucks were sure to be unobtainable). Probably they should look into hiring some.

Then on the 2nd of March Kalaw was bombed. I was with my Burmese hosts, high up overlooking the bazaar, and they didn't have an air raid shelter, so when the air raid siren sounded we just went out and watched.

We saw two planes fly low and drop their bombs. It was over in a couple of minutes. But we saw smoke rising from the bazaar. Mr. Yellappa was staying there, and I had a premonition. I rushed down. It was as I feared. Out of bravado or something he hadn't taken shelter, and a bomb fragment had got him in the leg.

The wound did not appear particularly serious. It was only later that she realized the bone had been shattered. Serious or not, if Kalaw was going to be attacked like this it was time to get out, hospital and all. Lakshmi and another officer went to Taunggyi, forty miles away, to see about transport. When they returned they found Yellappa doing poorly. The leg was inflamed, movement of any sort gave him agonizing pain, and it seemed unlikely he could survive being bumped and jolted all the way to Rangoon. So it was agreed that while the other patients went off in bullock carts, Yellappa should stay. Lakshmi and a few nursing orderlies would stay with him. They would move out of Kalaw itself, but that was all.

For several weeks she, her patient, and her little party took shelter at Yawnghwe, halfway to Taunggyi and close to lovely Inle Lake, where one of the Shan chiefs gave them a house. But even Yawnghwe wasn't safe. At the end of March British fighters strafed the place, *and somehow the people got it into their heads it was because of us—all those years they'd never been attacked.* So they moved four miles, to an isolated village. There, too, the locals obviously believed their presence meant danger, and kept their distance. But where else could Lakshmi and her party go? Besides, Yellappa wasn't getting any better. His leg had turned septic.

On the 6th of April a medical officer named Bawa appeared with a truck and medical supplies. Informed somehow of Yellappa's plight, he had come up by way of Mawchi to bring the party out. They waited several days to let the dressings and splints he had brought relieve Yellappa a little, then started off. At Taunggyi, which was full of Japanese troops hurrying south, they joined a truck convoy. Movement was safer that way, gasoline easier to get. But two nights later, when they were not far from Mawchi, word came that the British were about to seize Toungoo. Everyone knew that the only practicable route south for wheeled vehicles ran through that place. So the Japanese went no farther. They ditched their trucks and set off on foot for the Salween. Bawa and his party could come along if they wished. But this would have meant carrying Yellappa across miles of hill and jungle. Bawa declined.

They decided to stay in Mawchi, where the tungsten and tin mines are, in a beautiful bungalow that had been a mine engineer's.

We stayed in it for a few days. There were eight of us. Then two of our boys went reconnoitering and found a Gurkha village several miles away, off the main road. They asked the villagers if they would be willing to give us shelter, and the villagers said they would. So we went there, carrying Mr. Yellappa on a bamboo stretcher. They were very interesting, these Gurkhas. Their fathers had come to Burma to fight for the British, and been given land, but they did not intermarry with the Burmese. For wives the men somehow went back to Nepal.

By now the monsoon had begun. Mr. Yellappa was in a shocking state. What with the septicemia in his leg and repeated drenching from the rain, he was running a high fever and was often out of his mind. Major Bawa said it was not right for us to just sit where we were. The only hope of saving him was to go where he would get proper medical attention. We had heard that higher up in these Karen Hills there was a force of guerrillas with British officers. "I'm going to try to find these Britishers and surrender to them," Major Bawa said. He went off on the 1st of May.

Days went by. They noticed that the village was thinning out, this family leaving, that family leaving, and at last they asked why. A villager explained. There were lots of Japanese about, he said, stragglers trying to make their way east, and they were raiding the villages for food. They were armed, of course. The villagers were afraid of them. That was why they were leaving. But because of Yellappa, Lakshmi and her party couldn't.

We took it in turns to look after him. He was often delirious, and in his delirium was always planning new ways of raising money for Netaji. We were very low on food—we ate just one meal a day, a kind of congee or gruel made of maize flour or rice. Two of our party went away to surrender. Then one morning I woke up with a bayonet in my face.

Three Japanese were in the hut. They made signs to us to get out. One of our boys knew a little Japanese, and he tried to explain who we were, but these Japanese had never heard of the Indian National Army, or "Netaji

Bose" either. They let the boy stay in the hut with Mr. Yellappa. And they let me put on my uniform—I slept in just a longyi and shirt, you see. I put on my uniform, and my cap, as smartly as I could. Then I went out, and they tied me to a tree like the others.

All the time my mind was a blank. I wasn't particularly afraid. I could see they thought we were British spies, but I knew they couldn't do anything at once—they had to have an officer. At last a man who looked like one came walking along, whistling. He had a magazine in his hand. He came up and looked at me. Then he looked at something in the magazine. Then he looked at me, and again at something in the magazine. Suddenly he held the magazine up.

You remember I told you that all these Japanese journalists and photographers had come around to my Rani of Jhansi camp in Singapore when we were training. What this officer had in his hand was a magazine article with a picture of me. The officer knew a little English. "Is you?" he asked. I said it was. So he had the ropes cut, and I made the boy who spoke Japanese explain who we were—and they told us who they were. They had come down from the north, from facing the Chinese up along the old Burma Road, and they didn't know at all what the situation was here in the south. "But," the officer said, "don't stay in this village. It's too dangerous. There are lots of stragglers like us wandering in the area, and you may not be so lucky next time."

They didn't know where to go. But Lakshmi remembered that she had heard there was another Gurkha village higher up. So they gave poor Yellappa their last shot of morphine, strapped him to his stretcher, and walked for six hours, to this other village. There the villagers weren't at all happy to see them, and said they would have to find their own basha. They found one, and were beginning to make it habitable, when suddenly four armed men appeared: three Karens and a Gurkha. They were part of Force 136, the British guerrilla unit. "Come with us," they said, and relieved her of her pistol.

I asked, "can we bring Yellappa Sahib?" They said, "no, the camp is at a great height and the path is so narrow and steep a stretcher can't be got up it. You will have to leave him here with this boy. Later we'll see if something can be arranged, some kind of sling or hammock or something." So very reluctantly we left Mr. Yellappa.

We walked for two days. The second day we were climbing most of the time. At the end of the day we came to the camp. Major Bawa was there. The camp was commanded by a Colonel Peacock. He had two or three other British officers with him, but most of the soldiers were Karens. They had been evacuated to India during the retreat, trained, then brought back and dropped by parachute.

Now for the first time we heard that Germany had surrendered.

Colonel Peacock, it appeared, knew all about the Indian National Army, and about her as well. Technically she and her party were prisoners, he said, but unless instructed otherwise he was not going to put them behind wire; they would eat and live like everybody else. He was very nice, very courteous. She asked him to send men for Yellappa, but he said he couldn't spare any—the camp was swamped with people who had left their villages because of the Japanese. Then one day some refugees came in whom she recognized. They were from the place where she had left Yellappa. Did they know what had happened to him and the boy? They did.

They said that several days after we left, some Karen scouts came to the village, which by this time was completely deserted, and saw smoke coming out of a hut. It was the hut where Mr. Yellappa and the boy were, and the boy was cooking dinner. The scouts thought there must be Japanese in the hut. So they threw hand grenades. The hut caught fire. The boy rushed out and tried to tell the scouts that there was a sick man inside. They wouldn't listen. Then the boy ran in again and tried to bring Mr. Yellappa out, but he didn't have time, the hut fell in on them, and they were both burned to death.

Lakshmi spent three weeks with Peacock. It would be interesting to know what he thought of this confident young woman who began at once to care for the refugees, Gurkhas mostly—some Karens too. By the middle of June they numbered hundreds. All supplies came by air, but because of the monsoon the little plateau was often shrouded in mist or cloud. *We would hear the wretched planes circle and circle and go away because they couldn't find the drop zone. Colonel Peacock got quite worried. He didn't know how he was going to feed all these people. At last he sent a signal to ask what to do, and they said "march them all out"—to Toungoo, nearly a hundred miles away.*

They set out on the 22nd of June, perhaps five hundred souls escorted by a platoon of Karens under a British captain, their route not the Mawchi–Toungoo road (there was fighting there, 4 Corps trying to force its way up against determined Japanese resistance), but jungle tracks that took them through deserted villages. You could tell the Karen ones by the little churches. In these villages they sometimes took shelter for the night. It rained and rained, so that their clothes were always damp and smelled of mud and sweat, a thing no one but Lakshmi seemed to mind. Scouts went ahead, looking for Japanese. These were avoided if it was possible, but sometimes it wasn't. Once the whole column hid in the bush for what seemed an eternity, hands ready to clap over children's mouths, while a Japanese party far larger than the captain and his Karens could possibly handle forded a stream they too must negotiate—moving, however, in the opposite direction. On the 1st of July they reached Toungoo.

There the British captain turned her over to 4 Corps. Evidently she was expected—Colonel Peacock must have flashed word of her capture soon after she reached his hilltop. Someone in Toungoo, she noticed, had lettered "Rani of Jhansi" on the hood of a jeep. Certainly intelligence knew who she was. They had been following "S. Lakshmi" (they used the south Indian name order) since October of 1943, when she became a minister in Netaji's government. And after almost two years of enemy broadcasts out of Rangoon, Singapore, and other points east, broadcasts that made much of her regiment of women, broadcasts some of which she had made herself, the Indian war correspondents with 14th Army (now redesignated, for reasons that need not detain us, 12th Army) knew who she was too. But even if she hadn't been a celebrity, 4 Corps would hardly have put her into a POW cage. Instead they gave her a little tent with a sentry.

We had arrived late in the evening. Next morning I was coming out of my tent when some British other ranks came up and said, "oh miss, do you speak English?" I said I did. Then they said they would like to talk to me.

They asked me to tell them something about the Indian National Army. And I did. Now just at this time there was this election going on in England, the ballot papers had been flown out, and one of these fellows

said, "you know, I'm voting for Labour. If that so-and-so Churchill comes
back in, I'll join the INA."

"That's very strange," I said. "If it weren't for Churchill where would
you be? He led you to victory, didn't he?"

"Yes, miss," said the man. "He led us to victory. He's all right in times
of war. But," he went on, "we don't want him in times of peace."

Within a week Lakshmi was brought to Rangoon, which after
Herculean work on broken water mains, choked sewers, and uncol-
lected refuse, was livable once more. There she was put through a
normal interrogation, and that done was allowed to go to old Indian
friends in the city.

To the house of these friends, as August of 1945 advanced and word
spread of her presence, came all sorts of people.

There were the war correspondents I mention. A journalist named
Amritlal Seth spent a whole day with Lakshmi, and left bearing copious
notes, an account of the Rani of Jhansi Regiment she had scribbled on
the spot, and an implicit commitment to tell India all about her and her
women when he got back to Bombay. Officers of the victorious Indian
Army dropped by. Among them was K. S. Thimayya, an old family
friend. K. S had commanded a brigade (the first Indian to do so) in the
Arakan fighting. His older brother K. P. "Thimmy" Thimayya had
served with the 2/10th Baluch in Malaya. He had been captured there,
as Prem had (the reader may remember the little business of the forty
drums of stolen aviation fuel). He had joined the INA, moved to
Burma in command of the Reinforcement Group, and was in
Rangoon when the British recaptured the place. No doubt K. S. and
Lakshmi talked about him before K. S. went on to Singapore as
scheduled (this in early September), to help take the formal Japanese
surrender in that city. And there was Hugh Toye, the British intelligence
officer I have mentioned in connection with the Oaten affair and other
matters.

After a stint of several months with the Combined Services
Detailed Interrogation Centre (CSDIC) in Delhi, Major Toye (as he
then was) reached Rangoon in the middle of August. Like K. S.

Thimayya he was bound for Singapore, but for a different reason. Toye commanded a small intelligence detail. At Singapore he and his men were to interrogate INA men and their civilian associates. They were travelling by ship. At Rangoon they were obliged to wait for passage onward. During their stay they were billeted with the 2nd Forward Interrogation Unit. Not wishing to be idle, Toye did a number of interrogations for the 2nd, got to know its officers well, and discovered that it had recently interrogated Lakshmi. The consequence was that shortly before he sailed, Captain Rashid Yusuf Ali of this FIU arranged to have Major Toye meet her. Rashid took Toye around to her house and introduced him.

It was a curious thing to do, not in the line of duty for either of them. But then, neither were many of the visits Lakshmi was receiving—especially the visits by military men. It is true that by now the two atom bombs had had their effect. Hirohito had addressed his reluctant nation. The war was over. Moreover Lakshmi was a woman, an intelligent, captivating woman, and no longer in uniform (after the trek to Toungoo she cannot have had much of a uniform to stand up in). Nevertheless these visits constituted, by any reasonable standard, fraternization with the enemy—to be precise, fraternization with a turncoat. On the face of it, fraternizing was exactly what K. S. Thimayya, Rashid Yusuf Ali, Hugh Toye, and a dozen others were doing.

It was not as if Lakshmi had recanted. She hadn't, and everybody knew it. She was as committed to Subhas Chandra Bose (whose death had just been reported) as she had ever been. She was not abrasive about it, as some of her Burma-raised Rani of Jhansi women were. If reproached for having turned against the Raj, *they* were apt to shoot back that it was just what their interrogators ought to have done! Lakshmi did not flare up this way. But she was determined. She was determined, for one thing, to go right ahead with her marriage to Prem. She had made this plain to Rashid when, early in July, he told her it was true Prem was no longer in Burma. Rashid knew where Prem was because it was *he* who had conducted Prem's interrogation, early in May, shortly after the surrender north of Allanmyo. And Rashid talked to Lakshmi thus, because it was he who had interrogated *her*.

It is a pity these interrogation reports have not survived. Prem's, produced by this same 2nd Forward Interrogation Unit (it was then at Magwe), was the 2,885th in that series. Lakshmi's, two months later, was the 3,719th. Another FIU, the 3rd, through whose hands Shah Nawaz and Dhillon passed, also wrote reports. There must have been thousands of the things.

Of course the principal aim of forward interrogation is to supply the fighting forces with information of immediate operational use. So Japanese prisoners were interrogated too. But from the beginning the interrogation of INA prisoners had a second purpose. Your enemy you question, cage, and at war's end release. These Indians, however, were not enemies. They were something much worse. Even the Tamil laborers recruited in Malaya, for whom the only conceivable final disposition was a ticket home, were technically felons. What the Indian Army saw in the rest, the ex–Indian Army men, was a distorted mirror image of itself, men turned by some dreadful combination of circumstance, temptation, and duress into dupes, renegades, utterly faithless men. They could not simply be held until the war was over, then sent back to their families in India. Nor could they all, the many thousands of them, be quietly hanged or shot. A mix of reincorporation, rehabilitation, and punishment was required. To make this operative, some way had to be found of winnowing out the recoverable, then arranging the rest in groups ranked according to the severity of the proposed punishment. So a system was devised. In it, interrogation reports played an important part.

For the system began with a sorting. Much the largest part of the traitor army would, it was assumed, be found to consist of simple men who, overwhelmed by defeat and the abrupt withdrawal of their British officers, had lost their bearings and behaved like sheep. They were to be denominated "whites," sent back to their regimental depots, and readmitted into the ranks. Then there would be those who, while entitled to a measure of sympathy and understanding because of the pressure put upon them and the indoctrination they had undergone, nevertheless showed by their manner that they had bent to the one and listened to the other. These were "greys," bound for special "reconditioning" camps before being allowed, perhaps, to rejoin. Finally, there were those who exhibited by word, deed, or rank a fundamental disloyalty, compounded perhaps by criminal behavior. Let them be called "blacks." Blacks were *not* to be returned to their regiments. They were security risks, just as Japanese soldier prisoners were—but doubly so, since the war's end would not make them "safe" and therefore eligible for repatriation. For them there would remain the question of courts-martial and appropriate sentencing. Even while the war went on that process could begin.

So the system began with this sorting, which meant that recovered INA men had to be examined individually—exactly what forward interrogation was for. It was the Forward Interrogation Unit that determined whether a man was white, grey, or black. (If black, he was sent at once, if feasible, to CSDIC at Delhi, where he was questioned again with an eye to his probable trial.) If, then, these forward interrogation reports had survived, we would know a great deal about how and why thousands of men joined the INA. And the second round of interrogation, at Delhi, would have added to what we know. But they have not survived. Since battle intelligence has a very short useful life, there was nothing in the procedure to compel their preservation. Though all FIU reports were sent to CSDIC in Delhi, only those for blacks were of any interest, and then only as long as trial proceedings were still being considered. It was the same with the second round, the CSDIC interrogation reports. So everything was lost, with two exceptions.

I have said that it was Rashid Yusuf Ali who told Lakshmi about Prem's whereabouts, and who took Hugh Toye around to see her—and that these were not accidents: Rashid had interrogated Prem, and it was Rashid who interrogated Lakshmi two months later. Both interrogation reports, moreover, were reviewed (it was standard procedure) by the 2nd FIU's commanding officer, a Scots-Irishman by the name of W. P. G. Maclachlan. Major Maclachlan personally met both prisoners. As for Toye, he too knew a good deal about these two, and knew it long before Rashid took him around to see Lakshmi.[1] For Toye was still with CSDIC in Delhi when, towards the end of May, Prem was lodged in Delhi's Red Fort. (Of this, more in a moment.) Toye was given Prem's CSDIC report to edit (the actual interrogation was done by another), and this obliged him to go through Prem's file. In it he read what Rashid and Maclachlan had to say about Prem. He also met Prem. Perhaps he even wondered why this particular man had been snatched from the banks of the Irrawaddy and deposited in the Suspects and Escapees Wing so swiftly.

During the trial no one asked. No one remarked that while Dhillon and Shah Nawaz reached the Red Fort seven and eight weeks respectively after they surrendered, Prem was brought the twelve hundred miles in three. Surely it wasn't because Delhi wanted immediate operational intelligence. Prem had been out of touch with the other remnants of Bose's army for some time. Besides, who still took the INA seriously?

No doubt the Delhi people hoped to obtain information, which a former military secretary was in an excellent position to give, about Bose and his immediate entourage, how he stood with the Japanese, what he might be expected to do. But they must also have wanted Prem for himself, so to speak—because of who he was and what he had done. He was no stranger to them. The tales told by the five defecting staff officers in February had enabled intelligence to make a rough sketch of the person it had hitherto known only as a desk soldier. The diary seized in the March ambush had filled the sketch out. For over two months this sometime captain in the 10th Baluch Regiment had been, in the matter of renegade Indians, at the center of 14th Army's field of vision.

He commanded the INA's last substantial field force. He directed its raiding, led it in a brief but effective stand against an entire brigade, lost a third of it to desertion, extricated what was left, and held it together over a stubborn but hopeless retreat of some one hundred miles, before being cornered at last against the Irrawaddy. For more than two months 14th Army had had "the notorious commander of 2 Infantry Regiment," as they called him, in its sights.[2] Now it could send the man along. And it was more than happy to—because the man was troubling.

What was troubling about him is suggested, I think, by a little scene lodged in Prem's memory. The time is the evening of the 29th of April (next day he will sit under the tree and help the major with the crossword puzzle), and the place is a British brigade's field headquarters near Allanmyo. Prem is talking to the brigadier. Up comes Major General Douglas Gracey, commanding the 20th Indian Division, to which the brigade belongs. Prem is introduced. Gracey looks him up and down. "*So we've caught you,*" he says. "*Why didn't you come over sooner? You had plenty of time. You fought us at Popa, you fought us here, you fought us there—why didn't you come over sooner?*"

Prem tries to protest. He hasn't come over, he has been captured in battle. But Gracey, paying no attention, continues in an aggrieved and almost peevish manner. "*What did you mean, you people, by going on fighting? We had armor, artillery. You chaps had nothing. But instead of surrendering, you fought. It was madness. Why did you do it? Why didn't you come over?*" At last Prem gets in a few words. Of course it was madness, he says. A revolutionary army lives on the spirit of madness. How else could we have carried on against your numbers and your weapons? For a moment Gracey listens. He looks a little shaken. Then he turns to the brigadier, says a few words about placing a proper guard on this "*bad type,*" and walks off.

This is what Prem remembers. Gracey, if he has any recollection of the encounter, surely renders it differently. One can imagine him saying, "yes, I was curious to see what one of these Dehra Dun turncoats looked like, and Brigade happened to have one—cornered just the day before at the head of his little ragtag force. Asked him why the devil he hadn't given himself up sooner. Fellow babbled something about being part of a revolutionary army. All nonsense. Couldn't waste my time listening. Told my brigadier to lock him up, and went about my business." One can imagine Gracey saying this, or denying that he ever talked to Prem at all.

That something passed, however, between Prem and Gracey that evening; an exchange in which the one was perhaps less assured, and the other certainly less querulous, than Prem remembers; an encounter, nevertheless, in which it was the Indian who took and held the high ground, and the Englishman who was perplexed and even a little rattled—that this happened seems to me beyond doubt. Not only because Prem's memory, though it may play tricks on him, does not cut stories out of whole cloth. But also because Prem made an equivalent, though in its consequences different, impression on Maclachlan and Rashid Yusuf Ali. And this time we have more than Prem's recollections to go on. We have theirs.

I have said that to the proposition that all 14th Army forward interrogation reports have been lost, there are two exceptions. One is Rashid's report on Prem. The other is Rashid's report on Lakshmi. But these survive not in the the sense that they are lying in an archive somewhere. They survive in Rashid's memory. They are almost as vivid there as they were on the day when he wrote them. What follows are parts of these reports as Rashid gave them to me from memory in the course of an afternoon of conversation at Kanpur, late in 1988.

It was evidently Rashid's practice to begin an interrogation by taking name, date of birth, when and where captured, and the like. Evidently, too, he asked about childhood and education, for of Lakshmi he remarks that "she once gave her gold ornaments for an autograph of Gandhiji." But his questions and their answers dealt mostly with the war years. And from what Rashid remembers of these two interrogations, it is obvious he had no difficulty getting them to talk. Neither was trying to hide anything. Neither had anything to hide. Though Lakshmi may have been the readier of the two, both were clearly willing to tell Rashid almost anything he wanted to know about the army, the leader, and the movement. They did not act as if they had been defeated, because they did not believe they had. A battle, they seemed to imply, had been fought and lost. But the campaign was not over. It went on, not on the ground now but in the consciousness of the public. And the immediate object of the consciousness raising they were engaged in, Rashid must have felt, was Rashid himself.

So Lakshmi, for example, told Rashid what her regiment of women had proposed to accomplish. "She told me that if she had met me in Bengal or Assam, she would have greeted me as a brother. If I had resisted her sisterly embraces, she would have taken me prisoner. If I had tried to take *her* prisoner, she would have shot or bayoneted me." And he remembers thinking that the Indian Army should be thankful it had been saved the embarrassment of putting that scenario to the test.

She admitted to him that some of Prem's brother officers had joined the freedom army not from conviction but because they hadn't wanted to see their jawans (and themselves) shipped to Timor or beyond. But she made it clear this had been true only of some. Others were as committed to India's freedom as she was. It was nonsense to suppose that these freedom fighters had joined for rank, privilege, or easy living; and double nonsense to suppose they had done so under duress. Take her women again. Could anyone suppose that *they* had been coerced into joining, that someone had put pressure on *them*—or on their parents?

She laid out a great deal, all of it open, nothing so far as he could see contrived. And when the interrogation was over, when the report had been written and he turned to the summing up and the recommendation, Rashid found himself concluding that this remarkable woman would never go back to simple doctoring. The past two years had changed her. She would return to India a confirmed and ardent nationalist. "I can see no harm in this," he remembers writing, as if two years of active involvement in a frankly treasonable enterprise was nothing to cry shame about.

For color he recommended grey, and for her immediate disposal unsupervised house arrest in Rangoon. That is exactly what she got.

As for Prem, Rashid felt obliged to label him black. Here, after all, was a man who had violated (as Lakshmi had not) a formal oath of allegiance. But in the actual summing up the language had been rather different. "I cannot call him a traitor," Rashid believes he wrote. "He is a misguided patriot, one of the few sincere believers in the *Azad Hind Fauj*, scrupulous in the defense of Indian interests even against the Japanese. He surrendered because he had to, and is under no illusion as to his probable fate."

Rashid is Indian too, of course, though with a difference. His mother is English, he was schooled in England, he was actually commissioned there—though he went at once to India, first to the 7th Rajput Regiment, later to the Intelligence School at Karachi (which Toye also attended), and after independence commanded a battalion of Assam Rifles. Maclachlan, on the other hand, was British through and through. But his being so did not, apparently, make him insensible to the openness and sincerity of the two prisoners whose interrogations he oversaw. He did not quarrel with Rashid's summing up, though he did raise Lakshmi from grey to black (which pleased her). And he came to know Prem almost as well as Rashid did.

This was during Prem's interrogation, at Magwe in May, an interrogation spread over days like Lakshmi's. Together Maclachlan and Rashid studied the diary that had been recovered from the ambush. Delhi had already been told that it showed the writer to be "a competent commander who has the interests of his troops at heart, and is not in the movement for selfish ends."[3] With this Maclachlan and Rashid almost certainly agreed. Indeed, Prem believes that the diary pushed them past curiosity into a determination to help him in any way they could.

Of course they did not pretend that he was other than he was. "I do not hesitate to classify him black," wrote Maclachlan as he reviewed what Rashid had written. Prem's high position in the renegade army, the deaths for which he must ultimately be held responsible, above all his personal bearing of arms against the King-Emperor, allowed no alternative. But Maclachlan did not leave it at that.

He confessed that he had been struck by the frankness of the prisoner, "and by his moral courage in maintaining his views." It was perhaps this remark, coming as it did from a fellow European, that caught Hugh Toye's eye when the Sahgal file reached him in Delhi. (Something else caught his eye too. He and Prem were three days shy of being precisely the same age.)

It was possibly this remark that encouraged Toye—when circumstances dropped him in Rangoon—to listen to what Rashid had to say about Prem and go willingly to meet Prem's fiancée that August day. And on the other hand, perhaps Major Maclachlan had nothing to do with the business. It is nevertheless the case that Prem and Lakshmi made a great impression on Hugh Toye. By what they said, perhaps simply by being what they *were*, they opened his eyes a little to the validity and power of Indian patriotic feeling. And this began a process that, years later, drove Colonel Toye to write *The Springing Tiger*, the first sympathetic study by a westerner of Subhas Chandra Bose.

"One of the few sincere believers in the *Azad Hind Fauj*," Rashid had observed of Prem. This overdid it. Until almost the end of the war, 14th Army forward interrogators necessarily dealt with a skewed cross section of the INA, because the men who fell into their hands early on tended to be the insincere. Still, one can admit that Prem, Dhillon, Shah Nawaz, Lakshmi, and others were more fully committed to

Netaji's enterprise than was the ordinary INA man. It does not follow that the ordinary INA man felt no commitment at all.

Let enough of such men come in contact with the victors, let enough be brought back to India to mingle with the general public, and a new perception of what the freedom army was, and what it had tried to do, was sure to develop. Prem, Lakshmi, and their like might start the wagon rolling. Soon it would roll by itself.

❧

To return to Prem, there on the banks of the Irrawaddy just after his surrender at the end of April 1945.

For a time his life was quite agreeable. Mornings he had his interrogation sessions with Rashid. Toward noon Maclachlan appeared and the three had lunch together, occasionally with a drink. Eight or nine days passed in this way. *By this time we were calling each other Bill and Rashid and Prem.* (Maclachlan was not an ordinary Indian Army man. Lakshmi believes he had once worked for Burma Oil). *But India was sending messages that I should be sent back. So Rashid applied for leave. He had some coming and he wanted to escort me.* Apparently Maclachlan made no objection, for he went.

Rashid and Prem set off on the 12th of May. From Magwe they flew to Chittagong. From Chittagong they went by rail and ferry to Jhingergacha, sixty miles northeast of Calcutta, where the British had a camp to which captured INA men were brought. Prem stayed there four days. It was pleasant enough. Though the camp commander was British, his adjutant was not—he had been to Government College in Lahore, knew Rashid well, met their train, and that evening invited both to a party in the mess. At Jhingergacha, however, Rashid had to turn back. A young Englishman named Todd took Rashid's place. From that moment it was an open question who escorted whom.

For when they reached Calcutta's Howrah Station on the morning of the 18th and discoved that they were booked for the evening Delhi express, Todd chose to pass the day by killing a bottle of gin in the 1st Class refreshment room. Prem helped him kill it. In their two-berth compartment that evening, Todd produced a bottle of rum. Again Prem helped, but warned the younger man that mixing drinks was danger-ous. The warning went unheeded. Todd took far more than he could handle and was sick. Prem cleaned him up, got him into the lower berth, and accepted for safekeeping a manila envelope which held, he was told in a mumble, "*all the documents about you, please keep them safe.*" For the rest of the thirty-six-hour trip he as good as escorted himself.

At Delhi station the morning of May 20 he marched straight to the refreshment room and ordered an enormous European breakfast. Todd, protesting feebly at this contempt for form, found a telephone and called CSDIC. Then they drove to the Red Fort. *It was a Sunday,* Prem remembers. *The officer on duty was Indian. He didn't behave well—in fact he was pretty nasty. Later I discovered he had been a lawyer, and knew my father, and we became quite friendly. But at the time I suppose he didn't want Britishers to think he was on speaking terms with INA men.*

Prem was put in a cell. The cell was built right into the Red Fort's outer wall, which soaked up the heat (north India in May is fiercely hot), so that living in it was like living in an oven. There was nothing to read and no one to talk to. Outside lay the main road from New to Old Delhi. Prem could hear the traffic, though of course he could not see it. In the early morning particularly, it got so that he recognized certain cars by their horns (there were few cars in those days). *Number six,* he would tell himself, *is fifteen minutes late today.*

When CSDIC interrogation began, life improved a little. He was brought regularly to the interrogator's office, and this considerate man (his name was LeCheminat) *made it a point to keep me practically the whole day—so at least I was under a fan.* It was now that he met Hugh Toye. But the weeks went by without apparent point or limit, stretching mindlessly ahead. It would, in fact, be seven months before Prem was able to come and go again as a free man should.

More than a thousand miles away and several months later, Lakshmi's life took an unexpected turn. *In Mogul Street there was this medical shop. They wanted a doctor to examine patients.* Idleness had never suited Lakshmi, nor does it now. Besides, she was anxious to get on a paying basis with her hosts. So she asked permission to open a clinic.

This was in September. Early in November a newspaperman named Douglas Lackerseen came around to see her. "In a shoddy, fly-infested dispensary in downtown Rangoon, opposite the bomb-wrecked building of the former police headquarters," Lackerseen wrote, "sits Dr. Lakshmi Swaminadhan, treating poor Indian patients who look upon her as their ministering angel." Lakshmi hadn't been there when he put his head in the door, but the little waiting room was full of Indian mothers with children, and Lackerseen noticed that when she walked in "with a lively energetic step" their faces brightened. So, no doubt, did his. He got her age right—just turned thirty-one. "She wore a plain white saree with a green border, and had made up her eyes and lips. Dr. Lakshmi," he continued with something of an Englishman's inclination to understatement, "is an attractive woman." In fact she was stunning.

But she was not easy to talk to. "Always she seemed on guard against an unasked question, and most of her answers were short, sometimes monosyllabic." Lackerseen asked her whether she believed the report of Bose's death. She said she hoped he was still living. He asked her if she would agree that the defendants in the Red Fort trial (it had just begun) were war criminals. "How can I? In that case I myself am a war criminal." She had, she told him, been well treated by Peacock and his people. But when he wondered whether she had developed "British sympathies," she said quickly that she had not. "I shall never be pro-British. I still think of myself as a member of the Indian National Army." Lackerseen noticed that whenever Bose cropped up "her dark eyes sparkled."

Lackerseen persevered and filed his copy. In Madras the *Hindu*, which Lakshmi's family read, printed nine inches of it.[4] But Lackerseen never told his readers what the unasked question was. Perhaps Lakshmi had one of her own. Three weeks earlier she had done something much more likely to shake Rangoon, and India too, than anything that could possibly come out of a half hour's interview with a wire service man. Perhaps she was wondering what the consequences were going to be.

Though most of the ex–Indian Army men trapped in Burma had been shipped back to India, many INA recruits from Malaya were still around. They had been put to work on the great Rangoon cleanup, filling bullock carts with the accumulated rubbish of three years' neglect, taking it down to the river, dumping it where the tide could carry it away. That was over and done with now. They were free men— but at the same time "homeless and jobless," as another newspaperman observed. "Many are eking out an uncertain living doing various odd jobs as water carriers, *pan* vendors, and labourers. They still wear their ragged uniforms with badges of Bose's picture, and greet everyone with Jai Hind."[5]

They had not escaped Lakshmi's notice, these men, nor she theirs. Had it been appropriate for a doctor in a civil clinic to wear a uniform and cry Jai Hind, she would have done as they did. But she would not have stopped there. She wanted to do something that would really compel attention to the freedom movement. In October she found something that did.

It was two years since Netaji had announced the *Arzi Hukumat-e-Azad Hind*. The anniversary of that day was approaching, and properly celebrated it should cause a stir. Already she had begun to speak publicly. Somehow she had provided herself again with an INA uniform, which she wore on these occasions. She had spoken on Gandhi's birthday, October 2, and at a little meeting three days later during which she told some fifty listeners that the freedom struggle was not lost. But this had to be a real spectacle. What could she arrange?

There were, of course, resident Indians in the city, some of whom had courage. She had these men from Malaya. And she had herself. *I was the senior officer, I was the only one.* (She was a lieutenant colonel. Though India came to know her as "Captain Lakshmi," the last round of promotions had once more placed her one rung below Prem.) This was enough. How the business was managed is unclear. Lakshmi says nothing about committees, flyers, hiring a hall. As if by magic, when the 21st of October arrived, the thing was done.

> *In Rangoon whole streets had been very badly bombed. There was a space between two of these streets where the rubble was still lying, but which couldn't be seen from the main road. In that space we decided we would have our meeting.*
>
> *It happened there was an Indian newspaper correspondent, Jamal Kidwai, who came to see me that day. He said, "we've been hearing about the INA, but it's all in little pieces, we don't have the material that will make a real impact in India. And now there's this trial. We don't know what's going to happen. The men may be sentenced and hanged without anyone knowing. There must be some way we can put the INA across."*

So I said, "you'd better come to our meeting tonight." And he came. He saw in this bombed-out place a couple of thousand people. Some of my Rani of Jhansi girls were there. The men in their old tattered uniforms were there too. But there was nothing tattered in the way they stood to attention when I raised the flag. At the beginning of the meeting we sang Sukh Sukh Chain and shouted Netaji Zindabad and Jai Hind and Chalo Delhi. Then I spoke. Five or six others made fiery speeches too, in Hindustani or Tamil. And this Jamal Kidwai, he wrote it all up, adding a lot of his own, and in three or four days it was published in a number of Indian papers.

The police had been watching her. "It is high time this lady was returned to India," intelligence had observed early in October, adding sadly that "this has not yet been allowed."[6] Nor would it be, not after this *tamasha* just four days after Dorman-Smith's return to Rangoon aboard the cruiser *Cleopatra*. What this woman had done she would certainly attempt in Madras, Calcutta, Delhi itself, on a much grander scale, and at just the moment when the Army brought up for trial three defiant INA officers, one known to be her fiancé. It was an appalling prospect.

But neither could she be left where she was. So on the 15th of November, two days after Lackerseen's visit, her clinic was closed. She was flown to Meiktila, driven up to Kalaw, and put in a house with Burmese guards at the door. In that house she was to remain.

It was hardly durance vile. There were friends from her previous stay to bring her books, newspapers, eventually a gramophone. The Burmese couple she had been close to were right next door, and she found she could slip over and see them—the guards looked the other way. Young Indian officers sent up to Kalaw for rest and recreation discovered her and called in groups. And though she could not write or receive letters, by passing messages to visitors who were going to India and were willing to carry them, she was able to keep in touch with her family.

As time passed even these restrictions loosened. When an Indian newspaper reported, under the caption "S.O.S. From Captain Lakshmi," that she was in a desperate state, her mother cried nonsense. "I am in constant touch with my daughter," she wrote the *Hindu*. "She has had no complaints to make about the treatment given her."[7] Lakshmi agrees that this was so. *I was well looked after. I was in no danger. But I hardly saw anybody. Sometimes I was afraid they might forget me. Sometimes I was afraid I might sit here for the rest of my life.*

Early in March 1946 her detention ended at last. *I was sent back in one of those Dakotas. A British officer was detailed to escort me up to Burma's border with India. When we got into the plane he made me sit right next to him. The plane took off, we were flying, suddenly the pilot announced over the intercom, "we have now crossed the frontier and are over Indian territory"*—and this officer got up and sat down on the other side the plane. It was quite deliberate. Lakshmi thought of asking where were the parachutes, was she supposed to jump?

It was as if, by moving, he had washed his hands of her. It was as if he was telling her that for every Maclachlan and every Rashid Yusuf Ali there were a score like himself, a score who did not wish to have anything to do with her and her sort, a score who saw them for the nasty piece of work they were—these Jiffs.

CHAPTER 18

JIFFS

JIFC to be exact, standing for Japanese-Indian Fifth Column—or, if you preferred, Japanese-*Inspired* Fifth Column. But British intelligence, whose responsibility it was to track the traitors down, had not devised this acronym the instant it picked up the scent. It had been perfectly content to use the label the traitors used themselves, and might have gone right on using it, had not certain developments driven it to look for something pejorative, something plainly abusive.

Curiously, the intelligence service did not put its nose to the ground until mid-1942, well after these Jiffs got their start. Though Japanese shortwave stations in Saigon, Singapore, Bangkok, and Rangoon had for months beamed newscasts to India with word of the liberation force forming in Malaya, the service apparently knew nothing about it. Nothing of the happenings at Farrer Park. Nothing of the men abandoned by their British officers, turned over to the Japanese, handed on to Mohan Singh. Not until the 17th of July, five months after Singapore's fall, did intelligence acknowledge (in one of its Weekly Intelligence Summaries) the existence of an "Indian National Army."

It would be used, intelligence suspected, for sabotage, espionage, perhaps even for military operations of some sort. With respect to these last, "it has been suggested that the Japanese intend to use elements of the I.N.A. to precede their troops as they advance, with the object of exhorting Indian troops to lay down their arms. . . ."[1] That was the likelihood. But the service had very little hard information to go on. Much of what reached it was hearsay: for example, a tale of a division said to be forming in Indochina (of all places) clothed in "khaki shorts and shirts, black rubber shoes, and white Gandhi caps."[2] Besides, though intelligence had paid little attention to the Quit India resolution itself, from mid-August on it was much occupied with the disturbances that resolution had produced. Only when men bringing firsthand accounts of the renegade force began to arrive, did it take the matter seriously. And this was weeks into the autumn.

They came, these informants, a few all the way from Malaya (these were the most valuable), the rest from Burma itself. Their purpose in crossing the wild, thinly populated Burma-India border was a desperate desire to resume their old allegiance—or so they invariably said. By the end of 1942 the intelligence service had received scores of these fellows. And since what they told CSDIC promised to add greatly to the stock of information about the Indian National Army, the service ought to have been unreservedly delighted by their coming. It wasn't.

For not all of the arrivals were bona fide. "In a disquieting number of cases," complained a General Headquarters memorandum in March 1943, "individuals have managed to conceal from interrogators the fact that they have been in Japanese hands, and been sent back with specific instructions."[3] Some were locals, men "of Bengali or Chittagonian extraction." Others had come from a distance, among them Indian prisoners-of-war who had volunteered for Japanese "5th column" tasks (to use the language of the intelligence service) because it would get them out from behind barbed wire. They were not unwilling agents. They had been carefully coached. "Their duties, once behind our lines," intelligence believed, "comprise either the collection and passing back of information or the subversion of the army and the loyalty of civilians."[4] And there were many, intelligence suspected, whom the interrogators never saw at all because they did not turn themselves in. All were dangerous.

More dangerous, indeed, than the agents that were being turned out by the formal spy schools (Raghavan's was one) that had opened in Malaya. The graduates of these schools were given formal training in the use of codes, radios, explosives, and the like. They were then landed by submarine on the Indian coast or dropped in the interior by parachute, with instructions to make contact with the Congress underground, transmit information, spread rumors, blow things up. They had glamor, these fellows. They ought to have quite eclipsed the men who trudged the border. But it didn't work out that way. Some gave themselves up the moment they landed. Others, like the ex–havildar observed in a railroad station "taking a too obvious interest in troop trains,"[5] were quickly spotted. And though their quality improved, so that the proportion of those remaining at large grew higher, and some were never identified and caught at all, they disturbed the British much less than the men who were dispatched not to India but to the fighting on India's eastern frontier. In 1943 that meant the Arakan.

There, early in the year, half a dozen brigades of Lt. General N. M. S. Irwin's Eastern Army (the precursor of 14th Army), pushing down the Mayu Peninsula with Akyab their object, were stopped ten miles short of the peninsula's tip by numerically inferior Japanese forces, held motionless for seven weeks, then hit suddenly in the flank, cut up, and forced back with much loss of equipment to the point of departure. Spirits were low when the push began. (This was the *first* Arakan campaign, it was otherwise a year later with Briggs and Messervy's divisions.) They sank lower when the push came to a halt. Men were with difficulty persuaded to leave the beaten path and venture into the bush. And they dreaded the hours of darkness—Louis Allen gives the instance of an 8/13th Frontier Force company that abandoned a hilltop one fine morning because, having blazed away all night at suspicious noises, it discovered at dawn that it had shot off all its ammunition. It was a most unsoldierly show. Of some units the blunt post mortem opinion was that the men were gutless. But Irwin believed that INA agents had had a hand in the sorry business.

General Headquarters thought so too. Leaflets bearing appeals to desert were turning up in unexpected places. Some were directed by name to sepoys in forward units. They were carried by Indians in civilian dress who passed back and forth between the lines—intelligence came across a Japanese handbook that gave Japanese soldiers practical advice on how to recognize these fellows and avoid shooting them. Equally serious, drafts sent up from the regimental depots reached the Arakan already demoralized by tales fed them in line-of-communication camps. "It is now quite clear," the March memorandum continued, "that a double attack is being made on the morale and loyalty of Indian troops," one directed by the Congress underground that functioned in spite of the Quit India sweep, the other masterminded by the Japanese. Senior commanders were asked to review the problem and suggest what might be done.

Irwin's response is interesting, not least because it implies that the "double attack" is doing real damage. "In those units where collective disloyalty has occurred," it runs,[6] "the C.O. and Subadar Major were usually unaware of its advent, and I.N.A. and I.I.L. agents may easily escape their vigilance unless they are assisted by trained personnel." How many acts of "collective disloyalty" were actually occurring? Irwin does not say. Neither does Kirby, the official historian. Official historians rarely take note of such things. Nowhere in Kirby's two chapters on the first Arakan campaign does the word "desertion" appear. There *is*, however, written evidence of one spectacular instance.[7]

A platoon from the 1/15th Punjab went out on patrol one February day and vanished. The company's officers suspected nothing. They had no reason to suppose the platoon had deserted. It hadn't returned, that was all. But weeks went by. A formal inquiry was ordered. The company, it was discovered, had been "infected" with Congress party attitudes. There had been "contacts" with local "I.N.A. propagandists." Still, no one could say with assurance that the men had gone over. And then, ten months later, intelligence *found* the missing platoon.

It was attached to Company A of the INA's Special Service Group (about to be renamed the Bahadur Group), near Kalewa on the Chindwin. The men *had* deserted en masse. They had chosen, or somehow been induced, to join a body whose purpose was to do to other Indian Army platoons what had just been done to them. It was a dénouement that would have shocked and appalled Irwin had it come at once, not ten months later. But at the time his field commanders were quite disturbed enough by the relentless flow of less dramatic disappearances. "Recent desertions with arms include two parties of Mazbhi Sikhs, three from 10 Mule Company Bareilly, and two from 24 Indian Engineer Battalion Poona," ran the entry in one Weekly Intelligence Summary.[8] Notices of this sort appeared regularly in the first half of 1943, as in another kind of summary the weather might have, or the Dow Jones average.

ॐ

❧

On the last day of 1942 Lt. Colonel G. W. Wren, at MI 2 the War Office, Whitehall, circulated a warning about lost loyalty in another quarter. It was not sepoy desertion the Indian Army had most to fear, his warning (in the form of a memorandum) ran. It was the alienation of the officer, the Indian officer.

Colonel Wren did not deny that sepoy desertion might become serious. He knew what Mohan Singh and his renegades were up to because the Director of Military Intelligence in New Delhi had just sent him CSDIC reports on four men who had recently arrived from Malaya. One of these was a certain M. S. Dhillon, a major command-ing ammunition and transport companies in the Malayan campaign. Dhillon had been present at Farrer Park. Subsequently he had accompanied N. S. Gill to Burma for the express purpose of making contact with the British under the guise of spying for the Japanese. (His failure to reappear had moved the Japanese to arrest Gill on suspicion of having masterminded the defection, an act, the reader may remember, that so enraged Mohan Singh the Japanese were obliged to arrest him too.) Another recent arrival was Captain Pritam Singh of the 2/16th Punjab, not to be confused with the expatriate Pritam Singh whom Fujiwara had met in Bangkok. Reaching Singapore shortly before the surrender, this Pritam Singh had taken a bomb fragment in the shoulder and been hospitalized for several weeks. After a further interval during which he mingled with the other POWs, he had slipped away. Two other officers had gone with him. Together they had made their way to India, moving like Dhillon by way of the Chindwin, arriving almost exactly when Dhillon did. These were the men whose interrogation reports had been sent to Wren. And though the general drift of Wren's thinking may have been fixed before ever they reached his desk, when he wrote his memorandum the four reports were very much on his mind—particularly Pritam Singh's.[9]

Dhillon had provided CSDIC with the text of the Bangkok Resolutions, a list of Indian Independence League branches from Singapore to Tokyo, the INA's table of organization, material of that sort. Pritam Singh had preferred to talk. He had talked about Mohan Singh: the men, he said, thought him genuine, not acting a part. He had talked about Farrer Park: there had been wild excitement, he maintained, at the announcement of a national army. What particularly caught Wren's eye, however, were Pritam Singh's observations on the state of mind of the Indian officers, the Dehra Dun graduates like himself, who had been taken prisoner and had had to wrestle with the question, should they join the INA? and the other question, what should their men do?

They had been in a position, Pritam Singh said, to decide for these fellows. "The thing that struck one in Malaya"—this is CSDIC conveying in its own words what Pritam Singh had said during his interrogation—"was the tremendous power and influence of the ICOs over the men. If the officers were prepared to volunteer, then the whole unit would volunteer. And if the officers did not want to volunteer, then the men would also be disinclined."

Prem might have objected, if asked, that in the 2/10th Baluch this was not so. The three ICOs—himself, K. P. "Thimmy" Thimayya, and a Muslim officer named Burhan-ud-Din—had volunteered, while almost all the VCOs and other ranks had not. Prem might also have admitted that his battalion had been something of an exception. But what interested and troubled Wren was less the accuracy of Pritam Singh's proposition than the corollary. Once you granted that in the POW camps ICOs had great influence over the men, you raised the possibility that they had it in India as well. If they had it in India, you were led inevitably to a serious consideration of Indian officers distinct from British officers—to a consideration of ICOs in the Indian Army as a class: the level of their contentment, their loyalty. Pritam Singh evidently did not think that the one was high or the other secure.

Of course battalions in India still kept their British officers. There had been no Farrer Park *there*, no abandonment of the Indian by the Britisher. And British officers of the old school, who took pride in their knowledge of their men, their command of the vernacular, their standing *in loco parentis*, were not likely to lose overnight their hold over these men. Indianization, however, was rapidly changing the proportions between the races. When the war in Europe began, the 76,000 or so Indian other ranks (common soldiers) in the infantry component of the Indian Army had been led by a little over 1,000 British and some 200 Indian officers (there were 1,700 VCOs besides). By the end of the war the other ranks had multiplied fourfold, British officers threefold, Indian officers *ten*fold. Moreover, an emergency commissioned Englishman, often with little or no experience of India, was nothing like as close to his men as the pre–war regular had been. That, too, would draw the sepoy to the Indian. What, then, might happen if the swelling mass of Indian officers turned out to be unhappy with its state?

Pritam Singh had put his finger on a number of grievances. Among them was a small but galling one: Indian other ranks who passed British officers saluted as a matter of course, but no British soldier ever saluted an Indian. There were other grounds for ill feeling. They drove Pritam Singh to wonder whether your average Indian commissioned officer wasn't on the verge of shedding his fidelity. Colonel Wren did not argue the question. In his memorandum of warning he said flatly that the Indian already had.

"It is plain," the relevant portion begins, "that we have come to a parting of the ways. We have, by our policy toward India, bred up a new class of officer who may be loyal to India and perhaps to Congress but is not necessarily loyal to us. That spirit has not yet permeated through the rank and file, who still retain the old loyalty to the Sarkar." But "for the first time since the Mutiny this issue is making a major impact on the loyalty of the Indian Army." We cannot recover what has been lost. It is useless to try to educate ICOs, now, in the enduring virtues of the Raj. But neither dare we hesitate and do nothing. And Colonel Wren drove the point home with a brief cautionary tale.

In 1938 a group of junior staff officers attacked the new Army policy of Indianization by segregation. [By this Wren meant the practice of posting freshly commissioned Indian officers to Indianizing battalions only.] They wished to substitute for it Indianization up to a certain percentage on a man for man basis, and to give the Indian Commissioned Officer the pay, privileges, and position of the British. The risks were, and still are, obvious. But they wished for once to get ahead of events, to ride the storm rather than be submerged by it.

Colonel Wren continued.

They also held that the younger generation of British officer would stand it, that the Indian martial classes had earned it, and that the majority of serving officers of the Indian Army had reached the conclusion that it was the only possible course to adopt. They were defeated. But the war quickly accomplished what they could not do; and now, in December 1942, the last step in their plans has been taken, by giving ICOs powers of command over British troops.

Wren said nothing about Churchill having hotly objected to this last. Nor did he point out that Indian officers were still not paid what British officers were. (Not until April 1945 were Indian officers serving in Burma granted the same expatriation allowance that British officers received.) Colonel Wren turned, instead, to the cost of opportunity neglected. "The placing of the ICO on a par with the British officer is a concession that has been wrung out of a grudging Britain in the extremity of her peril." Whitehall's unwillingness to move until obliged to had soured relations, and rankled still. "As far as my experience in an Indianized unit goes, it is the cause of ninety percent of the trouble with the ICOs. Had we been less cautious in 1938, the danger from the I.N.A. in 1942 would have been a good deal smaller."

To ride the storm rather than be submerged by it—that was the moral. And intelligence, Wren pointed out, had a seaworthy boat in mind. "In every document that we see from India the D.M.I. raises at one stage or another the fact that the Army's problem would be helped by a more positive policy on the part of His Majesty's Government. In other words, the most effective counter to the I.N.A. and the I.I.L. must lie in any steps taken by His Majesty's Government which will transform our promises of independence for India into a reality in the minds of the politically minded younger generation. At present it is not a reality. . . ." Until it was, the Indian Army would be at risk.

Colonel Wren's analysis created a stir. In the India Office Library's file of INA-related papers there are a surprising number of references to it. Four months later Eastern Army made the same recommendation. Though the problem of suborned and deserting sepoys was mainly "a military one," observed Irwin in his response to GHQ's March cry of alarm,[10] he did not doubt that the surest road to its solution lay in "a declaration for a free or freer India similar to the U.S.A. declaration for the independence of the Philippines." If possible let such a declaration be made. But of course it wasn't possible. With Churchill at 10

Downing Street and Linlithgow in the Viceregal Palace, how could it be?

Colonel Wren did not credit Mohan Singh and his band of renegades with shifting the loyalty of the ICO. That was Britain's doing. Britain's treatment of India had "bred up" the new breed over a period of years. Yet it was clear, from the memorandum's timing and from the sources to which it referred, that what drove Wren to compose it, and Irwin to embrace or at least echo its one concrete proposal, was the immediate danger on India's eastern border.

The danger would pass, of course. One year later 14th Army, as Eastern Army would become when Slim took command, would be pushing down the Mayu Peninsula again, this time briskly. *Two* years later 14th Army would stand on the brink of total victory in Burma. The Weekly Intelligence Summaries would long since have ceased reporting "recent desertions with arms" because there would be none to report. The Bahadur Group (or what was left of it) would have been withdrawn to Rangoon and disbanded.

But for a time in late 1942 and early 1943, with memories of their being beaten in Malaya and pitchforked out of Burma still powerful and fresh, there was real fear among the British that the Indian National Army might weaken the sepoy's already diminished fighting spirit to the vanishing point just by showing itself and beckoning. And beyond this there was a realization in certain quarters that though the Indian Army might someday return in triumph to Burma and Malaya, it could never again be the sword and buckler of the Raj. Its Indian officers already served, in spirit, another master. Sooner or later they must be followed by the men.

Unable to adopt Colonel Wren's suggestion for a bold political démarche that should rob the INA of its appeal, New Delhi fell back on damage control. It set about ensuring that India learned as little as possible about the traitor army and its leader, and that what it did learn was as disparaging, as ugly, as it could be made to be.

The obvious first step was to keep all mention of both out of newspapers and books. With respect to the army this was easily arranged. Laws and practice, parts of which stretched back almost to the Sepoy Rebellion of 1857, allowed provincial governments to seize books, journals, even handbills, virtually at will. Allowed them to bind a newspaper publisher with a deposit, and pocket that deposit (while requiring a larger one) if something objectionable was printed. Allowed them, if the offense was repeated, to confiscate the second deposit *and* the printing plant as well. What constituted objectionable material varied with time and place. By the late 1930s the Government of India, which exercised general control over the business, had become increasingly reluctant to suppress political opinion. And though this reluctance vanished momentarily when Quit India began, so that for a time Congress party and its activities were quite blacked out, from late 1942 right through to the end of the war journalists were free to write more or less what they pleased about domestic politics. But tampering with the loyalty of the army was another matter. And the Indian *National* Army tampered simply by existing, simply by bearing that name. So from the moment the INA's existence became known, publishers were given to understand that not a word about it must reach the Indian reader. Foreign publications possibly aside (some may have escaped confiscation in the mail or at the ports), not a word, it is probably safe to say, did.

Even towards the end, when British arms were triumphant and there was seemingly no reason why the wretched remnants of Bose's renegade force should not be hauled before the public and pilloried, the ban held. Maymyo is recovered. Newspaper readers learn it is a "pleasant hill station" that for months harbored Mutaguchi's forward headquarters, they are not told it harbored Bose's too. Meiktila falls, an enemy force is "mopped up" near Mount Popa, a British column pushing south from Taungdwingyi approaches the Irrawaddy at Allanmyo. Never a suspicion that Prem and his regiment are anywhere about. On the front page of the *Hindu* appears an advertisement for Bombay's most recent screen thriller. The setting is Burma. An Indian girl stumbles upon a downed Indian pilot and at great risk to herself saves him from the Japanese. "From today's shackled Burma, ground to helplessness under the Jap's brutal heel, comes this matchless drama of a love no fear can crush." The name of the film is *Burma Rani*. But there is nothing in this issue, or in any other, about the real Ranis whom Lakshmi has organized and led.[11]

Bose was another matter. No one, of course, tried to publish his biography, a collection of his speeches, an article or two speculating about his movements and his intentions. The *Indian Year Book and Who's Who*, which in pre-war years had allotted him a substantial entry, capped the entry now with "mysteriously disappeared from his house in 1940, present whereabouts not known," and in the 1944 edition dropped it altogether—as if he were dead. Yet the publishers knew perfectly well that he was *not* dead. In fact they knew exactly where he was. So did the Indian public.

As early as November 1941, a month before Pearl Harbor, the Government of India itself had announced that Subhas Chandra had gone over to the Germans. What it announced, newspapers could print. When two years later Bose reached Malaya and took the INA in hand, the Japanese broadcast his doings—and many Indians listened. They were not supposed to, but how could they be prevented? "The usual question when an Indian buys a wireless set," a visiting BBC man remembers a Bombay dealer saying late in 1942, "is can I hear Germany and Japan on this?"[12] Evidently the answer, sotto voce, was "yes, you can," for a year and a half later intelligence was asking itself not *are* enemy broadcasts listened to, but *why*? For some buyers of radios the answer, surely, was that they wanted to hear Subhas Chandra Bose. It must have been particularly so during the great Bengal famine of 1943.

Famine in India, everyone supposed, was a thing of the past. In miserably mismanaged China enormous numbers perished periodically of hunger. In India they did not. Study and experience had taught the Government of India, when dearth on any scale threatened, to calculate where grain was needed, move it by rail, and make work for the poor so that they would have money with which to buy it. The government knew, in a word, how to administer famine away. It keeps the knowledge still.

The knowledge was effective, however, only if certain signals were given and properly received. Bengalis eat rice. Most of it is grown right in Bengal. By 1942, however, fewer than one in four Bengali rural families tilled their own paddy. The rest relied on the market, and the market that year was disturbed by the loss of the small but important Burma supply (the war cut Burma off, of course), and by a cyclone that flattened part of December's crop. When 1943 opened, therefore, there were grounds for alarm. Bengal faced no absolute scarcity of rice. Stocks were adequate. But they were barely so. Bengalis would eat only if what there was flowed smoothly to market—and the Bengal government behaved in such a way as to practically guarantee that it would not.[13]

For it began by intervening, by seizing all the rice it could find and fixing the price. Later it changed its mind, swung 180 degrees, lifted price control, and invited the market to do as it pleased. The dealers were dumbfounded. Then it occurred to them that a government that moved so suddenly and arbitrarily was entirely capable of applying a second confiscatory price freeze as soon as stocks in any quantity appeared. So stocks in any quantity did *not* appear; indeed, attracted by the prospect of the profits that should be theirs if they held back long enough, the dealers hid every bag they could.

Catastrophe was the result. Scarcity drove the price steadily upward, as the dealers knew it would. Wartime inflation had already put many common articles beyond the reach of the rural poor. Soon the poor could not afford to buy the very staple of their diet. In parts of Bengal rice disappeared from the shops, and for tens of thousands right across the province, it was starve where you were or find help somehow in the metropolis. Silently the hopeless and the helpless drifted to Calcutta. Even before the rains began, people there (Ian Stephens of the *Statesman* was among them) noticed, as they went about the city, unusual numbers of country folk squatting weak and bewildered in gutters and alleyways, lying in open spaces, curled up on the paved sidewalks of the well-to-do; without the means to buy rice even were it offered; quietly dying.

The Bengal government did nothing. It was confident there was rice out in the districts (there was), and that a policy of hands off would tease it out (which eventually it would). New Delhi, too, did nothing. It had not been asked to. It was nine hundred miles away and busy with the war—besides, in the north, the vigorous and martial north, they eat not rice but wheat. Linlithgow, very near the end of a record seven and a half years as viceroy, dutifully made trips to Bombay and Madras but stayed away from Calcutta. "Nothing is the matter" his absence seemed to say, and Ian Stephens noticed that the British public was fed the same message. "Cables from India were watched for references to conditions in Bengal," he remembered later, "and all such meaningful words as famine, corpse, starvation, methodically struck out."[14]

It was not until October, long after the rains had ended, and then only because men of influence in Calcutta beat the Government of India about the head (the *Statesman* led the way with photographic spreads and blistering editorials), that New Delhi woke to the disaster and moved. By then, of course, the damage was done. The starving had starved. The dying were dead. Their number, a Famine Commission eventually calculated, was 1,873,749—a neat and tidy figure, but one which inquirers since have had trouble with, because Bengal deaths in excess of normal mortality for that period come to three and a half million. Later Stephens was to write that the famine had been "a calamity which in sheer size exceeded any during the entire span of British imperial rule." At the time he was more cutting, calling it editorially "An All-India Disgrace."[15]

Angry as Stephens was, he wished Congressmen no profit from the Raj's embarrassment. When someone suggested it was time to release Gandhi, Nehru, and the others, he had the *Statesman* remind its readers of Quit India the previous August and the damage it had done. To bring the rebellion's instigators back into open political life would simply disturb the prosecution of the war—which Stephens, like Linlithgow, thought India's most pressing business. Indeed, this was one reason why the famine was so inexcusable. "A populace three parts starved is in no state to support armies or resist dangerous rumours."[16]

But Bose could not be muzzled. The disaster was soon public knowledge everywhere. It was, after all, much too big a thing for New Delhi to conceal from anybody except itself. Burmese rice might have prevented it. Burmese rice might even now alleviate it. From Rangoon in September 1943 (this was his second visit) Bose announced that his government, the newly created *Arzi Hukumat-e-Azad Hind*, was prepared to buy and ship—never mind how— one hundred thousand tons of rice as a gift to the people of Bengal.

The offer was made, as it had to be made, in a radio broadcast. It was received, as it was bound to be received, in stony silence.

Nevertheless it was heard. Just how many Bengali ears it reached it is impossible to say. No Calcutta newspaper, of course, said anything about it. "But at one of those now less frequent dinner-jacketed evening parties about this time, a British acquaintance of mine known for his Indian friendships made the ill-received remark that if a Japanese plane parachuted Subhas on to the Maidan next morning, ninety per cent of the city's Bengali inhabitants would rush forth to join him." Recollecting the incident a dozen years later, Stephens decided that perhaps the fellow had been right.[17]

So it was impossible to blot Subhas Chandra out. Nor could the Indian National Army's existence be kept wholly secret from the Indian public (Japanese radio made sure of that), or from battalions in the Arakan. Sepoys there were in daily danger of being approached by "contact parties" of the sort that had seduced the missing platoon. Something must be done about them. And the Indian Army as a whole must learn how to defend itself against subversion too. The problem appeared pressing. In May of 1943 there were discussions. By June there was a program.

It did not include attaching counter-intelligence agents to battalions in the Arakan that were believed to be particularly vulnerable, as Irwin had recommended. Nor was it agreed that, for a time, some should be sent to the rear, letting Gurkha battalions take their place. There *was* to be a change of name. Intelligence would no longer speak of the Indian National Army. (For one thing, doing so might unwittingly give it legal standing.) Indian Traitor Army was beyond reach because the Indian *Tea* Association had first call on the initials. Some people were already using Japanese-Indian Fifth Column and Japanese-*Inspired* Fifth Column. The labels were attractive because they conveyed so well what many hoped and half believed these traitor Indians were—not the vanguard of an army but a band of spies and mischief makers, cunning perhaps, unprincipled certainly, numerous never. So in June the two labels were officially adopted, in a form— JIFC—that when written answered for either, and when spoken rolled easily and contemptuously off the tongue. But the heart of the program was a campaign of "direct and intensive oral propaganda" that should prepare the sepoy to resist Jiffs no matter *what* they were called.[18]

Let company-grade officers collect their men in "josh groups" and talk frankly to them. (Eventually there would be a short Delhi course in how to run a josh group.) Let company-grade officers warn their men that they were going to run across Indians consorting with the enemy; explain to them that these fellows were traitors who, if caught, would be court-martialed, and if the charge was capital (killing or suborning a loyal jawan was capital) hanged; caution them that if they listened to the scoundrels, they risked coming to the same bad end. But above all, let these officers instruct their men in the evil qualities of the Japanese, bring Japanese behavior to life, make it real and vivid. To give them the means of doing this, intelligence combed its interrogation files for cases of barbarous behavior—of which the following, reported of Yenangyaung forty miles southwest of Mount Popa in early 1942, is a sample.

> A party of about 300 British and Indian prisoners of war was collected at this place on 18 and 19 March. The prisoners were stripped down to their vests and pants and, their hands having been tied behind their backs, they were beaten, kicked, and finally driven still bound into small rooms in which they were hopelessly overcrowded. They were then left for three days without food or water. Several died of thirst. A man of the 7th Rajput Regiment who begged for water was taken out and shot. . . . The traitor Ram Sarup then arrived and told the prisoners that the Japanese had intended to set fire to the building in which they were imprisoned and burn them alive. He urged them to join the so-called Indian National Army and promised food and water.

These lines, which for Englishmen could not fail to call up images of the Black Hole of Calcutta, appeared in a memorandum entitled "Japanese Treatment of Indian Prisoners of War in Burma." It was attached to a regular Weekly Intelligence Summary,[19] so that it went to all the persons in New Delhi and London who received that interesting serial. It was *not* released to the press, or otherwise made public; no weekly summaries were; but in some form or other it reached the troops. For the summary to which this memorandum was attached (it is June 1943) notes that while the material in it, including the passage just reproduced, is not to be quoted whole and verbatim, "commanding officers should with due regard to the temper of their men select instances to drive home specific points." There is a purpose here. It is "to instill hatred of the Japanese, contempt for traitors, and in general a desire to be 'up and at them'" into the men. From a separate catalogue of barbarous acts, this one devoted to "Japanese Treatment of Indian Prisoners of War in Malaya," enterprising commanding officers could obtain other material to lay before their josh groups. And as the weeks went by, they found still more.

How the groups responded it is impossible to say, there being no written record of the operation. Radio broadcasts are another matter. Intelligence not only produced them for GHQ, which sent them out over All-India Radio, it reported what they said, and how (so far as it could judge) they were received. By early 1944 programs directed at Indians in the places the Japanese had overrun, in particular Malaya and Burma, were being broadcast regularly on the 19 and 31 meter bands. And what listeners to these programs heard was essentially what sepoys in the josh groups were fed, racked up a notch or two: the Japanese in their true colors, their culture, religion, and society, unadorned and darkly unattractive.

A culture "anti-Hindu in its essence." A religion amounting to barely disguised worship of the state. A society in which prostitution was "a profession which even the most respectable women can take up." A people "overbearing and intolerant in their attitude towards all other people" who over the past six years had starved and murdered hundreds of thousands in China, were doing the same now in southeast Asia, and would for a certainty repeat the performance if ever they set foot in India. These were the characteristics of the Japanese as they truly were. These were the characteristics intelligence proposed to convey.[20] The work went so well that by mid-1944 talks to this effect were on the air in Bengali, Gujerati, Hindustani, Malayalam, Punjabi, and Tamil.

But Indians in India listened too. And as the message for external listeners was just what India too must hear if it was ever to be persuaded of the rightness of the war (intelligence was gloomily convinced that a great many politically conscious Hindus actually wanted Japan to win), no attempt was made to tell the home front one thing, the foreign front another. Both were treated to a heavy dose of Nippon-bashing in which those few Indians, those wretched few, who actually collaborated with the enemy were particular targets.

Bose got his share. He was pilloried for his transparent personal ambition, derided for being "an actor who loves to stand in the limelight and hear his own voice," jeered at for promising triumphs he did not deliver. He was ridiculed. One broadcast had for a centerpiece a faked radio interview in which Tojo talks to a fawning "Bose Babu." In another three cultivated Indian gentlemen exchange snide comments and a laugh or two over Netaji's flag-raising expedition to the Andaman Islands. Back issues of newspapers yielded cutting remarks about the sometime Congress leader, remarks ascribable to Gandhi, Nehru, Azad, and the like, and these were read over the air. The attention was unrelenting. "Pressure on Bose maintained" is the opening to more than one of the intelligence service's periodic reviews of the propaganda campaign.[21] But the harshest language was reserved for Bose's people.

Not for his battalions—not for the Indian National Army as such. There was no mention of it, under that name or any other; no mention of its formations, their estimated strength, the move to Burma, the actions in the Arakan and about the Manipur basin, the disaster at Imphal. The broadcasts made no mention of an army of any sort at all. But it was useless to pretend that *nothing* was happening. So intelligence did what in the circumstances came naturally to it. It granted the existence of Jiffs—a small class of Indians who out of fear, love of power, fondness for money and the good life, or motives more ignoble still, had hitched their fortunes to the puppet Bose and his brutal Japanese masters. And intelligence made sure that this last attribute stuck. It made sure that the charge of brutality blackened them to a fare-thee-well.

It did this by intimating a linkage. In the grim and sometimes lurid stories of injuries and death which it constructed out of the interrogations of defectors and escapees, stories which it passed on to GHQ, josh groups, and All-India Radio, it made no effort to distinguish Indians from Japanese, and to fix responsibility for these terrible things on the one or on the other. It allowed them to mingle.

The brief account just quoted of men penned for three days without food or water, then harangued by "the traitor Ram Sarup," stands cheek by jowl with accounts of the deliberate torching of trucks filled with wounded prisoners, of prisoners who could not keep up on the march pulled out of the line and shot, of a havildar deathly ill with dysentery thrown into the sea alive. And though it is not made explicit, the reader now—and surely the listener *then*—has a sense that there were Indians present at these barbarous acts, Indians who participated. These barbarities, he feels, were the work not just of the butcher, but of the butcher and his lackey. Butchers' lackeys. To the day he left India, and possibly beyond, Wavell never referred to the Indian National Army as other than a collection of cowards and weaklings. That, after all, is what butchers' lackeys can be expected to be.

This had consequences. One was that uninformed opinion in London and Delhi held the INA to be smaller and more prone to surrender than it actually was. Smaller because nastiness is not naturally abundant in any group. Prone to surrender because if the sepoy is a simple, sturdy fellow who remains loyal unless coerced or duped, he will revert to his original allegiance the moment he has a chance. Assume the active joiners, then, to be butchers' lackeys, and you assume a small body of committed rascals, a much larger body of the forced or misled, and a much larger body still of those who have, through all temptation and hardship, remained true to their salt. That is the configuration you will get, and that is the configuration intelligence allowed people to construct. With the result that when London and Delhi decided to go public about the renegade army—in late April 1945, their hand forced by war correspondents accompanying 14th Army in the plunge south—the press release explaining how that army came to be, told readers that when the Japanese and their lackeys tried to suborn the Indians in the POW camps, the great majority stood fast.

"But they didn't," somebody cried. For by this time intelligence knew very well that they hadn't.

Intelligence knew that within six months of Singapore's fall, three quarters of the 55,000 or so Indians in the POW camps had accepted Mohan Singh's invitation, or had tried to (there were not enough arms for all). Intelligence knew that though the December 1942 crisis and

Mohan Singh's arrest reduced the number, Netaji's arrival and the surge of civilian enlistments soon drove it above 40,000 again.[22] The imagined configuration was indeed imagined. "Of course I knew about the Jiffs," remarked Ian Stephens later. Still, "I'd no idea there were so many."[23]

There was a consequence of a more serious sort. Intelligence made much of Japanese barbarity, and implicated Jiffs in the same, because barbarous acts were reported and many no doubt occurred. But there was another reason. Eastern Army, as I have said, was worried about its men. The activity of even the few hundred Special Service Group Jiffs that Mohan Singh had managed to send from Malaya, or that had been collected locally, sapped the confidence of many sepoys and utterly demoralized some. The rot could be stopped, intelligence believed, if Jiffs were exposed as scum. This meant pointing the finger at more than their disloyalty. It meant showing what brutes they could be. So in mid-1943, at a moment when the sepoy still needed bucking up, and cautionary tales about what he would suffer if he imitated Jiffs or let them seduce him still seemed useful, the intelligence service set out to show him, and every Indian who would listen, just how brutal these Jiffs were.

Within months, however, two things changed. The sepoy began to shake off his low spirits. He became a member of 14th Army, which in the next year and a half stopped the Japanese cold, cut them up, and chased them all the way to Rangoon. Meanwhile it became apparent that the Indian National Army had ceased recruiting by methods that could be represented as brutal. Defectors were still making their way west. But they no longer brought tales of deprivation and physical cruelty, because in the Malayan camps where Bose made civilians into soldiers there wasn't any. Ill-treatment wasn't needed. There was no lack of willing volunteers. Even at the Red Fort trials none was ever alleged.

Once launched, however, the charge of brutality could not be recalled. No matter that it was no longer required to stoke the sepoy's hatred, no matter that it ceased to have any basis in actual behavior: it had a life of its own. The natural obscurity of war, compounded by censorship and normal information management, virtually guaranteed that the prevailing image of the INA officer would remain that of a man who was part traitor, part coward, and part bully, a lackey in the service of Nippon. And the prevailing image of his men, that of trapped sheep. When the war ended and the curtain lifted, these images might not easily be replaced.

✦

On the 10th of May, 1945, the curtain lifted a little though the war was not yet over.

Just a few days earlier Alan Humphreys, the Associated Press of India's special correspondent in Burma, describing Rangoon at the moment of its recapture, the waterfront "jammed with laughing brown, black, yellow faces," the streets filthy and neglected, had felt able to speculate about Ba Maw's last days in the place but had been careful not to mention Bose.[24] Just a few days *later* Humphreys was telling his readers that Bose too had been in Rangoon. Bose had left the city shortly after Ba Maw did. The men you saw along Dalhousie Street loading refuse into commandeered bullock carts were disarmed soldiers of the Indian National Army. In the interval between filings, the news ban on Jiffs and their leader had been revoked. Reporters could do what they pleased with the war winding down in Burma. And yet it was some time before readers of any of the great English-language dailies knew much about Netaji and the *Azad Hind Fauj*.

This was as true of the Congress leadership as of anybody else—truer, perhaps. Gandhi had been free for a year. But when the 10th of May came around, most of the other Congress leaders, including almost all the members of the Working Committee, were still where the mass arrests of August 1942 had put them. Not until June 15 were they released, and then only because without them the Simla Conference that Wavell had arranged could not be held. When they emerged from their prisons they knew next to nothing about what Subhas Chandra and his people had been doing. And for weeks and weeks thereafter, it might almost be said of them that they went on knowing little and caring less.

As he stepped from the Almora District Jail at eight that June morning, looking the *Hindu* thought "slightly aged" but well and in good humor, Jawaharlal Nehru told the small crowd waiting at the bottom of the steps that in the course of 1,041 days of incarceration (he was precise with the figure) he had quite lost touch with world affairs, as prisoners must. Newspapers had been his only resource, he said. He did not need to explain that prisoners, even political prisoners, were not allowed radios, and that their mail was regularly opened and sometimes withheld. What would happen in India now he did not know. Let there be no shouting of unnecessary slogans. Then he was driven off to his sister's Khali Estate close by, with its spectacular view of Himalayan peaks rising over the intervening Kumaon Hills.[25]

Three days later he was in his home town of Allahabad. Eight days later he was in Bombay. Through the remainder of the hot weather and the onset of the rainy season he was constantly on the move, picking up the threads three years of incarceration had severed. But he did not turn his gaze towards Burma and beyond, nor did the press ask him to.

In Bombay the reporters wanted to know what he thought of India's Communist Party. It had denounced the Quit India resolution even before it was passed, and thereafter supported the British war effort uncritically. Would Jawaharlal forgive it? He would not. In Lahore a month later, where he was met by an enormous crowd which he addressed "perspiring in awful heat," all attention was on the Simla Conference—it had just collapsed over Jinnah's insistence that all five Muslim members of the Viceroy's Council belong to the Muslim League—and both speech and questions were domestic. If asked about Bose, and occasionally he was, Nehru reminded the questioner that in 1942 there had been talk of Bose leading Indians against India side by side with the Japanese. Nehru had said he would fight him if he tried. He was of that conviction still. "Subhas Bose was quite wrong when he thought he could win the freedom of India with the help of the Japanese."[26] As for the Indian National Army, there is no record that he said anything about it at all.

Subsequently Nehru was to say that he had been been worried for some time by the uncertain fate of INA men captured during the fighting in Burma. If he worried now, he kept it to himself. There was little in the papers to draw his attention to the problem. The news releases from Rangoon were mostly about the fighting—in late July the Japanese who had been shouldered aside by 14th Army's dash for Rangoon made desperate efforts to break out across the Sittang—and as Jiff formations had ceased to exist, naturally they were never mentioned. Nor were Bose's broadcast objections to the Simla Conference much publicized. The *Hindu* noted them from time to time, but not directly, only reporting what Domei, the Japanese news agency, said that Bose had said, and never giving them more than a couple of inches. The reality was that the war in Southeast Asia and the Pacific was not over. As long as it continued it held the center of the stage, and kept everything else in the wings. And even now no one expected it to end soon.[27]

&

In Britain, it is true, there was the appearance of change. On the 26th of July Churchill, conceding defeat in the general election, advised the King to ask Attlee to form a government. Early in August Attlee did. But what difference would this make? Partway through his 1,041 days Nehru had relieved himself of surprisingly bitter feelings about the British in general, and the Labour party in particular. "There is an utter lack of decency, almost malice," in the British attitude towards India, he had written in his prison diary. "Often I think of the future—would I like to go to England again?" He would not. "Winston Churchill I consider an honourable enemy. He is implacable, but he obviously has fine qualities," and "one knows where he is. But what is one to do with the humbugs of the British Labour Party?—weak, ineffective, pedestrian and singularly ignorant."[28] The worst was Sir Stafford Cripps. Early in 1942 Sir Stafford had brought Indians an offer, the famous Cripps Offer, of dominion status at the end of the war and participation in an all-India government meanwhile. Subsequent negotiations had failed over defense. The British had insisted that defense remain their responsibility. Cripps had publicly blamed Congress Party for the failure, and Nehru had been furious. Now Cripps was in Attlee's cabinet. What could you expect of him, or of Attlee either?

Three years before it had fallen to Attlee, as Deputy Prime Minister in the coalition government (Churchill was temporarily absent), to chair the cabinet meeting that approved the arrests of 9 August and the proscription of Congress Party. Thereafter Attlee's remarks had dwelled less on the necessity of bringing independence to the subcontinent than on the difficulty of doing so. Now Nehru was suspicious that Labour in office would be no different. It was a suspicion the traditional speech from the throne at the opening of the new

Parliament—the speech the Sovereign delivers but the Prime Minister writes—did nothing to allay.

In this speech Indians looked, of course, for some considerable attention to themselves. Instead they were given, observed the *Hindu*, "a solitary sentence" assuring them that "in accordance with the promises already made to my Indian peoples, my Government will do their utmost to promote in conjunction with the leaders of Indian opinion the early realisation of full self-government in India."[29] *My Indian peoples*. India, then, was not a nation? His Majesty's Government saw only *peoples*?

The *Hindu* might have added that the single sentence came at the end of the speech, as if it were an afterthought, and was enormously overshadowed by remarks about Europe's problems, and by a review in many paragraphs of Labour's plans for the reconstruction of Britain. It might have added that in a brief mention of the newborn United Nations there was no hint that the fifty charter members would be joined soon, or ever, by countries formed through the progressive dismantling of colonial empires; and that the only mention of colonies at all occurred when George VI promised to "press on with the development of my Colonial Empire and the welfare of its peoples."

All these things the *Hindu* might have said, and didn't. It did ask readers to observe that the language of the solitary sentence was almost indistinguishable from the "progressive realisation of responsible government in India as an integral part of the British Empire" that Edwin Montagu had used when, in 1917, he committed Great Britain to India's eventual freedom. Almost thirty years had passed since Montagu rose in the House of Commons and announced the commitment. Had so little happened since that, with modest alterations of form but not substance, the same language could be used again?

If HMG was really keen on giving India her independence, it would have announced a date. But it wasn't. Hence the solitary sentence. What, then, *did* Labour have in mind? At this point the *Hindu* saw, or thought it saw, a cool political calculation.

The Conservatives were bound to oppose Attlee's legislative program, not because they thought it impossibly radical, but because they were determined to show the country that Labour did not have the overwhelming popular mandate it supposed it had. And indeed,

Labour didn't. Though the general election had given it a majority of almost 150 seats in the House of Commons, at the polls it had received only two million more votes than the Conservatives, a margin more than erased by the Liberal vote. Attlee, however, had won control of Parliament. He had won on the basis of his domestic program. He could not allow that program to be scuttled. Neither could he allow the country to suppose that Labour had moved wildly left. He would, therefore, "give battle on the field of domestic problems" while simultaneously demonstrating that "in the realm of colonial and foreign policy Labour . . . [is] more conservative than the Conservatives themselves."

This is how the *Hindu* regarded Labour. Freshly elected, secure in his command of Parliament, Attlee could if he wished treat India much as the Tories had treated her—and the *Hindu* was afraid that for reasons of domestic political expediency he might. The *Hindu* was not alone in thinking so. Nehru thought so too. Imagine, then, the war drifting on and on, with Congress party ever banned and politics impossible. It was a gloomy prospect. But the war, of course, did not.

⁂

The end, by sheer coincidence, came on the day Parliament opened. In the early hours of August 15, 1945, Attlee announced Japan's surrender over the BBC. Later that morning the King and Queen drove to the House of Lords to do the necessary, a part of which was the speech, and enormous crowds cheered as they passed. But the cheers were as much for the war's close (in one form or another it had lasted six years) as for the royal persons. In India there were not even cheers.

Lord Wavell broadcast a properly viceregal victory address complete with the inevitable (and in this case cryptic) "our real tasks are still ahead." Provincial governments declared holidays, two days in most places, three in Sind. "A wave of joy" swept Calcutta, the press said, but the joyful were mostly British and American servicemen eager to go home—Calcutta was the biggest leave and transit center in Mountbatten's command. Perhaps the city's underclass was briefly happy too, for on the coming Monday, rumor had it, food would be distributed to the poor. Otherwise it was hard to see what Japan's surrender could do for ordinary Indians, or be much noticed by them, unless they were moved by independence fever. Then they might notice, as the educated and politically sophisticated quickly did, that Japan's surrender precipitated things—things that quite early broke the political paralysis, and within months made independence a near, perhaps even immediate, prospect. Four things that transformed the landscape. The first of these was Subhas Chandra Bose's death on the 18th of the month.

It passed unnoticed for several days because the Japanese, in their confusion, did not at once announce it. Not until the 23rd of August did Domei broadcast the news that Bose had been killed in a plane crash. Picked up instantly, it created a stir right across the subcontinent. Schools closed, markets shut, in Bombay the cotton mills stopped working, in Ahmedabad there was a general *hartal*. At his prison quarters at Coonoor in the Nilgiri Hills, the last in a succession of prisons in which he had been confined since December 1941, Subhas Chandra's brother Sarat read about it in the *Hindu* and was devastated. Several nights before he had dreamt he saw Subhas. He was "very tall in stature. I jumped up to see his face." But before Sarat could move the figure disappeared. To a daughter he wrote at once about his agony—and her's, for he knew how fond of their uncle the children were. "How shall I console you all, how shall I console myself?" It comforted him a little to learn from the papers that "colleagues who had insulted him by their malevolence" were saying nice things about his brother now.[30]

Indeed they were. Though privately the members of the Congress High Command must have felt that in the matter of insults Bose had little to learn from anyone—over Singapore radio they had been called "Gandhi flunkeys" and much else—the news of his death gave them the opportunity to rearrange their feelings, and to speak about him in death as they had not been able to bring themselves to speak while he was living.

Gandhi contented himself with a gesture. When the news reached him at Poona, he had his volunteers omit the usual raising of the Congress flag at evening prayers. Vallabhbhai Patel, too, was at Poona. Though he believed it had been "a grievous mistake" to enlist Japan in India's struggle, he did not doubt that Bose had been moved "by the highest impulse of patriotism coupled with a sense of frustration." A thousand miles to the north, at the little hill station of Abbottabad,

Nehru, looking genuinely moved, told a public meeting that the dreadful news brought back fond memories of the days when he and Subhas had worked together. But it fell to Sarojini Naidu to put the nation's grief most forcefully. "To myriads of men and women," she wrote, "his death . . . is a deep personal bereavement." Those who, like herself, deplored his decision to seek the aid of foreign powers, nevertheless understood what had driven him to do so. "His proud, importunate and violent spirit was a flaming sword forever unsheathed in defence of the land he worshipped with such surpassing devotion. A greater love hath not man than this, that he lay down his life for his country and his people."[31]

The British reacted rather differently. Wavell was relieved. Bose alive would have presented "a most difficult problem." What on earth could one *do* with him?[32] It was a question the Viceroy had put to Sir Francis Mudie at the Home Department (India) at a time when Bose was *not* dead and no one expected him to be.

This was in the middle of August. Wavell was about to fly to London for talks. The *Hindu* had been mistaken when it read total inaction into the speech from the throne. Attlee was determined to resume the movement towards Indian self-government. His biographer believes his selection of Pethick-Lawrence, who was old, amiable, and did not rub Indians the wrong way, as the new Secretary of State for India, was intended as "a clear signal that he meant business" in this regard.[33] And Wavell himself, though distrustful of Attlee's judgment, was happy to have at 10 Downing Street a man who did not subject you as Churchill did to "diatribes" the moment India was mentioned, but took the matter seriously.[34]

It had for some time been generally understood that the resumption of normal political life in the subcontinent could not be postponed indefinitely. Japan's abrupt surrender forced the issue by depriving New Delhi of postponement's rationale—which, of course, was the war. So on the 21st of August, three days before he left for London (but with London's approval), Wavell gave public notice that come the cold weather there would be elections to the Central and Provincial legislatures, the first since 1937. And on the 22nd, it being obvious that you cannot have a soccer match if the players are unable to reach the field, he pronounced Congress Party's proscription over. That gave the party several months in which to collect its workers, reopen its offices, and campaign. What, meanwhile, should be done with Subhas Chandra were he to be captured?

Mudie's reply, transmitted actually the day India learned that Bose was dead, had not been encouraging.[35] The Bengali's influence over the INA was substantial, he wrote. "It affects all races, castes and communities." Men admired him for organizing India's first "National Army," and for so conducting himself and it that the Japanese had been forced to treat the Indians as allies. In the eyes of many he stood on a level with Gandhi. What to do with him? Half a dozen possibilities occurred to Sir Francis, none of them satisfactory. If Bose were returned for trial, he could not be hanged. "The pressure for his release would be too great" and the trial itself would give him enormous publicity. They might try him in Burma or Malaya; they might intern him in some distant place, the Seychelles perhaps; they might "leave him where he is, and don't ask for his surrender." Mudie had been happy with none of these. So it pleased Wavell immensely to discover, when he reached London on August 26, that the problem had been solved by an overloaded Japanese bomber on a distant Formosan airfield.

Congress leaders, too, must have been relieved. They too must have asked themselves how should they handle Subhas Chandra when he reappeared, behind bars of course, nevertheless alive—and bursting with reproaches. But *dead*? Dead he was no longer a loose cannon on the ship of independence politics. Dead he was simply the martyred leader of an army of freedom fighters whose existence, now that the censor could no longer conceal it, was beginning to be known. Forget that both leader and army had stooped to most un-Gandhian violence. That could be dealt with later. At the moment leader and army made a formidable stick with which to beat the British. What would catch India's attention more quickly, and rivet it more fully upon the independence struggle, than the Indian National Army living coupled with Subhas Chandra Bose dead?

If New Delhi had seen what was coming, it might have tried to ditch Netaji's jawans on the far side of the Burmese border. It might have plain abandoned them there. One can imagine a Mudie telegram to Kitson, Gracey, and the others advising "don't ask for their surrender," and one can imagine Gracey in particular taking the advice.

But the reestablished Government of Burma would have protested such a maneuver (Dorman-Smith could hardly have fancied Jiffs mingling with Aung San's people). Indian families anxious to recover their sons would have been wildly indignant. It would have made nonsense of the careful sorting into whites, greys, and blacks. And anyway, New Delhi did not see.

The movement of Netaji's men to India had begun long before Japan's surrender—a trickle in 1943, more than a trickle after Imphal. 14th Army's thrust down the great central valley, by scooping up entire INA battalions and depositing them at the port of Rangoon, had made shipping hundreds possible. By early July of 1945, half a dozen shiploads had already gone. When Japan surrendered, the Government of India had no option but to bring home the rest. So as the rains petered out and the cool weather approached, large bodies of Jiffs reached Chittagong and Calcutta by sea and and were carried thence to places all over north India. To Jhingergacha of course, and Nilganj (which is also near Calcutta). To Kirkee outside Poona, and Bahadurgarh close to Delhi. To Attock on the Indus two hundred miles northwest of Lahore, Multan on the Chenab two hundred miles southwest, Delhi itself (men likely to be tried or whose testimony might be needed were collected at the Red Fort), and other places, some named in the newspapers and some not—for the government never published a list.

With the exception of the camp at Bahadurgarh, which received blacks from Bose's German-sponsored Indian Legion (called Hiffs, of course), none were opened especially for the purpose. They were places where buildings or tents were available (district jails were sometimes used), and whose location bore some correspondence to the parts of India to which men would be released. For men *were* released, whites quickly, greys slowly, blacks not at all at first (though this would change). Here, too, the government was niggardly with information, and the figures the daily press picked up from press communiqués not always consistent. Nevertheless it is probably safe to say that by early September, some 7,000 Jiffs had reached India. By early November, the figure had risen to 12,000. Of these perhaps 3,000 had been allowed to rejoin their families. By December releases were averaging more than 600 a week.

Bose's fiery death had been the first thing Japan's sudden surrender precipitated. The call for elections and the lifting of Congress Party's proscription had been the second. The return of numbers of INA men and their dispersal across India were the third. It was left to the Red Fort trials to make the fourth.

CHAPTER 19

Auchinleck's Dilemma

Trials, too, had begun long before the surrender, though at the time the public was hardly aware that they had. In February 1946 Philip Mason, Joint Secretary to the War Department (India), told the newly elected and just convened Central Legislative Assembly that more than a score of men had been seized, tried by courts-martial, and sentenced *before* Rangoon was recovered. Nine, all deserters from Indian Army units in Burma, had been hanged. Exactly where and when they had been caught Mason did not say. Nor did he confirm the rumor, later known to be true, that a number of special agents dropped in India by plane or submarine had been summarily tried and hanged too. He was silent about these things, having made his point, which was that in wartime the capture and execution of spies and traitors "was an operational necessity."[1]

But now that the war was over, could not the whole dreary business be abandoned, and Jiffs set free the moment they stepped on Indian soil? Wasn't there precedent for this in the way the Burma National Army had been handled? *They* had been forgiven their transgressions. No penalties had been imposed on *them*. "Would it not be difficult to treat members of the Indian National Army who claimed to have been fighting on behalf of India, on a different basis?"

The question was asked and the suggestion made in London, at a meeting of the India and Burma Committee of the cabinet on the 17th of August, and Attlee, who chaired the committee himself, promptly knocked it on the head. Aung San and his men, he pointed out, "on finding that the Japanese were not, as they had at first thought, their deliverers, had got in touch with our military authorities and had been fighting on our side. That was quite different from the I.N.A."[2] This was true. It *had* been different. As soon as Aung San was sure Slim was winning, he had brought his battalions over. But how could the *Azad Hind Fauj* have done likewise? It wasn't Burma that Bose's army fought to free, it was India—which the Japanese did not occupy but which the British did. In such circumstances the Indian National Army could not possibly have joined Slim's 14th Army, and Attlee knew it.

Later in the same August meeting Attlee touched lightly upon the real reason why His Majesty's Government could not forgive the INA. A "general issue of principle" forbade it. Nothing could be worse for India and the Indian Army "than to let the impression grow that rebellion was an easy thing that need not be taken too seriously." That was all, Attlee did not elaborate, but if the committee had asked, the Prime Minister, with loyalty and disloyalty much on his mind, might have said something like this.

He might have invited the Committee to place Aung San beside almost any INA officer. Study them both, he might have said. Notice that both took up arms against the Raj. But one had accepted the King-Emperor's commission, while the other had not. Doesn't that make a difference?

Read the King-Emperor's commission. "George VI by the Grace of God, of Great Britain, Ireland and the British Dominions beyond the Seas, King, Defender of the Faith, Emperor of India," Prem's begins (Prem showed it to me once, a piece of parchment roughly twelve inches by fifteen slightly yellowed by age). "To Our trusty and well beloved Prem Kumar Sahgal, Greeting. We reposing especial Trust and Confidence in your Loyalty, Courage, and good Conduct, do by these Presents Constitute and Appoint you to be an Officer in Our Indian Land Forces. . . ."—and so on right through to the signature, appended at Simla (in peacetime the Government of India moved there during the hot season) on the 25th of June, 1939.[3] Our trusty and well beloved Prem Kumar Sahgal! In the end Prem had turned out to be faithless. But Aung San had not. No especial trust and confidence having been reposed in him, there was nothing he could be discovered to have been unfaithful to.

Juxtapose them once more, asking which of the two served the Raj longest and best? The answer, of course, must be Sahgal. Commissioned early in 1939, sent with his battalion to Malaya a year and a half later, commanding one company and sometimes two in often fierce fighting the length of the peninsula—Prem Sahgal served the Raj well. And since the Indian National Army clothed and armed itself with what it possessed when Singapore fell, it is a matter of record that from 1939 to the time he surrendered on the banks of the Irrawaddy, Sahgal never took the King-Emperor's uniform off. Aung San, on the other hand, never put it on. The disloyalty of the one was transparent—it fairly shouted at you. The disloyalty of the other, dressed as he was in the enemy's uniform, was not.

So there was no serious thought, at least at cabinet level, of forgetting who the renegades were and what they had done. The suggestion that they be treated like the Burmese died stillborn. And even less, to judge from Philip Mason's recollection of what he and others felt, was it entertained in New Delhi

Mason had been in India for more than fifteen years. He was of that class of Indian Civil Service officer who, though doing his share of district work, is also posted frequently to New Delhi, and can expect someday to be the governor of a province or, like Mudie, a member of the Viceroy's Council. Early in the war Mason had been made deputy secretary in the War Department. When Mountbatten became Supreme Allied Commander South-East Asia, and set up his headquarters at Kandy in the highlands of Ceylon, Mason went there to attend the planning sessions with which such headquarters abound, follow what was said and decided, and compose the daily minutes. Later he was brought back to Delhi and made joint secretary. On the staff ladder that put him only one rung below the secretary proper. In this capacity he was present at General Sir Claude Auchinleck's staff meetings, and did what he had done at Kandy. And because the secretary happened to be new to the War Department, far from familiar with its business, and wise enough to know it, Mason also drafted War Department communiqués and spoke generally for the department. So Mason was privy to what was thought and said about the returning Jiffs. He knew Auchinleck's mind in the matter. He had to. He couldn't have represented him to the Indian public if he hadn't.

Auchinleck wore two hats. He was the Member for War in the Viceroy's Council, and he was Commander-in-Chief. He had been C.-in-C. some years before, during those months in late 1940 and early

1941 when Wavell, commanding forces of almost unimaginable smallness against the Italians in East Africa and Libya, was giving England her
first ground victories of the war. Compelled to send part of his little
army to Greece, where it was lost, Wavell was unable to prevent
Rommel and the newly landed Afrika Corps from recovering all that
the Italians had given up along the North African coast; with the
consequence that Churchill, who sacked commanders with a readiness
that even Hitler thought extreme, sent him to Delhi to take Auchinleck's
place, and brought Auchinleck to Cairo to take his.

This was in July 1941. Thirteen months later, after several dramatic
shifts of fortune, the Germans once more stood on Egypt's border—
and once again the Prime Minister intervened, dismissing Auchinleck
and giving 8th Army to Montgomery. Meanwhile Wavell, by a turn of
events no one could have anticipated, found himself responsible for
defending Malaya, then Burma, against the Japanese. Both campaigns
went miserably, of course. And when they were followed by Eastern
Army's failure in the Arakan, an angry Churchill ordered Auchinleck to
India to command the Indian Army again. Wavell had hoped for the
South-East Asia Command. He was made Viceroy of India instead. That
meant minding the store in Delhi. And since, on Mountbatten's arrival,
the C.-in-C. India no longer directed India's armed forces in the field
but simply armed and trained them, Auchinleck in effect was asked to
stay behind and mind the store too.

Both Wavell and Auchinleck, then, were disappointed men, professional soldiers who had been passed over. In Wavell's case this was
particularly the case, for the post of viceroy carried no direct military
responsibilities; until now it had always been occupied by a civilian.
Nevertheless both men brought to their work energy, good humor,
and—with respect to India's future—a broadmindedness far greater
than either Linlithgow or Churchill possessed. Mason knew Wavell
well, so well that shortly before Wavell retired he made the Masons'
small son George a page at his daughter Felicity's wedding. Mason
knew Auchinleck even better because, as I have said, as joint secretary
he attended not only the formal discussions at which the Home
Member and others of his rank were present, but the C.-in-C.'s daily
ten o'clock staff meetings as well. At these "morning prayers" what to
do with the Jiffs was frequently discussed. And if Mason was well placed

to discover what Auchinleck thought on the matter, he was well placed, too, to hear what younger men were thinking, and to detect a contrary view if one existed.

For he was of an age with those "junior staff officers" whom Colonel Wren had introduced into his remarkable memorandum of three years before—men who had wanted to "get ahead of events, ride the storm rather than be submerged by it," men who had tried to anticipate ICO expectations and been unable to. If the question "shall we court-martial these Jiffs or release them?" called in anyone's mind for just such a getting-ahead-of-events response, Mason was likely to hear of it. If there were men of his age in the Army or the services who believed that it would be unwise to put the Zaman Kianis, Prem Sahgals, and Mahboob Ahmeds into the dock now that the war was over and self-government close, Mason was likely to catch wind of it. I knew that Mason had never expected, let alone wished, the Empire to continue forever. When asked at his ICS interview why he wanted to join the Service, he had replied that he hoped to participate in the process by which political power had been successfully devolved to Canada, Australia, and New Zealand. It was India's turn, he had said. And he had been lucky. "It was just the right thing," he remarks in his autobiography, "to say to that board of interviewers at that moment."

For this reason he never expected to become governor of a province or a member of the Viceroy's Council. He would not be in India long enough; the Empire would end, and with it the Service; he would go back to England and make a second life writing—which is exactly what he did.[4] I knew that Mason had attended innumerable meetings at which Jiffs had been discussed. It seemed to me that if anyone could explain how the trials came to be and why they took the course they took, it would be him; and that if any of the actors had toyed with the idea of not proceeding against the INA, he would have known—it was, after all, entirely possible that at the time his own thoughts traveled that road. So I wrote him and asked, "did such an idea cross your mind or anyone else's?" not putting the question directly, but leaving it implicit in a more general inquiry. And the answer, essentially, was that it had not.

Mason had believed, as Auchinleck (he assured me) had believed, that nothing should be allowed to undermine the principle that a soldier must remain true to his oath. He could not be sure, he wrote, how he would have behaved had he faced the choice Prem Sahgal and others faced when Singapore fell and an alternative loyalty was offered. It would have been difficult. But these young men had accepted the King-Emperor's commission. "I remember at the time recalling a story which had impressed me as a boy," he continued, "a story about a young officer who was captured by Muslims and ordered to renounce Christianity and adopt Islam, or face death. He was an agnostic, but was not prepared to give up outward allegiance to the faith he had ceased to believe in, and so he was killed." Thus would Philip Mason have behaved had he been in that predicament, he clearly hoped. Thus should Prem have, was the implication.[5]

And in a later letter Mason reached the same position by another road. I had asked him whether he knew Lakshmi's mother.

> Yes, I remember Ammu Swaminadhan very well. She wanted to get her daughter out of an internment camp in Burma, and I promised to make enquiries. I found that it was really only the force of inertia which prevented military intelligence from letting her daughter go, and I persuaded them to release her. I remember going to the Assembly to tell her that I had arranged this. I remember also that I said, thinking of my military friends: "Some people would say I was very weak about this." To which she replied: "That is not being weak, it is only being nice."
>
> She asked me to tea to meet her daughter, which I gladly accepted, but then discovered that I was also to meet one of the three accused in the first trial, and that I did not think I ought to do. I was perfectly prepared to shake hands with any Congressman who had honestly differed from us, but not with a soldier who had broken his oath of allegiance when in difficulties.[6]

If the likes of Philip Mason could not bring himself to shake hands with a Prem Sahgal in March, there can hardly have been a British man or woman anywhere about Delhi the preceding August who felt that the slate should be wiped clean. There *had* to be trials. And on Monday the 27th of August, 1945, in a press communiqué Mason himself drew up, the Government of India said there would be. Though most returning Jiffs would, in the spirit of mercy and generosity, gradually be released, "the leaders and those guilty of particularly heinous crimes" would be brought before courts-martial for all Indians to see.

༄

Nehru was quick to react. "The veil has at last been lifted," he told reporters next day. Soon the public would learn how the Indian National Army had been formed and grew, how many of its men were presently being held "in the various forts, camps and prisons of India," how many were to be charged and tried.[7]

It would not learn these things from the Government of India. Governments usually refuse information of this sort, and the GOI was no exception. But Congress Party was another matter. It was sure to show interest in the fate of these men as soon as it could pull itself out of the ditch into which the Quit India crackdown had flung it, and as August gave way to September it hurried to do just that.

District offices padlocked for three years were recovered. Arriving to reopen his, the Secretary of the Allahabad District Congress Committee found its contents "a sickening and disgusting sight. . . . Ninety per cent of the papers, files, writing pads, receipt books, pamphlets and other literature, were in such a condition as to be unrecognisable and useless for all practical purposes, mostly eaten by white ants."[8] Censorship ceased. Provincial Congress Committees reappeared. Though the ban on Subhas Chandra's Forward Bloc still held, on the 14th of September Sarat Bose, who had supported it but never formally belonged, was set free. Days later his son Sisir and two nephews were released. Calcutta gave them a tumultuous welcome. Tired, ill, much depressed by the reported death of his brother, Sarat declined to say anything about the freedom army. But that would not last.

Indeed, when the more than two hundred members of the All-India Congress Committee assembled in Bombay on the afternoon of September 21, he was there. The place was the same Gowalia Tank Maidan, in the shadow of the five Parsi towers of silence at the north end of Malabar Hill, where on an August evening thirty-seven months before this same AICC had demanded of the British that they pack their bags and go. The choice of site was deliberate. Politics must resume where it had left off. Azad once more presided. Gandhi was

present, though he was visibly less vigorous and his influence perceptibly less. "After more than three years of wanton suppression by the
British Government," a resolution prepared by the Working Committee began, "the A.I.C.C. desires to convey its greetings and congratulations to the nation for the courage and endurance with which it
withstood the fierce and violent onslaught of the British power, and its
deep sympathy to all those who suffered during these years of military,
police and ordinance rule."[9] Sarat was among those who had suffered.
He showed himself, and was wildly cheered by thirty thousand people
jammed into the huge, overpowering pandal (its main entrance was
modeled on the Sanchi Stupa), and by many more outside. The
Congress, it was clear, was not going to let India forget 1942. Hundreds
jailed that distant August were still behind bars.

Though the Indian National Army received less attention, it was far
from ignored. On reaching Bombay, Sarat had made a point of telling
the press that it was shameful to allege, as some did, that INA men had
toadied to the Japanese. Quite the opposite, when necessary they had
resisted them with great stubborness. For this and much else they
deserved their country's gratitude, yet many of them faced indefinite
imprisonment or worse. "Not a hair on the heads of the brave soldiers
of Indian freedom must be touched," he had said.[10] Now, on the last
day of the AICC meeting, Nehru moved a resolution that put Congress
Party squarely behind their instant release—or almost squarely: in one
respect Nehru hedged. It would be tragic, the resolution ran, if these
men were to be punished "for having laboured, however mistakenly, for
the freedom of India."[11] Someone spotted the "however mistakenly,"
and there was an amendment to delete. Would Pandit Nehru accept it?
He would not. But at the same session he announced something of
such importance to the prisoners at the Red Fort that his refusal was
hardly noticed. The Congress, he announced, would make itself
responsible for their defense.

Who else could possibly help these men? Netaji was dead. His
principal lieutenants were still in distant parts—Bhonsle in Bangkok,
Zaman Kiani in Singapore, Chatterji somewhere in French Indochina,
Ayer in Japan—and it would be months before they reached India. Had
they been in Delhi they could not have done much anyway, because

they would have been behind bars themselves. The only INA men who were free to come and go were simple jawans, whites released because they were sheep; and sheep do not hire lawyers or manage court proceedings. But the Congress could, and from it might draw political advantage. In mid-October, therefore, the Viceroy was formally advised that if the INA trials were not abandoned or at least postponed until after the elections, the Indian Army's prosecuting counsel would face a Defence Committee of the Congress.

It was for the moment a committee of seven, and several of the seven had names calculated to catch the public's eye. There was Sir Tej Bahadur Sapru, for the past quarter century a leading figure in moderate nationalist politics. There was K. N. Katju, a dozen years Sapru's junior but like him a star of the Allahabad bar; Jawaharlal Nehru, ready to put on a barrister's robes again after a lapse of almost twenty years; and Asaf Ali, a Muslim barrister from Delhi who, like Nehru, was a member of the Working Committee, and whose wife, the much younger Aruna Asaf Ali, had gone underground (the reader may remember) at the time of the Quit India sweep and was still gloriously at large. Committee offices were opened at No. 82 Daryaganj, just south of the Red Fort. Preparatory work for the trials could best be done there. And while this began, work of another sort came No. 82's way, work the Defence Committee did not expect; work that was, nevertheless, of great comfort and use to many INA families. It was to No. 82 Daryaganj that families whose men had been shipped to Malaya appealed if there had been no word from these men (or of them) since Percival's surrender, and if they were not among those returning now from the Japanese POW camps.

In 1942, when Malaya fell, some 55,000 Indians had passed into those camps. Through third parties the Japanese ought to have given New Delhi their names. After much prodding they had done so for the British and Australians prisoners, but they had not done so for the Indians—they had furnished no lists of them. And though field interrogation of recovered jawans, together with the interception at Indian ports of postcards sent from the POW camps, had enabled the War Department to track down many missing units, and on that basis assure many next of kin that their men were probably alive somewhere, to others it had been unable to say anything. "We are still without any information concerning 22,000," it had admitted early in 1945.[12] Families had had to be content with silence.

Now, however, with the war over and Indians returning by the shipload, finding the missing 22,000 suddenly seemed possible. Many *must* have accompanied Netaji to Burma. Many of these must have survived. So families whose men were still missing might conceivably find them if they searched Jhingergacha, Kirkee, Multan, and the other INA detention camps. But of course they couldn't, they couldn't actually search, they could only hope to be told. And if the Army did notify a Jiff's relatives that their man had reached India, it took its time about it, did not say whether he was white, grey, or black, did not say whether he was being considered for prosecution; did not even say to what camp he had been sent. What was more, until he reached India the Army said nothing at all—which, of course, allowed family to suppose that he was not even alive.

So when word got around that there were people trying to help Subhas Chandra's men, the predictable occurred. "Anxious enquiries from near relatives of the I.N.A. men are pouring into the office of the I.N.A. Defence Committee," the *Hindu* noted on October 25. One day later it had figures. Several *thousand* letters had already been received. Intelligence, which kept its ear to the ground as much now as ever, was alarmed. People were asking not only where were their men but whether the committee would defend them, and the committee seemed disposed to oblige. "There is little doubt," it warned, "that this is drawing numbers of hitherto loyal families into the Congress net."[13]

To handle the flood, an INA Enquiry Committee (later it would become the INA *Relief* and Enquiry Committee) appeared alongside the Defence Committee, while a third, a Funds Committee, raised money for the other two. It did not confine its canvassing to Delhi. Branches in other cities and towns added to the take. At Calcutta the movie houses donated one day's box office receipts. At Cuttack a benefit soccer match promised a handsome yield until the district magistrate, no friend to Jiffs or Subhas Chandra either, appeared suddenly and forbade the use of the field. In Bombay the local funds committee, which the mayor himself chaired, raised 15,000 rupees in the course of three weeks. At Lucknow Nehru personally auctioned oil paintings donated for the purpose, and collected 1,200 in one afternoon. In this way the Indian National Congress bound itself ever more closely to the uncertain fate of the rebel Bengali's defeated and caged men.

⁓✿⁓

Officially, it is true, the Congress continued to be neutral on the question, "should the Indian National Army have attempted what it attempted, should it have done what it did?" Election campaign literature did not mention Bose. It reaffirmed the party's commitment to nonviolence. As for independence, it simply repeated the Quit India resolution of three years before. The British, it said, must pack up and depart.

There was nothing neutral, however, about what party members did on the hustings. Though the speech with which Sarojini Naidu opened the Punjab campaign mentioned neither Netaji nor his army, she was well aware that as she spoke, young men and women wearing "Save the INA" badges moved through the audience obtaining signatures to a memorial that urged the Viceroy to abandon the trials. And she knew perfectly well that it was the Provincial Congress Committee that had framed it. Nehru was more forthright. Stepping from the Almora District Jail that distant June morning, he had asked that there be no shouting of unnecessary slogans. It was as if he had anticipated and wished to arm himself against mindless popular enthusiasms. Yet by late October he was urging every crowd he addressed to cry "Jai Hind" and "Chalo Delhi." He met some INA men and was impressed. "They are brave, stout-hearted and capable, and very politically minded," he wrote his close friend Krishna Menon. When in due course they passed into civilian life, "these thousands spreading out all over the country will make a difference, perhaps a great difference, for they are as hard as nails, very anti-British." His interest in them grew steadily. A day would come when, unhappy at the way a young man at a Patna election rally rendered the INA marching song, he would rise, seize the microphone, and sing it himself.[14]

His eye on the future and the realities thereof, Auchinleck unveiled a scheme for the complete Indianization of the Indian Army. Asked how long it would take, he said he wasn't sure, it would depend on how rapidly Indian youths came forward for officer training. A few days later Sardar Vallabhbhai Patel publicly mocked him. The general, he said, cannot tell us how long his scheme will take. "Does he not know that Mr. Subhas Chandra Bose organised an army of 60,000 and a women's brigade in under a year? It is this very army the British Government is trying to disband now." If the British were serious about giving India her independence, why did they not make the Indian *National* Army the nucleus of the army to be?[15]

This was disingenuous of the sardar. When after some months it began to look as if the British might be serious, the suggestion was not repeated. At the moment, however, it was politically effective, and so were warm references to Bose's men no matter what the context. "At most of the 160 political meetings held in the Central Provinces during the first half of October," observed the Director of the Intelligence Bureau in a confidential note to the Home Department, "demands were made for the abandonment of action against the I.N.A." It was the same in other provinces. Politicians found that if they wanted to hold a crowd, they had "to speak of the I.N.A. in appreciative terms."[16]

Gandhi joined the chorus. In late October, from the nature–cure clinic in Poona where he spent much of his time, he sent Wavell a short note "in fear and trembling, lest I may be overstepping my limit." He had been watching the preparations for the trials, he wrote. Though not at one with those who would resort to arms even in self-defense, he could not be blind to the courage and patriotism often displayed by persons who did, "as seems to be the case here." Could the Viceroy afford to ignore what Indians were thinking?

> India adores these men. . . . No doubt the Government have overwhelming might on their side. But it will be a misuse of that power if it is used in the teeth of universal Indian opposition.[17]

The note ended as self-deprecatingly as it had begun. It was not for him to say what the government should do. But the humility, as usual, was deceptive. Gandhi knew exactly what the Viceroy should do, he should cancel the trials and release the men.

But Wavell wasn't listening. Publicly he remained composed and calm. The Red Fort trials, like the political agenda—first elections to the Central Legislative Assembly, next provincial elections, then responsible ministries in the provinces, finally a constituent assembly to give self-governing India a constitution—must follow a settled, measured course. The Government of India would not be hurried. And no one watching the Viceroy on state occasions can have supposed it was likely to be. Addressing over a thousand spectacularly costumed guests at a durbar in Rawalpindi, he spoke only of his first visit to the place as a young subaltern thirty-eight years before, of the Indian Army's magnificent performance in the Middle East and Burma, of the Punjab's glorious reputation as the sword-arm of India. Nothing even faintly political passed his lips. In princely gatherings like this, of course, things political rarely did.

Privately, however, he was anxious. It was bad enough that Congress Party spoke warmly of these returning INA men, engaged lawyers to defend them, raised crowds to a frenzy by demanding their release. It would be worse if the men themselves refused to recognize what they had done, refused even to recognize that they had been beaten—and tried, perhaps, to resume the "march on Delhi" that their leader had made such a noise about.

Midway through the previous July, an officer who had mixed for some time with the four thousand or so INA men awaiting transport from Rangoon had submitted to intelligence, "as an instance of the degree to which Bose has taken possession of their minds," the case of a jawan who fell silent when his interrogator attempted to belittle that leader. He did not argue, this jawan. He simply stopped talking. It was his way of saying "you do not understand." The same officer, happening to chat one day with an INA man who, he knew, was carried in the Indian Army List as a captain, could hardly contain his astonishment when a soldier came up and addressed the fellow as "Colonel Sahib." How could you possibly allow yourself to be called by what you so obviously are not? he demanded, expecting at least a flustered look. But the Jiff was entirely unruffled. "I do not care what you think my rank is," he said. "To my men I am a colonel." His listener had to admit that to his men he certainly was.[18]

Bose, this officer warned, had filled his men with an ineradicable sense of mission. Defeated, dispersed, captured, they nevertheless remained so bitten by the independence bug as to be beyond rehabilitation. And the Viceroy had believed him. "This is the first occasion," he had written Pethick-Lawrence in August, "on which an anti-British politician has acquired a hold over a substantial number of men in the Indian Army, and the consequences are quite incalculable."[19] Now, in October, he did not require an intelligence briefing, he had only to read the daily papers, to discover that INA men were being welcomed by the Congress everywhere—at party rallies, party offices, in the homes of party leaders. Sixty Jiffs set free at Abbottabad, a news clipping told him, reached Lahore and were tendered a public reception by the local Congress committee before the district magistrate even realized they were in the city. An INA lieutenant who hurried to Allahabad after he was released from the Jubbulpore camp, stayed not with his own people but went directly to Anand Bhawan, the Nehru family home. Wavell found such associations disturbing—particularly the last.

In private Nehru could be quite reasonable. His public addresses, however, were something else. They were violent, and their violence threatened to make the peaceful pursuit of constitutional change impossible. Day by day the situation looked uglier. Before long the government might face disturbances on the scale of Quit India, with this difference: in 1942 a fair number of British battalions had been available for their suppression. Now the pressure for demobilization meant that with every passing month British battalions became fewer and fewer. The slack would have to be taken up by the Indian Army, parts of which had to be kept east of Calcutta to reoccupy Britain's colonial possessions and help the Dutch recover theirs. And the Indian Army was demobilizing too. What if it proved unequal to the task?

Almost three years before, at the time of the first Arakan campaign, GHQ had seen, or thought it saw, evidence that Congressmen, though shaken and left leaderless by the Quit India crackdown, were working with some success to undermine the fidelity of the Indian Army. It was apparent from the state of mind of drafts coming up to the fighting battalions. It helped explain the steady dribble of desertions. Later the campaign in Burma had gone so well, and the morale of the jawan had risen so high, that Headquarters had stopped worrying. But the war was over now, memories of the triumphal rush to Rangoon fading, demobilization in full swing. The Congress, fully legal once more and more bumptious than ever, rummaged openly for weapons to use against the Raj. That it would attempt once again the subversion of the armed forces seemed only too probable.

It would use Jiffs, intelligence believed. It would try to use Jiffs in other capacities, so why not in this as well. "Some people believe," Wavell wrote Pethick-Lawrence early in October, "that Nehru's plan is to make use of the I.N.A.—large quantities of arms are said to have been smuggled into India from the Burma front—both to train Congress volunteers and as a Congress striking force." *And*, he added, "to tamper with the Indian Army."[20] Two weeks passed and he raised the subject again. "This effort of Congress to suborn the Army," he wrote Pethick-Lawrence, "is likely to be the most dangerous development of the near future."[21] He had been told that it was the party's ambition to give jawans the vote and draw them into politics.

This was an alarming thought. But there was another side to Indian National Army men, the Viceroy reminded himself, the ugly side, the side loyal jawans had been kept informed of by their company-grade officers, in josh groups and out, and that returning prisoners of war— so often its victims—would be glad to talk about. Brutality in the service of the Japanese was the stock in trade of the committed Jiff, Wavell believed. He, personally, needed no instruction in that proposition, and he was heartened to discover that men returning from the Malayan prisoner-of-war camps seemed to need no instruction in it either.

At Dehra Dun one late September day he had inspected two Gurkha battalions just in from those camps. The men, he had been told by their officers, were "far more bitter about the I.N.A. than about the Japs," and looked for "stern justice" upon the former. Auchinleck had subsequently assured him that "this feeling is universal among the returned P.O.W., and that there are some very ugly cases to come for trial of torture and murder of loyal soldiers by the renegades."[22] Auchinleck had said this early in October. A few days later, at the final session of the National Defence Council, several Indian officers— among them Brigadier Thimayya, back from Singapore and soon to go to Japan to command the Indian Army's contribution to the Allied occupation force—had described at length their experiences in Burma and Malaya, and one, a major from the Hyderabad Regiment who had spent three and a half years in a Malayan POW camp, "sang a hymn of hate against the I.N.A." What the politicians and the press were saying about it, he protested, simply wasn't true. The joiners had joined "not from patriotic motives but because they were too weak or cowardly to stand up to their persecutors." The Council had listened intently. What the major said appeared to shock the members, and it occurred to Wavell that "when the courts-martial begin, other people may be shocked too."[23]

It was a pity they could not begin at once.

"I read the other day," Wavell wrote Pethick-Lawrence, "the summary of evidence against a Muslim officer who is charged among other things with having caused the death of a soldier serving under him in the I.N.A." The officer was Burhan-ud-Din, one of the three ICOs with the 2/10th Baluch (Prem and K. P. "Thimmy" Thimayya were the others) when Singapore surrendered. Early in 1944 Burhan-ud-Din had commanded a detachment of the Bahadur Group just outside Rangoon. The detachment had given him trouble. Men slipped into town without leave, looking for women. This had gone on for some time. And when at last five went missing in as many days, Burhan-ud-Din lost his temper, took out a search party, found all five, marched them back to the camp, and on the 5th of February, two days after Shah Nawaz left Rangoon for the north with Subhas Brigade, subjected them to as truly exemplary a punishment as any Captain Bligh might have contrived.

On an open space in one part of the camp stood two trees about twenty feet apart. Between these trees at a height of nine feet a stout rope was stretched, and under the rope a table was placed. The detachment paraded. The five were brought forward. They had not been tried. They had not been told what was going to happen to them. Burhan-ud-Din simply announced that they had deserted. Therefore they would be flogged. Turn by turn the five were made to stand upon the table. Their wrists were tied to the rope. The table was pulled away. Turn by turn, as ordered—Burhan-ud-Din promised a beating to any who held back—the watching men stepped forward and struck, one blow for each day of the culprit's absence. Joga Singh had been gone ten days. He was strung up first and received, it was alleged, twelve hundred strokes from 120 men, though at the trial the defense insisted that only 30 had ever paraded. Repeatedly he cried for mercy, and for water, and at times his body "contorted with pain to such an extent that it was bent double." At last his cries died away. But he continued to hang. It was only while they were flogging the fourth man that they noticed he had ceased moving, and cut him down. He had been dead for some time.

This was what the Viceroy read.[24] He would have loved to see it printed, hear it broadcast, have it shouted from the rooftops. About New Delhi and in civil lines and cantonments all across British India, there were any number of people who agreed with the *Statesman* that the government should long ago have given India the true story of the renegade army. Not the muted version that had been dished out during the war, all butchers and their lackeys with never a mention of the INA, but a frank, detailed account of the army's formation, growth, movements, use—and with it the treachery and the barbarity, driven home with such tales as the tale of Joga Singh's death by flogging.

> From failure to do so has resulted the present ludicrous position that, as a result of the Congress Party's energetic and deplorable propaganda, the real Indian Army is viewed by a large part of this country's politically-minded classes with little or none of the affectionate admiration and respect which it so richly deserves, and the remnants of a Japanese-sponsored body of expatriates have come to be undiscriminatingly regarded—to a man—as heroes.[25]

Auchinleck, too, was anxious to reverse the current of untruths. Even more than Wavell, however, he looked to the trials to do that work. He was confident, he had written the India Office in mid-October, "that when the evidence comes to be made public, as it will be made public because the trials are going to be open to the public, some of those gentlemen out there who have been so loud in their sympathy for the I.N.A. may sing a different tune. I think it will be difficult for them to defend murderers and torturers of people of their own race simply because they remained loyal to their salt."[26] The Red

Fort proceedings would be compellingly instructive. Meanwhile nothing must be done that could prejudice them in the eyes of the law, which leaking allegations before the trial could. So the Government of India must stand silent before the mounting gale of misinformation and abuse. The chilling tale of how Joga Singh had died would have to wait until it could be told properly—in court.

If this was the plan and the calculation, one might have expected the Army to pay close attention to the trials themselves, and manage them well. One might have expected it to have plenty of murderers and torturers on hand. One might at least have expected it to begin with Burhan-ud-Din.

～❀～

It is difficult, at first, to see why it didn't. The Army had picked Burhan-ud-Din up in Rangoon on May 3, the very day of the city's recapture. By early June it had him in the Red Fort along with "Thimmy" Thimayya, Prem, and almost two dozen other INA officers. That placed him within easy reach of Prosecution—Prosecution Section No. 7 of the Adjutant General's Branch, to be exact—which, as soon as it learned about the flogging death, could look for witnesses and build a case. And at some point, it appears, Section 7 did learn and did look. For when Burhan-ud-Din was at last brought to trial, five prosecution witnesses took the stand. Two had been flogged alongside Joga Singh that February day. Two had been made to join in the flogging. The fifth was the doctor who had pronounced the wretched man dead. In the face of their testimony there was little the defense could do except hunt for a technicality that might derail the proceedings; that, and trade on the defendant's reputation and character.

Burhan-ud-Din, however, did not have much to trade on. He was a strange man. He came from Chitral, a tiny princely state on the south slope of the Hindu Kush 150 miles north of Peshawar; an older brother was mehtar (ruler) of the place. His training was pukka enough (he received a Dehra Dun commission in 1936), and his commitment to the INA genuine. Both might have brought him respect, as they did Prem. But there was something odd about him, a touch of the fanatic, a whiff of suppressed rage; explaining, perhaps, the rope between the trees, the men paraded not to see justice done but to administer it, the flogging prolonged past all reason. Nor was he distinguished otherwise. He had done far less fighting in Netaji's service than Prem had, and less in the King-Emperor's too, reaching Singapore with other reinforcements only weeks before it fell. What kind of a man was he? I asked Prem once. *A man of moods,* was the reply. *He was a bit, well, mad.* Was he guilty of Joga Singh's death? *He did have the man beaten. The man did die.*

Neither the act nor the man had saving graces. From the Adjutant-General's point of view, then, it must have seemed an open-and-shut case, and one that would accomplish exactly what Auchinleck wished: to reestablish in the public's mind the true nature of the Jiff. A few more tales like the tale of Joga Singh, and "those gentlemen out there who have been so loud in their sympathy for the I.N.A." would indeed "sing a different tune."

Yet when the AG laid out the trials, he did not put Burhan-ud-Din at the top of the docket. Mason, who remembers the occasion—he routinely attended the conferences at GHQ during which decisions about courts-martial were made—believes he knows why. A court-martial proceeding had to be initiated within so many months or years of the alleged offense. Joga Singh had been flogged in the winter of 1944. It was now the autumn of 1945. The interval being greater than the statute of limitations allowed, Burhan-ud-Din's trial had to be dropped, at least until the limitation could be lifted, which might take months. This is why they did not begin with him, Mason says.[27]

But there is a problem with this explanation. The decision to set the Burhan-ud-Din case aside must have been made in mid-September.[28] Six weeks later, on the 31st of October, a viceregal ordinance removed the "limitation period" with regard to the trial of certain offenses under the Indian Army Act of 1911. Five days later still, on the day the first trial opened, Burhan-ud-Din was handed a charge sheet, which meant that he was going to be tried after all. The timing, however, was sheer coincidence. The section of the act made inoperative by the ordinance had disallowed proceedings begun more than three years after an alleged offense, and Joga Singh had been dead *for less than two.* We shall probably never know what the Burhan-ud-Din problem was. Perhaps he took ill. Perhaps a witness did. Perhaps a witness's mother died or his house fell in, all perfectly good reasons in the Indian Army for asking for leave; leave that had to be of indefinite duration because public transport went only so far, and in order to reach home a man might have to walk for a week. Whatever the problem, it was not a statute-of-limitations one.

There is this problem. And there is a more interesting question: why did the Adjutant-General make the substitution that he made, why did he bring Prem Sahgal, Dhillon, and Shah Nawaz to trial in Burhan-ud-Din's place?

Of this, too, Mason has a recollection—and a regret. It seems he had read Burhan-ud-Din's file. He knew that the flogging death of Joga Singh was indeed an arbitrary and brutal thing. As Mason remembers it, when the AG announced that he could not begin with Burhan-ud-Din but meant to try Sahgal, Dhillon, and Shah Nawaz instead, Mason asked whether the offenses with which they were charged were of the same order as Burhan-ud-Din's. Had *they*, also, committed acts of indisputable brutality? And Mason was assured that they had.

It crossed his mind, Mason says, to ask for their files. But he didn't. He took the AG's word for it. And that, he believes, was a mistake. For though these three, like Burhan-ud-Din, stood accused of murder or abetment of murder—in the matter of the five deserters allegedly shot at the base of Mount Popa eight months before—there was a difference. Sahgal, Dhillon, and Shah Nawaz had charged the five in accordance with the Indian National Army's own penal code, illegitimate though the court might pronounce it to be. Four had been properly tried. The fifth would have been had Legyi not intervened. Whereas for Joga Singh, Burhan-ud-Din had arranged little better than a lynching. Their proceedings had an air of due process about them. His did not. "I have always regretted not asking for these files," Mason says, "as I think I should have seen the difference."

That is the recollection, and that is the regret. But the regret is surely ex post facto. Had he read those files and seen the difference, would he have begged the AG to take Sahgal, Dhillon, and Shah Nawaz off the docket—then, in September? To suppose that he would is to suppose that he could have foreseen what the public effect of their trial was going to be. And it is also to suppose that he did not know how few genuine prospects for courts-martial, how pitifully few, the Adjutant-General had.

⁓

In his memoirs Mason says that when the government issued the press communiqué ("I drafted it myself") announcing its decision to put Indian National Army men on trial, people assumed it would be easy to find persons to proceed against. "No figures of course were mentioned," he remembers, "but it was thought at the time that there would be about a hundred trials which in law might lead to a death sentence,"[29] and many more leading to sentences that were less. This was in late August. Two months passed. And if Mason had anything to do with a paper that was laid, at this point, before the India and Burma Committee of the cabinet in London (he may have, for it presumably originated in his own War Department), he must have remarked to himself that in the interval the roster of triable Jiffs had grown even longer.

The paper begins by surveying the 43,000 men of whom the INA is believed to have been composed.[30] 20,000 of these are ex–Indian Army men. The rest are civilians recruited in Malaya. Of these, it continues, 16,000 have so far been "recovered," which means that they have been picked up and put into camps somewhere. Of these, a little more than 11,000 have been interrogated. The interrogation process has produced 2,565 blacks. (This is quite a drop from the figures, two to three times as large, current before Japan's surrender. Evidently many blacks have been redesignated greys.) And at this point the paper gets down to business. The Cabinet Committee wants to know how many blacks are likely to be convicted, and for what offenses. (It has possible clemency for convicted Jiffs in mind.) The paper proposes to answer with a detailed examination of those among the 2,565 who "as a result of interrogation . . . will be tried by court martial."

Will be tried, not could be or should be. The tone is categorical. There are some 800 of these people; and though the committee is told that Auchinleck means to postpone "for the present" the trials of a portion, it is clear this is not because the evidence against them is thought to be insufficient. The 800 are arranged by groups. "Officers Indian Army" makes one. Prem is undoubtedly there. "Those who deserted from our lines" is the label on another. Perhaps the platoon from the 1/15th Punjab that vanished while on patrol will be found here. There are ten of these groups. They are not accompanied by lists of names. But attached to each group is a number, the count of the actual, living bodies in that group. Does the India and Burma Committee want to know whether there are any more Burhan-ud-Dins upon whom justice must be done? The figure 92, appended to "those guilty of brutal conduct either to fellow Jifs/Hifs or to members of the Allied forces," informs it that there are ninety-one men who, like Burhan-ud-din (he is the ninety-second), are guilty of brutal conduct and will, indeed, be court-martialed. And so on, through the groups, the numbers, the general certitude.

And yet none of this, apparently, was of any use to the AG. In August, when Japan's unexpected surrender obliged responsible parties to think quickly and hard about the blackest of the blacks, the War Department (India) had cried out in alarm over their projected number, at that time thought to number some two thousand. 2,000 cases in twelve months, it had pointed out, would call for 250 officers just to man the courts-martial needed, and might lay upon Auchinleck as C.-in-C. the obligation of reviewing 40 sentences a week for fifty weeks! Where were those 2,000 cases now?

Since August, it was true, the standard by which blackness was judged had shifted. By mid-October Auchinleck was informing Whitehall that "we are only trying those Blacks who have been guilty . . . of crimes such as murder, torture, and things of that sort."[31] For this reason he wished to postpone proceedings against a portion of the 800. But postponement would affect only a portion. The more than four score brutes in Burhan-ud-Din's group were presumably as ready for trial as they had ever been. About Whitehall it must have been taken for granted that at the Red Fort dozens upon dozens of Jiffs were ready for the dock—all tagged, processed, charged or about to be. In India this was certainly the assumption.

Asaf Ali, the Defence Committee's convener, did not doubt for a moment that the War Department intended scores of trials. This was why he let reporters know that soon "new batches of senior and junior lawyers will be required," with clerks and peons to match;[32] this was why at No. 82 Daryaganj, where he spent a good deal of his time, the offices expanded steadily, almirah by almirah and room by room. Asaf Ali expected trials right through the cold season and into the hot. Yet during the six weeks that passed between the day Burhan-ud-Din's trial was put on the shelf, and the day courtoom proceedings of any sort began, Prosecution Section No. 7 did not offer the Adjutant-General so much as *one* scoundrel from the Burhan-ud-Din group in substitution. Prosecution did not present the AG with anybody from the other neatly prepared groups. For six weeks, even as Asaf Ali labored to get ready for trials that must go on well into 1946, only three Jiffs—Sahgal, Dhillon, and Shah Nawaz—stood charged with anything. Not until November did the number rise, and then only a little.

On the 5th Burhan-ud-Din was charged, making four where there had been three. On the same day Abdul Rashid, Singhara Singh, and Fateh Khan were served with charges too—which raised the count to seven. Like Burhan-ud-Din, they were accused of brutal acts: the fusillades at Kranji and Bidadari, the beatings that Rashid had had Nimbu the sweeper administer. But there the similarity ended. Abdul Rashid, Singhara Singh, and Fateh Khan had committed their brutalities not in Burma less than two years previously, but in Singapore more than three years back. In their case, then, there *had* been a statute-of-limitations problem. As matters stood that autumn, they could not have been brought to justice for what they had done; and so it must have been for them, and for a handful of others who would be charged in the months to come, that on the 31st of October, Section 67 of the Army Act of 1911 was set aside. The little exercise in limitation lifting that Philip Mason's memory associates with Burhan-ud-Din, must have been arranged for *them*. Indeed, when the trials of Rashid, Singhara Singh, and Fateh Khan finally opened, defense counsel objected that this was precisely the intent of the maneuver.

Was Auchinleck happy to see creatures of so little significance, and plucked from days so distant, marched on stage to teach India a lesson? He must have been asked, should steps be taken to set aside Section 67? He must have agreed. He may even have pushed the button. "I do not think myself," he remarked in the mid-October letter predicting a different tune when people learned the truth about the Jiffs, "that the lapse of three years is sufficient justification for not trying criminals of this sort." So he wanted them tried. Did he, perhaps, feel a little desperate?

Attached to a long late-November letter to Wavell is a list of "those who have so far been selected for trial by Court-Martial."[33] Selected! This is what we read when from among many contestants a happy few are chosen, so that for a moment we think we are about to discover who has been tapped for the varsity boat. But it isn't that way at all. Neither the choosers nor the chosen are happy. And the shortness of the list—it consists of the persons just named—is the shortness of failure, not success. Three months into a process that was to have exposed faithlessness and brutality by publicly trying renegades and rogues in handsome numbers, Auchinleck is able to present the Viceroy with just *seven* names.

Why there were so few it is not easy to explain. And why the fact of the scarcity took so long to sink in—for it did, the paper just referred to was not the only one that paraded figures with little relation to reality—is less explicable still. The mechanics of it all must have been part of the reason. It was probably easy enough to leaf through Forward Interrogation Unit reports, pick out likely prospects for prosecution, make lists, establish groups, and this no doubt was done. It was something else to carry an individual Jiff to the point of trial, particularly a public trial. For officers, before it would move, Prosecution routinely demanded the second or CSDIC interrogation, and a CSDIC interrogation took weeks. Then there were witnesses to be identified and brought to Delhi, perhaps from units in Java or places more distant still, perhaps from villages to which the men had returned, perhaps from INA detention camps. In the case of the men "recovered" in Malaya none of this, not even the quick scanning of FIU reports, could begin until Malaya itself had been reoccupied, which did not occur until September. Indeed, Hugh Toye once told me that in Singapore so many blacks and greys were crying for the interrogators' attention, or vying for it with whites who had to be identified and shipped home first, that looking back on the business he does not see how cases from his bailiwick could possibly have come to trial in Delhi before Christmas.

All this, too, at a time when personnel in the AG Branch (as in the services and the government at large) was stretched to the limit by the suddenness of the war's end, the accumulated weariness it was now possible to surrender to, the eagerness to get home to England. But it may be, also, that when Prosecution looked carefully at the men behind the numbers, it did not find what the information managers of earlier years had led it to believe it would find. It did not find the weaklings, cowards, torturers, and murderers that intelligence, by mingling Japanese with Indian behavior, had encouraged Auchinleck and Wavell to suppose the Jiff leadership consisted of.

It may be that among the men brought back from Burma there were other Burhan-ud-Dins who escaped attention because no one spoke, no one cried out, no one testified (as it were) to two trees, a stout rope, and five men dangling. It may be that a whole range of despicable acts should have been laid at the Indian National Army's door. It is more likely, I think, that Burhan-ud-Din was one of a kind; that there was no one else quite like him; that when Prosecution Section went through the files for the second time and studied the likes of R. M. Arshad, Mahboob Ahmed, and John Somasundaram (to name three among the dozens securely lodged in the Red Fort), it concluded that these were ordinary men: turncoats, of course, but otherwise about as decent as they come. Perceiving, then, that it had no one of Burhan-ud-Din's rank and Burma service to blacken the *Azad Hind Fauj* with, Prosecution was reduced to parading the three bullies from Mohan Singh's day. Scrapings from the bottom of the barrel.

❧

At this point it might have been wise to drop the trials altogether. But it is hard to see how Auchinleck could have drawn back now.

The reconquest of Burma had been the Indian Army's greatest triumph. That it should encounter there a force composed of men who had once belonged to it, constituted perhaps its greatest disgrace. The disgrace could be expunged, and the honor of the Indian Army made whole again, only by bringing to justice some, at least, of the leaders of this traitor force. A process for doing this had been set in motion. Buffeted from the outside by a rising public outcry that Congress Party orchestrated, half paralyzed on the inside by muddle, weariness, and the necessity of arranging in haste what would normally be done with magisterial deliberateness, the process faltered. It appeared, now, that there might be very little time left in which to carry it through, and few renegades of stature and substance at whom to direct it. But three men were securely in hand, men who had openly and frankly turned their coats. They had been taken arms in hand at the height of the great triumphant rush to Rangoon. There was not the slightest doubt about their guilt, no extenuating circumstances, nothing to blur the sharp outline of their treasonable acts. They could be dealt with properly. And there was an audience crowding round to see that they were, an audience it might be impossible to disappoint.

Sometime in the 1920s, at Moulmein in lower Burma, George Orwell, then a young officer in the Indian Police, was summoned one morning to do something about an elephant in must. An elephant in must is like a stag in rut but much more dangerous. Orwell got on his pony and rode to where the elephant had been reported. He came across the body of a coolie, lifeless, crushed into the mud by an enormous foot. Then he found the elephant. It was standing in a field tearing up bunches of grass, beating them against its knees to clean them as elephants do, stuffing them into its mouth. The elephant took no notice.

Orwell watched the elephant. He did not want to shoot it. It is a serious thing to kill a working elephant. Besides, it seemed to Orwell that the attack of must was already wearing off. In a while the mahout, who had gone off somewhere, would return and catch the beast. But he had sent for an elephant rifle, people had seen this, and now there was a crowd, "an immense crowd, two thousand at the least and growing every minute. It blocked the road for a long distance on either side. I looked at the sea of yellow faces above the garish clothes—faces all happy and excited over this bit of fun, all certain that the elephant was going to be shot." And suddenly Orwell realized that he would have to shoot the elephant. "The people expected it of me and I had got to do it; I could feel their two thousand wills pressing me forward, irresistibly. I had got to shoot the elephant. I had committed myself to doing it when I sent for the rifle. A sahib has got to act like a sahib; he has got to appear resolute, to know his own mind and do definite things. To come all that way, rifle in hand, with two thousand people marching at my heels, and then to trail feebly away, having done nothing—no, that was impossible. The crowd would laugh at me."

Except that the wills pressing irresistibly were British, it was not so very different with the court-martial of Sahgal, Dhillon, and Shah Nawaz.

CHAPTER 20

TRIAL AT THE RED FORT

Prem's family lost track of him when the war in the Pacific began. Until that moment, his sister Raj remembers, we knew where he was stationed. He was in a place called Kota Bharu. We used to get letters. But when the Japanese attacked, the letters ceased. That he had survived at all the family did not discover until well into 1942, and then (as Prem's father Achhru Ram explained to me one day) in a disconcertingly indirect and casual way.

> You see, the Japanese arranged to have some of their prisoners speak over the radio. And one day Prem spoke. He was heard by a lady in Jullunder District whose fiancé was also a prisoner of war, and who used to have the radio on almost all day. Later this was confirmed by others. But we did not hear him.
>
> I was then practising before the High Court of Lahore. The court closed about the 15th of July and remained closed until early October. We went to Mussoorie. We took our radio with us, so that if possible we might hear him. In August there is a Hindu festival called Raksha Bandhan, when the sisters tie the sacred thread round their brothers' wrists. Prem was missed very much that day. To turn their minds to something else, my wife and my two daughters and my two other sons—we all went to the cinema. I generally never go to the cinema. There the electricity failed, so we were not able to see the film. But that day again Prem spoke, and again we did not hear him. I was very much disappointed, so disappointed that I actually cried.

It was not until early 1944, by which time Achhru Ram had become a judge of the Lahore High Court, that the family discovered where Prem was. A friend had a son with the army in Burma. He came home one day on leave, and in the course of his stay told his father that Prem was military secretary to Subhas Chandra Bose. The news troubled Achhru Ram. *I knew what would happen to these boys. I had no doubt about the final victory of the British. They were bound to be tried, and the minimum sentence that could be passed upon them was transportation for life.* It did not follow, however, that he and the family knew much about the Indian National Army, how large it was and what it was trying to do. That came only when the war was over and the newspapers, suddenly, were full of the subject.

1945 arrived. Burma was recovered. If he was still alive, would Prem be court-martialed in Burma and perhaps shot there, or would they bring him home? Toward the end of May, Achhru Ram received word that a distant cousin had happened upon Prem in a Calcutta railroad station, recognized him, and exchanged a few words with him. Instantly Achhru Ram hurried to Delhi and there, with the help of an old friend who had contacts, tried to find out where his son was. It was useless. No one would tell him anything. Nevertheless he suspected that he was in the Red Fort, and of course he was.

It was the period when Prem lived in a cell in the fort's outer wall. He had nothing to do. It was very dull. He remembers almost nothing except a curious little brush that relieved the dullness a little.

One day the cell door opened and an American general *not from the fighting services, some sort of economist chap,* was ushered in. Prem was lying on his back in his bunk. He didn't see any reason to get up.

"*Do you speak English?*" asked the American.

"*No,*" replied Prem.

"*That's a silly answer,*" said the American.

"*That was a silly question,*" said Prem.

The other was silent a moment.

"*What do you know about the Azad Hind Bank?*" he asked.

Prem guessed he wanted to know what its assets were, how big it was, that kind of thing.

"*Not much,*" he said.

"*But you used to share a room with this man Yellappa.*"

"*I've shared rooms with lots of people. I don't ask them their business, and they don't ask me mine.*"

Another silence. Prem was still lying on his back.

"So you won't tell me anything about the Azad Hind Bank?"

"I won't," said Prem.

The American turned on his heel and walked out. Prem thought, *that's that. But a moment later the Britisher who had brought the man in came back and said, "My God! How you handled that chap!" He was very pleased. You see, the Americans pushed them around a lot. He said, "can I do anything for you?"* Prem asked him to bring him something to read. *And he did. From then on I had plenty of old magazines.*

Coincidence though it may be, Prem remembers no unpleasant encounters with his captors thereafter. When his CSDIC interrogation was complete, he was put with the other prisoners in Salimgarh, a small ruined fort a stone's throw northeast of the Red Fort proper. There he found Arshad, Mahboob Ahmed, and other old friends. Nights they were locked in their barracks. During the day, however, they could mingle, talk, play badminton, even order from the canteen. The guards were General Service, men deemed not fit for fighting, very friendly. When, after a time, they grew too friendly, Gurkhas took their place.

Weeks went by. Shah Nawaz, his interrogation finished, was brought over to Salimgarh too. Dhillon followed. Then, one September day, all three were told they were going to be court-martialed. This meant they were free now to get in touch with their families.

Prem did not know where his people were. They might be at a hill station somewhere, it was that time of year. So he got in touch with a woman in Delhi who came from a Jullundur family. They had grown up together and she was like a sister to him. She wired his father. From a place near Simla to which he had taken the family while the High Court was closed, Achhru Ram rushed down to Delhi and saw his son—for the first time in almost five years.

Colonel Walsh, the military prosecutor, arranged the meeting. Achhru Ram knew him slightly because Walsh had once appeared before the Lahore High Court. Achhru Ram listened to Prem's story. Then, with Walsh's help, he saw Dhillon and Shah Nawaz. He had already made up his mind that he would drop everything and bring his legal talents and reputation to his son's defense. They talked. He told Dhillon and Shah Nawaz that he would help them too.

He did more. He decided that

nothing should happen that may cause any rupture between these three. Their defense should be common. They were happy to meet me. You see, Shah Nawaz didn't expect his people to come to his assistance. His closest relation was an uncle, a retired subadar-major. Dhillon's father was a farmer, and he, too, didn't expect any help. So they were happy to have me take charge. One more decision I took. I decided that I would be more interested in their cases than in Prem's. Only in this way could we keep together.

Then I returned to Lahore and spoke to my chief justice. He was an exceedingly nice Englishman. I told him I wanted to defend these three boys, not as a lawyer, but to make every other arrangement and be present and advise them. "It may embarrass you," I said, "so you had better accept my resignation." He said, "let me speak to the Governor." Next day he told me what the Governor had said. "If the defense of the three is common, then he has as much right to arrange for the defense of the two others as for his own son."

For a while Achhru Ram made it his practice, since the High Court did not sit on Saturdays, to come down to Delhi by the night train Friday, do his business over the next thirty-six hours, and return to Lahore by the night train Sunday. This, however, was wearisome. So he asked his chief justice for a month's leave, rented a house in the Karol Bagh section of Delhi three miles west of the Red Fort, and moved there with Ratan Devi, his wife. After a time his daughter Raj joined them from Poona. Another daughter and his two younger sons visited occasionally. But the Karol Bagh house was more than a home away from home. From Lahore, Achhru Ram drew friends and colleagues down to Delhi to help with the defense. First to come was Inder Duo Dua, a young man he was training up himself; then Badri Das, much older and very distinguished; later still two former High Court judges, Bakshi Sir Tek Chand and Kanwar Sir Dalip Singh. The house became their base. Achhru Ram paid the bills and hired cars and drivers for their common use.

He knew about the Congress party's Defence Committee, of course. He had known about it from the beginning, and though he could not join it (his position as a serving judge would not allow this), his Lahore people could and did. It was Achhru Ram, moreover, who so managed things that when the first trial opened, Bhulabhai Desai took charge in the courtroom, examining and cross-examining witnesses, raising objections when objections were opportune, delivering the mandatory final address.

Bhulabhai was a well known Bombay advocate, as Indian lawyers not called to the bar from one of the London Inns of Court were called. He was also a prominent member of the Congress. In 1941, like many Congress leaders, he offered individual *satyagraha* and was briefly jailed. Subsequently he served the party as floor leader in the Central Legislative Asembly—in that arena the Congress, curiously, remained alive and functioning throughout the war. Achhru Ram knew Bhulabhai well. The moment he met his son and learned that a trial was imminent, he got in touch with him. Independently Lakshmi's mother, Ammu, did the same. Bhulabhai and her husband had been good friends.

Bhulabhai was out of favor with many members of the Working Committee because, some months before, he had made overtures to the Muslim League, on the party's behalf it was true, but without their consent (they were then behind bars). Gandhi was known to disapprove of him, believing he drank. So the Working Committee made Sir Tej Bahadur Sapru senior defense counsel designate. Sapru, however, was almost seventy, tired and ill. Come the trial he would, it was known, make one appearance and withdraw. Bhulabhai was not a young man. He had just turned sixty-eight, and his health, too, was poor. But no one could match him in courtroom advocacy. Achhru Ram felt the three accused *must* have him. Prem believes it was he who saw to it that Bhulabhai sat on the committee from the beginning and, when the time came, took Sapru's place.

The trial was scheduled to open October 8. But when Colonel Walsh asked for the list of defense witnesses, Achhru Ram saw his chance, told him it would take weeks to locate and bring in all that were going to be needed, and got a month's respite. To Prem he said, *"make as long a list as you can. We will not be examining many witnesses. But if you give the names of officers whose whereabouts you do not know, even though we do not need them, they will be flown here."* And it happened. Scores of officers were brought to Delhi and lodged in the Red Fort. Only Lakshmi did not come. Her reputation as a firebrand had preceded her, and the British thought it wiser to bury her quietly in the Shan Highlands.

October advanced. From time to time the committed members of the Defence Committee met—Bhulabhai, Asaf Ali, Badri Das, one or two others, usually with Achhru Ram present. Someone suggested they try to get the trial transferred to a civil court. Achhru Ram objected, pointing out that courts-martial give the defense great advantages, and his voice prevailed. Nehru stopped in to see the three defendants. Prem remembers saying to him, "*look, Panditji, if you have any embarrassment about the Congress not believing in violence and that sort of thing. . . ,*" and remembers Nehru saying emphatically that he did not. Perhaps it was now that Nehru let Krishna Menon know how impressed he was becoming with INA men. Meanwhile a courtroom was being readied at the Red Fort.

⁂

The Lal Qila ("Red Fort") is actually less a fort than a walled city, a small walled city, with sturdy walls of rich red sandstone. The great Mogul emperor Shah Jahan, who also gave India the Taj Mahal, built it in the middle of the seventeenth century, and next to it a much, much larger walled city. It was in Shahjahanabad, as this was called, that his subjects were to live. He, his court, and his administration were to occupy the Red Fort, just to its east against the River Jumna (Yamuna). Together these would make Delhi what Agra heretofore had been, the capital of the Mogul Empire. And for half a century the business prospered.

But in the eighteenth and early nineteenth centuries Shahjahanabad suffered heavily from neglect and repeated sackings, the last by the British in 1857. Such was the destruction and decay that after a time, though the city within remained, only fragments of its walls and a handful of its gates still stood. The area lost all connection with Shah Jahan's name, and became simply Delhi—called Old Delhi today, to distinguish it from New. The much smaller Red Fort, however, survived. Though deprived of some of their proudest ornaments, the exquisite marble halls and pavilions that Shah Jahan had built along the fort's eastern edge remained intact. (It is to them that the tourist, Indian or foreign, automatically gravitates.) And as these halls and pavilions had never come close to filling the more than one hundred acres within the Red Fort's walls, in the latter part of the nineteenth century the

British put portions of them to military and administrative use. Barracks were constructed along the fort's north-south axis, gaunt buildings (they still stand) of grey brick and stone pierced by tall narrow openings to let light and air into the verandahs that encircle each floor. It was in one of these barrack blocks that the INA courts-martial, it had been decided, should be held.

The grounds for the decision were practical. The trials had to be public, and the Red Fort was a known and public place. There had to be means of controlling access, of admitting some (the press, the families of the accused) without admitting all, and this a walled enclosure made possible. Add the clerical and logistical support that the fort's staff could be expected to supply, and GHQ would have had to search hard and long to do better. There was no guile in the business, no hidden agenda. Just as Sahgal, Dhillon, and Shah Nawaz were singled out to be tried first, not because one was a Hindu, one a Sikh, and one a Muslim (though to this day some suppose this to have been the reason), but because they were at hand and eminently triable, so the Red Fort was picked because it was right for the job. Auchinleck did not mean to send a signal. Nevertheless it was a curious, and in the end unfortunate, choice.

For in the Red Fort, eighty-eight years before, Auchinleck's forebears had inflicted a great indignity upon India. When the Sepoy Rebellion broke out, Shah Jahan's Mogul Empire still lingered within its walls—in the person of Bahadur Shah II, nineteenth of his line. There was no substance to this imperial remnant. The emperors had long since handed the *diwani* (revenue collecting authority) to the British, surrendered all practical power, and kept only the title. But neither did there seem any harm in the arrangement. Like his father before him, Bahadur Shah passed his days in the Red Fort's halls and pavilions enjoying the generous monthly allowance the British paid him, and unlike his father, writing verse.

Then in May 1857, the rebel sepoys suddenly appeared. They took what is now Old Delhi and the Red Fort too—there were no British troops in the vicinity. They declared Bahadur Shah India's true emperor once more, though at eighty-two he might have preferred to be left alone, and propped him up to encourage the other rebels fighting to the south and east. In September, however, a small British force that had made its way down from the Punjab, and for months had clung precariously to a ridge north of Delhi, went over to the attack and after bloody fighting recovered and sacked the city. That put an end to the arrangement. From the British point of view it had proved unexpectedly dangerous. Bahadur Shah's sons were seized and shot out of hand. Bahadur Shah himself was brought before a military court, charged with treason and abetment of murder (several score Europeans including women and children had been killed in the May rising), sentenced to transportation for life, and shipped to Rangoon, where he died four years later alone and unattended. As for the Red Fort, it had been damaged, but not beyond repair. It was now that it became wholly and unashamedly British.

Indians remembered this. What had been done to the last of the Mogul emperors, never mind that he and his father had been no more than cardboard figures, was shameful. In Rangoon, Netaji had Bahadur Shah's tomb cleaned and repaired. When his regiments started for the front, he reminded them that the march to Delhi would not be complete until the tricolor flag flew over the Viceregal Palace and they stood at the gates of the Red Fort. Bahadur Shah's trial had been held in the Diwan-i-Khas or hall of private audience, perhaps the most elegant of the Red Fort's public buildings, and from there to the barracks where the British prepared to try Sahgal, Dhillon, and Shah Nawaz, on the same charges of treason and abetment of murder, it was no distance at all. You could easily hit a cricket ball that far. The parallel was striking, so striking that when this second trial was over, and a journalist named Moti Ram rushed into print with the proceedings, he added to it those of January 1858, and called the whole *Two Historic Trials in Red Fort.*

"No more suitable venue for it . . . could have been found," wrote Nehru in the foreword he dashed off for Moti Ram's book. Before the trial was over, Auchinleck may have doubted how suitable it had turned out to be. But in October no one worried. Carpenters cleared a third-floor room some sixty feet by twenty-five, laid a low coir-matted platform across one end, and placed a line of tables on it for the court to sit behind. Prosecution and defense faced each other from tables set at right angles to the court. The press had its own roped enclosure in the body of the room. That left perhaps 150 seats for the families and relatives of the accused and for other legitimately interested persons, all of whom had to apply in advance for passes. In a room below were phones and a telegraph line for the use of the press. The whole was simple, cramped, and at any time from April through September would have been unbearable even with ceiling fans whirling. But it was November now, and such winter as north India gets had begun.

The 5th of November drew near. Nehru reached Delhi and spent an hour with the Viceroy, at the latter's invitation, for Wavell wished to warn him that no government could tolerate indefinitely such incitements to violence as he allowed himself to make. "I cannot help liking him," Wavell remarked afterwards in a note to Pethick-Lawrence. "But he seems to have reached the state of mind of a fanatic. . . ."[1] Certainly the warning had little perceptible effect. In two public addresses, one before factory workers, the other at the kick-off to Asaf Ali's campaign for a seat in the Central Legislative Assembly, Nehru mingled harsh criticism of the way the Quit India rebellion had been suppressed with a savage attack on the management of the Bengal famine. Only when he spoke about the approaching trial did he show restraint. The premise on which the trial rested, namely, that Britishers might sit in judgment on men who had simply done what they thought necessary for India's freedom, was false. "The people of India should be the final court and arbiter of the case."[2] But he hoped his listeners would allow the Defence Committee to carry the burden of the young patriots' defense. If you must hold demonstrations, he said, do not hold them at the Red Fort. And apparently they listened.

Monday the 5th arrived. A small crowd carrying "Save INA Patriots" placards (in English) collected across the road from the Lahore Gate, the fort's principal entrance, and met official cars with shouts of "Jai Hind." Pass holders made their way along roped paths to the barracks block, up the narrow stairs, and into the courtroom, which they packed.. At ten o'clock an NCO bawled for silence. The Judge-Advocate entered. The court followed, four senior British officers (the president of the court was a major general) and three distinctly less senior Indian officers, none in wigs or gowns of course. Counsel for both sides trouped in. Press photographers were given a moment to snap the scene and did their best, standing on chairs and tables (no one had thought to provide anything stable), until a table went down with a crash. The accused were produced, in uniform but without badges of rank. Their INA badges had long since been taken from them, and they had made it clear that they would not disgrace (and, incidentally, demote) themselves by resuming their Indian Army ones. Oaths were administered. The charges were read. Asked how they pleaded, all three pleaded "not guilty." Then they were directed to sit down, one behind the other, to the left of their counsel. Before they sat they turned and gave Nehru "a smart salute."

The smallness of the hall, the meanness of its furnishings, the clutter and the crush, do not suggest an occasion of any great importance. But the *Hindustan Times*, from which I have taken these bits of description, was prepared to make a great deal of the event. Its Tuesday issue appeared under the headline "I.N.A. Trial Opens in Red Fort" in letters three quarters of an inch high. It had managed to collect photographs of Sahgal, Dhillon, and Shah Nawaz and a shot of "Women Warriors of the Rani of Jhansi Regiment" marching with rifles on their shoulders. It carried a long story about Monday's proceedings, a story that ran for pages. The story began with the statement that here was a trial "unprecedented in British Indian history." And if you look at the photographs that were taken before the table crashed, photographs that subsequently found their way into the papers, you will find one that suggests that "unprecedented" is, indeed, the appropriate term.

The photograph shows the members of the Congress Defence Committee, in their capacity as counsel for the defense, collected for the first time in the courtroom—and what is striking is their number. There they are (see photo section), not two or three but *thirteen* gentlemen of the law, in the white shirt fronts and black robes of their trade. Sapru is there. (He will withdraw shortly to Allahabad to celebrate his 70th birthday.) Nehru and Katju are there. So are the four whom Achhru Ram has brought down from Lahore (Sir Dalip Singh is on Nehru's right). In front row center Bhulabhai Desai and Asaf Ali are conferring, Bhulabhai his nose almost on the table, Asaf Ali whispering earnestly in his ear. It is extraordinary. This is no ordinary band. These are legal luminaries. The photographer has captured here as great a concentration of legal talent as has come together in India on any one case. The fact that they are squeezed elbow to elbow and two deep behind plain wooden tables not three feet across, does not lessen the significance of that.

One person is missing. Achhru Ram is absent. *I wanted to sit with the lawyers, but I was told I was not a lawyer, I was a judge.* He had been put in the visitors' section with his wife and his daughter Raj, and there, it was plain, the court expected him to remain.

It was intolerable. When the Prime Minister of the Punjab, an old client, phoned Achhru Ram from Lahore that evening to ask how things had gone, Achhru Ram surprised him by telling him that he had not been a lawyer that day. *"But I will be a lawyer tomorrow, because I am going to resign my judgeship."* And he prepared to do just that. At which wheels turned, phone calls were made, and when, next morning, Achhru Ram stepped out of his Karol Bagh house for a short walk in the park, a huge Pathan came up and handed him a letter from the president of the court. He might sit, it read, with the defense.

✑

The trial lasted eight weeks. If Sir Naushirwan P. Engineer, Advocate-General of India and chief counsel for the prosecution (Walsh was his deputy) had had his way, it would not have lasted two.

There had already been a four weeks' postponement. Prosecution was as ready, now, to bring Sahgal, Dhillon, and Shah Nawaz to trial as it would ever be; and anxious to do so; for with elections to the Central Legislative Assembly approaching and the temper of the country what it was, further delay was bound to play into the hands of persons who wished to make a spectacle of the proceedings. But no sooner were Monday morning's formalities over than Bhulabhai Desai was on his feet asking for a further adjournment. Few of his 112 available defense witnesses had been interviewed, he said, and there were dozens more he wished brought to Delhi, some from distant places. Sir Naushirwan objected. He was allowed to deliver his opening address. He was allowed to call his first witness. Beyond this, however, Colonel Kerin the Judge Advocate would not let him go. It was Kerin's job to guide the court in matters both procedural and substantive, and he was determined, it seems, to be evenhanded. So when the first witness finished testifying late Tuesday afternoon, the court on Kerin's advice voted to adjourn for two weeks. It resumed on Wednesday the 21st, met for eight working days, and on the afternoon of Friday the 30th broke off again until December 7.

Stretching the trial out in this way no doubt *did* feed the growing popular excitement and tumult, as some had feared it would. But what defeated the Government of India's attempt to demonize the Indian National Army, and with it these three men, was less Engineer's inability to keep the proceedings brief than the direction the proceedings took. And this followed from what Engineer wanted the opening days' testimony to accomplish. The direction was established by the first witness, by the man he chose to bring in first. Engineer's first witness did the damage—though, looking back at the matter, it is hard to see how the Advocate-General could have made any other choice.

There were two arrows in Sir Naushirwan's quiver, the treason charge, and the charge of murder and/or abetment of murder—and it made a difference in what order he fitted them to his bow. Justice must be done, and be *seen* to be done. But it had to be done upon turncoats who happened to be brutes, not upon brutes who happened to be turncoats: the treason charge had to be addressed first. And since Sahgal, Dhillon, and Shah Nawaz had pleaded innocent to all the charges, not just to some of them, their treason could not be taken for granted. It had to be proved.

To prove it, Sir Naushirwan had in hand a heterogeneous collection of such Indian National Army papers as had somehow survived its defeat, escaped burning, been picked up, and reached Delhi. They were papers of the sort any army will generate—supply indents, interoffice memoranda, intelligence summaries, tables of organization, situation reports, field orders, the like. Spread out and examined, they gave even the casual reader some sense of who had been doing what. In this case they demonstrated beyond doubt or the possibility of contradiction that there had indeed been an organized force of turncoats, that it had attempted to break into India, and that the three defendants had been part of it. So Engineer proposed to have these papers laid before the court at the very start of the trial. To do this, Prosecution Section 7 groomed and presented a certain D. C. Nag.

Nag was a sometime civil magistrate who, in mid-career, had entered the Adjutant-General's Branch of the Indian Army and, happening to be in Malaya when the Pacific war began, became at Singapore's surrender a POW. Nag's legal talents and experience (he was forty-seven) made him attractive to Mohan Singh's recruiters. He was invited to join the INA, did so (probably more out of prudence than patriotic feeling), and went to work drafting an INA Act on the model of the Indian Army Act—with which, of course, he was thoroughly familiar. Later he accompanied Bose to Burma. He was with Bose at Maymyo, he returned with him to Rangoon; everywhere he went he did headquarters staff work, met officers who were similarly engaged or who were passing through, came to know faces and the signatures that went with them, and in this way developed an easy familiarity with all parts of Netaji's enterprise. By the time Rangoon fell and an Indian Army Forward Interrogation Unit found him, he was a walking repository of information about the renegades. And now, on this Monday and Tuesday of early November 1945, it all came tumbling out, in the shape of some seventy documents each of which he was asked to identify and swear to, seventy read into the record as exhibits A to Z, AA to ZZ, and so on. Where, before, there had been only hints, rumors, and imaginings, now there was a paper trail. And suddenly the Indian National Army began to be credible.

For up to this point what India knew about the freedom army's performance in the field had hardly risen above the level of hearsay. A few newspapermen, it is true, had managed to catch the odd INA man before he was caged, and on the basis of what he said had written general accounts of the Arakan venture, the attempt at Imphal, the fighting along the Irrawaddy, whatever. But these accounts were thin and unsubstantial. And as 1945 drew to a close they were overshadowed and cheapened by increasing numbers of frankly fanciful pieces, of which Amritlal Seth's *Jai-Hind: The Diary of a Rebel Daughter of India with the Rani of Jhansi Regiment* was perhaps the earliest, and certainly the type.

Amritlal Seth had spent an August day with Lakshmi, in Rangoon shortly after she came out of the hills. He had departed with a bundle of notes; he had left behind an implied promise to put her story into print; and three months later, at the very moment the first Red Fort trial began (the timing was not accidental), out from a Bombay publisher came the piece he had promised—for while Lakshmi's name appears nowhere in *Jai-Hind's* pages, it is clear from the context and the photographs that the diarist is supposed to be her.

As a diary, parts of *Jai-Hind* are plausible enough. Many of the entries correspond exactly with what Lakshmi has subsequently written or said, and allowances can be made for some that do not. It is perhaps forgivable that Seth gives Lakshmi a husband and has him die in an attempt on a British ammunition dump. Perhaps Lakshmi actually knew enough shorthand to take down Netaji's Berlin broadcasts as they came over the radio; perhaps she really did wonder, when Singapore fell, what she would do were a Japanese to molest her, though I doubt she kept potassium cyanide handy to swallow should one try. But when the women of the regiment, tired of nursing the sick and wounded, beg to be sent to the front, and are; when they meet the enemy and, after a brief skirmish, force some to surrender; the credibility index drops to zero. I once asked Lakshmi whether she and her women ever hurled themselves downhill at the British crying "Azad Hind Zindabad" as they ran (an entry said they had), and she laughed, that brief, delightful laugh she has. "*When we were being trained in bayonet fighting,*" she said, "*we were taught to shout that shout.*" But that was as far as it went.

Flights of the imagination did not end with *Jai-Hind,* they began there. Kusum Nair's *The Story of the I.N.A.* (years later Kusum Nair became well known for her books on Indian agriculture and village life) has Lakshmi's Ranis clear British armor from the road over which Bose is trying to reach Moulmein by sustained and accurate rifle fire. This is pure fantasy. British intelligence is a model of sobriety by comparison. Anxious for some reason to demonstrate the effectiveness of the Ranis' training, intelligence reports that on a certain October day in 1944 "a detachment passing through a suburb in Rangoon came across a minor street brawl between Indians and Burmans. The girls charged with fixed bayonets, cordoned off the two parties, and kept order till the police arrived."[3] Though intelligence does not say how it came by this interesting tidbit, it has the smell of truth about it. Kusum Nair's skirmish on the road to Moulmein does not. Well into 1946 there was far too much of the latter.

Had Prem, too, and his battalions, been served up in this way, the Indian National Army might never have escaped from the shadows and come out into the light. But Prem, luckily for him, had not talked to a journalist. Nor had he given or even shown his diary to one. He had lost it during the night ambush on the 29th of March. Shah Nawaz's diary had fallen into British hands at his capture May 17. "Legyi Operations," the battle report filed by Prem with the 2nd INA Division on April 6, had been picked up when division headquarters was overrun somewhere on the road to Magwe. Now, during the first two days of the trial, parts of the diaries and the whole of the Legyi account were trotted out, authenticated by Nag, and placed in evidence along with other like papers. No journalists got to them and prettied them up. They were as they were. They told things as they had actually happened. Nothing is quite so matter-of-fact as a pocket diary kept day by day by a busy person without literary pretensions, and a battle report *has* to be concrete. From the Red Fort courtroom, moreover, these documents passed at once, with much else besides, into the great dailies, which reported them at length and sometimes reproduced them verbatim. Interested persons then read them. In this way a window opened, for the first time, upon the reality of the INA.

Right through the trial this process continued. When Kitson of the 4/2nd Gurkha Rifles arrived and gave his account of Prem's surrender (it was for him that the trial was adjourned a second time), the headline over the *Statesman*'s account of that day's proceedings read "Story of Surrender on the Irrawaddy." Readers learned from the colonel's own lips that "approximately 40 officers and 500 other ranks of the Indian National Army, of whom about 50 were wounded," had executed a retreat of more than one hundred miles with no better than bullock carts for transport, only to be trapped at last against a river by a force in every respect superior that had been overtaking them for weeks.[4] There was nothing romantic about the picture. Defeat is defeat, and a surrender is a surrender. But it was clear that the encounter had been, for Kitson, a normal military one. He had followed—or bumped into, it is not clear which—a battalion of the enemy. Nothing in his manner or in what he said suggested that when the colonel met these Jiffs on the banks of the Irrawaddy, he took them for players in some romantic tragedy. Nor did he recognize them for the dupes and weaklings, the cowards and the bullies, that intelligence represented Jiffs to be. They were just plain men.

Prem remembers that on the way from the waiting room to the courtroom on that December 7, he passed Kitson, *and he gave me a big broad smile.* Later, Kitson testified that though he had not preserved Prem's surrender note, to the best of his recollection it said that those laying down their arms expected to be treated as prisoners of war. This was just what Prem had maintained the note said. This was not, however, what the prosecution wished to hear. Engineer had summoned Kitson all the way from Java expecting him to testify that Prem had used the demeaning language of the surrender leaflets, the language of sheep begging to be readmitted to the fold. Kitson disappointed him. "I asked Sahgal," Kitson continued,

> if he liked the British, and he said that he had two or three very great friends among British officers, but that the reason why he was fighting was that he disliked the system of British imperialism in India. He told me that he had fought for what he considered to be right, and that now that he had lost he was prepared to take the consequences.[5]

The smile, then, had been in the nature of a salute, one officer acknowledging another, as winners and losers do in the honorable sport of war.

Two days of Nag and Exhibits A to ZZ drove home the treason charge. Their diary entries convicted Prem and Shah Nawaz of waging war against the King-Emperor, as the prosecution knew they would. Field orders and reports did the same for Dhillon. No more need have been said about the subject. But when the trial resumed on November 21, more was.

Engineer insisted. His opening address had dealt at length with the pressure put upon men to follow Mohan Singh. He went back to this now. Though recruiting for war was not waging war, it was preparation for war right enough. Everyone knew that INA recruiters had done terrible things to reluctant jawans. The defendants had been aware of these "atrocities" and had condoned them. To know and to condone was, in the circumstances, to make war under another name. Therefore he was going to produce witnesses who would testify to the shameful barbarities that stained the character of the renegade army, and the character of these three too.

Bhulabhai objected. "I have never yet heard of any law that merely because you know that somebody has done something, that knowledge constitutes an offence." It was "an extraordinary argument, and I know the reason. . . . It is to create a prejudice against honourable men, who on their own showing took no part in any of the atrocities."[6] But this time he did not have his way. He could shut Dhargalkar up in the matter of the seven-by-six-by-five-foot cage, the court agreeing that though this Sandhurst man with the "carefully-cultivated English accent" might have a grievance against the Japanese who put him in one, that grievance ought not to be aired here. He could not bar the witnesses Engineer proposed to parade. Perhaps this was because Engineer was at his most persuasive. The defendants, he argued, had made speeches urging jawans to join or risk "hardships," and it was certainly relevant to ask what those hardships had been. Perhaps it was because Colonel Kerin himself was of two minds. In any case, toward the end of November the court listened for four straight days while a string of witnesses told their tales of being fed rice mixed with gravel, of being made to run carrying sacks of earth slung on bamboo poles, of being beaten senseless, of things worse.

But as the tales were told, it became more and more apparent that they had nothing to do with Sahgal, Dhillon, and Shah Nawaz. In his closing address Engineer admitted as much. Kerin made it explicit. "There is not and never has been," he advised the court, which as required listened to him before it retired to reach a verdict, "the least suggestion that these three accused before you were ever personally engaged in the ill-treatment of prisoners, or even that they were at any time present when men were tortured or ill-treated."[7] Why, then, had so much been made of it, if not to "create a prejudice against honourable men" as Bhulabhai had charged?

And what made telling these tales even more curious and irrelevant was the bringing to trial, not many days after the tales were told, of three genuinely brutal Jiffs.

Burhan-ud-Din came first. On the 3rd of December he stood at last in the dock. There was a pause of several days to argue a procedural matter, and on the 6th the court listened to the prosecution's case. Its core was, of course, poor Joga Singh. Instantly the details were in all the dailies. Then, on the 15th, Singhara Singh and Fateh Khan took their turn—without Abdul Rashid, who asked to be tried separately. Again there was a pause for procedural maneuvering. On the 18th the prosecution laid out the stories of the Kranji and Bidadari firing. These, too, were reported in the papers, though briefly, since they had already been used by Engineer. The repetition cannot have been lost upon thoughtful readers. There was, anyway, not much to say about Singhara Singh and Fateh Khan, their alleged brutalities aside. Of Burhan-ud-Din, once the tale of the flogging had been told, there was hardly more. But Sahgal, Dhillon, and Shah Nawaz were public figures, attractive public figures, before ever they stepped into a courtroom. The first two days of the trial had added to their visibility. Now they and Bose's government and army—the *Arzi Hukumat-e-Azad Hind* and *Azad Hind Fauj* of Netaji's day not Mohan Singh's—continued to draw the lion's share of public attention, in part because of the witnesses Bhulabhai fetched to Delhi on their behalf.

He asked for Percival, and was refused. He asked for certain of Wavell's papers, and again he was refused. But the authorities were willing to give him S. A. Ayer. Ayer and Habib-ur-Rahman were flown in from Japan (they had followed Bose's ashes there). Five Japanese of rank followed: two career Foreign Office men, a former vice-minister for foreign affairs, Ambassador Hachiya, and the major general who planned the Imphal campaign. For three December days Bhulabhai passed Ayer and these Japanese before the court. Their testimony continued the process of establishing the reality of Bose's government and army.

This is apparent from the newspaper coverage. "I.N.A.'s Role in Imphal Battle" announced the *Hindu* over a long account of the December 10 proceedings. "Stockily built impetuous General Katakura spoke in Japanese exuberantly and with a wealth of picturesque gestures which kept the Judges and the audience interested and sometimes amused."[8] The gist of his remarks, the story continued, was that though INA troops had come under Japanese overall command, they did not mingle with the Japanese but had their own operational assignments. The Foreign Office people (one of whom spoke excellent English) assured court and audience that Tojo had meant it when he said he wished to see India independent, and that Tokyo's recognition of Bose's government was genuine. But Ayer's testimony was the most useful. Almost two years' continuous personal contact with Subhas Chandra and the Provisional Government's staff allowed him to talk more knowingly about League membership, raising money, the rice offer to Bengal, and the like, than anybody else in the trial. And though he was not necessarily believed—Engineer repeatedly insisted that activities Ayer called voluntary had in fact been compelled—no one who listened can have helped but know a great deal more about the enterprise after Ayer finished testifying, than he had known before Ayer began.

These were witnesses for the defense. Bhulabhai had named over one hundred and interviewed more than seventy, wrote the *Hindu*'s trial correspondent on the last day of testimony, "but it is understood that Mr. Desai decided against calling more than 11 because he felt that the 28 prosecution witnesses had made statements which served his purpose equally well."[9] Indeed they had. So far as I can tell, none of the Indian prosecution witnesses (and all the prosecution witnesses except Colonel Kitson *were* Indian), not even the six men called to give evidence in the matter of the four deserters allegedly shot at Mount Popa's base, wished the three defendants ill. Often it was quite the other way around. Prosecution had collected these men because they could testify to certain things. Once produced, however, they could not be managed—as in a civil trial, Achhru Ram explained to me, they could. Moreover, the defense knew pretty accurately what the prosecution was going to do. *The first day I met the prosecutor, he gave me a summary of the prosecution evidence and I had a hundred copies printed.* So a shrewd cross-examiner, which Bhulabhai certainly was, could turn prosecution witnesses to his advantage.

Again and again the court and the audience heard them say things that helped rather than damaged a defendant's case. "'No Subservience to Japanese.' What Capt. Shah Nawaz Told His Brigade," ran the heading over the *Hindu*'s account of the courtroom proceedings on the last Wednesday in November.[10] That was the day when Dilasa Khan, pressed to admit that Bose's officers were clay in the hands of the Japanese, reconstructed from memory the caution Shah Nawaz had given his men before he brought them up from Malaya. If they noticed a Japanese soldier mistreating an Indian woman, Dilasa Khan remembered Shah Nawaz saying, that soldier was to be told to stop. But if he persisted, "we are at liberty to use force and even shoot him in order to prevent it. Because the fight which we are making now is for the freedom and well-being of India, and not for the benefit of the Japanese." Prosecution had not produced Dilasa Khan to have him say this. Once on the stand, however, he could not be silenced. And meanwhile the public grew more and more excited.

❧

Ayer later wrote, of his arrival in Delhi on the 22nd of November, that he "straightaway attacked a pile of newspapers. They carried pages and pages of reports of the trial, which had opened on 5th November and then adjourned for a few days." As he went from paper to paper, "my excitement knew no bounds. The I.N.A. had literally burst on the country. . . . From the Himalayas to Cape Cormorin [it] was aflame with an enthusiastic fervour unprecedented in its history."[11]

For once Netaji's Minister of Publicity and Propaganda may not have overstated the case. India *was* aflame. "There has seldom been a matter which has attracted so much Indian public interest and, it is safe to say, sympathy." Thus Sir Norman Smith, Director of the Intelligence Bureau, in a confidential note to the Home Department on November 20. Had Ayer seen the note, he would have protested that the DIB did not measure the clamor adequately. *Never* has a matter so stirred the public, he would have said. But at the same time he would have been pleased to learn that in Sir Norman's opinion "the general Nationalist Press," meaning the newspapers he himself devoured, was encouraging that clamor marvelously. "The effect the publications in question have is undoubted, for many of them are most popular and widely-read even in rural areas." Sir Norman did not see what could be done about it now. It was too late. "The country's ear has largely been captured."[12]

In Lahore tension was palpable long before the trial itself began. Diwali, the Hindu festival, was near (Lahore then was almost as much a Hindu as a Muslim city), and students went about begging householders not to set out the usual Diwali lights—little clay cups holding oil and a floating wick which, when placed along walls and parapets, give residential quarters at night a magical appearance. Out of respect for the patriots whose trial would soon begin, Lahore must remain dark. When Diwali evening came, dark it remained. "Only at isolated points tiny earthen lamps faintly flickered."[13]

The Lahore papers were full of pieces about the Indian National Army, and photographs too: of the three defendants, of Subhas Chandra in uniform, of jawans entering a Manipur village carrying Netaji's portrait (this was the photo Sivaram had identified as fake). Children roamed the lanes and alleys chanting "Azad Fauj Chhor Do, Lal Qila Tor Do." Let the freedom fighters go, tear down the Red Fort. And on November 5, the day the trial began, there was a general *hartal*. All the shops and offices closed. Thousands of students took to the streets. If a school was reluctant to shut, they shamed it into doing so, or compelled it to. Elsewhere in the Punjab there was *hartal* too, at Lyallpur to the west, at Rawalpindi to the north. And at Karachi, way to the southwest, the municipal corporation anounced an INA day soon.

Simple to organize—it was just a matter of parading with tricolor banners, shouting "Chalo Delhi", demanding the release of the Red Fort prisoners—INA days multiplied right across the country. And right across the country, sub-divisional magistrates attempted to anticipate and stop them, usually by publishing orders that forbade (to use the stock phrase) "processions, meetings, and demonstrations in sympathy with the Indian National Army." One late November edition of the *Hindu* reported ten such prohibitory orders in the course of forty-eight hours for Madras Province alone. In Vellore the prohibition was to last for one day only. In Salem it was to hold for fifteen. In Cocanada, three hundred miles up the coast, it was to remain in force for an entire month. One would love to know whether the magistrate there was able to make his prohibition stick. It may have been difficult when elections to the Central Legislative Assembly reached the town.

As usual these elections were to be held not simultaneously but strung out over weeks. They were due in the Punjab on November 23. They were due in Delhi, where Asaf Ali was running, on the 24th, and in Bombay and the United Provinces a few days later. Madras Province would go to the polls on the 1st of December. (Ammu was contesting the Madras City general constituency with a man whose brother-in-law had joined the INA. But Ammu had the advantage, she had Lakshmi, and by this time Lakshmi's name was on everybody's lips.) Last would come Calcutta, on December 10, the polling delayed there by the Puja holidays. And this was not all. Close behind were the elections to the provincial legislative assemblies, scheduled to begin with Assam and Sind in January, and not likely to be over in the Central Provinces until April. India was in for months and months of the most intense political activity. Auchinleck would have preferred to keep the Red Fort trials out of politics. He couldn't. As for Nehru and Congress Party, the closer the connection the better—at least for the moment.

In mid-November Nehru campaigned furiously through the Punjab. Then he came to Delhi (Achhru Ram flew down from Lahore with him in an Indian National Airways Beechcraft), and spent half a day with defense counsel at the trial—it had resumed after its two weeks' adjournment. He went to Meerut District next, where he toured for three days at an average rate, the newspapermen with him reported, of ten public addresses a day. In Assam a month later it was the same. At one point Nehru covered four hundred miles in three days and spoke fourteen times. And these were only his scheduled addresses. Villagers determined to have *darshan* of the Pandit found that if they blocked the road he would stop, get out of his automobile, and say a few words.

His speeches, as usual, were passionate. To a sense of enormous impatience with British rule he added an implied appeal to violence, an appeal felt particularly by students in any audience. When, therefore, students took out processions (as the Indian expression goes) to protest the Red Fort trials, they were not easily checked, turned back, or dispersed. They stood their ground and threw rocks. A collision of this sort occurred at Madura, deep in the south (it was Ayer's home town), the day after the first trial began. The police there fired, leaving two dead and more wounded. Over the next two weeks there were similar encounters in half a dozen places. But it was at Calcutta, on the afternoon of November 21, that a really serious confrontation erupted.

It, too, started with an attempt by university students to observe an INA Day. The plan was to assemble at Wellington Square and march the half mile to Dalhousie Square, which, with its tank (as India calls an artificial stone or brick-lined pond); its gardens; the General Post

Office on one corner, the Writers' Buildings across the north face; was as central and important an open space as Calcutta possessed. Police, however, stopped the column halfway up Dhurrumtolla Street. Dalhousie Square was a prohibited area, they pointed out. The students nevertheless persisted. There were more than a thousand of them. Onlookers swelled their number. They surged forward and were received with lathi charges, some delivered on horseback, until at last the police, who were being pelted unmercifully with brickbats, fired. Three persons fell. But the demonstrators did not scatter.

All night a hard core of students faced the police across the disputed stretch of roadway. In the morning they withdrew, then returned to resume the attempt, though Sarat Bose sent a note (and his brother Sunil came in person) urging them not to. This time they moved simultaneously up Bow Bazar and Dhurrumtolla. And this time, with enormous crowds at their back, they could not be stopped. The police gave way. Tens of thousands swept triumphantly into Dalhousie Square. But it was only the beginning. Already tram and bus drivers had quit work to show their support. Now the muncipal sweepers and water workers, who had labor grievances anyway, came out too. Shops and offices closed, less in sympathy than from necessity—it was difficult to get to work. Mobs leavened with the professional thugs India knows as *goondas* roamed the city, compelling Indians in European dress to take off their hats and ties, stopping British and American military vehicles at improvised barricades and setting fire to them, committing general mayhem. Outnumbered and savagely stoned, the police fired another dozen times. For three days Calcutta lived without transport, water, refuse collection, or order. Then, on the evening of the 24th, just as troops were about to be brought in, quiet unaccountably returned. But several score had been killed, hundreds injured, and some 150 burnt-out vehicles littered the streets.

If only, lamented the *Hindu*, the authorities understood what a wretched pattern these INA trials impose. Everywhere the cycle of protest leading to repression has been the same, "from Madura, where two young men died of gun-shot wounds early this month, to Calcutta, where the toll has been frightful. It begins with a procession or other demonstration to which the police object, tempers rise, there is a precipitate lathi charge followed by stone throwing, and then the police open fire with regrettable loss of innocent lives and the public more embittered than ever."[14]

But though the Calcutta police action prompted demonstrations in Dacca, Patna, and Benares; in Allahabad, Karachi, Bombay (where the police fired and several persons were killed), and in lesser places besides; this was the end of serious threats to law and order from students. The danger they posed had never been great. Even the Calcutta riots, as riots go, had not been serious. What *was* disturbing was a less visible phenomenon, an undercurrent of anti-European—and particularly anti-British—feeling below and outside student life. It could have been flowing there always. The Red Fort trials seemed to bring it to the surface.

Sir Norman Smith was aware of this, and paid it some attention. "So far the campaign in favour of the I.N.A.," he wrote in the note already mentioned in connection with Ayer's arrival, "has not resulted in any overt action against Indian Army men or Europeans. In respect of the former, there has been no hint of social boycott or anything of the kind, and it may be that nothing of this character is intended." He did admit that "the appearance of threatening posters"—posters promising twenty English deaths for every INA man hanged had been seen in Delhi and Calcutta—"does not make the position in respect of Europeans as satisfactory as could be wished."[15] But it is probably safe to say he did not lie awake at night over this, or similar dark gestures. It was otherwise with Enid Candlin.

Enid's husband Stanton was a metallurgist. They had met and married in Shanghai, where she was born. Early in 1941 they had come to India because Stanton was offered a position in a steel fabrication plant near Calcutta. In 1944 they moved to Bombay, where he took a job in an armaments factory just outside the city. But already life was growing hard for them, as it was growing hard generally for Europeans not in the services and without private means. Prices rose steadily. Salaries stayed where they were. Home leave was impossible, and technicians of Stanton Candlin's sort could rarely afford to send their families to the hills in the hot weather. Now the "natives" were turning ugly, and it was this business of the Indian National Army that made them so. Enid had not known the army existed "until the press was allowed to tell the public that the leaders were to be tried for treason."

"One of Stanton's best clerks," her recollections continue,[16] "a man of whom we were genuinely fond, who was both intelligent and good and who was personally always friendly to the British as individuals, told us that Subhas Chandra Bose was the George Washington of India." In his house he had hung pictures of three INA men. They were the leaders who were being tried for treason. He called them "India's heroes."

You could go into town to do some shopping and discover that the shops were observing "*hartal*, a boycott against the English." You could go into a shop that was obviously open, and stand there, and wait. And no one would serve you.

And then there was the open hostility.

> Even in our little station there was a series of incidents, which were multiplied a thousand times all over the country. Bricks were thrown at Europeans in the dark, windows were smashed, women's handbags snatched and thrown away, and most of these acts were unpunished. In the military hospital which belonged to our transit camp an English nurse had her face slapped by a sweeper in full view of an Indian ward—and the authorities dared do nothing. Any spark, it was thought, might start a conflagration.

Sir Henry Twynam, Governor of the Central Provinces, was neither as calm as Sir Norman nor as agitated as Mrs. Candlin. In a late November letter to the Viceroy he dwelt at some length on what the trials and the Congress election campaign might be doing to the Army. "I am bound to say that I do feel some uneasiness as to the attitude which Indian troops may adopt if called upon to fire on mobs. The disposition towards a sudden change of attitude in a tense political atmosphere is present now, I think, as it was in the days of the mutiny." He meant, of course, *the* Mutiny—the 1857 business. He had been reading in that regard, he continued, "some of the original reports printed in select State documents,"

> and extremely interesting they are. It is extraordinary how Units which were thought to be perfectly loyal suddenly decided to throw in their lot with the mutineers. I do not for one moment suggest that there is any widespread disposition on these lines, but

a slight uneasiness remains in my mind when I envisage the possibility of the Province being completely denuded of British troops.

At present in this Province I have 3 European Commissioners, 5 Deputy Commissioners, no Sessions Judges, no Assistant Commissioners, and 7 District Superintendents of Police. Altogether I have available 17 European I.C.S. officers, including 3 Judicial officers, and 19 European members of the Indian Police. These figures exclude people serving in the Government of India but include people on leave. This handful of Europeans has to deal with a population of 18 or more millions over an area of 100,000 square miles. It will be readily appreciated how difficult it will be for the administration if the present "hymn of hate" leads to the retirement of any substantial proportion of this handful of officers.[17]

Fortunately for Enid Candlin's peace of mind she did not, of course, see this letter.

In the Red Fort the first trial moved towards its appointed end. There was no doubt what that must be.

The defense had one small victory. On the charge sheets Dhillon stood accused of murdering Hari Singh, Duli Chand, Daryao Singh, and Dharam Singh, because—it was alleged—he had had them shot in a *nullah* at the base of Mount Popa on the 6th of March. And Prem stood accused of abetment of murder because he had awarded the sentences. It was useless to argue that the four had been tried and convicted following procedures laid down by the *Azad Hind Fauj's* own INA Act, the act Nag had drafted. The court did not acknowledge the legitimacy of army or act. So the defendants, as we have seen, could only deny that the four men had actually been shot. Sentence had been passed as a warning to others, then quietly remitted.

All hung on the testimony of the six men who said they had witnessed the shooting. It was Prem's father who saw how their testimony could be defeated. A *nullah* is a narrow thing. It may vary in width, as any ditch will, but if it is to be of any use as a refuge from roaming aircraft, its width will be measured in yards—not more. All the witnesses agreed that during those March days everyone routinely took cover in *nullah*s, and that the four men were shot in one. But when Achhru Ram studied what the witnesses had said about the shooting, who stood where, who saw what, what each person *could* have seen—the testimony here was crucial, for it was not enough that there had been shots and then bodies—it dawned on him that if the *nullah* was as constricted as some of the witnesses said it was, testimony to the actual shooting might be thrown in doubt. He put this to Bhulabhai, Bhulabhai argued it in court, and it worked. The same tactic could not be employed to save Shah Nawaz because the shooting of Muhammad Hussain on March 29 occurred under different circumstances. But it worked for Prem and Dhillon. Left uncertain, the court acquitted them of these charges.

It was otherwise with treason. Of treason, Prem, Dhillon, and Shah Nawaz stood convicted not only by their diaries and the other exhibits, and by what witnesses (Colonel Kitson among them) had told the court, but by their own statements, written out in advance as court-martial procedure required, and read aloud to the court by each—Shah Nawaz first, Prem second, Dhillon last—one December afternoon. "Freedom For India: I.N.A.'s Objective Explained," ran the heading in the *Hindu*'s rendering of that day. The paper reproduced at length what the three defendants had said. It noted, too, that "there were more spectators in the audience than at any time since the opening days of the trial a month ago."[18] Freedom for India! It would have been idle of the three to pretend, now, that they had not deliberately fought to obtain it.

On a Monday and Tuesday, speaking extemporaneously as was his habit, Bhulabhai delivered the closing address for the defense. The following Saturday Sir Naushirwan read the address for the prosecution. A week passed. On the morning of Saturday the 29th the Judge Advocate summed up, and the court adjourned. It met again on Monday the 31st, briefly, to allow Walsh to give evidence as to the character and particulars of service of the accused. Then the trial was over.

Bhulabhai was not there. He was on a train bound for Bombay. Achhru Ram was not there either. He had left for Lahore the day before. Raj had gone back to Poona to be with her small child. Only Prem's mother and another sister stayed on. They hoped to catch sight of Prem. During the trial that had been possible. Family could get passes to the trial sessions, and they and Dhillon's wife (who came every day on her bicycle) had attended regularly. They could visit the accused, not in the Salimgarh barracks but in a special enclosure to which they were brought. *The guards would be there,* Raj told me, *but they would turn their faces, they didn't interfere.*

But Prem's mother and sister were not allowed to see him that Monday. Achhru Ram had not thought they would be, which was one reason he had left for Lahore. He knew what, perhaps, his wife did not know: that when, at the end of a court-martial, the court asks for evidence of character and particulars of service, it is because it has found the accused guilty and has only to decide how heavy the punishment shall be. He had discovered, somehow, that this short final session was going to take place; he knew what its purpose must be; and he knew that days then pass before the sentence is confirmed and announced. He had wanted his wife to come away with him at once, not wait for the Monday. *We were all very upset,* Raj remembers. *And we thought there was no point our staying in Delhi. Besides, my father had taken so much of leave.* He could not absent himself from the High Court indefinitely.

Nevertheless these two stayed. But they did not get to see Prem. So on Monday afternoon they, too, left for Lahore. Raj says that, in the train, *my mother broke down and said she did not know whether she would ever see her son again.*

CHAPTER 21

THE TRIUMPH OF THE INA

Tuesday and Wednesday passed. On Thursday afternoon the three accused were called to the Red Fort proper. They went, and stood before an officer. The officer told them that they had been found guilty of waging war against the King, but not guilty of murder—or, Shah Nawaz excepted, abetment of murder. The sentence on all three was cashiering (dismissal from the service), forfeiture of pay and allowances, and transportation for life. Then the officer added, in a low matter-of-fact voice, that with respect to transportation for life, but not the other parts, the sentence had been remitted by the Commander-in-Chief.

They were confused and remained standing.

"That's all," said the officer.
"What do we do now?" we said.
"You're free," he said. "You can go."
"Where to?"
"If you have people in Delhi, go there. Otherwise we'll make a booking for you on a train to Lahore."

Prem thought of the woman from Jullundur who had been like a sister to him. Her name was Raksha Saran, and her husband was a member of the Defence Committee and managed the office at 82 Naryaganj. So they went to her house. The servants didn't recognize Prem. He had visited the Sarans when he came to Delhi to take the Dehra Dun entrance exam, but that had been ten years ago. Nevertheless they called Mrs. Saran, and she came at once, and the news spread. After a while they went to Asaf Ali's house, where the *Hindu's* man, ever alert, had preceded them. "Joyously they marched in, followed by a crowd of friends and admirers loaded with sweets and garlands," his account reads.[1] First, however, someone must have phoned Lahore.

As Raj tells the story, secondhand for she was in Poona at the time, her parents had gone that evening to visit a sick friend. Her two brothers were at a movie. Only her sister was at home when somebody rang and said, "*congratulations, your brother has been released.*"

> My sister couldn't believe it. "Don't be silly," she said. But he said "we have just got the news from Delhi."
>
> She had been lying down when the telephone rang. Barefoot and crying she ran to a neighbor's house and told them what she had heard. Then one of our servants came and said there were calls coming from other people. So my sister sent this servant on a cycle to find our parents. He was in tears— many of our servants had been with us for years and years and were very attached to the family—and when they asked him what was the matter, he could hardly speak. But at last he said Prem had been released. Our mother said, "don't talk rot. What are you saying?" But they came back to the house. And by the time they got there, there were hundreds and hundreds of people gathered.

Word was sent to the movie house. *The manager didn't want to announce what had happened for fear of losing everybody. But someone went in to find my brothers, it got out anyway, and most of the people left and came to our house. So there was an enormous crowd.* Later that night her brothers boarded a train for Delhi.

In Delhi Friday evening the Provincial Congress Committee organized a rally at the Gandhi Grounds, opposite the main railroad station. Asaf Ali presided and more than a hundred thousand people came. They filled the open spaces, jammed all the approaches, spilled into side streets, watched from the balconies of houses. Even on the dais the crush was so great that Dhillon's wife fainted. Asaf Ali spoke. He was followed by the three officers. When the loudspeakers failed, the crowd amused itself by shouting "Azad Hind Fauj Zindabad" (long live the Indian National Army), "Hamara Nara Jai Hind" (Jai Hind is our battle cry), and other slogans. Eventually it dispersed. Late that night the three, with Prem's two brothers, boarded the Frontier Mail for Lahore. It should bring them there early Saturday morning.

But long before it neared the city it was running late, for at every station, even during the small hours of the morning, crowds insisted on getting a glimpse of the three and would not let the train continue until they had. How it was to enter Lahore's main station at all, and how the three were to be extricated if it did, were questions the railroad people solved by arranging to take them off at the Cantonment station, several miles short of the city proper, and bring them on by car. This worked, up to a point. At the main station an enormous crowd waited, thick on the ground, in trees, on roofs, perched on the portico of the station itself. It was good-natured, as Indian crowds generally are. Through it the car inched. But when the car roof began to buckle under the weight of people pressing from all sides, Prem and his two comrades moved to the back of a truck. There they could stand and be seen. A young woman, perceiving her opportunity, worked her way over, climbed up, deliberately cut her finger, and with her blood applied tilak to their foreheads. The crowd roared.

Somewhere close by, though probably not close enough to see the woman apply the tilak, stood John Percival Morton, Senior Superintendent of Police, Lahore District. Under him were two superintendents of police (both British), one for the urban sub-division of the district and one for the rural; a handful of Anglo-Indian inspectors and sergeants; and four thousand men. "At that time," Morton explains in a typed memoir that sits today in the India Office Library in London,[2] "Lahore was held in check by Section 144 orders prohibiting the gathering of five or more persons in any one place." (He refers to Section 144 of the Criminal Procedure Code.) But on this January morning Morton found himself staring at far more than five persons. Before him was "a seething mass of humanity stretching back into the heart of the City," tens of thousands collected to welcome "the three heroes of the Delhi Trial . . . and celebrate their victory." To attempt to apply Section 144 to a body so large and obviously so worked up would, he recognized, be worse than foolhardy. It would be ludicrous. "There was nothing I could do but withdraw the Police and keep a low profile." And that was what he did.

He cannot have been happy about it. To Morton it did not matter how ecstatically Lahore received these three. To Morton they were renegades, then and forever, and what was going on at the station meant nothing—a bad taste in the mouth. But to Prem Sahgal, Dhillon, and Shah Nawaz the tumult and the shouting, in the very heart of the province from which they came, meant a great deal. Victorious armies are granted ceremonial triumphs. Defeated armies are not. At the Lahore railroad station on Saturday the 5th of January, 1946, three gallant officers received a triumphant welcome home. It was possibly the only triumphant welcome they were going to get. But it was genuine. And it was implicitly accorded them as representatives of the larger body of which they were a part. It was the triumph of the INA.

﷽

There we might leave it. But there are loose ends to tie. There are two grave disappointments to record. And there is the question how to situate the Indian National Army in the coming of Indian independence, what part to assign it, what credit to give.

The British reaction to Auchinleck's quite startling remittal of sentence—Englishmen anxious to comfort Achhru Ram had not dared suggest that his son could expect anything less than five years—was in some quarters violent. The *Statesman*, it turned out, had from the beginning followed the trial "with amazement and disgust." Staging the trial in the Red Fort betrayed an "astonishing lack of tactical and historical sense." Why open the proceedings to the public? Why hadn't the first officers accused been those who had committed "acts of gross brutality?" It had been in sum "a sorry business" from which the Indian Army was bound to suffer.[3] But no one publicly urged Auchinleck to abandon the trials. Two more had opened. Others were in preparation. In Bangkok, Saigon, and other distant places there were still Jiffs to be identified and picked up, and as late as February some three thousand lingered in Malayan camps, waiting to be brought home. The machinery had a certain momentum, and also a certain justification. To stop it dead would be wrenching. Let it continue turning, then. But let the product—courts-martial—be delivered at some place more out of the way.

This was arranged. The second and third trials, which had already begun, were moved to Delhi Cantonment on the southwest edge of the city. All subsequent trials opened there. Press and public could still attend, but it was less likely that they would, and increasingly they didn't. Warned that the charge of treason was inflaming public opinion, Auchinleck instructed the Adjutant General to bring in brutalities only. "By upholding the finding of waging war against the King in the first trial," he observed to Wavell, "we have achieved our object, which was, as you will remember, to establish the fact that failure to his allegiance is a crime which cannot be condoned in a soldier."[4] One finding had been enough. Never mind that the guilty had only had their knuckles rapped. It was the best that could be done.

Burhan-ud-Din's trial was interrupted so successfully by legal maneuvers that February was almost over before the court found him guilty, and dispatched him to seven years' rigorous imprisonment. Legal maneuvers did the same for the joint trial of Singhara Singh and Fateh Khan. Not until the middle of March did these two begin (but not finish, at independence all sentences were quashed) their *fourteen* years. Other trials followed or proceeded concurrently, each less significant than the last. Eventually the press lost interest. The dailies and the wire services ceased sending reporters. With the curious consequence that today, no one is quite sure how many trials had been completed (my private count is ten) when, early in May, a terse press communiqué announced the end. There were to be no more trials. At roughly the same time the last of the detained INA men, at the Red Fort and elsewhere, were released.

But one trial, the trial of Abdul Rashid, must be looked at again, because it contributed to the first of the two grave disappointments that Prem and others were meanwhile encountering.

Rashid was an emergency commissioned captain in the 1/14th Punjab Regiment. Sometime in 1942 Mohan Singh put him in charge of the Bidadari concentration camp. There he had men beaten— Rashid is the big Pathan of whom Prem remarks, *he did ill-treat people, he had them beaten up, he had a sweeper named Nimbu who used to do the beating.* For this and for taking up arms against the King-Emperor, Rashid was charged along with Singhara Singh and Fateh Khan. Prosecution thought it reasonable to try all three together. Rashid objected. He did not want to be defended by Congress Party's defense committee. He wanted to be defended by the Muslim League, which had a defense committee too. So on January 9 he went on trial separately in Delhi Cantonment. Thus far what he had contrived was simply a little peculiar. The Congress committee was hardly sectarian. Asaf Ali, its convener, was Muslim. Then two things happened.

Rashid denied that he had joined the INA to fight the British. He had joined, he said, because he could see that Mohan Singh and his Sikh and Hindu friends intended to ride into India on the backs of the Japanese and, once there, make it a place where no decent Muslim could hold up his head. He had joined, as other Muslims he assured the court had joined, so that they could arm themselves against this conspiracy. Privately, Prem was very angry. He knew Rashid for a coward and a bully. When the first INA collapsed he had helped get him, Singhara Singh, and Fateh Khan out of the Provost Marshal's office (*we didn't want a crowd like that there*). Now this, a deliberate attempt to blacken the freedom army in order to save his own skin!

But when, towards the end of January, Rashid's defense failed; when, on the evidence that he had once beaten a fellow POW unconscious and left him tied all day to the trunk of a tree, he was given (this on February 4) seven years' rigorous imprisonment; the whole complexion of the case changed. Nehru pronounced the sentence unwise. Prem mastered his personal distaste for the man and objected that, whatever offences might be alleged against him, as an officer of the Indian National Army, Rashid ought not to have been brought before a British court at all. Already the Muslim League was taking a different tack. Burhan-ud-Din's trial would not end for another three weeks, Fateh Khan's for another six, so the League's attention (and the public's too) was fixed upon Rashid. That its own defense committee could not obtain for him, what Bhulabhai's Congress committee had snatched for Sahgal, Dhillon, and Shah Nawaz, was insufferable. So the League cried foul. Rashid, it protested, was the victim of deliberate religious discrimination. In this dirty business the hand of the Hindu was visible, the hand of the Hindu Congress Party—Congress had the Government of India in its pocket. This was the line the League took and the press reported. Nevertheless it looked, for a moment, as if League bitterness might soften or even melt in the presence of the mass protest that erupted, once again, in Calcutta.

In Calcutta, on February 11, students once again left their classes, gathered in Wellington Square, and attempted to march to Dalhousie Square. Once again their route was barred, and students and police alike turned violent. Mobs formed, roads were barricaded, vehicles were torched, shop windows on fashionable Chowringhee Road smashed. There was firing, with dozens dead and scores wounded. But the violence was not as severe as it had been the previous November, nor did it go on as long—troops appeared much sooner. And there was something else. Rashid's sentence did more than send students into the streets, it sent Muslim students alongside Hindu. On February 12 a column a mile long again made for Dalhousie Square, and was allowed to pass. It was a column extraordinary for the number of people in it, "over one lakh" the *Hindu* said, meaning not so much that it exceeded one hundred thousand as that it defied counting. It was even more extraordinary for its composition. "Hindus and Muslims, Congressmen, Leaguers, Communists, students and women" composed it, the *Hindu* continued.[5] Many of the participants shouted slogans urging Hindu-Muslim unity. For a few hours it seemed as if in Calcutta Hindus and Muslims were forging a common front. And where Calcutta led, India might follow.

But the seeming was illusion. There was tension behind the harmony, as the *Hindu* reported a day or so later from its own city of Madras. In Madras, too, Hindu and Muslim students came together— or more precisely met, there was no question of a street procession—to demand Rashid's release. The meeting had hardly begun, however, when some students from Muhammadan College said they would not join in the shouting of "Jai Hind" unless they were permitted to shout their own war cry too. There was discussion. There was argument. "Jai Hind," it was pointed out, was not something Hindus had invented. It was the slogan, the call to battle, of an army in which Rashid and many other Muslims had served. But this was the first time in Madras that Hindu and Muslim students had come together on a common platform. No one wished to spoil the occasion. So when the Muslim students persisted, a way around the difficulty was found. Hindus would not shout "Jai Hind." Muslims would not shout "Pakistan Zindabad" (long live Pakistan). All would instead shout "Release INA Prisoners," a cry so very much less exciting than either of the others that, while the *Hindu* does not say anything about it, one suspects there was very little shouting at all that day.[6]

Pakistan—the land of the clean, the pure, the chaste (the Urdu word *pak* embraces all three). Coined more than a decade before by an Indian law student at Cambridge, it had had for years little currency. And Jinnah, the cold, confident, political tactician who spoke English better than he spoke the language of this homeland he was determined to carve out of the subcontinent, had for years made little headway with his All-India Muslim League. Then came the war. The war gave Jinnah his opportunity. Congress helped, by shooting itself in the foot not once but twice: the first time when, annoyed over the way Linlithgow pitchforked India into hostilities, it abandoned office in half a dozen provinces; the second when it embarked on Quit India—which, besides putting the leadership behind bars, closed Congress Party offices and furloughed party workers right across the subcontinent.

For three years the Congress was proscribed and almost dormant. The Muslim League was not. Its membership swelled. Its organization hardened. It announced that it alone spoke for Muslims, and torpedoed Wavell's Simla Conference by insisting that all five Muslim seats on the Viceroy's Council be filled by League men. It entered the Central and Provincial elections of late 1945 and early 1946 determined to make the point again, this time at the polls, and took every Muslim seat in the Central Legislative Assembly and nine out of every ten seats reserved for Muslims in the Provincial Legislative Assemblies. Though Congress Muslims survived (Asaf Ali entered the Central Assembly with a handy win in his Delhi open constituency), it was clear, now, that in most provinces they would continue to do so only if Hindus voted for them. By the time Abdul Rashid came up for sentencing and the Madras college students had their little argument about what shouts to shout, the League could claim to speak for virtually all the Muslims in India. And Jinnah, whose every second word now was "Pakistan," spoke for the League.

Of all this the men of the Indian National Army had been modestly aware, especially during the months of formation and training in Malaya. They were not politically minded. They were, however, conscious of the communities from which they came—Hindu, Muslim, Sikh—and of the links these communities had with parties. Quit

India had given them the license they needed to fight their way into India. And Quit India, they knew, had been Gandhi's doing, hence Congress Party's doing, therefore assignable chiefly to Hindus. But their geographical isolation (at INA Headquarters nobody read Jinnah's *Dawn* or the *Hindustan Times*), the routine of military life (which is a life essentially apolitical), above all their commander's deliberate and adroit smoothing of communal differences, had made of them—by the time they reached Burma—as truly a band of brothers as an observer could hope to see. And when the fighting in Burma was over and they were brought back to India, they carried this spirit with them into the Red Fort. We do not have to take their word for it. It is what visitors saw.

Toward the end of that November a group of journalists were given a tour of Salimgarh. "A more cheerful or determined set of men it would be impossible to find anywhere," the *Hindu's* correspondent reported. Asked what proportion were Muslims, what proportion Hindus or from other communities, the prisoners grew impatient. "How does that worry you? We never think of such things." One of the visitors wrote Sir Stafford Cripps, whom he knew personally, about the experience. "There is not the slightest feeling among them of Hindu and Moslem. They told us yesterday that in their army they had abolished all such distinctions. Hindus and Moslems had to eat the same food cooked by the same people, and no questions were asked." And the writer was driven to a wider conclusion. "I am more than ever convinced that this trial is a first-class blunder."[7]

But the realities of the Indian political scene broke this communal harmony even before the first trial ended. Ten days before this November press visit, it was reported that the Punjab Provincial Congress Party was going to ask Shah Nawaz to run for a seat in the Punjab Legislative Assembly. The idea was not illogical. It would have been hard to find three men who were better known than Sahgal, Dhillon, and Shah Nawaz. Running for office from prison was by now a commonplace—Subhas Chandra could have given anyone tips on how to do it. And for all that Prem had the connections, it was the older Shah Nawaz whom the public held to be the leader.

December came. A Muslim reserved constituency embracing Rawalpindi was chosen. The filing date approached. Then, suddenly, Shah

Nawaz's name was withdrawn. The League, it seemed, had decided to put up a candidate of its own. It would not allow Shah Nawaz to go to the Assembly unopposed. "We did not like that such a personality should be dragged into the arena of an election fight," explained the Chairman of the Provincial Congress Parliamentary Board (himself a Muslim) as he announced the withdrawal.[8] Privately he may have doubted whether even Shah Nawaz could carry Rawalpindi against a Jinnah man.

Shah Nawaz persevered. (In his modest way he seems to have had political ambitions, for in later years he sat in the Lok Sabha—India's lower house—and held minor ministerial positions.) In January 1946 he went to Calcutta to attend Subhas Chandra Bose's birthday celebration. He stayed with Sarat, gave a press conference, and rode in the two-mile-long birthday procession. Calcutta was Bose country, of course. Nobody thought the procession or the celebration would be threatened, and they weren't. In Bombay the police were less sure. They told a similar procession not to pass through a Muslim quarter lest there be trouble, and when it tried to anyway, stopped it with lathi charges and tear gas, though subsequent inquiry failed to establish that the Muslim quarter would have objected. In Jhansi a Bose birthday procession that passed through the Muslim quarter *was* attacked. Even Calcutta was not completely safe. As he left a mosque after Friday prayers one day, Shah Nawaz had his car windows broken by hooligans throwing stones and shouting "Pakistan Zindabad." From then on the divisiveness over Pakistan could only increase.

·❦·

So from the beginning the pleasure Prem took in the cheering crowds, in the sense of national unity and purpose he thought he detected in them, was disturbed by the discovery to what end Jinnah proposed to lead those Indians who could be persuaded—it was clear many could—that they were Muslims before they were anything else. About the Congress, too, Prem harbored misgivings.

It, too, had done well at the polls, its strength in the Central Legislative Assembly rising by half, and in the Provincial Legislative Assemblies proportionately—though at the expense of local, secular, or frankly Hindu parties. And it had accomplished this by adopting the language and the posture of Netaji and his men. By crying "Jai Hind" and "Chalo Delhi," which were *his* gifts to the lexicon of independence politics. By threatening the British with just such a Quit India rebellion on a massive scale as *they* had proposed to ignite by forcing their way across India's eastern border. Congress Party had prospered by embracing the Indian National Army and its leader. Or was the verb more appropriately *hitched*? Had the Congress simply hitched its wagon to this engine of popular excitement, and would it, now that the trials were over and the elections won, cast loose?

From the 7th to the 11th of December the Working Committee had met in Calcutta to draft the party manifesto for the provincial elections that were soon to begin. Gandhi had taken up station at Sodepur, close by. Nehru and the others had repeatedly gone to him there. The text that resulted had reaffirmed Congress Party's commitment to nonviolence in language that suggested that casting loose was exactly what the Party would do—even, that the Party believed it had never been hitched. Sardar Patel put the matter at its infuriating best a few days before the manifesto was published.

The occasion was the inaugural meeting of INA week. Sarat Bose presided. A hundred men just released from the Nilganj detention camp paraded. A portrait of Subhas Chandra twelve feet by sixteen was unveiled. Then Patel rose and explained to the crowd assembled in a south Calcutta park why the men and women of the Indian National Army deserved to be recognized. Was it for their courage and self-sacrifice? The Sardar allowed that it was. Was it because they had taken up arms and fought for India's freedom? The Sardar was silent. Their greatest accomplishment, he said, had been the suppression of communal divisions. Because of this the Congress welcomed them and had a place for them. But there was a condition to meet. If they wished to enter the Congress fold they would have to adhere to the Congress creed—"and put their swords back into the scabbard."[9]

Prem was still shut up in Salimgarh when Patel spoke. But the air of mingled condescension and indifference, the implication that we are happy to defend you but care nothing for your uniform, became apparent to him over the succeeding months and gradually put his back up. He was not unprepared, then, when Lakshmi went farther and developed a positive distaste for the Congress and its leaders.

This was after her return from Burma. On the 3rd of March her Dakota crossed the Burma–India line, and the British officer escorting her rose and took a seat on the opposite side of the aisle. To her great disappointment, no one met her at Calcutta's Dum Dum airport. Ammu, it turned out, had come down from Delhi a week before, waited in vain for three days, and gone back. So she caught a taxi into the city. *While we were driving along,* she remembers, *the taxi driver suddenly turned and asked me if I was the Rani of Jhansi. I told him that I was not, I had only commanded a regiment of that name. That was enough for him. He told me how the whole of India was thrilled by the INA and Subhash Babu's exploits.* And by her own, no doubt. Though she had been out of the country while the trials were taking place, the rumor of what she and her women had done (*The Diary of a Rebel Daughter of India* surely helped) already occupied the public imagination to a degree that none of the three who had been released in January could match. And not simply in the south. A Lucknow man once told me that at his college the chant ran:

Sahgal Dhillon Shah Nawaz
Inquilab Zindabad
Captain Lakshmi Zindabad
Jhanski Rani Zindabad
Captain Lakshmi Zindabad[10]

Which gave her three times the exposure of those three young men combined.

From Calcutta she flew to Delhi, where her mother and Prem met her. There was a rally on the Gandhi Grounds at which she was supposed to speak, but couldn't, she was shaking so from a malaria attack. Then she flew down to Madras with her mother.

What she and Prem did over the next few months has about it a certain atmosphere of anticlimax and disillusionment. Lakshmi was besieged by journalists who wanted to know all about her and her regiment. *I could quite understand their eagerness, and I tried to answer their questions.* But what they were after was *the glamor stuff about Netaji and his officers, myself included,* while she wanted to make them understand what Subhas Chandra had attempted, what an enormous undertaking his army and his provisional government had been, what he and they had meant to do once they broke into India. Ordinary people were more willing to listen. So she tried public speaking. There were times when she traveled almost constantly (Prem sometimes went with her), talking to crowds, covering a good deal of ground. On one April swing down the Kerala coast she touched Cannanore, Tellichery, Calicut, Cochin, Quilon, and Trivandrum—and spoke a dozen times—in just six days. She hoped she was succeeding. She wasn't sure she was.

And there was practical work to be done. At Delhi, Prem for some time had been the moving force in the INA Relief and Enquiry Committee. Nehru chaired it, Patel was the treasurer, Sarat Bose and Prem's prospective mother-in-law Ammu were members, but he was the joint general secretary. Its task was to find jobs for released INA men, and to support them and their families until jobs were found. The men were overwhelmingly north India born, with villages to go back to, so their problems were soluble provided there was money enough, and a good deal of money was being raised. But the Committee paid no attention to the south. And that, Lakshmi discovered when she went there, was insupportable. Men of south Indian origin who had been recruited from civilian life into Netaji's army, were being repatriated from Malaya by the boatload. When they landed they often had nobody to go to. So she pitched in and, with the help of others, set up temporary camps, raised money, found jobs.

But this could not go on indefinitely. Prem and she could not forever be picking up the pieces, as it were. Congress leaders were kind but patronizing. *They looked upon us as good little boy scouts and girl guides whom they had saved, and who now ought to obey and serve them.* Were she and Prem to go into politics? Whenever they saw Nehru, Lakshmi remembers, *he was very affectionate and patted us and all that, and said, "I've got big things in store for you. Just be patient. Be quiet. Don't disturb me now because I'm in the process of. . . . You see, the British are handing over. Let things get settled and then I'll attend to you."*

That was what struck her. The British were handing over. And Congressmen, confident that their hour had come, were beginning to behave like the men they expected to replace, brown sahibs taking the place of white. She wanted no part of that. Nor was there any serious prospect that INA officers would be asked to reenter the Indian Army. A disinclination to see these fellows competing for senior ranks in what was bound to be a smaller peacetime force, would by itself make a man like K. S. Thimayya think twice before he wished his brother back. So Prem, who surely would have risen some day to the command of a division or a corps in the army of independent India, who might even have become, like Thimayya, Chief of the Army Staff—Prem had no future in that quarter either. What else? If you kept on good terms with the Congress and rocked no boats, you might get a lesser embassy some day, Helsinki perhaps, or the like. Already some of his INA colleagues were angling for such appointments. But this was not for Prem.

In September 1946 he took a job with Sir J. P. Srivastava, an industrialist and member of the Viceroy's Council. "*You must be surprised to be asked to lunch by a toady,*" Prem remembers him saying. "*But I have read your file, and I think you are the sort of chap who doesn't give up when things are black.*" Would Prem come to Kanpur, where Sir J. P. had mills? Prem would, and went.

In March 1947 he and Lakshmi were married in Lahore. It was a quiet ceremony, for communal riots had broken out and Prem's father was ill. Then Lakshmi too came to Kanpur. For the independence celebrations on August 15, she remembers, *the city had been illuminated. There were fireworks and music, and a banquet in the City Hall to which we were invited.* It would be quite a bash. What the INA had fought to obtain was about to become a reality. But they couldn't bear to go. "India's Millions Rejoice" ran the headline in the *Hindustan Times*, but only the day before it had been "Fires Raging All Over Lahore." So she and Prem and two friends from the old days in Burma went to *one of the very few restaurants Kanpur boasted of—Valerio's—a sleazy place which had gone to seed now that the British were leaving.* Walls and woodwork were crumbling, the lights were dim, cobwebs hung from the corners. *The waiter was shabby, and seemed surprised to find that anyone could patronise such a place. But it suited our mood.* She ate very little. The men had a few beers.

Prem and Lakshmi have lived in Kanpur ever since.

❧

Did they ask themselves whether the freedom army had been of any use?

Only two weeks after Prem and his two comrades reached Lahore in triumph, Bhulabhai spoke precisely to that question. He, too, had observed, even before the trials ended, that there was perceptible movement in London. The Labour government was beginning to take Indian independence seriously. "We are on the threshold of freedom," he told businessmen assembled in Bombay's Taj Mahal hotel, "and it may be that you have not to launch a struggle." But Prem, Lakshmi, and the others *had* launched a struggle. If, now, it appeared that the struggle had been unnecessary, how should they reckon these last several years, how could they justify the pain and the effort?

Bhulabhai had an answer. It was important, he said, to give a signal, to give evidence of intent.

> It is good to know that at least two and a half million people of India owed their allegiance to a Government of Free India established at Singapore by Netaji Subhas Chandra Bose. He had the imagination, the foresight and courage. That is an historical event. We are proud to be able to say that there were men able to organise at the risk of their lives an army to free our country. You cannot have an objective more decent than this.[11]

It was good to know. It was good to be able to say that there were men (and women too, he might have added) who were willing to risk their lives for India. But Bhulabhai was wrong if he supposed that Britain's sudden willingness to consider a swift passage to complete independence had nothing to do with the Indian National Army and the Red Fort trials. Army and trials gave that willingness a powerful, perhaps decisive, boost. The case for saying so begins with an extraordinary note that the Viceroy, Lord Wavell, sent the Secretary of State for India, Pethick-Lawrence, on the 6th of November 1945, one day after the first court-martial convened.

Wavell, of course, had been disturbed for some time by Congress Party's direction. Nehru's speeches particularly bothered him. He had met the Pandit briefly on November 3, and though their conversation had been pleasant enough, he had come away convinced that the man's public posture was not going to change. Congressmen would use the trials to inflame India. Never mind that riot and storm were no part of their creed. "Either there is a secret policy which includes use of violence, or the more extreme leaders are out of control." Gandhi had been expected to moderate their behavior, "but he has said and done practically nothing for weeks, and his friends are believed to be seriously worried about his health."

"I must accordingly," Wavell had continued, "warn H.M.G. to be prepared for a serious attempt by the Congress . . . to subvert by force the present administration in India." The rising would come in the spring, or "quite possibly earlier." It would mean an organized assault upon the fabric of government, attacks on railroads, telegraph offices, police stations, public buildings generally. Government servants would be hunted down and killed. It would be 1942 all over again, though on a much larger scale. And its object would be "the expulsion of the British."

What was to be done? Half measures would not answer. The Government of India should ready itself to suppress Congress agitation instantly and "with great thoroughness." On the information already available, the GOI would be justified in arresting the leaders at once. This the Viceroy did not recommend. To clap Nehru and the others in jail would destroy all confidence in the sincerity of Britain's commitment to constitutional advance. But His Majesty's Government, Wavell believed, must make the Congress—and all India too—understand that any attempt on the part of a political party to use force would be met with force. Normal channels would not suffice for such a message. HMG must be seen to be in earnest. This was possible only if the warning took the shape of a formal statement in Parliament. Only a statement there, direct and unequivocal, could "bring Congress to its senses" and prevent the rising "which I apprehend." And Wavell closed by asking Pethick-Lawrence to arrange such a statement "at some very early date."[12]

A week went by. In London Pethick-Lawrence passed the note on to the India and Burma Committee of the cabinet. "I cannot take the Viceroy's warning lightly," he observed, "particularly as I am told for the first time that there are signs of a demoralising effect not only among the civil services but also in the Indian Army." Still, this was no time to wave threats in Congress Party's face. The things His Majesty's Government had in mind for India ought to be the subject of a formal statement in Parliament (there had been none since September), but a determination to crush violent protest was not properly one of them. "To make personal contact with Indian politicians and remove their suspicions," was. A statement would be drafted. In it the warning Wavell wanted would appear. The warning would be muted, however, and not occupy the center of the stage.[13]

Wavell objected. "From our point of view here," he wrote Pethick-Lawrence on the 27th, "the primary object of the statement should be to announce His Majesty's Government's determination not to permit violence." The statement should be crisp, cover little but the warning, and put the warning first.[14] But his objection reached Whitehall too late to be effective. In the India and Burma Committee, and in the full cabinet too (Attlee chaired both), it was the consensus that the thrust of the statement must be conciliation, not threats. A draft to this effect was discussed and approved on the very day Wavell transmitted his objection. Next day it was initialed. Six days later, on the 4th of December, it was read in both Houses of Parliament. It was hardly what the Viceroy wanted.

The warning was present, right enough. It was couched, however, in language quite the opposite of crisp, and buried in a late paragraph, so no one paid it much attention. What *did* catch Indian eyes was the information that in January a dozen Members of Parliament would leave England for India, M.P.'s charged with transmitting "the general wish and desire of the people of this country that India should speedily attain her full and rightful position as an independent partner State in the British Commonwealth."[15] A Parliamentary delegation would shortly be on the way. Simply by existing it would convey to Indians an implicit promise of freedom soon. So the effect of the December 4 statement was almost the opposite of what Wavell had asked for one month earlier.

No doubt he was disappointed, though in his letters to Pethick-Lawrence he did not show it. He remained uneasy. There was trouble down the road, and it would be the worse for not having been anticipated and met with a clear warning. Nevertheless he did not renew his request. If Whitehall declined to draw a line, so be it.

Restoring order when an insurrection did break out would simply be that much more difficult. It perhaps did not occur to him that if things dragged on, a time might come when a force capable of restoring order was no longer available. But Auchinleck, who as Commander-in-Chief would have to do the actual restoring, was bound to consider that possibility. In fact he was already thinking hard about it.

❧

The November 6 note had not gone unnoticed by the Chiefs of Staff in London. Perhaps this was because Field Marshal Lord Alanbrooke, Chief of the Imperial General Staff, happened to visit Delhi the day before Wavell sent it on, read it, and agreed with it, but remarked that in the event of serious disorders he had "no idea where the troops would come from."[16] Indeed, where *would* they come from? On the 16th of November the Chiefs put that question formally to Auchinleck. Were a second and more powerful Quit India rising to break out, did he have enough British battalions to suppress it? If not, how many more would he require? And as finding more was certain to be difficult, perhaps impossible, could he rely on his Indian battalions to do the job?

The Commander-in-Chief's response was prompt. It took the form of an "appreciation", or general review of the situation, very different from one he had sent Pethick-Lawrence on the 31st of October, just a few weeks earlier. In October he had been asked, how will the Red Fort trials (then about to begin) affect the Indian Army? How will your jawans take the process, how will your Indian officers respond? Auchinleck's answer had been that there was nothing to worry about. "The Army as a whole," he had said, "will accept the policy of limited trials." By this he meant not that his men felt trying a few Jiffs was permissible though trying them all was not. He meant the reverse. If all could not be brought to justice, some at least must be. "The majority view," he had written, "is that they are all traitors."[17] The Army would understand that for practical reasons only the blackest could be prosecuted, and would not make a fuss about it. But it would regret the necessity of letting so many off.

This was what Auchinleck had believed, and said, *on the last day of October.* In the weeks since, however, his estimate had been seriously shaken by a strong current of opinion from the Punjab. What the

Punjab thought about the Red Fort trials was not what he had expected it to think. And what it thought mattered.

For there, on the great north Indian plain cut by the five famous rivers, the Indian Army recruited the greater part of its fighting men. When Prem and the 2/10th Baluch sailed for Malaya in November 1940, *half* the army—some two hundred thousand men divided almost evenly between Muslims on the one hand, Sikhs and Hindus on the other—were Punjab born. (Among them, of course, were Prem himself, Dhillon, and Shah Nawaz.) Only one tenth came from Bengal, Bihar, and the United Provinces combined—came, that is, from the entire valley of the Ganges. And though by the end of the war the Punjab's share of the then more than two million had dropped proportionately, because the expanding administrative and technical services drew more successfully from other provinces, the Punjab still supplied most of the fighting men. How, then, the Punjab viewed the Red Fort trials was of the greatest importance. And what it thought, conveyed on November 17 by Sir Bertrand Glancy the Punjab's governor, and supported by what Punjab Government representatives said at a New Delhi conference several days later, was startling.[18]

In the eyes of most Punjabis, Sir Bertrand's memorandum declared, Sahgal, Dhillon, and Shah Nawaz are heroes. The public does not take their murder and abetment of murder charges seriously. Calling them traitors simply feeds their popularity. If a sentence of death is pronounced, and actually carried out, we shall face agitation worse than that which preceded the Amritsar massacre of 1919, violence more serious than any seen during the Quit India troubles of 1942. Its forcible suppression will prejudice for years any hope of a constitutional settlement in India.

What purpose, moreover, do these trials serve? Except for a few who have suffered at the hands of Jiffs, the men who know anything about the Indian National Army are sympathetic. A sentence of death upon some for being false to their allegiance will carry no lesson to jawans generally because jawans know that hundreds of equally guilty INA men are being released every day. The trial just beginning cannot, of course, be abandoned. If it is, Congress will sniff weakness. Future trials, however, ought to be few and—it was the most surprising of Glancy's proposals—*not for treason*. It is the treason charge that inflames feelings so, and makes the situation in the Punjab more threatening than any in living memory.

This was Glancy's message. To it was added what his representatives, one from the ICS and one from the Police, said at the November 19 through 20 conference that the Home Department put together in New Delhi to consider what was likely to happen when Jiffs went home. It had been assumed that as they were released from the detention camps, greys first, blacks later and more slowly, they would sink unnoticed into the villages from which they came. It had been assumed that even if they talked the Congress line—and not many, given their simplicity, would be able to do so—there would not be enough of them to have much effect. As Philip Mason pointed out (he was sitting in for the War Department), close to one million Indian Army men were scheduled for demobilization over the next eight months. Almost one million loyal jawans would scatter to their villages. But of Jiffs there would be at most twenty thousand. The one would quite swamp the other. The loyals would drown out the disloyals. So there was nothing to worry about.

But few of the conferees were so easily persuaded. Loyals and Jiffs, after all, were cut from the same cloth. There had been a time when they served together, saluted the regimental colors together, ate (as the saying went) the same salt. And many loyals had relatives in the traitor army—nephews, uncles, cousins; perhaps even, like Brigadier Thimayya, a brother. If, now, these Jiffs returned to their villages with tales of an army, a freedom army, that had fought for what even villagers were beginning to believe India must have, could anyone be sure that loyals would refuse to listen? When one day the subject of the detention camps happened to come up, "Home Secretary [the minutes read] pointed out that the longer the I.N.A. personnel were kept together, the worse they became." In Burma senior officers begged New Delhi to ship the last Jiffs home before the blacks finished infecting the whites. Translate this to the Punjab, traditional recruiting ground of the Indian Army, and what did you have? You had thousands of committed INA veterans settling down in precisely the places to which jawans went regularly on furlough, and from which recruits were regularly sought. Let this go on long enough and the whole army might be contaminated.

To call this a bombshell does not overstate the case. Auchinleck knew about the desertions, some years back, from Eastern Army. He knew that in the Arakan jawans had gone over to the enemy, and that they had done so not just because their morale was low but because they found Jiff appeals attractive. But he did not suppose that Jiffs had many friends in the Punjab. His years with the Indian Army had taught him that Bengalis were objects of derision and contempt to the martial classes everywhere—especially in the Punjab. Bose was a Bengali. Would any soldier of caliber wish to serve under a babu, a speech maker, a politician in Sam Browne belt and boots? Bose must have dragooned a few and then turned to the cowards and the weaklings to fill out his ranks. But the cowards and the weaklings could never win the sympathy, let alone the respect, of Punjabis—particularly Punjabis who had served with 14th Army.

Perhaps Auchinleck had in his mind's eye the snapshot, already well known, of Slim's 4th and 33rd Corps linking up one June 1944 day on the Imphal–Kohima road. Two tankers, one an Englishman and one a Sikh, greet each other. The Englishman has his back to the camera. The Sikh leans from the turret of his tank to grip the other's hand. Bearded, turbanned, smiling broadly, he is the perfect picture of vigor, assurance, and good humor. So stouthearted a son of the Punjab as this can have no use, surely, for quitters and turncoats. Yet Glancy and his people say that he has.

Glancy's memorandum together with the conference minutes reached Auchinleck on November 21. On the 24th he wrote Wavell proposing an end to treason trials—exactly what Glancy had recommended. Two army area commanders protested. "I have no information here which leads me to suspect that the I.N.A. issue is yet really serious in the Army," objected one. "How can we expect to keep loyalty if we don't condemn disloyalty?" inquired the other.[19] But Auchinleck, the Punjab presumably on his mind, was not to be turned. "With the existing Armed Forces recruited from all parts and all classes of India," and given "the growth of nationalist feeling," it was "quite impossible to isolate the Armed Forces from the rest of the country." He believed, now, that there was "no general resentment" in the Indian Army against Jiffs, and that most Indian officers would approve of what he was going to do.[20] If area commanders thought otherwise, it was because they listened too readily to their own kind. He, for his part, had for some time been attempting to estimate what *Indian* officers thought, and he did so now with a special urgency.

Sir George Cunningham, Governor of the North-West Frontier Province (which meant Peshawar and beyond), was making the same effort, and on the 27th suggested something that Glancy had stopped short of. Auchinleck, he wrote, ought to announce that "as Indian opinion is opposed to the trial of these persons [he meant Sahgal, Dhillon, and Shah Nawaz], he wipes the whole thing out and takes no further proceedings against anyone." Announce it now, he urged the C.-in-C. Halt the first trial and cancel any that are scheduled to follow. Do not let your subordinates tell you that this will be resented in the Army. Some Indian officers and men whose relations or close friends have suffered at the hands of Jiffs are no doubt thirsting for their blood, but they are few in number. "Most Indian soldiers who have said to me 'Hang the lot' have, in my opinion, said so because they thought it was what I wanted to hear."[21]

Auchinleck dug in his heels. He stuck to his proposal of November 24: Jiffs to continue to be charged, but with brutal acts only, not treason. Once the court-martial proceedings in the first batch were fully under way, this was done. But he did not instantly free Sahgal, Dhillon, and Shah Nawaz. Nor did he find fault with his protesting area commanders. "I know from my long experience of Indian troops," he wrote Wavell, "how hard it is even for the best and most sympathetic British officer to gauge the inner feelings of the Indian soldier."

Nevertheless he wanted that officer to try. And he very much wanted to discover for himself just how jawans viewed the Indian National Army. "I have set up a special organisation in G.H.Q.," he told the Viceroy, "with the sole object of trying to find out the real feeling of Indian ranks on this subject." He himself suspected, "from my own instincts largely, but also from the information I have had from various sources," that in the ranks

> there is a growing feeling of sympathy for the I.N.A., and an increasing tendency to disregard the brutalities committed by some of its members, as well as the forswearing by all of them of their original allegiance. It is impossible to apply our standards of ethics

to this problem, or to shape our policy as we would had the I.N.A. been men of our own race.[22]

It was a statement that mingled the preconceptions of his youth with an extraordinary sensitivity, a statement he was to repeat often in one form or another over the next several months.

🕉

Meanwhile there was the Chiefs' 16th of November inquiry still to meet. Should a rising occur, the Chiefs had asked, could the Indian Army be relied upon? On the 24th, the very day Auchinleck proposed an end to all trials for treason, he sent his answer. As usual it took the form of an appreciation, but in tone and content it was very different from the "do not worry" appreciation he had sent Pethick-Lawrence three weeks before.[23]

Were violent disturbances likely? Not at once, Auchinleck wrote, not before April; it wouldn't be in Congress Party's interest to interrupt the voting by encouraging any. Come April, however, and a rising might easily occur—and on a formidable scale. The Party would have learned from Quit India how easily rail, road, and telegraph communications could be disrupted. There were lots of unlicensed arms about, and many released INA men (as well as demobilized jawans who had caught the Congress bug) to use them. The principal danger areas would be Bengal, Bihar, and the United Provinces. But the government could expect serious agitation in other parts of India too, and would find that the people as a whole were a good deal more alive and rebellious than they had been in 1942.

Was the Indian Army capable of meeting disturbances on such a scale? Here Auchinleck's train of thought took a direction rather different from Wavell's. What troubled the Viceroy was the noise and fury Congress deliberately fomented. He wanted a plain statement of his government's determination, if provoked, to use the Indian Army against the Party, because he believed that only the threat of force could bring it to its senses. What troubled the Chiefs, however, was the Indian Army *itself*, not how or when—or if—it should be used, but whether it would prove usable. And it was to this concern that Auchinleck spoke on November 24.

In paragraph after paragraph the C.-in-C. reviewed the strains and influences to which the army was exposed, its commitments (noting not for the first time that using Indian divisions to help the Dutch recover Java was wildly unpopular), its distribution and strength. The conclusion he reached and transmitted to the Chiefs was that should a rising occur, everything would hang upon the army's confidence, its resolution, its state of mind. Given the troubling currents of the day—and Auchinleck put the INA and the trials high among these currents—this could best be secured by letting the Army know exactly what might be expected of it. That in turn called for a declaration by His Majesty's Government that armed force would be used if armed force was needed. It was just what the Viceroy had asked for.

"In the absence of a firm declaration," Auchinleck added, "the loyalty of the Indian Forces is likely progressively to deteriorate. . . ." If the rot went far enough and an insurrection occurred, it would be up to British battalions to suppress it. But there were very few British battalions in India. The task would be beyond them. They would not even be able to protect the lines of communication over which reinforcements from abroad would have to move. What then? "To regain control of the situation," Auchinleck confessed, "nothing short of an organised campaign for the reconquest of India is likely to suffice." He could not immediately "compute the air and land forces" that such a campaign would require. And as the Chiefs knew perfectly well that the British public would never support one, they did not ask him to work the figures up.

So Auchinleck urgently wanted what Wavell wanted, though for a different reason. No more than Wavell did he get it. The Chiefs had his appreciation on the 1st of December. Attlee read it a few days later and, while he waited for the Chiefs' report, wrote Pethick-Lawrence that it was clear everything depended upon "the reliability and spirit of the Indian Army."

> Provided that they do their duty, armed insurrection in India would not be an insoluble problem. If, however, the Indian Army were to go the other way, the picture would be very different. It is therefore clear that all possible steps should be taken to foster the loyalty of the Indian Forces, to show them that they have the solid backing of His Majesty's Government.

A variety of ways in which this might be accomplished occurred to him. Victory parades. Welcome home parades. Pay increases. Handouts of land. "Good propaganda to the villages in which the bulk of the fighting men live."[24] The Prime Minister said nothing about a "firm declaration." The statement on the floor of the two Houses, the statement that fell so far short of what Wavell had asked for on the 6th of November, had just been made, and it was soon apparent that nothing further would follow. In Downing Street they did not listen to what Auchinleck was saying. Or if they listened, they did not understand.

Auchinleck did not allow his thoughts to escape into any letter or memorandum that I have seen, but it is a fair guess that he knew now that the Indian Army would shortly cease to be the sharp sword obedient to the hand of the wielder that the Raj required. For almost a century he and his people had been the wielders. Soon His Majesty's Government would have no sharp sword to wield. And so when the time came, he remitted the sentences on Sahgal, Dhillon, and Shah Nawaz, explaining later, in a justly famous "personal and secret" letter to all senior British officers, that there had been no alternative. Though the great majority of Indian officers admitted the "gravity" of the offense, "practically all are sure that any attempt to enforce the sentence would have led to chaos in the country at large, and probably to mutiny and dissension in the Army, culminating in its dissolution."[25]

That, happily, had been avoided. It would be his and every responsible person's object "to maintain the reliability, stability, and efficiency of the Indian Army for the future, whatever Government may be set up in India." Auchinleck knew, however, that the shape this government took, and the manner of its establishment, could no longer be determined by Whitehall or New Delhi, by a cabinet mission (at the time he wrote one had been announced) or Act of Parliament—in a word, by the Raj. It would be determined by Indians, politely if they had their way, violently if they did not. For the Indian Army, which for almost a century had been the ultimate enforcing agency of the Raj, no longer had the capacity to compel.

This, indeed, was how it went. Independence came a year and a half later. What delayed it was not concern for process and consensus but the Hindu-Muslim (or Congress-League) struggle, resolved in the end by Partition peacefully pronounced but bloodily executed. That agony went on for months. The Indian Army, with some exceptions, was not employed to stop it. It, too, was breaking up.

What might have happened if, after all, His Majesty's Government had declared its willingness to use armed force against the Congress? What might have happened if Auchinleck, ordered to send in the Indian Army, had discovered that it was still, in spite of all, a sharp sword obedient to the hand of the wielder? It is impossible to say. The occasion did not develop. The Army was never put to the test. Three days before Christmas, Auchinleck telegraphed the Chiefs that there were "signs of a definite change in the attitude of the Congress High Command. Election speeches and propaganda of political leaders have become more sober and less inflammatory."[26] He dated the change from the Working Committee's Calcutta meeting early in December. (It was then, though Auchinleck knew nothing about this, that Patel gave INA men the little lecture about putting swords back into scabbards.) Wavell, too, noticed a mellowing. "There has been no real change of heart in Congress," he wrote the King, "but I think they have changed their tactics. . . ."[27] Neither the C.-in.-C nor the Viceroy thought this would be more than a lull. Yet it lasted.

The heat and fury of October and November did not resume. The prospect of a second 1942 steadily receded. Auchinleck supposed this was because Nehru and Patel were beginning to realise that they would wish to find a disciplined and obedient army at hand—should they assume power. Exactly so, except that for Congress Party the operative word, by late December, was not should but *when*. The Congress had threatened violence as long as it saw no other way of bending the British to its will. By early 1946 it knew that the British were bending and would bend further, and that *purna swaraj* was within India's grasp. On the 26th of January Nehru told an enthusiastic Allahabad crowd that freedom was not far off. For fifteen years, ever since the first public declaration of India's independence at Lahore on the 26th of January 1930, patriots had come together on this day to repeat the aspiration. "But soon we will be assembling to pledge ourselves to maintain the independence that we will have won," he said.[28] The Raj was handing over. And the Congress, of which he was now the undisputed leader, would be the legatee.

It was no longer necessary, therefore, to look for ways and means of disarming the Raj. It was no longer necessary to hail the defendants in the Red Fort trials and make much of the freedom army from which they had come. That work was done. But it does not follow that this army and these trials had nothing to do with Britain's now irreversible bending.

Auchinleck did not say, and probably did not believe, that the Raj had ceased to be the object of the Indian officer's loyalty simply because Bose and his renegades had come along. Colonel Wren had not supposed so either. Both believed that the shifting of allegiance was bound to happen, and would have happened sooner or later no matter what. Nevertheless it did not happen later. It happened then. In the autumn of 1945 India was swept by a storm of excitement and indignation, a storm that Bose and his renegades ignited. It was a storm the Indian officer, and the jawan too, could not ignore. They did not ignore it. We have it on the authority of the Commander-in-Chief that they djd not ignore it. In 1942, at the time of Quit India, there had been no question of their reliability. Now their own commander doubted it. Three years of campaigning, three years climaxed by battlefield victories in Europe and on the Irrawaddy, do not explain the change. Only that autumn storm can. It was the Indian National Army that forced Britain's hand.

⚜

One small scene, and a suggestion, remain. On the 11th of February Philip Mason rose in the newly elected and recently convened Central Legislative Assembly (where Lakshmi's mother Ammu had a seat) to defend the government's handling of the first Red Fort trial. By his own account Mason was an effective speaker. He had rehearsed what he meant to say so often—the debate, on a hostile Congress motion, had been postponed several times—that he had it by heart. And in his memoirs he says that he held the Members in the palm of his hand. "There was no barracking; they listened with absolute attention. I have spoken a good deal since then, but never to an audience so hushed and so attentive." But what he said, not many can have believed.

The trial, he said, had had a purpose. That purpose was "to maintain the integrity and reliability of the Indian Army" so that it could be passed on in form and spirit as it had always been, "a sharp sword obedient to the hand of the wielder whoever he might be." (The phrase, which I have let Auchinleck borrow, is in fact Mason's.) Who, he asked rhetorically, might that future wielder be? "An autonomous Government" he replied, coming as close to "independent India" as under the circumstances he dared come. When would such a government appear? In the not very distant future. And by what process? By "a transfer of power."[29]

What an imperious phrase. How marvelously cemented in the historical imagination, how massive and immovable on the library shelf. Not by struggle would India become free, Mason was saying. Not by struggle *did* she, the twelve volumes of *India: The Transfer of Power* announce. The instruments of governance were not won, they were delivered, in the manner of the father handing the car keys to his son.

Among those instruments, perhaps chief among them, was the Indian Army. It was to be passed on as it stood, regimental flags, battle honors, the full range of practice and tradition, untouched and inviolate. It was because Bose and his Jiffs had by their very presence threatened to bring the structure down, that it had been thought necessary (Bose being dead) to put Jiffs on trial. At the Red Fort, however, no one asked, was it the *Indian-ness* of the Indian Army that Bose and his men had particularly challenged? It would have occurred to no one to ask that question because the Indian Army, everyone knew, though Indian in name and overwhelmingly in composition, was not really India's at all. It was a mercenary army (in unguarded moments it used the term) in the service of the Raj.

Now, on that February day, Philip Mason assured his listeners that this "sharp sword obedient to the hand of the wielder" was in due course to pass into the service of an independent India. In due course. Mason made it clear that there would be nothing precipitate about the process. Britain had its hand upon the hilt. Britain would keep its hand there a good while longer.

But many of his listeners, Ammu among them, knew without being privy to Auchinleck's thoughts or memoranda that even as Philip Mason spoke, Britain's hand was slipping. Already the Indian Army was ceasing to be Britain's to dispose of. The autumn storm provoked by Subhas Chandra dead and Red Fort defendants living had made the Indian Army aware that it was no longer obedient, at least in spirit, to the Raj. Much less would it remain obedient to the hands of the wielder *whoever he might be*. Already *India* was the wielder. The Indian Army could choose no other, it served the nation; it would not wait to be conveyed when the British were ready to convey it, because it was already in the process of conveying itself. It was the same, or soon would be, with other organs and institutions of governance, even with the Central Legislative Assembly. For when Mason spoke, the assembly's Speaker was no longer the nominee of the Government of India. In open balloting Congress Party had just captured the chair.

What are we to make, then, of the premise enshrined in the title of those twelve fat volumes and assumed in much that has been said and written about Indian independence over the past fifty years? Shall we continue to believe that in India, power was not seized; that power, instead, was transferred? Shall we continue to entertain the image of power passing, when the proper moment has arrived and the parties are ready, from hand to hand, just as a set of car keys may pass from a father to a son? Or shall we consign this interpretation to some lower level, to the status of a thing comparatively true and useful in some respects and circumstances, but otherwise in the nature of a fancy—a fiction even. A happy fiction, but hardly more than that.

Subhas Chandra Bose's sudden death did nothing to erase his memory. For years many people, including an older brother, believed that he was not dead at all. He had survived the crash or had never been near the Sally bomber, and lived on somewhere, preparing for the moment when, like the Mahdi, he would return to sweep away the rubbish and lead the nation out of its torpor and muddle. A dozen false sightings and two exhaustive official inquiries did little to dampen this popular conviction. With the passage of time it dissolved, at last, by itself.

But he is remembered still, particularly in Calcutta. There his birthday, which falls shortly before the nation's Republic Day, is greeted with almost as much enthusiasm as that day itself. Processions are taken out, speeches made. His equestrian statue at the north end of the Maidan is covered with flowers. And at Netaji Bhawan, the Bose family house on Lala Lajpat Rai Road that serves as museum, archive, and memorial rolled into one, people from all over India and beyond come together on this 23rd of January for a gathering half commemorative, half scholarly (papers are given), that goes on for three or four days.

What he is remembered for is his vigor, his militancy, his readiness to trade blood (his own if necessary) for nationhood. In large parts of Uttar Pradesh, the historian Gyanendra Pandey has recently remarked, independence is popularly credited not to "the quiet efforts at self-regeneration initiated by Mahatma Gandhi," but to "the military daring of Netaji Subhas Chandra Bose."[30] Prem and Lakshmi believe that had he brought his government and army across the Burmese border, had he simply managed to survive the war and return to India, he might have given her both independence without Partition and the revolution she needed and still lacks. *Indians regret,* they say, *that freedom did not come directly as a result of armed struggle. Things then would have been different, and better—no compromises, no maneuvering for office, no encouragement to the divisive forces now so rampant.* To this day people invoke his name when times are bad.

So there is hardly a city anywhere in India that does not have its Subhas Chandra Bose Avenue, its Netaji Marg. It is otherwise with the soldiers he commanded. If there are public thoroughfares honoring the *Azad Hind Fauj,* they must be few for I have yet to run across one. No holiday honors the army, no statue preserves an officer's face; there is no archive, no museum (though Netaji Bhawan houses some photographs and other memorabilia), and with one modest exception no monument. Prem and the two other accused in the first trial speak briefly (their voices have been recorded) at the conclusion of the daily son et lumière at the Red Fort. But the tourists who come of an evening to enjoy that production expect to be entertained with Mogul court doings, not India's struggle for independence. And Mogul court doings are what they mostly get.

Not even a plaque informs the curious in which building the three were tried. If you want signs of a determination to keep the memory of the INA alive, you must go to the Manipur basin. There, I am told, the state government has built a replica of the Singapore waterfront memorial the sappers blew up, and maintains a small INA museum and library. Manipur, however, is far away on India's border. In India proper, outside of Bengal, the army appears to be largely forgotten. And the clincher, for me, is this. At the place where I teach I sometimes ask young Indian students whether they have ever heard of Subhas Chandra Bose. Almost invariably they reply "of course"—and are amused or even a little indignant that I should ask. But with the Indian National Army it is different. When I make my inquiry about it, explaining perhaps the when and where of the force, often they look blank.

This is odd. Subhas Chandra began life as a politician. He did not finish it that way. The figure on horseback at the north end of the Maidan is a martial figure, and it is for his military daring that he is remembered, Gyanendra Pandey says. The two years in Southeast Asia, from the July morning when the men brandished their rifles and roared their assent, to the August afternoon when the Sally crashed in flames, were the climactic years of his life. Remove those two years—imagine Subhas unable to make the submarine journey, languishing idle and neglected in a contracting Reich, at last captured and put away in some distant place—and he is seriously, perhaps fatally, diminished. Those years were crucial.

But Bose the soldier (for a soldier he was determined to be) did not move through them solitary and alone. He had an army. It was there in Singapore, alive but marking time, when he arrived. He brought it quite literally to its feet, added a regiment of women, more than doubled its numbers, took it to Burma, and led it in the months of promise and in the months of defeat. It became his indispensable partner. With it, raising India against the British on the ground—or, as it turned out, in the forum of public opinion—was possible. Without it, raising India was not. Had the Indian National Army in its several tens of thousands not existed, Subhas Chandra would have been reduced to making radio addresses, arranging photo opportunities, shuffling portfolios in a provisional government that had no credibility because it had no prospects. He would have been reduced to posturing. And had he persisted, he would be remembered now as the puppet British intelligence said he was at the time.

The men and women of the Indian National Army made all the difference. *Without Netaji*, Prem once said to me, *we would have been nothing*. But what, one may reasonably ask, would he have been without them?

Prem died suddenly on the 17th of October, 1992, eight weeks after this book went to press.

INA Strength

Because INA papers in both Burma and Malaya were for the most part scattered, lost, or deliberately destroyed on Bose's order, it is not easy to establish the strength, composition, or disposition of the army at any given moment during its life. The most convincing estimates of strength are those made by British intelligence, in particular one made by Lt. Colonel G. D. Anderson and his staff when, in May 1946, they prepared—in some haste, for CSDIC Delhi which he commanded was about to close down—a series of "monographs" on aspects of the INA.

There were seventeen of these monographs (most but not all are preserved in the India Office Library under the heading L/WS/2/45). One dealt with recruitment and training, another with awards and decorations. There was a monograph on the several spy schools the army ran, there was a monograph on army finance. Monograph no. 3 is entitled "The Incidence of Volunteers and Non-Volunteers." It was written in an effort to determine once and for all just how many there had been of each. How Anderson and his people arrived at their figures is not clear. I suppose they used the estimates they had been making and adjusting for years. These rested in part on the interrogation of captured or surrendering Jiffs, but there must always have been guesswork involved.

Colonel Anderson begins with the 55,000 Indian soldiers who passed alive into Japanese hands during the Malayan campaign, some during the fighting, most when Singapore fell. 45,000 of these assembled at Farrer Park on February 17, he believes, though such a large number, given the confusion in the days immediately following Percival's surrender, strikes me as unlikely. Most of these volunteered. "Only 5,000 PW remained staunch non-volunteers," the monograph reads. Add to these the 10,000 on the mainland, who were not approached, he says (though we have it on the authority of Shah Nawaz that they were), and that gives us 40,000 volunteers and 15,000 non-volunteers in the autumn of 1942.

The Japanese, however, provided arms for only 16,000. Of these, some 4,000 withdrew when the first INA collapsed. "The second INA thus started off with only 12,000 members." But "through the demagogic oratory of S. C. Bose" between 8,000 and 10,000 ex–Indian Army men were brought into the ranks during 1943–45. There would conceivably have been thousands more had not so many POWs been shipped off to labor for the Japanese in distant places. Meanwhile some 18,000 Indian civilians enlisted. In early 1945, then, the INA by Anderson's count consisted of approximately 40,000 men raised in Malaya, to which add an indeterminate but small number recruited and trained in Burma, and perhaps some of the 5,000 Indian soldiers who had been defending Hong Kong. From these Anderson might have been expected to subtract the losses from wounds, hunger and disease, capture, and desertion, but he does not.

Colonel Anderson's round figure is precisely what D. C. Nag of the INA comes up with at the first Red Fort trial. "The final strength of the Indian National Army was about 40,000," he tells the court (Moti Ram, *Trials in Red Fort*, 28). At almost the same moment Whitehall puts the total at 43,000 (memorandum dated 20 Oct 1945, in *Transfer of Power*, 6:369, doc. 154). It does so by raising Anderson's estimate of civilian recruits by several thousand.

NOTES

Introduction

1. See the foreword to the first volume of Nicholas Mansergh, ed., *The Transfer of Power 1942–47* (London: H. M. Stationery Office, 1970–83), ix. Mansergh gives a longer account of the venture (incorporating, however, the language I quote here) in the India Office Library's annual report for 1982–83, 8–17.

2. The quotation, from page 11 of the India Office Library's annual report for 1983–84, is part of a piece by Hugh Tinker appropriately called "Burma: Power Transferred or Exacted?" 7–13. Tinker says frankly that he wanted to "escape" from the transfer-of-power concept, and was delighted when Mansergh suggested that the Burma set receive a different title.

3. *Hindu*, 22 Feb 1946.

Chapter 1

1. Quoted in Geoffrey Ashe, *Gandhi* (New York: Stein and Day, 1969), 296.

2. Philip Mason, *A Matter of Honour* (New York: Holt, Rinehart and Winston, 1974).

3. Raja Rampal Singh, quoted in Stephen P. Cohen, *The Indian Army* (Berkeley: University of California Press, 1971), 66.

Chapter 2

1. "Subharama Swaminadhan was M.A. Madras and in 1898 L.L.B. Edinburgh and in 1899 B.Sc. (Pure) Edinburgh," writes Dr. A. R. Mills of that university (letter to me of 20 Feb 1979). The three Gilchrist Scholarships, he explains, were open "to natives of India (note the Victorian language!) who had passed the competitive exams at the Presidential Colleges of India." The stipend of one hundred pounds a year is worth so little today, Mills adds, that it purchases not Indian M.A.'s but scientific apparatus.

2. *Swaminadhan: A Memoir* (privately printed, n.d.). Much of the information on Swaminadhan comes from this little book, which Mrinalini kindly lent me.

3. Throughout I have done my best to test Lakshmi's memory, and Prem's, against published accounts and the recollections of others. That this particular incident occurred is confirmed in its general outlines by Margaret Cousins herself, in James H. Cousins and Margaret Cousins, *We Two Together* (Madras: Ganesh, 1950), 581.

4. From the recollections of N. S. Gill, recorded Oct 1973 (Nehru Memorial Library, New Delhi).

Chapter 3

1. This war diary, WO 17 2/108 in the Public Record Office, London, runs from late October 1940, when the battalion left Bareilly, to the end of December 1941. November is missing, with the explanation "diary destroyed by enemy action." As for January and February, perhaps things were so frantic it wasn't even kept.

2. The Indian Army List for January 1942 carries Prem Kumar Sahgal as an acting captain from April 1940, as a temporary captain from March 1941. His permanent rank is lieutenant. Among the 60 lieutenants on the 10th Baluch Regiment list he appears 42nd in order of seniority. G. G. Bewoor, two years his senior at Dehra Dun, is 23rd. It is perhaps an index of Indianization that of these 60 officers, about 25 (to judge by their names) are Indian. It is perhaps another that among the 2nd lieutenants, all but a handful of whom are emergency commissioned, only 20 out of 136 are.

3. Bisheshwar Prasad, ed., *Campaigns in South-East Asia, 1941–42* (New Delhi: Combined Inter-Services Historical Section, 1960), 130–31.

Chapter 4

1. This and subsequent quotations are from Kate Caffrey, *Out in the Midday Sun* (New York: Stein and Day, 1973), 142, 164, 186, and 187.

2. It is Joyce Lebra's opinion, developed after meeting the man and reading his published accounts, and communicated to the author verbally and in correspondence, that Fujiwara's sympathy for Indian independence was genuine and immediate.

3. From Shah Nawaz's written statement at the first Red Fort trial, quoted in Moti Ram, ed., *Two Historic Trials in Red Fort* (New Delhi: Roxy Printing Press, 1946), 104.

4. This and subsequent quotations are drawn from his account of his early life and career, reproduced in Durlab Singh, ed., *The I.N.A. Heroes* (Lahore: Hero Publications, 1946), 140–53.

5. Moti Ram, *Trials in Red Fort*, 141. Subsequent quotations come from other parts of Bhulabhai's address, which occupies pages 140l [*sic*] through 219.

6. Arshad's account of Farrer Park appears in ibid., 140–40a.

7. Hunt *was* interviewed in Delhi early in October 1945, by Prem's father Achhru Ram and by his colleague Badri Das. Hunt had paused there en route to England for medical

treatment. But "no statement was taken from him," Badri Das later explained. It would have been unusable in court "because the statement would have to be taken before the accused," and as the trial was still a month away, the accused weren't available. Though the defense would have liked Hunt to testify, it did not (given his physical condition) press for his detention in Delhi. Nor did the prosecution show any interest. Ibid., 37–38.

8. Ibid., 51.

9. Ibid., 105, 118.

10. Ibid., 51. It is Baboo Ram who puts these words into Mohan Singh's mouth, but they correspond closely with other accounts.

Chapter 5

1. Mohan Singh, *Soldier's Contribution to Indian Independence* (New Delhi: Army Educational Stores, n.d. [1974?]), 109.

2. Shah Nawaz Khan, *My Memories of I.N.A. & Its Netaji* (Delhi: Rajkamal Publications, 1946), 20–21.

3. Moti Ram, *Trials in Red Fort*, 140b. The quotations immediately following are from the same page.

4. "A Forgotten Long March: The Indian Exodus from Burma, 1942," *Journal of Southeast Asian Studies* 6, no. 1 (Mar 1975): 5.

5. Moti Ram, *Trials in Red Fort*, 7.

6. Ibid., 10. The reference to "gross atrocities" occurs on page 228.

7. *Hindu*, 20 Dec 1945.

8. Moti Ram, *Trials in Red Fort*, 281–82.

9. Ibid., 45.

10. *Hindu*, 24 Nov 1945.

11. Ibid., 25 Nov 1945.

12. Hugh Toye, *The Springing Tiger* (London: Cassell, 1959), 113.

13. Colonel Toye offers no evidence for the truth of Durrani's tale. Nor has he been willing to show me any, or allow me to refer to the correspondence between us in which he makes the case. It is reasonable to assume, however, that Toye once had, or at least once saw, such evidence.

14. The phrase "heroic personal story" appears as the subtitle to Mahmood Khan Durrani, *The Sixth Column* (London: Cassell, 1955). The finger pressing and the water treatment appear on pages 249–51.

15. Shah Nawaz, *I.N.A. & Its Netaji*, 32.

16. Moti Ram, *Trials in Red Fort*, 94.

17. Mohammad Zaman Kiani, "India's Freedom and the Great INA Movement," *The Oracle* 6 no. 1 (Jan 1984): 106.

18. Shah Nawaz, *I.N.A. & Its Netaji*, 49.

Chapter 6

1. Linlithgow to Churchill, 31 Aug 1942, in *Transfer of Power*, 2:853, doc. 662.

2. Francis G. Hutchins, *India's Revolution: Gandhi and the Quit India Movement* (Cambridge: Harvard University Press, 1973), 67.

3. Ibid., 137.

4. Philip Woodruff, *The Men Who Ruled India: The Guardians* (London: Jonathan Cape, 1963), 242. At the time Philip Mason wrote under this pen name.

5. Ashe, *Gandhi*, 319.

6. Jawaharlal Nehru, *The Discovery of India*, 3rd ed. (London: Meridian Books, 1951), 414.

7. Ibid., 403.

8. Reginald Coupland, *The Indian Problem: Report on the Constitutional Problem in India* (New York: Oxford University Press, 1944), 2:242. The word *totalitarian* appears frequently in British official correspondence and speeches about the Congress. Gandhi is often termed *dictatorial*.

9. Linlithgow to Amery, 19 Feb 1943, in *Transfer of Power*, 3:690, doc. 486.

10. Quoted in Gowher Rizvi, *Linlithgow and India* (London: Royal Historical Society, 1978), 121.

11. Winston S. Churchill, *A Roving Commission* (New York: Charles Scribner's Sons, 1951), 104.

12. This phrase occurs toward the end of his Mansion House speech on 10 Nov 1942, reproduced among other places in *Keesing's Contemporary Archives*, 5450.

13. Quoted in Rizvi, *Linlithgow and India*, 162.

14. Hutchins, *India's Revolution*, 199, 200.

15. *The Collected Works of Mahatma Gandhi* (New Delhi: Ministry of Information and Broadcasting, 1958–84), 76:291.

16. Ibid., 400.

17. Ibid., 96.

18. Ibid., 159.

19. Quoted in Sarvepalli Gopal, *Jawaharlal Nehru: A Biography* (Cambridge: Harvard University Press, 1976), 1:292.

20. *Collected Works of Gandhi*, 76:160.

21. Quoted in Coupland, *The Indian Problem*, 2:294.

22. *Collected Works of Gandhi*, 76:295.

23. Ibid., 379.

24. Quoted in Maulana Abul Kalam Azad, *India Wins Freedom: An Autobiographical Narrative* (Bombay: Orient Longmans, 1959), 85.

25. Hutchins, *India's Revolution*, 241.

26. Ian Stephens, *Monsoon Morning* (London: Ernest Benn, 1966), 5.

27. Churchill to Amery, 14 Sept 1942, in *Transfer of Power*, 2:961, doc. 743.

28. Gyanendra Pandey, "The Revolt of August 1942 in Eastern UP and Bihar," in *The Indian Nation in 1942*, edited by himself (Calcutta: K. P. Bagchi, 1988), 136.

29. "Repression of a Civil Rebellion in Bengal 1942–44" (paper delivered at the 14th Annual Conference on South Asia, Madison, Wisconsin, Nov 1985).

30. So Professor Pandey argues, in his introduction to the collection of essays (notice the title) mentioned in note 28 this chapter.

31. Linlithgow quoting L. Brander in a letter to Amery 28 Feb 1943, in L/PO/3/3C, India Office Library.

32. Quoted in K.K. Ghosh, *The Indian National Army: Second Front of the Indian Independence Movement* (Meerut: Meenakshi Prakashan, 1969), 83 note 16.

33. *Collected Works of Gandhi*, 76:311.

Chapter 7

1. Moti Ram, *Trials in Red Fort*, 307.

2. Ibid., 53.

3. Mohan Singh, *Soldier's Contribution*, 122.

4. Ibid., 135.

5. Quoted in Ghosh, *Indian National Army*, 98.

6. Personal correspondence with the author.

7. Joyce Lebra has talked to Fujiwara, to Suzuki's son, and to Yanagawa, a Japanese on the staff of the intelligence agency *Beppan*, which trained the officer corps of the Java Defense Volunteer Army (*Peta*). "All three," she remembers, "were struck by parallels between their own missions and that of the legendary Lawrence of Arabia." Joyce C. Lebra, *Japanese-Trained Armies in Southeast Asia* (New York: Columbia University Press, 1977), 7–8, 91–92, 100; and personal correspondence with the author.

8. Quoted in K. R. Palta, *My Adventures with the I.N.A.* (Lahore: Lion Press, 1946), 41.

9. The scene is described at length in Kesar Singh Giani, *Indian Independence Movement in East Asia* (Lahore: Singh Brothers, 1947), 1:93–98. Giani apparently was present.

10. Ibid., 102.

11. Ibid.

12. Quoted in ibid., 131.

13. Palta, *My Adventures*. For the quotation, see page 19.

14. Shah Nawaz, *I.N.A. & Its Netaji*, 58.

Chapter 8

1. Nirad C. Chaudhuri, *The Autobiography of An Unknown Indian* (London: Macmillan, 1951), 377.

2. I have Paul Greenough to thank for this suggestion, and for much else on the subject of Bengal and the Bengalis.

3. Dilip Kumar Roy, *The Subhash I Knew* (Bombay: Nalanda Publications, 1946), 51–52.

4. Ibid., 54.

5. Harindranath Chattopadhyaya, *Life and Myself* (Bombay: Nalanda, 1948), 179.

6. Subhas Chandra Bose, *An Indian Pilgrim: An Unfinished Autobiography 1897–1921* (New York: Asia Publishing House, 1965), 170, 172.

7. Ibid., 88.

8. Ibid., 65.

9. Hemendranath Das Gupta, *Subhas Chandra* (Calcutta: Jyoti Prokasalaya, 1946), 72.

10. This and subsequent quotations are from Edward Oaten, "The Bengal Student As I Knew Him 1909–1916", in *Netaji and India's Freedom*, edited by Sisir K. Bose (Calcutta: Netaji Research Bureau, 1975), 29–34.

11. Das Gupta, *Subhas Chandra*, 15.

12. Quoted in ibid., 16. .

13. Sir John Strachey, *India: Its Administration & Progress*, 4th ed. rev. (London: Macmillan, 19ll), 2. Subsequent quotations are from pages 5, 6, 10, 8, 548, and 552–53, in that order.

14. Quoted in John Clive, *Macaulay: The Shaping of the Historian* (New York: Random House, 1973), 383.

15. K. M. Panikkar, *Asia and Western Dominance* (London: George Allen & Unwin, 1959), 247–48.

16. Clive, *Macaulay*, 381.

17. Quoted in Sir George Trevelyan, *The Competition Wallah* (London: Macmillan, 1895), 323 (first published 1865). The full text of the minute occupies pages 319–30.

18. The committee's report is appended to Oaten's account (see note 10 this chapter). The lines quoted appear on page 48.

19. Bose, *An Indian Pilgrim*, 68.

20. Roy, *The Subhash I Knew*, 45.

21. Das Gupta, *Subhas Chandra*, 26. Five years later Subhas wrote his brother Sarat that he ought to have admitted assaulting Oaten. At roughly the same time he told fellow ICS candidate C. C. Desai that "he had no hand in this particular incident." Subhas to Sarat, 23 Apr 1921, in Sisir K. Bose, ed., *Netaji Collected Works* (Calcutta: Netaji Research Bureau, 1980–), 1:233. Kewal L. Panjabi, ed., *The Civil Servant In India* (Bombay: Bharatiya Vidya Bhavan, 1965), 71.

22. Bose, *An Indian Pilgrim*, 70.

23. Ibid., 70–71.

24. Sisir Bose, *Netaji and India's Freedom*, 49.

25. Hugh Toye, *Springing Tiger*, 18–19.

26. Roy, *The Subhash I Knew*, 53.

27. Strachey, *India*, 544–45.

28. Rabindranath Tagore, "Indian Students and Western Teachers," *The Modern Review* (Calcutta) Apr 1916: 416–22.

29. Subhas Chandra Bose, *The Indian Struggle 1920–1942* (New York: Asia Publishing House, 1964), 132, 134, 141, 216; *An Indian Pilgrim*, 69 note 1.

Chapter 9

1. From a letter to his mother, in *An Indian Pilgrim*, 119–20.

2. Ibid., 40.

3. Ibid., 3.

4. Bose, *Indian Struggle*, 301.

5. Thomas Babington Macaulay, "Warren Hastings," in *Macaulay: Prose and Poetry*, ed. G. M. Young (Cambridge: Harvard University Press, 1967), 386 (first published 1841).

6. From the letter cited in note 1 this chapter.

7. "The Fear of Cowardice" serves as chapter heading for an entire section of Lloyd I. Rudolph and Susanne Hoeber Rudolph, *The Modernity of Tradition* (Chicago: University of Chicago Press, 1967).

8. From an 1891 issue of *The Vegetarian*, quoted in ibid., 167.

9. Ibid., 164.

10. Strachey, *India*, 451.

11. Roy, *The Subhash I Knew,* 77.

12. Ibid., 171.

13. Leonard A. Gordon, *Brothers Against the Raj: A Biography of Sarat & Subhas Chandra Bose* (New Delhi: Viking Penguin, 1990), 41, 134.

14. Nirad C. Chaudhuri, *The Continent of Circe* (New York: Oxford University Press, 1966), 89.

15. From a letter to Hementa, in *An Indian Pilgrim*, 167.

16. Ibid., 82.

17. Ibid., 102.

18. Ibid., 95.

19. Mihir Bose, *Lost Hero: A Biography of Subhas Bose* (London: Quartet Books, 1982), 67–68.

20. Bose, *Indian Struggle*, 141.

21. Quoted in Mihir Bose, *Lost Hero*, 33.

22. Bose, *Indian Struggle*, 131.

23. The quotations are from Gordon, *Brothers Against the Raj*, 244–45.

24. Ibid., 159.

25. Gopal, *Nehru*, 1:28.

26. Bose, *Indian Struggle*, 229.

27. Ibid., 231.

28. Quoted in William Manchester, *The Last Lion* (Boston: Little Brown, 1983), 815.

29. Quoted in Milan Hauner, *India in Axis Strategy* (Stuttgart: Ernst Klett, 1981), 62.

30. Bose, *Indian Struggle*, 293, 294.

31. Ibid., 250.

32. Ibid., 296.

33. Quoted in Gordon, *Brothers Against the Raj*, 308.

34. Mihir Bose, *Lost Hero*, 116. Leonard Gordon has no single compelling explanation.

35. Netaji Research Bureau, comp. *Crossroads: Being the Works of Subhas Chandra Bose 1938–1940* (New York: Asia Publishing House, 1962), 11.

36. Ibid., 105, 106.

37. Ibid., 107.

38. Ibid., 133.

39. M. A. H. Ispahani, quoted in Mihir Bose, *Lost Hero*, 143.

40. Ibid., 129.

41. Quoted in N. G. Jog, *In Freedom's Quest* (Bombay: Orient Longmans, 1969), 176.

Chapter 10

1. Mihir Bose, *Lost Hero*, 210.

2. M. Sivaram, *The Road To Delhi* (Rutland: Charles E. Tuttle, 1966), 126.

3. S. A. Ayer, *Unto Him A Witness* (Bombay: Thacker, 1951), 212–13.

4. Sivaram, *Road To Delhi*, 140.

5. Mamoru Shinozaki, *Syonan: My Story* (Singapore: Asia Pacific, 1975), 66.

6. What follows I have reconstructed from a long conversation I had with J. Athi Nahappan (as she now is) in Calcutta, Jan 1989.

7. Recollections of K. P. K. Menon, recorded Nov 1971, Nehru Memorial Library, New Delhi.

Chapter 11

1. From a radio broadcast, 9 July 1943, transcribed in "Arun," *Testament of Subhas Bose 1942–1945* (Delhi: Rajkamal, 1946), 192.

2. Durlab Singh, *I.N.A. Heroes*, 18.

3. Ibid., 21.

4. Ibid., 14.

5. Moti Ram, *Trials in Red Fort*, 109.

6. Ayer, *Unto Him A Witness*, xvii, xx.

7. James Grant, *History of India* (London: Cassell Petter & Galpin, n.d.), 1:344.

8. G. A. Grierson, *Encyclopedia Britannica*, 11th ed. (1910–11), 13:480.

9. Netaji Research Bureau, *Crossroads*, 13–14.

10. The song begins "*Subh sukh chain ki barkha barse Bharat bhag hai jaga,*" which translates "may there be showers of welfare and happiness now that India has woken to her destiny." The second and third lines pass in review the parts of the subcontinent from the Punjab, Sind, and Gujarat to the Himalayas and "black Yamuna and Ganga." The chorus is the expected repetition of the word *victory.*

11. Abid Hasan Safrani, *The Men from Imphal* (Calcutta: Netaji Research Bureau, 1971), 14.

12. A. C. Chatterji, *India's Struggle for Freedom* (Calcutta: Chuckervertty Chatterjee, 1947), 148–49.

13. *Greater Asia*, 15 Jan 1944.

Chapter 12

1. Dorothy Hess Guyot, "The Political Impact of the Japanese Occupation of Burma" (Ph.D. diss., Yale University, 1966), 182.

2. U Khin, *U Hla Pe's Narrative of the Japanese Occupation of Burma* (Ithaca: Cornell University Southeast Asia Program, 1961), 55.

3. Ayer, *Unto Him A Witness,* 224.

4. J. S. Furnivall, *Colonial Policy and Practice* (New York: New York University Press, 1956), 183.

5. Guyot, "Japanese Occupation of Burma," 341.

6. Quoted in M. B. K., "Burmese Attitude in the Burma Campaign," *The Guardian* 8, No. 4 (Apr 1961): 26.

7. Maung Htin Aung, *A History of Burma* (New York: Columbia University Press, 1967), 264.

8. Ibid., 294.

9. From "Snapshots of Aung San," in *Aung San of Burma*, ed. Maung Maung (The Hague: Martinus Nyhoff, 1962), 8, 10, 12. Bo Let Ya's real name was Hla Pe. Like most of his fellows, on becoming one of the Thirty Comrades he took a high-sounding pseudonym. *Bo* simply signifies a military officer. The Hla Pe of note 2, this chapter, is another person.

10. Maung Maung, "On the March with Aung San," in ibid., 61.

11. Dr. Tha Hla, "Editor of the `Oway' Magazine," in ibid., 26.

12. Aung San, "Self-Portrait," in ibid., 4

13. Guyot, "Japanese Occupation of Burma," 263.

14. Thakin Nu, *Burma under the Japanese* (London: Macmillan, 1954), 73–74, 85.

15. U Khin, *U Hla Pe's Narrative,* 60–61.

16. Khin Myo Chit, *Three Years under the Japs* (Sanchaung: Khin Myo Chit, 1945), 4–5.

17. Sir Reginald Dorman-Smith to L. S. Amery, 8 Apr 1943, quoted in Hugh Tinker, ed., *Burma: The Struggle for Independence 1944–1948* (London: H. M. Stationery Office, 1983), 1:23, doc. 11.

18. Bose, *Indian Struggle*, 131.

19. Ba Maw, radio speech of 30 Mar 1944, as reported five days later in *Greater Asia*.

20. Moti Ram, *Trials in Red Fort*, 77.

21. An appendix to Weekly Intelligence Summary no. 109, 3 Dec 1943, in L/WS/1/1433, reproduces in full the British translation of this pamphlet, entitled "About the

Indian National Army," and published for the *Hikari Kikan* the previous September. (Note: the L/WS papers are housed in the India Office Library, London.)

22. Monograph 7, L/WS/2/45.

23. *Greater Asia*, 28 Mar 1944.

24. Sivaram, *Road To Delhi*, 196. The same picture appeared about this time in *Greater Asia*.

25. Ibid., 198. Chin Kee Onn, *Malaya Upside Down* (Singapore: Jitts, 1946), 140.

26. Toye, *Springing Tiger*, 109.

Chapter 13

1. Quoted in Raymond Callahan, *Burma 1942–1945* (Newark: University of Delaware Press, 1978), 93.

2. Quoted in Louis Allen, *Burma: The Longest War 1941–45* (New York: St. Martin's, 1984), 154.

3. Sir William Slim, *Defeat into Victory* (London: Cassell, 1956), 299.

4. Allen, *Longest War,* 230.

5. Ibid., 327.

6. Callahan, *Burma 1942–1945,* 137.

7. Fujiwara Iwaichi, *F. Kikan* (Hong Kong: Heineman Asia, 1985), 259.

8. From "a verbatim extract from an English letter written by the officer commanding No. 1 Guerilla Regiment to S. C. Bose in April, 1944, shortly after the regiment arrived in the Falam/Haka area" (appendix A, Weekly Intelligence Summary no. 163, 15 Dec 1944, L/WS/1/1433).

9. Moti Ram, *Trials in Red Fort,* 330.

10. Ibid., 331.

11. Quoted in Allen, *Longest War,* 221.

12. Weekly Intelligence Summary no. 138, 23 June 1944.

13. Slim, *Defeat into Victory,* 327–28.

14. Sir Francis Tuker, *While Memory Serves* (London: Cassell, 1950), 555–57.

15. Colonel Toye's narrative account of "Yamamoto Force and the 1st I.N.A. Division" occupies appendix 3 of *Springing Tiger.* The quotations are from page 229.

16. Weekly Intelligence Summary no. 140, 7 July 1944.

17. Shah Nawaz, *I.N.A. & Its Netaji,* 124.

18. E. D. Smith, *Battle for Burma* (New York: Holmes & Meier, 1979), 110.

19. Shah Nawaz, *I.N.A. & Its Netaji,* 121.

20. Weekly Intelligence Summary no. 142, 21 July 1944; and no. 153, 6 Oct 1944.

21. The officer was Eric Lanning, of the 4th Battalion, 6th Gurkha Rifles—Slim's old regiment. I am much indebted to him for copies of these leaflets, and to Amita Shastri for their translation. Most are in romanized Hindustani, some in English, a few in Hindustani using the Devanagari script. The one quoted here is actually a composite of several.

22. Monograph 5, L/WS/2/45.

23. Shah Nawaz, *I.N.A. & Its Netaji*, 126.

24. Weekly Intelligence Summary no. 129, 21 Apr 1944.

25. Kiani, "India's Freedom," 119. For the full reference see note 17 chapter 5.

26. Weekly Intelligence Summary no. 150, 15 Sept 1944.

27. Geoffrey Tyson, *Forgotten Frontier* (Calcutta: W. H. Targett, 1945), 85.

28. Allen, *Longest War*, 194.

29. *Burma Handbook* (Simla: Government of India, 1943), 124.

30. Abid Hasan Safrani, *Men From Imphal*, 3.

31. Fujiwara, *F. Kikan*, 264.

32. Moti Ram, *Trials in Red Fort*, 331.

33. Fujiwara, *F. Kikan*, 264–65.

34. Eric Lanning again. See note 21 this chapter.

35. Abid Hasan Safrani, *Men From Imphal*, 12.

Chapter 14

1. Moti Ram, *Trials in Red Fort*, 337.

2. *Greater Asia*, 4 July 1944.

3. Ibid., 4 July 1944; 11 July 1944.

4. Giani, *Indian Independence Movement*, 2:139.

5. *Greater Asia*, 3 Aug 1944.

6. Ibid., 15 Aug 1944.

7. Moti Ram, *Trials in Red Fort*, 314–15.

8. Ibid., 337–38.

9. Shah Nawaz, *I.N.A. & Its Netaji*, 127–28.

10. Moti Ram, *Trials in Red Fort*, 349.

11. Ghulam Mohammad, in ibid., 85.

Chapter 15

1. Slim, *Defeat into Victory*, 393.

2. S. Woodburn Kirby, *The War Against Japan*, vol. 4 (London: H. M. Stationery Office, 1965), 266; Slim, *Defeat into Victory*, 424. Raymond Callahan repeats Slim's mistake, with a twist. "The INA division guarding the eastern shore collapsed," he writes, adding that this was "the only significant contribution of that force to the Burma campaign" (*Burma 1942-1945*, 158). Yet British intelligence knew *within weeks* that Dhillon had nothing like a division with him. "More than 250 Jifs of Nehru Brigade, 2 Division, have surrendered to our troops in the bridgehead over the Irrawaddy at Pagan-Nyaungu," observed Weekly Intelligence Summary no. 173 of 23 Feb 1945. "These Jifs state that there are 700 more in the area. Preliminary interrogation reveals that the Japanese apparently entrusted the defence of the important area opposite our bridgehead to these Jifs with only a small Japanese backing, located in their rear. . . . The other two brigades, or guerilla regiments, of 2 Division are reported to have left Rangoon and reached Kyaukpadaung. . . ." Kyaukpadaung is, of course, miles from both Nyaungu and the river.

3. Slim, *Defeat into Victory*, 425.

4. G. S. Dhillon, "The Nehru Holds the Irrawaddy," *The Oracle* 6 no. 1 (Jan 1984): 93–94.

5. Ibid., 94.

6. Prem Sahgal diary entry for 19 Feb, in Moti Ram, *Trials in Red Fort*, 349.

7. Entry for 8 Feb, ibid.

8. Entry for 22 Feb, ibid.

9. Shah Nawaz has him say this in *I.N.A. & Its Netaji*, 144.

10. Prem Sahgal diary entry for 2 Mar, in Moti Ram, *Trials*, 350.

11. Shah Nawaz diary entry for 3 Mar, in ibid., 332.

12. The quotations that follow come not from the speech itself (the text has not survived) but from two Orders of the Day, both dated 13 Mar, in which Bose conveys succinctly his anger and concern, and what he proposes to do. See ibid., 318–20. Ayer's account is from *Unto Him a Witness*, 200–203.

13. Kirby, *War Against Japan*, 4: 269.

14. The diary entries, dated 14–17 Mar, are from Moti Ram, *Trials*, 351. I have amended Prem's hasty prose to make it fully intelligible.

15. Entry for 26 Mar, ibid., 352.

16. So Ghulam Mohammad remembers him saying. Ibid., 90.

17. Entry for 1 Mar, ibid., 350.

18. Testimony of Jaghri Ram, 29 Nov, ibid., 94.

19. From Prem's end-of-trial written statement, in ibid., 116.

20. One of the six prosecution witnesses, Abdul Hafiz Khan, deserted from Dhillon's 7th Battalion two weeks later (or so he testified), and toward the end of March a lieutenant named Iltaf Razak "escaped" from Prem's regiment taking four men with him (ibid., 98, 57). It would be surprising if during March Dhillon in particular did not lose others.

21. Slim, *Defeat into Victory*, 488.

22. Shah Nawaz diary entry for 31 Mar, in *Trials*, 333.

23. Prem's typed version follows exactly Exhibit LLL in ibid., 342–47.

24. Kirby's account lists 5 Brigade's supporting arms, reports that its first objective was Legyi, and covers the fighting there from 2 Apr on in three sentences. It acknowledges the presence of "an I.N.A. battalion" alongside an indeterminate number of Japanese, and says that though the brigade "surrounded" Legyi and repeatedly attacked, it made no progress for five days (Kirby, *War Against Japan*, 4:363). The account in Prasad is briefer still and mentions no INA men at all, only Japanese. See Bisheshwar Prasad, ed., *The Reconquest of Burma*, vol. 2 (Calcutta: Orient Longmans, 1959), 374.

25. John Masters, *The Road Past Mandalay* (New York: Harper & Brothers, 1961), 306–8.

Chapter 16

1. I can establish accurately neither the size nor the organization of the Burma National Army. Five to ten thousand men in seven battalions are the figures commonly advanced. Dorothy Guyot gives us precisely 11,480 men "on the eve of the resistance." "Impossible to estimate accurately," is Hugh Tinker's verdict. See Guyot, "Japanese Occupation of Burma," 316; and Hugh Tinker, *The Union of Burma* (London: Oxford University Press, 4th ed., 1967), 17 note 2.

2. *Greater Asia*, 20 Mar 1945. Subsequent excerpts are from 31 Mar, 7 Apr, and 14 Apr.

3. Kya Doe, "The Bogyoke," in Maung Maung, *Aung San of Burma*, 75–76.

4. Linlithgow to Amery, 16 Mar 1943, in Mansergh, *Transfer of Power*, 3:821, doc. 596.

5. Dorman-Smith to Amery, 16 Dec 1944, in Tinker, ed., *Burma: The Struggle for Independence*, 1:135, doc. 70.

6. Ibid., 1:xxv.

7. Mountbatten to Leese, 27 Feb 1945, in ibid., 1:171, doc. 96.

8. Philip Ziegler, *Mountbatten* (New York: Alfred A. Knopf, 1985), 299.

9. Quotations in the three paragraphs preceding are from Mountbatten to Chiefs of Staff, 27 Mar 1945 (by coincidence the very day of the rising); and from the minutes of a meeting held 5 Apr at Mountbatten's headquarters in Kandy. See *Burma: The*

Struggle for Independence, 1:197–99, doc. 108; and 1:209–14, doc. 116. The arguments in the two are much of a piece.

10. Advanced Hqs ALFSEA to Mountbatten, 9 May 1945, and Mountbatten's reply the same day, in ibid., 1:238, docs. 133 and 134. Just how you wire *no* in capital letters I cannot imagine, but there in the printed record it stands.

11. Slim to Advanced Hqs ALFSEA, 15 May 1945, in ibid., 1:250–51, doc. 144.

12. Slim, *Defeat into Victory*, 516–18.

13. From Mountbatten's telegram of 27 Mar (see note 9 this chapter), page 199.

14. Slim, *Defeat into Victory*, 505.

15. The two firsthand accounts of Bose's departure from Rangoon, by S. A. Ayer (*Unto Him a Witness*, 14–21), and Janaki Davar (reproduced in Shah Nawaz, *I.N.A. & Its Netaji*, 204–11), give few clues as to his state of mind; and Leonard Gordon does not ask what it may have been. But Gordon calls the chapter in which he covers Bose's INA days "An Indian Samurai: Subhas Bose in Asia" (*Brothers Against the Raj*, chapter 11), and observes that Japanese who knew Bose well remark that he kept the promises he made—a samurai trait.

16. Ayer, *Witness*, 17.

17. "The records of the I.N.A. Headquarters were destroyed by the end of April, 1945," testified D. C. Nag, the officer in charge of the INA's legal department, without elaboration, at the first Red Fort Trial (Moti Ram, *Trials in Red Fort*, 36). When else but at this time?

18. See note 15 this chapter. I have rearranged and conflated some of the entries.

19. Nu, *Burma under the Japanese*, 122.

20. This, and the diary entries to do with surrender that follow, appear in Moti Ram, *Trials*, 335.

21. Ibid., 92.

22. The passages quoted are from one of these, delivered 21 May 1945. See S. A. Ayer, ed., *Selected Speeches of Subhas Chandra Bose* (New Delhi: Ministry of Information and Broadcasting, 1962), 247. Part of the argument Bose gave directly, part is implicit in what he said.

23. On the basis of Japanese sources, Joyce Lebra believes that Bose seriously considered asking the Russians to help him liberate India from the north, and once, while in Tokyo, tried to see the Soviet ambassador. Leonard Gordon, too, has him trying to see this person, not once but repeatedly. See Joyce Lebra, *Jungle Alliance: Japan and the Indian National Army* (Singapore: Asia Pacific Press, 1971), 194–96; and Leonard Gordon, *Brothers Against the Raj*, 517–18, 538. But the only direct evidence for the attempts to make contact appears to be six lines in a book-length ramble apparently written by General Kawabe in the 1950s, extensive excerpts from which in "a free

English translation" were used by K. K. Ghosh and later published in Sisir Bose, ed., *Netaji and India's Freedom*, under the title "Subhas Chandra Bose and Japan" (the lines appear on page 404). Though Kawabe's book, Ghosh avers, is based on official Japanese records, the looseness and occasional inaccuracy of its narrative, and the fact that Kawabe devotes to Netaji's Russian approach only these lines, with no specificity of date or place, suggest that he wrote not from the evidence but from his recollection of what people *said* Bose had done or tried to do. I do not believe Bose ever approached the Russians with a proposal for common action against Britain. Russia as shelter, that August, is another matter.

24. Sivaram, *Road to Delhi*, 253.

25. Ayer remained with Bose until the afternoon of August 17. His account of these days occupies pages 47–73 of *Unto Him a Witness*.

26. P. N. Oak, *Rani of Zanshi: A Play in Three Acts* (Singapore: Indian Independence League, 1944), 17.

27. *Unto Him a Witness*, 72.

28. Ibid, 114.

Chapter 17

1. For what Colonel Toye was doing at this time I depend largely upon what he told me in conversations over a period of years, and upon what Prem and Lakshmi remember of their contact with him.

2. Weekly Intelligence Summary no. 185, 18 May 1945.

3. Ibid., no. 183, 4 May 1945.

4. *Hindu*, 15 Nov 1945.

5. Ibid., 27 Oct 1945.

6. Weekly Intelligence Summary (Civil Affairs, Burma) no. 100, 6 Oct 1945, L/WS/1/738.

7. *Hindu*, 22 Feb 1946.

Chapter 18

1. Weekly Intelligence Summary no. 37, 17 July 1942.

2. Ibid., no. 53, 6 Nov 1942.

3. "Subversive Activities Directed Against the Indian Army," 18 Mar 1943, in L/WS/1/1711.

4. Weekly Intelligence Summary no. 76, 16 Apr 1943.

5. Ibid., no. 58, 11 Dec 1942.

6. The memorandum in response, 8 Apr 1943 (in L/WS/1/1576), bears the same subject heading as GHQ's.

7. The tale of the platoon, which follows, is drawn from the GHQ memorandum of 18 Mar (see note 3 this chapter); from Linlithgow to Provincial Governors, 7 May 1943, in Mansergh, *Transfer of Power*, 3:951, doc. 690; and from Weekly Intelligence Summary no. 116, 21 Jan 1944.

8. Weekly Intelligence Summary no. 81, 21 May 1943.

9. Pritam Singh's CSDIC report appears in appendix C to CSDIC No. 2 Section, Report No. 19, 6 Nov 1942, in L/WS/1/1572. Wren's memorandum, "Indian National Army," dated 31 Dec 1942, is in L/WS/1/1711. That Wren read Pritam Singh's report I deduce from his saying he received four reports, "the most important" of which (because it brought information about the INA's organization) "is the last one of Major M. S. Dhillon." Pritam Singh was accompanied by two officers, and was interrogated just before Dhillon. If the four whose interrogation reports Wren refers to are not *these* four, who were they?

10. See note 6 this chapter.

11. *Hindu*, 15 Mar 1945, 30 Mar, 18 Apr, 28 Apr.

12. See note 31 in chapter 6.

13. This is Paul Greenough's judgment. The account that follows is based largely on his *Prosperity and Misery in Modern Bengal: The Famine of 1943–1944* (New York: Oxford University Press, 1982).

14. Stephens, *Monsoon Morning*, 187–88.

15. Ibid., 193; *Statesman* editorial of 19 Aug 1943, reproduced in ibid., 260–64.

16. Ibid., 180.

17. Ibid., 148.

18. The elements of this program are given in an MI2 memorandum dated June 1943, in L/WS/1/1576. Though intelligence spelled it Jifs, I prefer (as do Paul Scott, Ian Stephens, and others) Jiffs.

19. Weekly Intelligence Summary no. 83, 4 June 1943.

20. "A Useful Propaganda Objective," appended to ibid., no. 76, 16 Apr 1943.

21. Ibid., nos. 93, 13 Aug 1943; 94, 20 Aug 1943; 98, 17 Sept 1943; 106, 12 Nov 1943; and 119, 11 Feb 1944.

22. See the Appendix: INA Strength.

23. Stephens, *Monsoon Morning*, 220.

24. *Hindu*, 8 May 1945.

25. Ibid., 16 and 17 June, 1945.

26. Ibid., 19 July and 25 June, 1945.

27. In May, when the war in Europe ended, I was a young second lieutenant with an 8-inch howitzer battalion near Bologna, on the edge of the Po Valley. Asked if I wished to transfer to our occupation forces in Austria (I had some German), I said, no, I wanted to accompany my battalion to the Pacific. We thought we would be needed there, but of course we weren't and never went.

If, by the way, I had learned that an Indian Army officer named Prem Sahgal, a man not much older than myself, would soon stand accused in Delhi of having fought with the Japanese against the British, and could be hanged for it, I would have been appalled—but not at what might happen to the man. At what he had done. I look at the matter very differently today.

28. Sarvepalli Gopal, ed., *Selected Works of Jawaharlal Nehru* (New Delhi: Orient Longman, 1980), 8:311.

29. *Hindu*, 17 Aug 1945. The text of the speech is available in *Keesing's Contemporary Archives*, 7374.

30. Sarat Bose, from a diary entry and letter quoted in Gordon, *Brothers Against the Raj*, 544.

31. *Hindu*, 26 and 29 Aug 1945.

32. Penderel Moon, ed. *The Viceroy's Journal* (London: Oxford University Press, 1973), 164.

33. Kenneth Harris, *Attlee* (London: Weidenfeld and Nicolson, 1982), 365.

34. "Diatribes" is Wavell's own term. Moon, *Viceroy's Journal*, 168.

35. Mudie to Jenkins (Wavell's private secretary), 23 Aug 1945, in *Transfer of Power*, 6:138–40, doc. 57.

Chapter 19

1. *Hindu*, 9 Feb 1946; *Statesman*, 20 Feb 1946.

2. *Transfer of Power*, 6:78–79, doc. 33. The minutes of such meetings do not always report who said what when, and the reporting is never verbatim.

3. The reader, observing that this commission issues from George VI, may wonder why I have called Prem an ICO, not a KCO. The answer is that his commission was issued and signed in India, not England, and brought him less than a Sandhurst graduate's pay and less command power: he could give orders to but not punish British troops.

4. Not all Mason has written has India for its subject. But a good deal has, and in its combination of grace, sweep, sympathy for both sides of the Anglo-Indian equation, and general good sense, puts Philip Mason (or Philip Woodruff, briefly his nom de plume), in the very front rank of those Englishmen who, having had experience of India, undertake to review the several centuries of British presence there for those who have not. The quotation is from *A Shaft of Sunlight* (London: Andre Deutsch, 1978), 67.

5. Mason to author, 2 June 1983. Explicit permission to quote.

6. The same, 16 June 1983.

7. *Hindu*, 30 Aug 1945.

8. Ibid., 29 Aug 1945.

9. From the *Statesman*, 15 Sept 1945, quoted in *Transfer of Power*, 6:274–75, doc. 115. The Working Committee had met a full week before the Bombay AICC meeting.

10. *Hindu*, 22 Sept 1945.

11. *Sunday Statesman*, 16 Sept 1945, quoted in *Transfer*, 6:279, doc. 115. Again, the resolution dates from the Working Committee meeting more than a week earlier.

12. Undated memo in A. G. Liaison Letters 1945, L/WS/1/902.

13. Fortnightly Security Intelligence Summary no. 6, 26 Oct 1945, L/WS/1/1506.

14. Letter to Krishna Menon, 27 Oct 1945, in Gopal, ed., *Selected Works of Nehru*, 14:343–44. That Nehru sang the marching song sounds improbable, but the *Hindu* (27 Dec 1945) cannot have made it up.

15. *Hindu.*, 2 Nov 1945.

16. Enclosure with Home Department to India Office, 20 Nov 1945, in *Transfer*, 6:513, doc. 222. The reader will perhaps forgive me for not having explained that civil and military intelligence were two different things. Most of the references so far have been to military intelligence. Sir Norman Smith, the DIB in question, directed civil intelligence, the province of the Indian Police.

17. Gandhi to Jenkins, 29 Oct 1945, in *Transfer*, 6:418, doc. 175.

18. Weekly Security Intelligence Summary no. 194, 20 July 1945, L/WS/1/1506.

19. Wavell to Pethick-Lawrence, 20 Aug 1945, in *Transfer*, 6:107, doc. 47.

20. Wavell to Pethick-Lawrence, 9 Oct 1945, in ibid., 6:319, doc. 135.

21. Wavell to Pethick-Lawrence, 22 Oct 1945, in ibid., 6:375, doc. 157.

22. Wavell to Pethick-Lawrence, 1 Oct 1945, in ibid., 6:305–6, doc. 127.

23. See letter cited in note 20 this chapter, page 322; and Moon, *Viceroy's Journal*, 175.

24. The summary of evidence is not attached to Wavell's letter of 22 Oct (cited in note 21 this chapter). Presumably it resembled closely the prosecution statements at Burhan-ud-Din's trial (see the *Hindu*, 8 Dec 1945 and 11 Jan 1946) from which I have constructed this account.

25. *Statesman*, 9 Nov 1945.

26. Auchinleck to Mayne, 14 Oct 1945, L/WS/1/1577.

27. Philip Mason gave me his account of how Burhan-ud-Din's case was passed over in the letter referred to in note 5 this chapter. An earlier version with key explanations omitted appears in his foreword to Toye, *Springing Tiger*, xi.

28. No in-house account of the courts-martial process exists, or if it does I do not know where it is hiding. And Mason does not say when the GHQ conference at which the decision was announced took place. But it cannot have been earlier than September 11, because Prosecution did not prepare to take a man to trial until it had his CSDIC report—and Dhillon's, last of the three, wasn't done until that date. Nor much later, because on the 18th the newspapers had it on good authority that the first trial would begin soon, and on the 21st named these three as the defendants—something the press could not have known unless the AG had made his decision.

29. Mason, *Shaft of Sunlight*, 192–93.

30. The paper, in the form of a memorandum dated 20 Oct 1945, is in *Transfer*, 6:368–71, doc. 154.

31. See note 26 this chapter.

32. *Hindu*, 13 Nov 1945.

33. Auchinleck to Wavell, 24 Nov 1945, in *Transfer*, 6:536, doc. 233.

Chapter 20

1. Wavell to Pethick-Lawrence, 4 Nov 1945, in *Transfer*, 6:441, doc. 188.

2. *Hindu*, 5 Nov 1945.

3. Weekly Intelligence Summary no. 49, 25 May 1945.

4. *Statesman*, 8 Dec 1945.

5. Moti Ram, *Trials in Red Fort*, 102.

6. Ibid., 44–45.

7. Ibid., 280.

8. *Hindu*, 12 Dec 1945.

9. Ibid., 15 Dec 1945. The true figures were 12 and 29.

10. Ibid., 29 Nov 1945.

11. Ayer, *Unto Him A Witness*, 129.

12. From the enclosure, Home Department to India Office, cited in note 16 chapter 19, pages 512–13.

13. *Hindu*, 6 Nov 1945.

14. Ibid., 29 Nov 1945.

15. From the enclosure cited in note 12 this chapter, page 514.

16. Enid Saunders Candlin, *A Traveler's Tale* (New York: Macmillan, 1974), 352–53.

17. Twynam to Wavell, 26 Nov l945, in *Transfer*, 6:542–43, doc. 239.

18. *Hindu*, 9 Dec 1945.

Chapter 21

1. *Hindu*, 5 Jan 1946.

2. Mss. Eur. D 1003.

3. *Statesman*, 5 Jan 1946.

4. Auchinleck to Wavell, 22 Jan 1946, in *Transfer*, 6:835, doc. 374.

5. *Hindu*, 14 Feb 1946.

6. Ibid., 15 Feb 1946.

7. Ibid., 23 Nov 1945; B. Shiva Rao to Cripps, 20 Nov 1945, in *Transfer*, 6:564, doc. 248.

8. *Hindu*, 15 Dec 1945.

9. Ibid., 10 Dec 1945.

10. "Jhanski Rani Zindabad" translates "long live the Rani of Jhansi." "Inquilab Zindabad" becomes "long live the revolution." Like Americans, Indians meant by revolution not social transformation or upheaval, but something much simpler and less disturbing—independence.

11. *Hindu*, 19 Jan 1946.

12. Wavell to Pethick-Lawrence, 6 Nov 1945, in *Transfer*, 6:450–54, doc. 194.

13. The papers that passed between Pethick-Lawrence and Wavell, and about Whitehall, on the matter of the Viceroy's 6 November note, occupy more than a dozen "documents" in *Transfer*, volume 6. The two quotations are from a memorandum dated 14 Nov, page 482, doc. 210; and from a telegram dated 21 Nov, page 516, doc. 223.

14. Ibid., 6:553, doc. 246.

15. Ibid., 6:561, doc. 247.

16. Moon, *Viceroy's Journal*, 181.

17. Enclosure in Wavell to Pethick-Lawrence 2 Nov 1945, in *Transfer*, 6:436, doc. 185.

18. The paragraphs that follow draw upon Glancy's memorandum of 17 November (in Auchinleck to Wavell, 24 Nov 1945, *Transfer*, 6:535–36, doc. 233), and upon the minutes of the conference, entitled "Record of a Conference Held on 19th and 20th November at New Delhi, to Discuss . . . Policy towards Jifs, Hifs, and Other Traitors or Collaborators," in L/WS/1/1577. For a brief parallel account of how and when the Indian Army became aware of the INA's appeal, based on Auchinleck and Cariappa papers with which I am not familiar, see Partha Sarathi Gupta, "Imperial Strategy and the Transfer of Power 1939–51," in Amit Kumar Gupta, ed., *Myth and Reality: The Struggle for Freedom in India 1945–47* (New Delhi: Manohar, 1987), 7–8.

19. Scoones to Auchinleck 24 Nov, and O'Connor to Auchinleck 24 Nov; both in John Connell, *Auchinleck* (London: Cassell, 1959), 803–5.

20. Auchinleck to Wavell, 24 Nov 1945, in *Transfer*, 6:532, doc. 233.

21. Cunningham to Wavell, 27 Nov 1945, in ibid., 6:546–47, doc. 243.

22. Auchinleck to Wavell, 26 Nov 1945, in ibid., 6:544–45, doc. 241.

23. The appreciation appears in full in ibid., 6:576–84, doc. 256.

24. Attlee to Pethick-Lawrence, 6 Dec 1945, in ibid., 6:616, doc. 271.

25. Enclosure in Auchinleck to Wavell, 13 Feb 1946, in ibid., 6:939-46, doc. 425.

26. Auchinleck to Chiefs, 22 Dec 1945, in ibid., 6:674, doc. 309.

27. Wavell to George VI, 31 Dec 1945, in ibid., 6:714, doc. 322.

28. *Hindu*, 28 Jan 1946.

29. Ibid., 12 Feb 1946; Mason, *Shaft of Sunlight*, 193–94.

30. From page 159 of the essay cited in note 28, chapter 6.

GLOSSARY

ahimsa	nonviolence
AICC	All-India Congress Committee
ashram	place of religious retreat
Azad Hind	Free India
babu	term of respect attached to a gentleman's name; also, clerk
bhadralok	in Bengal, persons of high birth; respectable people
BNA	Burma National Army; successor to the BIA or Burma Independence Army
Brahmin	a person of the highest Hindu caste
chappal	sandal, usually made of leather
chappati	pancake-shaped unleavened bread of north India, rather like a Mexican tortilla, but made of wheat flour not corn
charkha	light hand-held spinning wheel
communal	of or pertaining to a community—in India, usually a racial or religious community. Thus, communal violence between Hindus and Muslims
CSDIC	Combined Services Detailed Interrogation Center
dal	the yellow split pea of northern India

darshan	sight of a person or place that bestows a blessing upon the viewer
dhoti	loin cloth, usually voluminous, worn by men
ECO	emergency commissioned officer
fauj	army
GHQ	General Headquarters
GOI	Government of India
guru	holy man, teacher
hartal	stoppage of all activity, usually to exert pressure
havildar	noncommissioned officer, roughly the equivalent of a sergeant
HMG	His Majesty's Government
ICO	Indian commissioned officer, i.e., a graduate of Dehra Dun
ICS	Indian Civil Service
INA	Indian National Army
jawan	common soldier
jemadar	Viceroy's commissioned officer, roughly the equivalent of a lieutenant
Jiff	derogatory name applied to men of the INA; meaning, "Japanese-Indian Fifth Column"
KCO	King's commissioned officer, i.e., a graduate of Sandhurst
khadi	hand-spun, hand-woven cloth
lathi	metal-tipped stave used by police
lungi	skirtlike garment worn by south Indian men
maidan	a grassy open space for sports and recreation
netaji	beloved and respected leader

NCO	noncommissioned officer
nullah	ditch
other ranks	ordinary soldiers, what Americans call "enlisted men"
padang	Malayan equivalent of a maidan
pandal	large temporary tent structure used for ceremonies and meetings
pandit	a particularly learned Brahmin; hence, an honorific prefix to a name
POW	prisoner of war
puja	worship
pukka	genuine, real, substantial
raj	kingdom, rule, sovereignty
sadhu	Hindu wandering holy man
sardar	chief, headman, commander; hence, an honorific prefix to a name
sarkar	government
sarong	Malayan equivalent of a lungi
satyagraha	truth force, soul force
sepoy	the old term for a common Indian soldier, replaced now by jawan
subadar	Viceroy's commissioned officer, roughly the equivalent of a captain
subadar-major	Viceroy's commissioned officer, roughly the equivalent of a major
swaraj	self-rule, independence
sweeper	one who cleans by sweeping; in India, applied to untouchables who do general indoor and outdoor cleaning, including the removal of human waste

thakin	Burmese word meaning lord, prince, master
tilak	ornamental spot, usually red, worn on the forehead by Hindu men and women, sometimes with caste significance
VCO	Viceroy's commissioned officer, invariably Indian
Whitehall	a street off Parliament Square, London, bordered by government offices; hence, figuratively, the British government

A Note on Sources

"The story of the I.N.A.," remarks Sarvepalli Gopal midway in his life of Nehru, "has been told often and at length." In fact it hasn't. Over the half century since that army surrendered, only four books—two by Indians, one by an Englishman, one by an American—have seriously addressed the topic.

In 1946 Shah Nawaz (sometimes styled Shah Nawaz Khan), fresh from the first Red Fort trial, published "the entire and uncoloured story of the I.N.A." under the title *My Memories of I.N.A. & Its Netaji* (Delhi: Rajkamal Publications). Shah Nawaz served from the army's beginning to its end. What he did not see or experience, he reconstructed from conversations with fellow officers. His book is the fullest report by any of the participants, and for parts of the army's performance it is the only thing we have. But Shah Nawaz wrote in a hurry, at a moment when INA men were anxious to tell their story and enshrine their leader. What he was told, he reproduced. What he was not told, he left out. The result is a narrative incomplete in substance and uncomfortably devotional in manner.

A dozen years later, Hugh Toye's enduring recollection of personal involvement drove him, too, to publish. It was an unexpected activity for a career Royal Artillery officer, but Toye is no ordinary gunner: partway through his thirty years of service he added an Oxford D.Phil. to his Queen's College, Cambridge, B.A. Posted to the Intelligence School at Karachi, then to CSDIC in Delhi, Toye did intelligence work from mid-1943 well past VJ Day. His duties brought him into contact with the INA. Contact bred surprise, surprise gave way to interest. Eventually Colonel Toye wrote a book. Short, beautifully written, obviously based upon papers accumulated in the course of his intelligence work (though he rarely cites anything and supplies no reference when he does), *The Springing Tiger* (London: Cassell, 1959) anticipates the Granada documentary by a quarter of a century in its determination to give these reputed renegades their rightful place in India's independence movement.

And it is effective, as effective as the film (for which Toye served as a consulting expert) is not. But Toye puts Bose at the center of his story (the Indian paperback edition, from Jaico of Bombay, is called *Subhash Chandra Bose*). Bose's prewar career, his months of disappointment in Germany, the escape eastward, building an army and a provisional government, taking both to Burma and losing both there—these command the reader's attention. Characteristically, Netaji's last days and death occupy twice the space allotted to the Red Fort trials. This is a pity. Toye never met Subhas Chandra. He did meet a number of INA men and one extraordinary INA woman. He read scores of interrogation reports; he had access to other intelligence material, much of it, like the reports, since lost. His biography of Bose is not, and does not purport to be, definitive. The book he failed to write about the Indian National Army might have been.

And on the other hand he probably did not think it worth doing. For if it is clear that Toye developed a considerable respect for Subhas Chandra, it is equally clear that he thought the manner in which his army was formed disgraceful. It is otherwise with Joyce Lebra. Perhaps because she is American, more probably because she brings to the subject a scholar's interest in Japan and a different set of questions, *Jungle Alliance: Japan and the Indian National Army* (Singapore: Asia Pacific Press, 1971) takes for granted the possibility that the Indians of Percival's defeated army did not have to be suborned. An invitation was extended that many chose to accept. It was extended, of course, by the Japanese. Lebra asks why.

Using Japanese as well as English-language sources, supplementing these with personal interviews—of Japanese mostly, though in India she knows Mohan Singh and Dhillon well—Professor Lebra reaches the conclusion that while there was much hesitation and more than a touch of calculation in the Japanese approach to the Indians of Percival's defeated army, some Japanese genuinely wanted to help India obtain her freedom. Fujiwara was the chief of these. Fujiwara becomes Lebra's hero. *Jungle Alliance* begins with him, ends with him, and throughout reminds us that the INA did not move in a vacuum, but was rather the most vigorous among the several Japanese-supported independence forces in that part of the world—a subject Lebra has explored further in *Japanese-Trained Armies in Southeast Asia* (New York: Columbia University Press, 1977).

No one pursues the Japanese connection more thoroughly than Lebra, not even Fujiwara himself, for his *F. Kikan: Japanese Army Intelligence Operations in Southeast Asia During World War II* (Hong Kong: Heinemann Asia, 1983) is actually a memoir not a study, and dwindles to nothing when Iwakuro takes his place. There is, it is true, Louis Allen. British like Toye, Allen too was attached to intelligence in Southeast Asia. Unlike Toye, he speaks and reads Japanese. In *Burma: The Longest War 1941–45* (New York: St. Martin's, 1984) he narrates the several campaigns in that area (with a masterfulness and wealth of detail that delight the reader) as much from the Japanese side as from the British. Of Nippon's relations with the INA, however, he says almost nothing. Though his preface ranges widely over war and politics, over soldiers and politicians, over British, Japanese, Burmese, Chinese, Karens, Americans, and, of course, Indians of the Indian Army, neither Bose nor his men are so much as mentioned—and in the body of the book receive short shrift. Presumably Allen, if he noticed these Indians at all, set them down as rascals, and thought it prudent to exclude them as much as possible from the honorable company of everybody else. Lebra's attitude is different. For her the INA is at once real, respectable, and inconceivable without Japanese sponsorship. *Jungle Alliance* gives this a scrupulous examination. In doing so it necessarily follows what is going on in Malaya and Burma, but its chief focus is always the Japanese connection. It remained for K. K. Ghosh to direct a book at the army itself.

The Indian National Army (Meerut: Meenakshi Prakashan, 1969) is the product of as thorough a search of INA material east of Suez as anyone is ever likely to make. Ghosh went everywhere, talked to or corresponded with everyone, read everything. His narrative, in places almost crowded off the page by footnotes of a quite bewildering complexity, carries the army from its beginnings in 1942 through the disaster at Imphal. Ghosh says little, however, about actual field operations. After Imphal he says nothing at all. Mount Popa is never mentioned. With a hop, skip, and a jump he carries the reader directly to India and the Red Fort trials. He supplies a reason. The furor these trials produced, he explains, tells us that India would have risen in violent rebellion had the army managed to break into Assam and Bengal in 1944. Because it did not manage to, there is no need to follow it further. Its political raison d'être (touching off a second '42) having ceased to be viable in Rangoon, our attention may turn to Delhi—where, by offering up martyrs to the vengeful court-martial proceedings of the British, it will secure in the arena of public opinion what it failed to win on the frontier.

Ghosh is largely right about this last. But to suppose that what took place in Burma in early 1945 had no influence on Indian public opinion, is to forget who the defendants in the first trial were. Though beaten, they had kept on fighting. And this made all the difference. It was the battling with no hope along the Irrawaddy, not the battling with high hope about the Manipur basin, that justified the freedom army and gave it in the end such moral leverage.

Perhaps, though, Ghosh pursued his military narrative so unenthusiastically, and abandoned it so lightly, because he found he did not have much to work from. To be fair, no one does. It is the nature of the case. There exists no "official" history of the Indian National Army. The provisional government for which it fought did not survive to commission one. Independent India inherited, of course, the army of the Raj, and could hardly have been expected to sponsor a formal account of its defeated rival. Besides, there were no archives from which to write such a history. There are none now. One does not have to look far to discover why.

A revolutionary army directed by a revolutionary government is not likely to have the will, let alone the means, to preserve its records through the torment of defeat on foreign soil. Persuading the victor to assume loving custody of those records will be harder still. Bose did not try. "Destroy all files" was among his last injunctions. It was of a piece with his determination not to be taken prisoner himself.

So Netaji's wartime correspondence such as it was, the minutes of cabinet meetings, interoffice memoranda, INA operations orders, indents for arms and ammunition, the "war diaries" or logs that battalions kept, are missing. The loss was not complete. Towards the end the British stumbled upon an indeterminate number of papers from which they extracted what could be used in courts-martial. Those used in the first trial have survived because Moti Ram got his hands on them. But even they are fragmentary.

Consider Prem's diary, seized in the night ambush. From this diary the prosecution submitted only entries January 24 through March 28. What happened to the rest of it? It was certainly in Delhi in the summer of 1945 because Hugh Toye remembers reading it (a dog-eared, pocket-sized notebook) before editing Prem's CSDIC report. Once Prem's trial was over, however, and Exhibit OOO (which proved that Prem took up arms against the King-Emperor) had done its work, it cannot have seemed worth preserving. To build an archive of such papers would have been to imply that the INA was a thing of substance, permanence, legitimacy even. No one has seen the diary lately. It is a fair guess no one ever will.

A word more about Moti Ram. Neither at the time nor later were official transcripts of the trial proceedings published. The public, however, was intensely curious, the proceedings open to the press, so reporters from the wire services and the dailies crowded the courtroom daily, and among them was a staff correspondent for the *Hindustan Times*—our Moti Ram. Helped, he says, by "official copies of day-to-day proceedings" passed to him (and perhaps to others) by General Headquarters, Moti Ram wrote up what went on. But he did more. He saved what he wrote, added to it the texts of such exhibits as defense counsel chose to give him (they knew what he was up to), appended an account of the 1858 trial of Bahadur Shah—a little flourish this, to remind people of past wrongs and indignities—and just weeks after the close of the first trial, rushed the whole into print.

Though the haste is transparent—in the fractured pagination, and in the failure to reproduce what witnesses were asked in cross-examination (we read only their answers)—*Two Historic Trials in Red Fort* (New Delhi: Roxy Printing Press, 1946) is invaluable. The nearly three dozen witnesses, most of them ex-Indian Army other ranks, NCOs, and VCOs, tell us about Farrer Park; about how and why they joined the army; about the training, the move to Burma, the action there, their individual experiences of capture or surrender; never whole, never even in sequence, for they have been summoned to answer questions not reminisce; nevertheless to much cumulative effect. Sahgal, Dhillon, and Shah Nawaz answer questions too but also read prepared statements. The concluding address for the defense, the concluding address for the prosecution, the Judge-Advocate's summing up—together their delivery took almost twenty hours and lasted four days—are given in full. And among the exhibits printed, along with the piece of Prem's diary and two pieces from the diary of Shah Nawaz, there are enough situation reports, special orders, unit tables, and the like to convey some sense of how the army was put together and what it attempted. A rival compilation by V. S. Kulkarni and K. S. N. Murty, *First Indian National Army Trial* (Poona: Mangal Sahitya Prakashan, 1946), is far, far less complete. The official transcript of the proceedings, if it still exists, has yet to surface. Without Moti Ram it would be difficult to prepare any account of the Indian National Army at all.

None of the subsequent trials, however, produced a Moti Ram, probably because none caused the stir the first did. Indeed, as public interest dwindled, newspaper coverage dwindled too, until at last it quite dried up, leaving us oddly uncertain just how many trials there were. Meanwhile, however, books, pamphlets, and lesser ephemera had begun to flow (Amritlal Seth's and Kusum Nair's I have mentioned in the text), many thrown together by persons with little firsthand knowledge of the movement and even less concern with getting the story straight. A few, however, were written by men who had actually served under Bose, and over the next forty years several more of this sort have appeared. As a class they leave something to be desired. Serious in purpose, they are nevertheless often inexact factually, and their tone (which can be far from measured or modest) frequently troubles a western ear. Yet it would be difficult to write the story of the INA without them.

First to appear, Durlab Singh's *The I.N.A. Heroes* (Lahore: Hero Publications, 1946), is a collection of brief autobiographical accounts by Sahgal, Dhillon, and Shah Nawaz, accounts that, while repetitive of things said during the trial, also add to them. A. C. Chatterji's *India's Struggle for Freedom* (Calcutta: Chuckervertty Chatterjee, 1947) provides much detail on the freedom government and army's Malayan period. *Indian Independence Movement in East Asia* (Lahore: Singh Brothers,

1947), by an administrator named Kesar Singh Giani (the *Giani* is equivalent to *Reverend*), has the same focus. K. R. Palta's *My Adventures with the I.N.A.* (Lahore: Lion Press, 1946) is confined, by contrast, to Burma. Almost thirty years after the events he records, Mohan Singh reworked a much earlier version of his diary into Soldier's Contribution to Indian Independence (New Delhi: Army Educational Stores, n.d. [probably 1974]), but his contribution stops with 1942. Two newspapermen in Bose's service, S. A. Ayer and M. Sivaram, have left personal accounts. Ayer's *Unto Him A Witness* (Bombay: Thacker, 1951), though somewhat hagiographical in manner, conveys a great deal about how Bose lived and worked (Ayer was almost constantly with him). Sivaram's *The Road to Delhi* (Rutland: Charles E. Tuttle, 1966) gives an interesting picture of the movement's publicity work, which Sivaram both managed and had reservations about. Over the past fifteen years the *Oracle* (Calcutta) has carried short but useful autobiographical pieces by Dhillon, Abid Hasan, Zaman Kiani, C. J. Stracey, and two Rani of Jhansi women, Maya Banerjee and Shanti Majumdar. Abid Hasan Safrani (as he sometimes styles himself) has also written a little booklet called *The Men From Imphal* (Calcutta: Netaji Research Bureau, 1971). From the same house in the same year comes John A. Thivy's equally slight *The Struggle in East Asia*. And that, so far as personal reminiscenses by civil and military participants are concerned, is all we have—except for what Prem and Lakshmi remember.

I taped most of what they have to say in the course of five weeks spent with them in their Kanpur bungalow many years ago. (As Prem's father, the late Achhru Ram, was living with them at the time, and Prem's younger sister Raj Sethi paid a visit while I was there, I was able to talk to them as well. Much later I met Lakshmi's brother Govind in Madras and her sister Mrinalini in Ahmedabad.) My wife and I made further visits to Kanpur, and in the intervals we corresponded. Prem and Lakshmi have made a deliberate effort to preserve and cultivate their recollections, of the war years particularly, so as I worked I tested much of what I was writing against those recollections. When I wanted to lay something out using language I had picked from the tapes, I passed the passage to them for review. And of course many observations, stories, stretches of narrative, were theirs from the beginning. The consequence is that everything in *italics* in this book may with perfect confidence be taken to be what they actually remember or think. To this extent the book is their memoir, their contribution to the corpus of personal recollections upon which a movement so lacking in records of a normal sort must necessarily depend.

For what went on in India, from the hot weather of 1945 up to the hot weather of the following year, I have relied chiefly on the *Hindu* of Madras. *Greater Asia* (Rangoon), the thrice-weekly sponsored by the Japanese, was extremely useful as much for what the Indian community in Burma was asked to believe, as for what actually happened there. Students of Britain's terminal relations with India and Burma have been so spoiled by Nicholas Mansergh's enormous *India: The Transfer of Power 1942–47* and Hugh Tinker's lesser *Burma: The Struggle for Independence 1944–48* (for some observations about each see the Introduction to this book), that they rarely go beyond the documents selected, to documents that weren't. Nor have I. It is the same with the official military histories (Britain's, by S. Woodburn Kirby and others, runs to five volumes); it is the same with the splendid collections of Gandhi and Nehru papers. Indeed, in the case of the more than eighty Gandhi volumes it is probably safe to assume there is nothing left to find.

It is otherwise with Bose. His collected works, edited under the direction of his nephew Sisir Bose, did not begin to appear until 1980, consist in part of autobiographical pieces already published, and will not run beyond ten volumes. This seems curiously sparse, considering the vigorous political life Bose led. But perhaps his unusually long spells of Indian imprisonment and European exile, capped by almost five wartime years during which there can have been little correspondence with anyone, have meant fewer letters waiting to be published than are normal for a figure of his stature. There are no end of books and booklets that touch upon him in one way or another, among them half a dozen lives—I found Mihir Bose's *The Lost Hero: A Biography of Subhas Bose* (London: Quartet Books, 1982) particularly lively. It has been left to an American, however, to write the definitive work. Leonard Gordon of Columbia University has been examining Bengali nationalism and the particular Bengali family of which Subhas was a part for a quarter of a century. *Bengal: The Nationalist Movement 1876–1940* (New York: Columbia University Press, 1974) has been succeeded by *Brothers Against The Raj: A Biography of Sarat & Subhas Chandra Bose* (New

Delhi: Viking Penguin, 1990). A more thorough examination of the intertwined public lives of these two remarkable men it is difficult to imagine. And if Gordon does less with the younger brother's last two years than one might expect, and does almost nothing with the army upon whose success in battle his fortunes, reputation, life even, hung—why, perhaps it is because he, too, discovered when he reached that period how little there was to build upon.

The literature bearing on the mainstream—the Gandhi-cum-Nehru mainstream—of India's independence movement is large, and bibliographies abound: for example, in Sarvepalli Gopal's two-volume *Jawaharlal Nehru: A Biography* (Cambridge: Harvard University Press, 1976); in Judith M. Brown's *Gandhi: Prisoner of Hope* (New Haven: Yale University Press, 1989); and in the several books by D. A. Low, R. J. Moore, and Sumit Sarkar. The notes to Sucheta Mahajan's "British Policy, Nationalist Strategy and Popular National Upsurge 1945–46," in *Myth and Reality: The Struggle for Freedom in India 1945–47*, edited by Amit Kumar Gupta (New Delhi: Manohar, 1987), are themselves a treasure chest of references for that short but crucial period, and the article itself so substantial and compelling one hopes she will expand it into a book. But one stretch is poorly charted. Aside from Francis G. Hutchins's *India's Revolution: Gandhi and the Quit India Movement* (Cambridge: Harvard University Press, 1973), and the essays collected by Gyanendra Pandey in *The Indian Nation in 1942* (Calcutta: K. P. Bagchi, 1988), there is little (and that hardly worth reading) about the August upheaval. Can this be because the episode, which was unmistakably Gandhi's doing while at the same time unmistakably violent, suggests that in the river that carried India to freedom, there were more rapids and rough white water than many looking back care to be shown or to remember?

More surprising still is the shortness of the shelf where Burma's independence is concerned. Aung San is almost faceless. Cut down young by assassins' bullets, he left no autobiography and few papers. *Aung San* (Queensland: University of Queensland Press, 1984), by his gallant daughter the Nobel Prize-winning Aung San Suu Kyi, is too thin and (oddly) colorless to constitute a true biography, and in U Maung Maung's *Burmese Nationalist Movements 1940–1948* (Honolulu: University of Hawaii Press, 1990) he is hardly to be found. So another Maung Maung's thirty-year-old collection of tributes and reminiscences, published under the title *Aung San of Burma* (The Hague: Martinus Nyhoff, 1962), remains the best source for this extraordinary man. Ba Maw's *Breakthrough in Burma* (New Haven: Yale University Press, 1968) is elegant, self-serving, and eventually tedious. Thakin Nu's brief *Burma Under the Japanese* (London: Macmillan, 1954) has the immediacy of a memoir, but Dorothy Hess Guyot's impressive unpublished 1966 Yale University Ph.D. dissertation, "The Political Impact of the Japanese Occupation of Burma," covers more ground and is decidedly more useful.

Gerard H. Corr's *The War of the Springing Tigers* (London: Osprey, 1975) is short, breezy, and does nothing that Hugh Toye does not do better. There is more substance to A. L. Barker's *The March on Delhi* (London: Faber and Faber, 1963). But for narrative of this sort it makes sense to go directly to Louis Allen, or to Field-Marshal Sir William Slim. Few can beat the British at the writing of military memoirs. What they may lose on the battlefield they will more than recover at the bookstall. And Slim's *Defeat into Victory* (London: Cassell, 1956) has the added advantage of being the work not of one among many field commanders in Burma, but of the man who ran the show. No one can lay the book down without feeling that, pointless though the rush for Rangoon was from a strategic point of view, it gave Britain in the evening of her empire, in a part of the world where British forces had suffered defeats without parallel in British history, a desperately needed triumph. And the instrument of that triumph was that most peculiarly imperial construct, the Indian Army; the old *British* Indian Army; for almost one hundred years the sword and buckler of the now terminal Raj. On the Irrawaddy, in the first half of 1945, the Indian Army achieved what will by any measure be accounted not simply its last but its greatest victory. And it was Slim, of course, who led it.

Lord Louis Mountbatten's *Report to the Combined Chiefs of Staff by the Supreme Allied Commander South East Asia 1943–45* (London: H. M. Stationery Office, 1951) contains among other things the reasoning that led the Supremo to welcome (cautiously) Aung San and his Burma National Army into the war against Japan. Burma's place in the strategic plans and disputes of the Allies can be teased out of Christopher Thorne's encyclopedic *Allies of a Kind* (New York: Oxford University

Press, 1978), but Raymond Callahan explores the subject quite as ably and far more lucidly in his short *Burma 1942–1945* (Newark: University of Delaware Press, 1978). For India's place in the strategic plans of the Germans and the Japanese the authoritative study is Milan Hauner's *India in Axis Strategy* (Stuttgart: Ernst Klett for the German Historical Institute of London, 1981). Unfortunately Hauner follows the German end of the equation much more closely than the Japanese.

Filed under the heading L/WS in the India Office Library, London, are a fair number of papers bearing on the INA, among them a hurried review of that army function by function, department by department, compiled by G. D. Anderson of CSDIC Delhi, and a collection of intelligence summaries prepared weekly for New Delhi's use. From the first you can learn a good deal about the army's strength and structure (the appendix to this book draws heavily upon it). From the second it is possible to establish what the Government of India knew about the INA operationally, from Rash Behari's time to Subhas Chandra's death and beyond. As the reader will see from a glance at the notes, I have made much use of the second in particular, and of miscellaneous press clippings, telegrams, and memoranda filed under other L/WS headings. Some of these are of great interest (I am thinking particularly of the remarkable Wren memorandum of late 1942). Most are the fruit of, or were prompted by, British intelligence work. To attempt the story of the INA from such material is a bit like trying to write the history of the Army of Northern Virginia from the reports of Pinkerton agents. But the sources for a proper narrative account of Subhas Chandra Bose's freedom force are beggarly. And beggars can't be choosers.

Index

In the text Subhas Chandra Bose is referred to variously as Subhas, Subhas Chandra, Bose, or Netaji. In this index he will be referred to only as Bose.